Operations Management

R. Dan Reid

University of New Hampshire

Nada R. Sanders

Wright State University

John Wiley & Sons, Inc.

ACQUISITIONS EDITOR	Beth Lang Golub
DEVELOPMENTAL EDITOR	Marian D. Provenzano
SUPPLEMENT EDITOR	Cynthia Snyder
EDITORIAL ASSISTANTS	Lili Kalish, Jennifer Battista
MARKETING MANAGER	Jessica Garcia
SENIOR PRODUCTION EDITOR	Ken Santor
SENIOR DESIGNER	Karin Kincheloe
TEXT DESIGNER	Meryl Levavi
COVER DESIGNER	David Levy
ILLUSTRATION EDITOR	Anna Melhorn
ILLUSTRATIONS	ECL Art
PHOTO RESEARCHER	Elyse Reider
PHOTO EDITOR	Hilary Newman
COVER PHOTOGRAPH	© Charly Franklin/FGP International

This book was set in 10.5/12 Minion by Progressive Information Technologies, Inc., and printed and bound by Von Hoffmann Press. The cover was printed by Von Hoffmann Press.

This book is printed on acid free paper.∞

To order books or for customer service please call 1(800)225-5945.

ISBN 0-471-32011-0

Printed in the United States of America

10 9 8 7 6 5 4 3 2 1

Dedicated to all of our students

past, present, and future. May the insights and lessons learned from past students enable all of us to better travel through the world of operations management.

ABOUT THE AUTHORS

R. Dan Reid is Associate Professor of Operations Management at the Whittemore School of Business and Economics at the University of New Hampshire. He holds a Ph.D. in Operations Management from The Ohio State University, an M.B.A. from Angelo State University, and a B.A. in Business Management from the University of Maryland. During the past twenty years he has taught at The Ohio State University, Ohio University, Bowling Green State University, Otterbein College, and the University of New Hampshire.

Dr. Reid's research publications have appeared in numerous journals such as the *Production and Inventory Management Journal, Mid-American Journal of Business, Cornell Hotel and Restaurant Administration Quarterly, Hospitality Research and Education Journal, Target,* and the *OM Review.* His research interests include manufacturing planning and control systems, quality in services, purchasing, and supply chain management. He has worked for, or consulted with, organizations in the telecommunications, consumer electronics, defense, hospitality, and capital equipment industries. Dr. Reid has served as Program Chair and President of the Northeast Region of the Decision Sciences Institute (NEDSI) and as Associate Program Chair and Proceedings Editor of the First International DSI Conference, and held numerous positions within DSI. He has been the Program Chair and Chair of the Operations Management Division of the Academy of Management. Dr. Reid has also served as President of the Granite State Chapter of the American Production and Inventory Control Society. He has been a board member of the Operations Management Association and the Manchester Manufacturing Management Center. Dr. Reid is a Past Editor of the *OM Review.*

Dr. Reid has designed and taught courses for undergraduates, graduates, and executives on topics such as resource management, manufacturing management, introduction to operations management, purchasing management, and manufacturing planning and control systems.

Nada R. Sanders is Professor of Operations Management at the Raj Soin College of Business at Wright State University. She holds a Ph.D. in Operations Management from The Ohio State University, an M.B.A. from The Ohio State University, and a B.S. degree in Mechanical Engineering from Franklin University. She has taught for over twenty years at a variety of academic institutions including The Ohio State University, Capital University, and Wright State University in addition to lecturing to various industry groups. She has designed and taught classes for undergraduates, graduates, and executives on topics such as operations management, operations strategy, forecasting, and supply chain management. She has received a number of teaching awards including the College of Business Outstanding Teacher Award.

Dr. Sanders has extensive research experience and has published in numerous journals such as *Decision Sciences, Journal of Operations Management, Sloan Management Review, Omega, Interfaces, Journal of Behavioral Decision Making, Journal of Applied Business Research, Production & Inventory Management Journal.* She has authored chapters in books and encyclopedias such as the *Forecasting Principles Handbook* (Kluwer Academic Publishers), *Encyclopedia of Production and Manufacturing Management* (Kluwer Academic Publishers) and the *Encyclopedia of Electrical and Electronics Engineering* (John Wiley & Sons). Dr. Sanders has served as Vice President of Decision Sciences Institute (DSI), President of the Midwest Decision Sciences Institute, and has held numerous other positions within the Institute. In addition to DSI, Dr. Sanders is active in the Production Operations Management Society (POMS), APICS, INFORMS, Council of Logistics Management (CLM), and the International Institute of Forecasters (IIF). She has served on review boards and/or as a reviewer for numerous journals including *Decision Sciences, International Journal of Production Research, OM Review, Omega,* and others. In addition, Dr. Sanders has worked and/or consulted for companies in the telecommunications, pharmaceutical, steel, automotive, warehousing, retail, and publishing industries, and is frequently called upon to serve as an expert witness.

PREFACE

Something different is going on in the world of operations management. Rapid economic changes such as global competition, e-business, the Internet, and advances in technology have placed operations management in the limelight of business. Today companies are competing in a very different environment than they were only a few years ago, and operations management is the function through which companies can succeed in this competitive economic landscape.

Instead of being confined to one department, operations management concepts are far reaching, affecting every aspect of the organization. Wether if one's area of expertise is accounting, finance, human resources, information technology, management, marketing, or purchasing, students need to understand the critical impact operations management has on any business.

We each have over 20 years of teaching experience and understand the challenges inherent in teaching and taking the introductory OM course. The vast majority of students taking this course are not majoring in operations management. Rather, classes are typically composed of students from various business disciplines or students who are undecided about their major and have little knowledge of operations management. The challenge is not only to teach the foundation of the field, but also to help students understand the impact operations has on the business as a whole, and the close relationship of operations management with other business functions. We were motivated to write this book to help students understand operations management and to make it easier for faculty to teach the introductory operations management course. We have three major goals for this book:

GOALS OF THE BOOK ■

1. Provide a Solid Foundation in Operations Management

Our book is standard in terms of the concepts and techniques that are covered, but also covers emerging topics such as supply chain management, enterprise resource planning, and electronic data interchange. We give equal time to strategic and tactical decisions and provide coverage of both service and manufacturing organizations. We look closely at some of the unique challenges service organizations face in OM.

2. Demonstrate Cross Functional Relevance

While several excellent textbooks provide appropriate foundation coverage, we believe that few provide sufficient motivation for students. We are aware that a major teaching challenge in OM is that students aren't motivated to study OM because they don't understand its relevance to their majors. We think the course textbook can greatly support the professor in this area; therefore, a chief goal of this book is to integrate coverage of why and how OM is integral to all organizations. Interfunctional coordination and decision making have become the norm in today's business environment. Throughout every chapter we discuss information flow between business functions and the role of each function in the organization.

3. Provide an Accessible and Engaging Learning Package

A good textbook is not just a repository of everything about the subject. In addition to providing relevance for business students, the third main goal of our textbook is to help students learn the material in an engaging and accessible way. Our textbook supports professors by providing the right amount of depth and useful pedagogy—with the ultimate goal of reducing lines during office hours.

■ FEATURES OF THE BOOK

We have developed our pedagogical features to implement and reinforce the goals discussed above and address the many challenges in this course.

Streamlined Presentation

We have streamlined the treatment and coverage of OM topics. Through our teaching experience we have found that many OM texts present material in a manner difficult to understand by students completely unfamiliar with the topic. Over the years we had been inundated with students who needed clarification on text material which was confusing and unclear. To meet students' needs we focused on presenting the basics of OM concepts with extensive use of practical and relevant business examples. We eliminated from the printed book coverage of topics less frequently covered at the introductory level, such as Linear Programming, the Transportation Method, and Simulation Analysis. However, the complete chapters of these topics are available on the CD provided in each textbook.

Links to Practice

Many OM texts have many boxes and sidebars, which make it difficult for students to understand what they need to know. Furthermore, the many examples frequently interrupt the flow of the text and make a chapter difficult to read and assimilate. We recognize the importance of including "real world" examples, but believe they should be integrated into the stream of the text instead of interrupting the text. Therefore, we have developed "embedded boxes" called *Links To Practice* which provide brief examples of specific companies in every chapter. Embedded by both content and design into the general text discussion, each provides a concise and relevant example without interrupting the flow of the text. The examples chosen range from large multinational organizations to small local businesses.

Consider how Lands' End uses technology in its business. Lands' End went on-line in 1995. The company sold only $160 worth of gear the first month. Today, Lands' End sells over $10 million per month on-line. The company has a live chat room that allows customers to ask questions about merchandise. It also offers a "shopping with a friend" service that allows a customer, his or her friend or friends, and a customer service representative to be linked together. However, Lands' End's "virtual model" highlights how far technolgy has advanced. A few strokes on the keyboard and the shopper is able to produce an on-screen model with his or her body measurements. Even though this virtual model is not perfect, over 1 million shoppers have built their own models at the Lands' End site.

LINKS TO PRACTICE
Lands' End, Inc.
www.landsend.com

"OM Across the Organization" and "Cross Functional" Icons

Unique to this book is an end-of-chapter summary titled "OM Across the Organization" that highlights the relationship between OM and key business functions such as accounting, finance, human resources, information technology, management, marketing, and purchasing. This section is designed to help students understand the close relationship of operations management with other business functions and appreciate the critical impact OM has on other business functions. In addition, a cross-

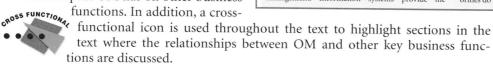

OM ACROSS THE ORGANIZATION

Supply chain management changes the way companies do business. Consider how supply chain management affects different functional areas in the organization.

Accounting shares some of the benefits and responsibilities of supply chain management. As inventory levels decrease, customer service increases. Manufacturing is using its capacity more effectively. Accounting is exposed to the risks of information sharing and of developing partnerships. With information sharing comes the need for increased confidentiality.

Marketing benefits by improved customer service levels achieved by POS data collection. A shared database gives marketing current demand trends and eliminates demand filtering between levels of the supply chain. POS data also facilitates quick customer response time.

Information systems are critical for supply chain management. Information systems provide the means for collecting relevant demand data, developing a common database, and providing a means for transmitting order information. Information systems enable information sharing through POS data and EDI.

Purchasing has an elevated role in supply chain management within organizations. Purchasing facilitates and manages a strong supplier base through partnering.

Operations uses timely demand information to effectively plan production schedules and use its capacity. Operations responds to customer demand data, improving customer service.

Who is responsible for supply chain management within an organization? In a manufacturing company this is usually the materials manager, who is familiar with external suppliers, internal functions, and external distributors. The person who does supply chain management must see the big picture so that local priorities do not overshadow global priorities.

functional icon is used throughout the text to highlight sections in the text where the relationships between OM and other key business functions are discussed.

Relevant Business Examples

Current textbooks typically do not use business examples students can relate to. The typical examples provided are those of large corporations such as General Motors, IBM, or Xerox. Primarily using these types of examples creates the impression for the students that this is a field that is either beyond their reach or irrelevant to their needs. We have found that students understand the concepts better when these concepts are also presented in a context that is smaller in scale, including more on small and medium-sized business examples. Our text also uses selected big business examples where appropriate.

Chapter Opening Vignettes and "OM Is Everywhere"

To help students intuitively understand the topic, each chapter begins with a description of a personal problem that can be solved using the concepts discussed in the chapter. Our objective is to attract the attention of the student by starting with a personal example they can relate to. We demonstrate that OM is not just about operating a plant or a business, but that it is relevant in everything that we do. An end-of-chapter section called "*OM Is Everywhere*" relates back to the chapter-opening vignette and describes how the

Buying a product used to mean getting dressed, leaving home, and shopping at stores or malls until you found what you wanted. Today, most of us can go online 24 hours a day, 7 days a week and buy just about anything over the Internet. You can shop while sitting at your computer and never leave home. You can order food from a supermarket or a restaurant online, or buy clothing and household goods. You can buy books, videos, CDs—the Internet has revolutionized the way we do business.

In this chapter we look at supply chains: the connected links of external suppliers, internal processes, and external distributors. We also learn how advances in information technology help companies coordinate their supply chains.

We will begin with the effect of supply chain management on organizations.

chapter topic impacts the student's personal life. It addresses the issue of why this is important even outside the business organization and helps summarize the concepts in the chapter.

Integrated Technology Perspective

E-commerce and the Internet are transforming the business environment, and we integrate these concepts in every chapter. We discuss a range of topics from enterprise resource planning (ERP) and electronic data interchange (EDI) to quality issues of buying goods on-line.

Pedagogy

Before Studying This Chapter   Before the start of each chapter students are provided with a short statement of what they need to either know or review from previous material, referring students to specific topic and page information. This enables the student to review previous material necessary to understand the topic being covered.

> **Before studying this chapter you should know or, if necessary, review**
> 1. The implications of competitive priorities Chapter 2, pages 28–32.
> 2. Product design considerations Chapter 3, pages 48–52.
> 3. Process selection considerations Chapter 3, pages 52–58.

Before You Go On   Sections strategically placed within every chapter summarize key material the student should know before continuing. Often the material in chapters can be overwhelming. We felt that breaking up the chapter with a brief summary of key material is highly beneficial in aiding learning and comprehension. Finally, key terms and concepts are highlighted in boldface when they are first explained in the text and are listed at the end of the chapter with page references.

> **Before You Go On**
> Make sure you understand the structure of the supply chain, the bullwhip effect, and some of the challenges to supply chain management in today's marketplace: (1) A supply chain consists of external suppliers, internal functions of the company, and external distributors. (2) The bullwhip effect causes erratic replenishment orders placed on different levels in the supply chain that have no apparent link to final product demand. (3) Customers demand more value from their suppliers. Added value to the customer can take the form of higher quality, quicker response, or lower prices. Consumer expectations, globalization, information technology, and environmental needs can affect the future of supply chain management.

Solved Problems   Numerous solved problems are provided complete with step by step explanations to ensure students understand the process and why the problem is solved in a particular way. Where appropriate we provide a series of steps for problem solving and offer *Problem Solving Tips*.

> ### SOLVED PROBLEMS
>
> **■ Solved Problem 1**
> Jack Smith, owner of Jack's Auto Sales, is deciding whether his company should process its own auto loan applications or outsource the process to Loans Etc. If Jack processes the auto loan applications internally, he faces an annual fixed cost of $2500 for membership fees, allowing him access to the TopNotch credit company, and a variable cost of $25 each time he processes a loan application. Loans Etc. will process the loans for $35 per application but Jack must lease equipment from Loans Etc. at a fixed annual cost of
>
> $1000. Jack estimates processing 125 loan applications per year. What do you think Jack should do?
>
> **Solution**
> First, set the total costs of each alternative equal to each other, or $1000 + ($35 ∗ Q) = $2500 + ($25 ∗ Q). Solving for Q, we have $10Q = $1500, or Q = 150 loan applications. Since the costs are equal at 150 loan applications and Jack expects to need 125 applications processed, he is better off outsourcing the loan applications to Loans Etc.

Cases   Each chapter ends with a case that reinforces the issues and topics discussed in the chapter. The cases can provide the basis for group discussion or can be assigned as individual exercises for the student. Many cases conclude with a list of questions for students to answer.

In addition, each chapter offers a unique interactive learning exercise titled *Internet Challenge* where students are provided with a short case and given specific Internet assignments.

Interactive Learning Using the Text, the Interactive CD, and the Web Site We have created a number of interactive learning activities for students which will help them learn the material in a dynamic and interesting way. At the end of each chapter, there is a list of activities which are available on the CD and the web site. Students can work on these activities on their own, and instructors have the flexibility to assign material for individual or group study. The activities include:

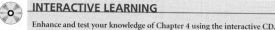

INTERACTIVE LEARNING

Enhance and test your knowledge of Chapter 4 using the interactive CD.

1. **Video** *Cisco Systems, Inc.*
2. **Spreadsheet** *The Bullwhip Effect*
3. **Company Tour**
   Finkel & Sons, Inc.
   Reynolds Metal Company
4. **Additional Web Resources**
   nummi,www.nummi.com
   IBM, http://houns54.clearlake.ibm.com

   Visit our dynamic Web site, www.wiley.com/college/reid, for more cases, Web links, and additional information.
5. **INTERNET CHALLENGE** *Global Shopping*

Since the Internet provides access to products around the world, your challenge involves some global shopping. This year you have been given a budget of $10,000 to furnish and decorate your off-campus apartment. You have chosen a global theme. Your job is to find items from as many different parts of the world as you can to use in your apartment. You can spend up to $10,000 but you cannot exceed your budget. Do not forget that shipping must be included not need to worry about major appliances (computer, television, stereo, oven, refrigerator, dishwasher, etc.) but you do need everything else. Since you plan to host a major party in your new apartment, everything you buy must be delivered within six weeks.

(b) Provide a list of all of the items you would buy, the cost of each item, and the total money spent. Organize your list by the room the item is intended for. Be sure

- **Interactive Simulations**
- **NBR Videos**
- **Interactive Spreadsheets**
- **Company Tours**
- **Internet Challenge**
- **Virtual Company Consulting Case**
- **Additional Web Resources**

ORGANIZATION OF THE BOOK ■

We have arranged the topics in the book in progressive order from strategic to tactical. Early in the book we cover operations topics that require a strategic perspective and a cultural change within the organization, such as supply chain management, total quality management, and just-in-time systems. Progressively we move to more tactical issues, such as work management, inventory management, and scheduling concerns. We recognize that most faculty will select the chapters relevant to their needs. To make it easier for students and faculty each chapter can stand alone. Any specific knowledge needed for a chapter is summarized immediately prior to the chapter, with specific topic and page references for the student to review.

INSTRUCTIONAL SUPPORT PACKAGE ■

Our supporting material has been designed to make learning OM easier for students and teaching OM easier for faculty.

Instructor Resources

1. The Instructor's Resource CD A comprehensive resource guide designed to assist professors in preparing lectures and assignments. The resource guide provides:

- **Instructor's Manual:** Includes a suggested course outline, teaching tips and strategies, war stories, answers to all end-of-chapter material, brief description of the additional resources in the Interactive Learning box, additional in-class exercises, and tips on integrating the Theory of Constraints.

• **Solutions Manual:** A complete set of detailed solutions is provided for all problems.

• **Video Guide:** A guide to help instructors use the NBR videos includes a brief description of each video clip, additional discussion questions, and suggested answers to all the discussion questions.

• **Test Bank:** A comprehensive Test Bank comprised of approximately 1700 questions that consists of multiple choice, true-false, essay questions, and open-ended problems for each chapter. The Test Bank is also available in a computerized version that allows instructors to customize their exams.

• **PowerPoint Slides:** PowerPoint Slides are available for use in class. Full-color slides highlight key figures from the text as well as many additional lecture outlines, concepts, and diagrams. Together, these provide a versatile opportunity to add high-quality visual support to lectures.

2. Nightly Business Report Video The comprehensive Video package offers video selections from the highly respected business news program, *Nightly Business Report (NBR).* These video clips tie directly to the theme of operations management and bring to life many of the examples used in the text.

3. eGrade: eGrade is a web-based student quizzing program that enhances academic productivity by providing immediate scoring and feedback. For each chapter of the text, students can test their knowledge with these interactive quizzes that give hints for solving the problem. eGrade quizzes contain a variety of problem types, and specialize in quantitative problems. The quiz questions are randomized so that students can take the quiz multiple times.

4. Student Resource CD-ROM: Included in each copy of the book, this CD-ROM includes various resources including selected video cases, simulations, and Excel spreadsheets, for personal student use and study.

5. Wiley Business Extra and Xanedu: The Business Extra Program, a partnership between Wiley and the Dow Jones Company, offers an exciting new way to extend your textbook beyond the walls of the classroom. The Business Extra Program includes a special password to Wiley's *Business Extra* web site, through which your students get instant access to a wealth of current articles, as well as a special offer for the *Wall Street Journal* and wsj.com. The *Business Extra Password Card* can be packaged with the text. Another way to extend the boundaries of the classroom is by combining Xanedu with the textbook. The Xanedu web site includes millions of articles from thousands of publications. Wiley's partnership with Xanedu allows us to offer a portion of these vast resources to students at a minimal cost. Students receive a password to access a special portion of the Reid & Sanders web site that contains links to articles related to a variety of operations management topics.

Student Resources

Student Resource CD Included in each copy of the book, the CD contains the following resources:

• **NBR Videos:**   Students will have the ability to view selected Nightly Business Report videos before or after class. They can view the videos and link to video overviews and questions on the text web site. The questions prompt students to think critically about the issues described in the video.

• **Simulations:**   Simulations have been created using Extend LT to illustrate the functioning of intermittent (job shop) and continuous (flow shop) operations that students typically have difficulty visualizing. Students can not only see the flow (line versus jumbled), speed of production, and product variety; they can also change numerous variables in the operation (e.g. number of products produced, layout arrangement) and directly view the consequences. Using Extend LT, students can create their own simulations.

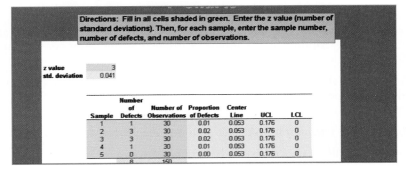

Department	Hourly arrivals	Number of servers	Customers served per hour	Average number waiting	Server utilization	Number served
Radiology	10	1	8	5.3	0.91	23
Lab	8	1	12	0.52	0.72	25
Lobby	15	2	8	1.4	0.77	39
Examination	18	3	7	1.4	0.86	57
Surgery	6	3	3	0.028	0.59	16
Therapy	11	2	6	1.5	0.85	31

• **Excel Spreadsheets:**   Templates are provided so that students can model and solve problems presented in the textbook. Step-by-step directions are provided. Directions prompt students as they work through each spreadsheet. Expected outcomes and questions are also given.

Directions: Fill in all cells shaded in green. Enter the z value (number of standard deviations). Then, for each sample, enter the sample number, number of defects, and number of observations.

| | z value | 3 |
| | std. deviation | 0.041 |

Sample	Number of Defects	Number of Observations	Proportion of Defects	Center Line	UCL	LCL
1	1	30	0.01	0.053	0.176	0
2	3	30	0.02	0.053	0.176	0
3	3	30	0.02	0.053	0.176	0
4	1	30	0.01	0.053	0.176	0
5	0	30	0.00	0.053	0.176	0
	8	150				

Operations Management Web site

An extensive web site has been developed in support of *Operations Management*. The site is available at **http://www.wiley.com/college/reid**, and offers a range of information for both the instructor and the student. The web site includes the following resources:

1. **Instructor Web Site**

• **Company Tours:**   Web links to the tours of various companies. Each tour includes a brief description of the company and discussion questions for students to consider after viewing the tour.

• **Current Articles:**   Current articles are provided to aid instructor in linking lectures to business practice.

• **Updates and Corrections:**   Any corrections and updates to the text will be communicated to the instructor via this web site.

• **Additional Cases:**   Additional cases for use in class.

• **Additional Problems:**   Additional solved problems for use in class.

• **Excel Data Sets:**   End-of-chapter problem data inserted into Excel spreadsheets to avoid errors from copying.

2. **Student Web Site**

• **Virtual Company Consulting Case:**   A web-based company features an Intranet site for a simulated company. Students are "hired" as interns and are

asked to complete assignments that require them to use information from the online cases and Intranet site to develop recommended solutions. These exercises get the students into active, hands-on learning to complement the concepts discussed in the chapter.

• **Company Tours:**   Web links to the plant tours of various companies along with a brief description of the tour and discussion questions for students to consider after viewing the tour.

• **Current Articles:**   Articles discussing current events are provided by topic. Students can perform a search allowing them to research an OM topic of interest.

• **Web Links:**   Direct links to related web sites are provided.

• **Updates:**   Allows us to directly communicate changes in either the text or the field directly to the students.

ACKNOWLEDGMENTS ◼

During the development of *Operations Management* we benefited greatly from the comments, suggestions, and evaluations from many of our colleagues who teach the OM course throughout North America. We would like to acknowledge the contributions made by the following individuals:

David Alexander
Angelo State University

Stephen L. Allen
Truman State University

Jerry Allison
University of Central Oklahoma

Suad Alwan
Chicago State University

Tony Arreola-Risa
Texas A&M University

Gordon F. Bagot
California State University–Los Angeles

Brent Bandy
University of Wisconsin–Oshkosh

Joseph R. Biggs
California Polytechnic State University at San Luis Obispo

Jean-Marie Bourjolly
Concordia University

Ken Boyer
DePaul University

Karen L. Brown
Southwest Missouri State University

Linda D. Brown
Middle Tennessee State University

James F. Campbell
University of Missouri–St. Louis

Cem Canel
University of North Carolina at Wilmington

Chin-Sheng Chen
Florida International University

Louis Chin
Bentley College

Sidhartha R. Das
George Mason University

Greg Dobson
University of Rochester

Ceasar Douglas
Grand Valley State University

Shad Dowlatshahi
University of Missouri–Kansas City

L. Paul Dreyfus
Athens State University

Lisa Ferguson
Hofstra University

Mark Gershon
Temple University

William Giauque
Brigham Young University

Greg Graman
Wright State University

Jatinder N.D. Gupta
Ball State University

Peter Haug
Western Washington University

Daniel Heiser
DePaul University

Ted Helmer
F. Theodore Helmer and Associates, Inc.

Lew Hofmann
The College of New Jersey

Lisa Houts
California State University–Fresno

Tim C. Ireland
Oklahoma State University

Peter T. Ittig
University of Massachusetts–Boston

Jayanth Jayaram
University of Oregon

Robert E. Johnson
University of Connecticut

Mehdi Kaighobadi
Florida Atlantic University

Yunus Kathawala
Eastern Illinois University

Basheer Khumawala
University of Houston

Thomas A. Kratzer
Malone College

Ashok Kumar
Grand Valley State University

Cynthia Lawless
Baylor University

Raymond P. Lutz
University of Texas at Dallas

Satish Mehra
University of Memphis

Brad C. Meyer
Drake University

Abdel-Aziz M. Mohamed
California State University–Northridge

Charles L. Munson
Washington State University

Kenneth E. Murphy
Florida International University

Jay Nathan
St. Johns University

Harvey N. Nye
University of Central Oklahoma

Susan E. Pariseau
Merrimack College

Carl J. Poch
Northern Illinois University

Claudia H. Pragman
Minnesota State University

Willard Price
University of the Pacific

Feraidoon Raafat
San Diego State University

William D. Raffield
University of St. Thomas

Ranga Ramasesh
Texas Christian University

Paul H. Randolph
Texas Tech University

Robert M. Saltzman
San Francisco State University

George O. Schneller IV
Baruch College–City University of New York

A. Kimbrough Sherman
Loyola College in Maryland

William R. Sherrard
San Diego State University

Chwen Sheu
Kansas State University

Sue Perrott Siferd
Arizona State University

Samia M. Siha
Kennesaw State University

Natalie Simpson
State University of New York–Buffalo

Barbara Smith
Niagara College

Victor E. Sower
Sam Houston State University

Linda L. Stanley
Our Lady of the Lake University

Donna H. Stewart
University of Wisconsin–Stout

Manouchehr Tabatabaei
University of Tampa

Nabil Tamimi
University of Scranton

Larry Taube
University of North Carolina–Greensboro

Giri K. Tayi
State University of New York at Albany

Charles J. Teplitz
University of San Diego

Timothy L. Urban
The University of Tulsa

Michael L. Vineyard
Memphis State University

John Visich
University of Houston

Robert Vokurka
Texas A&M University

George Walker
Sam Houston State University

John Wang
Montclair State University

Theresa Wells
University of Wisconsin–Eau Claire

T.J. Wharton
Oakland University

Barbara Withers
University of San Diego

Steven A. Yourstone
University of New Mexico

SPECIAL THANKS ▪

We would also like to acknowledge the work of our supplements authors who worked to create a variety of support materials for both instructors and students: Linda Stanley, Our Lady of the Lake University, created Excel spreadsheets for the text and the CD; Nabil Tamimi, University of Scranton, prepared the Solutions Manual and also provided an accuracy check of all the worked examples and solved problems in the text; Lisa Ferguson, Hofstra University, prepared the Instructor's Manual; Chuck Munson, Washington State University, and Brent Bandy, University of Wisconsin–Oshkosh, co-authored the Test Bank; Dan Heiser, DePaul University, created the PowerPoint presentation slides; Mehdi Kaighobadi, Florida Atlantic University, provided Excel data sets; Jay Nathan, St. Johns University, and Harvey Nye, University of Central Oklahoma, prepared extra problem sets; Ranga Ramasesh, Texas Christian University, wrote the NBR Video Guide; Yunus Kathawala, Eastern Illinois University, and Barbara Smith, Niagara College, helped to develop content for the Web site; and Gordon Bagot, California State University–Los Angeles coordinated the Business Extra/Xanedu articles. The Virtual Company Consulting Case is based on cases developed by Ted Helmer, Theodore Helmer and Associates, Inc. and Jon Ozmun, Northern Arizona University.

We would like to offer special acknowledgment to the publishing team at Wiley for their creativity, talent, and hard work. Their great personalities and team spirit have made working on the book a pleasure. Special thanks go to Beth Golub, Acquisitions Editor, Marian Provenzano, Developmental Editor, and Jessica Garcia, Marketing Manager, for all their effort. We really appreciate it.

Other Wiley staff who contributed to the text and media are: Cynthia Snyder, Supplement Editor; David Kear, New Media Editor; Ken Santor, Senior Production Editor; Karin Kincheloe, Senior Designer; Anna Melhorn, Illustration Editor; Hilary Newman, Photo Editor; Lili Kalish and Jennifer Battista, Editorial Assistants; and Elyse Ryder, Photo Researcher. We would also like to thank David Krahl of Imagine That, Inc. for developing the Extend simulations.

BRIEF CONTENTS

CONTENTS

CHAPTER 7 JUST-IN-TIME
■ SYSTEMS 175

CHAPTER 8
■ FORECASTING 205

CHAPTER 14 MASTER SCHEDULING AND ROUGH-CUT CAPACITY PLANNING 426

CHAPTER 15 MATERIAL REQUIREMENTS PLANNING 451

CHAPTER 16 SCHEDULING 480

Introduction to Operations Management

LEARNING OBJECTIVES

After completing this chapter you should be able to:

1. Define operations management.
2. Explain the role of operations management in business.
3. Describe decisions that operations managers make.
4. Describe the differences between service and manufacturing operations.
5. Identify major historical developments in operations management.
6. Identify current trends in operations management.
7. Describe the flow of information between operations management and other business functions.

CHAPTER OUTLINE

Many of you reading this book may think that you don't know what operations management (OM) is or that it is not something you are interested in. However, once we begin you will realize that you already know quite a bit about operations management. You may even be working in an operations management capacity and have used certain operations management techniques. You will also realize that operations management is probably the most critical business function today. If you want to be on the frontier of business competition, you want to be in operations management.

Today companies are competing in a very different environment than they were only a few years ago. To survive they must focus on quality, time-based competition, efficiency, and international perspectives. Global competition, e-business, the Internet, and advances in technology require flexibility and responsiveness. This new focus has placed operations management in the limelight of business, because it is the function through which companies can achieve this type of competitiveness.

The purpose of this book is to help prepare you to be successful in this new business environment. Operations management will give you an understanding of how to help your organization gain a competitive advantage in the marketplace. Regardless of whether your area of expertise is marketing, finance, MIS, or operations, the techniques and concepts in this book will help you in your business career. The material in this book will teach you how your company can offer products and services cheaper, better, and faster. You will also learn that operations management concepts are far reaching, affecting every aspect of the organization and even everyday life.

■ WHAT IS OPERATIONS MANAGEMENT?

CROSS FUNCTIONAL

▶ **Operations management**
The business function responsible for planning, coordinating, and controlling the resources needed to produce a company's products and services.

Every business is managed through three major functions: finance, marketing, and operations management. The vice president for each of these functions reports directly to the president or CEO of the company, as shown in Figure 1-1. Other business functions—such as accounting, purchasing, human resources, and engineering—support these three major functions. Finance is the function responsible for managing cash flow, current assets, and capital investments. Marketing is responsible for sales, generating customer demand, and understanding customer wants and needs. Most of us have some idea of what finance and marketing are about, but what does operations management do?

Operations management (OM) is the business function that plans, coordinates, and controls the resources needed to produce a company's products and services. Operations management is a *management* function. It involves managing people, equipment, technology, information, and many other resources. Operations management is

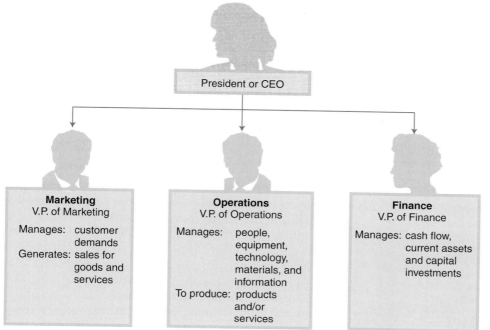

Figure 1-1

Organizational chart showing the three major business functions

the central core function of every company. This is true whether the company is large or small, provides a physical product or a service, is for profit or not for profit. Every company has an operations management function. Actually, all the other organizational functions are there primarily to support the operations function. Without operations, there would be no products or services to market.

The role of operations management is to transform a company's inputs into the finished products or services. Inputs include human resources (such as workers and managers), facilities and processes (such as buildings and equipment), as well as materials, technology, and information. Outputs are the goods and services a company produces. Figure 1-2 shows this **transformation process**. At a factory the transformation is the physical change of raw materials into products, such as transforming leather and rubber into sneakers, denim into jeans, or plastic into toys. At an airline it is the efficient movement of passengers and their luggage from one location to an-

▶ **Role of operations management**
To transform organizational inputs into outputs.

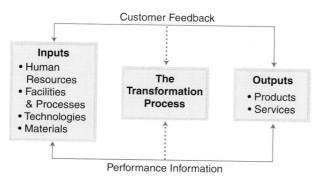

Figure 1-2

The transformation process

other. At a hospital it is organizing resources such as doctors, medical procedures, and medications to transform sick people into healthy ones.

Operations management is responsible for orchestrating all the resources needed to produce the final product. This includes designing the product; deciding what resources are needed; arranging schedules, equipment, and facilities; managing inventory; controlling quality; designing the jobs to make the product; and designing work methods. Basically, operations management is responsible for all aspects of the process of transforming inputs into outputs. As shown in Figure 1-2, this transformation process is always changing in order to adapt to changes in the environment, particularly in response to customer feedback.

LINKS TO PRACTICE
The E-tailers
www.Amazon.com

The Web-based age has created a highly competitive world of on-line shopping that poses special challenges for operations management. The Web can be used for on-line purchasing of everything from CDs, books, and groceries, to prescription medications and automobiles. While the Internet has given consumers flexibility, it has also created one of the biggest challenges for companies: delivering exactly what the customer ordered at the time promised. Ensuring that orders are delivered from "mouse to house" is the job of operations and is much more complicated than might seem. Companies must forecast what customers want and maintain adequate inventories of products, manage distribution centers and warehouses, operate fleets of trucks, and schedule deliveries, while keeping costs low and customers happy. Many companies like Amazon.com manage almost all aspects of their operation. Other e-tailers hire outside firms for certain functions, such as using couriers like Kozmo and Urbanfetch for deliveries. Competition among e-tailers has become intense as customers demand increasingly shorter delivery times. Same-day service has become common in metropolitan areas. Barnesandnoble.com provides same-day delivery in Manhattan, Los Angeles, and San Francisco, and couriers such as Urbanfetch offer one-hour delivery. Understanding and managing the operations function of an online business has become essential in order to remain competitive.

▶ **Value added**
The amount of value added to inputs to create the final value of a product.

For operations management to be successful, it must add value during the transformation process. We use the term **value added** to describe the difference between the final value of a product and the value of all the inputs. The greater the value added, the more productive a business is. An obvious way to add value is to reduce the cost of activities in the transformation process. Activities that do not add value are considered a waste; these includes certain jobs, equipment, and processes. An important function of operations is to analyze all activities, eliminate those that do not add value, and restructure processes and jobs to achieve greater efficiency. Today's business environment is more competitive than ever, and the role of operations management has become the focal point of efforts to increase competitiveness by improving efficiency.

■ DIFFERENCES BETWEEN MANUFACTURING AND SERVICE ORGANIZATIONS

Organizations can be divided into two broad categories: **manufacturing organizations** and **service organizations.** There are two primary distinctions between these categories. First, manufacturing organizations produce a physical, tangible product that can be stored in inventory before it is needed. By contrast, service organizations produce an intangible product that cannot be produced ahead of time. Second, in manufacturing operations most customers have no direct contact with the operation. Customer contact is made through distributors and retailers. For example, a customer buying a car at a car dealership never comes into contact with the automobile factory. However, in service organizations the customers are typically present during the creation of the service. Hospitals, colleges, theaters, and barber shops are examples of service organizations in which the customer is present during the creation of the service.

The differences between manufacturing and service organizations are not as clear-cut as they might appear, and there is much overlap between them. Most manufacturers provide services as part of their offering, and many service firms manufacture physical products that they deliver to their customers or consume during service delivery. For example, a manufacturer of furniture may also provide shipment of goods and assembly of furniture. On the other hand, a barber shop may sell its own line of hair care products. The differences between manufacturing and services are shown in Figure 1-3, which focuses on the dimensions of product tangibility and degree of customer contact. Pure manufacturing and pure service extremes are shown, as well as the overlap between them.

Even in pure service companies some segments of the operation may have low customer contact while others have high customer contact. The former can be thought of as "back room" or "behind the scenes" segments. Think of a fast-food operation such as Wendy's, for which customer service and customer contact are important parts of the business. However, the kitchen segment of Wendy's operation has no direct customer contact and can be managed like a manufacturing operation. Similarly, a hospital is a high-contact service operation, but the patient is not present in certain segments, such as the lab where specimen analysis is done.

In addition to pure manufacturing and pure service, there are companies that have some characteristics of each type of organization. For these companies it is hard

▶ **Manufacturing organizations**
Organizations that primarily produce a tangible product and typically have low customer contact.

▶ **Service organizations**
Organizations that primarily produce an intangible product, such as ideas, assistance, or information, and typically have high customer contact.

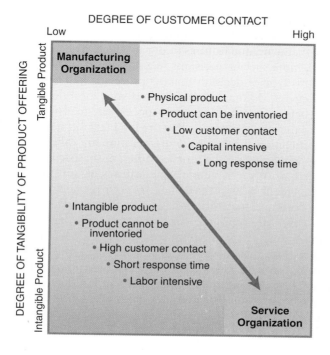

Figure 1-3

Characteristics of manufacturing and service organizations

to tell whether they are actually manufacturing or service organizations. Think of a post office, an automated warehouse, or a mail order catalog business. These companies have low customer contact and are capital intensive, yet they provide a service. We call these companies *quasi-manufacturing organizations.*

LINKS TO PRACTICE
US Postal Service
www.usps.com

The US Postal Service is an example of a quasi-manufacturing type of company. It provides a service: speedy, reliable delivery of letters, documents and packages. Its output is intangible and cannot be stored in inventory. Yet most operations management decisions made at the Postal Service are similar to those that occur in manufacturing. Customer contact is low, and at any one time there is a large amount of inventory. The Postal Service is capital intensive, having its own fleet of trucks and relying on scanners to sort packages and track customer orders. Scheduling enough workers at peak processing times is a major concern, as is planning delivery schedules. Note that although the output of the US Postal Service is a service, inputs include labor, technology, and equipment. The responsibility of OM is to manage the conversion of these inputs into the desired outputs. Proper management of the OM function is critical to the success of the US Postal Service.

■ OPERATIONS MANAGEMENT DECISIONS

In this section we look at some of the specific decisions operations managers have to make. The best way to do this is to think about decisions we would need to make if we started our own company—say, a company called Gourmet Wafers that produces praline–pecan cookies from an old family recipe. Think about the decisions that would have to be made to go from the initial idea to actual production of the product—that is operations management. Table 1-1 breaks these down into the generic decisions that would be appropriate for almost any product or service, the specific decisions required for our example, and the formal terms for these decisions that are used in operations management.

Note in the Gourmet Wafers example that the first decisions made were very broad in scope (e.g., the unique features of our product). We needed to do this before we could focus on more specific decisions (e.g., worker schedules). Although our example is simple, this type of decision-making process is followed by every company, including IBM, General Motors, Lands' End, and your local floral shop. Also note in our example that before we can think about specific day-to-day decisions, we need to make decisions for the whole company that are long term in nature. Long-term decisions that set the direction for the entire organization are called **strategic decisions**. They are broad in scope and set the tone for other, more specific decisions. They address questions such as: What are the unique features of our product? What market do we plan to compete in? What is the demand for our product?

▶ **Strategic decisions**
Decisions that set the direction for the entire company; they are broad in scope and long term in nature.

▶ **Tactical decisions**
Decisions that are specific and short term in nature and are bound by strategic decisions.

Short-term decisions that focus on specific departments and tasks are called **tactical decisions**. Tactical decisions focus on more specific day-to-day issues, such as the quantities and timing of specific resources. Strategic decisions are made first and determine the direction of tactical decisions, which are made more frequently and routinely. Therefore, we have to start with strategic decisions and then move on to tactical decisions. This relationship is shown in Figure 1-4. Tactical decisions must be aligned with strategic decisions, because they are the key to the company's effectiveness in the long run. Tactical decisions provide feedback to strategic decisions, which can be modified accordingly.

Table 1-1 Operations Management Decisions for Gourmet Wafers

General Decisions To Be Made	Decisions Specific for Cookie Production	Operations Management Term
What are the unique features of the business that will make it competitive?	The business offers freshly baked cookies "home-made" style, in a fast-food format.	Operations strategy
What are the unique features of the product?	The unique feature of the cookies is that they are loaded with extra-large and crunchy pecans, and are fresh and moist.	Product design
What are the unique features of the process that give the product its unique characteristics?	A special convection oven is used to make the cookies in order to keep them fresh and moist. The dough is allowed to rise longer than usual to make the cookies extra light.	Process selection
What sources of supply should we use to ensure regular and timely receipt of the exact materials we need? How do we manage these sources of supply?	The key ingredients, pecans and syrup, will be purchased from only one supplier located in South Carolina because it offers the best products. A relationship is worked out in which the supplier sends the ingredients on the exact schedule that they are needed.	Supply chain management
How will managers ensure the quality of the product, measure quality, and identify quality problems?	A quality check is made at each stage of cookie production. The dough is checked for texture; the pecans are checked for size and freshness; the syrup is checked for consistency.	Quality management
What is the expected demand for the product?	Expected sales for each day of the week have been determined; for example, it is expected that more cookies will be sold during the weekday and most during the lunch hour. Expected cookie sales for each month and for the year have also been determined.	Forecasting
Where will the facility be located?	After looking at locations of customers and location costs, it is decided that the facility will be located in a shopping mall.	Location analysis
How large should the facility be?	The business needs to be able to produce 200 cookies per hour, or up to 2000 cookies per day.	Capacity planning
How should the facility be laid out? Where should the kitchen and ovens be located? Should there be seating for customers?	Decisions are made about where the kitchen will be located and how the working area will be arranged for maximum efficiency. The business is competing on the basis of speed and quality; therefore, the facility should be arranged to promote these features. There will be a small seating area for customers and a large counter and display case for buying.	Facility layout
What jobs will be needed in the facility, who should do what task, and how will their performance be measured?	Two people will be needed in the kitchen during busy periods and one during slow periods. Their job duties are determined. One person will be needed for ordertaking at all times.	Job design and work measurement
How will the inventory of raw materials be monitored? When will orders be placed and how much will be kept in stock?	A different policy is developed for common ingredients, such as flour and sugar. These ingredients will be ordered every two weeks for a two-week supply. A special purchasing arrangement is worked out with the supplier of specialty ingredients.	Inventory management
Who will work on what schedule?	Two people will work the counter in split shifts. One kitchen employee will work a full shift, with a second employee working part time.	Scheduling

Figure 1-4

The relationship between strategic and tactical decisions

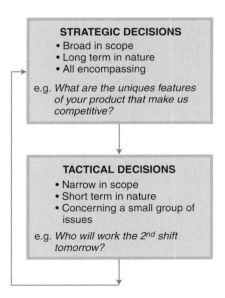

STRATEGIC DECISIONS
- Broad in scope
- Long term in nature
- All encompassing

e.g. *What are the uniques features of your product that make us competitive?*

TACTICAL DECISIONS
- Narrow in scope
- Short term in nature
- Concerning a small group of issues

e.g. *Who will work the 2nd shift tomorrow?*

You can see in the example of Gourmet Wafers how important OM decisions are. OM decisions are critical to all types of companies, large and small. In large companies these decisions are more complex because of the size and scope of the organization. Large companies typically produce a greater variety of products, have multiple location sites, and often use domestic and international suppliers. Managing OM decisions and coordinating efforts can be a complicated task, yet the OM function is critical to the company's success.

LINKS TO PRACTICE
Texas Instruments Incorporated
www.ti.com

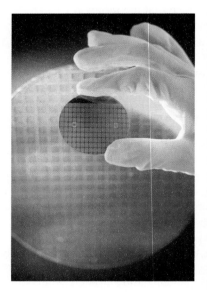

We can illustrate this point by looking at operations management decisions made by Texas Instruments (TI) in order to position itself for global collaboration with customers, distributors, and suppliers. TI found its business growing exponentially, with more than 120,000 monthly orders received and processed electronically. The coordination effort included 56 factories, including subcontractors, and the management of over 45,000 products. To succeed, the company needed to develop a system to generate better forecasts, coordinate manufacturing of products, manage orders, and track deliveries. Managing and coordinating global operations management functions was considered paramount to the company's success. TI adopted a comprehensive software package called enterprise resource planning (ERP) that integrates information throughout the organization, manages forecasts, and coordinates factory operations. Designing and implementing the ERP system at TI required an understanding of all the strategic and tactical operations decisions; otherwise the system would not be effective. The system has proved to be a success, and TI considers it a major achievement to be able to consistently manage factory operations across the globe.

Before You Go On

You should understand that operations management (OM) is the business function responsible for planning, coordinating, and controlling the resources needed to produce a company's products and services. OM is directly responsible for managing the transformation of a company's inputs (e.g., materials, technology, and information) into finished products and services. OM requires a wide range of strategic and tactical decisions. Strategic decisions are long range and very broad in scope (e.g., unique features of the company's product and process). They determine the direction of tactical decisions, which are more short term and narrow in scope (e.g., policy for ordering raw materials). All organizations can be separated into manufacturing and service operations, which differ based on product tangibility and degree of customer contact. Service and manufacturing organizations have very different operational requirements.

PLAN OF THIS BOOK ■

The purpose of this book is to provide concepts and techniques that give you the ability to efficiently plan, order, and control the resources needed to produce a company's products and services. The topics progress from strategic to tactical, similar to the order of decisions used in the Gourmet Wafers example. The plan of this book is shown in Figure 1-5. We begin with broad, overarching issues such as product design and process selection. Also early in the book we cover operations topics that require a strategic perspective and a cultural change within the organization, such as supply chain management, total quality management, and just-in-time systems. Progressively we move to more tactical issues, such as work measurement, inventory management, and scheduling concerns.

We have designed the chapters to provide relevant operations management concepts and techniques that are important to business professionals regardless of field of study. Throughout the chapters we show how the discussed tools and concepts relate to other functions in the organization. We show that operations management concepts are far reaching, affecting every aspect of the organization.

HISTORICAL DEVELOPMENT ■

When we think of what operations management does—namely, managing the transformation of inputs into goods and services—we can see that as a function it is as old as time. Think of any great organizational effort, such as organizing the first Olympic

Type of Decision	Operations Management Topic	Chapter
Strategic	Operations Strategy	Ch. 2
↑	Product Design and Process Selection	Ch. 3
	Supply Chain Management	Ch. 4
	Quality Management	Ch. 5 and 6
	Just-in-Time Systems	Ch. 7
	Forecasting	Ch. 8
	Capacity Planning and Location Analysis	Ch. 9
	Facility Layout	Ch. 10
	Work Measurement	Ch. 11
	Inventory Issues	Ch. 12, 13, 14, and 15
Tactical	Scheduling Issues	Ch. 16 and 17

Figure 1-5

Plan of the book

Table 1–2 Historical Development of Operations Management

Concept	Time	Explanation
Industrial Revolution	Late 1700s	Brought in innovations that changed production by using machine power instead of human power.
Scientific management	Early 1900s	Brought concepts of analysis and measurement of the technical aspects of work design, and development of moving assembly lines and mass production.
Human relations movement	1930s to 1960s	Focused on understanding human elements of job design, such as worker motivation and job satisfaction.
Management science	Mid-1900s	Focused on the development of quantitative techniques to solve operations problems.
Computer age	1970s	Enabled processing of large amounts of data and allowed widespread use of quantitative procedures.
Just-in-time systems (JIT)	1980s	Designed to achieve high-volume production with minimal inventories.
Total quality management (TQM)	1980s	Sought to eliminate causes of production defects.
Reengineering	1980s	Required redesigning a company's processes in order to provide greater efficiency and cost reduction.
Flexibility	1990s	Offered customization on a mass scale.
Time-based competition	1990s	Based on time, such as speed of delivery.
Supply chain management	1990s	Focused on reducing the overall cost of the system that manages the flow of materials from suppliers to final customers.
Global competition	1990s	Designed operations to compete in the global market.
Environmental issues	1990s	Considered waste reduction, the need for recycling, and product reuse.
Electronic commerce	Late 1990s; early twenty-first century	Used the Internet for conducting business activity.

games, building the Great Wall of China, or erecting the Egyptian pyramids, and you will see operations management at work. Of course, back then, this function did not have a name. Operations management did not emerge as a formal field of study until the late 1950s and early 1960s, when scholars began to recognize that all production systems face a common set of problems and stressed the systems approach to viewing operations processes.

Many events helped shape operations management. We will describe some of the most significant of these historical milestones and explain their influence on the development of operations management. Later we will look at some current trends in operations management. These historical milestones and current trends are summarized in Table 1-2.

The Industrial Revolution

▶ **Industrial Revolution**
An industry movement that changed production by substituting machine power for labor power.

The **Industrial Revolution** had a significant impact on the way goods are produced today. Prior to this movement, products were made by hand by skilled craftspeople in their shops or homes. Each product was unique, painstakingly made by one person. The Industrial Revolution changed all that. It started in the 1770s with the development of a number of inventions that relied on machine power instead of human

Today's modern work environment

Steamboat and railroad forging during the Industrial Revolution

power. The most important of these was the steam engine, which was invented by James Watt in 1764. The steam engine provided a new source of power that was used to replace human labor in textile mills, machine-making plants, and other facilities. The concept of the factory was emerging.

About the same time, the concept of *division of labor* was introduced. First described by Adam Smith in 1776 in *The Wealth of Nations*, this important concept would become one of the building blocks of the assembly line. Division of labor means that the production of a product is broken down into a series of small, elemental tasks, each of which is performed by a different worker. The repetition of the task allows the worker to become highly specialized in that task.

A few years later, in 1790, Eli Whitney introduced the concept of *interchangeable parts*. Prior to that time, every part used in a production process was unique. With interchangeable parts, parts are standardized so that every item in a batch of items fits equally. This concept meant that we could move from one-at-a-time production to volume production, for example, in the manufacture of watches, clocks, and similar items.

Scientific Management

Scientific management was an approach to management created by Frederick W. Taylor at the turn of the century. Taylor was an engineer with an eye for efficiency. Through scientific management he sought to increase worker productivity and organizational output. This concept had two key features. First, it was assumed that workers are motivated only by money and are limited only by their physical ability. Taylor believed that worker productivity was governed by scientific laws, and that it was up to management to discover these laws through measurement, analysis, and observation. Workers were to be paid in direct proportion to how much they produced. The second feature of this approach was separation of the planning and doing functions in a company, which means the separation of management and labor. Management was responsible for designing productive systems and determining acceptable worker output. Workers had no input into this process—they were permitted only to work.

Many people did not like the scientific management approach. This was especially true of workers, who thought that management used these methods to unfairly increase output without paying them accordingly. Still, many companies adopted the scientific management approach. Today many see scientific management as a major milestone in the field of operations management. Scientific management has had many influences on operations management. For example, *piece rate incentives*, in

▶ **Scientific management**
An approach to management that focused on improving output by redesigning jobs and determining acceptable levels of worker output.

which workers are paid in direct proportion to their output, came out of this movement. Also, a widely used method of work measurement, *stopwatch time studies*, was introduced by Frederick Taylor. In stopwatch time studies, observations are made and recorded of a worker performing a task over many cycles. This information is then used to set a time standard for performing the particular task. This method is still used today to set a time standard for short, repetitive tasks.

The scientific management approach was popularized by Henry Ford, who used the techniques in his factories. Combining technology with scientific management, Ford introduced the *moving assembly line* to produce Ford cars. Ford also combined scientific management concepts with division of labor and interchangeable parts to develop the concept of *mass production*. These concepts and innovations helped him increase production at his factories.

The Human Relations Movement

▶ **Hawthorne studies**
The studies responsible for creating the human relations movement, which focused on giving more consideration to workers' needs.

The early twentieth century was dominated by the scientific management movement and its philosophy. However, this changed with the publication of the results of the **Hawthorne studies**. The Hawthorne studies were conducted at a Western Electric plant in Hawthorne, Illinois, in the 1930s. The purpose was to study the effects of environmental changes, such as changes in lighting and room temperature, on the productivity of assembly line workers. The findings from the study were unexpected; the productivity of the workers continued to increase regardless of the environmental changes made. Elton Mayo, a sociologist from Harvard, analyzed the results and concluded that the workers were actually motivated by the attention they were given. The idea of workers responding to the attention they are given came to be known as the *Hawthorne effect*.

Many sociologists and psychologists went to Hawthorne to study these findings, which led to the **human relations movement**, an entirely new philosophy based on the recognition that factors other than money can contribute to worker productivity. The impact of these findings on development of operations management has been tremendous. The influence of this new philosophy can be seen in the implementation of a number of concepts that motivate workers by making their jobs more interesting and meaningful. For example, the Hawthorne studies showed that scientific management had made jobs too repetitive and boring. *Job enlargement* is an approach in which workers are given a larger portion of the total task to do. Another approach used to give more meaning to jobs is *job enrichment*, in which workers are given a greater role in planning.

Management Science

▶ **Management science**
A field of study that focuses on the development of quantitative techniques to solve operations problems.

While one movement was focusing on the technical aspects of job design and another on the human aspects, a movement called **management science** was developing that would make its own unique contribution to operations management. Management science focused on developing quantitative techniques for solving operations problems. The first mathematical model for inventory management was developed by F. W. Harris in 1915. Shortly thereafter, procedures were developed for statistical sampling theory and quality control.

World War II created an even greater need for the ability to quantitatively solve complex problems of logistics control, weapons system design, and deployment of missiles. Consequently, management science grew during the war and continued to grow after the war was over. Many quantitative tools were developed to solve problems in forecasting, inventory control, project management, and other areas. Management science is a mathematically oriented field that provides operations management with tools that can be used to assist in decision making. A popular example of such a tool is linear programming.

The Computer Age

The 1970s witnessed the advent of widespread use of computers in business. With computers, many of the quantitative models developed by management science could be used on a larger scale. Data processing was made easier, with important effects in areas such as forecasting, scheduling, and inventory management. A particularly important computerized system, material requirements planning (MRP), was developed for inventory control and scheduling. Material requirements planning was able to process huge amounts of data to compute inventory requirements and develop schedules for the production of thousands of items. This type of processing was impossible before the age of computers.

Just-in-Time

Just-in-time (JIT) is a major operations management philosophy, developed in Japan in the 1980s, that is designed to achieve high-volume production using minimal amounts of inventory. This is achieved through coordination of the flow of materials so that the right parts arrive at the right place in the right quantity; hence the term, *just-in-time*. However, JIT is much more than the coordinated movement of goods. It is an all-encompassing organizational philosophy that employs teams of workers to achieve continuous improvement in processes and organizational efficiency by eliminating all organizational waste. Although JIT was first used in manufacturing, it has seen use in the service sector—for example, in the food service industry. JIT has had a profound impact on changing the way companies manage their operations. It is credited with helping turn many companies around and is used in companies including Honda, Toyota, and General Motors. JIT promises to continue to transform businesses in the future.

> ▶ **Just-in-time**
> A philosophy designed to achieve high-volume production through elimination of waste and continuous improvement.

Total Quality Management

As customers demand ever higher quality in their products and services, companies have been forced to focus on improving quality in order to remain competitive. **Total quality management (TQM)** is a philosophy that aggressively seeks to improve product quality by eliminating causes of product defects and making quality an all-encompassing organizational philosophy. With TQM everyone in the company is responsible for quality. TQM was practiced by some companies in the 1980s, and has become pervasive in the 1990s with the help of "quality gurus" like W. Edwards Deming. This is an area of operations management that no competitive company has been able to ignore. The importance of this movement is demonstrated by the number of companies joining the ranks of those achieving ISO 9000 certification. ISO 9000 is a set of quality standards developed for global manufacturers by the International Organization for Standardization. Today many companies require their suppliers to meet these standards as a condition for obtaining contracts.

> ▶ **Total quality management**
> A philosophy that seeks to improve quality by eliminating causes or product defects and making quality the responsibility of everyone in the organization.

Business Process Reengineering

Business process reengineering means redesigning a company's processes to increase efficiency, improve quality, and reduce costs. In many companies things are done in a certain way that has been passed down over the years. Often managers say, "Well, we've always done it this way." Reengineering requires asking why things are done in a

> ▶ **Reengineering**
> Redesigning a company's processes to make them more efficient.

certain way, questioning assumptions, and then redesigning the processes. Operations management is a key player in a company's reengineering efforts.

Flexibility

▶ **Flexibility**
An organizational strategy in which the company attempts to offer a greater variety of product choices on a mass scale.

Traditionally companies competed by either mass-producing a standardized product or offering customized products in small volumes. One of the current competitive challenges for companies is the need to offer a greater variety of product choices to customers of a traditionally standardized product. This is the challenge of **flexibility**, which basically means being able to offer customization on a mass scale. For example, Procter and Gamble offers 13 different product designs in the Pampers line of diapers. Although diapers are a standardized product, the product designs are customized to the different needs of customers, such as the age, sex, and development of the child using the diaper.

Time-Based Competition

▶ **Time-based competition**
An organizational strategy focusing on efforts to develop new products and deliver them to customers *faster* than competitors.

One of the most important trends in companies today is **competition based on time**. This includes developing new products and services faster than the competition, reaching the market first, and meeting customer orders most quickly. For example, two companies may produce the same product, but if one is able to deliver it to the customer in two days whereas the other delivers it in five days, the first company will make the sale and win over the customer.

Supply Chain Management

▶ **Supply chain management**
Management of the flow of materials from suppliers to customers in order to reduce overall cost and increase responsiveness to customers.

Supply chain management involves managing the flow of materials from suppliers and buyers of raw materials all the way to the final customer. The objective is to have everyone in the chain work together to reduce overall cost and improve quality and service delivery. Supply chain management requires a team approach, with functions such as marketing, purchasing, operations, and engineering all working together. This approach has been shown to result in more satisfied customers, and everyone in the chain profits.

Global Marketplace

▶ **Global marketplace**
A trend in business focusing on customers, suppliers, and competitors from a global perspective.

Today businesses must think in terms of a global marketplace in order to compete effectively. This includes the way they view their customers, competitors, and suppliers. Key issues are meeting customer needs and getting the right product to markets as diverse as the Far East, Europe, or Africa. Operations management is responsible for most of these decisions. OM decides whether to tailor products to different customer needs, where to locate facilities, how to manage suppliers, and how to meet local government standards. Also, global competition has forced companies to reach higher levels of excellence in the products and services they offer. Regional trading agreements, such as the North American Free Trade Agreement (NAFTA), the European Union (EU), and the General Agreement on Tariffs and Trade (GATT), guarantee continued competition on the global level.

Environmental Issues

There is increasing emphasis on the need to reduce waste, recycle, and reuse products and parts. Society has placed great pressure on business to focus on air and water quality, waste disposal, global warming, and other **environmental issues**. Operations management plays a key role in redesigning processes and products in order to meet and exceed environmental quality standards. The importance of this issue is demonstrated by a set of standards termed ISO 14000. Developed by the International Organization for Standardization (ISO), these standards provide guidelines and a certification program documenting a company's environmentally responsible actions.

▶ **Environmental issues**
A trend in business to consciously reduce waste, recycle, and reuse products and parts.

Electronic Commerce

Electronic commerce is the use of the Internet for conducting business activities, such as communication, business transactions, and data transfer. The Internet developed from a government network called ARPANET, which was created in 1969 by the U.S. Defense Department. Since the late 1990s the Internet has become an essential business medium, enabling efficient communication between manufacturers, suppliers, distributors, and customers. Use of the Internet continues to change the way business functions, including operations management, are performed.

CURRENT TRENDS ◼

Operations management has changed over time and continues to change as we learn more about performing tasks more efficiently. The advent of computers in the 1970s accelerated this development. Today the Internet and World Wide Web promise to further accelerate this development. Certain concepts that were widely accepted as recently as 20 years ago are considered obsolete today. For example, we used to believe that extra quality measures meant higher costs. Today we know that improving quality leads to lower costs, because we have less scrap, less rework, and more satisfied customers. Operations management is changing rapidly as organizations are under ever increasing pressure to be more competitive.

Today's global and Internet-based business environment poses special challenges for operations management, including complexities of managing on-line operations, and global supplier and distribution networks. As customers increasingly expect greater product choices, operations must develop ways for effective mass customization and delivery of a larger variety of products to a global customer base. Capabilities of information technologies such as broadband and wireless are rapidly increasing. New opportunities and challenges arise daily for the operations function in managing all its resources to achieve the firm's competitiveness.

OPERATIONS MANAGEMENT IN PRACTICE ◼

Of all the business functions, operations is the most diverse in terms of the tasks performed. If you think about all the issues involved in managing a transformation process, you can see that operations managers are never bored. Let's look at who operations managers are and what they do.

The head of the operations function in a company usually holds the title of vice president of operations or vice president of manufacturing, and generally reports directly to the president or chief operating officer. Below the vice president level are midlevel managers: manufacturing manager, operations manager, quality control manager, plant manager, and others. Below these managers are a variety of entry-level positions such as quality specialist, production analyst, inventory analyst, and production supervisor. These people perform a variety of functions, such as analyzing production problems, developing forecasts, making plans for new products, measuring quality, monitoring inventory, and developing employee schedules. Thus, starting with entry-level positions and moving up to the top levels of operations, there are many job opportunities in operations management. In addition, operations jobs tend to offer high salaries, interesting work, and excellent opportunities for advancement.

As you can see, all business functions need information from operations management in order to perform their tasks. At the same time, operations managers are highly dependent on input from other areas. This process of information sharing is dynamic, requiring that managers work in teams and understand each other's roles.

OM ACROSS THE ORGANIZATION

Now that we know the role of the operations management function and the decisions operations managers make, let's look at the relationship between operations with other business functions. As mentioned earlier, most businesses are supported by three main functions: operations, marketing, and finance. Although these functions involve different activities, they must interact to achieve the goals of the organization. They must also follow the strategic direction developed at the top level of the organization. Figure 1-6 shows the flow of information from the top to each business function, as well as the flow between functions.

Many of the decisions made by operations managers are dependent on information from the other functions. At the same time, other functions cannot be carried out properly without information from operations. Figure 1-7 shows these relationships.

Marketing is not fully capable of meeting customer needs if marketing managers do not understand what operations can produce, what due dates it can and cannot meet, and what types of customization operations can deliver. The marketing department can develop an exciting marketing campaign, but if operations cannot produce the desired product, sales will not be made. In turn, operations managers need information about customer wants and expectations. It is up to them to design products with characteristics that customers find desirable, and they cannot do this without regular coordination with the marketing department.

Finance cannot realistically judge the need for capital investments, make-or-buy decisions, plant expansions, or relocation if finance managers do not understand operations concepts and needs. On the

Figure 1-6

Organizational chart showing flow of information

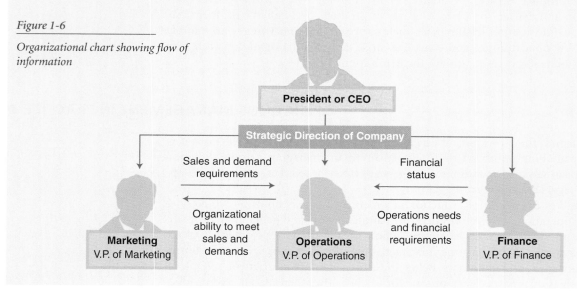

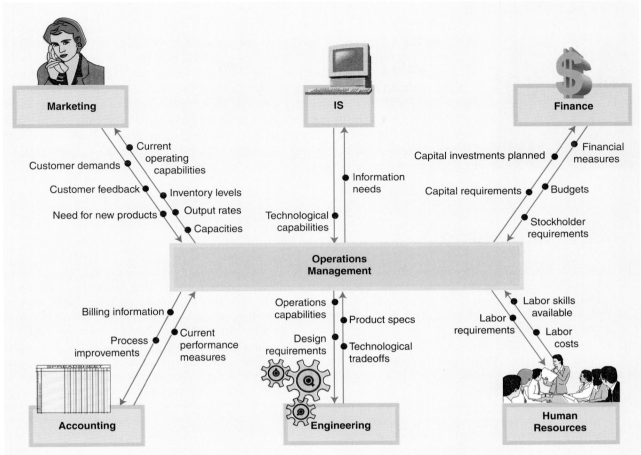

Figure 1-7

Information flow between operations and other business functions.

other hand, operations managers cannot make large financial expenditures without understanding financial constraints and methods of evaluating financial investments. It is essential for these two functions to work together and understand each other's constraints.

Information systems (IS) is a function that enables information to flow throughout the organization and allows OM to operate effectively. OM is highly dependent on information such as forecasts of demand, quality levels being achieved, inventory levels, supplier deliveries, and worker schedules. IS must understand the needs of OM in order to design an adequate information system. Usually, IS and OM work together to design an information network. This close relationship needs to be ongoing. IS must

be capable of accommodating the needs of OM as they change in response to market demands. At the same time, it is up to IS to bring the latest capabilities in information technology to the organization to enhance the functioning of OM.

Human resource managers must understand job requirements and worker skills if they are to hire the right people for available jobs. To manage employees effectively, operations managers need to understand job market trends, hiring and layoff costs, and training costs.

Accounting needs to consider inventory management, capacity information, and labor standards in order to develop accurate cost data. In turn, operations managers must communicate billing information and process improvements to accounting.

■ OM IS EVERYWHERE

When we think about what operations management is, we realize that this function is applicable not only to a business but to everyday life. Any time we organize resources we are using operations techniques. The "product" we are creating may be organizing a party, studying for final exams, planning a vacation, organizing a weekend schedule packed with activities, or planning a trip to the supermarket. The tools of operations management can help us perform even ordinary tasks more efficiently. As you proceed through this course you will see that operations management is not found only in big corporations. It also occurs in small offices, pizza shops, the local gym, hair salons, grocery stores, and many other areas of everyday life.

CHAPTER HIGHLIGHTS

1 Operations management is the business function that is responsible for managing and coordinating the resources needed to produce a company's products and services. Without operations management there would be no products or services to sell.

2 The role of operations management is to transform organizational inputs—human resources, facilities, materials, technology, and information—into a company's finished products or services.

3 Operations management is responsible for a wide range of decisions. They range from strategic decisions, such as designing the unique features of a product and process, to tactical decisions, such as planning worker schedules.

4 Organizations can be divided into manufacturing and service operations, which differ in the tangibility of the product and the degree of customer contact. Manufacturing and service operations have very different operational requirements.

5 A number of historical milestones have shaped operations management into what it is today. Some of the more significant of these are the Industrial Revolution, scientific management, the human relations movement, management science, and the computer age.

6 OM is a highly important function in today's dynamic business environment. Among the trends that have had a significant impact on business are just-in-time, total quality management, reengineering, flexibility, time-based competition, supply chain management, a global marketplace, and environmental issues.

7 Operations managers need to work closely with all other business functions in a team format. Marketing needs to provide information about customer expectations. Finance needs to provide information about budget constraints. In turn, OM must communicate its needs and capabilities to the other functions.

KEY TERMS

operations management (OM) 2
transformation process 3
value added 4
manufacturing organizations 5
service organizations 5
strategic decisions 6
tactical decisions 6

industrial revolution 10
scientific management 11
human relations movement 11
management science 12
just-in-time systems (JIT) 13
total quality management (TQM) 13
reengineering 13

flexibility 14
time-based competition 14
supply chain management 14
global marketplace 14
environmental issues 15

DISCUSSION QUESTIONS

1. Define the term *operations management*.
2. Explain the decisions operations managers make and give three examples.
3. Describe the transformation process of a business. Give two examples.
4. What are the three major business functions, and how are they related to one another?
5. What are the differences between strategic and tactical decisions, and how are they related to each other?

6. Identify the two major differences between service and manufacturing organizations.
7. What are the three historical milestones in operations management? How have they influenced management?
8. Identify three current trends in operations management and describe them.
9. Define the terms total quality management, just-in-time, and reengineering.

CASE: *Hightone Electronics, Inc.*

George Gonzales, Operations Director of Hightone Electronics, Inc., sat quietly at the conference table overlooking the lobby of the corporate headquarters office in Palo Alto, California. He reflected on the board meeting that had just adjourned, and the challenge that lay ahead for him. The Board had just announced their decision to start an Internet based division of HEI. Web based purchasing in the electronics industry had been growing rapidly. The Board felt that HEI needed to offer on-line purchasing to their customers in order to maintain its competitive position. The Board looked to George to outline the key operations management decisions that needed to be addressed in creating a successful Internet based business. The next board meeting was just a week away. He had his work cut out for him.

Hightone Electronics Inc. was founded in Palo Alto, California over fifty years ago. Originally, the company provided radio components to small repair shops. Products were offered for sale through a catalogue that was mailed to prospective customers every four months. The company built its reputation on high quality and service. As time passed, HEI began supplying more than just radio parts, adding items such as fuses, transformers, computers, and electrical testing equipment. The expansion of the product line had been coupled with an increase in the number and type of customers the company served. While the traditional repair shops still remained a part of the company's market, technical schools, universities, and well known corporations in the Silicon Valley were added to the list of customers.

Today HEI operates the Palo Alto facility with the same dedication to supplying quality products through catalogue sales that it had when it was first founded. Customer service remains the top priority. HEI stocks and sells over 22,000 different items. Most customers receive their orders within 48 hours of placing an order, and all components are warranted for a full year.

Expanding HEI to include web based purchasing seemed to be a natural extension of catalogue sales that the company already does successfully. Charles Gonzales agreed that the company has no choice but to move in this competitive direction. However, Charles did not agree with the opinion of the Board that this would be "business as usual." He believed that there were many operations decisions that needed to be identified and addressed. As he stated in the meeting, "Having a slick web site is one thing, but making sure the right product is delivered to the right location is another. Operations is the key to making this happen." His challenge for the next board meeting was to identify the key operations decision and persuade the Board that these issues needed serious consideration.

Case Questions:

1. Explain why operations management is critical to the success of a business. Why would developing of an Internet based business require different operations considerations for HEI? Is Charles Gonzales correct in his assessment that this would not be "business as usual"?

2. Recall that HEI wishes to continue its reputation of high quality and service. Identify key operations management decisions that need to be considered. How different will these decisions be for the Internet business?

INTERACTIVE LEARNING

Enhance and test your knowledge of Chapter 1 using the interactive CD.

1. Video *Amazon.com*

   Visit our dynamic Web site, www.wiley.com/college/reid, for more cases, web links, and additional information.

2. **Additional Web Resources**
   APICS, www.apics.org
   http://www.superfactory.com/Resources/tours.htm
   Council of Logistics Management, www.clm1.org

3. **INTERNET CHALLENGE** *Demonstrating Your Knowledge of OM*

Visit the Web sites of at least one service and one manufacturing company. For each company, identify at least five characteristic OM decisions and show your results in a table. Which decisions are strategic and which are tactical? How do these decisions differ between the two companies?

Web sites to consider:
  www.sprint.com (Sprint Corporation)
  www.logisticspro.com (Logistics Pro)
  www.yellowcorp.com (Yellow Corporation)
  www.milliken.com (Milliken & Company)
  www.kmart.com (Kmart Corporation)

BIBLIOGRAPHY

Beach, R, Muhlemann, A.P., Price, D.H.R., Paterson, A., and Sharp, J.A., "Manufacturing Operations and Strategic Flexibility: Survey and Cases," *International Journal of Operations and Production Management*, 20, 1, 2000, 7–30.

Berry, W.L. and Cooper, M.C., "Manufacturing Flexibility: Methods for Measuring the Impact of Product Variety on Performance in Process Industries," *Journal of Operations Management*, 17, 1999, 163–178.

Chase, R.B., Aquilano, N.J., and Jacobs, F.B., *Operations Management for a Competitive Advantage*, Ninth Edition, McGraw-Hill Irwin, 2001.

Dornier, P., Ernst, R., Fender, M., and Kouvelis, P., *Global Operations and Logistics*, John Wiley & Sons, 1998.

Klassen, R.D. and Whybark, D.C., "Environmental Management in Operations: The Selection of Environmental Technologies," *Decision Sciences*, 30, 3, 1999, 601–631.

Koste, L.L. and Malhotra, M.K., "Trade-offs Among the Elements of Flexibility: A Comparison from the Automotive Industry," *Omega*, 28, 2000, 693–710.

Skinner, W., *Manufacturing in the Corporate Strategy*, John Wiley & Sons, NY, 1978.

Skinner, W., "Manufacturing Strategy on the 'S' Curve," *Production and Operations Management*, Spring, 1996, 3–14.

Operations Strategy and Competitiveness

Before studying this chapter you should know or, if necessary review

1. The role of the OM function in organizations, Chapter 1, pp. 3–4.
2. Differences between strategic and tactical decisions, Chapter 1, pp. 6–8.

LEARNING OBJECTIVES

After studying this chapter you should be able to

1. Define the role of business strategy.
2. Explain how a business strategy is developed.
3. Explain the role of operations strategy in the organization.
4. Explain the relationship between business strategy and operations strategy.
5. Describe how an operations strategy is developed.
6. Identify competitive priorities of the operations function.
7. Define productivity and identify productivity measures.
8. Compute productivity measures.

CHAPTER OUTLINE

To maintain a competitive position in the marketplace, a company must have a long-range plan. This plan needs to include the company's long-term goals, an understanding of the marketplace, and a way to differentiate itself from its competitors. All other decisions made by the company must support this long-range plan. Otherwise, each person in the company would pursue goals that he or she considered important, and the company would quickly fall apart.

The functioning of a football team on the field is similar to the functioning of a business and provides a good example of the importance of a plan or vision. Before the plays are made, the team prepares a game strategy. Each player must perform a particular role on the team to support this strategy. The strategy is a "game plan" designed so that the team can win. Imagine what would occur if individual players decided to do plays that they thought were appropriate. Certainly the team's chance of winning would not be very high. A successful football team is a unified group of players using their individual skills in support of a winning strategy. The same is true of a business.

The long-range plan of a business is called the **business strategy.** The role of each of the individual business functions, such as operations, finance, and marketing, is to find ways to best support the business strategy. Just as the players on a football team support the team's strategy, the role of everyone in the company is to do his or her job in a way that supports the business strategy.

In today's highly competitive, Internet based, and global marketplace, it is more important than ever for companies to have a clear plan for achieving their goals. In this chapter we discuss the role of operations strategy, its relationship with the business strategy, and the ways in which the operations function can best support the business strategy. Because strategy is about competitiveness, we will also learn ways to measure the competitiveness of a business by measuring its productivity.

▶ **Business strategy**
A long-range plan or vision for a business.

■ THE ROLE OF OPERATIONS STRATEGY

▶ **Operations strategy**
A long-range plan for the operations function that specifies the design and use of resources to support the business strategy.

The role of **operations strategy** is to provide a plan for the operations function so that it can make the best use of its resources. Operations strategy specifies the policies and plans for using the organization's resources to support its long-term competitive strategy Figure 2-1 shows this relationship.

Remember that the operations function is responsible for managing the resources needed to produce the company's products or services. Operations strategy is the plan that specifies the design and use of these resources to support the business strategy. This includes the location, size, and type of facilities available; worker skills and talents required; use of technology, special processes needed, special equipment; and quality control methods. It is the role of operations strategy to provide an overall plan for the use of all these resources. The operations strategy must be aligned with

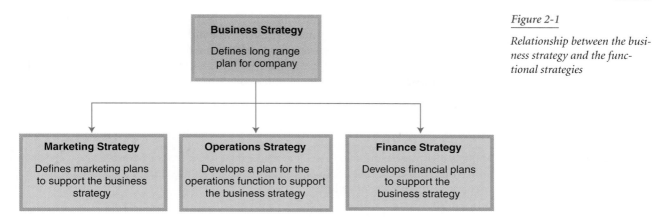

Figure 2-1

Relationship between the business strategy and the functional strategies

the company's business strategy and enable the company to achieve its long-term plan.

The Importance of Operations Strategy

Operations strategy did not come to the forefront until the 1970s. Up to that time U.S. companies emphasized mass production of standard product designs. There were no serious international competitors, and U.S. companies could pretty much sell anything they wanted to. However, that changed in the 1970s and 1980s. Japanese companies began offering products of superior quality at lower cost, and U.S. companies lost market share to their Japanese counterparts. In an attempt to survive, many U.S. companies copied Japanese approaches. Unfortunately, merely copying these approaches often proved unsuccessful; it took time to really understand Japanese approaches. It became clear that Japanese companies were more competitive because of their operations strategy; that is, all their resources were specifically designed to directly support the company's overall strategic plan.

Harvard Business School professor Michael Porter says that companies often do not understand the differences between *operational effectiveness* and *strategy*. Operational effectiveness is the ability to perform operations tasks more efficiently than competitors. Strategy, on the other hand, is a plan for competing in the marketplace. Running a race very efficiently is an example of operational effectiveness. However, it is not enough to be efficient. Strategy is defining what race you will run in. Without strategy, you could be running efficiently in the wrong race. Operational effectiveness and strategy must be aligned; otherwise you may be *very efficiently performing the wrong task*. The role of operations strategy is to make sure that all the tasks performed by the operations function are the *right tasks*.

Now that we know the meaning of *business strategy* and *operations strategy* and their importance, let's look at how a company would go about developing a business strategy. Then we will see how an operations strategy would be developed to support the company's business strategy.

DEVELOPING A BUSINESS STRATEGY ■

A company's business strategy is developed after its managers have considered many factors and made some strategic decisions. These include developing an understanding of what business the company is in (the company's *mission*), analyzing and developing an understanding of the market (*environmental scanning*), and identifying the company's strengths (*core competencies*). These three factors are critical to the development of the company's long-range plan, or business strategy. In this section, we describe each of these factors in detail and show how they are combined to formulate the business strategy.

Mission

The first decision a company needs to make is to identify its mission. Every organization, from IBM to the Boy Scouts, has a mission. The **mission** is a statement that answers three overriding questions:

- ◆ *What* business will the company be in ("selling personal computers," "operating an Italian restaurant")?
- ◆ *Who* will the customers be, and what are the expected customer attributes ("homeowners," "college graduates")?
- ◆ *How* will the company's basic beliefs define the business ("gives the highest customer service," "stresses family values")?

Following is a list of some well-known companies and parts of their mission statements:

Dell Computer Corporation: "to be the most successful computer company in the world"
Delta Airlines: "worldwide airlines choice"
IBM: "translate advanced technologies into values for our customers as the world's largest information service company"
Lowe's: "helping customers build, improve and enjoy their homes"
Ryder: "offers a wide array of logistics services, such as distribution management, domestically and globally"

You can see that identifying the mission is a very important part of developing a business strategy. The mission basically defines the company. In order to develop a long-term plan for a business, you must first know exactly what business you are in, what customers you are serving, and what your company's values are. If a company does not have a well-defined mission it may pursue business opportunities about which it has no real knowledge or that are in conflict with its current pursuits, or it may miss opportunities altogether.

For example, Dell Computer Corporation has become a leader in the computer industry in part by following its mission. If it did not follow its mission Dell might decide to pursue other opportunities, such as producing mobile telephones similar to those manufactured by Motorola and Nokia. Although there is a huge market for mobile telephones, it is not consistent with Dell's mission of focusing on computers.

Environmental Scanning

A second factor that must be considered when developing a business strategy is the external environment in which the business is operating. This environment includes trends in the market, in the economic and political environment, and in society. These trends must be analyzed to determine business opportunities and threats. This process of monitoring the external environment is called **environmental scanning.** To remain competitive, companies have to continuously monitor their environment and be prepared to change their business strategy, or long-range plan, in light of environmental changes.

What Does Environmental Scanning Tell Us? Environmental scanning allows a company to identify *opportunities* and *threats*. For example, through environmental scanning we could see gaps in what customers need and what competitors are doing to meet those needs. A study of these gaps could reveal an opportunity for our company, and we could design a plan to take advantage of it. On the other hand, our company may currently be a leader in its industry, but environmental scanning could reveal competitors that are meeting customer needs better—for example, by offering a wider array of services. In this case, environmental scanning would reveal a threat and we would have to change our strategy so as not to be left behind. Just because a company is an industry leader today, does not mean they will continue to be a leader in the future. In the 1970s Sears Roebuck was a retail leader, but fell behind the pack in the 1990s.

What Do We Mean by Trends in the Environment? The external business environment is always changing. To stay ahead of the competition, a company must constantly look out for trends or changing patterns in the environment, such as *marketplace trends*. These might include changes in customer wants and expectations, and ways in which competitors are meeting those expectations. For example, in the computer industry customers are demanding speed of delivery, high quality, and low price. Dell Computer Corporation has become a leader in the industry because of its speed of delivery and low price. Other computer giants, such as Compaq, have had to redesign their business and operations strategies to compete with Dell. Otherwise, they would be left behind. It is through environmental scanning that companies like Compaq can see trends in the market, analyze the competition, and recognize what they need to do to remain competitive.

There are many other types of trends in the marketplace. For example, we are seeing changes in the use of technology, such as point-of-scale scanners, automation, computer-assisted processing, electronic purchasing, and electronic order tracking. One rapidly growing trend is e-commerce. For retailers like the GAP, Eddie Bauer, F.A.O. Schwarz, Fruit of the Loom, Inc., Barnes & Noble, and others, e-commerce has become a significant part of their business. Victoria's Secret has even used the Internet to conduct a fashion show in order to boost sales. Some companies began using e-commerce early in its development. Others, like Sears Roebuck, waited and then found themselves working hard to catch up to the competition.

In addition to market trends, environmental scanning looks at economic, political, and social trends that can affect the business. *Economic trends* include recession,

Pepsi seeks customers and suppliers all over the globe.

inflation, interest rates, and general economic conditions. Suppose that a company is considering obtaining a loan in order to purchase a new facility. Environmental scanning could show that interest rates are particularly favorable and that this may be a good time to go ahead with the purchase.

Political trends include changes in the political climate—local, national, and international—that could affect a company. For example, the creation of the European Union has had a significant impact on strategic planning for global companies such as IBM, Hewlett Packard, and PepsiCo. Similarly, changes in trade relations with China have opened up opportunities that were not available earlier. There has been a change in how companies view their environment—a shift from a national to a global perspective. Companies seek customers and suppliers all over the globe. Many have changed their strategies in order to take advantage of global opportunities, such as forming partnerships with international firms, called *strategic alliances*. For example, companies like Motorola and Xerox want to take advantage of opportunities in China and are developing strategic alliances to help them break into that market.

Finally, *social trends* are changes in society that can have an impact on a business. An example is the awareness of the dangers of smoking, which has made smoking less socially acceptable. This trend has had a huge impact on companies in the tobacco industry. In order to survive, many of these companies have changed their strategy to focus on customers overseas where smoking is still socially acceptable, or have diversified into other product lines.

Core Competencies

▶ **Core competencies**
The unique strengths of a business.

The third factor that helps define a business strategy is an understanding of the company's strengths. These are called **core competencies**. In order to formulate a long-term plan, the company's managers must know the competencies of their organization. Core competencies could include special skills of workers, such as expertise in providing customized services or knowledge of information technology. Another example might be flexible facilities that can handle the production of a wide array of products. To be successful, a company must compete in markets where its core competencies will help it win. Table 2-1 shows a list of some core competencies that companies may have.

Table 2-1 Organizational Core Competencies	
1. Workforce	Highly trained Responsive in meeting customer needs Flexible in performing a variety of tasks Strong technical capability Creative in product design
2. Facilities	Flexible in producing a variety of products Technologically advanced An efficient distribution system
3. Market Understanding	Skilled in understanding customer wants and predicting market trends
4. Financial Know-how	Skilled in attracting and raising capital
5. Technology	Use of latest production technology Use of information technology Quality control techniques

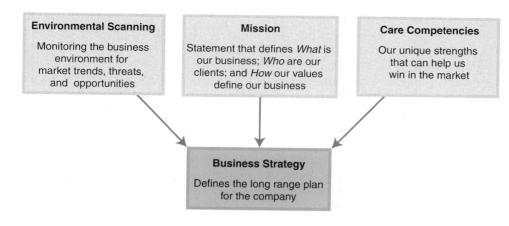

Figure 2-2

Three inputs in developing a business strategy

Highly successful firms develop a business strategy that takes advantage of their core competencies or strengths. To see why it is important to use core competencies, think of a student developing plans for a successful professional career. Let's say that this student is particularly good at mathematics but not as good in verbal communication and persuasion. Taking advantage of core competencies would mean developing a career strategy in which the student's strengths could provide an advantage, such as engineering or computer science. On the other hand, pursuing a career in marketing would place the student at a disadvantage because of a relative lack of skills in persuasion.

Putting It Together

Figure 2-2 shows how the mission, environmental scanning, and core competencies help in the formulation of the business strategy. Note that the figure shows a dynamic, ongoing process that is constantly allowed to change. As environmental scanning reveals changes in the external environment, the company may need to change its business strategy to remain competitive while taking advantage of its core competencies and staying within its mission.

Let's look at how Dell Computer Corporation combined its mission, environmental scanning, and core competencies to develop a highly successful business strategy. Dell's mission is to "be the most successful computer company in the world at delivering the best customer experience in markets we serve. In doing so, Dell will meet customer expectations of: highest quality, leading technology, competitive pricing, individual and company accountability, best-in-class service and support, flexible customization capability, superior corporate citizenship, and financial stability." The mission defined what business Dell is in: highest quality, leading technology, computer company. It also defined Dell's customers: focus on markets served. Finally, it defined how Dell would do this: through competitive pricing, best-in-class service and support, flexible customization capability. You can see how this mission defines Dell as a company.

An environmental scan revealed that competing computer manufacturers, such as IBM and Compaq, used inter-

LINKS TO PRACTICE
Dell Computer Corporation
www.dell.com

mediate resellers to sell computers. This led to higher inventory, higher costs, and slower responsiveness to customer wants. Michael Dell's idea was to sell directly to the customer and be able to put together exactly the system the customer wanted within a short time. Dell defined its core competencies as flexible manufacturing and the latest technological offering. Together, the mission, environmental scan, and core competencies were used to develop a competitive business strategy that provides customized computer solutions to customers within 36 hours at a highly competitive price.

Dell's business strategy was to take advantage of an opportunity in the market. However, to implement this strategy, the company needed to develop an operations strategy that arranged all the resources in ways that would support the business strategy. Operations strategy designs a plan for resources in order to take the business strategy from concept to reality. In the next section we look at how an operations strategy is developed.

Before You Go On

Make sure that you understand the role of the *business strategy* in defining a company's long-term plan. Without a business strategy the company would have no overriding plan. Such a plan acts like a compass, pointing the company in the right direction. To be effective, a long-range plan must be supported by each of the business functions. The *operations strategy* looks at the business strategy and develops a long-range plan specifically for the operations function. In the next section we will see how the operations strategy is developed.

■ DEVELOPING AN OPERATIONS STRATEGY

▶ **Competitive priorities**
Capabilities that the operations function can develop in order to give a company a competitive advantage in its market.

Once a business strategy has been developed, an operations strategy must be formulated. This will provide a plan for the design and management of the operations function in ways that support the business strategy. The operations strategy relates the business strategy to the operations function. It focuses on specific capabilities of the operation that give the company a competitive edge. These capabilities are called **competitive priorities**. By excelling in one of these capabilities, a company can become a winner in its market. These competitive priorities and their relationship to the design of the operations function are shown in Figure 2-3.

Competitive Priorities

Operations managers must work closely with marketing in order to understand the competitive situation in the company's market before they can determine which competitive priorities are important. There are four broad categories of competitive priorities:

▶ **Cost**
A competitive priority focusing on low cost.

1. Cost Competing based on cost means offering a product at a low price relative to the prices of competing products. The need for this type of competition emerges from the business strategy. The role of the operations strategy is to develop a plan for the use of resources to support this type of competition. Let's look at some specific characteristics of the operations function we might find in a company competing on cost.

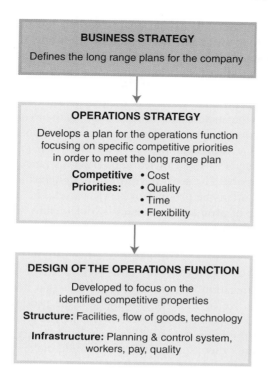

Figure 2-3

Operations strategy and the design of the operations function

To develop this competitive priority, the operations function must focus primarily on cutting costs in the system, such as costs of labor, materials, and facilities. Companies that compete based on cost study their operations system carefully to eliminate all waste. They might offer extra training to employees to maximize their productivity and minimize scrap. Also, they might invest in automation in order to increase productivity. Generally, companies that compete based on cost offer a narrow range of products and product features, allow for little customization, and have an operations process that is designed to be as efficient as possible.

One company that successfully competes on cost is Southwest Airlines. Southwest's entire operations function is designed to support this strategy. Facilities are streamlined: only one type of aircraft is used, and flight routes are generally short. This serves to minimize costs of scheduling crew changes, maintenance, inventories of parts, and many administrative costs. Unnecessary costs are completely eliminated: there are no meals, printed boarding passes, or seat assignments. Employees are trained to perform many functions and use a team approach to maximize customer service. Because of this strategy, Southwest has been a model for the airline industry for a number of years.

LINKS TO PRACTICE
Southwest Airlines Company
www.southwest.com

▶ **Quality**
A competitive priority focusing on product and service quality.

2. Quality Many companies claim that quality is their top priority, and many customers say that they look for quality in the products they buy. Yet quality has a subjective meaning; it depends on who is defining it. For example, to one person quality could mean that the product lasts a long time, such as a Volvo, a car known for its longevity. To another person quality might mean high performance, such as a BMW. When companies focus on quality as a competitive priority, they are focusing on the dimensions of quality that are considered important by their customers.

Quality as a competitive priority has two dimensions. The first is *high-performance design*. This means that the operations function will be designed to focus on aspects of quality such as superior features, close tolerances, high durability, and excellent customer service. The second dimension *is product and service consistency*, which measures how often the product or service meets the exact design specifications. A good example of product consistency is McDonald's, where we know we can get the same product every time at any location. Companies that compete on quality must deliver not only high-performance design but product and service consistency as well.

A company that competes on this dimension needs to implement quality in every area of the organization. One of the first aspects that needs to be addressed is *product design quality*, which involves making sure the product meets the requirements of the customer. A second aspect is *process quality*, which deals with designing a process to produce error-free products. This includes focusing on equipment, workers, materials, and every other aspect of the operation to make sure it works the way it is supposed to. Companies that compete based on quality have to address both of these issues: the product must be designed to meet customer needs, and the process must produce the product exactly as it is designed.

To see why product and process quality are both important, let's say that your favorite fast-food restaurant has designed a new sandwich called the "Big Yuck." The restaurant could design a process that produces a perfect "Big Yuck" every single time. But if customers find the "Big Yuck" unappealing, they will not buy it. The same would be true if the restaurant designed a sandwich called the "Super Delicious" to meet the desires of its customers. Even if the "Super Delicious" was exactly what the customers wanted, if the process did not produce the sandwich the way it was designed, often making it soggy and cold instead, customers would not buy it. Remember that the product needs to be designed to meet customer wants and needs, and the process needs to be designed to produce the exact product that was intended, consistently without error.

▶ **Time**
A competitive priority focusing on speed and on-time delivery.

3. Time Time or speed is one of the most important competitive priorities today. Companies in all industries are competing to deliver high-quality products in as short a time as possible. Companies like Federal Express, LensCrafters, UPS, and Dell Computer compete based on time. Today's customers don't want to wait, and companies that can meet their need for fast service are becoming leaders in their industries.

Making time a competitive priority means competing based on all time-related issues, such as rapid delivery and on-time delivery. Rapid delivery refers to how quickly an order is received; on-time delivery refers to the number of times deliveries are made on time. When time is a competitive priority, the job of the operations function is to critically analyze the system and combine or eliminate processes in order to save time. Often companies use technology to speed up processes, rely on a flexible workforce to meet peak demand periods, and eliminate unnecessary steps in the production process.

Federal Express, the world's largest provider of expedited delivery services, is an example of a company that competes based on time. To support this strategy, the operation function had to be designed to promote speed. For example, bar code technology is used to speed up processing and handling, and the company uses its own fleet of airplanes. Federal Express also relies on a very flexible part-time workforce, such as college students who are willing to work a few hours at night. This allows Federal Express to cover workforce requirements during peak periods without having to schedule full-time workers.

LINKS TO PRACTICE
FedEx Corporation
www.federalexpress.com

4. Flexibility As a company's environment changes rapidly, including customer needs and expectations, the ability to readily accommodate these changes can be a winning strategy. This is **flexibility.** There are two dimensions of flexibility. One is the ability to offer a wide variety of products or services and customize them to the unique needs of clients. This is called *product flexibility*. A flexible system can quickly add new products that may be important to customers or easily drop a product that is not doing well. Another aspect of flexibility is the ability to rapidly increase or decrease the amount produced in order to accommodate changes in the demand. This is called *volume flexibility*.

    You can see the meaning of flexibility when you compare ordering a suit from a custom tailor to buying it off the rack at a retailer. Another example would be going to a fine restaurant and asking to have a meal made just for you, versus going to a fast-food restaurant and being limited to items on the menu. The custom tailor and the fine restaurant are examples of companies that are flexible and will accommodate customer wishes. Another example of flexibility is Empire West, Inc., a company that makes a variety of products out of plastics, depending on what customers want. Empire West makes everything from plastic trays to body guards for cars.

    Companies that compete based on flexibility often cannot compete based on speed, because it generally requires more time to produce a customized product. Also, flexible companies typically do not compete based on cost, because it may take more resources to customize the product. However, flexible companies often offer greater customer service and can meet unique customer requirements. To carry out this strategy, flexible companies tend to have more general-purpose equipment that can be used to make many different kinds of products. Also, workers in flexible companies tend to have higher skill levels and can often perform many different tasks in order to meet customer needs.

▶ **Flexibility**
A competitive priority focusing on offering a wide variety of products or services.

Why Not Focus on All Priorities?

You may be wondering why the operations function needs to give special focus to some priorities and not all. Aren't all the priorities important? The reason is that as more resources are dedicated toward one priority, fewer resources are left for others. This is called a **trade-off**. For example, our restaurant might be known for making a "home-made" pizza with the freshest ingredients. However, because of the ingredients we use, we may not be able to offer the pizza at the lowest price. Also, since we are

▶ **Trade-off**
The need to focus more on one competitive priority than on others.

making each pizza individually, we may not be able to produce pizzas very quickly. So we have to make a trade-off.

It is important to know that any business must achieve a basic level of each of these priorities. In our pizza example, even though we are not competing based on price, we still cannot offer the pizza at such a high price that customers would not want to pay for it. Also, even though we are not competing based on time, we still have to produce the pizza within a reasonable amount of time; otherwise, customers will not be willing to wait for it.

To help us decide which competitive priorities to focus on, we can distinguish between *order winners* and *order qualifiers*. **Order qualifiers** are those competitive priorities that we have to meet if we want to do a business in a particular market. **Order winners,** on the other hand, are the competitive priorities that help us win orders in the market. Using our pizza example, order qualifiers might be low price (say, less than $10.00) and quick delivery (say, under 15 minutes), because this is a standard that has been set by competing pizza restaurants. Our order winner may be "fresh ingredients" and "home-made taste." This may be what makes us different from all the other pizza restaurants. Knowing the order winners and order qualifiers in a particular market is critical to focusing on the right competitive priorities.

Translating Competitive Priorities into Production Requirements

Operations strategy makes the needs of the business strategy specific to the operations function by focusing on the right competitive priorities. Once the competitive priorities have been identified, a plan is developed to support those priorities. The operations strategy will specify the design and use of the organization's resources; that is, it will set forth specific operations requirements. These can be broken down into two categories:

1. **Structure**—Operations decisions related to the design of the production process, such as characteristics of facilities used, selection of appropriate technology, and the flow of goods and services through the facility.
2. **Infrastructure**—Operations decisions related to the planning and control systems of the operation, such as the organization of the operations function, the skills and pay of workers, and quality control approaches.

Together, the structure and infrastructure of the production process determine the nature of the company's operations function.

The structure and infrastructure of the production process must be aligned to enable the company to pursue its long-term plan. Suppose we determined that *time* or *speed* of delivery is the order winner in the marketplace and the competitive priority we need to focus on. We would then design the production process to promote speedy product delivery. This might mean having a system that does not necessarily produce the product at the absolutely lowest cost, possibly because we need costlier or extra equipment to help us focus on speed. The important thing is that every aspect of production of a product or delivery of a service needs to focus on supporting the competitive priority. However, we cannot neglect the other competitive priorities. A certain level of order qualifiers must be achieved just to remain in the market. The issue is not one of focusing on one priority to the exclusion of the others. Rather, it is a matter of degree.

Let's return to the example of Dell Computer Corporation. Earlier we explained how Dell used its mission, environmental scanning, and core competencies to develop its business strategy. But to make this business plan a reality, the company

---

▶ **Order qualifiers**
Competitive priorities that must be met for a company to qualify as a competitor in the marketplace.

▶ **Order winners**
Competitive priorities that win orders in the marketplace.

▶ **Structure**
Operations decisions related to the design of the production process, such as facilities, technology, and the flow of goods and services through the facility.

▶ **Infrastructure**
Operations decisions related to the planning and control systems of the operation, such as organization of workers and their pay, management policies, and quality measures.

needed to develop an operations strategy to create its structure and infrastructure. The focus was on customer service, cost, and speed. Dell set up a system in which customers could order computers directly from the company, without going through an intermediary, such as a retailer. An operations system was designed so that ordering of components and assembly of computers did not occur until an order was actually placed. This kept costs low because Dell did not have computers sitting in inventory. A warehousing system was designed so that when components were needed, suppliers would deliver them to the plant within 15 minutes; in contrast, competitors like IBM and Compaq must wait hours or even days to receive needed components. To further increase speed, Dell set up a shipping arrangement with United Parcel Service (UPS). With this structure and infrastructure, Dell was able to implement its business plan.

Before You Go On

By now you should have a clear understanding of how an operations strategy is developed and its role in helping the organization decide which competitive priorities to focus on. There are four categories of competitive priorities: *cost, quality, time,* and *flexibility*. A company must make trade-offs in deciding which priorities to focus on. The operations strategy and the competitive priorities dictate the design and plan for the operations function, which includes the structure and infrastructure of the operation. This is a dynamic process, and as the environment changes, the organization must be prepared to change accordingly. Operations strategy plays a key role in an organization's ability to compete. In the next section we discuss a way to measure a company's competitive capability.

PRODUCTIVITY ■

A sound business strategy and supporting operations strategy make an organization more competitive in the marketplace. But how does a company measure its competitiveness? One of the most common ways is by measuring productivity. In this section we will look at how to measure the productivity of each of a company's resources as well as the entire organization.

Measuring Productivity

Recall that operations management is responsible for managing the transformation of many inputs into outputs, such as products or services. A measure of how efficiently inputs are being converted into outputs is called **productivity**. Productivity measures how well resources are used. It is computed as a ratio of outputs (goods and services) to inputs (e.g., labor and materials). The more efficiently a company uses its resources, the more productive it is:

▶ **Productivity**
A measure of how efficiently an organization converts inputs into outputs.

$$\text{Productivity} = \text{output/input} \tag{2-1}$$

We can use this equation to measure the productivity of one worker or many, as well as the productivity of a machine, a department, the whole firm, or even a nation. The possibilities are shown in Table 2-2.

When we compute productivity for all inputs, such as labor, machines, and capital, we are measuring **total productivity**. Total productivity describes the productivity of an entire organization. For example, let's say that the weekly dollar value of a company's output, such as finished goods and work in progress, is $8,600 and that the

▶ **Total productivity**
Productivity computed as a ratio of output to all organizational inputs.

Table 2-2 Productivity Measures	
Total Productivity Measure	Output produced/all inputs used
Partial Productivity Measure	Output/labor *or*
	Output/machines *or*
	Output/materials *or*
	Output/capital
Multifactor Productivity Measure	Output/(labor + machines) *or*
	Output/ (labor + materials) *or*
	Output/(labor + capital + energy)

value of its inputs, such as labor, materials, and capital is $10,200. The company's total productivity would be computed as follows:

$$\text{Total productivity} = \frac{\text{output}}{\text{input}} = \frac{\$8,600}{\$10,200} = .84$$

Often it is much more useful to measure the productivity of one input variable at a time in order to identify how efficiently each is being used. When we compute productivity as the ratio of output relative to a single input, we obtain a measure of **partial productivity**. Following are two examples of the calculation of partial productivity:

▶ **Partial productivity**
Productivity computed as a ratio of output to only one input (e.g., labor, materials, machines)

1. Our new cookie oven produced 346 cookies in 4 hours. What is its productivity?

$$\text{Machine productivity} = \text{number of cookies/oven time}$$
$$= \frac{346 \text{ cookies}}{4 \text{ hours}} = 86.5 \text{ cookies/hour}$$

2. We hired two new workers to paint small tables in our furniture shop. If the workers painted 22 tables in 8 hours, what was their productivity?

$$\text{Labor productivity} = \frac{22 \text{ tables}}{2 \text{ workers} \times 8 \text{ hours}} = 1.4 \text{ tables/hour}$$

▶ **Multifactor productivity**
Productivity computed as a ratio of output to several, but not all, inputs.

Sometimes we need to compute productivity as the ratio of output relative to a group of inputs, such as labor and materials. This is a measure of **multifactor productivity**. For example, let's say that output is worth $382 and labor and materials costs are $168 and $98, respectively. A multifactor productivity measure of our use of labor and materials would be

$$\text{Multifactor productivity} = \text{output/(labor + materials)}$$
$$= \$382/(\$168 + \$98) = 1.43$$

Interpreting Productivity Measures

To interpret the meaning of a productivity measure, it must be compared with a similar productivity measure. For example, if one worker at a pizza shop produces 17 pizzas in 2 hours, the productivity of that worker is 8.5 pizzas per hour. This number by itself does not tell us very much. However, if we compare it to the productivity of two other workers, one who produces 7.2 pizzas per hour and another 6.8 pizzas per hour, it is much more meaningful. We can see that the first worker is much more productive than the other two workers. But how do we know whether the productivity of all three workers is reasonable? What we need is a standard. In Chapter 11 we will discuss ways to set standards and how those standards can help in evaluating the performance of our workers.

It is also helpful to measure and compare productivity over time. Let's say that we want to measure the total productivity of our three pizza makers (our "labor") and we compute a labor productivity measure of 7.5 pizzas per hour. This number does not tell us much about the workers' performance. However, if we compared our weekly productivity measures for the last four weeks, we would get much more information:

Week	1	2	3	4
Productivity (pizzas/labor hour)	5.4	6.8	7.1	7.5

Now we can see that the workers' productivity is improving over time. But what if we find out that our main competitor, a pizzeria down the street, has a productivity of 9.5 pizzas per labor hour? Suddenly we know that even though our productivity is going up, it should be much higher. We will have to analyze how we are making pizzas and increase our productivity in order to be competitive. By comparing our productivity over time and against similar operations, we have a much better sense of how high our productivity really is.

When evaluating productivity and setting standards for performance, we also need to consider our strategy for competing in the marketplace—namely, our competitive priorities. A company that, competes based on speed would probably measure productivity in units produced over time. However, a company that competes based on cost might measure productivity in terms of costs of inputs such as labor, materials, and overhead. The important thing is that our productivity measure provides information on how we are doing relative to the competitive priority that is most important to us.

OM ACROSS THE ORGANIZATION

The business strategy defines the long-range plan for the entire company and guides the actions of each of the company's business functions. Those functions, in turn, develop plans to support the business strategy. However, in defining their individual strategies, it is important for the functions to work together and understand each other's needs.

Marketing identifies target markets, studies competition, and communicates with customers. In developing its own strategy, marketing needs to fully understand the capabilities of the operations function, the types of resources being used, and the way those resources are utilized. Otherwise, marketing's strategy could entail making promises that operations cannot deliver. In turn, marketing needs to communicate to operations all observed and anticipated market changes.

Finance develops financial plans to support the business strategy. However, since it is the operations function that manages all the organization's resources, the financial plans in effect support operations activities. Before it can develop its own strategy, finance needs to communicate with operations in order to understand the financial requirements of planned resources. In turn, operations managers cannot fully develop a strategy until they have a clear understanding of financial capabilities.

The strategies of all the business functions need to support each other in achieving the goals set by the business strategy, and are best developed through a team approach.

■ OM IS EVERYWHERE

This chapter has focused on competitiveness and winning in the marketplace. But how does this apply to everyday life? Let's look first at the notion of strategy. Most of us have a *personal strategy* similar to a business strategy; that is, we have a long-range plan that governs the things we do. This personal strategy is based on our personal mission, our understanding of the environment we live and work in, and our core competencies or strengths. Since you are reading this book, you are probably a student in an operations management course. Your personal strategy is probably to have a successful career in business. Let's see how implementing the concept of operations strategy can help in everyday life.

Figure 2-4 shows the development of our personal strategy and its relationship to our "functional" strategies. In developing our personal strategy, we first have to consider our *mission*, which defines us and our core beliefs (e.g., "ethics in business rules" versus "win at all cost"). We also consider our strengths or core competencies (e.g., "excellent writer" versus "winning technical skills"). Finally, we have to study the environment for job opportunities and market trends (e.g., "growing opportunities in operations management").

Once we have developed our personal strategy, we focus on the strategies for each "function" in order to support the strategy. Our "finance strategy" is to develop a plan to finance our college education. Our "marketing strategy" is to develop a plan to sell our skills through networking, working with the university's employment office, and constantly monitoring the market for new job opportunities and skills required. As far as our "operations strategy" is concerned, it is not only to attend classes and study hard but also to make decisions about electives and activities that will make us more competitive. These could include joining student chapters of professional organizations or an internship program to gain experience.

In developing our "operations strategy" we also have to make trade-offs, such as deciding whether to take more courses and focus on *speed* or take fewer courses and

Figure 2-4

Development of a personal strategy

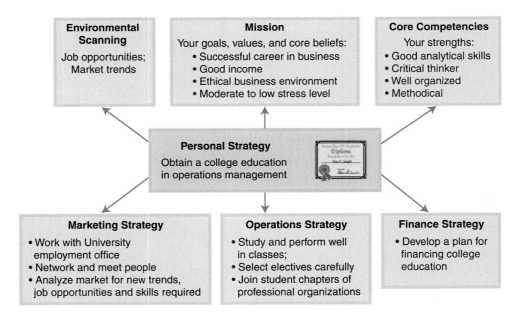

focus on *quality*. Our decision has to do with our personal strategy as well as the information provided by the other functional strategies. "Finance" might say that we need to focus on speed and finish school quickly. "Marketing" might say that we need to focus on quality, but that current job opportunities are excellent and we should hurry to take advantage of them. "Operations," on the other hand, might say that we cannot get through school that fast and that "finance" may need to develop a new plan and "marketing" should be looking for future opportunities.

In this example you can see that managing the complexities of a career is not too different from managing the complexities of a business. We have to consider many "functional" strategies in order to carry out our personal strategy. If these plans do not work together, we may run out of money or pursue a career that has poor job prospects. An organization works in much the same way, and the strategies must work together if the company is to meet its goals. Finally, just as a business needs a strategy to succeed in the long run, so does a person's career. Without a plan, a student can take courses randomly only to find that after years of schooling he or she still does not have a degree. A plan is needed to run a successful career as well as a successful business.

CHAPTER HIGHLIGHTS

1. A business strategy is a long-range plan and vision for a business. Each of the individual business functions needs to support the business strategy.

2. An organization develops its business strategy by doing environmental scanning and considering its mission and its core competencies.

3. The role of operations strategy is to provide a long-range plan for the use of the company's resources.

4. The role of business strategy serves as an overall guide for the development of the organization's operations strategy.

5. The operations strategy focuses on developing specific capabilities called competitive priorities. In designing its operation, an organization is governed by the operations strategy and the specific competitive priorities it has chosen to develop.

6. There are four categories of competitive priorities: cost, quality, time, and flexibility.

7. Productivity is a measure that indicates how effectively an organization is using its resources.

8. It is computed as the ratio of organizational outputs divided by inputs.

KEY TERMS

business strategy 22
operations strategy 22
mission 24
environmental scanning 24
core competencies 26
competitive priorities 28
cost 28

quality 30
time 30
flexibility 31
trade-off 31
order qualifiers 32
order winners 32
structure 32

infrastructure 32
productivity 33
total productivity 33
partial productivity 34
multifactor productivity 34

FORMULA REVIEW

$$\text{Productivity} = \frac{\text{output}}{\text{input}}$$

SOLVED PROBLEMS

1. Bluegill Furniture is a small furniture shop that focuses on making kitchen chairs. The weekly dollar value of its output, including finished goods and work in progress, is $14,280. The value of inputs, such as labor, materials, and capital is approximately $16,528. Compute the total productivity measure for Bluegill Furniture.

   Solution

   $$\text{Total productivity} = \frac{\text{output}}{\text{input}} = \frac{\$14,280}{\$16,528} = .864$$

2. Bluegill has just purchased a new sanding machine that processes 17 chairs in 8 hours. What is the productivity of the sanding machine?

   Solution

   $$\text{Machine productivity} = \frac{\text{number of chairs}}{\text{processing time}}$$
   $$= \frac{17 \text{ chairs}}{8 \text{ hours}}$$
   $$= 2.125 \text{ chairs/hour}$$

3. Bluegill has hired two new workers to paint chairs. They have painted 10 chairs in 4 hours. What is their productivity?

   Solution

   $$\text{Labor productivity} = \frac{10 \text{ chairs}}{2 \text{ workers} \times 4 \text{ hours}}$$
   $$= 1.25 \text{ chairs/hour}$$

DISCUSSION QUESTIONS

1. Explain the importance of a business strategy.
2. Explain the role of operations strategy in a business.
3. Describe how a business strategy is developed.
4. Describe how an operations strategy is formulated from the business strategy.
5. Explain what is meant by the term *competitive priority* and describe the four categories of competitive priorities discussed in the chapter.
6. Find an example of a company that makes quality its competitive priority. Find another company that makes time its competitive priority. Compare these strategies.
7. What is meant by the terms *order qualifiers* and *order winners*? Explain why they are important.
8. Describe the meaning of productivity. Why is it important?
9. Explain the three types of productivity measures.

PROBLEMS

1. Two workers have the job of placing plastic labels on packages before the packages are shipped out. The first worker can place 1000 labels in 30 minutes. The second worker can place 850 labels in 20 minutes. Which worker is more productive?

2. Last week a painter painted 3 houses in 5 days. This week she painted 2 houses in 4 days. In which week was the painter more productive?

3. One type of bread-making machine can make 6 loaves of bread in 5 hours. A new model of the machine can make 4 loaves in 2 hours. Which model is more productive?

4. A company that makes kitchen chairs wants to compare productivity at two of its facilities. At facility #1, 6 workers produced 240 chairs. At facility #2, 4 workers produced 210 chairs, during the same time period. Which facility was more productive?

5. A painter is considering using a new high-tech paint roller. Yesterday he was able to paint 3 walls in 45 minutes using his old method. Today he painted 2 walls of the same size in 20 minutes. Is the painter more productive using the new paint roller?

6. Aztec Furnishings makes hand-crafted furniture for sale in its retail stores. The furniture maker has recently installed a new assembly process, including a new sander and polisher. With this new system, production has increased to 90 pieces of furniture per day from the previous 60 pieces of furniture per day. The number of defective items produced has dropped from 10 pieces per day to 1 per day. The production facility operates strictly eight hours per day. Evaluate the change in productivity for Aztec using the new assembly process.

7. Howard Plastics produces plastic containers for use in the food packaging industry. Last year their average monthly

production included 20,000 containers produced using one shift 5 days a week with an 8-hour-a-day operation. Of the items produced 15% were deemed defective. Recently Howard Plastics has implemented new production methods and new quality improvement program. Their monthly production has increased to 25,000 containers with 9% defective.

(a) Compute productivity ratios for the old and new production system.

(b) Compare the changes in productivity between the two production systems.

8. Med-Tech labs is a facility that provides medical tests and evaluations for patients, ranging from analyzing blood samples to performing magnetic resonance imaging (MRI). Average cost to patients is $60 per patient. Labor costs average $15.00 per patient, materials costs are $20.00 per patient, and overhead costs are averaged at $20.00 per patient.

(a) What is the *multifactor* productivity ratio for Med-Tech? What does your finding mean?

(b) If the average lab worker spends 3 hours for each patient, what is the *labor* productivity ratio?

9. Handy-Maid Cleaning Service operates 5 crews with 3 workers per crew. Different crews clean a different number of homes per week and spend differing amount of hours. All the homes cleaned are about the same size. The manager of Handy-Maid is trying to evaluate the productivity of each of the crews. The following data has been collected over the past week.

Work Crew	Hours	Homes Cleaned
Anna, Sue, and Tim	35	10
Jim, Jose, and Andy	45	15
Dan, Wendy, and Carry	56	18
Rosie, Chandra, and Seth	30	10
Sherry, Vicky, and Roger	42	18

Assuming the quality of cleaning was consistent between crews, which crew was most productive?

CASE: *Prime Bank of Massachusetts*

Prime Bank of Massachusetts was started in 1964 with James Rogers as CEO and now Chairman of the Board. Prime Bank had been growing steadily since its beginning and has developed a loyal customer following. Today there are 45 bank locations throughout Massachusetts, with corporate headquarters in Newbury, Massachusetts. The bank offers a wide array of banking services to commercial and non-commercial customers.

Prime Bank has considered itself to be a conservative, yet innovative organization. Its locations are open Monday–Friday 9–4 and Saturday 9–12. Most of the facilities are located adjacent to well-established shopping centers, with multiple ATM machines and at least three drive-through windows. However, Prime Bank's growth has brought on certain problems. Having the right amount of tellers available in the bank as well as in the drive-through window has been a challenge. Some commercial customers had recently expressed frustration due to long waiting time. Also, the parking lot has often become crowded during peak periods.

While Prime Bank was going through a growth period, the general banking industry had been experiencing tougher competition. Competitors were increasingly offering lower interest rates on loans with higher yields on savings accounts and certificates of deposit. Also, Prime Bank was experiencing growing pains, and something needed to be done soon or they would begin losing customers to competition.

The Board, headed by James Rogers, decided to develop a more aggressive strategy for Prime Bank. While many of their competitors were competing on *cost,* the Board decided that Prime Bank should focus on *customer service* in order to differentiate itself from the competition. The Bank had already begun moving in that direction by offering a 24-hour customer service department to answer customers' banking

questions. Yet, there were difficulties with this effort, such as poor staffing and not enough telephone lines. James Rogers wanted Prime Bank to aggressively solve all customer service issues, such as staffing, layout, and facilities. He also wanted greater creativity in adding improvements in customer service, such as on-line banking, and special services for large customers. He believed that improving most aspects of the Bank's operation would give them a competitive advantage.

The Board presented their new strategy to Victoria Chen, Vice President of Operations. Victoria had recently been promoted to the V.P. level and understood the importance of operations management. She was asked to identify all changes that should be made in the operation function that would support this new strategy and present them at the next board meeting. Victoria had been hoping for an opportunity to prove herself since she began with the bank. This was her chance.

Case Questions:

1. Why is the operations function important in implementing the strategy of an organization? Explain why the changes put in place by Victoria Chen and her team could either hurt or help the Bank.

2. Develop a list of changes for the operations function that should be considered by the Bank. Begin by identifying operations management decisions that would be involved in operating a bank, e.g. layout of facility, staff, drive-through service. Then identify ways that they can be improved at Prime Bank in order to support the strategy focused on customer service?

3. Think of the improvements identified in answering question #2. How different would these improvements be if the Bank had a strategy of cutting cost rather than supporting customer service?

INTERACTIVE LEARNING

Enhance and test your knowledge of Chapter 2 using the interactive CD.

1. **Video** *The Walt Disney Company*

   Visit our dynamic Web site, www.wiley.com/college/reid, for more cases, Web links, and additional information.

2. **Company Tour**
   The Boeing Company
   Sensenich Propeller Manufacturing Company

3. **Additional Web Resources**
   Association for Manufacturing Excellence, www.ame.org

4. **INTERNET CHALLENGE** *Understanding Strategic Differences*

Select two companies in the same industry, either in service or manufacturing. You can select industries such as fast food, banking, health care, computer manufacturing, or auto manufacturing. Use the Internet to visit the selected companies' Web sites and collect the following information: their mission statement, target market, and specifics of their product and service offerings. Explain the differences between the companies' business strategies and target markets. How do their product and service offerings differ relative to their target markets and their overall strategies? Finally, how does their operations function support their business strategies? Try to explain how operations utilizes specific organizational resources to support the business strategy.

Web sites to consider:
www.lhcargo.com (Lufthansa Cargo)
www.ualcargo.com (United Airlines Cargo)

BIBLIOGRAPHY

Ahlstrom, P. and Westbrook, R. "Implications of Mass Customization for OM: An Exploratory Survey," *International Journal of Operations and Production Management*, 19, 3,1999, 262–274.

Fine, Charles H. *Clock Speed, Winning Industry Control in the Age of Temporary Advantage*, New York: Perseus Books, 1998.

Gagnon, S. "Resource Based Competition and the New Operations Strategy," *International Journal of Operations and Production Management*, 19, 2, 1999, 135–138.

Grover, V., and Malhotra, M. K., "A Framework for Examining the Interface Between Operations and Information Systems: Implications for Research in the New Millennium," *Decision Sciences*, 30, 4,1999, 901–919.

Hayes, Robert H., and Steven C. Wheelwright, *Restoring our Competitive Edge: Competing through Manufacturing*, New York: John Wiley & Sons, 1984.

Hill, Terry, *Manufacturing Strategy Text and Cases*, Irwin McGraw-Hill, 2000.

Porter, Michael E. "What is Strategy?" *Harvard Business Review* 74 (November-December 1996), 61–78.

Rondeau, P.J., Vonderembse, M. S., and Raghunathan, T. S., "Exploring Work System Practices for Time-Based Manufacturers: Their Impact on Competitive Capabilities," *Journal of Operations Management*, 18, 2000, 509–529.

Robert, Michel, *Strategy Pure and Simple II*, Mc Graw-Hill, 1998.

Spring, M., and Dalrymple, J.F., "Product Customization and Manufacturing Strategy," *International Journal of Operations and Production Management*, 20, 2000, 4, 441–467.

Vickery, S., Droge, C., and Germain, R., "The Relationship between Product Customization and Organizational Culture," *Journal of Operations Management*, 17, 1999, 377–301.

Vokurka, R.J., and O'Leary-Kelly, S.W, "A Review of Empirical Research on Manufacturing flexibility," *Journal of Operations Management*, 18, 2000, 485–501.

Ward, P.T. and Duray, R., "Manufacturing Strategy in Context: Environment, Competitive Strategy, and Manufacturing Strategy," *Journal of Operations Management*, 18, 2000, 123–138.

Product Design and Process Selection

Before studying this chapter you should know or, if necessary, review

1. Differences between manufacturing and service organizations, Chapter 1, pp. 4–6.
2. Differences between strategic and tactical decisions, Chapter 1, pp. 6–8.
3. Competitive priorities, Chapter 2, pp. 28–33.

LEARNING OBJECTIVES

After completing this chapter you should be able to

1 Define product design and explain its strategic impact on the organization.

2 Describe the steps used to develop a product design.

3 Use break-even analysis as a tool in deciding between alternative products.

4 Identify different types of production processes and explain their characteristics.

5 Describe the steps used in process design and selection.

6 Understand how to use a process flowchart.

7 Understand current technological advancements and how they impact process design.

8 Understand issues of designing service operations.

CHAPTER OUTLINE

Have you ever been with a group of friends on a Friday night and decide to order pizzas? One person wants pizza from Pizza Hut because he likes the taste of stuffed-crust pizza made with cheese in the crust. Someone else wants Donato's pizza because she likes the unique crispy-thin crust. A third wants pizza from Spagio's because of the wood-grilled-oven taste. Even a simple product like a pizza can have different features unique to its producer. Different customers have different tastes, preferences, and product needs and the variety of product designs on the market appeal to the preferences of a particular customer group. This is what product design is all about.

In this chapter we will learn about *product design,* which is the process of deciding on the unique characteristics and features of the company's product. We will also learn about *process selection,* which is the development of the process necessary to produce the designed product. Product design and process selection decisions are typically made together. Pizza Hut's stuffed-crust pizza dictated a certain design of the manufacturing process. The product design team had to ask questions like "Can we do it?" How will we do it?" How much longer will it take?" "Do we need special cheese, a different temperature setting, a special oven?" "How much will it cost?" Similarly, when Spagio was designing their wood-grilled pizza or Donato's their crispy-thin pizza, they too were thinking about the special techniques and equipment they would need to make their product. This step—process selection—is necessary to realize the product design. A company can have a highly innovative design for its product, but if it has not figured out how to make the product cost effectively, the product will stay a design forever.

Product design and process selection affect product quality, product cost, and customer satisfaction. If the product is not well designed or if the manufacturing process is not true to the product design, the quality of the product may suffer. Further, the product has to be manufactured using materials, equipment, and labor skills that are efficient and affordable; otherwise, its cost will be too high for the market. We call this the product's manufacturability—the ease with which the product can be made. Finally, if a product is to achieve customer satisfaction, it must have the combined characteristics of good design, competitive pricing, and the ability to fill a market need. This is true whether the product is pizzas or cars.

■ PRODUCT DESIGN

Most of us might think that the design of a product is not that interesting. After all, it probably involves materials, measurements, dimensions, and blueprints. When we think of design we usually think of car design or computer design and envision engineers working on diagrams. However product design is much more than that. Product design brings together marketing analysts, art directors, sales forecasters, engineers, finance experts, and other members of a company to think and plan strategically. It is exciting and creative, and it can spell success or disaster for a company.

Product design is the process of defining all the features and characteristics of just about anything you can think of, from Starbuck's cafe latte or Jimmy Dean's sausage to GM's Saturn or HP's DeskJet printer. Product design also includes the design of services, such as those provided by Salazar's Beauty Salon, La-Petite Academy Day Care Center, or Federal Express. Consumers respond to a product's appearance, color, texture, performance. All of its features, summed up, are the product's design. Someone came up with the idea of what this product will look like, taste like, or feel like so that it will appeal to you. This is the purpose of product design. **Product design** defines a product's characteristics, such as its appearance, the materials it is made of, its dimensions and tolerances, and its performance standards.

Tangible versus Intangible Products

The design elements just discussed are typical of industries such as manufacturing and retail in which the product is tangible. For the service industries, in which the product is intangible, the design elements are equally important, but they have an added dimension.

Service design is different from product design in that we are designing both the service and the entire *service concept*. As with a tangible product, the service concept is based on meeting customer needs. The service design, however, adds to this the esthetic and psychological benefits of the product. These are the service elements of the operation, such as promptness and friendliness. They also include the ambiance, image, and "feel-good" elements of the service. Consider the differences in service design of a company like Canyon Ranch, which provides a pampering retreat for health conscious but overworked professionals, versus Gold's Gym, which caters to young athletes. As with a tangible product, the preference for a service is based on its product design. **Service design** defines the characteristics of a service, such as its physical elements, and the esthetic and psychological benefits it provides.

Strategic Importance of Product Design

Product design is strategically important to a company. We learned in Chapter 2 that every business needs a long-range plan or vision, called a business strategy. A company's business strategy maps out its business, customers, and competitors. The activities a company engages in and the decisions a company makes must support this business strategy. A company's product designs must also support the company's business strategy.

Suppose you are a software engineer at a startup software company. Your company's product is database management software geared to large clients with substantial banks of data. Now there is talk about changing directions and making a "lite" version of the product for smaller clients with much less data. This could be a danger signal for your company. Why? The answer is that a company's products define the company's customers. Together, a company's products and customers define the company's image, competition, future growth, and position in the marketplace. For these reasons, product design is a major factor in a company's ability to keep and build its customer base. Every company targets a particular customer group. Think about retailers like The Gap, which caters to a young, modern clientele versus Talbots, which caters to a slightly older and more conservative clientele. What would happen if Talbot's and

This photo shows Allegro electronic portfolio by software developer Vadem. This is the latest product design in handheld computers that combines portability, power and features.

▶ **Product design**
The process of defining all of the product's characteristics.

▶ **Service design**
The process of establishing all the characteristics of the service, including physical, sensual, and psychological benefits.

The Gap started sharing the same concept in clothes design? They certainly would not meet the needs of their customer group and so might risk losing their market position.

To summarize: a company's product design must match the needs and preferences of the customer group targeted by the company's business strategy. Otherwise, the company will lose its customer base and erode its market position.

■ STEPS IN PRODUCT DESIGN

Certain steps are common in the development of most product designs. They are the following:

Step 1   Idea Development.
All product designs begin with an idea. Someone thinks of a need and a product design that would satisfy it.

Step 2   Product Screening.
Once an idea is developed, it needs to be evaluated. Often a business comes up with numerous product ideas. At this stage we need to screen the ideas and decide which ones have the greatest chance of succeeding.

Step 3   Preliminary Design and Testing.
This is the stage where preliminary design of the product is made and market testing and prototype analysis are performed.

Step 4   Final Design.
This is the last stage, where the final design of the product is made.
Next we look at these steps in a little more detail.

Idea Development

All product designs begin with an idea. The idea might come from a product manager who spends time with customers and has a sense of what customers want, from an engineer with a flare for inventions, or from anyone else in the company. To remain competitive, companies must be innovative and bring out new products regularly. In some industries, the cycle of new product development is predictable. We see this in the auto industry, where new car models come out every year, or the retail industry, where new fashion is designed for every season.

In other industries, new product releases are less predictable but just as important. The Body Shop, retailer of plant-based skin care products, periodically comes up with new ideas for their product lines. The timing often has to do with the market for a product, and whether sales are declining or continuing to grow.

Ideas from Customers and Competitors The first source of ideas are customers, the driving force in the design of products and services. Marketing is a vital link between customers and product design. Market researchers collect customer information by studying customer buying patterns and using tools such as customer surveys and focus groups. Management may love an idea, but if market analysis shows that customers do not like it, the idea is not viable. Analyzing customer preferences is an ongoing process. Customer preferences next year may be quite different from what they are today. For this reason, the related process of forecasting future consumer preferences is important, though difficult.

Competitors are another source of ideas. A company learns by observing its competitors' products and services and the success rate of these products and services.

This includes looking at product design, pricing strategy, and other aspects of the operation. Studying the practices of companies considered "best in class" and comparing the performance of our company against theirs is called **benchmarking**. We can benchmark against a company in a completely different line of business and still learn from some aspect of that company's operation. For example, Lands' End is well known for its successful catalog business, and companies considering catalog sales often benchmark against Lands' End. Similarly, American Express is a company known for its success at resolving complaints and it too is used for benchmarking.

▶ **Benchmarking**
The process of studying the practices of companies considered "best in class" and comparing your company's performance against theirs.

The importance of benchmarking can be seen by the efforts taken by IBM to improve its distribution system. In 1997 IBM found its distribution costs increasing, while customers were expecting decreasing cycle times from factory to delivery. It appeared that IBM's supply chain practices were not keeping up with those of its competitors. To evaluate and solve this problem IBM hired Mercer Management Consultants, who performed a large benchmarking study. IBM's practices were compared to those of market leaders in the PC industry, as well as to the best logistics practices outside the technology area. The objective was to evaluate IBM's current performance, that of companies considered best-in-class, and identify the gaps. Through the study, IBM discovered which specific costs exceeded industry benchmarks and which parts of the cycle time were excessively long. It also uncovered ways to simplify and reorganize its processes to gain efficiency. Based on findings from the benchmarking effort, IBM made changes in its operations. The results were reduced costs, improved delivery, and improved relationships with suppliers. IBM found benchmarking so beneficial that it plans to perform similar types of studies on an ongoing basis in the future.

LINKS TO PRACTICE
IBM Corporation
www.ibm.com

Reverse Engineering Another way of using competitors' ideas is to buy a competitor's new product and study its design features. Using a process called **reverse engineering,** a company's engineers carefully disassemble the product and analyze its parts and features. This approach was used by the Ford Motor Company to design its Taurus model. Ford engineers disassembled and studied many other car models, such as BMW and Toyota, and adapted and combined their best features. Product design ideas are also generated by a company's R & D department, whose role is to develop product and process innovation. Other sources of ideas are suppliers, the company's employees, and new technological developments.

▶ **Reverse engineering**
The process of disassembling a product to analyze its design features.

Product Screening

After a product idea has been developed it needs to be evaluated to determine its likelihood of success. This is called *product screening*. The company's product screening team evaluates the product design idea according to the needs of the major business functions. In their evaluation, executives from each functional area may explore issues such as the following:

◆ **Operations** What are the production needs of the proposed new product and how do they match our existing resources? Will we need new facilities and equipment? Do we have the labor skills to make the product? Can the material for production be readily obtained?

◆ **Marketing** What is the potential size of the market for the proposed new product? How much effort will be needed to develop a market for the product and what is the long-term product potential?

◆ **Finance** The production of a new product is a financial investment like any other. What is the proposed new product's financial potential, cost, and return on investment?

Unfortunately, there is no magic formula for deciding whether or not to pursue a particular product idea. Managerial skill and experience, however, are key. Companies generate new product ideas all the time, whether for a new brand of cereal or a new design for a car door. Approximately 80% of ideas do not make it past the screening stage. Management analyzes operations, marketing, and financial factors, and then makes the final decision. Fortunately, we have decision-making tools to help us evaluate new product ideas. A popular one is break-even analysis, which we will look at next.

▶ **Break-even analysis**
A technique used to compute the amount of goods a company would need to sell to cover its costs.

Break-Even Analysis: A Tool for Product Screening **Break-even analysis** is a technique that can be useful when evaluating a new product. This technique computes the quantity of goods a company needs to sell just to cover its costs, or break even, called the "break-even" point. When evaluating an idea for a new product it is helpful to compute its break-even quantity. An assessment can then be made as to how difficult or easy it will be to cover costs and make a profit. A product with a break-even quantity that is hard to attain might not be a good product choice to pursue. Next we look at how to compute the break-even quantity.

The total cost of producing a product or service is the sum of its fixed and variable costs. A company incurs **fixed costs** regardless of how much it produces. Fixed costs include overhead, taxes, and insurance. For example, a company must pay for overhead even if it produces nothing. **Variable costs,** on the other hand, are costs that vary directly with the amount of units produced, and include items such as materials and labor. Together, fixed and variable costs add up to total cost:

$$\text{Total cost} = \text{fixed cost} + \text{variable cost}$$

Using symbols, we have the following equation:

$$\text{Total cost} = F + (VC)Q$$

where F = fixed cost
VC = variable cost per unit
Q = number of units sold

Figure 3-1 shows a graphical representation of these costs as well as the break-even quantity. The quantity produced is shown on the horizontal axis and dollars are shown on the vertical axis. Fixed cost is represented by a horizontal line and is the same regardless of how much is produced. The diagonal line above fixed cost is total cost, which is the sum of fixed and variable costs. When $Q = 0$, total cost is only equal to fixed cost. As Q increases, total cost increases through the variable cost component. The blue diagonal in the figure is revenue. Revenue is the amount of money brought in from sales:

$$\text{Revenue} = (SP)Q$$

where SP = selling price per unit.

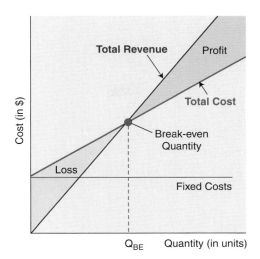

Figure 3-1

Graphical approach to break-even analysis

When $Q = 0$, revenue is zero. As sales increase, so does revenue. Remember, however, that to cover all costs we have to sell the break-even amount. This is the quantity Q_{BE}, where revenue equals total cost. If we sell below the break-even point we will incur a loss, since costs exceed revenue. To make a profit, we have to sell above the break-even point. Since revenue equals total cost at the break-even point, we can use the above equations to compute the value of the break-even quantity:

$$\text{Total cost} = \text{total revenue}$$
$$F + (VC)\,Q = (SP)\,Q$$

Algebraically solving for Q, we get the following equation:

$$Q_{BE} = \frac{F}{SP - VC}$$

Note that we could also find the break-even point by drawing the graph and finding where the total cost and revenue lines cross.

■ Example 3.1 Computing the Break-Even Quantity

Fred Boulder, owner of Sports Feet Manufacturing, is considering whether to produce a new line of footwear. Fred has considered both the processing needs for the new product as well as the market potential. He has also estimated that the variable cost for each product manufactured and sold is $9 and the fixed cost per year is $52,000.

(a) If Fred offers the footwear at a selling price of $25, how many pairs must he sell to break even?

(b) If Fred sells 4000 pairs at the $25 price, what will be his contribution to profit?

Solution
(a) To compute the break-even quantity:

$$Q = \frac{F}{SP - VC}$$
$$= \frac{\$52,000}{\$25 - \$9} = 3250 \text{ pairs}$$

The break-even quantity is 3250 pairs. This is how much Fred would have to sell to cover his costs.

(b) To compute the contribution to profit with sales of 4000 pairs we can go back to our basic relationship between cost and revenue:

$$\text{Profit} = \text{total revenue} - \text{total cost}$$
$$= (SP)\,Q - [F + (VC)\,Q]$$

Now we can substitute the appropriate numerical values:

$$\text{Profit} = \$25\,(4000) - [\$52,000 + \$9\,(4000)]$$
$$= \$12,000$$

The contribution to profit is $12,000 if Fred can sell 4000 pairs from his new line of footwear.

Break-even analysis is an excellent tool for more than simply deciding between different products. It can be used to make many other decisions, such as evaluating different processes or deciding whether it is better to make or buy a product.

Preliminary Design and Testing

Once a product idea has passed the screening stage, it is time to begin preliminary design and testing. At this stage, design engineers translate general performance specifications into technical specifications. Prototypes are built and tested. Changes are made based on test results and the process of revising, rebuilding a prototype, and testing continues. For service companies this may entail testing the offering on a small scale and working with customers to refine the service offering. Fast-food restaurants are known for this type of testing, where a new menu item may be tested in only one particular geographic area. Product refinement can be time consuming and there may be a desire on the part of the company to hurry through this phase to rush the product to market. However, rushing creates the risk that all the "bugs" have not been worked out, which can prove very costly.

Final Design

Following extensive design testing the product moves to the final design stage. This is where final product specifications are drawn up. The final specifications are then translated into specific processing instructions to manufacture the product, which include selecting equipment, outlining jobs that need to be performed, identifying specific materials needed and suppliers that will be used, and all the other aspects of organizing the process of product production.

■ FACTORS TO CONSIDER IN PRODUCT DESIGN

Here are some additional factors that need to be considered during the product design stage.

Design for Manufacture

When we think of product design we generally first think of how to please the customer. However, we also need to consider how easy or difficult it is to manufacture

Table 3-1 Guidelines for DFM
DFM guidelines include the following:
1. Minimize parts.
2. Design parts for different products.
3. Use modular design.
4. Avoid tools.
5. Simplify operations.

the product. Otherwise, we might have a great idea that is difficult or too costly to manufacture. **Design for manufacture (DFM)** is a series of guidelines that we should follow to produce a product easily and profitably. DFM guidelines focus on two issues:

▶ **Design for manufacture (DFM)**
A series of guidelines to follow in order to produce a product easily and profitably.

1. **Design simplification** means reducing the number of parts and features of the product whenever possible. A simpler product is easier to make, costs less, and gives us higher quality.
2. **Design standardization** refers to the use of common and interchangeable parts. By using interchangeable parts we can make a greater variety of products with less inventory and significantly lower cost and provide greater flexibility. Table 3-1 shows guidelines for DFM.

An example of the benefits of applying these rules is seen in Figure 3-2. We can see the progression in the design of a toolbox using the DFM approach. All of the pictures show a toolbox. However, the first design shown requires 20 parts. Through simplification and use of modular design the number of parts required has been reduced to 2. It would certainly be much easier to make the product with 2 parts versus 20 parts. This means fewer chances for error, better quality, and lower costs due to shorter assembly.

Product Life Cycle

Another factor in product design is the stage of the life cycle of the product. Most products go through a series of stages of changing product demand called the

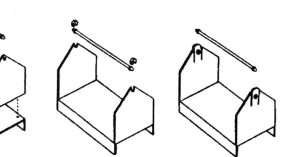

Figure 3-2

Progressive design of a toolbox using DFM

48 mm

Figure 3-3

Stages of the product life cycle

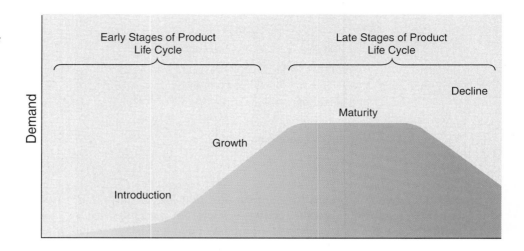

▶ **Product life cycle**
A series of stages that products pass through in their lifetime, characterized by changing product demands.

product life cycle. There are typically four stages of the product life cycle: introduction, growth, maturity, and decline. These are shown in Figure 3-3.

Products in the introductory stage are not well defined and neither is their market. Often all the "bugs" have not been worked out and customers are uncertain about the product. In the growth stage, the product takes hold and both product and market continue to be refined. The third stage is that of maturity, where demand levels off and there are usually no design changes. The product is predictable at this stage and so is its market. Many products, such as toothpaste, can stay in this stage for many years. Finally, there is a decline in demand, because of new technology, better product design, or market saturation.

The first two stages of the life cycle can collectively be called the early stages of the product life cycle because the product is still being improved and refined, and the market is still in the process of being developed. The last two stages of the life cycle can be referred to as the later stages because here the product and market are both well defined.

Understanding the stages of the product life cycle is important for product design purposes, such as knowing at which stage to focus on design changes. Also, when considering a new product, the expected length of the life cycle is critical in order to estimate future profitability relative to the initial investment. The product life cycle can be quite short for certain products, as seen in the computer industry. For other products it can be extremely long, as in the aircraft industry. A few products, such as paper, pencils, nails, milk, sugar, and flour, do not go through a life cycle. However, almost all products do and some may spend a long time in one stage.

Concurrent Engineering

▶ **Concurrent engineering**
An approach that brings together multifunction teams in the early phase of product design in order to simultaneously design the product and the process.

Concurrent engineering is an approach that brings many people together in the early phase of product design in order to simultaneously design the product and the process. This type of approach has been found to achieve a smooth transition from the design stage to actual production in a shorter amount of development time with improved quality results.

The old approach to product and process design was to first have the designers of the idea come up with the exact product characteristics. Once their design was complete they would pass it on to operations who would then design the production process needed to produce the product. This was called the "over-the-wall" approach, because the designers would throw their design "over-the-wall" to operations who then had to decide how to produce the product.

There are many problems with the old approach. First, it is very inefficient and costly. For example, there may be certain aspects of the product that are not critical for product success but are costly or difficult to manufacture, such as a dye color that is difficult to achieve. Since manufacturing does not understand which features are not critical, it may develop an unnecessarily costly production process with costs passed down to the customers. Because the designers do not know the cost of the added feature, they may not have the opportunity to change their design or may do so much later in the process, incurring additional costs. Concurrent engineering allows everyone to work together so these problems do not occur. Figure 3-4 shows the difference between the "over-the-wall" approach and concurrent engineering.

A second problem is that the "over-the-wall" approach takes a longer amount of time than when product and process design work together. As you can see in Figure 3.4, when product and process design work together much of the work is done in parallel rather than in sequence. In today's markets, new product introductions are expected to occur faster than ever. Companies do not have the luxury of enough time to follow a sequential approach and then work the "bugs" out. They may eventually get a great product, but by then the market may not be there!

The third problem is that the old approach does not create a team atmosphere, which is important in today's work environment. Rather, it creates an atmosphere where each function views its role separately in a type of "us versus them" mentality. With the old approach, when the designers were finished with the designs, they considered their job done. If there were problems, each group blamed the other. With concurrent engineering the team is responsible for designing and getting the product to market. Team members continue working together to resolve problems with the product and improve the process.

(a) Sequential design: Walls between functional areas

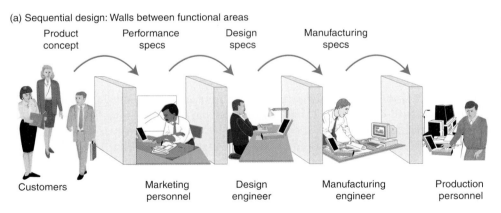

Figure 3-4

The first illustration shows sequential design with walls between functional areas. The second illustration shows concurrent design with walls broken down.

(b) Concurrent design: Walls broken down

Design team

Remanufacturing

▶ Remanufacturing
The concept of using components of old products in the production of new ones.

Remanufacturing is a concept that has been gaining increasing importance, as our society becomes more environmentally conscious and focuses on efforts such as recycling and eliminating waste. **Remanufacturing** uses components of old products in the production of new ones. In addition to the environmental benefits, there are significant cost benefits because remanufactured products can be half the price of their new counterparts. Remanufacturing has been quite popular in the production of computers, televisions, and automobiles.

■ PROCESS SELECTION

So far we have discussed issues involved in product design. Though product design is very important for a company, it cannot be done separately from the **selection of the process.** In this section we will look at issues involved in process design. Then we will see how product design and process selection issues are related.

Types of Processes

When you look at different types of companies, ranging from a small coffee shop to IBM, it may seem like there are hundreds of different types of processes. Some are small, like your local Starbuck's, and some are very large, like a Ford Motor Company plant. Some produce standardized "off-the-shelf" products, like Pepperidge Farm's frozen chocolate cake, and some work with customers to customize their product, like a gourmet bakery that makes cakes to order. Though there seem to be large differences between the processes of companies, many companies have certain processing characteristics in common. In this section we will divide these processes into groups with similar characteristics, allowing us to understand problems inherent with each type of process.

All processes can be grouped into two broad categories: intermittent operations and continuous operations. These two categories differ in almost every way. Once we understand these differences we can easily identify organizations based on the category of process they use.

▶ Intermittent operations
Processes used to produce many different products with varying processing requirements in lower volumes.

Intermittent Operations   **Intermittent operations** are used to produce many different products with varying processing requirements in lower volumes. Examples are an auto body shop, a tool and dye shop, or a health-care facility. Because different products have different processing needs, there is no standard route that all products take through the facility. Instead, resources are grouped by function and the product is routed to each resource as needed. Think about a health-care facility. Each patient, "the product," is routed to different departments as needed. One patient may need to get an x-ray, go to the lab for blood work, and then go to the examining room. Another patient may need to go to the examining room and then to physical therapy.

To be able to produce products with different processing requirements, intermittent operations tend to be labor intensive rather than capital intensive. Workers need to be able to perform different tasks depending on the processing needs of the products produced. Often we see skilled and semiskilled workers in this environment with a fair amount of worker discretion in performing their jobs. Workers need to be flexible and able to perform different tasks as needed for the different products that are being produced. Equipment in this type of environment is more general purpose to satisfy different processing requirements. Automation tends to be less common, because automation is typically product specific. Given that many products are being produced with different processing requirements, it is usually not cost efficient to invest in automation for only one product type. Finally, the volume of goods produced is directly tied to the number of customer orders.

Continuous Operations **Continuous operations** are used to produce one or a few standardized products in high volume. Examples are a typical assembly line, cafeteria, or automatic car wash. Resources are organized in a line flow to efficiently accommodate production of the product. Note that in this environment it is possible to arrange resources in a line because there is only one type of product. This is directly the opposite of what we find with intermittent operations.

> ▶ **Continuous operations**
> Processes used to produce one or a few standardized products in high volume.

To efficiently produce a large volume of one type of product these operations tend to be capital intensive rather than labor intensive. An example is "mass production" operations, which usually have much invested in their facilities and equipment to provide a high degree of product consistency. Often these facilities rely on automation and technology to improve efficiency and increase output rather than on labor skill. The volume produced is usually based on a forecast of future demands rather than on direct customer orders.

The most common differences between intermittent and continuous operations relate to two dimensions: (1) the amount of product volume produced, and (2) the degree of product standardization. Product volume can range from making a single unique product one at a time to producing a large number of products at the same time. Product standardization refers to a lack of variety in a particular product. Examples of standardized products are Fruit-of-the-Loom white undershirts, calculators, toasters, and television sets. The type of operation used, including equipment and labor, is quite different if a company produces one product at a time to customer specifications instead of mass production of one standardized product. Specific differences between intermittent and continuous operations are shown in Table 3-2.

The Continuum of Process Types Dividing processes into two fundamental categories of operations is helpful in our understanding of their general characteristics. To be more detailed, we can further divide each category according to product volume and degree of product standardization as follows. Intermittent operations can be di-

Designing a custom-made cake is an example of an intermittent operation.

An assembly line is an example of a continuous operation.

Table 3-2 Differences between Intermittent and Continuous Operations

Decision	Intermittent Operations	Continuous Operations
Product variety	Great	Small
Degree of standardization	Low	High
Organization of resources	Grouped by function	Line flow to accommodate processing needs
Path of products through facility	In a varied pattern, depending on product needs	Line flow
Factor driving production	Customer orders	Forecast of future demands
Critical resource	Labor-intensive operation (worker skills important)	Capital intensive operation (equipment, automation, technology import)
Type of equipment	General purpose	Specialized
Degree of automation	Low	High
Throughput time	Longer	Shorter
Work-in-process inventory	More	Less

vided into *project processes* and *batch processes.* Continuous operations can be divided into *line processes* and *continuous processes.* Figure 3-5 shows a continuum of process types. Next we look at what makes these processes different from each other.

▶ **A project process**
A type of process used to make a one-at-a-time product exactly to customer specifications.

◆ **Project processes** are used to make one-at-a-time products exactly to customer specifications. These processes are used when there is high customization and low product volume, because each product is different. Examples can be seen in construction, shipbuilding, medical procedures, creation of artwork, custom tailoring, and interior design. With project processes the customer is usually involved in deciding on the design of the product. The artistic baker you hired to bake a wedding cake to your specifications uses a project process.

▶ **A batch process**
A type of process used to produce a small quantity of products in groups or batches based on customer orders or specifications.

◆ **Batch processes** are used to produce small quantities of products in groups or batches based on customer orders or product specifications. The volumes of each product produced are still small and there can still be a high degree of customization. Examples can be seen in bakeries, education, and printing shops. The classes you are taking at the university use a batch process.

▶ **A line process**
A type of process used to produce a large volume of a standardized product.

◆ **Line processes** are designed to produce a large volume of a standardized product for mass production. With line processes the product that is produced is made in high volume with little or no customization. Think of a typical assembly line that produces everything from cars, computers, television sets, shoes, candy bars, even food items.

▶ **Continuous process**
A type of process that operates continually to produce a high volume of a fully standardized product.

◆ **Continuous processes** operate continually to produce a very high volume of a fully standardized product. Examples include oil refineries, water treatment plants, and certain paint facilities. The products produced by continuous processes are usually in continual rather than discrete units, such as liquid or gas. Also, these facilities are usually highly capital intensive and automated.

Note that both project and batch processes have low product volumes and offer customization. The difference is in the volume and degree of customization. Project processes are more extreme cases of intermittent operations compared to batch processes. Also, note that both line and continuous processes primarily produce large

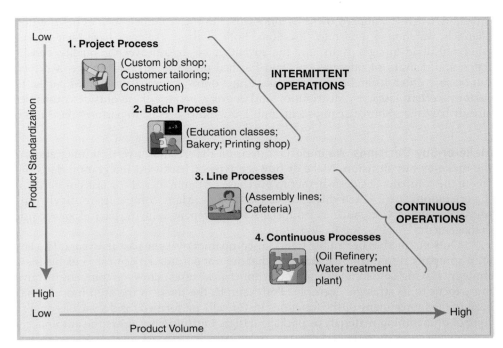

Source: Adapted from Robert H. Hayes and Steven C. Wheelwright, "Link Manufacturing Process and Product Life Cycles," Harvard Business Review, *January-February, 1979, pp. 133–140.*

volumes of standardized products. Again, the difference is in the volume and degree of standardization. Continuous processes are more extreme cases of high volume and product standardization than are line processes.

Figure 3-5 positions these four process types along the diagonal to show the best process strategies relative to product volume and product customization. Companies whose process strategies do not fall along this diagonal may not have made the best process decisions. Bear in mind, however, that not all companies fit into only one of these categories: a company may use both batch and project processing to good advantage. For example, a bakery that produces breads, cakes, and pastries in batch may also bake and decorate cakes to order.

Process Decisions

Vertical Integration A major strategic decision involving process selection relates to the amount of vertical integration of the company. **Vertical integration** refers to the segments in the chain from acquisition of raw materials to final delivery of finished products that the company owns. Some companies are highly vertically integrated, and own their own raw material facilities, manufacturing plants, and fleets of trucks for delivery to customers. An example is Dole Pineapple, which owns and controls most of the canned pineapple production from pineapple farms to the processing plant. Other companies choose the opposite strategy, and use outside suppliers of materials and subassemblies and distributors of their products.

There are two types of vertical integration strategies. One is called **backward integration,** where a company owns or acquires sources of supply, raw materials, or subassemblies. **Forward integration,** on the other hand, is integration in the opposite

▶ **Vertical integration**
The amount of segments owned by a company in the chain from raw materials to final product delivery.

direction, where a company owns facilities closer to the customer, such as distribution channels, warehouses, and retail locations. Both of these strategies have their advantages and disadvantages. Both have the advantage of control over the quality, consistency, and delivery of raw materials and finished products. A disadvantage, however, can be cost. Often it can be much cheaper to use outside suppliers and third parties to perform certain tasks, like distribution and delivery, because these outside companies already have the resources, equipment, and "know-how" needed to perform these tasks.

► A make-or-buy-decision
The decision on whether a company should purchase certain materials or tasks, or perform the operations in house.

Make-or-Buy Decisions An important decision that relates to vertical integration is the **make-or-buy decision.** Make or buy is a type of backward integration decision, where the company decides whether to purchase certain materials or tasks or perform the operations itself. Often this is called *outsourcing*. Many companies routinely outsource certain services, such as janitorial services, repair, security, payroll, or records management.

Outsourcing has been a big trend for companies over the past few years. The key for a company is to outsource activities that are not considered critical to its business strategy. Having someone else perform noncritical tasks allows a company to give more focus to its strategic decisions. For example, the trend in the auto industry has been to outsource many of the functions historically performed inside, such as quality control of incoming materials or package design. Outsourcing allows the automakers to focus more on product and process design, which are much more critical to their success. The importance of outsourcing is evidenced by the growth of companies that perform many noncritical tasks for other firms. For example, Grainger Industrial Supply is a company that performs purchasing and inventory control of noncritical items for companies such as American Airlines and Procter & Gamble, which frees up these companies to focus on what they do best.

Many factors must be considered in the make-or-buy decision. They include the following:

1. **Strategic impact.** Probably the most important factor in the make-or-buy decision is the strategic impact of outsourcing certain tasks. Once tasks are outsourced, a company usually has much less control over them. Customers may not be as satisfied with the product. Also, outsourcing certain tasks now makes it more difficult to bring them back at a later date due to cost and loss of expertise. Companies need to identify functions that are critical and noncritical to their success, as identified through the company's business strategy. Critical functions that have strategic impact should not be outsourced. Noncritical functions, on the other hand, should be outsourced whenever possible in order to free up the company to focus on its main tasks.

2. **Available capacity.** A factor in favor of making products in-house is available capacity. Capacity refers to the output capability of a facility, such as the number of products it can produce over a period of time. If a company has available capacity, as well as skills and equipment required, it is often a good business decision to produce the items in-house.

3. **Expertise.** When considering outsourcing, a company should evaluate whether it has the expertise necessary to perform a job or the costs necessary to acquire the expertise. In many cases it is more efficient to hire somebody else who is proficient in performing certain tasks. For example, many companies will hire outside advertising firms for large promotions and advertising campaigns.

4. **Quality considerations.** As we saw in Chapter 2, quality is an important competitive priority and needs to be given consideration when making the make-or-buy decision. By making products in-house the firm has more control over quality. However, if special expertise is required the company may not be able to achieve the level of quality available from an outside expert. In that case it may be better to outsource.

5. **Speed.** Specialized suppliers can often provide parts more quickly than the manufacturer can produce. This is especially important for products that have fluctuating or unpredictable demands. Suppliers can also be more flexible in accommodating rapid design changes.

6. **Cost.** The last factor to consider is the cost of manufacturing the item in-house versus buying it from the outside. However, cost should not be the most important factor and needs to be balanced with the other factors discussed. A more expensive alternative that is strategically sound can prove to be a far better alternative in the long run.

Designing Processes

Process Flow Analysis **Process flow analysis** is a tool for evaluating an operation in terms of the sequence of steps from inputs to outputs with the goal of improving its design. One of the most important tools in process flow analysis is a process flowchart. A **process flowchart** is used for viewing the flow of the processes involved in producing the product. It is a very useful tool for seeing the totality of the operation and for identifying potential problem areas. There is no exact format for designing the chart. The flowchart can be very simple or very detailed. Figure 3-6 shows a flowchart for Antonio's Take-Out Pizza Shop that includes the steps involved in placing and processing a customer order. The points in the process for potential problems are indicated. Management can then take care to monitor these problem areas. The chart could be even more detailed, including information such as frequency of errors or approximate time to complete a task.

> ▶ **A process flowchart**
> Shows the flow of all the process steps involved in producing the product or service.

Another way of using a process flowchart is to overlay it on a facility layout to visually represent movement through the physical plant or store, as shown in Figure 3-7 for Antonio's Take-Out Pizza Shop. Arrows indicate the direction of movement, with blue arrows indicating movement of the customer and red arrows indicating movement of the product, from order placement to delivery. The chart allows Antonio to analyze the flow. If one of the problem areas is experiencing difficulty, such as long wait for the order, Antonio can look at the layout to see whether there are ways to correct that, such as with an additional oven and workstation.

Process Reengineering **Reengineering** means redesigning the company's processes. Reengineering is a drastic measure of analyzing the company's processes and redeveloping them from scratch. The process requires teamwork from many areas of the company and good communication. Hard questions need to be asked and old ways of doing things questioned. Reengineering is usually applied to the core processes of a company, such as filling customer orders. Reengineering can produce dramatic improvements in quality, cost, and customer service. Many companies such as Bell Atlantic and Kodak have been able to achieve large benefits through reengineering. However, it does not always work. Reengineering is a radical measure that focuses on drastic changes rather than incremental changes. It usually means layoffs or shifts in job duties and a very different way of doing things for the company's employees. Reengineering is usually applied as a last resort for companies that are either in trouble or foresee trouble in the future. When other measures for a company have failed, reengineering may be the last resort.

> ▶ **Reengineering**
> Redesigning the company's processes from scratch.

Figure 3-6

Process flowchart for Antonio's take-out-pizza

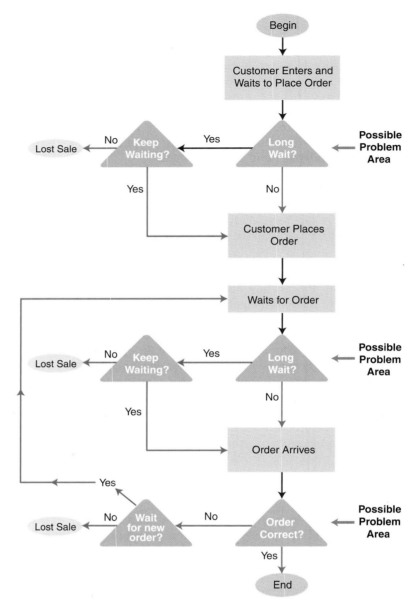

Make sure that you understand the key issues in product design. Be familiar with the different stages of the product life cycle. Recall that products in the early stages of the life cycle are still being refined based on the needs of the market. This includes product characteristics and features. At this stage the market for the product has not yet been fully developed and product volumes have not reached their peak. By contrast, products in the later stages of their life cycle have well-developed characteristics and demand volumes are fairly stable.

Review the different types of processes and their characteristics. Recall that intermittent processes are designed to produce products with different processing requirements in smaller volumes. Continuous operations, on the other hand, are designed for one or a few types of products produced in high volumes.

Next we discuss how product design and process selection decisions are interrelated.

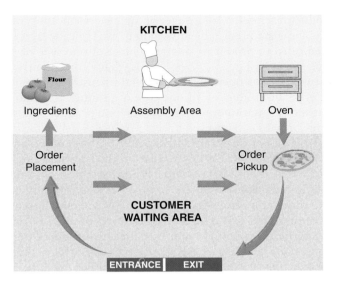

Figure 3-7

Process flowchart with facility layout for Antonio's take-out pizza

RELATIONSHIP BETWEEN PRODUCT DESIGN AND PROCESS SELECTION ■

Decisions of product design and process selection are directly linked and cannot be made independently of one another. The type of product a company produces defines the type of operation needed. The type of operation needed, in turn, defines many other aspects of the organization. This includes how a company competes in the marketplace (competitive priorities), the type or equipment and its arrangement in the facility, the type of organizational structure, and future types of products that can be produced by the facility. Table 3-3 summarizes some key decisions and how they differ for intermittent and continuous types of operations. Next we look at each of these decision areas.

Product Design Decisions

Intermittent and continuous operations typically focus on producing products in different stages of the product life cycle. Intermittent operations focus on products in the early stage of the life cycle because facilities are general purpose and can be adapted to the needs of the product. As products in the early stage of the life cycle are still being refined, intermittent operations are ideally suited for these types of products. Also, demand volumes for these products are still uncertain and intermittent operations are designed to focus on producing lower volumes of products with differing characteristics.

Table 3-3 Differences in Key Organizational Decisions for Different Types of Operations		
Decision	**Intermittent Operations**	**Continuous Operations**
Product design	Early stage of product life cycle	Later stage of product life cycle
Competitive priorities	Delivery, flexibility, and quality	Cost and quality
Facility layout	Resources grouped by function	Resources arranged in a line
Vertical integration	Low	High

Once a product reaches the later stages of the life cycle both its product features and its demand volume are predictable. As volumes are typically larger at this stage, a facility that is dedicated to producing a large volume of one type of product is best from both efficiency and cost perspectives. This is what a continuous operations provides. Recall that continuous operations are capital intensive with much automation dedicated to the efficient production of one type of product. It would not be a good decision to invest such a large amount of resources for a product that is uncertain relative to its features or market. However, once a product is well defined with a sizable market, continuous types of operations are a better business alternative. This is why continuous operations tend to focus on products in the later stages of their life cycle.

The product focus of both types of operations has significant implications for a company's future product choices. Once a company has an intermittent operation in place, designed to produce a variety of products in low volumes, it is a poor strategic decision to pursue production of a highly standardized product in the same facility. The same holds true for attempting to produce a newly introduced product in a continuous operation.

The differences between the two types operations are great, including the way they are managed. Not understanding the differences between the two types of operations and the products they are designed to produce is a mistake often made by companies. A company may be very successful at managing a continuous operation that produce a standardized product. Management may then see an opportunity involving products in the early stage of the life cycle. Not understanding the differences in the operational requirements, management may decide to produce this new product by applying their "know-how." The results can prove disastrous.

LINKS TO PRACTICE
Babcock & Wilcox Company
www.babcock.com

The problems that can arise when a company does not understand the differences between intermittent and continuous operations are illustrated by the experience of the Babcock & Wilcox Company in the late 1960s. B & W was very successful at producing fossil fuel boilers, a standardized product made via a continuous operation. Then the company decided to pursue production of nuclear pressure vessels, a new product in the early stages of its life cycle requiring an intermittent operation. B & W saw the nuclear pressure vessels as a wave of the future. Because they were successful at producing boilers, they believed they could apply those same skills to production of the new product. Unfortunately, B & W failed miserably and almost went out of business at that time.

Competitive Priorities

The decision of how a company will compete in the marketplace—its competitive priorities—is largely affected by the type of operation it has in place. Intermittent operations are typically less competitive on cost than continuous operations. The reason is that continuous operations mass produce a large volume of one product. The cost of the product is spread over a large volume, allowing the company to offer that product at a comparatively lower price.

Think about the cost difference you would incur if you decided to buy a business suit "off the rack" from your local department store (produced by a continuous operation) versus having it custom made by a tailor (an intermittent operation). Certainly a custom-made suit would cost considerably more. The same product produced by a continuous operation typically costs less than one made by an intermittent operation. However, intermittent operations have their own advantages. Having a custom-made suit allows you to choose precisely what you want in style, color, texture, and fit. Also, if you were not satisfied you could easily return it for adjustments and alterations. Intermittent operations compete more on flexibility and delivery compared to continuous operations.

Today all organizations understand the importance of quality. However, the elements of quality that a company focuses on may be different depending on the type of operation used. Continuous operations provide greater consistency between products. The first and last products made in the day are almost identical. Intermittent operations, on the other hand, offer greater variety of features and workmanship not available with mass production.

It is important that companies understand the competitive priorities best suited for the type of process that they use. It would not be a good strategic decision for an intermittent operation to try to compete primarily on cost, as it would not be very successful. Similarly, the primary competitive priority for a continuous operation should not be variety of features, because this would take away from the efficiency of the process design.

Facility Layout

Facility layout, covered in Chapter 10, is concerned with the arrangement of resources of a facility to enhance the production process. If resources are not arranged properly, a company will have inefficiency and waste. The type of process a company uses directly affects the facility layout of the organization and the inherent problems encountered.

Intermittent operations group their resources based on similar processes or functions. There is no one typical product that is produced; rather, a large variety of items are produced in low volumes, each with their own unique processing needs. Since no one product justifies the dedication of an entire facility, resources are grouped based on their function. Products are then moved from resource to resource, based on their processing needs. The challenge with intermittent operations is to arrange the location of resources to maximize efficiency and minimize waste of movement. If the intermittent operation has not been designed properly, many products will be moved long distances. This type of movement adds nothing to the value of the product and contributes to waste. Any two work centers that have much movement between them should be placed close to one another. However, this often means that another work center will have to be moved out of the way. This can make the problem fairly challenging.

Intermittent operations are less efficient and have longer production times due to the nature of the layout. Material handling costs tend to be high and scheduling resources is a challenge. Intermittent operations are common in practice. Examples include a doctor's office or a hospital. Departments are grouped based on their function, with examining rooms in one area, lab in another, and x-rays in a third. Patients are moved from one department to another based on their needs. Another example is a bakery that makes custom cakes and pastries. The work centers are set up to perform different functions, such as making different types of dough, different types of fillings, and different types of icing and decorations. The product is routed to different workstations depending on the product requirements. Some cakes have the filling in the center (i.e., Boston cream pie), others only on top (i.e., sheet cake), and some have no filling at all (i.e., pound cake).

Continuous operations have resources arranged in sequence to allow for efficient production of a standardized product. Since only one product or a few highly similar products are being produced, all resources are arranged to efficiently meet production needs. Examples are seen on an assembly line, in a cafeteria, or even a car wash. Numerous products, from breakfast cereals to computers, are made using continuous operations.

Though continuous operations have faster processing rates, lower material handling costs, and greater efficiency than intermittent operations, they also have their shortcomings. Resources are highly specialized and the operation is inflexible relative to the market. This type of operation cannot respond rapidly to changes in market needs for the products wanted or the changes in demand volume. The challenge is to arrange workstations in sequence and designate the jobs that will be performed by each to produce the product in the most efficient way possible.

Vertical Integration

The larger the number of processes performed by a company in the chain from raw materials to product delivery, the higher is the vertical integration. Vertical integration is a strategic decision that should support the future growth direction of the company. Vertical integration is a good strategic option when there are high volumes of a small variety of input materials, as is the case with continuous operations. The reason is that the high volume and narrow variety of input material allows task specialization and cost justification. Recall the example of Dole Pineapple. The company's product is canned pineapple. The input material is fresh pineapple. Since one input material is needed in large volume the company has chosen to be vertically integrated so as to have greater control of costs and product quality.

It is typically not a good strategic decision to vertically integrate into specialized processes that provide inputs in small volumes. This would be the case for intermittent operations. For example, let's consider a bakery that makes a variety of different types of cakes and pies. Maybe the bakery purchases different fillings from different sources, such as apple pie filling from one company, chocolate filling from another, and cream filling from a third. If the company were to purchase production of the apple filling, it would not gain much strategically because it still relies on other suppliers. However, if the bakery shifted its production to only making apple pies, then the vertical integration may be a good choice.

In summary, vertical integration is typically a better strategic decision for continuous operations. For intermittent operations it is generally a poor strategic choice.

■ MANUFACTURING TECHNOLOGY DECISIONS

Advancements in technology have had the greatest impact on process design decisions. Technological advances have enabled companies to produce products faster, with better quality, at a cheaper rate. Many processes that were not imaginable only a few years ago have been made possible through the use of technology. In this section we look at some of the greatest impacts technology has had on process design.

Automation

An important decision in designing processes is deciding whether the firm should automate, to what degree, and the type of automation that should be used. **Automation** is machinery that is able to perform work without human operators. Automation can be a single machine or an entire factory. Although there are tremendous advantages to automation, there are also disadvantages. Companies need to consider these carefully before making the final decision.

Automation has the advantage of product consistency and ability to efficiently produce large volumes of product. With automated equipment the last part made in the day will be exactly like the first one made. Because automation brings consistency, quality tends to be higher and easier to monitor. With automation, production can flow uninterrupted throughout the day, without breaks for lunch, and there is no fatigue factor.

However, automation does have its disadvantages. First, automation is typically very costly. These costs can be justified only through a high volume of production. Second, automation is typically not flexible in accommodating product and process changes. Therefore, automation would probably not be good for products in the early stages of their life cycle or for products with short life cycles. Automation needs to be viewed as another capital investment decision and financial payback is critical. For all these reasons automation is typically less present in intermittent than in continuous operations.

Next we look at different types of automation.

▶ **Automation**
Machinery that is able to perform work without human operators.

Automated Material Handling

Material handling devices are used to move and store products. Historically the primary method of moving products used conveyors in the form of belts or chains. Today's material handling devices can read bar codes that tell them which location to go to and are capable of moving in many directions. One such device is an **automated guided vehicle (AGV)**. This is a small battery-driven truck that moves materials from one location to the other. The AGV is not operated by a human and takes its directions from either an on-board or central computer. Even AGVs have become more sophisticated over time. The older models followed a cable that was installed under the floor. The newer models follow optical paths and can go anywhere there is aisle space.

One of the biggest advantages of AGVs is that they can pretty much go anywhere, as compared to traditional conveyor belts. Managers can use them to move materials wherever they are needed, avoiding huge piles of inventory in one area.

Another type of automated material handling are **automated storage and retrieval system (AS/RSs)**, which are basically automated warehouses. AS/RSs use AGVs to move material and computer-controlled racks and storage bins. The storage bins can typically rotate like a carousel, so that the desired storage bin is available for either storage or retrieval. All this is controlled by a computer that keeps track of the exact location and quantity of each item. The computer controls how much will be stored or retrieved in a particular area. AS/RSs can have great advantages over traditional warehouses. Though they are much more costly to operate, they are also much more efficient and accurate.

Hand held scanner reading shipping barcode on wood crate.

Computer-Aided Design (CAD)

Computer-aided design (CAD) is a system that uses computer graphics to design new products. Gone are the days of drafting designs by hand. Today's powerful desk-

▶ **Computer-aided design (CAD)**
A system that uses computer graphics to design new products.

Automated cheese warehouse

top computers combined with graphics software allow the designer to create drawings on the computer screen and then manipulate them geometrically to be viewed from any angle. With CAD the designer can rotate the object, split it to view the inside, and magnify certain sections for closer view.

CAD can also perform other functions. Engineering design calculations can be performed to test the reactions of the design to stress and evaluate strength of materials. This is called **computer-aided engineering (CAE)**. For example, the designer can test how different dimensions, tolerances, and materials respond to different conditions such as rough handling or high temperatures. The designer can use the computer to compare alternative designs and determine the best design for a given set of conditions. The designer can also perform cost analysis on the design, evaluating the advantages of different types of materials.

Another advantage of CAD is that it can be linked to manufacturing. We already discussed the importance of linking product design to process selection. Through CAD this integration is made easy. **Computer-aided manufacturing (CAM)** is the process of controlling manufacturing through computers. Since the product designs are stored in the computer database, the equipment and tools needed can easily be simulated to match up with the processing needs. Efficiencies of various machine choices and different process alternatives can be computed.

As you can imagine, there are numerous advantages to CAD. It has dramatically increased the speed and flexibility of the design process. Designs can be made on the computer screen and printed out when desired. Electronic versions can be shared by many members of the organization for their input. Also, electronic version can be archived and compared to future versions. The designer can catalogue features based on their characteristics—a very valuable feature. As future product design are being considered, the designer can quickly retrieve certain features from past designs and test them for inclusion in the design being currently developed. Overall, it is estimated that CAD can speed up the design process by up to 50%.

Flexible Manufacturing Systems (FMS)

▶ **A flexible manufacturing system (FMS)**
A type of automated system that provides the flexibility of intermittent operations with the efficiency of continuous operations.

A **flexible manufacturing system (FMS)** is a type of automation system that provides the flexibility of intermittent operations with the efficiency of continuous operations. As you can see by the definition, this is a *system* of automated parts not only one machine. An FMS consists of groups of computer-controlled machines and/or robots, automated handling devices for moving, loading, and unloading, and a computer control center.

Based on the instructions from the computer control center, parts and materials are automatically moved to appropriate machines or robots. The machines perform their tasks and the parts are then moved to the next set of machines with the parts automatically loaded and unloaded. The routes taken by each product are determined with the goal of maximizing efficiency of the operation. Also, the FMS "knows" when one machine is down due to maintenance or if there is a backlog of work on a machine, and it will automatically route the materials to an available machine.

Flexible manufacturing systems are still fairly limited in the variety of products that they handle. Usually they can only produce similar products from the same family. Flexible manufacturing systems are not very widespread. One of the primary reasons is their high cost. A decision to use an FMS needs to be long term and strategic, requiring a sizable financial outlay.

Robotics

When most of us think of robots we think of something like the robot from the old television show "Lost In Space," which resembles humans. However, in manufacturing a robot is usually nothing more than a mechanical arm with a power supply and a computer control mechanism that controls the movements of the arm. The arm can be used for many tasks, such as painting, welding, assembly, loading, and unloading of machines. Robots are excellent for physically dangerous jobs such as working with radioactive or toxic materials. Also, robots can work 24 hours a day to produce a highly consistent product.

Robots range in their degree of sophistication. Some robots are fairly simple and follow a repetitive set of instructions. Other robots follow complex instructions, and some can be programmed to recognize objects and even make simple decisions. One type of automation that is similar to simple robotics is the **numerically controlled (NC) machine**. NC machines are controlled by a computer and can do a variety of tasks such as drilling, boring, or turning parts of different sizes and shapes. Factories of the future will most likely be composed of a number of robots and NC machines working together.

The use of robots has not been very widespread in U.S. firms. However, this is an area that can provide a competitive advantage for a company. Cost justification should not only consider reduction in labor costs but also the increased flexibility of operation and improvement in quality. The cost of robots can vary greatly and depends on the robots' size and capabilities. Generally, it is best for a company to consider purchasing multiple robots or forms of automation to spread the costs of maintenance and software support. Also, the decision to purchase automation such as robotics needs to be a long-term strategic decision that considers the totality of the production process. Otherwise, the company may have one robot working 24 hours a day and piling up inventory while it waits for the other processes to catch up.

▶ **A numerically controlled (NC) machine**
Controlled by a computer and can perform a variety of tasks.

Production line robot placing windshield on car

Robots can be used to improve operations of almost any business—even literal "operations." Recently robots have begun to be used in performing certain medical surgeries. The first minimally invasive robotic surgery on a human heart valve was performed by three robot arms at the New York University Medical center in April 2000. To perform the surgery, doctors at NYU used the robot arms to cut a 6-centimeter incision between the ribs and send an endoscope that would allow the surgeons to see what they were doing. The robot arms controlled through a complex robotic surgical system. The doctors, seated at a workstation, can manipulate conventional surgical instruments while the robotic surgical system mirrors these movements on an ultra-fine scale. The advantage of using robots is that they can perform delicately fine, small, motor movements, have consistent finger dexterity, and require only tiny incisions. The prediction is that robots will become involved in performing many surgeries, such as eye surgery, neurosurgery, and cosmetic surgery.

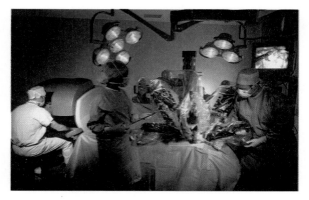

LINKS TO PRACTICE
Performing Robotic Surgery

Computer-Integrated Manufacturing

► Computer-integrated manufacturing (CIM)
A term used to describe the integration of product design, process planning, and manufacturing using an integrated computer system.

Computer-integrated manufacturing (CIM) is a term used to describe the integration of product design, process planning, and manufacturing using an integrated computer system. Computer-integrated manufacturing systems vary greatly in their complexity. Simple systems might integrate computer-aided design (CAD) with some numerically controlled machines (NC machines). A complex system, on the other hand, might integrate purchasing, scheduling, inventory control, and distribution, in addition to the other areas of product design.

The key element of CIM is the integration of different parts of the operation process to achieve greater responsiveness and flexibility. The purpose of CIM is to improve how quickly the company can respond to customer needs of product design and availability, as well as quality, productivity, and improve overall efficiency.

■ DESIGNING SERVICES

Most of the issues discussed in this chapter are as applicable to manufacturing as they are to service organizations. However, there are issues unique to services that pose special challenges for service design.

Most of us think we know what is needed to run a good service organization. After all, we encounter services almost every day, at banks, fast-food restaurants, doctor's offices, barber shops, grocery stores, and even the university. We have all experienced poor service quality and would gladly offer advice as to how we think it could be run better. However, there are some very important features of services you may have not thought about. Let's see what they are.

How Are Services Different from Manufacturing?

In Chapter 1 we learned about two basic features that make service organizations different from manufacturing. These are the intangibility of the product produced and the high degree of customer contact. Next we briefly review these and see how they impact service design.

Intangible Product Service organizations produce an intangible product, which cannot be touched or seen. It cannot be stored in inventory for later use or traded in for another model. The service produced is *experienced* by the customer. The design of the service needs to specify exactly what the customer is supposed to experience. For example, it may be relaxation, comfort, and pampering such as offered by Canyon Ranch Spa. It may be efficiency and speed, such as offered by Federal Express. Defining the customer experience is part of the service design. It requires identifying precisely what the customer is going to feel and think, and consequently how he or she is going to behave. This is not always as easy as it might seem.

The experience of the customer is directly related to customer expectations. For services to be successful the customer experience needs to meet or even exceed these expectations. However, customer expectations can greatly vary depending on the type of customer and customer demographic. This includes customer age, gender, background, and knowledge. The expectation is made through product marketing to a particular market segment. It is highly important in designing the service to identify the target market the service is geared to and create the correct expectation.

High Degree of Customer Contact Service organizations have a high degree of customer contact. The customer is often present while the service is being delivered, such as at a theater, restaurant, or bank. Also, the contact between the customer and service provider is often the service itself, such as what you experience at a doctor's office. For a service to be successful this contact needs to be a positive experience for the customer, and this depends greatly on the service provider.

Unfortunately, since services often have multiple service providers, there can be great variation in the type of service delivered. We have all had experiences where the service of one organization varied greatly depending on the skills of the service provider. This could be a hairdresser at a hair salon, a food server at a restaurant, or a teller at a bank. We have all heard people say something similar to "I often have dinner at Aussie Steak Grill and I insist that Jenny be my server." Similarly, someone might say "I go to Olentangy Family Physicians, but I won't see Dr. Jekyl because he is rude and unfriendly." For a service to be successful, the service experience must be consistent at all times. This requires close quality management to ensure high consistency and reliability. Many of the procedures we use in manufacturing to ensure high quality, such as standardization and simplification, are used in services as well. Fast-food restaurants such as McDonald's and Wendy's are known for their consistency. The same is true of hotel chains such as Holiday Inn and Embassy Suites.

To ensure that the service contact is a positive experience for the customer, employees of the service need to have training that encompasses a great array of skills that include courtesy, friendliness, and overall disposition. The service company also needs to structure the proper incentive system to motivate employees. For example, studies have shown that employee performance is motivated more by monetary incentives rather than by their belief in the idea of the service.

The Service Package

The really successful service organizations do not happen spontaneously. They are carefully thought out and planned, down to every employee action. To design a successful service we must first start with a service concept or idea, which needs to be very comprehensive. We have learned that when purchasing a service, customers actually buy a **service package** or bundle of goods. The service package is a grouping of features that are purchased together as part of the service. There are three elements of the service package: (1) the physical goods, (2) the sensual benefits, and (3) the psychological benefits. The physical goods of the service are the tangible aspects of the service that we receive, or are in contact with, during service delivery. In a fine-dining restaurant the physical goods are the food consumed, as well as facilities such as comfortable tables and chairs, table cloths, and fine china. The sensual benefits are the sights, smell, and sounds of the experience—all the items we experience through our senses. Finally, the psychological benefits include the status, comfort, and well-being of the experience.

It is highly important that the design of the service specifically identify every aspect of the service package. When designing the service we should not focus only on the tangible aspects; it is often the sensual and psychological benefits that are the deciding factors in the success of the service. The service package needs to be designed to precisely meet the expectations of the target customer group.

Once the service package is identified it can then be translated into a design using a process that is not too different from the one used in manufacturing. Details of the service, such as quality standards and employee training, can later be defined in keeping with the service concept. The service providers—the individuals who come in

▶ **A service package**
A grouping of physical, sensual, and psychological benefits that are purchased together as part of the service.

CROSS FUNCTIONAL

direct contact with the customers—must be trained and motivated to precisely understand and satisfy customer expectations.

Imagine going to a fast-food restaurant and having the server take his time asking you how you want your hamburger cooked and precisely what condiments you would like to accompany it, then waiting a long time to receive your food. Similarly, imagine going to an expensive hair salon and having the staff rush you through the process. In both cases, you as the customer would not be satisfied because the service delivery did not meet your expectations. Next time you might choose to go somewhere else. These examples illustrate what happens when there is a mismatch between the service concept and the service delivery.

Differing Service Designs

There is no one model of successful service design. The design selected should support the company's service concept and provide the features of the service package that the target customers want. Different service designs have proved successful in different environments. In this section we look at three very different service designs that have worked well for the companies that adopted them.

Substitute Technology for People Substituting technology for people is an approach to service design that was advocated some years ago by Theodore Levitt.[1] Levitt argued that one way to reduce the uncertainty of service delivery is to use technology to develop a production line approach to services. One of the most successful companies to use this approach is McDonald's. Technology has been substituted wherever possible to provide product consistency and take the guesswork away from employees. Some examples of the use of technology include the following:

◆ Buzzers and lights are used to signal cooking time for frying perfect french fries.
◆ The size of the french fryer is designed to produce the correct amount of fries.
◆ The french fry scoop is the perfect size to fill an order.
◆ "Raw materials" are received in usable form (e.g., hamburger patties are premade; pickles and tomatoes are presliced; french fries are precut).
◆ There are 49 steps for producing the perfect french fries.
◆ Steps for producing the perfect hamburger are detailed and specific.
◆ Products have different colored wrappings for easy identification.

In addition to the use of technology in the production of the product, there is consistency in facilities and a painstaking focus on cleanliness. For example, the production process at McDonald's is not left to the discretion of the workers. Rather, their job is to follow the technology and preset processes.

Today, we are all accustomed to the product consistency, speed of delivery, and predictability that are a feature of most fast-food restaurants. However, this concept was very new in the early 1970s. It is this approach to services that has enabled McDonald's to establish its global reputation.

Substituting technology for people is an approach we have seen over the years in many service industries. For example, almost all gas stations have reduced the number of cashiers and attendants with the advent of credit card usage at self-serve pumps. Also, many hospitals are using technology to monitor patient heart rate and blood pressure without relying exclusively on nurses. As technologies develop in different

[1]Theodore Levitt, "Production Line Approach To Services," *Harvard Business Review* 50, no. 5 (September–October 1972), pp. 41–52.

service industries we will continue to see an ever increasing reliance on its use and the elimination of workers.

Get the Customer Involved A different approach to service design was proposed by C. H. Lovelock and R. F. Young.[2] Their idea was to take advantage of the customer's presence during the delivery of the service and have him or her become an active participant. This is different from traditional service designs where the customer passively waits for service employees to deliver the service. Lovelock and Young proposed that since the customers are already there, "get them involved."

We have all seen a large increase in the self-serve areas of many service firms. Traditional salad bars have led to self-serve food buffets of every type. Many fast-food restaurants no longer fill customer drink orders, but have the customers serve themselves. Grocery stores allow customers to select and package baked goods on their own. Many hotels provide in-room coffee makers and prepackaged coffee, allowing customers to make coffee at their convenience.

This type of approach has a number of advantages. First, it takes a large burden away from the service provider. The delivery of the service is made faster and costs are reduced due to lowered staffing requirements. Second, this approach empowers customers and gives them a greater sense of control in terms of getting what they want. This approach provides a great deal of customer convenience and increases satisfaction. However, as different types of customers have different preferences, many facilities are finding that it is best to offer full-service and self-service options. For example, many breakfast bars still allow a request for eggs cooked and served to order, and most gas stations still offer some full-service pumps.

High Customer Attention Approach A third approach to service design is providing a high level of customer attention. This is in direct contrast to the first two approaches we discussed. The first approach discussed automates the service and makes it more like manufacturing. The second approach requires greater participation and responsibility from the customer. The third approach is different from the first two in that it does not standardize the service and does not get the customer involved. Rather, it is based on customizing the service needs unique to each customer and having the customer be the passive and pampered recipient of the service. This approach relies on developing a personal relationship with each customer and giving the customer precisely what he or she wants.

There are a number of examples of this type of approach. Nordstrom Department Stores is recognized in the retail industry for its attention to customer service. Salespeople typically know their customers by name and keep a record of their preferences. Returns are handled without question and the customer is always right without questions asked. Another example of this is a midwestern grocer called Dorothy Lane Market. Dorothy Lane prides itself on its ability to provide unique cuts of specialty meats precisely to customer order. Like at Nordstrom, a list is kept of primary customers and their preferences. Customers are notified of special purchases, such as unique wines, specialty chocolates, and special cuts of meat.

Whereas the first two approaches to service design result in lowered service costs, this third approach is geared toward customers that are prepared to pay a higher amount for the services they receive. As you can see, different approaches are meant to serve different types of customers. The design chosen needs to support the specific service concept of the company.

[2]C. H. Lovelock and R. F. Young, "Look to Customers to Increase Productivity," *Harvard Business Review* 57, no. 2 (month year), pp. 168–178.

OM ACROSS THE ORGANIZATION

The strategic and financial impact of product design and process selection mandates that operations work closely with other organizational functions to make these decisions. Operations is an integral part of this decision because it understands issues of production, ease of fabrication, productivity, and quality. Now let's see how the other organizational functions are involved with product design and process selection.

Marketing is impacted by product design issues because they determine the types of products that will be produced and affect marketing's ability to sell them. Marketing's input is critical at this stage because marketing is the function that interfaces with customers and understands the types of product characteristics customers want. It is marketing that can provide operations with information on customer preferences, competition, and future trends.

Process selection decisions impact marketing as well. Process selection decisions typically require large capital outlays. Once in place, process decisions are typically difficult to change and are in place for a long time. Process decisions affect the types of future products that the company can produce. Because of this, marketing needs to be closely involved in ensuring that the process can meet market demands for many years to come.

Finance plays an integral role in product design and process selection issues because these decisions require large financial outlays. Finance needs to be a part of these decisions to evaluate the financial impact on the company. Process selection decisions should be viewed as any other financial investment, with risks and rewards. Finance must ensure that the tradeoff between the risks and rewards is acceptable. Also, it is up to finance to provide the capital needed for this investment and balance that against future capital requirements.

Information systems needs to be part of the process selection decision. Operations decisions, such as forecasting, purchasing, scheduling, and inventory control differ based on the type of operation the company has. Information systems will be quite different for intermittent versus continuous operations. Therefore, the information system has to be developed to match the needs of the production process being planned.

Human resources provides important input to process selection decisions because it is the function directly responsible for hiring employees. If special labor skills are needed in the process of production, human resources needs to be able to provide information on the available labor pool. The two types of operations discussed, intermittent and continuous, typically require very different labor skills. Intermittent operations usually require higher-skilled labor than continuous operations. Human resources needs to understand the specific skills that are needed.

Purchasing works closely with suppliers to get the needed parts and raw materials at a favorable price. It is aware of product and material availability, scarcity, and price. Often certain materials or components can use less expensive substitutes if they are designed properly. For this reason it is important to have purchasing involved in product design issues from the very beginning.

Engineering needs to be an integral part of the product design and process selection decision because this is the function that understands product measurement, tolerances, strength of materials, and specific equipment needs. There can be many product design ideas, but it is up to engineering to evaluate their manufacturability.

As you can see, product design and process selection issues involve many functions and affect the entire organization. For this reason, product design and process selection decisions need to be made using a team effort with all these functions working closely together to come up with a product plan that is best for the company.

OM IS EVERYWHERE ■

Product and process design affect your everyday life in more ways than you might realize. Every time you are dissatisfied with the features of a product or the delivery or a service, you can blame product and process design. Your loyalty toward a particular product, like the pizza preferences we discussed in the beginning of the chapter, are all because of product and process design.

Product and process design are a big part of your life in other ways too. Often you "design" products and processes even when you are not aware of it. Suppose you decide to be creative in the kitchen and create a recipe for your own chocolate cream pie. You base your "design" on the best ideas from old recipes, including an Oreo-cookie crust and marshmallow cream topping. You purchase all the ingredients and proceed to "produce" your product. However, halfway through "production" you realize that the recipe calls for a double-boiler to make the cream filling and you do not have one. This means that you will have to stop what you are doing and go to a store to buy a double-boiler. In the meantime, some of the ingredients might get stale and your pie will not be as good as you hoped. Also, the cost of the pie might be more than you bargained for. Had you designed your "process" while you were designing the product you would not have this problem. Next time you are "designing" a product you might want to use the concept of concurrent engineering and design the process along with the product.

CHAPTER HIGHLIGHTS

1 Product design is the process of deciding on the unique characteristics and features of a company's product. Process selection, on the other hand, is the development of the process necessary to produce the product we design. Product design is a big strategic decision for a company, because the design of the product defines who the company's customers will be, as well as the company's image, its competition, and its overall future growth.

2 Steps in product design include idea generation, product screening, preliminary design and testing, and final design. A useful tool at the product-screening stage is break-even analysis.

3 Break-even analysis is a technique used to compute the amount of goods we would have to sell just to cover our costs.

4 Production processes can be divided into two broad categories: intermittent and continuous operations. Intermittent operations are used when products with different characteristics are being produced in smaller volumes. These types of operations tend to organize their resources by grouping similar processes together and having the product routed through the facility based on their needs. Continuous operations are used when one or a few similar products are produced in high volume. These operations arrange resources in sequence to allow for an efficient build-up of the product. Both intermittent and continuous operations have their advantages and disadvantages. Intermittent operations provide great flexibility but have high material handling costs and challenges scheduling resources. Continuous operations are highly efficient but inflexible.

5 Product design and process selection decisions are linked. The type of operation a company has in place is defined by the product the company produces. The type of operation then affects other organizational decisions, such as competitive priorities, facility layout, and degree of vertical integration.

6 A process flowchart is used for viewing the flow of the processes involved in producing the product. It is a very useful tool for seeing to totality of the operation and for identifying potential problem areas. There is no exact format for designing the chart. The flowchart can be very sample or very detailed.

7 Different types of technologies can significantly enhance product and process design. These include automation, automated material handling devices, computer-aided design (CAD), numerically controlled (NC) equipment, flexible manufacturing systems (FMS), and computer-integrated manufacturing (CIM).

8 Designing services has a few more complexities then manufacturing, because services produce an intangible product and typically have a high degree of customer contact. Different service designs include substituting technology for people, getting the customer involved, and the high customer attention approach.

KEY TERMS

product design 43
service design 43
benchmarking 45
reverse engineering 45
break-even analysis 46
design for manufacture (DFM) 49
product life cycle 49
concurrent engineering 50
remanufacturing 52

intermittent operations 52
continuous operations 53
project process 54
batch process 54
line process 54
continuous process 54
vertical integration 55
make-or-buy decision 56
process flowchart 57

reengineering 57
automation 63
computer-aided design (CAD) 63
flexible manufacturing system (FMS) 64
numerically controlled (NC)
   machine 65
computer-integrated manufacturing
   (CIM) 66
service package 67

FORMULA REVIEW

1. Total cost = fixed cost + variable cost

2. Revenue = $(SP) Q$

3. $F + (VC) Q = (SP) Q$

4. $Q_{BE} = \dfrac{F}{SP - VC}$

SOLVED PROBLEMS

■ Problem 1

Joe Jenkins, owner of Jenkins Manufacturing, is considering whether to produce a new product. He has considered the operations requirements for the product as well as the market potential. Joe estimates the fixed costs per year to be $40,000 and variable costs for each unit produced to be $50.

(a) If Joe sells the product at a price of $70, how many units of product does he have to sell in order to break even? Use both the algebraic and graphical approach.
(b) If Fred sells 3000 units at the product price of $70, what will be his contribution to profit?

Solution
(a) To compute the break-even quantity we follow our basic equation and substitute the appropriate numbers:

$$Q = \frac{F}{SP - VC} = \frac{\$40,000}{\$70 - \$50} = 2000 \text{ units}$$

The break-even quantity is 2000 units. This is how much Fred would have to sell in order to cover his costs.

Graphically we can obtain the same result. This is shown in Figure 3-8.
(b) To compute the contribution to profit with sales of 3000 units:

$$\text{Profit} = \text{total revenue} - \text{total cost}$$
$$= (SP) Q - [F + (VC) Q]$$

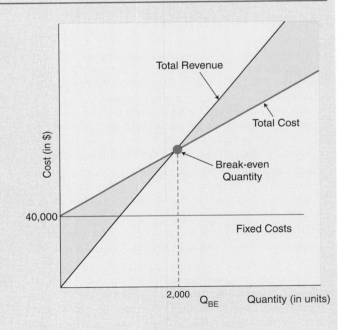

Now we can substitute numerical values:

$$\text{Profit} = \$70 (3000) - [\$40,000 + \$50 (3000)]$$
$$= \$20,000$$

The contribution to profit is $20,000 if Joe can sell 3000 units of product.

DISCUSSION QUESTIONS

1. Define product design and explain its relationship to business strategy.

2. What are the differences between product and service design?

3. Explain the meanings of benchmarking and reverse engineering.

4. Explain the meaning of design for manufacture (DFM) and give some examples.

5. Describe the stages of the product life cycle. What are demand characteristics at each stage?

6. Explain the term concurrent engineering. Why is it important?

7. Identify the two general types of operations. What are their characteristics?

8. What is meant by the term vertical integration? What types of companies are more likely to become vertically integrated?

9. What is a process flow chart and what is it used for?

10. Give some examples of automation. How has automation changed the production process?

11. Discuss the benefits of computer-aided design (CAD).

12. What is meant by the term *service package?*

13. Name three service companies and describe their service package.

14. Give examples of services that have a good match between customer expectations and service delivery. Give examples of services that do not have a good match.

PROBLEMS

1. See-Clear Optics is considering producing a new line of eyewear. After considering the costs of raw materials and the cost of some new equipment, the company estimates fixed costs to be $40,000 with a variable cost of $45 per unit produced.

(a) If the selling price of each new product is set at $100, how many units need to be produced and sold to break even? Use both the graphical and algebraic approaches.

(b) If the selling price of the product is set at $80 per unit, See-Clear expects to sell 2000 units. What would be the total contribution to profit from this product at this price?

(c) See-Clear estimates that if it offers the price at the original target of $100 per unit, the company will sell about 1500 units. Will the pricing strategy of $100 per unit or $80 per unit yield a higher contribution to profit?

2. Med-First is a medical facility that offers outpatient medical services. The facility is considering offering an additional service, mammography screening tests on site. The facility estimates the annual fixed cost of the equipment and skills necessary for the service to be $120,000. Variable costs for each patient processed are estimated at $35 per patient. If the clinic plans to charge $55 for each screening test, how many patients must it process a year in order to break even?

3. Tasty Ice Cream is a year-round take-out ice cream restaurant that is considering offering an additional product, hot chocolate. Considering the additional machine it would need plus cups and ingredients, it estimates fixed cost per year to be $200 per year and the variable cost at $.20. If it charges $1.00 for each hot chocolate, how many hot chocolates does it need to sell in order to break even?

4. Slick Pads is a company that manufactures laptop notebook computers. The company is considering adding its own line of computer printers as well. It has considered the implications from marketing and financial perspectives and estimates fixed costs to be $500,000. Variable costs are estimated at $200 per unit produced and sold.

(a) If the company plans to offer the new printers at a price of $350, how many printers does it have to sell to break even?

(b) Describe the types of operations considerations that the company needs to consider before making the final decision.

5. Perfect Furniture is a manufacturer of kitchen tables and chairs. The company is currently deciding between two new methods for making kitchen tables. The first process is estimated to have a fixed cost of $80,000 and a variable cost of $75 per unit. The second process is estimated to have a fixed cost of $100,000 and a variable cost of $60 per unit.

(a) Graphically plot the total costs for both methods. Identify which ranges of product volume are best for each method.

(b) If the company produces 500 tables a year, which method provides a lower total cost?

6. Harrison Hotels is considering adding a spa to its current facility in order to improve their list of amenities. Operating the spa would require a fixed cost of $25,000 a year. Variable cost is estimated at $35.00 per customer. The Hotel wants to break even if 12,000 customers use the spa facility. What should be the price of the spa services?

7. Kaizer Plastics produces a variety of plastic items for packaging and distribution. One item, container #145, has had a low contribution to profits. Last year, 20,000 units of container #145 were produced and sold. The selling price of the container was $20.00 per unit, with a variable cost of $18 per unit and a fixed cost of $70,000 per year.

(a) What is the break-even quantity for this product? Use both graphic and algebraic methods to get your answer.

(b) The company is currently considering ways to improve profitability by either stimulating sales volumes or reducing variable costs. Management believes that sales can be increased by 35 percent of their current levels or that variable cost can be reduced to 90 percent of their current level. Assuming all other costs equal, identify which alternative would lead to a higher profit contribution.

8. George Fine, owner of Fine Manufacturing, is considering the introduction of a new product line. George has considered factors such as costs of raw materials, new equipment, and requirements of a new production process. He estimates that the variable costs of each unit produced would be $8 and fixed cost would $70,000.

(a) If the selling price is set at $20 each, how many units have to be produced and sold for Fine Manufacturing to break even? Use both graphical and algebraic approaches.

(b) If the selling price of the product is set at $18.00 per unit, Fine Manufacturing expects to sell 15,000 units. What would be the total contribution to profit from this product at this price?

(c) Fine Manufacturing estimates that if it offers the price at the original target of $20 per unit, the company will sell about 12,000 units. Which pricing strategy–$18.00 per unit or $20.00 per unit–will yield a higher contribution to profit?

(d) Identify additional factors the George Fine should consider in deciding whether to produce and sell the new product.

9. Handy-Maid Cleaning Service is considering offering an additional line of services to include professional office cleaning. Annual fixed costs for this additional service are estimated to be $9,000. Variable costs are estimated at $50.00 per unit of service. If the price of the new service is set at $80.00 per unit of service, how many units of service are needed for Handy-Maid to break even?

10. Easy-Tech software corporation is evaluating the production of a new software product to compete with the popular word processing software currently available. Annual fixed costs of producing the item are estimated at $150,000 while the variable costs is $10.00 per unit. The current selling price of the item is $35.00 per unit, and the annual sales volume is estimated at 50,000 units.

(a) Easy-Tech is considering adding new equipment that would improve software quality. The negative aspect of this new equipment would be an increase in both fixed and variable costs. Annual fixed cost would increase by $50,000 and variable cost by $3.00. However, marketing expects the better quality product to increase demand to 70,000 units. Should Easy-Tech purchase this new equipment and keep the price of their product the same? Explain your reasoning.

(b) Another option being considered by Easy-Tech is the increase in the selling price to $40.00 per unit to offset the additional equipment costs. However, this increase would result in a decrease in demand to 40,000 units. Should Easy-Tech increase their selling price if they purchase the new equipment? Explain your reasoning.

CASE: *Biddy's Bakery (BB)*

Biddy's Bakery was founded by Elizabeth McDoogle in 1984. Nicknamed "Biddy," Elizabeth started the home-style bakery in Cincinnati, Ohio as a alternative to commercially available baked goods. The mission of Biddy's Bakery was to produce a variety of baked goods with old-fashioned style and taste. The goods produced included a variety of pies and cakes, and were sold to the general public and local restaurants.

The operation was initially started as a hobby by Elizabeth and a group of her friends. Many of the recipes they used had been passed down for generations in their families. The small production and sales facility was housed in a mixed commercial and residential area on the first floor of "Biddy's" home. Elizabeth ("Biddy") and three of her friends worked in the facility from 6 AM to 2 PM making and selling the pies. The operation was arranged as a job-shop with work stations set up to perform a variety of tasks as needed. Most of the customers placed advanced orders and Biddy's Bakery took pride in accepting special requests. The Bakery's specialty was the McDoogle Pie, a rich chocolate confection in a cookie crust.

Meeting Capacity Needs

Initially sales were slow and there were periods when the business operated at a loss. However, after a few years Biddy's Bakery began to attract a loyal customer following. Sales continued to grow slowly but steadily. In 1994, a first floor storage area was expanded to accommodate the growing business. However, Biddy's Baker quickly outgrew its current capacity. In May of 2000 Elizabeth decided to purchase the adjacent building and move the entire operation into the much large facility. The new facility had considerably more capacity than needed, but the expectation was that business would continue to grow. Unfortunately, by the end of 2000 Elizabeth found that her sales expectations had not been met and she was paying for a facility with unused space.

Getting Management Advice

Elizabeth knew that her operations methods, though traditional, were sound. A few years ago she had called upon a team of business students from a local university for advice, as part of their course project. They had offered some suggestions, but were most impressed with the efficient manner with which she ran her operation. Recalling this experience she decided to contact the same university for another team of business students to help her with her predicament.

After considerable analysis the team of business students came up with their plan: Biddy's Bakery should primarily focus on production of the McDoogle Pie in large volumes, with major sales to go to a local grocery store. The team of business students discussed this option with a local grocery store chain that was pleased with the prospect. Under the agreement Biddy's Bakery would focus its production on the McDoogle Pie, which would be delivered in set quantities to one store location twice a week. The volume of pies required would use up all of the current excess capacity and take away most of capacity from production of other pies.

Elizabeth was confused. The alternative being offered would solve her capacity problems, but it seemed that the business would be completely different though she did not understand how or why. For the first time in managing her business she did not know what to do.

Case Questions:

1. Explain the challenge faced by Elizabeth in meeting her capacity needs. What should she have considered before moving into the larger facility?
2. What is wrong with the proposal made by the team of business students? Why?
3. What type of operation does Biddy's Bakery currently have in place? What type of operation is needed to meet the proposal made by the team of business students? Explain the differences between these two operations.
4. Elizabeth senses that the business would be different if she accepts the proposal, but does not know how and why. Explain how it would be different.
5. What would you advise Elizabeth?

INTERACTIVE LEARNING

Enhance and test your knowledge of Chapter 3 using the interactive CD.

1. **Simulation** *Understanding Intermittent and Continuous Operations*

2. **Video** *Xerox Corporation*

   Visit our dynamic Web site, www.wiley.com/college/reid, for more cases, Web links, and additional information.

3. **Company Tour** *Ercol Furniture*

4. **Additional Web Resources** *National Association of Purchasing Managers, www.napm.org*

5. **INTERNET CHALLENGE** *Country Comfort Furniture*

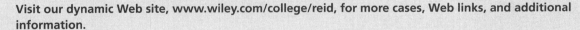

You have just taken a position with Country Comfort Furniture, a furniture manufacturer known for its custom-designed country furniture. The primary focus of the company has been on kitchen and dining room furniture in the upper portion of the high-price range. Due to competitive pressures and changes in the market, Country Comfort is now considering production of prefabricated kitchen and dining room furniture in the medium-price range.

You have been asked to help Country Comfort evaluate the new product design it is considering. Perform an Internet search to identify at least two major competitors that Country Comfort would have if it chooses to pursue the new product line. Next, identify key product design features of each competitor's products, their target market, and price range. Based on your search, what are your recommendations to Country Comfort on product design and current competition?

BIBLIOGRAPHY

Boyer, K.K. "Evolutionary Patterns of Flexible Automation and Performance: A Longitudinal Study," *Management Science*, 45, 6, 1999, 824–842.

D'Souza, D.E. and Williams, F.P., "Toward a Taxonomy of Manufacturing Flexibility Dimensions," *Journal of Operations Management*, 18, 2000, 577–593.

Flynn, B.B., Schroeder, R.G., and Flynn, E.J., "WCM: An Investigation of Hayes and Wheelwright's Foundation," *Journal of Operations Management*, 17, 1999, 249–269.

Golden, W., and Powell, P. "Toward a Definition of Flexibility: In Search of the Holy Grail?" **28**, *Omega*, 2000, 373–384.

Hayes, R. H. and S.C. Wheelwright. *Restoring Our Competitive Edge: Competing Through Manufacturing*, New York: Wiley, l984.

Hayes, R. H. and S.C. Wheelwright. "Link Manufacturing Process and Product Life Cycles," *Harvard Business Review*, **57**, (January-February l979), pp. 133–140.

Hill, Terry. *Manufacturing Strategy: Text and Cases*. 3rd ed New York: McGraw-Hill, 2000.

Klassen, R.D., and Whybark, D.C., "Environmental Management in Operations: The Selection of Environmental Technologies," *Decision Sciences*, **30**, 3, 1999, 601–631.

Pannirselvam, G.P., Ferguso L.A., Ash, R.C. and Sifered, S.P., "Operations Management Research: An Update for the 1990's," *Journal of Operations Management*, **18**, 1999, 95–112.

Rondeau, P.J., Vonderembse, M.A., and Raghunathan, T.S., "Exploring Work System Practices for Time-Base Manufacturers: Their Impact on Competitive Capabilities," *Journal of Operations Management*, 18, 2000, 509–529.

Ward, P.C., McCreery, T.K., Ritzman, L.P. and Sharma, D., "Competitive Priorities in Operations Management," *Decision Science*, **29**, 4, 1998, 1035–1046.

Supply Chain Management

Before studying this chapter you should know or, if necessary, review

1. The implications of competitive priorities Chapter 2, pages 28–32.
2. Product design considerations Chapter 3, pages 48–52.
3. Process selection considerations Chapter 3, pages 52–58.

LEARNING OBJECTIVES

After studying this chapter, you should be able to

1 Describe supply chains and supply chain management.

2 Describe the bullwhip effect.

3 Describe supply chain management factors.

4 Describe the role of vertical integration.

5 Solve insourcing or outsourcing problems.

6 Describe the role of purchasing in supply chain management.

7 Describe the role of information sharing in supply chain management.

8 Describe different technologies used in information sharing.

9 Describe how to implement supply chain management.

10 Describe the role of warehouses in supply chains.

11 Describe supply chain performance measurements.

12 Describe current and future trends in supply chain management.

CHAPTER OUTLINE

Buying a product used to mean getting dressed, leaving home, and shopping at stores or malls until you found what you wanted. Today, most of us can go on-line 24 hours a day, 7 days a week and buy just about anything over the Internet. You can shop while sitting at your computer and never leave home. You can order food from a supermarket or a restaurant online, or buy clothing and household goods. You can buy books, videos, CDs—the Internet has revolutionized the way we do business.

In this chapter we look at supply chains: the connected links of external suppliers, internal processes, and external distributors. We also learn how advances in information technology help companies coordinate their supply chains.

We will begin with the effect of supply chain management on organizations.

■ WHAT IS A SUPPLY CHAIN?

▶ **Supply chain**
A network of all the activities involved in delivering a finished product to the customer.

▶ **Supply chain management**
Coordinates and manages all the activities of the supply chain.

A **supply chain** is the network of activities that deliver a finished product or service to the customer. These include sourcing raw materials and parts, manufacturing and assembling the products, warehousing, order entry and tracking, distribution through the channels, and delivery to the customer. An organization's supply chain is facilitated by an information system that allows relevant information such as sales data, sales forecasts, and promotions to be shared among members of the supply chain. Figure 4-1 shows a basic supply chain structure.

At the beginning of the chain are the external suppliers who supply and transport raw materials and components to the manufacturers. Manufacturers transform these materials into finished products that are shipped either to the manufacturer's own distribution centers or to wholesalers. Next, the product is shipped to retailers who sell the product to the customer. Goods flow from the beginning of the chain through the manufacturing process to the customer. Relevant information flows back and forth among members of the supply chain.

Supply chain management is the vital business function that coordinates and manages all the activities of the supply chain linking suppliers, transporters, internal departments, third-party companies, and information systems. Supply chain management entails

- ◆ Coordinating the movement of goods through the supply chain from suppliers to manufacturers to distributors
- ◆ Sharing relevant information such as sales forecasts, sales data, and promotional campaigns among members of the chain

A prime example of operations management (OM), supply chain management provides the company with a sustainable, competitive advantage, such as quick response time, low cost, state-of-the-art quality design, or operational flexibility.

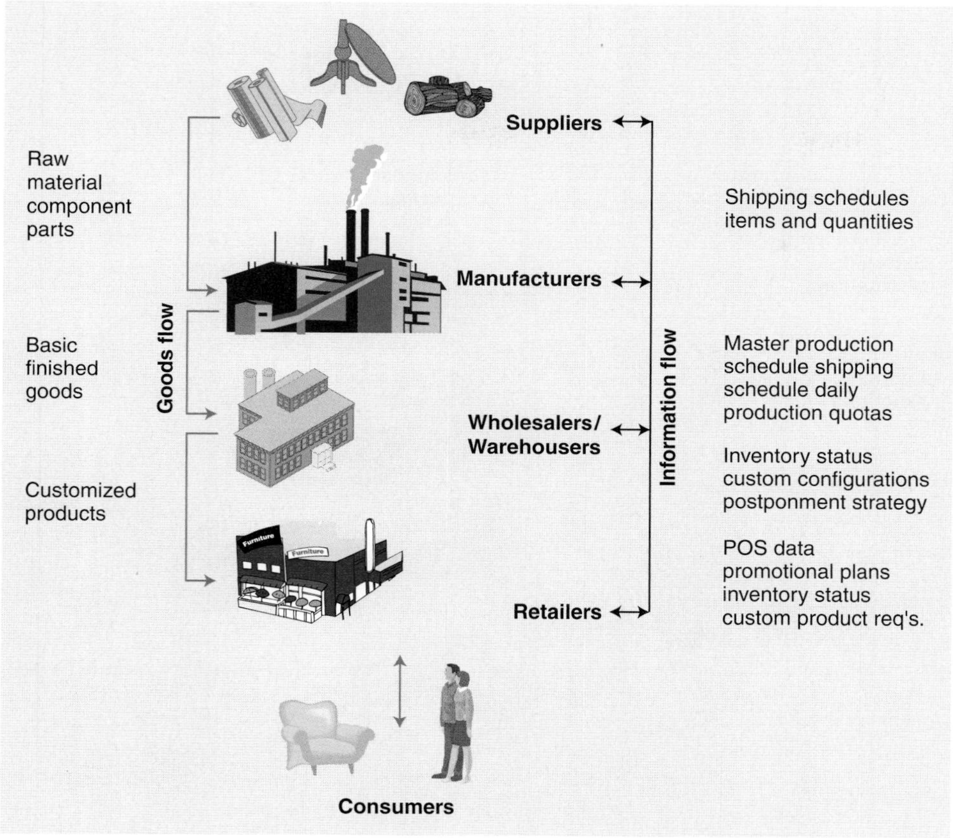

Figure 4-1

Basic supply chain

Dell Computer is a good example of a company using its supply chain to achieve a sustainable competitive advantage. Quick delivery of customized computers at prices 10–15% lower than the industry standard is Dell's competitive advantage.

A customized Dell computer can be enroute to the customer within 36 hours. This quick response allows Dell to reduce its inventory level to approximately 13 days of supply compared to Compaq's 25 days of supply. Dell achieves this in part through its warehousing plan. Most of the components Dell uses are warehoused within 15 minutes travel time to an assembly plant. Dell does not order components at its Austin, Texas, facility, instead, suppliers restock warehouses as needed and Dell is billed for items only after they are shipped. The result is better value for the customer.

COMPONENTS OF A SUPPLY CHAIN ■

A company's supply chain structure has three components: external suppliers, internal functions of the company, and external distributors. Figure 4-2 shows a simplified supply chain for packaged milk products.

Figure 4-2

Milk products supply chain

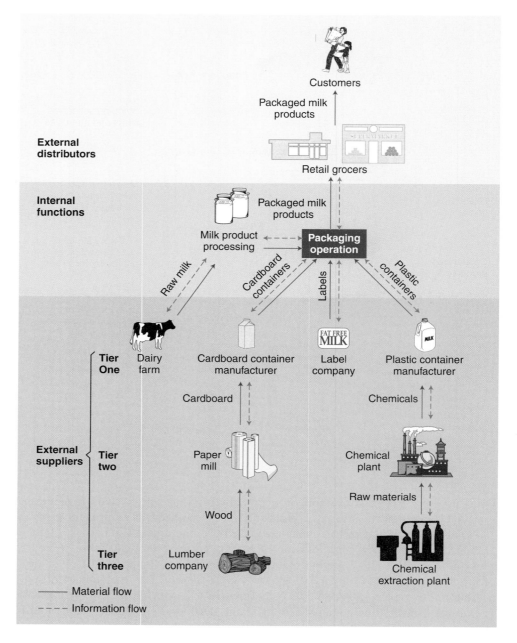

External suppliers include the dairy farmer, cardboard container manufacturer, label company, plastic container manufacturer, paper mill, chemical processing plant, lumber company, and chemical extraction plant. Internal functions include the processing of the raw milk into consumer milk products and packaging milk products for distribution to retail grocery outlets. The external distributors transport finished products from the manufacturer to retail grocers, where the products are sold to the customer. The supply chain includes every activity, from collecting the raw milk, producing the consumer milk products, packaging the milk products, distributing the packaged milk products to retail grocers, to selling the finished milk products to the customer.

Let's look at each component of the supply chain in detail.

External Suppliers

Milk products manufacturing involves several companies, as shown in Figure 4-2. The milk is packaged either in cardboard or plastic containers by **tier one suppliers.** Note that a tier one supplier provides materials directly to the processing facility and that the labels supplier is also a tier one supplier.

The paper mill and the chemical processing plant are **tier two suppliers** because they directly supply tier one suppliers but do not directly supply the packaging operation. The lumber company that provides wood to the paper mill is a **tier three supplier**, as is the chemical extraction plant that supplies raw materials to the chemical processing plant.

Companies put substantial effort into developing the external supplier portion of the supply chain because the cost of materials might represent 50–60% or even more of the cost of goods sold. A company is typically involved in a number of supply chains and often in different roles. In the supply chain for the plastics container manufacturer shown in Figure 4-2 for example, the chemical plant is now a tier one supplier and the chemical extraction facility is a tier two supplier. Even though the plastics container manufacturer was a tier one supplier to the milk processing facility, the plastic container manufacturer still has its own unique supply chain. Now consider the supply chain for a retail grocer: the tier one suppliers are providers of packaged consumer products and the grocer has no external distributors because the customers buy directly from the store. As you can see, supply chains come in all shapes and sizes.

Remember that tier one suppliers (the cardboard container manufacturer, dairy farm, label company, and plastics container manufacturer in Figure 4-2) directly supply the consumer product manufacturer (packaged milk products), whereas tier two suppliers (paper mill and chemical processing plant) directly supply tier one suppliers. To summarize: supply chains are a series of linked suppliers and customers in which each customer is a supplier to another part of the chain until the product is delivered to the customer.

Internal Functions

Internal functions in a milk production supply chain, for example, are as follows:

- ◆ Processing, which converts raw milk into milk products and packages these products for distribution to retail grocery outlets
- ◆ Purchasing, which selects appropriate suppliers, ensures that suppliers perform up to expectations, administers contracts, and develops and maintains good supplier relationships
- ◆ Production planning and control, which schedules the processing of raw milk into milk products
- ◆ Quality assurance, which oversees the quality of the milk products
- ◆ Shipping, which selects external carriers and/or a private fleet to transport the product from the manufacturing facility to its destination

External Distributors

External distributors transport finished products to the appropriate locations for eventual sale to customers. Logistics managers are responsible for managing the movement of products between locations. **Logistics** includes *traffic management* and *distribution mangement*. **Traffic management** is the selection and monitoring of external carriers (trucking companies, airlines, railroads, shipping companies, and

▶ **Tier one supplier**
Supplies materials or services directly to the processing facility.

▶ **Tier two supplier**
Directly supplies materials or services to a tier one supplier in the supply chain.

▶ **Tier three supplier**
Directly supplies materials or services to a tier two supplier in the supply chain.

CROSS FUNCTIONAL

▶ **Logistics**
Activities involved in obtaining, producing, and distributing material and product in the proper place and in proper quantities.

▶ **Traffic management**
Responsible for arranging method of shipment for both incoming and outgoing products or materials.

▶ **Distribution management**
Responsible for movement of material from the manufacturer to the customer.

couriers) or internal fleets of carriers. **Distribution management** is the packaging, storing, and handling of products at receiving docks, warehouses, and retail outlets.

Next, we will look at a common challenge to supply chain managers called the bullwhip effect.

■ THE BULLWHIP EFFECT

▶ **Bullwhip effect**
Inaccurate or distorted demand information created in the supply chain.

Sharing product demand information between members of a supply chain is critical. However, inaccurate or distorted information can travel through the chain like a bullwhip uncoiling. The **bullwhip effect**, as this is called, causes erratic replenishment orders placed on different levels in the supply chain that have no apparent link to final product demand. The results are excessive inventory investment, poor customer service levels, ineffective transportation use, misused manufacturing capacity, and lost revenues. We will discuss the causes of the bullwhip effect, and how they send inaccurate or distorted information down the supply chain. First, however, let's look at the traditional supply chain shown in Figure 4-3 and follow the product demand information flow from the final seller back to the manufacturer of the product:

1. The final seller periodically places replenishment orders with the next level of the supply chain, which could be a local distributor. The timing and order quantity—for example, monthly orders in varying amounts—are determined by the final seller. The timing and quantity can be fixed or variable.

2. The local distributor has many customers (final sellers) placing replenishment orders. Each final seller uses its own product demand estimates and quantity rules. Based on these replenishment orders, the local distributor places replenishment orders with its supplier, which could be a regional distribution center (RDC).

3. As before, the customers (the local distributors) determine the timing and quantity of orders placed with the RDC. Each RDC periodically places orders based on demand at the RDC. The RDC orders from the manufacturer of the finished good.

4. In turn, the manufacturer develops plans and schedules production orders based on orders from the RDCs. The manufacturer does not know what the demand is for the finished good by the final customer but knows only what the RDCs order.

Figure 4-3

Traditional supply chain information flow

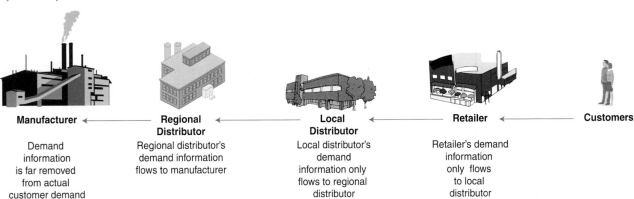

Manufacturer	Regional Distributor	Local Distributor	Retailer	Customers
Demand information is far removed from actual customer demand	Regional distributor's demand information flows to manufacturer	Local distributor's demand information only flows to regional distributor	Retailer's demand information only flows to local distributor	

The greater the number of levels in the supply chain, the further away the manufacturer is from final customer demand. Since suppliers in the chain do not know what customer demand is or when a replenishment order might arrive, suppliers stockpile inventory.

Causes of the Bullwhip Effect

The causes of the bullwhip effect are demand forecast updating, order batching, price fluctuation, and rationing and gaming. Let's look at each of these causes.

Each member in the supply chain, beginning with the retailers, does *demand forecast updating* with every inventory review. Based on actual demand, the retailers update their demand forecast. The retailers review their current inventory level and based on their inventory policies determine whether a replenishment order is needed. The wholesalers repeat the process, updating their demand forecast based on demand from the retailers. Note that the demand is from the retailers' inventory replenishments and may not reflect actual customer demand at the retail level. The wholesalers update their demand forecast and place appropriate replenishment orders with the distribution centers. The distributors repeat the process again, updating their demand forecasts based on demand from the wholesalers. The distributors review their inventory levels and place the appropriate orders with the manufacturer. These orders are determined by the inventory policies at the distributors. Orders placed with the manufacturer end up replenishing each level in the supply chain rather than being directly linked to end-customer demand.

A company does *order batching* when instead of placing replenishment orders right after each unit is sold it waits some period of time, sums up the number of units sold, and then places the order. This eliminates constant product demand and replaces it with lumpy demand: certain levels in the supply chain can experience periods of no demand. Order batching policies amplify variability in order timing and size.

Price fluctuations cause companies to buy products before they need them. Price fluctuations follow special promotions like price discounts, quantity discounts, coupons, and rebates. Each of these price fluctuations affects the replenishment orders placed in the supply system. When prices are lower, members of the supply chain tend to buy in larger quantities. When prices increase, order quantities decrease. Price fluctuations create more demand variability within the supply chain.

Rationing and shortage gaming result when demand exceeds supply and products are rationed to members of the supply chain. Knowing that the manufacturer will ration items, customers within the supply chain often exaggerate their needs. For example, if you know the company is only supplying 50% of the order quantity, you double the order size. If you really need 100 pieces, you order 200 so you are sure to get what you need. Such game-playing distorts true demand information in the system.

Counteracting the Bullwhip Effect

Here are four ways of counteracting the bullwhip effect:

1. Change the way suppliers forecast product demand by making this information from the final seller level available to all levels of the supply chain. This allows all levels to use the same product demand information when making

replenishment decisions. Companies can do this by collecting point-of-sale (POS) information, a function available on most cash registers.

2. Eliminate order batching. Companies typically use large order batches because of the relatively high cost of placing an order. Supply chain partners can reduce ordering costs by using electronic data interchange (EDI) to transmit information. Lower ordering costs in turn eliminate the need for batch orders.

3. Stabilize prices. Manufacturers can eliminate incentives for retail forward buying by creating a uniform wholesale pricing policy. In the grocery industry, for example, major manufacturers use an everyday low-price policy or a value pricing strategy to discourage forward buying.

4. Eliminate gaming. Instead of filling an order based on a set percentage, manufacturers can allocate products in proportion to past sales records. Customers then have no incentive to order a larger quantity to get the quantity they need.

■ FACTORS AFFECTING SUPPLY CHAIN MANAGEMENT

In a roundtable discussion following a joint research effort by Mercer Management Consulting, the MIT Center for Transportation Studies, and *Logistics Management & Distribution Report* magazine, leading corporate supply chain executives included the following business and economic factors among those having a significant impact on supply chain management.

Consumer Expectations and Competition

Consumer expectations reflect the shift in power from the supplier to the customer. This shift in power is partially due to the increased number of suppliers available to customers. Since customers have so many choices among suppliers, companies differentiate themselves by providing their customers with excellent value.

Dell Computers, Gateway 2000, L.L. Bean, Lands' End, Amazon.com, UPS, and FedEx are all good examples of companies that put a premium on values such as preferred customer service, short lead times, or quality guarantees. Dell Computer differentiates itself with short lead times. The company does this by warehousing most of the components used within 15 minutes of the assembly plant. Because companies like Dell have raised customer expectations, organizations failing to provide similar value lose market share. Advances in industrial technology, increased globalization, shorter product life cycles, greater access to information, plentiful venture capital, and creative new business designs further challenge supply chain management to provide competitive value to the customer.

Globalization

Experts predict shifts in global demographics and economic power in the medium term. The world is changing and new markets are emerging—for example, in Latin American, Africa, Asia, and Eastern Europe. These new markets force companies to rethink how to provide value to customers worldwide. Consumers in new markets will not accept hand-me-downs in product design and service but will instead demand value equal to what is delivered to consumers in established markets. One good example of globalization is the success of artisans in Kenya, who by marketing their goods over the Internet have increased annual export earnings to $2 million from only $10,000.

Information Technology

Information technology has changed the way products are bought and distributed. Some companies producing consumer products estimate that at least half of their business will be done over the Internet. Given the market presence facilitated by e-commerce, as Internet-based business is called, companies are competing everywhere in the world. E-commerce allows consumers to comparison shop for suppliers around the world, view color pictures in an on-line catalog and get all the information needed about an item, use a credit card or electronic funds transfer, and buy the item on-line. In the future, we may be able to buy just about anything on-line.

Consider how Lands' End uses technology in its business. Lands' End went on-line in 1995. The company sold only $160 worth of gear the first month. Today, Lands' End sells over $10 million per month on-line. The company has a live chat room that al-lows customers to ask questions about merchandise. It also offers a "shopping with a friend" service that allows a customer, his or her friend or friends, and a customer service representative to be linked together. However, Lands' End's "virtual model" highlights how far technolgy has advanced. A few strokes on the keyboard and the shopper is able to produce an on-screen model with his or her body measurements. Even though this virtual model is not perfect, over 1 million shoppers have built their own models at the Lands' End site.

LINKS TO PRACTICE
Lands' End, Inc.
www.landsend.com

Government Regulations

Another possible factor in the way products are bought and distributed is government regulations. Of particular concern is whether any trade barriers may be erected in the future. Given that the Internet allows access to markets worldwide, leading corporate supply chain executives believe that it is important that governments not erect barriers to limit free trade. It is unknown what the future will bring in terms of government involvement.

Environment

Recycling, sustainable eco-efficiency, and waste minimization are already affecting supply chain management. According to the European Union's packaging requirements, cardboard boxes must be removed from consumption sites and recycled. U.S. automobile parts producers ship their parts in reusable containers rather than disposable containers. Supply chains need to spend more attention on the final disposition of products and packaging and develop ways to make money by successfully recycling product materials. Companies need to find ways of generating income from successful recycling programs.

Before You Go On

Make sure you understand the structure of the supply chain, the bullwhip effect, and some of the challenges to supply chain management in today's marketplace: (1) A supply chain consists of external suppliers, internal functions of the company, and external distributors. (2) The bullwhip effect causes erratic replenishment orders placed on different levels in the supply chain that have no apparent link to final product demand. (3) Customers demand more value from their suppliers. Added value to the customer can take the form of higher quality, quicker response, or lower prices. Consumer expectations, globalization, information technology, and environmental needs can affect the future of supply chain management.

■ VERTICAL INTEGRATION

▶ **Vertical integration**
A measure of how much of the supply chain is actually owned or operated by the manufacturing company.

▶ **Insource**
Refers to processes or activities that are completed in-house.

▶ **Outsource**
Refers to processes or activities that are completed by suppliers.

▶ **Backward integration**
Owning or controlling sources of raw materials and components.

▶ **Forward integration**
Owning or controlling the channels of distribution.

Which products or services are provided in-house by the manufacturer and which are provided to the manufacturer by other members of the supply chain? **Vertical integration** is a measure of how much of the supply chain is owned or operated by the manufacturer. Products or services provided by the manufacturer are **insourced**. Products or services not provided by the manufacturer are **outsourced**. Outsourcing means that the manufacturer pays suppliers or third-party companies for their products or services, a practice that is on the rise. A recent survey reported that 35% of more than 1000 large companies have increased their outsourcing. Another survey of large companies reported that 86% outsourced at least some materials or services. The activity most frequently outsourced was manufacturing.

Backward integration is a company's acquisition or control of sources of raw materials and component parts: the company acquires, controls, or owns the sources that were previously external suppliers in the supply chain. **Forward integration** is a company's acquisition or control of its channels of distribution—what used to be the external distributors in the supply chain.

A company bases its level of vertical integration on its objectives. The greater the vertical integration, the lower is the level of outsourcing. Conversely, the higher the level of outsourcing, the lower is the level of vertical integration. Some factors favor vertical integration. For example, companies needing a high volume of a product or service can sometimes achieve economies of scale by providing the product or service in-house. Companies with special skills may find that it is cheaper to provide certain products or services in-house. Other factors encourage outsourcing. For example, companies with low volumes generally find it cheaper to outsource a product or service rather than provide it in-house. Sometimes a company can get a better quality product or service from a supplier than it can provide itself.

Now let's look at the financial calculations behind insourcing and outsourcing decisions.

■ INSOURCING VERSUS OUTSOURCING DECISIONS

It may be easy to calculate the costs of insourcing versus outsourcing and make the right financial decision. But such decisions involve more than financial calculations. Is a particular product or service critical to your company's success? Is the product or service one of your company's core competencies? Is it something your company must do to survive? If the answer is yes to any of these questions, your company will provide the product or service in-house. If the product or service is not one of its core competencies, the company needs to decide whether it should make or buy the product or service. Other considerations are, for example, whether the products or services provided in-house are identical to those outsourced. Is product quality in-house comparable to product quality in the marketplace. Is product functionality comparable, or does one product have an advantage in terms of quality or functionality? Finally, does the company have the capital needed for any up-front costs to provide the product or service in-house?

Now let's look at how a company might make the financial calculations. To make a financial calculation, we look at the total costs involved in either producing the entire quantity in-house or buying the entire quantity from a supplier. The total cost of buying the item is any fixed annual cost associated with buying the product plus a variable cost for each item bought during the year, or

$$TC_{Buy} = FC_{Buy} + (VC_{Buy} \times Q)$$

where TC_{Buy} = total costs of buying the item from a supplier
FC_{Buy} = fixed costs associated with buying the item from the supplier
VC_{Buy} = variable costs associated with buying the item from the supplier
Q = quantity of units bought

Similarly, we calculate the total cost of making the item in-house as

$$TC_{Make} = FC_{Make} + (VC_{Make} \times Q)$$

where TC_{Make} = total costs of making the item in-house
FC_{Make} = fixed costs associated with making the item in-house
VC_{Make} = variable costs associated with making the item in-house
Q = quantity of units made in-house

The first step in solving the make or buy decision is to determine at what quantity the total costs of the two alternatives are equal. To do this, we set the total cost of buying equal to the total cost of making.

$$FC_{Buy} + (VC_{Buy} \times Q) = FC_{Make} + (VC_{Make} \times Q)$$

Solving this tells us the *indifference point*—that is, how many units we must buy or produce when the total costs are equal. If we need this exact amount, we would be indifferent to whether we bought the item or produced it in-house. If we need less than this quantity, we choose the alternative with the lower fixed cost and the higher variable cost. If we need more than this quantity, we choose the alternative with the lower variable costs.

Let's look at a numerical example.

Remember that when the quantity needed exceeds the indifference point, use the alternative with the lower variable cost. If the usage quantity is below the indifference point, then choose the alternative with the lower fixed cost.

■ Example 4.1 MS Bagel Shop: A Make-or-Buy Decision

Two recent college graduates, Mary and Sue, have decided to open a bagel shop. Their first decision is whether they should make the bagels on-site or buy the bagels from a local bakery. They do some checking and learn the following.

◆ If they buy from the local bakery, they will need new airtight containers in which to store the bagels delivered from the bakery. The fixed cost for buying and maintaining these containers is $1000 annually.

◆ The bakery has agreed to sell the bagels for $0.40 each.

◆ If they make the bagels in-house, they will need a small kitchen with a fixed cost of $15,000 annually and a variable cost per bagel of $0.15.

◆ They believe they will sell 60,000 bagels in the first year of operation.

Should Mary and Sue make or buy the bagels?

Solution
First, we set the total costs equal to each other using the formula from above.

$$FC_{Buy} + (VC_{Buy} * Q) = FC_{Make} + (VC_{Make} \times Q)$$

or $1000 + ($0.40 \times Q) = $15,000 + ($0.15 \times Q)$. Solving for Q, we have $(0.25Q) = $14,000$, or $Q = 56,000$ bagels. Since the costs are equal at 56,000 bagels and Mary and Sue expect to use 60,000 bagels, they should make the bagels in-house rather than buy them from the local bakery. By making the bagels, the cost for each additional bagel above 56,000 is $0.15 instead of the $0.40 they would pay the bakery for each bagel.

■ THE ROLE OF PURCHASING

A company's purchasing department plays an important role in supply chain management decisions. Purchasing is typically responsible for selecting suppliers, negotiating and administering long-term contracts, monitoring supplier performance, placing orders to suppliers, developing a responsive supplier base, and maintaining good supplier relations. Since material costs may represent at least 50–60% of the cost of goods sold, purchasing significantly affects profitability. Moreover, changes in product cost structure, with materials comprising the bulk of the cost of goods sold, has elevated the role of purchasing in many organizations.

Outsourcing requires decisions about which supplier to contract with for products or services. These decisions in turn depend on the criticality and frequency of the product or service, and they determine the relationship the company forms with the supplier. For example, if the purchase is one-time only, the company does not need to develop a relationship with the supplier. However, if the company wants a reliable supplier for a critical product or service, it needs to develop a long-term relationship with the supplier.

Developing Supplier Relationships

A strong supplier base is essential to the success of many organizations. Choosing a supplier is like choosing where to shop for something you want to buy. The first thing you decide is which merchants have the product or service you want. Adequate quality for the product or service is usually a prerequisite for even considering a merchant. What else is important to you when choosing a merchant? Availability, perhaps size and color for clothing, freshness and appearance for produce, and physical proximity so you can see the product or try it on. Also relevant are quick response time, such as overnight shipping or rapid alterations; price, of course; ease of doing business; reputation; and warranty or service agreements are all considerations.

What is important to you as an individual when choosing a merchant is also important for your company when choosing a supplier. In general, we want merchants or suppliers who give us good value. Several studies report that the top three criteria for selecting suppliers are price, quality, and on-time delivery. Even more important, however, is that the choice of suppliers be consistent with a company's mission. For example, if your company is competing on the basis of quick response time, your suppliers must offer minimal lead times and be able to respond quickly.

How Many Suppliers?

Once your company has chosen its suppliers, the next question is: Should you give a single supplier all your business for a particular product or service? Or should you use multiple suppliers? Table 4-1 lists arguments in favor of single supplier and multiple suppliers.

For some operations, like make-to-order products, it is easier to deal with a single supplier. This is especially true for scheduling deliveries, resolving problems, mini-

TABLE 4-1 Arguments in Favor of One Supplier and Multiple Suppliers	
Pros of One Supplier	**Pros of Multiplier Suppliers**
• The supplier may be the exclusive owner of essential patents and/or processes and thus be the only possible source.	• Competition among suppliers may provide better service and price.
• By using one supplier, quantity discounts may be achieved.	• Probability of assured supply is better. Multiple suppliers spreads the risks.
• The supplier will be more responsive if it has all of your business for the item.	• It eliminates supplier dependence on the purchaser.
• Contractual agreements may prohibit the splitting of an order.	• It provides greater flexibility of volume.
• The supplier is so outstanding that no other supplier is a serious contender.	• No single supplier may have sufficient capacity.
• Single sourcing is a prerequisite for partnering.	• It allows for testing of new suppliers without jeopardizing flow of materials.
• The order is too small to split between suppliers.	• Government regulations may require multiple sources.
• When the purchase involves a die, tool, mold, or expensive setup, the cost of duplicating may be prohibitive.	
• Deliveries can be scheduled more easily.	
• Supports just-in-time manufacturing and EDI.	
• It allows better supplier relations.	
• The just-in-time philosophy can be better utilized.	

mizing the cost of dies or tools, developing computer links, and so forth. In addition, using a single supplier can improve the quality of your finished product by ensuring the consistency of the input materials.

On the other hand, multiple suppliers reduce the risk of a disrupted supply—that is, if one supplier suffers a disaster, other suppliers can pick up the slack. Further, multiple suppliers can more easily support changing quantity requirements. For example, if you need a larger quantity than a single supplier can supply, the order can be split between multiple suppliers. This is referred to as flexibility of volume. Finally, government regulations may require the use of multiple suppliers for some operations.

The answer of how many suppliers depends on your supply chain structure. If your company wants to integrate its supply chain, partnering or using a single supplier makes sense. For example, the trend in industry is toward a smaller supply base. A benchmarking study of 24 industries done by the Center for Advanced Purchasing Studies in 1994 reported a 6.5% average decrease in the number of active suppliers.

Developing Partnerships

▶ **Partnering**
A process of developing a long-term relationship with a supplier based on mutual trust, shared vision, shared information, and shared risks.

One compelling argument in support of using single suppliers is that it is a prerequisite for developing a partnering relationship. **Partnering** with a supplier needs a commitment from both the company and the supplier. The goal is to establish an ongoing relationship in which both parties benefit from the arrangement—what is called a "win-win situation."

The two kinds of partnerships are *basic* and *expanded*. A basic partnership is built on mutual respect, honesty, trust, open and frequent communications, and a shared understanding of each partner's role in helping the supply chain achieve its objectives. Expanded partnerships are reserved for a few key suppliers. These are long-term relationships built on mutual strategic goals. Expanded partners must be committed to helping each other succeed. They must place a high priority on maintaining the relationship and on sharing information, risks, opportunities, and technologies.

LINKS TO PRACTICE
The Timken Company
www.timken.com

The Timken Company produces high-quality, antifriction, tapered roller bearings, and specialty alloy steels for global consumption. In 1987, Timken started a coordinated sourcing strategy aimed at improving the value of purchased products and reducing the supplier base. A cross-functional team at Timken initiated the process.

At a supplier conference, Timken executives explained to prospective suppliers the company's concept of total value. Timken defines total value as quality, delivery, price, and responsiveness. Timken chose Wayne Steel, a steel service center, as its provider of strip steel. Wayne Steel has leading-edge equipment and is known for its response to customers' quality and service requirements. In addition, Wayne is a leader in close-tolerance, just-in-time programs. Because of this, Wayne can ship small quantities quickly to its customers—a major competitive advantage. Timken and Wayne struggled for three years establishing the partnership. This partnership enabled Timken to save $1 million because of a fixed price clause during the first year of the contract and another $350,000 annually through reduction in freight and slitting costs. Wayne was able to reduce Timken's lead time from 3 months to 5 days for cut-to-length flats and 48 hours for coils.

Wayne delivered exact requirements (no minimum quantity requirements) to Timken. This eliminated the need for 7500 square feet of warehouse space. Inventory turns went from 4 to 40 and inventory investment was reduced by $1.5 million. Wayne's use of better material improved the yield rate at Timken by 4%.

For Wayne Steel, the benefits of the partnership are also obvious. With long-term commitments, Wayne was able to invest in the equipment and systems needed to differentiate itself from other steel service centers. Long-term relationships also support Wayne Steel's business philosophy. Wayne has a no-layoff policy because achieving its corporate objectives requires loyal and committed personnel. Long-term relationships also ensure a continuous level of business. This stability allows Wayne to invest in its workforce.

The Timken–Wayne partnership illustrates the need for both partners to benefit if the partnership is to survive.

Critical Factors in Successful Partnering

Impact, intimacy, and vision are critical factors in successful partnering. Impact means attaining levels of productivity and competitiveness that are not possible through normal supplier relationships. Intimacy means the working relationship between partners. Vision means the mission or objectives of the partnership. Let's look at each of these factors.

Impact comes through mutual change. The supplier and the customer must be willing to make changes. Studies suggest that the three sources of impact are reduction of duplication and waste, leveraging core competence, and creating new opportunities.

Duplication can involve any activity by both the supplier and the customer. For example, suppliers count items before shipping and customers count the same items after receipt. What value is added by having both parties count the same items?

Waste reduction means eliminating any activity that does not add value. For example, moving items into and out of storage adds no value. It makes sense to have items delivered to and stored where they are used.

Duplication can also be eliminated in paperwork and administration. Sweetheart, a manufacturer of paper drinking cups, faced price-cutting demands from a major customer. Sweetheart was told prices needed to be reduced 10% or the customer would use a different supplier. To meet this challenge, Sweetheart partnered with paperboard producer Georgia-Pacific. Shared electronic data interface reduced paperwork and administration,

LINKS TO PRACTICE
Sweetheart Cup Company
www.sweetheart.com
Georgia-Pacific Corporation
www.gp.com

and cut expensive inventory. Joint planning optimized production plans, giving Sweetheart a more consistent product from Georgia-Pacific at a better price. Sweetheart can satisfy its high-volume customers and Georgia-Pacific benefits through more business.

Leveraging core competence is about sharing knowledge. Different companies have different strengths or competencies. Instead of making the supplier or the customer reinvent the wheel, all partners can benefit from shared expertise. Following is an example.

Hillenbrand, a manufacturer of hospital room equipment products, has six geographically dispersed manufacturing facilities. The company uses its own 400-truck fleet, and both domestic and international carriers. Hillenbrand decided to partner with UPS to improve the cost, quality, and responsiveness of Hillenbrand's overall logistics. For UPS, fleet management is a core competence; for Hillenbrand, fleet management is an expensive, noncore requirement. Hillenbrand does not want to incur the expense of building a world-class core competence in fleet management. By partnering with UPS, Hillenbrand can leverage and benefit from its partner's expertise. Hillenbrand was able to create $1.5 million in cost improvements during the first year of the partnership. UPS revenues with Hillenbrand have grown by almost $2 million. Both the supplier and the customer have benefited.

Creating new opportunities means partners working together to produce something that neither could have achieved alone. Let's look at an example involving a tier one supplier to an automobile manufacturer.

This supplier used to make daily truckload deliveries of a major subassembly to the auto assembly plant some 1200 miles away. Every day, four trucks left the supplier filled with subassemblies and every day four of the supplier's empty trucks left the auto assembly plant. The supplier was wasting significant transport capacity with empty trucks returning to its facility. To remedy the problem, the supplier worked with the automobile manufacturer to develop a new truck trailer that carried subassemblies to the automaker and also hauled new autos back to a major metropolitan area. Thus, the auto manufacturer could send new cars to market and eliminate wasted transport capacity. Because the supplier transported the cars to market in an enclosed truck, protected from weather and road hazards, the cars arrived customer-ready. By using the empty trucks to haul the new autos to this market, the supplier eliminated the wasted transport capacity, provided a valuable service to the auto manufacturer, and generated cost savings for both partners. The partnership created a win-win situation that neither could have created alone.

Intimacy comes from the working relationship between partners. Because partners share confidential information, trust between them is critical. Intimacy means eliminating surprises: sharing daily information with partners prevents surprises. For example, a tier one supplier to the automotive industry needs to know how many autos are produced daily, any planned changes in production rates, and the current number of days of finished goods inventory. This information shows the supplier near-term demand and facilitates better customer service to the auto producer.

Vision is the mission or objectives of the partnership. The partners must articulate and share their vision. This shared vision provides the structure for the partnership and the role each partner plays in achieving success for the supply chain.

Successful partnering needs a substantial commitment by both partners. Many companies try to reduce the number of their suppliers and develop a smaller, highly focused supplier base. The emphasis is on finding viable suppliers and developing long-term partner relationships.

Table 4-2 summarizes the different aspects of partner relationships.

Benefits of Partnering

▶ **Early supplier involvement (ESI)**
Involvement of critical suppliers in new product design.

Early supplier involvement (ESI) is a natural result of partnering relationships and is one way to create impact. Critical suppliers become part of a cross-functional, new-

Table 4-2 Characteristics of Partnership Relations

- Have a long-term orientation
- Are strategic in nature
- Share information
- Share risks and opportunities
- Share a common vision
- Share short- and long-term plans
- Are driven by end-customer expectations

product design team. These suppliers provide technical expertise in the initial phases of product design. Early involvement by suppliers often shortens new product development time, improves competitiveness, and reduces costs. One example of early supplier involvement is Whirlpool Corporation's partnership with Eaton, a supplier of gas valves and regulators. Whirlpool used Eaton's design expertise to bring a new gas range to market several months sooner than it could have using Whirlpool's in-house design skills.

Third-Party Service Providers

A 1996 study by the Council for Logistics Management (CLM) of the third-party logistics industry reports that third-party partnerships add value to the supply chain. In this study, 72% of the respondents use third-party logistic services, with outbound transportation and warehousing leading the list. Freight consolidation and distribution were reported most likely to be outsourced in the future. Also companies engaged in international business use third-party logistic services to handle most of their logistics needs.

Partnerships provide the benefits of vertical integration through the sharing of information without the disadvantage of ownership. Next, we will look at what information sharing means for partner relationships.

INFORMATION SHARING ■

To operate efficiently, supply chain members need to share information. This information includes sales data collected at the point of sale; order change notices such as additional orders or cancellations; global inventory management, both quantity and location; and global sourcing opportunities so that supply chain members can improve purchase leveraging and component standardization.

The benefits of information sharing can be significant. When Osram, Inc. bought GTE's Sylvania lighting division, it initiated a supply chain integration program. Within six months, fill rates were at 95% and climbing; individual stock keeping unit (SKU) forecast accuracy had improved by 16%; obsolete inventory was down 10%; and the company had saved more than $300,000 on transportation costs.

Let's look at the risk and power of information sharing within a supply chain. The risk for a member of a supply chain is the member's partial dependence on the whole supply chain for its success or failure rather than on that member's individual performance.

The greater the amount of business generated by the supply chain for an individual company, the greater that company's risk and the higher its dependency on the success of the supply chain. So if most of the member's business supports the supply chain and the supply chain fails, then the member's business is in trouble.

Supermarkets use barcode scanners for obtaining point-of-sale information.

Through information sharing, the power has shifted from the manufacturers to the customers. This is due in part to the impact of a few giant retail conglomerates controlling the majority of dollars in this industry. Major retailers have achieved this power through the use of technologies such as point-of-sale scanners and bar codes, large sales volume, and their location next to the customer in the supply chain.

Wal-Mart is an good example of successful information sharing. Wal-Mart shares point-of-sale information from its retail outlets directly with its major suppliers. These major suppliers are then responsible for replenishing their products. This practice eliminates the need for Wal-Mart to manage its suppliers and gives suppliers responsibility for the sales and marketing of their products in Wal-Mart stores. As a result, suppliers get information more quickly and can resupply the stores more quickly. Also real-time data on what is being sold around the country gives Wal-Mart and its suppliers a competitive advantage.

■ THE ROLE OF TECHNOLOGY

▶ **Electronic data interface (EDI)**
A computer-to-computer link using a standard data format.

One method for exchanging information is **electronic data interface** (**EDI**), a computer-to-computer link using a standard data format. EDI links supply chain members together for order processing, inventory levels, accounting data, manufacturing schedules, and shipping dates. EDI reduces paperwork and allows members of the supply chain to share information. The benefits of EDI are shown in Table 4-3.

EDI improves productivity throughout the supply chain. It provides fast information transmission, eliminates entering data repetitively, and improves data accuracy by minimizing human error.

Table 4-3 Benefits of EDI	
◆ Quick access to standardized information	◆ Improved communications
◆ Reduced paperwork	◆ Reduced clerical costs
◆ Improved data accuracy	◆ Reduced telephone and fax transmissions
◆ Improved tracking capability	

Bar coding and **electronic scanning** allow members of the supply chain to more accurately track sales of items through point-of-sale (POS) systems similar to those used by major retailers. Companies like UPS and FedEx, use bar coding and scanners to track movements of packages. Manufacturing companies use these technologies to track production of items through the plant. They use bar code scanners as a quick and accurate means of collecting data. Another use of bar code scanning and EDI is a quick response program of just-in-time replenishment between suppliers and retailers.

▶ **Bar coding**
A method of encoding data using bar codes for fast and accurate readability.

▶ **Electronic scanning**
Electronic scanning of bar code information.

INTEGRATED SUPPLY CHAIN MANAGEMENT ■

Implementing integrated supply chain management needs considerable effort on the part of the initiating company. This strategic change often is a result of external pressures on the company, such as global competitors, industry consolidation, the switch to e-commerce, or major technological changes within the industry.

A company's first step in improving performance is to analyze the supply chain. Typically, a small cross-functional team leads the effort and may reveal that some functional areas are performing at suboptimal levels.

Most companies start by integrating internal functions because they are under the company's direct control. These functions include production planning and control, and purchasing and distribution. The focus is on improving system performance through shared information using a common database and compatible computer software.

The next step is to integrate external suppliers through partner relationships, first by establishing the characteristics of a desired partner and then by evaluating potential partners. Table 4-4 shows possible objectives for the manufacturer and the supplier.

A company evaluating potential partners looks at the following aspects of the potential partner's business:

◆ History, sales volume, product lines, market share, number of employees, major customers, and major suppliers
◆ Current management team in terms of past performance, stability, and strategic vision
◆ Labor force in terms of skill, experience, commitment to quality, and relations with the supplier
◆ Internal cost structure, process and technology capabilities, financial stability, information system compatibility, supplier sourcing strategies, and long-term relationship potential

Table 4-4 Possible Partnership Objectives	
Manufacturer's Goals	**Supplier's Goals**
◆ Reduce costs	◆ Increase sales volume
◆ Reduce duplication of effort	◆ Increase customer loyalty
◆ Improve quality	◆ Reduce costs
◆ Reduce lead time	◆ Improve demand data
◆ Implement cost reduction program	◆ Improve profitability
◆ Involve suppliers earlier	◆ Reduce inventory
◆ Reduce time to market	
◆ Reduce inventory	

The company reduces the selection pool to a few potential partners, identifies a single partner, and commits to the partnership. At this point, both parties agree on how to measure the performance of the partnership. The partners set time frames for the frequency and methods of performance assessment, and to decide how problems will be resolved. When they reach agreement on these issues, the partners develop supply chain operating procedures and put the partnership into motion.

■ THE ROLE OF WAREHOUSES

Warehouses include plant, regional, and local warehouses. They can be owned or operated by the supplier or wholesaler, or they can be public warehouses. A further classification is general warehouse or distribution warehouse.

▶ **General warehouse**
Used for long-term storage.

▶ **Distribution warehouse**
Used for short-term storage, consolidation, and product mixing.

A **general warehouse** is used for storing goods for long periods with minimal handling. A **distribution warehouse** is used for moving and mixing goods. Within the supply chain, warehouses have three roles: transportation consolidation, product mixing or blending, and service.

The business of a general warehouse is storage. The business of a distribution warehouse is movement and handling; therefore, the size of the facility is less important than its throughput. At a distribution warehouse, goods are received in large-volume lots and broken down into small individual orders.

LINKS TO PRACTICE
Fingerhut Corporation
www.fingerhut.com

A good example of the importance of distribution warehousing in support of e-commerce is Fingerhut's warehouse in St. Cloud, Minnesota. Employees rush through the warehouse on forklifts and cargo haulers filling orders for on-line retailers. Every item is encoded to speed packing. Red lasers scan each package as it rushes down the conveyor, verifying the actual package weight against expected package weight. Packages that do not match are pushed aside for a human to further inspect. The crew at this warehouse can process as many as 30,000 item per hour.

Transportation Consolidation

Warehouses can consolidate less-than-truckload (LTL) quantities into truckload (TL) quantities. This consolidation can be both in supplier shipments to the manufacturer and in finished goods shipped to distant warehouses. The goal is to use TL shipments for as much of the distance as possible because TL shipments are cheaper than LTL shipments.

For inbound supplier shipments, a manufacturer can have small LTL deliveries from several suppliers consolidated at a convenient warehouse and then shipped to the manufacturer in TL shipments. For outbound shipments, the manufacturer can send TL deliveries to distance warehouses that break down the shipment for LTL delivery to local markets.

Product Mixing

Transportation consolidation is typically done to reduce transportation costs, whereas product mixing is a value-added service for customers. With product mixing, the customer places an order to the warehouse for a variety of products. The warehouse groups the items together and ships the mixture of items directly to the customer. Without product mixing, the customer would have to place individual orders for each item and pay shipping for each item. Instead, product mixing enables quicker customer service and reduces transportation costs.

Services

Warehouses improve customer service by moving the goods closer to the customer and thus reducing customer response time. The warehouse can also customize basic products before they are shipped to the customer. For example, an electronics appliance manufacturer can send almost finished products to the warehouse. When the warehouse gets an order for the product, the warehouse can insert the product directions in the appropriate language inside the container. The warehouse can also insert the correct power cord for such an appliance. This service allows the company to provide a customized product for the customer without requiring prepackaging; this maximizes the flexibility of its inventory.

SUPPLY CHAIN PERFORMANCE MEASUREMENT ■

When dealing with a number of independent suppliers, a company needs to measure the performance of the supply chain. A performance measurement system is the basis for understanding how the supply chain works, for influencing behavior by members of the supply chain, and for informing members about the overall performance of the supply chain.

Performance improves when people know that their performance will be measured. As a result, companies perform differently when they know someone is keeping score.

Companies using supply chain management respond to pressures from customers for better quality, quicker response, and lower costs. Customers demand value, so it makes good business sense for your company to measure activities that add value to the supply chain.

What does customer satisfaction mean to your customers? Does it mean filling their whole order? Does it mean your quick response to their requests? Or is it more important to have the product arrive on time? Answering these questions identifies the activities that support the supply chain's objectives.

The supply chain needs to measure product quality—by warranty costs, products returned, and cost reductions allowed because of product defects. And the supply chain needs to measure its costs, including inventory investment, inventory obsolescence, capacity utilization, and total supply chain costs.

In a study of U.S.–Mexican maquiladora operations, performance improvements were measured in order cycle-time reduction, routing and scheduling, and outbound cross-border transportation. The bottom line in this example is that companies have to measure performance of the supply chain and the measurements must support behavior that is consistent with the supply chain objectives.

■ THE FUTURE OF SUPPLY CHAIN MANAGEMENT

Consumer expectations will continue to increase, parts and products will need to be shipped worldwide in a timely manner, competition will continue to intensify, and information technology will continue to evolve. How does the supply chain manager respond to these pressures?

Supply chain managers must design fully integrated supply chains. Future supply chains will be agile, flexible, and integrated. Key factors will be coordinating across the whole supply chain and choosing activities based on customer needs.

One method of satisfying rising consumer expectations is already in use: household replenishment, via the Internet, with freeze-point delay. **Household replenishment** is the automated fulfillment of consumer demand at the point of use (the home). **Freeze-point delay or postponement** means that the manufacturer customizes the product as late in the process as possible. For example, a producer of global desktop PCs stores its completed components (monitors, printers, disk drives, keyboards, and power cords at the warehouse. Once the order is placed, the warehouse workers combine the components for the computer system and insert the power cord for that particular country. Instead of prepackaging products for specified markets, the company makes generic products that can be customized at the warehouse for any country. The benefit for the company is to make better use of its inventory investment. It also gives the company's inventory a high degree of flexibility, and the warehouse is now adding value to the supply chain. To make this happen, however, product designers need to rethink their design so that features can be added at the final stage.

Consider the impact of potential inventory reduction on e-commerce: no inventory needed for product displays at thousands of retail outlets around the world; inventory held in warehouses awaiting an electronic order for direct delivery to the customer.

Here's a scenario for a new third-party logistics provider spawned by home replenishment combined with freeze-point delay: the replenishment service specialist. Such a provider would receive full-truckload quantities of consumer products at convenient locations nationwide and do the final product blending, packaging, and labeling in response to electronic orders received from customers. The provider would then provide periodic replenishment deliveries to the homes of customers.

Another way for supply chains to meet future needs is through virtual organizations. A virtual organization provides core functions and outsources everything else. The supply chain manager of a virtual organization oversees third-party providers and ensures a smooth-functioning supply chain.

Beyond e-commerce and virtual organizations, we can make some reasonable predictions for the future. Companies will continue to identify their core competencies, keep those activities in-house, and outsource noncore activities. Purchasing will assume a more strategic role, adding value rather than handling tactical activities such as procuring and managing low-value goods and services. Companies will develop performance measurements for supply chains.

Companies will continue to reduce inventory levels, at the same time improving customer service. Freeze-point delay or postponement will allow maximum customer choice while simultaneously reducing inventory investment.

More third parties are likely to become involved as companies outsource noncore activities. Companies will continue to reduce their supplier base. Purchasing will continue to develop strong, highly-focused, long-term suppliers.

Improvements in technology will continue to facilitate rapid, accurate data collection and sharing. Above all, supply chain management will play a more central role as we enter the twenty-first century.

▶ **Household replenishment** The automated fulfillment of consumer demand at the point of use (the home).

▶ **Freeze-point delay** Allows the manufacturer to customize the product as late in the process as possible.

CROSS FUNCTIONAL

OM ACROSS THE ORGANIZATION

Supply chain management changes the way companies do business. Consider how supply chain management affects different functional areas in the organization.

Accounting shares some of the benefits and responsibilities of supply chain management. As inventory levels decrease, customer service increases. Manufacturing is using its capacity more effectively. Accounting is exposed to the risks of information sharing and of developing partnerships. With information sharing comes the need for increased confidentiality.

Marketing benefits by improved customer service levels achieved by POS data collection. A shared database gives marketing current demand trends and eliminates demand filtering between levels of the supply chain. POS data also facilitates quick customer response time.

Information systems are critical for supply chain management. Information systems provide the means for collecting relevant demand data, developing a common database, and providing a means for transmitting order information. Information systems enable information sharing through POS data and EDI.

Purchasing has an elevated role in supply chain management within organizations. Purchasing facilitates and manages a strong supplier base through partnering.

Operations uses timely demand information to effectively plan production schedules and use its capacity. Operations responds to customer demand data, improving customer service.

Who is responsible for supply chain management within an organization? In a manufacturing company this is usually the materials manager, who is familiar with external suppliers, internal functions, and external distributors. The person who does supply chain management must see the big picture so that local priorities do not overshadow global priorities.

OM IS EVERYWHERE ■

Most of us buy goods and services so we have some ideas about choosing a supplier and developing a relationship with a supplier. Getting to know your grocer may mean that you have access to the freshest produce, the leanest meats, or the nicest pastries. Frequent buyer, frequent flyer, and frequent traveler programs are designed to reward customer loyalty.

E-commerce is changing the way business is done. You can buy almost anything electronically, 24 hours a day, and often more cheaply because e-commerce allows companies to reduce their distribution inventory. Companies can produce customized products quickly and reasonably using the Internet as a vehicle for information processing. In the future, customers will get better value, quicker response time, customized products, and reasonable costs from e-commerce companies in all parts of the world.

CHAPTER HIGHLIGHTS

1 Every organization is part of a supply chain, either as a customer or a supplier. Supply chains include all the processes to make a finished product, from the extraction of raw materials through to the sale to the end user. Supply chain management is the integration of all these activities to complete the product.

2 The bullwhip effect distorts product demand information passed between levels of the supply chain. The more levels, the more the distortion possible. Variability results from updating demand estimates at each level, order batching, price fluctuations, and rationing.

3 Many factors affect supply chain management. Consumer expectations have risen significantly. Customers demand better service, better product quality, and quicker response at a reasonable price. New markets are creating a global marketplace. Competition within markets is forcing improved value for the customer. The evolution of information and communications has changed business. The Internet provides global market access.

4 Organizations determine the appropriate level of vertical integration based on corporate objectives. Typically, standardized, high-volume products or services have greater integration than customized, low-volume products or services.

5 Companies make insourcing and outsourcing decisions. Make-or-buy decisions are based on financial and strategic criteria. Companies outsource activities that are not part of their core competencies.

6 Purchasing manages supplier selection and develops the supplier relationship. Developing the supplier base can include forming partnerships—long-term relationships with mutual strategic goals. Partners share information, risks, technologies, and opportunities. Impact, intimacy, and vision are critical to successful partnering. Impact means attaining higher levels of productivity and competitiveness that are not possible through normal supplier relationships. Impact comes from reducing duplication and waste, leveraging core competencies, and creating new opportunities. Vision is a shared objective.

7 Information sharing is critical to supply chain management. Two major issues are risk and power. Risk occurs because individual company success or failure is partially due to the success of the supply chain. Power has moved more toward the customer.

8 Technology advancements such as electronic scanners, bar coding, EDI, and POS terminals have facilitated demand data collection. Technology has greatly reduced the cost of developing a common database for supply chain management.

9 A company implements supply chain management as a major strategic change toward improving performance. Companies typically integrate internal functions first, then integrate external suppliers and distributors. It must be in everyone's best interests to be a part of an integrated system.

10 Within the supply chain, warehouses have three roles: transportation consolidation, product mixing or blending, and service. Warehouses consolidate less-than-truckload (LTL) quantities into truckload (TL) quantities. Product mixing adds value for the customers. Customers place orders to the warehouse for a variety of products. The warehouse groups the items and ships them directly to the customer. Warehouses improve customer service by placing goods closer to the customer to reduce response time or by customizing basic products before they are shipped to the customer.

11 Companies need to evaluate the performance of their supply chains. The measurements must reflect the objectives of the supply chain.

12 The future of supply chain management is bright. The information and communications evolution is likely to change the way companies do business. The concept of household replenishment and freeze-point delay are viable near-term possibilities. Selling through the Internet will allow companies to reduce distribution channel inventory and provide quicker response time to the customer. The timely managing of sales information will be critical to success in the twenty-first century.

KEY TERMS

supply chain 78
supply chain management 78
tier one supplier 81
tier two supplier 81
tier three supplier 81
logistics 81
traffic management 81
distribution management 82

bullwhip effect 82
vertical integration 86
insource 86
outsource 86
backward integration 86
forward integration 86
partnering 90
early supplier involvement 92

electronic data interface (EDI) 94
bar coding 95
electronic scanning 95
general warehouse 96
distribution warehouse 96
household replenishment 98
freeze-point delay 98

FORMULA REVIEW

For insourcing or outsourcing:

$$FC_{Buy} + (VC_{Buy} \times Q) = FC_{Make} + (VC_{Make} \times Q)$$

SOLVED PROBLEMS

■ Solved Problem 1

Jack Smith, owner of Jack's Auto Sales, is deciding whether his company should process its own auto loan applications or outsource the process to Loans Etc. If Jack processes the auto loan applications internally, he faces an annual fixed cost of $2500 for membership fees, allowing him access to the TopNotch credit company, and a variable cost of $25 each time he processes a loan application. Loans Etc. will process the loans for $35 per application but Jack must lease equipment from Loans Etc. at a fixed annual cost of $1000. Jack estimates processing 125 loan applications per year. What do you think Jack should do?

Solution

First, set the total costs of each alternative equal to each other, or $1000 + ($35 * Q) = $2500 + ($25 * Q)$. Solving for Q, we have $10Q = 1500, or $Q = 150$ loan applications. Since the costs are equal at 150 loan applications and Jack expects to need 125 applications processed, he is better off outsourcing the loan applications to Loans Etc.

DISCUSSION QUESTIONS

1. For the next item you buy, determine its supply chain.
2. How do supply chains for service organizations differ from supply chains for manufacturing organizations?
3. How can increased customer expectations be satisfied?
4. Think of your last major purchase. What criteria did you use to choose the supplier?
5. Explain the concept of partnering, including advantages and disadvantages.
6. Explain the benefits of using a single supplier as opposed to multiple suppliers.

7. Describe how technology facilitates information sharing.
8. Describe the kinds of information that are necessary in a supply chain.
9. Describe the role of warehouses in a supply chain.
10. Explain how a company could implement supply chain management.
11. Describe what you think will be the future of supply chain management.

PROBLEMS

1. Gabriela Manufacturing must decide whether to insource or outsource a new toxic-free miracle carpet cleaner that works with its Miracle Carpet Cleaning Machine. If it decides to insource the product, the process would incur $300,000 of annual fixed costs and $1.50 per unit of variable costs. If it is outsourced, a supplier has offered to make it for an annual fixed cost of $120,000 and a variable cost of $2.25 per unit in variable costs.

(a) Given these two alternatives, determine the indifference point (where total costs are equal).
(b) If the expected demand for the new miracle cleaner is 300,000 units, what would you recommend that Gabriela Manufacturing do?

2. Gabriela Manufacturing was able to find a new supplier that would provide the item for $1.80 per unit with an annual fixed cost of $200,000. Should Gabriela Manufacturing insource or outsource the item?

3. Downhill Boards (DB), a producer of snow boards, is evaluating a new process for applying the finish to their snow boards. Durable Finish Company (DFC) has offered to apply the finish for $170,000 in fixed costs and a unit variable cost of $0.65. Downhill Boards currently incurs a fixed annual cost of $125,000 and has a variable cost of $0.90 per unit. Annual demand for the snow boards is 160,000.

(a) Calculate the annual cost of the current process used at Downhill Boards.
(b) Calculate the annual cost if Durable Finish Company applies the finish.
(c) Find the indifference point for these two alternatives.
(d) How much of a change in demand is needed to justify outsourcing the process?

4. Fast Finish, Inc. (FFI) has made a technological breakthrough in finish application. FFI will apply the finish for $0.23 per unit in variable costs plus a fixed annual cost of $230,000. Use the cost and demand information given in problem 3 for Downhill Boards to evaluate this proposal.

(a) What will it cost Downhill Boards to outsource the finishing process?
(b) At what demand level does it make sense economically to outsource the finishing process?
(c) What additional factors should be considered when making this outsourcing decision?

5. Henri of Henri's French Cuisine (HFC), a chain of 12 restaurants, is trying to decide if it makes sense to outsource the purchasing function. Currently Henri employs two buyers at an annual fixed cost of $85,000. Henri estimates that the variable cost of each purchase order placed is $15. Value-Buy (VB), a group of purchasing specialists, will perform the purchasing function for a fixed annual fee of $100,000 plus $5 for each purchase order placed. Last year, HFC placed 1450 purchase orders.

(a) What was the cost last year to HFC when doing the purchasing in-house?
(b) What would the cost have been last year had HFC used Value-Buy?
(c) What is the indifference point for the two alternatives?
(d) If HFC estimates they will place 1600 purchase orders next year, should they use VB?
(e) What additional factors should be considered by HFC?

CASE: *Electronic Pocket Calendars Supply Chain Management Game*

In this supply chain game, retailers sell electronic pocket calendars to their customers and place replenishment orders to their wholesaler. The wholesaler sells the pocket calendars to the retailers and orders the calendars from a distributor. The distributor sells the pocket calendars to the wholesalers and orders calendars directly from the factory. The distribution system is shown in the figure. For each period the game is played, participants must follow the same sequence:

1. Receive any shipments into inventory.
2. Ship calendars to satisfy new customer demand and any backorders, as long as sufficient product is available.

3. Determine the ending inventory (a negative value indicates backorders exist).
4. Determine the inventory position (ending inventory plus any quantity already ordered).
5. Place replenishment orders.

For this game, inventory holding costs will be $10.00 per case per week and backorder costs of $15.00 per case per week.

Each person must keep track of his or her own costs. The weekly demand at the retailers will be provided by your professor. Once the demand is known by the retailers, the retailers place the appropriate replenishment orders with the wholesalers. The wholesalers update their inventory records and place the necessary orders with the distributor. At this point, the distributor updates its inventory records and places the appropriate replenishment order with the factory. Lead time throughout the supply chain is two weeks. For example, once the factory releases an order to be manufactured it is two weeks before it is available, or when the distributor orders pocket calendars from the factory it is two weeks before they arrive.

A number of participants are needed in this game. One person manages the factory (1). There are three distribution centers, each needing a manager (3). Each distribution center supplies two different wholesalers (6), and each wholesaler supplies two unique retailers (12). In some cases a location may have co-managers to speed up the transactions. The accompanying table provides' information regarding each location in the supply chain.

For each period of the game, retailers follow these procedures.

1. The retailer accepts into stock any orders due to arrive during the current period. The beginning inventory plus the arriving order determine how much inventory the location has available to satisfy demand during that period.

2. Next, the professor provides each retailer with actual demand data for that period. The demand is given to the retailer on a paper order form. The data are not shown to other members of the supply chain but are treated as confidential information.

3. Retailers fill orders as long as sufficient inventory (calculated in Step 1) is available.

4. Retailers calculate their ending inventory level. If sufficient inventory is available, ending inventory is beginning inventory minus that period's actual demand. If there is not sufficient inventory then backorders occur. When a backorder occurs, your ending inventory value is negative. For example, if you only have 30 units available and demand is 32 units, your inventory balance is −2 units.

5. Retailers calculate their inventory position. Inventory position is the ending inventory plus any quantity already ordered that has not yet arrived. For example, if your ending inventory is −2 but you have placed an order for 90 additional cases, your inventory position is 88 cases (−2 + 90).

6. If the retailer's inventory position is at or below its reorder point, the retailer places an order with its wholesaler. Retailers A11 and A12 order from wholesaler A1, retailers A21 and A22 order from wholesaler A2, and so on. These orders are made in writing and delivered to the appropriate wholesaler. No other communication is permitted.

For the wholesalers, the procedure each period is:

1. The wholesaler accepts into stock any orders due to arrive during the current period. The beginning inventory plus the arriving order determine how much inventory the location has available to satisfy demand during that period.

2. Next, the wholesalers look at the replenishment orders from the retailers for that period. These data are not shown to other members of the supply chain but are treated as confidential information.

3. Wholesalers fill orders as long as sufficient inventory (calculated in Step 1) is available.

4. Wholesalers calculate their ending inventory level. If sufficient inventory is available, ending inventory is beginning inventory minus that period's actual demand. If there is not sufficient inventory then backorders occur. When a backorder occurs, your ending inventory value is negative.

5. Wholesalers calculate their inventory position. Inventory position is the ending inventory plus any quantity already ordered that has not yet arrived.

6. If the wholesaler's inventory position is at or below its reorder point, the wholesaler places an order with its distributor. Wholesalers A1 and A2 order from distributor A, wholesalers B1 and B2 order from distributor B, and so on. These orders are in writing and delivered to the appropriate distributor. No other communication is permitted.

For the distributors, the procedure followed each period is:

1. The distributor accepts into stock any orders due to arrive during the current period. The beginning inventory plus the arriving order determine how much inventory the location has available to satisfy demand during that period.

2. Next, the distributor looks at the replenishment orders

Electronic Pocket Calendar Supply Chain.

Individual Location Information

	Replenishment Order Quantity (cases)	Reorder Point (cases)	Beginning Inventory (cases)	Average Weekly Demand (cases)
Factory	350	190	277	175
Distributor A	120	125	185	60
Distributor B	180	190	280	90
Distributor C	100	52	77	25
Wholesaler A1	90	95	140	45
Wholesaler A2	60	31	46	15
Wholesaler B1	105	110	163	52.5
Wholesaler B2	75	80	118	37.5
Wholesaler C1	60	31	46	15
Wholesaler C2	40	21	31	10
Retailer A11	60	62	92	30
Retailer A12	30	31	46	15
Retailer A21	45	24	35	11.25
Retailer A22	15	8	13	3.75
Retailer B11	75	78	116	37.5
Retailer B12	60	31	46	15
Retailer B21	40	42	62	20
Retailer B22	35	37	55	17.5
Retailer C11	40	21	31	10
Retailer C12	20	11	16	5
Retailer C21	20	12	18	5.5
Retailer C22	20	10	15	4.5

from its wholesalers for that period. These data are not shown to other members of the supply chain but are treated as confidential information.

3. Distributors fill orders as long as sufficient inventory (calculated in Step 1) is available.

4. Distributors calculate their ending inventory level. If sufficient inventory is available, ending inventory is beginning inventory minus that period's actual demand. If there is not sufficient inventory then backorders occur.

5. Distributors calculate their inventory position. Inventory position is the ending inventory plus any quantity already ordered that has not yet arrived.

6. If the distributor's inventory position is at or below its reorder point, the distributor places an order with the factory. These orders are in writing and delivered to the appropriate distributor. No other communication is permitted.

The factory follows these procedures each period:

1. The factory accepts into stock any manufacturing orders completed for the current period. The beginning inventory plus the arriving order determine how much inventory the location has available to satisfy demand during that period.

2. Next, the factory looks at the replenishment orders from the distributors for that period.

3. The factory fills orders as long as sufficient inventory (calculated in step 1) is available.

4. Factory calculates its ending inventory level. If sufficient inventory is available, ending inventory is beginning inventory minus that period's actual demand. If there is not sufficient inventory then backorders occur. When a backorder occurs, your ending inventory value is negative.

5. The factory calculates its inventory position. Inventory position is the ending inventory plus any quantity already ordered that has not yet arrived.

6. If the factory's inventory position is at or below its reorder point, the factory releases an order to manufacturing.

Procedures for all locations include the following:

1. At the end of each period record the amount of actual inventory you have left, the actual number of backorders, the cost of holding the inventory, the cost of the backorders, and the total cost.

2. Update your total statistics; that is, keep a running total of the cases of inventory, the number of backorders, and the cumulative holding costs, cumulative backorder costs, and total costs.

End of Game Discussion Questions

1. How well does the distribution system seem to work? Talk about it in terms of customer service, costs, effective use of inventory, and information flows.

2. Given the amount of inventory in the system, why did backorders occur?

3. In this distribution chain, what happened to customer demand data?

4. How should customer demand data be communicated through the system?

5. What would you recommend be done differently?

INTERACTIVE LEARNING

Enhance and test your knowledge of Chapter 4 using the interactive CD.

1. **Video** *Cisco Systems, Inc.*

2. **Spreadsheet** *The Bullwhip Effect*

3. **Company Tour**
   Finkel & Sons, Inc.
   Reynolds Metal Company

4. **Additional Web Resources**
   nummi,www.nummi.com
   IBM, http://houns54.clearlake.ibm.com

Visit our dynamic Web site, www.wiley.com/college/reid, for more cases, Web links, and additional information.

5. **INTERNET CHALLENGE** *Global Shopping*

Since the Internet provides access to products around the world, your challenge involves some global shopping. This year you have been given a budget of $10,000 to furnish and decorate your off-campus apartment. You have chosen a global theme. Your job is to find items from as many different parts of the world as you can to use in your apartment. You can spend up to $10,000 but you cannot exceed your budget. Do not forget that shipping must be included in your budget. You can choose more than a single item from any country.

(a) Visit the Internet to find products for your apartment. You need to furnish a one-bedroom apartment. You do not need to worry about major appliances (computer, television, stereo, oven, refrigerator, dishwasher, etc.) but you do need everything else. Since you plan to host a major party in your new apartment, everything you buy must be delivered within six weeks.

(b) Provide a list of all of the items you would buy, the cost of each item, and the total money spent. Organize your list by the room the item is intended for. Be sure to identify the country of origin for each item. Have fun shopping!

BIBLIOGRAPHY

Bovet, David, and Yossi Sheffi. "The Brave New World of Supply Chain Management." *Supply Chain Management Review* (Spring 1998), p. 14.

Davis, Mark M., Nicholas J. Aquilano, and Richard B. Chase. *Fundamentals of Operations Management*, 3rd ed. Irwin McGraw-Hill, 1999.

Fawcett, Stanley E., and Steven R. Clinton, "Enhancing Logistics Performance to Improve the Competitiveness of Manufacturing Operations." *Production & Inventory Management Journal* 37, no.1 (1996), p. 40.

Handfield, Robert B., and Ernest L. Nichols. *Introduction to Supply Chain Management.* Englewood Cliffs, N.J.: Prentice-Hall, 1999.

Krajewski, Lee J., and Larry P. Ritzman. *Operations Management Strategy and Analysis*, 5th ed. Reading, Ma.: Addison-Wesley, 1999.

Lee, Hau L., V. Padmanabhan, and Seungjin Whang. "The Bullwhip Effect in Supply Chains." *Sloan Management Review* (Spring 1997), pp. 93–102.

Leenders, Michiel R., and Harold E. Fearon. *Purchasing and Supply Management*, 11th ed. Burr Ridge, Ill.: Irwin, 1997.

Quick, Rebecca. "Behind Doors of a Warehouse: Heavy Lifting of E-commerce." *Wall Street Journal*, (September 3, 1999).

Rackham, Neil, Lawrence Friedman, and Richard Ruff. *Getting Partnering Right.* New York: McGraw-Hill, 1996.

Schmitz, J. M., Frankel R., and Frayer. D. J. "ECR Alliances: A Best Practice Model." Washington, D.C.: Grocery Manufacturers Association, 1995.

Sullivan, Allanna. "From a Call to a Click." *Wall Street Journal*, June 27, 2000.

"Who Wins in the New Economy?" *Wall Street Journal*, July 17, 2000.

Total Quality Management

Before studying this chapter you should know or, if necessary, review

1. Trends in total quality management (TQM), Chapter 1, page 13.
2. Quality as a competitive priority, Chapter 2, page 30.

LEARNING OBJECTIVES

After studying this chapter you should be able to

1. Explain the meaning of total quality management (TQM).
2. Identify features of the TQM philosophy.
3. Describe the four dimensions of quality.
4. Identify costs of quality.
5. Describe tools for identifying and solving quality problems.
6. Describe quality awards and quality certifications.
7. Identify key leaders in the field of quality and their contributions.

CHAPTER OUTLINE

Everyone has had experiences of poor quality when dealing with business organizations. These experiences might involve an airline that has lost a passenger's luggage, a dry cleaner that has left clothes wrinkled or stained, poor course offerings and scheduling at your college, a purchased product that is damaged or broken, or a pizza delivery service that is often late or delivers the wrong order. The experience of poor quality is exacerbated when employees of the company either are not empowered to correct quality inadequacies or do not seem willing to do so. We have all encountered service employees who do not seem to care. The consequences of such an attitude are lost customers and opportunities for competitors to take advantage of the market need.

In this chapter you will learn that making quality a priority means putting customer needs first. It means meeting and exceeding customer expectations by involving everyone in the organization through an integrated effort. **Total quality management (TQM)** is an integrated organizational effort designed to improve quality at every level. In this chapter you will learn about the philosophy of TQM, its impact on organizations, and its impact on your life. You will learn that TQM is about meeting quality expectations as defined by the customer; this is called **customer-defined quality.** However, defining quality is not as easy as it may seem, because different people have different ideas of what constitutes high quality. Let's begin by looking at different ways in which quality can be defined.

▶ **Total quality management (TQM)** An integrated effort designed to improve quality performance at every level of the organization.

▶ **Customer-defined quality** The meaning of quality as defined by the customer.

■ DEFINING QUALITY

The definition of quality depends on the role of the people defining it. Most consumers have a difficult time defining quality, but they know it when they see it. For example, although you probably have an opinion as to which manufacturer of athletic shoes provides highest quality, it would probably be difficult for you to define your quality standard in precise terms. Also, your friends may have different opinions regarding which athletic shoes are of highest quality. The difficulty in defining quality exists regardless of product, and this is true for both manufacturing and service organizations. Think about how difficult it may be to define quality for products such as airline services, child day-care facilities, college classes, or even OM textbooks. Further complicating the issue is that the meaning of quality has changed over time.

Today, there is no single universal definition of quality. Some people view quality as "performance to standards." Others view it as "meeting the customer's needs" or "satisfying the customer." Let's look at some of the more common definitions of quality.

▶ **Conformance to specifications** How well product or service meets the targets and tolerances determined by its designers.

◆ **Conformance to specifications** measures how well the product or service meets the targets and tolerances determined by its designers. For example, the dimensions of a machine part may be specified by its design engineers as $3 \pm .05$ inches. This would mean that the target dimension is 3 inches but the dimensions can vary between 2.95 and 3.05 inches. Similarly, the wait for hotel room service may be specified as 20 minutes, but there may be an acceptable delay of an additional 10 minutes. This definition of quality is directly measurable, though it may not be directly related to the consumer's idea of quality.

◆ **Fitness for use** focuses on how well the product performs its intended function or use. For example, a Mercedes Benz and a Jeep Cherokee both meet a fitness for use definition if one considers transportation as the intended function. However, if one becomes more specific and assumes that the intended use is for transportation on mountain roads and carrying fishing gear, the Jeep Cherokee has a greater fitness for use. You can also see that fitness for use is a user-based definition in that it is intended to meet the needs of a specific user group.

◆ **Value for price paid** is a definition of quality that consumers often use for product or service usefulness. This is the only definition that combines economics with consumer criteria; it assumes that the definition of quality is price sensitive. For example, suppose that you wish to sign up for a personal finance seminar and discover that the same class is being taught at two different colleges at significantly different tuition rates. If you take the less expensive seminar, you will feel that you have received greater value for the price.

◆ **Support services** provided are often how the quality of a product or service is judged. Quality does not apply only to the product or service itself; it also applies to the people, processes, and organizational environment associated with it. For example, the quality of a university is judged not only by the quality of staff and course offerings, but also by the efficiency and accuracy of processing paperwork.

◆ **Psychological criteria** is a subjective definition that focuses on the judgmental evaluation of what constitutes product or service quality. Different factors contribute to the evaluation, such as the atmosphere of the environment or the perceived prestige of the product. For example, a hospital patient may receive average health care, but a very friendly staff may leave the impression of high quality. Similarly, we commonly associate certain products with excellence because of their reputation; Rolex watches and Mercedes-Benz automobiles are examples.

> ▶ **Fitness for use**
> A definition of quality that evaluates how well the product performs for its intended use.

> ▶ **Value for price paid**
> Quality defined in terms of product or service usefulness for the price paid.

> ▶ **Support services**
> Quality defined in terms of the support provided after the product or service is purchased.

> ▶ **Psychological criteria**
> A way of defining quality that focuses on judgmental evaluations of what constitutes product or service excellence.

Differences Between Manufacturing and Service Organizations

Defining quality in manufacturing organizations is often different from that of services. Manufacturing organizations produce a tangible product that can be seen, touched, and directly measured. Examples include cars, CD players, clothes, computers, and food items. Therefore, quality definitions in manufacturing usually focus on tangible product features.

The most common quality definition in manufacturing is *conformance*, which is the degree to which a product characteristic meets preset standards. Other common definitions of quality in manufacturing include *performance*–such as acceleration of a vehicle; *reliability*–that the product will function as expected without failure; and *features*–the extras that are included beyond the basic characteristics. The relative importance of these definitions are based on the preferences of each individual customer. It is easy to see how different customers can have different definitions in mind when they speak of high product quality.

In contrast to manufacturing, service organizations produce a product that is intangible. Usually, the complete product cannot be seen or touched. Rather, it is experienced. Examples include delivery of health care, experience of staying at a vacation resort, and learning at a university. The intangible nature of the product makes defining quality difficult. Also, since a service is experienced, perceptions can be highly subjective. Quality of services is often defined by perceptual factors such as *courtesy* and *friendliness* of staff, *promptness* in resolving complaints, and *atmosphere*. Other definitions of quality in services include *time*–the amount of time a customer has to wait for the service; and *consistency*–the degree to which the service is the same each time. For these reasons, defining quality in services can be especially challenging.

LINKS TO PRACTICE
General Electric Co.
www.ge.com
Motorola, Inc.
www.motorola.com

Today's customers demand and expect high quality. Companies that do not make quality a priority risk long-run survival. World-class organizations such as General Electric Co. and Motorola attribute their success to having one of the best quality management programs in the world. General Electric considers quality so important that it has a designation called "Black Belt" for individuals highly trained in quality improvement principles and techniques. The full-time job of Black Belts is to identify and solve quality problems. Motorola, the leading manufacturer of products such as cell phones, pagers, and semiconductors, has set up similar quality initiatives. Motorola was one of the first companies to win the prestigious Malcolm Baldrige National Quality Award in 1988. The primary goal for both organizations has been to achieve total customer satisfaction. To this end, the efforts of these organizations have included eliminating almost all defects from products, processes, and transactions. Both companies consider quality to be the critical factor that has resulted in significant increases in sales and market share, as well as cost savings in the range of millions of dollars.

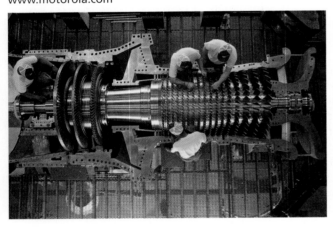

■ THE EVOLUTION OF TOTAL QUALITY MANAGEMENT

The concept of quality has existed for many years, though its meaning has changed and evolved over time. In the early twentieth century, quality management meant inspecting products to ensure that they met specifications. In the 1940s, during World War II, quality became more statistical in nature. Statistical sampling techniques were used to evaluate quality, and quality control charts were used to monitor the production process. In the 1960s, with the help of so-called "quality gurus," the concept took on a broader meaning. Quality began to be viewed as something that encompassed the entire organization, not only the production process. Since all functions were responsible for product quality and all shared the costs of poor quality, quality was seen as a concept that affected the entire organization.

TIME:	Early 1900s	1940s	1960s	1980s and Beyond
FOCUS:	Inspection	Statistical sampling	Organizational quality focus	Customer driven quality

|←——————————————————————————→| |←————————————→|

Old Concept of Quality:
Inspect for quality after production.

New Concept of Quality:
Built quality into the process.
Identify and correct causes of
quality problems.

Figure 5-1

Timeline showing the differences between old and new concepts of quality

The meaning of quality for businesses changed dramatically in the late 1970s. Before then quality was still viewed as something that needed to be inspected and corrected. However, in the 1970s and 1980s many U.S. industries lost market share to foreign competition. In the auto industry, manufacturers such as Toyota and Honda became major players. In the consumer goods market, companies such as Toshiba and Sony led the way. These foreign competitors were producing lower-priced products with considerably higher quality.

To survive, companies had to make major changes in their quality programs. Many hired consultants and instituted quality training programs for their employees. A new concept of quality was emerging. One result is that quality began to have a strategic meaning. Today, successful companies understand that quality provides a competitive advantage. They put the customer first and define quality as meeting or exceeding customer expectations.

Since the 1970s, competition based on quality has grown in importance and has generated tremendous interest, concern, and enthusiasm. Companies in every line of business are focusing on improving quality in order to be more competitive. In many industries quality excellence has become a standard for doing business. Companies that do not meet this standard simply will not survive. As you will see later in the chapter, the importance of quality is demonstrated by the national quality awards and quality certifications that are coveted by businesses.

The term used for today's new concept of quality is **total quality management** or **TQM.** Figure 5-1 presents a timeline of the old and new concepts of quality. You can see that the old concept is *reactive*, designed to correct quality problems after they occur. The new concept is *proactive*, designed to build quality into the product and process design. Next, we look at the philosophy of TQM in more detail.

THE PHILOSOPHY OF TQM ■

What makes TQM different from the old concept of quality is the focus on identifying the root causes of quality problems and correcting them, as opposed to inspecting the product after it has been made. Not only does TQM encompass the entire organization, it stresses that quality is customer driven. TQM attempts to embed quality in every aspect of the organization. It is concerned with technical aspects of quality as well as the involvement of people, such as customers, company employees, and suppliers. Several specific features make up the philosophy of TQM.

Customer Focus

The first, and overriding, feature of TQM is the company's focus on its customers. The goal is to first identify and then meet customer needs. TQM recognizes that a perfectly produced product has little value if it is not what the customer wants. Therefore, we can say that quality is customer driven. However, it is not always easy to determine what the customer wants, because tastes and preferences change. For example, in the auto industry trends change relatively quickly, from small cars to sports utility vehicles and back to small cars. The same is true in the retail industry, where styles and fashion are short lived. Companies need to continually gather information by means of focus groups, market surveys, and customer interviews in order to stay in tune with what customers want. They must always remember that they would not be in business if it were not for their customers.

Continuous Improvement

▶ **Continuous improvement**
A philosophy of never-ending improvement.

A second feature of the TQM philosophy is the focus on **continuous improvement.** Traditional systems operated on the assumption that once a company achieved a certain level of quality, it was successful and further improvements were unnecessary. We tend to think of improvement in terms of plateaus that are to be achieved, such as passing a certification test or reducing the number of defects to a certain level. Traditionally, change for American managers involves large magnitudes, such as major organizational restructuring. The Japanese, on the other hand, believe that the best and most lasting changes come from gradual improvements. To use an analogy, they believe that it is better to take frequent small doses of medicine than to take one large dose. Continuous improvement, called kaizen by the Japanese, requires that the company continually strive to be better through learning and problem solving. Because we can never achieve perfection, we must always evaluate our performance and take measures to improve it.

Quality at the Source

▶ **Quality at the source**
The belief that it is best to uncover the source of quality problems and eliminate it.

Quality at the source is another integral part of TQM. It is far better to uncover the source of quality problems and correct it than to discard defective items after production. If the source of the problem is not corrected, the problem will continue. For example, if you are baking cookies you might find that some of the cookies are burned. Simply throwing away the burned cookies will not correct the problem. You will continue to have burned cookies and will lose money when you throw them away. It will be far more effective to see where the problem is and correct it. For example, the temperature setting may be too high; the pan may be curved, placing some cookies closer to the heating element; or the oven may not be distributing heat evenly.

Quality at the source exemplifies the difference between the old and new concepts of quality. The old concept focused on inspecting goods after they were produced or after a particular stage of production. If an inspection revealed defects, the defective products were either discarded or sent back for reworking. All this cost the company money and these costs were passed on to the customer. The new concept of quality focuses on identifying quality problems at the source and correcting them.

Employee Empowerment

Directly related to quality at the source is the role of employees in the organization. Part of the TQM philosophy is to empower all employees to seek out quality problems and correct them. With the old concept of quality, employees were afraid to identify problems for fear that they would be reprimanded. Often poor quality was passed on to someone else, in order to make it "someone else's problem." The new concept of quality, TQM, provides incentives for employees to identify quality problems. Employees are rewarded for uncovering quality problems, not punished.

In TQM, the role of employees is very different from what it was in traditional systems. Workers are empowered to make decisions relative to quality in the production process. They are considered a vital element of the effort to achieve high quality. Their contributions are highly valued, and their suggestions are implemented. In order to perform this function, employees are given continual and extensive training in quality measurement tools.

To further stress the role of employees in quality, TQM differentiates between *external* and *internal customers*. *External customers* are those that purchase the company's goods and services. *Internal customers* are employees of the organization who receive goods or services from others in the company. For example, the packaging department of an organization is an internal customer of the assembly department. Just as we would not pass a defective item to an external customer, we must not pass a defective item to an internal customer.

Understanding Quality Tools

As you can see, TQM places a great deal of responsibility on every worker. If employees are to identify and correct quality problems, they need proper training. They need to understand how to assess quality by using a variety of quality control tools, how to interpret findings, and how to correct problems. Continuous improvement tells us that one-time training is not enough. Rather, training needs to be done on an ongoing basis. Since quality management is an activity that permeates all levels of the organization, it is necessary for employees at all levels to understand how to use quality control tools for quality assessment.

Team Approach

TQM stresses that quality is an organizational effort. To facilitate the solving of quality problems, it places great emphasis on teamwork. The use of teams is based on the old adage that "two heads are better than one." Using techniques such as brainstorming, discussion, and quality control tools, teams work regularly to correct problems. The contributions of teams are considered vital to the success of the company. For this reason, companies set aside time in the workday for team meetings.

Teams vary in their degree of structure and formality, and different types of teams solve different types of problems. One of the most common types of teams is the **quality circle,** a team of volunteer production employees and their supervisors whose purpose is to solve quality problems. The circle is usually composed of eight to ten members, and decisions are made through group consensus. The teams usually meet weekly during work hours in a place designated for this purpose. They follow a preset process for analyzing and solving quality problems. Open discussion is

▶ **Quality circle**
A team of volunteer production employees and their supervisors who meet regularly to solve quality problems.

promoted, and criticism is not allowed. Although the functioning of quality circles is friendly and casual, it is serious business. Quality circles are not mere "gab sessions." Rather, they do important work for the company and have been very successful in many firms.

The importance of exceptional quality is demonstrated by The Walt Disney Company in operating its theme parks. The focus of the parks is customer satisfaction. This is accomplished through meticulous attention to every detail, with particular focus on the role of employees in service delivery. Employees are viewed as the most important organizational resource and great care is taken in employee hiring and training. All employees are called "cast members," regardless of whether they are janitors or performers. Employees are extensively trained in customer service, communication, and quality awareness. Continual monitoring of quality is considered important and employees meet regularly in teams to evaluate their effectiveness. All employees are shown how the quality of their individual jobs contributes to the success of the park.

Benchmarking

▶ **Benchmarking**
Studying the business practices of other companies for purposes of comparison.

Another important aspect of TQM is studying business practices of companies considered "best in class." This is called **benchmarking.** The ability to learn and study how others do things is an important part of continuous improvement. The benchmark company does not have to be in the same business, as long as it excels at something that the company doing the study wishes to emulate. For example, many companies have used Lands' End to benchmark catalog distribution and order filling, because Lands' End is considered a leader in this area. Similarly, many companies have used American Express to benchmark conflict resolution.

Managing Supplier Quality

TQM extends the concept of quality to a company's suppliers. Traditionally, companies tended to have numerous suppliers that engaged in competitive price bidding. When materials arrived, an inspection was performed to check their quality. TQM views this practice as contributing to poor quality and wasted time and cost. The philosophy of TQM extends the concept of quality to suppliers and ensures that they engage in the same quality practices. If suppliers meet preset quality standards, materials do not have to be inspected upon arrival. Today, many companies have a representative residing at their supplier's location, thereby involving the supplier in every stage from product design to final production.

DIMENSIONS OF QUALITY ■

Traditionally, manufacturers have defined quality as how well the product conforms to preset specifications. For example, an inexpensive frozen pizza that has met all the standards set by its producer would be considered high quality. Yet, most customers do not know or even care about the manufacturing standards set for a product. As we have already seen, customers define quality in very different terms.

Today's concept of quality is customer driven. Quality is defined as *meeting or exceeding customer expectations*. Customer expectations, however, often vary from one customer to the next. Also, the expectations of customers today may not be satisfied tomorrow as customer tastes and preferences change. To achieve customer-oriented quality, a company must stay abreast of the needs and wants of its customers.

Four dimensions of quality must be addressed in developing a product that provides a high level of customer satisfaction. These dimensions are

- ◆ Quality of product or service design
- ◆ Quality of conformance to the design
- ◆ Ease of use
- ◆ Post-sale service

Quality of Design

Achieving **quality of design** entails determining which features will be included in the final product or service. It starts with customer wants and culminates in the development of either a blueprint with a list of components for a tangible product or a set of detailed service specifications. Quality of design typically originates with market research, since the marketing department is generally responsible for assessing customer needs. Information about customer preferences can be collected through market surveys, focus groups, and customer interviews. This type of data collection should be done continually in order to keep pace with changes in consumer preferences.

▶ **Quality of design**
The determination of which features will be included in the final design of a product.

The process of developing quality of design includes forming a cross-functional team with members from many disciplines. Certainly the marketing department is involved due to its close contact with customers. Also involved are the operations and engineering departments in order to translate marketing concepts into specific operational requirements. Often, suppliers are involved as well because they can provide suggestions for parts design and usage. Collectively, these teams work together to define a product that meets customer needs.

CROSS FUNCTIONAL

Quality of Conformance to Design

Once the product has been designed, the production process must be set up to meet the specifications of the design. Called **quality of conformance,** it is the degree to which the product meets, or conforms to, the specifications of the product design. For example, product designs specify dimensions such as width, length, or height. How well the produced product meets these preset requirements is the critical element at this stage. For example, quality of conformance for a bottle of soft drink relates to how close its volume comes to the preset 16 ounces.

▶ **Quality of conformance**
The degree to which the product meets, or conforms to, its design specifications.

Ease of Use

Once a product has been produced and sold, an important dimension of quality is its ease of use. This means that the instructions for use are simple, what the product is used for and what it is not used for is clear, the product is easy to operate, it does not break down frequently, and it is easy to maintain. For example, a vacuum cleaner can be designed to have many uses, such as cleaning as well as vacuuming carpets. However, if customers perceive that it is difficult to operate, it will be considered to have low quality.

Legal issues can come into play if difficulty of operation impinges on safety. Companies that have been involved in product litigation have found that many problems result from incorrect operation of the product or unclear instructions. To protect themselves, companies place clear and simple warning labels on their products. For example, umbrella-type strollers have a warning label reminding the user to remove the baby before folding the stroller, and hair dryers have a tag warning the user not to use the dryer in water. Precautions may be obvious to any user with common sense, but companies have found the labels to be necessary.

Ease of use is also important for services. For example, many manufacturers of prescription medications such as antibiotics have focused on drugs that can be taken once a day compared to older versions that had to be taken four or six times a day. In health-care delivery, ease of use includes providing clear instructions for taking medications or performing certain tests, such as taking one's own blood pressure. For example, a patient who is told to monitor his or her blood pressure needs to be given clear instructions on how to perform the measurement, read the results, and interpret them. Similar situations occur in other services. Hotels may offer coffee makers in their rooms, but if the instructions for use are complicated, the quality of service will be perceived as poor.

Post-Sale Service

The last dimension of quality is post-sale service, which consists of all the issues that arise after the product has been purchased. It includes responsiveness of service personnel, rapid repair, flexible preventive maintenance, and short lead times for ordering spare parts. In services, it may take the form of a telephone call by a physician or nurse to check on a patient, the responsiveness of hotel staff to a guest inquiry, or even the care of a professor in answering a student's question. In the past, companies frequently overlooked this dimension. It was felt that once the product or service was sold, the company's responsibility ended. Today, many companies specifically compete on this last dimension of quality, promising full service after the sale.

You can see from this discussion that providing high quality involves much more than the production of the product itself. It involves much planning, from the design phase all the way to providing customer support long after the sale. Now, let's look at what poor quality actually costs the organization.

■ COST OF QUALITY

The reason quality has gained such prominence is that organizations have gained an understanding of the high cost of poor quality. Quality affects all aspects of the organization and has dramatic cost implications. The most obvious consequence occurs when poor quality creates dissatisfied customers and eventually leads to loss of business. However, quality has many other costs, which can be divided into two categories. The first category consists of costs necessary for achieving high quality, which are called *quality control costs*. These are of two types: *prevention costs* and *appraisal costs*. The second category consists of the cost consequences of poor quality, which are called *quality failure costs*. These include *external failure costs* and *internal failure costs*. These costs of quality are shown in Figure 5-2. The first two costs are incurred in the hope of preventing the second two.

Prevention costs are all costs incurred in the process of preventing poor quality from occurring. They include quality planning costs, such as the costs of developing and implementing a quality plan. Also included are the costs of product and process design, from collecting customer information to designing processes that achieve conformance to specifications. Employee training in quality measurement is included as part of this cost, as well as the costs of maintaining records of information and data related to quality.

Appraisal costs are incurred in the process of uncovering defects. They include the cost of quality inspections, product testing, and performing audits to make sure that quality standards are being met. Also included in this category are the costs of worker time spent measuring quality and the cost of equipment used for quality appraisal.

Internal failure costs are associated with discovering poor product quality before the product reaches the customer site. One type of internal failure cost is rework, which is the cost of correcting the defective item. Sometimes the item is so defective that it cannot be corrected and must be thrown away. This is called *scrap*, and its costs include all the material, labor, and machine cost spent in producing the defective product. Other types of internal failure costs include the cost of machine downtime due to failures in the process and the costs of discounting defective items for salvage value.

External failure costs are associated with quality problems that occur at the customer site. These costs can be particularly damaging because customer faith and loyalty can be difficult to regain. They include everything from customer complaints, product returns, and repairs, to warranty claims, recalls, and even litigation costs resulting from product liability issues. A final component of this cost is lost sales and lost customers. For example, manufacturers of lunch meats and hot dogs whose products have been recalled due to bacterial contamination have had to struggle to regain consumer confidence. Other examples include auto

▶ **Prevention costs**
Costs incurred in the process of preventing poor quality from occurring.

▶ **Appraisal costs**
Costs incurred in the process of uncovering defects.

▶ **Internal failure costs**
Costs associated with discovering poor product quality before the product reaches the customer.

▶ **External failure costs**
Costs associated with quality problems that occur at the customer site.

Prevention costs.	Costs of preparing and implementing a quality plan.
Appraisal costs.	Costs of testing, evaluation, and inspecting quality.
Internal failure costs.	Cost of scrap, rework, and material losses.
External failure costs.	Costs of failure at customer site, including returns, repairs, and recalls.

Figure 5-2

Costs of quality

manufacturers whose products have been recalled due to major malfunctions such as problematic braking systems and airlines that have experienced a crash with many fatalities. External failure can sometimes put a company out of business almost overnight.

Companies who consider quality important invest heavily in prevention and appraisal costs in order to prevent internal and external failure costs. External failure costs tend to be particularly high for service organizations. The reason is that with a service the customer spends much time in the service delivery system, and there are fewer opportunities to correct defects than there are in manufacturing. Examples of external failure in services include an airline that has overbooked flights, long delays in airline service, and lost luggage.

Before You Go On

Today's concept of quality, called total quality management (TQM), focuses on building quality into the process as opposed to simply inspecting for poor quality after production. TQM is customer driven and it encompasses the entire company. Before you go on, you should understand the eight features of total quality management: *customer focus, continuous improvement, quality at the source, employee empowerment, understanding quality tools, a team approach, benchmarking,* and *managing supplier quality.* You also need to understand the four dimensions of quality: *quality of design, quality of conformance to design, ease of use,* and *postsales service.* To be successful, a company needs to address all four of these dimensions of quality. You should also know the four categories of quality costs. These are *prevention and appraisal costs,* which are costs that are incurred to prevent poor quality, and *internal and external failure costs,* which are costs that the company hopes to prevent.

■ WAYS OF IMPROVING QUALITY

The Plan–Do–Study–Act Cycle

▶ **Plan–do–study–act cycle**
A diagram that describes the activities that need to be performed to incorporate continuous improvement into the operation.

The plan–do–study–act (PDSA) cycle describes the activities a company needs to perform in order to incorporate continuous improvement in its operation. This cycle, shown in Figure 5-3, is often called the *Deming wheel* after its originator, W. Edwards Deming. The circular nature of this cycle shows that continuous improvement is a never-ending process. Next we look at the specific steps in the cycle.

Figure 5-3

The plan–do–study–act cycle

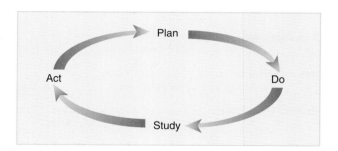

Plan   The first step in the PDSA cycle is to *plan*. Managers must evaluate the current process and make plans based on any problems they find. They need to document all current procedures, collect data, and identify problems. This information should then be studied and used to develop a plan for improvement as well as specific measures to evaluate performance.

Do   The next step in the cycle is implementing our plan (*do*). During the implementation process managers should document all changes made and collect data for evaluation.

Study   The third step is to *study* the data collected in the previous phase. The data are evaluated to see whether the plan is achieving the goals established in the *plan* phase.

Act   The last phase of the cycle is to *act* on the basis of the results of the first three phases. The best way to accomplish this is to communicate the results to other members in the company and then implement the new procedure if it has been successful. Note that this is a cycle; the next step is to plan again. After we have acted, we need to continue evaluating the process, planning, and repeating the cycle again.

Quality Function Deployment

A critical aspect of building quality into a product is to ensure that the product design meets customer expectations. This typically is not as easy as it seems. Customers often speak in everyday language. For example, a product can be described as "attractive," "strong," or "safe." However, these terms can have very different meaning to different customers. What one person considers to be strong, another may not. To produce a product that customers want, we need to translate customers' everyday language into specific technical requirements. However, this can often be difficult. A useful tool for translating the voice of the customer into specific technical requirements is **quality function deployment (QFD)**. Quality function deployment is also useful in enhancing communication between different functions, such as marketing, operations, and engineering.

▶ **Quality function deployment (QFD)**
A tool used to translate the preferences of the customer into specific technical requirements.

QFD enables us to view the relationships among the variables involved in the design of a product, such as technical versus customer requirements. This can help us analyze the big picture—for example, running tests to see how changes in certain technical requirements of the product affect customer requirements. An example is an automobile manufacturer evaluating how changes in materials used affect customer safety requirements. This type of analysis can be very beneficial in developing a product design that meets customer needs yet does not create unnecessary technical requirements for production.

QFD begins by identifying important customer requirements, which typically come from the marketing department. These requirements are numerically scored based on their importance, and scores are translated into specific product characteristics. Evaluations are then made of how the product compares with its main competitors relative to the identified characteristics. Finally, specific goals are set to address the identified problems. The resulting matrix looks like a picture of a house and is often called the *house of quality*. Next we use the example of manufacturing a backpack to show how we would use QFD. We will start with a relationship matrix that ties customer requirements to product characteristics, shown in Figure 5-4.

CROSS FUNCTIONAL

Figure 5-4

Relationship matrix

Customer Requirements	Relative Importance	No. of Zippers & Compartments	Weight of Backpack	Strength of Backpack	Grade of Dye Color	Cost of Materials	Competitive Evaluation
Durable	25	✓	✓	✓(strong)	✓	✓(strong)	1 2 3(B) 4(A) 5(US)
Lightweight	20	X(strong)	X(strong)	X		✓	1 2(A) 3(US/B) 4 5
Roomy	25	✓	X				1 2 3(US/A) 4(B) 5
Looks Nice	20	✓			✓(strong)	✓	1(US) 2 3(B) 4(A) 5
Low Cost	10	X	X	X	X	X(strong)	1(US) 2 3(B) 4(A) 5
TOTAL	100						

Product Characteristics

Relationship

✓(circled) Strong Positive
✓ Positive
X Negative
X(circled) Strong Negative

US = Our Backpack
A = Competitor A
B = Competitor B

Customer Requirements

Remember that our goal is to make a product that the customer wants. Therefore, the first thing we need to do is survey our customers to find out specifically what they would be looking for in a product—in this case, a backpack for students. To find out precisely what features students would like in a backpack, the marketing department might send representatives to talk to students on campus, conduct telephone interviews, and maybe conduct focus groups. Let's say that students have identified five desirable features: the backpack should be durable, lightweight and roomy, look nice, and not cost very much. These are shown in Figure 5-4. The importance customers attach to each of these requirements is also determined and shown in the figure. This part of the figure looks like the chimney of the "house." You can see that durability and roominess are given the greatest importance.

Competitive Evaluation

On the far right of our relationship matrix is an evaluation of how our product compares to those of competitors. In this example there are two competitors, A and B. The evaluation scale is from one to five—the higher the rating, the better. The important thing here is to identify which customer requirements we should pursue and how we fare relative to our competitors. For example, you can see that our product excels in durability relative to competitors, yet it does not look as nice. This means that in designing our product, we could gain a competitive advantage by focusing our design efforts on a more appealing product.

Product Characteristics

Specific product characteristics are on top of the relationship matrix. These are technical measures. In our example these include the number of zippers and compartments, the weight of the backpack, strength of the backpack, grade of the dye color, and the cost of materials.

The Relationship Matrix

The strength of the relationship between customer requirements and product characteristics is shown in the relationship matrix. For example, you can see that the number of zippers and compartments is negatively related to the weight of the backpack. A negative relationship means that as we increase the desirability of one variable we decrease the desirability of the other. At the same time, roominess is positively related to the number of zippers and compartments, as is appearance. A positive relationship means that an increase in desirability of one variable is related to an increase in the desirability of another. This type of information is very important in coordinating the product design.

The Trade-off Matrix

You can see how the relationship matrix is beginning to look like a house. The complete house of quality is shown in Figure 5-5. The next step in our building process is to put the "roof" on the house. This is done through a trade-off matrix, which shows how each product characteristic is related to the others and allows to see what trade-offs we need to make. For example, the number of zippers is negatively related to the weight of the backpack.

Setting Targets

The last step in constructing the house of quality is to evaluate competitors' products relative to the specific product characteristics and to set targets for our own product. The bottom row of the house is the *output* of quality function deployment. These are specific, measurable product characteristics that have been formulated from general customer requirements.

The house of quality has been found to be a very useful. You can see how it translates everyday terms like "lightweight," "roominess," and "nice looking," into specific product characteristics that can be used in manufacturing the product. Note also how the house of quality can help in the communication between marketing, operations, and design engineering.

Figure 5-5

House of quality

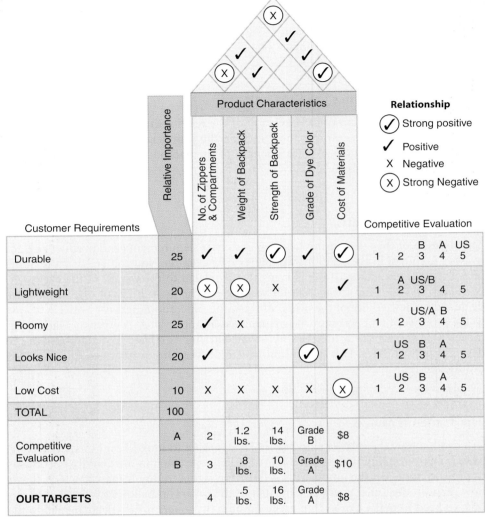

US = Our Backpack
A = Competitor A
B = Competitor B

■ TOOLS FOR PROBLEM SOLVING

To identify, study, and solve quality problems we need certain tools. In this section we will look at seven different tools. These are often called the seven tools of quality control and are shown in Figure 5-6. They are easy to understand yet extremely useful in identifying and analyzing quality problems. Sometimes workers use only one tool at a time, but often a combination of tools is most helpful.

▶ **Cause-and-effect diagram**
A chart that identifies potential causes of particular quality problems.

Cause-and-Effect Diagrams

Cause-and-effect diagrams are charts that identify potential causes for particular quality problems. They are often called fishbone diagrams because they look like the

1. Cause and Effect Diagram

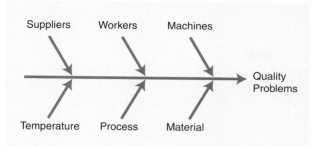

2. Flow Chart

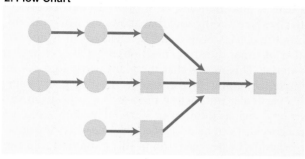

3. Check List

Defect Type	No. of Defects	Total
Broken zipper	✓✓	3
Ripped material	✓✓✓✓✓✓	7
Missing buttons	✓✓	3
Faded color	✓✓	2

Figure 5-6

The seven tools of quality control

4. Control Chart

5. Scatter Diagram

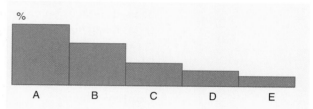

6. Pareto Chart

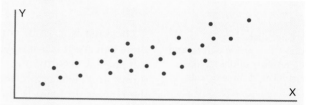

7. Histogram

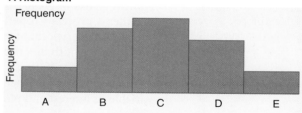

bones of a fish. The "head" of the fish is the quality problem, such as damaged zippers on a garment or broken valves on a tire. The diagram is drawn so that the "spine" of the fish connects the "head" to the possible cause of the problem. These causes could be related to the machines, workers, measurement, suppliers, materials, and many other aspects of the production process. Each of these possible causes can then have smaller "bones" that address specific issues that relate to each cause. For example, a problem with machines could be due to a need for adjustment, old equipment, or tooling problems. Similarly, a problem with workers could be related to lack of training, poor supervision, or fatigue.

Cause-and-effect diagrams are problem-solving tools commonly used by quality control teams. Specific causes of problems can be explored through brainstorming. The development of a cause-and-effect diagram requires the team to think through all the possible causes of poor quality.

Flowcharts

▶ **Flowchart**
A schematic of the sequence of steps involved in an operation or process.

A **flowchart** is a schematic diagram of the sequence of steps involved in an operation or process. It provides a visual tool that is easy to use and understand. By seeing the steps involved in a operation or process, everyone develops a clear picture of how the operation works and where problems could arise.

Checklists

▶ **Checklist**
A list of common defects and the number of observed occurrences of these defects.

A **checklist** is a list of common defects and the number of observed occurrences of these defects. It is a simple yet effective fact-finding tool that allows the worker to collect specific information regarding the defects observed. The checklist in Figure 5-6 shows four defects and the number of times they have been observed. It is clear that the biggest problem is ripped material. This means that the plant needs to focus on this specific problem—for example, by going to the source of supply or seeing whether the material rips during a particular production process. A checklist can also be used to focus on other dimensions, such as location or time. For example, if a defect is being observed frequently, a checklist can be developed that measures the number of occurrences per shift, per machine, or per operator. In this fashion we can isolate the location of the particular defect and then focus on correcting the problem.

Control Charts

▶ **Control charts**
Charts used to evaluate whether a process is operating within set expectations.

Control charts are a very important quality control tool. We will study the use of control charts at great length in the next chapter. These charts are used to evaluate whether a process is operating within expectations relative to some measured value such as weight, width, or volume. For example, we could measure the weight of a sack of flour, the width of a tire, or the volume of a bottle of soft drink. When the production process is operating within expectations, we say that it is "in control."

To evaluate whether a process is in control or not, we regularly measure the variable of interest and plot it on a control chart. The chart has a line down the center representing the average value of the variable we are measuring. Above and below the center line are two lines, called the upper control limit (UCL) and the lower control limit (LCL). As long as the observed values fall within the upper and lower control limits, the process is in control and there is no problem with quality. When a measured observation falls outside of these limits, there is a problem.

Scatter Diagrams

▶ **Scatter diagrams**
Graphs that show how two variables are related to each other.

Scatter diagrams are graphs that show how two variables are related to one another. They are particularly useful in detecting the amount of correlation, or the degree of linear relationship, between two variables. For example, increased production speed and number of defects could be positively correlated; as production speed increases, so does the number of defects. Two variables could also be negatively correlated, so that an increase in one of the variables is associated with a decrease in the other. For example, increased worker training might be associated with a decrease in the number of defects observed.

The greater the degree of correlation, the more linear are the observations in the scatter diagram. On the other hand, the more scattered the observations in the diagram, the less correlation exists between the variables. Of course, other types of relationships can also be observed on a scatter diagram, such as an inverted U. This may be the case when one is observing the relationship between two variables such as oven temperature and number of defects, since temperatures below and above the ideal could lead to defects.

Pareto Analysis

Pareto analysis is a technique used to identify quality problems based on their degree of importance. The logic behind Pareto analysis is that only a few quality problems are important, whereas many others are not critical. The technique was named after Vilfredo Pareto, a nineteenth-century Italian economist who determined that only a small percentage of people controlled most of the wealth. This concept has often been called the 80–20 rule and has been extended to many areas. In quality management the logic behind Pareto's principle is that most quality problems are a result of only a few causes. The trick is to identify these causes.

▶ **Pareto analysis**
A technique used to identify quality problems based on their degree of importance.

One way to use Pareto analysis is to develop a chart that ranks the causes of poor quality in decreasing order based on the percentage of defects each has caused. For example, a tally can be made of the number of defects that result from different causes, such as operator error, defective parts, or inaccurate machine calibrations. Percentages of defects can be computed from the tally and placed in a chart like those shown in Figure 5-6. We generally tend to find a few causes account for most of the defects.

Histograms

A **histogram** is a chart that shows the frequency distribution of observed values of a variable. We can see from the plot what type of distribution a particular variable displays, such as whether it has a normal distribution and whether the distribution is symmetrical.

▶ **Histogram**
A chart that shows the frequency distribution of observed values of a variable.

In the food service industry the use of quality control tools is important in identifying quality problems. Grocery store chains, such as Kroger and Meijer, must record and monitor quality of incoming produce, such as tomatoes and lettuce. Quality tools can be used to evaluate acceptability of product quality and to monitor product quality from individual suppliers. They can also be used to evaluate causes of quality problems, such as long transit time or poor refrigeration. Similarly, restaurants use quality control tools to evaluate and monitor quality of delivered goods, such as meats, produce, or baked goods.

LINKS TO PRACTICE
The Kroger Company
www.kroger.com
Meijer, Inc.
www.meijer.com

■ QUALITY STANDARDS

▶ **Malcolm Baldrige National Quality Award**
An award given annually to companies that demonstrate quality excellence and establish best-practice standards in industry.

The Malcolm Baldrige Award

The Malcolm Baldrige National Quality Award was established in 1987, when Congress passed the Malcolm Baldrige National Quality Improvement Act. The award was named after the former Secretary of Commerce, Malcolm Baldrige, and is intended to reward and stimulate quality initiatives. It is designed to recognize companies that establish and demonstrate high quality standards. The award is given to no more than two companies in each of three categories: manufacturing, service, and small business. Past winners include Motorola Corporation, Xerox, Federal Express, 3M, IBM, and Ritz-Carlton.

To compete for the Baldrige Award, companies must submit a lengthy application, which is followed by an initial screening. Companies that pass this screening move to the next step, in where they undergo a rigorous evaluation process conducted by certified Baldrige examiners. The examiners conduct site visits and examine numerous company documents. They base their evaluation on seven categories, which are shown in Figure 5-7. Let's look at each category in more detail.

The first category is *leadership*. Examiners consider commitment by top management, their effort to create an organizational climate devoted to quality, and their active involvement in promoting quality. They also consider the firm's orientation toward meeting customer needs and desires, as well as those of the community and society as a whole.

Categories		Points
1 Leadership		**110**
1.1 Leadership System	80	
1.2 Company responsibility and citizenship	30	
2 Strategic Planning		**80**
2.1 Strategy Development Process	40	
2.2 Company Strategy	40	
3 Customer and Market Focus		**80**
3.1 Customer and Market Knowledge	40	
3.2 Customer Satisfaction and Relationship Enhancement	40	
4 Information and Analysis		**80**
4.1 Selection and Use of Information and Data	25	
4.2 Selection and Use of Comparative Information & Data	15	
4.3 Analysis and Review of Company Performance	40	
5 Human Resource Development and Management		**100**
5.1 Work Systems	40	
5.2 Employee Education, Training, and Development	30	
5.3 Employee Well-Being and Satisfaction	30	
6 Process Managment		**100**
6.1 Management of Product and Service Processes	60	
6.2 Management of Support Processes	20	
6.3 Management of Supplier and Partnering Processes	20	
7 Business Results		**450**
7.1 Customer Satisfaction Results	130	
7.2 Financial and Market Results	130	
7.3 Human Resource Results	35	
7.4 Supplier and Partner Results	25	
7.5 Community-specific Results	130	
TOTAL POINTS		**1000**

Figure 5-7

Malcolm Baldrige Award criteria

Ritz-Carlton is one of the past winners of the Malcolm Baldrige National Quality Award.

The second category is *strategic planning*. The examiners look for a strategic plan that has high quality goals and specific methods for implementation. The next category, *customer and market focus*, addresses how the company collects market and customer information. Successful companies should use a variety of tools toward this end, such as market surveys and focus groups. The company then needs to demonstrate how it acts on this information.

The fourth category is *information and analysis*. Examiners evaluate how the company obtains data and how it acts on the information. The company needs to demonstrate how the information is shared within the company as well as with other parties, such as suppliers and customers.

The fifth and sixth categories deal with management of human resources and management of processes, respectively. These two categories together address the issues of people and process. *Human resource development and management* addresses issues of employee involvement. This entails continuous improvement programs, employee training, and functioning of teams. Employee involvement is considered a critical element of quality. Similarly, *process management* involves documentation of processes, use of tools for quality improvement such as statistical process control, and the degree of process integration within the organization.

The last Baldrige category receives the highest points and deals with *business results*. Numerous measures of performance are considered, from percentage of defective items to financial and marketing measures. Companies need to demonstrate progressive improvement in these measures over time, not only a one-time improvement.

The Baldrige criteria have evolved from simple award criteria to a general framework for quality evaluation. Many companies use these criteria to evaluate their own performance and set quality targets even if they are not planning to formally compete for the award.

ISO 9000 Standards

The *International Organization for Standardization* (ISO) is an international organization whose purpose is to establish agreement on international quality standards. It currently has members from 90 countries, including the United States. To develop and promote international quality standards, **ISO 9000** has been created. ISO 9000 consists of a set of standards and a certification process for companies. By receiving ISO 9000 certification, companies demonstrate that they have met the standards specified by the ISO. The standards are applicable to all types of companies and have gained global acceptance. In many industries ISO certification has become a requirement for doing business. Also, ISO 9000 standards have been adopted by the European Community as a standard for companies doing business in Europe.

To receive ISO certification, a company must provide extensive documentation of its quality processes. This includes methods used to monitor quality, methods and frequency of worker training, job descriptions, inspection programs, and statistical process control tools used. High-quality documentation of all processes is critical. The company is then audited by an ISO 9000 examiner, who visits the facility to make sure the company has a well-documented quality management system and that the process meets the standards. If the examiner finds that all is in order, certification is received. However, companies have to be recertified by ISO every three years.

One of the shortcomings of ISO certification is that it focuses only on the process used and conformance to specifications. In contrast to the Baldrige criteria, ISO certification does not address questions about the product itself and whether it

▶ **ISO 9000**
A set of international quality standards and a certification demonstrating that companies have met all the standards specified.

meets customer and market requirements. Also, there are no standards for design quality, leadership and organizational climate, structure, and organizational strategy. Rather, ISO certification focuses strictly on procedures, employee training, and documentation of the quality management system. Therefore, even though ISO 9000 certification has become pervasive, it should be viewed as a basic standard of quality and a first step towards achieving the overall goals of total quality management.

Other Quality Standards

ISO 14000   The need for standardization of quality created an impetus for the development of other standards. In 1996 the International Standards Organization introduced standards for evaluating a company's environmental responsibility. These standards, termed **ISO 14000,** focus on three major areas:

▶ **ISO 14000**
A set of international standards and a certification focusing on a company's environmental responsibility.

- ◆ **Management systems** standards measure systems development and integration of environmental responsibility into the overall business.
- ◆ **Operations** standards include the measurement of consumption of natural resources and energy.
- ◆ **Environmental systems** standards measure emissions, effluents, and other waste systems.

With greater interest in green manufacturing and more awareness of environmental concerns, ISO 14000 may become an important set of standards for promoting environmental responsibility.

▶ **QS 9000**
A set of quality standards and certification developed specifically for the auto industry.

QS 9000   **QS 9000** is a set of quality standards developed by the big three automobile manufacturers—Ford, Chrysler, and General Motors—in 1994. QS 9000 is based on ISO 9000, but has been modified specifically for automotive suppliers. The big three automakers require all their first-tier suppliers to receive QS 9000 certification. Like the ISO 9000 standards, these standards focus on continuous improvement, prevention of defects, and elimination of waste. However, they go beyond ISO 9000 and include many concepts that enhance the standing of the auto industry, such as manufacturing capability and production part approval. The goal is to standardize quality in the entire auto industry in order to reduce the cost of doing business, eliminate waste in the supply chain, and enhance the industry's competitive position.

■ QUALITY GURUS

To fully understand the TQM movement, we need to look at the philosophies of individuals who are considered "gurus" of TQM. Their philosophies and teachings have contributed to our knowledge and understanding of quality today.

W. Edwards Deming

W. Edwards Deming is often referred to as the father of quality control. He was a statistics professor at New York University in the 1940s. After World War II he assisted many Japanese companies in improving quality. The Japanese regarded him so highly that in 1951 they established the *Deming Prize,* an annual award given to firms that demonstrate outstanding quality. It was almost 30 years later that American businesses began adopting Deming's philosophy.

A number of elements of Deming's philosophy depart from traditional notions of quality. The first is the role management should play in a company's quality improvement effort. Historically, poor quality was blamed on workers—on their lack of productivity, laziness, or carelessness. However, Deming pointed out that only 15% of quality problems are actually due to worker error. The remaining 85% are caused by processes and systems, including poor management. Deming said that it is up to management to correct system problems and create an environment that promotes quality and enables workers to achieve their full potential. He believed that managers should drive out any fear employees have of identifying quality problems, and that numerical quotas should be eliminated. Proper methods should be taught, and detecting and eliminating poor quality should be everyone's responsibility.

Other element of Deming's philosophy are continuous improvement and reduction in process variability. Deming identified two types of causes of process variability. The first type consists of common causes, such as poor employee training or poor process design. The second type consists of special causes, such as a malfunctioning machine or a poor supplier. Identifying and eliminating both types of causes is one of the keys to improving system quality. To achieve these goals, Deming stressed the use of statistical quality control tools. He believed that improving the system, rather than inspecting for defects at the end, is the key to improving quality.

Joseph M. Juran

After W. Edwards Deming, Dr. Joseph Juran is considered to have had the greatest impact on quality management. Juran originally worked in the quality program at Western Electric. He became better known in 1951, after the publication of his book *Quality Control Handbook*. In 1954 he went to Japan to work with manufacturers and teach classes on quality. Though his philosophy is similar to Deming's, there are some differences. Whereas Deming stressed the need for an organizational "transformation", Juran believes that implementing quality initiatives should not require such a dramatic change and that quality management should be embedded in the organization.

One of Juran's significant contributions is his focus on the definition of quality and the cost of quality. Juran is credited for defining quality as fitness for use rather than simply conformance to specifications. As we have learned in this chapter, defining quality as fitness for use takes into account customer intentions for use of the product, instead of only focusing on technical specifications. Juran is also credited with developing the concept of cost of quality, which allows us to measure quality in dollar terms rather than on the basis of subjective evaluations.

Juran is well known for originating the idea of the quality trilogy: quality planning, quality control, and quality improvement. The first part of the trilogy, quality planning, is necessary so that companies identify their customers, product requirements, and overriding business goals. Processes should be set up to ensure that the quality standards can be met. The second part of the trilogy, quality control, stresses the regular use of statistical control methods to ensure that quality standards are met and to identify variations from the standards. The third part of the quality trilogy is quality improvement. According to Juran, quality improvements should be continuous as well as breakthrough. Together with Deming, Juran stressed that to implement continuous improvement workers need to have training in proper methods on a regular basis.

Phillip Crosby

Phillip B. Crosby is a third recognized guru in the area of TQM. He worked in the area of quality for many years, first at Martin Marietta and then, in the 1970s, as the vice president for quality at ITT. He developed the phrase "Do it right the first time" and the notion of *zero defects*, arguing that no amount of defects should be considered acceptable. He scorned the idea that a small number of defects is a normal part of the operating process because systems and workers are imperfect. Instead, he stressed the idea of prevention.

To promote his concepts, Crosby wrote a book titled *Quality Is Free*, which was published in 1979. He became famous for coining the phrase "quality is free" and for pointing out the many costs of quality, which include not only the costs of wasted labor, equipment time, scrap, rework, and lost sales, but also organizational costs that are hard to quantify. Crosby stressed that efforts to improve quality more than pay for themselves because these costs are prevented. Therefore, quality is free. Like Deming and Juran, Crosby stressed the role of management in the quality improvement effort and the use of statistical control tools in measuring and monitoring quality.

■ WHY TQM EFFORTS FAIL

In this chapter we have discussed the meaning of TQM and the great benefits that can be attained through its implementation. Yet there are still many companies that attempt a variety of quality improvement efforts and find that they have not achieved any or most of the expected outcomes. The most important factor in the success or failure of TQM efforts is the genuineness of the organization's commitment. Often companies look at TQM as another business change that must be implemented due to market pressure without really changing the values of their organization. Recall that TQM is a complete philosophy that has to be embraced with true belief, not mere lip service. Looking at TQM as a short, term financial investment is a sure recipe for failure.

Another mistake is the view that the responsibility for quality and elimination of waste lies with employees other than top management. It is a "let the workers do it" mentality. A third common mistake is over- or under-reliance on statistical process control (SPC) methods. SPC is not a substitute for continuous improvement, teamwork, and a change in the organization's belief system. However, SPC *is* a necessary tool for identifying quality problems. Some common causes for TQM failure are

- ◆ Lack of a genuine quality culture
- ◆ Lack of top management support and commitment
- ◆ Over- and under-reliance on statistical process control (SPC) methods

Companies that have attained the benefits of TQM have created a quality culture. These companies have a developed processes for identifying customer-defined quality. In addition, they have a systematic method for listening to their customers, collecting and analyzing data pertaining to customer problems, and making changes based on customer feedback. You can see that in these companies there is a systematic process for putting the customer needs first that encompasses the entire organization.

OM ACROSS THE ORGANIZATION

As we have seen, total quality management has impacts on every aspect of the organization. Every person and every function is responsible for quality and is affected by poor quality. For example, recall that Motorola implemented its six-sigma concept not only in the production process but also in the accounting, finance, and administrative areas. Similarly, ISO 9000 standards do not apply only to the production process; they apply equally to all departments of the company. A company cannot achieve high quality if its accounting is inaccurate or the marketing department is not working closely with customers. TQM requires the close cooperation of different functions in order to be successful. In this section we look at the involvement of these other functions in TQM.

Marketing plays a critical role in the TQM process by providing key inputs that make TQM a success. Recall that the goal of TQM is to satisfy customer needs by producing the exact product that customers want. Marketing's role is to understand the changing needs and wants of customers by working closely with them. This requires a solid identification of target markets and an understanding of whom the product is intended for. Sometimes apparently small differences in product features can result in large differences in customer appeal. Marketing needs to accurately pass customer information along to operations, and operations needs to include marketing in any planned product changes.

Finance is another major participant in the TQM process because of the great cost consequences of poor quality. General definitions of quality need to be translated into specific dollar terms. This serves as a baseline for monitoring the financial impact of quality efforts and can be a great motivator. Recall the four costs of quality discussed earlier. The first two costs, prevention and appraisal, are preventive costs; they are intended to prevent internal and external failure costs. Not investing enough in preventive costs can result in failure costs, which can hurt the company. On the other hand, investing too much in pre-

ventive costs may not yield added benefits. Financial analysis of these costs is critical. You can see that finance plays a large role in evaluating and monitoring the financial impact of managing the quality process. This includes costs related to preventing and eliminating defects, training employees, reviewing new products, and all other quality efforts.

Accounting is important in the TQM process because of the need for exact costing. TQM efforts cannot be accurately monitored and their financial contribution assessed if the company does not have accurate costing methods.

Engineering efforts are critical in TQM because of the need to properly translate customer requirements into specific engineering terms. Recall the process we followed in developing quality function deployment (QFD). It was not easy to translate a customer requirement such as "a good looking backpack" into specific terms such as materials, weight, color grade, size, and number of zippers. We depend on engineering to use general customer requirements in developing technical specifications, identifying specific parts and materials needed, and identifying equipment that should be used.

Purchasing is another important part of the TQM process. Whereas marketing is busy identifying what the customers want and engineering is busy translating that information into technical specifications, purchasing is responsible for acquiring the materials needed to make the product. Purchasing must ensure that the parts and materials needed are of sufficiently high quality, locate sources of supply, and negotiate a purchase price that meets the company's budget as identified by finance.

Human resources is critical to the effort to hire employees with the skills necessary to work in a TQM environment. That environment includes a high degree of teamwork, cooperation, dedication, and customer commitment. Human resources is also faced with challenges relating to reward and incentive systems. Rewards and incentives are different in

TQM than those found in traditional environments that focus on rewarding individuals rather than teams.

Information systems (IS) is highly important in TQM because of the increased need for information accessible to teams throughout the organization. IS should work closely with a company's TQM development program in order to understand exactly the type of information system best suited for the firm, including the form of the data, the summary statistics available, and the frequency of updating.

■ OM IS EVERYWHERE

The concepts of total quality management may seem foreign to you. After all, this is something companies that deal with customers have to think about, not students or individuals. Actually, you use many elements of total quality management in your everyday life. Remember that much of TQM comes from the Japanese, and they approach the company the same way they approach life. For example, think about the concept of continuous improvement. Aren't you more successful in a course when you study regularly rather than cramming for an exam? How about exercising moderately on a regular basis, rather than spending an entire day at the gym after a long hiatus? These are precisely the differences between implementing continuous improvement versus a large one-time change. Continuous improvement leads to more significant and meaningful change in the long run, which is something you can apply to every aspect of your life.

Other TQM concepts that we can apply in everyday life include quality at the source and Pareto analysis. Many of the daily problems and frustrations we experience have only a few main causes. If we are smart, we will try to identify and eliminate these causes. Eliminating only one cause, might make several problems disappear. For example, we may be getting poor grades in a few courses and may not be keeping up with certain team assignments. We can focus on each individual course or team, but the real problem may be poor time management. Perhaps putting ourselves on a detailed schedule will solve our problems both in our courses and in our teams.

Another important TQM concept that has worked well for companies and can work well for you is benchmarking. Benchmarking involves studying the practices of someone who is very successful and emulating that person. Companies emulate other companies that are considered "world class." You can emulate a role model, whether in your professional or your personal life. This would mean studying what he or she does well and learning from it. All of us can learn from others who are more successful than we are.

CHAPTER HIGHLIGHTS

1 Total quality management (TQM) is different from the old concept of quality because the focus is on serving customers, identifying the causes of quality problems, and building quality into the production process.

2 Eight features of TQM combine to create the TQM philosophy: customer focus, continuous improvement, quality at the source, employee empowerment, understanding quality tools, team approach, benchmarking, and managing supplier quality.

3 Quality can be described by four dimensions, all of which must be addressed by companies in their quest to improve quality. These dimensions are quality of product and service design, quality of conformance to design, ease of use, and post-sales support.

4 There are four categories of quality costs. The first two are prevention and appraisal costs, which are incurred by a company in attempting to improve quality. The last two costs are internal and external failure costs, which are the costs of quality failures that the company wishes to prevent.

5 Quality function deployment (QFD) is a tool used to translate customer needs into specific engineering re-

quirements. Seven problem-solving tools are used in managing quality. Often called the seven tools of quality control, they are cause-effect diagrams, flowcharts, checklists, scatter diagrams, Pareto charts, control charts, and histograms.

6 The Malcolm Baldrige Award is given to companies to recognition of excellence in quality management. Companies are evaluated in seven areas, including quality leadership and performance results. These criteria have become a standard for many companies that seek to improve quality. ISO 9000 is a certification based on a set of quality standards established by the International Organization for Standardization. Its goals is to ensure that quality is built into production processes, and it focuses mainly on quality of conformance.

7 The three best-known quality gurus are W. Edwards Deming, Joseph M. Juran, and Phillip Crosby. Deming is considered the father of quality control. Juran developed the concept of the quality trilogy. Crosby is known for the saying "quality is free."

KEY TERMS

total quality management (TQM) 108
customer-defined quality 108
conformance to specifications 108
fitness for use 109
value for price paid 109
support services 109
psychological criteria 109
continuous improvement 112
quality at the source 112
quality circle 113
benchmarking 114

quality of design 115
prevention costs 117
appraisal costs 117
internal failure costs 117
external failure costs 117
plan–do–study–act cycle 118
quality function deployment 119
cause–effect diagram 122
flowchart 124
checklist 124
control charts 124

scatter diagrams 124
Pareto analysis 125
histogram 125
Malcolm Baldrige Award 126
ISO 9000 127
ISO 14000 128
QS 9000 128
W. Edwards Deming 128
Joseph M. Juran 129
Phillip Crosby 130

DISCUSSION QUESTIONS

1. Define quality for the following products: a university, an exercise facility, spaghetti sauce, and toothpaste. Compare your definitions with those of others in your class.

2. Describe the TQM philosophy and identify its major characteristics.

3. Explain how TQM is different from the traditional notions of quality. Also, explain the differences between traditional organizations and those that have implemented TQM.

4. Find three local companies that you believe exhibit high quality. Next, find three national or international companies that are recognized for their quality achievements.

5. Describe the four dimensions of quality. Which do you think is most important?

6. Describe each of the four costs of quality: prevention, appraisal, internal failure, and external failure. Next, describe how each type of cost would change (increase, decrease, or remain the same) if we designed a higher quality product that was easier to manufacture.

7. Think again about the four costs of quality. Describe how each would change if we hired more inspectors without changing any other aspects of quality.

8. Explain the meaning of the Plan–do–act–study cycle. Why is it described as a cycle?

9. Describe the use of quality function deployment (QFD). Can you find examples in which the voice of the customer was not translated properly into technical requirements?

10. Describe the seven tools of quality control. Are some more important than others? Would you use these tools separately or together? Give some examples of tools that could be used together.

11. What is the Malcolm Baldrige National Quality Award? Why is this award important, and what companies have received it in the past?

12. What are ISO 9000 standards? Who were they set by and why? Can you describe other certifications based on the ISO 9000 certification?

13. Who are the three "gurus" of quality control? Name at least one contribution made by each of the them.

CASE: *Gold Coast Advertising (GSA)*

George Stein sat in his large office overlooking Chicago's Michigan Avenue. As CEO of Gold Coast Advertising he seemed to always be confronted with one problem or another. Today was no exception. George had just come out of a long meeting with Jim Gerard, head of the Board for the small advertising agency. Jim was concerned about a growing problem with lowered sales expectations and a decreasing customer base. Jim warned George that something had to be done quickly or Jim would have to go to the Board for action. George acknowledged that sales were down but attributed this to general economic conditions. He assured Jim that the problems would be addressed immediately.

As George pondered his next course of action, he admitted to himself that the customer base of GSA was slowly decreasing. The agency did not quite understand the reason for this decrease. Many regular customers were not coming back and the rate of new customers seemed to be slowly declining. GSA's competitors seemed to be doing well. George did not understand the problem.

What do Customers Want?

GSA was a Chicago based advertising agency that developed campaigns and promotions for small and medium sized firms. Their expertise was in the retail area, but they worked with a wide range of firms from the food service industry to the medical field. GSA competed on price and speed of product development. Advertising in the retail area was competitive and price had always been important. Also, as retail fashions change rapidly speed in advertising development was thought to be critical.

George reminded himself that price and speed had always been what customers wanted. Now he felt confused that he really didn't know his customers. This was just another crisis that would pass, he told himself. But he needed to deal with it immediately.

Case Questions:

1. What is wrong with how Gold Coast Advertising measures its quality? Explain why Gold Coast should ask its customers about how they define quality.

2. Offer suggestions to George Stein on ways of identifying quality dimensions GSA's customers consider important.

3. Develop a short questionnaire to be filled out by GSA's customers that evaluates how customers define quality.

INTERACTIVE LEARNING

Enhance and test your knowledge of Chapter 5 using the interactive CD.

1. **Video** *Nordstrom Inc.*

    Visit our dynamic Web site, www.wiley.com/college/reid, for more cases, Web links, and additional information.

2. **Company Tour**
    Harsco Corporation
    Steinway & Sons
    Artesyn Communication Products, LLC

3. **Additional Web Resources**
    American Society for Quality, www.asqc.org
    NIST quality program-Baldrige Award, www.quality.nist.gov

4. **Virtual Company Consulting Case**

5. **INTERNET CHALLENGE** *Snyder Bakeries (A)*

You have recently taken a position with Snyder Bakeries, a producer of a variety of different types of baked goods that are packaged and sold directly to grocery chains. Snyder Bakeries has been in business since 1978. It is a small company with 95 employees, earning roughly $2.5 million annually. Competition in the baked goods market has been increasing steadily and Snyder Bakeries is being forced to look at its operations. In addition, turnover and dissatisfaction among Snyder employees have been high. Mr. Lowell Snyder, President of Snyder Bakeries, is looking to you for help in redesigning the company's quality program. He would like you to focus on helping Snyder Bakeries develop a team approach among its employees as part of implementing principles of total quality management.

To help Mr. Snyder, use the Internet as a valuable source of information. Perform an Internet search to identify at least two companies that Snyder Bakeries can use as a benchmark for developing a team approach among employees. Explain how each of these competitors uses teams, how the teams are developed, how incentives are provided, and how employees are motivated. Also, identify the benefits these companies have gained from using the team approach. Finally, outline a plan for Mr. Snyder based on the information you have gathered.

BIBLIOGRAPHY

Crosby, Philip. *Quality Without Tears: The Art of Hassle-Free Management*. New York: McGraw-Hill, 1984.

Deming, W. Edwards. *Out of Crisis,* Cambridge, Ma. MIT Center for Advanced Engineering Study, 1986.

Evans, James R. and William M. Lindsay. *The Management and Control of Quality*. 4th ed. Cincinnati: South-Western, 1999.

Garvin, David A. *Managing Quality*. New York: Free Press, 1988.

Goetsch, David L., and Stanley Davis. *Implementing Total Quality*. Upper Saddle River, N.J.: Prentice-Hall, 1995.

Hall, Robert. *Attaining Manufacturing Excellence*. Burr Ridge, Ill.: Dow-Jones Irwin, 1987.

Juran, Joseph M. "The Quality Trilogy," *Quality Progress* 10, no. 8(1986), pp. 19–24.

Juran, Joseph M. *Quality Control Handbook,* 4th edition, New York: McGraw-Hill, 1988.

Juran, Joseph M. *Juran on Planning for Quality,* New York: Free Press, 1988.

Kitazawa, S., and Sarkis, J., "The Relationship Between ISO 14001 and Continuous Source Reduction Programs," *International Journal of Operations and Production Management*, 20, 2, 2000, 225–248.

Medori, D., and Steeple, D., "A Framework for Auditing and Enhancing Performance Measurement Systems," *International Journal of Operations and Production Management*, 20, 5, 2000, 520–533.

Rosenberg, Jarrett, "Five Myths about Customer Satisfaction," *Quality Progress* 29, 12(December), 1996, 57–60.

Zimmerman, R.E., Steinmann, L. and V. Schueler, "Designing Customer Surveys that Work," *Quality Progress,* (October), 1996, 22–28.

6

Statistical Quality Control

Before studying this chapter you should know or, if necessary, review

1. Quality as a competitive priority, Chapter 2, page 30.
2. Total quality management (TQM) concepts, Chapter 5, pages 111–114.

LEARNING OBJECTIVES

After studying this chapter you should be able to

1. Describe categories of statistical quality control (SQC).

2. Explain the use of traditional statistical tools in measuring quality characteristics.

3. Identify and describe causes of variation.

4. Describe the use of control charts.

5. Identify the differences between x-bar, R-, p-, and c-charts.

6. Explain the meaning of process capability and the process capability index.

7. Explain the term six-sigma.

8. Explain the process of acceptance sampling and describe the use of operating characteristic (OC) curves.

9. Describe the challenges inherent in measuring quality in service organizations.

CHAPTER OUTLINE

We have all had the experience of purchasing a product only to discover that it is defective in some way or does not function the way it was designed to. This could be a new backpack with a broken zipper or an "out of the box" malfunctioning computer printer. Many of us have struggled to assemble a product the manufacturer has indicated would need only "minor" assembly, only to find that a piece of the product is missing. As consumers, we expect the products we purchase to function as intended. However, producers of products know that it is not always possible to inspect every product and every aspect of the production process at all times. The challenge is to design ways to maximize the ability to monitor the quality of products being produced and eliminate defects.

In Chapter 5 we learned that total quality management (TQM) addresses organizational quality from managerial and philosophical viewpoints. TQM focuses on customer-driven quality standards, managerial leadership, continuous improvement, building quality into product and process design, identifying quality problems at the source, and making quality everyone's responsibility. However, talking about solving quality problems is not enough. We need specific tools that can help us make the right quality decisions. These tools come from the area of statistics and are used to help us identify quality problems in the production process as well as in the product itself. Statistical quality control is the subject of this chapter.

Statistical quality control (SQC) is the term used to describe the set of statistical tools used by quality professionals. Statistical quality control can be divided into three broad categories:

1. **Traditional statistical tools** are used to describe quality characteristics and relationships. Included are various descriptive statistics, such as the mean, standard deviation, and range.
2. **Acceptance sampling** is the process of randomly inspecting a sample of goods and deciding whether to accept the entire lot based on the results. Acceptance sampling determines whether a batch of goods should be accepted or rejected.
3. **Statistical process control (SPC)** involves inspecting a random sample of the output from a process and deciding whether the process is producing products with characteristics that fall within a predetermined range. SPC answers the question of whether the process is functioning properly or not.

The tools in each of these categories provide different types of information for use in analyzing quality. Traditional statistical tools are common descriptive statistics that have been used for many years. They describe certain quality characteristics, such as the central tendency and variability of observed data. Although descriptions of certain characteristics are helpful, they are not enough to help us evaluate whether qual-

CROSS FUNCTIONAL

▶ **Statistical quality control (SQC)**
The general category of statistical tools used to evaluate organizational quality.

▶ **Traditional statistical tools**
Statistics used to describe quality characteristics and relationships.

▶ **Acceptance sampling**
The process of randomly inspecting a sample of goods and deciding whether to accept the entire lot based on the results.

▶ **Statistical process control (SPC)**
A statistical tool that involves inspecting a random sample of the output from a process and deciding whether the process is producing products with characteristics that fall within a predetermined range.

ity is good or bad. Acceptance sampling can help us do this. Acceptance sampling helps us decide whether desirable quality has been achieved for a batch of products, and whether to accept or reject the items produced. Although this information is helpful in making the quality acceptance decision *after* the product has been produced, it does not help us identify and catch a quality problem *during* the production process. For this we need tools in the statistical process control (SPC) category.

All three of these statistical quality control categories are helpful in measuring and evaluating the quality of products or services. However, statistical process control (SPC) tools are used most frequently because they identify quality problems during the production process. For this reason, we will devote most of the chapter to this category of tools. The quality control tools we will be learning about do not only measure the value of a quality characteristic. They also help us identify a *change* or variation in some quality characteristic of the product or process. We will first see what types of variation we can observe when measuring quality. Then we will be able to identify specific tools used for measuring this variation.

LINKS TO PRACTICE
R~x~ on the Internet

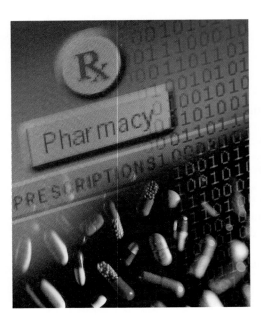

In the age of Web-based purchasing, product quality is more important than ever. This is particularly true when purchasing items such as prescription drugs over the Internet. Web pharmacies offer conveniences that brick-and-mortar facilities cannot. Prescriptions can be phoned in, faxed, or e-mailed at any time, and the medications can be sent directly to your home. However, buying prescriptions on-line is not as simple as buying books or CDs. Problems can arise relative to product quality and safety. These problems range from concerns over correct medications and improper storage to outdated ingredients and counterfeit medicines. The use of statistical quality control tools can help to maintain high quality standards.

■ SOURCES OF VARIATION: COMMON AND ASSIGNABLE CAUSES

If you look at bottles of a soft drink in a grocery store, you will notice that no two bottles are filled to exactly the same level. Some are filled slightly higher and some slightly lower. Similarly, if you look at blueberry muffins in a bakery, you will notice that some are slightly larger than others and some have more blueberries than others. These types of differences are completely normal. No two products are exactly alike because of slight differences in materials, workers, machines, tools, and other factors. These are called **common causes of variation.** Common causes of variation are based on random causes that we cannot identify. These types of variation are unavoidable and are due to slight differences in processing.

► **Common causes of variation**
Random causes that cannot be identified.

An important task in quality control is to find out the range of natural random variation in a process. For example, if the average bottle of a soft drink called Cocoa

Fizz contains 16 ounces of liquid, we may determine that the amount of natural variation is between 15.8 and 16.2 ounces. If this were the case, we would monitor the production process to make sure that the amount stays within this range. If production goes out of this range—say, bottles are found to contain 15.6 ounces—this would lead us to believe that there is a problem with the process because the variation is greater than the natural random variation.

The second type of variation that can be observed involves variations where the causes can be precisely identified and eliminated. These are called **assignable causes of variation.** Examples of this type of variation are poor quality in raw materials, an employee who needs more training, and a machine in need of repair. In each of these examples the problem can be identified and corrected. Also, if the problem is allowed to persist, it will continue to create a problem in the quality of the product. In the example of the soft drink bottling operation, bottles filled with 15.6 ounces of liquid would signal a problem. The machine may need to be readjusted. This would be an assignable cause of variation. We can assign the variation to a particular cause (machine needs to be readjusted) and we can correct the problem (readjust the machine).

▶ **Assignable causes of variation**
Causes that can be identified and eliminated.

TRADITIONAL STATISTICAL TOOLS ■

Traditional statistical tools can be helpful in describing certain characteristics of a product and a process. The most important descriptive statistics are measures of central tendency, such as the mean, and measures of variability, such as the standard deviation and range. We first review these traditional statistical tools and then see how we can measure their changes.

The Mean

In the soft drink bottling operation we stated that the average bottle is filled with 16 ounces of liquid. The average, or the **mean,** is a statistic that measures the central tendency of a set of data. Knowing the central point of a set of data is highly important. Just think how important that number is when you receive test scores!

To compute the mean we simply sum all the observations and divide by the total number of observations. The equation for computing the mean is

▶ **Mean (average)**
A statistic that measures the central tendency of a set of data.

$$\overline{X} = \frac{\sum\limits_{i=1}^{n} x_i}{n}$$

where $\overline{X}$ = the mean
x_i = observation i
n = number of observations

The Range and Standard Deviation

In the bottling example we also stated that the amount of natural variation in the bottling process is between 15.8 and 16.2 ounces. This information provides us with the amount of variability of the data. It tells us how spread out the data is around the mean. There are two measures that can be used to determine the amount of variation

▶ **Range**
The difference between the largest and smallest observations in a set of data.

▶ **Standard deviation**
A statistic that measures the amount of data dispersion around the mean.

in the data. The first measure is the **range,** which is the difference between the largest and smallest observations. In our example, the range for natural variation is 0.4 ounces.

Another measure of variation is the **standard deviation.** The equation for computing the standard deviation is

$$\sigma = \sqrt{\dfrac{\sum\limits_{i=1}^{n}(x_i - \overline{x})^2}{n-1}}$$

where σ = standard deviation of a sample
$\overline{x}$ = the mean
x_i = observation i
n = the number of observations in the sample

Small values of the range and standard deviation mean that the observations are closely clustered around the mean. Large values of the range and standard deviation mean that the observations are spread out around the mean. Figure 6-1 illustrates the differences between a small and a large standard deviation for our bottling operation. You can see that the figure shows two distributions, both with a mean of 16 ounces. However, in the first distribution the standard deviation is large and the data are spread out far around the mean. In the second distribution the standard deviation is small and the data are clustered close to the mean.

Distribution of Data

A third traditional statistical tool used to measure quality characteristics is the shape of the distribution of the observed data. When a distribution is symmetric, there are the same number of observations below and above the mean. This is what we commonly find when only normal variation is present in the data. When a disproportionate number of observations are either above or below the mean, we say that the data has a *skewed distribution.* Figure 6-2 shows symmetric and skewed distributions for the bottling operation.

Figure 6-1

Normal distributions with varying standard deviations

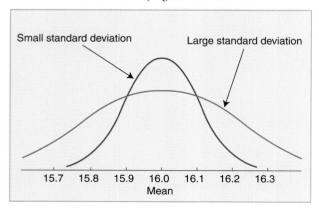

Figure 6-2

Differences between symmetric and skewed distributions

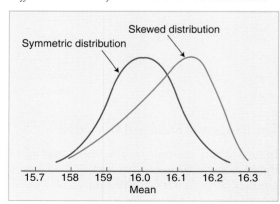

STATISTICAL PROCESS CONTROL METHODS ■

Statistical process control methods extend the use of traditional statistical tools to monitor the quality of the product and process. As we have learned so far, there are common and assignable causes of variation in the production of every product. Using statistical process control we want to determine the amount of variation that is common or normal. Then we monitor the production process to make sure production stays within this normal range. That is, we want to make sure the process is in a *state of control*. The most commonly used tool for monitoring the production process is a control chart. Different types of control charts are used to monitor different aspects of the production process. In this section we will learn how to develop and use control charts.

Developing Control Charts

A **control chart** (also called process chart or quality control chart) is a graph that shows whether a sample of data falls within the common or normal range of variation. A control chart has upper and lower control limits that separate common from assignable causes of variation. The common range of variation is defined by the use of control chart limits. We say that a process is **out of control** when a plot of data falls outside the control limits.

▶ **Control chart**
A graph that shows whether a sample of data falls within the common or normal range of variation.

Figure 6-3 shows a control chart for the Cocoa Fizz bottling operation. The *x* axis represents samples (#1, #2, #3, etc.) taken from the process over time. The *y* axis represents the quality characteristic that is being monitored (ounces of liquid). The center line (CL) of the control chart is the mean, or average, of the quality characteristic that is being measured. In Figure 6-3 the mean is 16.0 ounces. The upper control limit (UCL) is the maximum acceptable variation from the mean for a process that is in a state of control. Similarly, the lower control limit (LCL) is the minimum acceptable variation from the mean for a process that is in a state of control. In our example, the upper and lower control limits are 16.2 and 15.8 ounces, respectively. You can see that if a sample of observations falls outside the control limits we need to look for assignable causes.

▶ **Out of control**
The situation in which a plot of data falls outside preset control limits.

The upper and lower control limits on a control chart are usually set at ±3 standard deviations from the mean. If we assume that the data exhibit a normal distribution, these control limits will capture 99.74% of the normal variation. Control limits can be set at ±2 standard deviations from the mean. In that case, control limits would capture 95.44% of the values. Figure 6-4 shows the percentage of values that fall within a particular range of standard deviation.

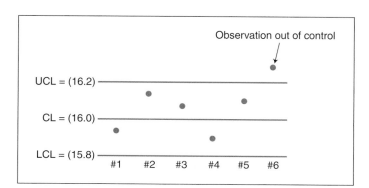

Figure 6-3

Quality control chart for Cocoa Fizz

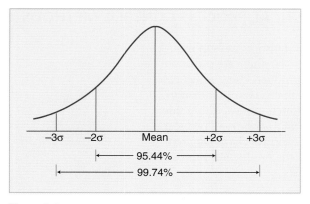

Figure 6-4

Percentage of values captured by different ranges of standard deviation

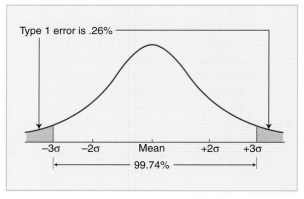

Figure 6-5

Chance of Type I error for ±3σ (sigma standard deviations)

Looking at Figure 6-4, we can conclude that observations that fall outside the set range represent nonnormal or assignable causes of variation. However, there is a small probability that a value that falls outside the limits is still due to normal variation. This is called Type I error, with the error being the chance of concluding that there are assignable causes of variation when only normal variation exists. Another name for this is alpha risk (α), where alpha refers to the sum of the probabilities in both tails of the distribution that falls outside the confidence limits. The chance of this happening is given by the percentage or probability represented by the shaded areas of Figure 6-5. For limits of ±3 standard deviations from the mean, the probability of a Type I error is .26% (100% − 99.74%), whereas for limits of ±2 standard deviations it is 4.56% (100% − 95.44%).

Types of Control Charts

Control charts are one of the most commonly used tools in statistical process control. They can be used to measure any characteristic of a product, such as the weight of a cereal box, the number of chocolates in a box, or the volume of bottled water. The different characteristics that can be measured by control charts can be divided into two groups: **variables** and **attributes**. A *control chart for variables* is used to monitor characteristics that can be measured and have a continuum of values, such as height, weight, or volume. A soft drink bottling operation is an example of a variable measure, since the amount of liquid in the bottles is measured and can take on a number of different values. Other examples are the weight of a bag of sugar, the temperature of a baking oven, or the mean diameter of a plastic tubing.

A *control chart for attributes*, on the other hand, is used to monitor characteristics that have discrete values and can be counted. Often they can be evaluated with a simple yes or no. Examples include color, taste, or smell. The monitoring of attributes usually takes less time than that of variables because a variable needs to be measured (e.g., the bottle of soft drink contains 15.9 ounces of liquid). An attribute requires only a single decision, such as yes or no, good or bad, acceptable or unacceptable (e.g., the apple is good or rotten, the meat is good or stale, the shoes have a defect or do not have a defect, the lightbulb works or it does not work) or counting the number of de-

▶ **Variable**
A product characteristic that can be measured and has a continuum of values (e.g., height, weight, or volume).

▶ **Attribute**
A product characteristic that has a discrete value and can be counted.

fects (e.g., the number of defective cookies in the sample, the number of dents in the car, the number of barnacles on the bottom of a boat).

Statistical process control is used to monitor many different types of variables and attributes. In the next two sections we look at how to develop control charts for variables and control charts for attributes.

CONTROL CHARTS FOR VARIABLES ■

Control charts for variables monitor characteristics that can be measured and have a continuous scale, such as height, weight, volume, or width. When an item is inspected, the variable being monitored is measured and recorded. For example, if we were producing candles, height might be an important variable. We could take samples of candles and measure their height. Two of the most commonly used control charts for variables monitor both the central tendency of the data (the mean) and the variability of the data (either the standard deviation or the range). Note that each chart monitors a different type of information. When observed values go outside the control limits, the process is assumed not to be in control. Production is stopped, and employees attempt to identify the cause of the problem and correct it. Next we look at how these charts are developed.

Mean (x-Bar) Charts

A mean control chart is often referred to as an *x-bar chart.* It is used to monitor changes in the mean of a process. To construct a mean chart we first need to construct the center line of the chart. To do this we take multiple samples and compute their means. Usually these samples are small, with about four or five observations. Each sample has its own mean, $\bar{x}$. The center line of the chart is then computed as the mean of all the samples:

▶ **X-bar chart**
A control chart used to monitor changes in the mean value of a process.

$$\bar{\bar{x}} = \frac{\bar{x}_1 + \bar{x}_2 + \cdots \bar{x}_n}{n}$$

To construct the upper and lower control limits of the chart, we use the following formulas:

Upper control limit (UCL) $= \bar{\bar{x}} + z\sigma_{\bar{x}}$
Lower control limit (LCL) $= \bar{\bar{x}} - z\sigma_{\bar{x}}$

where $\bar{\bar{x}} =$ the average of the sample means
  $z =$ standard normal variable
  $\sigma_{\bar{x}} =$ standard deviation of the distribution of sample means, computed as $\sigma/\sqrt{n}$

Example 6.1 shows the construction of a mean (x-bar) chart.

Another way to construct the control limits is to use the sample range as an estimate of the variability of the process. Remember that the range is simply the difference between the largest and smallest values in the sample. The spread of the range can tell us about the variability of the data. In this case control limits would be constructed as follows:

Upper control limit (UCL) $= \bar{\bar{x}} + A_2 \bar{R}$
Lower control limit (LCL) $= \bar{\bar{x}} - A_2 \bar{R}$

■ Example 6.1 Constructing a Mean (x-bar) Chart

A quality control inspector at the Cocoa Fizz soft drink company has taken three samples with four observations each of the volume of bottles filled. The data and the computed means are shown in the table. If the standard deviation of the bottling operation is .2 ounces, use the above information to develop control limits of 3 standard deviations for the bottling operation.

	Samples of Bottle Volume in Ounces		
Observation	1	2	3
1	15.8	16.1	16.0
2	16.0	16.0	15.9
3	15.8	15.8	15.9
4	15.9	16.0	15.8
Mean ($\bar{x}$)	15.875	15.975	15.9

Solution

The center line of the control data is the average of the samples:

$$\bar{\bar{x}} = \frac{15.875 + 15.975 + 15.9}{3} = \frac{47.75}{3} = 15.92$$

The control limits are

$$UCL = \bar{\bar{x}} + z\sigma_{\bar{x}} = 15.92 + 3\left(\frac{.2}{\sqrt{4}}\right) = 16.22$$

$$LCL = \bar{\bar{x}} - z\sigma_{\bar{x}} = 15.92 - 3\left(\frac{.2}{\sqrt{4}}\right) = 15.62$$

Following is the associated control chart:

UCL = (16.22) _____

CL = (15.92) _____

LCL = (15.62) _____

where A_2 is a constant that includes three standard deviations of ranges. The value of A_2 can be obtained from Table 6-1, depending on the sample size being considered. R is the average of the sample ranges and is computed as follows:

$$\bar{R} = \frac{\Sigma R_i}{n}$$

where R_i = the range of each sample i

n = number of sample ranges

■ Example 6.2 Constructing a Mean (X-bar) Chart from the Sample Range

A quality control inspector at Cocoa Fizz has taken four samples with five observations each of the volume of bottles filled. If the average range for the four samples is .2 ounces and the average mean of the observations is 16.0 ounces, develop three-sigma control limits for the bottling operation.

Solution:

$$\bar{\bar{X}} = 16 \text{ ounces} \qquad \bar{R} = .2$$

The value of A_2 is obtained from Table 6.1. For $n = 5$, $A_2 = .58$. This leads to the following limits:

The center of the control chart = CL = 16 ounces

$$UCL = \bar{\bar{x}} + A_2\bar{R} = 16 + (.58)(.2) = 16.12$$

$$LCL = \bar{\bar{x}} - A_2\bar{R} = 16 - (.58)(.2) = 15.88$$

TABLE 6-1 Factors for control limits of X and R charts

Sample Size n	Factor for x-Chart A_2	Factor for R-Chart D_3	Factor for R-Chart D_4
2	1.88	0	3.27
3	1.02	0	2.57
4	0.73	0	2.28
5	0.58	0	2.11
6	0.48	0	2.00
7	0.42	0.08	1.92
8	0.37	0.14	1.86
9	0.34	0.18	1.82
10	0.31	0.22	1.78
11	0.29	0.26	1.74
12	0.27	0.28	1.72
13	0.25	0.31	1.69
14	0.24	0.33	1.67
15	0.22	0.35	1.65
16	0.21	0.36	1.64
17	0.20	0.38	1.62
18	0.19	0.39	1.61
19	0.19	0.40	1.60
20	0.18	0.41	1.59
21	0.17	0.43	1.58
22	0.17	0.43	1.57
23	0.16	0.44	1.56
24	0.16	0.45	1.55
25	0.15	0.46	1.54

Source: Factors adapted from the *ASTM Manual on Quality Control of Materials.*

Range (R) Charts

Range (R) charts are another type of control chart for variables. Whereas x-bar charts measure shift in the central tendency of the process, range charts monitor the dispersion or variability of the process. The method for developing and using R-charts is the same as that for x-bar charts. The center line of the control chart is the average range, and the upper and lower control limits are computed as follows:

$$CL = \overline{R}$$
$$UCL = D_4 \overline{R}$$
$$LCL = D_3 \overline{R}$$

where values for D_4 and D_3 are obtained from Table 6-1.

▶ **Range (R) chart**
A control chart that monitors changes in the dispersion or variability of process.

■ **Example 6.3 Constructing a Range (R) Chart**

Ten samples of five observations each have been taken from the Cocoa Fizz soft drink bottling plant in order to test for volume dispersion in the bottling process. The average sample range was found to be .5 ounces. Develop control limits for the sample range.

Solution:

$$\overline{R} = .5 \text{ ounces}$$
$$n = 5$$

From Table 6-1 for $n = 5$:

$$D_4 = 2.11$$
$$D_3 = 0$$

Therefore,

$$\text{UCL} = D_4 \overline{R} = 2.11\,(.5) = 1.055$$
$$\text{LCL} = D_3 \overline{R} = 0\,(.5) = 0$$

Using Mean and Range Charts Together

You can see that mean and range charts are used to monitor different variables. The mean or x-bar chart measures the central tendency of the process, whereas the range chart measures the dispersion or variance of the process. Since both variables are important, it makes sense to monitor a process using both mean and range charts. It is possible to have a shift in the mean of the product but not a change in the dispersion. For example, at the Cocoa Fizz bottling plant the machine setting can shift so that the average bottle filled contains not 16.0 ounces, but 15.9 ounces of liquid. The dispersion could be the same, and this shift would be detected by an x-bar chart but not by

Figure 6-6

Process shifts captured by x-charts and R-charts

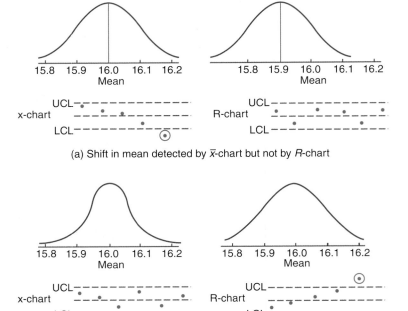

(a) Shift in mean detected by $\overline{x}$-chart but not by *R*-chart

(b) Shift in dispersion detected by *R*-chart but not by $\overline{x}$-chart

a range chart. This is shown in part (a) of Figure 6-6. On the other hand, there could be a shift in the dispersion of the product without a change in the mean. Cocoa Fizz may still be producing bottles with an average fill of 16.0 ounces. However, the dispersion of the product may have increased, as shown in part (b) of Figure 6-6. This condition would be detected by a range chart but not by an x-bar chart. Because a shift in either the mean or the range means that the process is out of control, it is important to use both charts to monitor the process.

CONTROL CHARTS FOR ATTRIBUTES ■

Control charts for attributes are used to measure quality characteristics that are counted rather than measured. Attributes are discrete in nature and entail simple yes-or-no decisions. For example, this could be the number of nonfunctioning lightbulbs, the proportion of broken eggs in a carton, the number of rotten apples, the number of scratches on a tile, or the number of complaints issued. There are two types of control charts for attributes: p-charts and c-charts.

P-charts are used to measure the proportion of items in a sample that are defective. Examples are the proportion of broken cookies in a batch and the proportion of cars produced with a misaligned fender. P-charts are appropriate when both the number of defects measured and the size of the total sample can be counted. A proportion can then be computed and used as the statistic of measurement.

C-charts count the actual number of defective items. However, with c-charts the total sample size is unknown. These charts are used when the number of defects can be measured but the proportion of defects in a sample cannot. For example, we can count the number of complaints from customers in a month, the number of bacteria on a petri dish, or the number of barnacles on the bottom of a boat. However, we *cannot* compute the proportion of complaints from customers, the proportion of bacteria on a petri dish, or the proportion of barnacles on the bottom of a boat.

Problem-Solving Tip: The primary difference between using a p-chart and a c-chart is as follows. A p-chart is used when both the total sample size and the number of defects can be computed. A c-chart is used when we can compute *only* the number of defects but not the total sample size.

P-Charts

P-charts are used to measure the proportion of defects in a sample. The computation of the center line as well as the upper and lower control limits is similar to the computation for the other kinds of control charts. The center line is computed as the average proportion of defects in the population, $\bar{p}$. This is obtained by taking a number of samples of n observations at random and computing the average value of p across all samples.

▶ **P-chart**
A control chart that monitors the *proportion* of defects in a sample.

To construct the upper and lower control limits for a p-chart, we use the following formulas:

$$\text{UCL}_p = \bar{p} + z\sigma_p$$
$$\text{LCL}_p = \bar{p} - z\sigma_p$$

where z = standard normal variable

As with the other charts, z is selected to be either 2 or 3 standard deviations, depending on the amount of data we wish to capture in our control limits. Usually, however, they are set at 3.

The sample standard deviation is computed as follows:

$$\sigma_p = \sqrt{\frac{\bar{p}(1 - \bar{p})}{n}}$$

■ Example 6.4 Constructing a p-Chart

A production manager at a tire manufacturing plant has inspected the number of defective tires in five random samples with 20 observations each. Following are the number of defective tires found in each sample:

Sample	Number of Defective Tires	Number of Observations Sampled
1	2	20
2	2	20
3	1	20
4	2	20
5	2	20
Total	9	100

Construct a three-sigma control chart ($z = 3$) with this information.

Solution
The center line of the chart is

$$CL = \bar{p} = \frac{\text{number of defectives tires}}{\text{number of observation}} = \frac{9}{100} = .09$$

$$\sigma_p = \sqrt{\frac{\bar{p}(1 - \bar{p})}{n}} = \sqrt{\frac{(.09)(.91)}{20}} = 0.64$$

$$UCL = \bar{p} + z\,(\sigma_p) = .09 + 3\,(.064) = .282$$
$$LCL = \bar{p} - z\,(\sigma_p) = .09 - 3\,(.064) = -.102$$

In this example the lower control limit is negative, which sometimes occurs because the computation is an approximation of the normal distribution. When this occurs, the LCL is rounded up to zero because we cannot have a negative control limit.
    Following is the control chart:

UCL = (.282) _____

CL = (.09) _____

LCL = (0) _____

C-Charts

▶ **C-chart**
A control chart used to monitor the *number* of defects per unit.

C-charts are used to monitor the number of defects per unit. Examples are the number of returned meals in a restaurant, the number of trucks that exceed their weight limit in a month, the number of discolorations on a square foot of carpet, and the number of bacteria in a milliliter of water. Note that the types of units of measurement we are considering are a period of time, a surface area, or a volume of liquid.

The average number of defects, $\bar{c}$, is the center line of the control chart. The upper and lower control limits are computed as follows:

$$UCL_c = \bar{c} + z\sqrt{\bar{c}}$$
$$LCL_c = \bar{c} - z\sqrt{\bar{c}}$$

■ Example 6.5 Computing a C-Chart

The number of weekly customer complaints are monitored in a large hotel using a c-chart. Complaints have been recorded over the past ten weeks. Develop three-sigma control limits using these data:

Week	Number of Complaints
1	0
2	2
3	3
4	1
5	0
6	0
7	2
8	1
9	0
10	1
	10

Solution:
The average number of complaints per week is $10/10 = 1$. Therefore, $\bar{c} = 1$.

$$UCL_c = \bar{c} + 3\sqrt{\bar{c}} = 1 + 3\sqrt{1} = 4$$
$$LCL_c = \bar{c} - 3\sqrt{\bar{c}} = 1 - 3\sqrt{1} = -2 \rightarrow 0$$

As in the previous example, the LCL is negative and should be rounded up to zero. Following is the control chart for this example:

UCL = (4) _____
CL = (1) _____
LCL = (0) _____

Before You Go On

We have discussed several types of statistical quality control (SQC) techniques. One category of SQC techniques consist of traditional statistical tools such as the mean, range, and standard deviation. These tools are used to describe quality characteristics and relationships. Another category of SQC techniques consists of statistical process control (SPC) methods that are used to monitor changes in the production process. To understand SPC methods you must understand the differences between common and assignable causes of variation. Common causes of variation are based on random causes that cannot be identified. A certain amount of common or normal variation occurs in every process due to differences in materials, workers, machines, and other factors. Assignable causes of variation, on the other hand, are variations that can be identified and eliminated. An important part of statistical process control (SPC) is monitoring the production process to make sure that the only variations in the process are those due to common or normal causes. Under these conditions we say that a production process is in a *state of control*.

You should also understand the different types of quality control charts that are used to monitor the production process: x-bar charts, range charts, p-charts, and c-charts.

PROCESS CAPABILITY ■

So far we have discussed ways of monitoring the production process to ensure that it is in a *state of control* and that there are no assignable causes of variation. A critical aspect of statistical quality control is evaluating the ability of a production process to meet or exceed preset specifications. This is called **process capability.** To understand exactly what this means, let's look more closely at the term *specification*. **Product specifications,** often called *tolerances*, are preset ranges of acceptable quality characteristics, such as product dimensions. For a product to be considered acceptable, its

▶ **Process capability**
The ability of a production process to meet or exceed preset specifications.

▶ **Product specifications**
Preset ranges of acceptable quality characteristics.

characteristics must fall within this preset range. Otherwise, the product is not acceptable. Product specifications, or tolerance limits, are usually established by design engineers or product design specialists.

For example, the specifications for the width of a machine part may be specified as 15 inches ± .3. This means that the width of the part should be 15 inches, though it is acceptable if it falls within the limits of 14.7 inches and 15.3 inches. Similarly, for Cocoa Fizz, the average bottle fill may be 16 ounces with tolerances of ±.2 ounces. Although the bottles should be filled with 16 ounces of liquid, the amount can be as low as 15.8 or as high as 16.2 ounces.

Specifications for a product are preset on the basis of how the product is going to be used or what customer expectations are. As we have learned, any production process has a certain amount of natural variation associated with it. To be capable of producing an acceptable product, the process variation cannot exceed the preset specifications. Process capability thus involves evaluating process variability relative to preset product specifications in order to determine whether the process is capable of producing an acceptable product. In this section we will learn how to measure process capability.

Measuring Process Capability

Simply setting up control charts to monitor whether a process is in control does not guarantee process capability. To produce an acceptable product, the process must be *capable* and *in control* before production begins. Let's look at three examples of process variation relative to design specifications for the Cocoa Fizz soft drink company. Let's say that the specification for acceptable volume of liquid is preset at 16 ounces ± .2 ounces, which is 15.8 and 16.2 ounces. In part (a) of Figure 6-7 the process produces 99.74% (three sigma) of the product with volumes between 15.8 and 16.2 ounces. You can see that the process variability closely matches the preset specifications. Almost all the output falls within the preset specification range.

In part (b) of Figure 6-7, however, the process produces 99.74% (three sigma) of the product with volumes between 15.7 and 16.3 ounces. The process variability is outside the preset specifications. A large percentage of the product will fall outside the specified limits. This means that the process is *not capable* of producing the product within the preset specifications.

Part (c) of Figure 6-7 shows that the production process produces 99.74% (three sigma) of the product with volumes between 15.9 and 16.1 ounces. In this case the process variability is within specifications and the process exceeds the minimum capability.

▶ **Process capability index:** an index used to measure process capability.

Process capability is measured by the **process capability index,** C_p, which is computed as the ratio of the specification width to the width of the process variability:

$$C_p = \frac{\text{specification width}}{\text{process width}} = \frac{\text{USL} - \text{LSL}}{6\sigma}$$

where the specification width is the difference between the upper specification limit (USL) and the lower specification limit (LSL) of the process. The process width is computed as 6 standard deviations (6σ) of the process being monitored. The reason we use 6σ is that most of the process measurement (99.74%) falls within ±3 standard deviations, which is a total of 6 standard deviations.

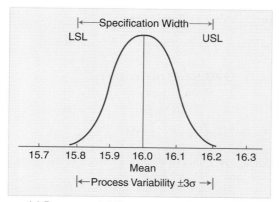

(a) Process variability meets specification width

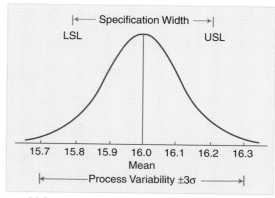

(b) Process variability outside specification width

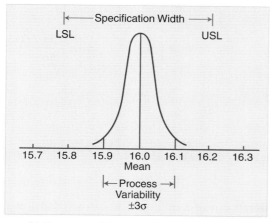

(c) Process variability within specification width

Figure 6-7

Relationship between process variability and specification width

There are three possible ranges of values for C_p that also help us interpret its value:

$C_p = 1$: A value of C_p equal to 1 means that the process variability just meets specifications, as in Figure 6-7(a). We would then say that the process is minimally capable.

$C_p \leq 1$: A value of C_p below 1 means that the process variability is outside the range of specification, as in Figure 6-7(b). This means that the process is not capable of producing within specification and the process must be improved.

$C_p \geq 1$: A value of C_p above 1 means that the process variability is tighter than specifications and the process exceeds minimal capability, as in Figure 6-7(c).

A C_p value of 1 means that 99.74% of the products produced will fall within the specification limits. This also means that .26% of the products will not be acceptable (100 − 99.74). Although this percentage sounds very small, when we think of it in terms of parts per million (ppm) we can see that it can still result in a lot of defects. The number .26% corresponds to 2600 parts per million (ppm) defective (.026 × 1,000,000). That number can seem very high if we think of it in terms of 2600 wrong prescriptions out of a million, or 2600 incorrect medical procedures out of a million,

■ **Example 6.6 Computing the C_p Value at Cocoa Fizz**

Three bottling machines at Cocoa Fizz are being evaluated for their capability:

Bottling Machine	Standard Deviation
A	.05
B	.1
C	.2

If specifications are set between 15.8 and 16.2 ounces, determine which of the machines are capable of producing within specifications.

Solution:
To determine the capability of each machine we need to divide the specification width (USL − LSL = 16.2 − 15.8 = .4) by 6σ for each machine:

Bottling Machine	σ	USL − LSL	6σ	$C_p = \dfrac{USL - LSL}{6\sigma}$
A	.05	.4	.3	1.33
B	.1	.4	.6	0.67
C	.2	.4	1.2	0.33

Looking at the C_p values, only machine A is capable of filling bottles within specifications, because it is the only machine that has a C_p value at or above 1.

or even 2600 malfunctioning aircraft out of a million. You can see that this number of defects is still high. The way to reduce the ppm defective is to increase process capability.

The C_p measure is very valuable. However, it has one shortcoming: it assumes that process variability is centered on the specification range. Unfortunately, this is not always the case. Figure 6-8 shows data from the Cocoa Fizz example. In the figure the specification limits are set between 15.8 and 16.2 ounces, with a mean of 16.0 ounces. However, the process variation is not centered; it has a mean of 15.9 ounces. Because of this, a certain proportion of products will fall outside the specification range.

The problem illustrated in Figure 6-8 is not uncommon, but it can lead to mistakes in the computation of the C_p measure. Because of this, another measure for process capability is used more frequently:

$$C_{pk} = \min\left(\frac{USL - \mu}{3\sigma}, \frac{\mu - LSL}{3\sigma}\right)$$

where μ = the mean of the process
σ = the standard deviation of the process

This measure of process capability helps us address a possible lack of centering of the process over the specification range. To use this measure, the process capability of each half of the normal distribution is computed and the minimum of the two is used.

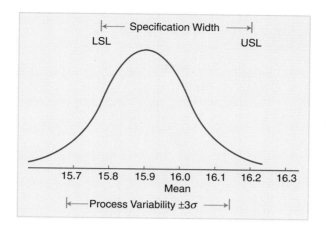

Looking at Figure 6-8, we can see that the computed C_p is 1:

Process mean: $\mu = 15.9$

Process standard deviation $\sigma = .1$

LSL $= 15.8$

USL $= 16.2$

$$C_p = \frac{.6}{6(.1)} = 1$$

This means that the process is fully capable. However, from the graph you can see that the process is *not* capable because it is not fully centered. Only using the C_p measure would lead to an incorrect conclusion. Computing C_{pk} gives us a different answer:

$$C_{pk} = \min\left(\frac{\text{USL} - \mu}{3\sigma}, \frac{\mu - \text{LSL}}{3\sigma}\right)$$

$$C_{pk} = \min\left(\frac{16.2 - 15.9}{3(.1)}, \frac{15.9 - 15.8}{3(.1)}\right)$$

$$C_{pk} = \frac{.1}{.3} = .33$$

The C_{pk} value is less than 1, showing that the process is not capable.

■ **Example 6.7 Computing the C_{pk} Value**

Compute the C_{pk} measure of process capability for the following machine and interpret the findings. What value would you have obtained with the C_p measure?

Machine Data: USL $= 110$

LSL $= 50$

Process $\sigma = 10$

Process $\mu = 60$

Solution:
To compute the C_{pk} measure of process capability:

$$C_{pk} = \min\left(\frac{USL - \mu}{3\sigma}, \frac{\mu - LSL}{3\sigma}\right)$$

$$= \min\left(\frac{110 - 60}{3(10)}, \frac{60 - 50}{3(10)}\right)$$

$$= \frac{10}{30} = .33$$

This means that the process is not capable. The C_p measure of process capability gives us the following measure,

$$C_p = \frac{60}{6(10)} = 1$$

leading us to believe that the process is capable. The reason for the difference in the measures is that the process is not centered on the specification range, as shown in Figure 6-9.

Figure 6-9

Process variability not centered across specification width for Example 6.7

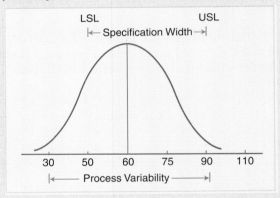

Process capability of machines is a critical element of statistical process control.

Six-Sigma Quality

The term **six-sigma** was coined by the Motorola Corporation in the 1980s to describe the high level of quality the company was striving to achieve. Sigma (σ) stands for the number of standard deviations of the process. Recall that ± 3 sigma (σ) means that 2600 ppm are defective. The level of defects associated with six-sigma is approximately 3.4 ppm. Figure 6-10 shows a process distribution with quality levels of ± 3 sigma (σ) and ± 6 sigma (σ). You can see the difference in the number of defects produced.

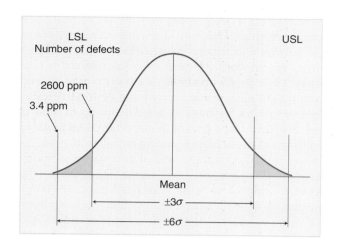

Figure 6-10

PPM defective for $\pm 3\sigma$ versus $\pm 6\sigma$ quality

To achieve the goal of six-sigma, Motorola has instituted a quality focus in every aspect of its organization. Before a product is designed, marketing ensures that product characteristics are exactly what customers want. Operations ensures that exact product characteristics can be achieved through product design, the manufacturing process, and the materials used. The six-sigma concept is an integral part of other functions as well. It is used in the finance and accounting departments to reduce costing errors and the time required to close books at the end of the month. Other companies, such as General Electric and Texas Instruments, have followed Motorola's leadership and have also instituted the six-sigma concept.

LINKS TO PRACTICE
Motorola, Inc
www.motorola.com

ACCEPTANCE SAMPLING ■

Acceptance sampling, the third branch of statistical quality control, refers to the process of randomly inspecting a certain number of items from a lot or batch in order to decide whether to accept or reject the entire batch. What makes acceptance sampling different from statistical process control is that acceptance sampling is performed either *before* or *after* the process, rather than during the process. Acceptance sampling *before* the process involves sampling materials received from a supplier, such as randomly inspecting crates of fruit that will be used in a restaurant, boxes of glass dishes that will be sold in a department store, or metal castings that will be used in a machine shop. Sampling *after* the process involves sampling finished items that are to be shipped either to a customer or to a distribution center. Examples include randomly testing a certain number of computers from a batch to make sure they meet operational requirements, and randomly inspecting snowboards to make sure that they are not defective.

Sampling involves randomly inspecting items from a lot.

You may be wondering why we would only inspect some items in the lot and not the entire lot. Acceptance sampling is used when inspecting every item is not physically possible or would be overly expensive, or when inspecting a large number of items would lead to errors due to worker fatigue. This last concern is especially important when a large number of items are processed in a short period of time. Another example of when acceptance sampling would be used is in destructive testing, such as testing eggs for salmonella or vehicles for crash testing. Obviously, in these cases it would not be helpful to test every item! However, 100% inspection does make sense if the cost of inspecting an item is less than the cost of passing on a defective item.

As you will see in this section, the goal of acceptance sampling is to determine the criteria for acceptance or rejection based on the size of the lot, the size of the sample, and the level of confidence we wish to attain. Acceptance sampling can be used for both attribute and variable measures, though it is most commonly used for attributes. In this section we will look at the different types of sampling plans and at ways to evaluate how well sampling plans discriminate between good and bad lots.

Sampling Plans

> ▶ **Sampling plan**
> A plan for acceptance sampling that precisely specifies the parameters of the sampling process and the acceptance/rejection criteria.

A **sampling plan** is a plan for acceptance sampling that precisely specifies the parameters of the sampling process and the acceptance/rejection criteria. The variables to be specified include the size of the lot (N), the size of the sample inspected from the lot (n), the number of defects above which a lot is rejected (c), and the number of samples that will be taken.

There are different types of sampling plans. Some call for *single sampling*, in which a random sample is drawn from every lot. Each item in the sample is examined and is labeled as either "good" or "bad." Depending on the number of defects or "bad" items found, the entire lot is either accepted or rejected. For example, a lot size of 50 cookies is evaluated for acceptance by randomly inspecting 10 cookies from the lot. The cookies may be inspected to make sure they are not broken or burned. If 4 or more of the 10 cookies inspected are bad, the entire lot is rejected. In this example, the lot size $N = 50$, the sample size $n = 10$, and the maximum number of defects at which a lot is accepted is $c = 4$. These parameters define the acceptance sampling plan.

Another type of acceptance sampling is called *double sampling*. This provides an opportunity to sample the lot a second time if the results of the first sample are inconclusive. In double sampling we first sample a lot of goods according to preset criteria for definite acceptance or rejection. However, if the results fall in the middle range, they are considered inconclusive and a second sample is taken. For example, a water treatment plant may sample the quality of the water ten times in random intervals throughout the day. Criteria may be set for acceptable or unacceptable water quality, such as .05% chlorine and .1% chlorine. However, a sample of water containing between .05% and .1% chlorine is inconclusive and calls for a second sample of water.

In addition to single and double-sampling plans, there are *multiple sampling plans*. Multiple sampling plans are similar to double sampling plans except that criteria are set for more than two samples. The decision as to which sampling plan to select has a great deal to do with the cost involved in sampling, the time consumed by sampling, and the cost of passing on a defective item. In general, if the cost of collecting a sample is relatively high, single sampling is preferred. An extreme example is collecting a biopsy from a hospital patient. Because the actual cost of getting the sample is high, we want to get a large sample and sample only once. The opposite is true when the cost of collecting the sample is low but the actual cost of testing is high. This may be the case with a water treatment plant, where collecting the water is inexpensive but the chemical analysis is costly. In this section we will focus primarily on single sampling plans.

Operating Characteristic (OC) Curves

As we have seen, different sampling plans have different capabilities for discriminating between good and bad lots. At one extreme is 100% inspection, which has perfect discriminating power. However, as the size of the sample inspected decreases, so does the chance of accepting a defective lot. We can show the discriminating power of a sampling plan on a graph by means of an **operating characteristic (OC) curve.** This curve shows the probability or chance of accepting a lot given various proportions of defects in the lot.

Figure 6-11 shows a typical OC curve. The *x* axis shows the percentage of items that can be defective in a lot. This is called "lot quality." The *y* axis shows the probability or chance of accepting a lot. You can see that if we use 100% inspection we are certain of accepting only lots with zero defects. However, as the proportion of defects in the lot increases, our chance of accepting the lot decreases. For example, we have a 90% probability of accepting a lot with 5% defects and an 80% probability of accepting a lot with 8% defects.

Regardless of which sampling plan we have selected, the plan is not perfect. That is, there is still a chance of accepting lots that are "bad" and rejecting "good" lots. The steeper the OC curve, the better our sampling plan is for discriminating between "good" and "bad." Figure 6-12 shows three different OC curves, A, B, and C. Curve A

▶ **Operating characteristic (OC) curve**
A graph that shows the probability or chance of accepting a lot given various proportions of defects in the lot.

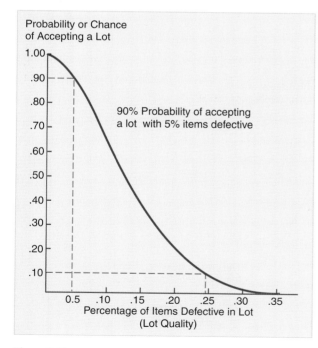

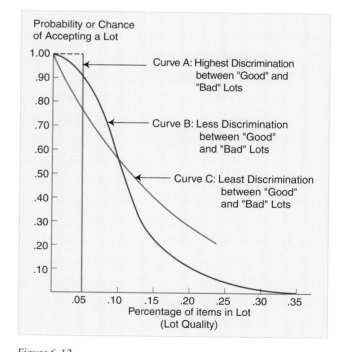

Figure 6-11

Example of an operating characteristic (OC) curve

Figure 6-12

OC curves with different steepness levels and different levels of discrimination

is the most discriminating and curve C the least. You can see that the steeper the slope of the curve, the more discriminating is the sampling plan. When 100% inspection is not possible, there is a certain amount of risk for consumers in accepting defective lots and a certain amount of risk for producers in rejecting good lots.

There is a small percentage of defects that consumers are willing to accept. This is called the **acceptable quality level (AQL)** and is generally in the order of 1–2%. However, sometimes the percentage of defects that passes through is higher than AQL. Consumers will usually tolerate a few more defects, but at some point the number of defects reaches a threshold level beyond which consumers will not tolerate them. This threshold level is called the **lot tolerance percent defective (LTPD)**. The LTPD is the upper limit of the percentage of defective items consumers are willing to tolerate.

Consumer's risk is the chance or probability that a lot will be accepted that contains a greater number of defects than the LTPD limit. This is the probability of making a Type II error—that is, accepting a lot that is truly "bad." Consumer's risk or Type II error is generally denoted by beta (β). The relationships among AQL, LTPD, and β are shown in Figure 6-13. **Producer's risk** is the chance or probability that a lot containing an acceptable quality level will be rejected. This is the probability of making a Type I error—that is, rejecting a lot that is "good." It is generally denoted by alpha (α). Producer's risk is also shown in Figure 6-13.

We can determine from an OC curve what the consumer's and producer's risks are. However, these values should not be left to chance. Rather, sampling plans are usually designed to meet specific levels of consumer's and producer's risk. For example, one common combination is to have a consumer's risk (β) of 10% and a producer's risk (α) of 5%, though many other combinations are possible.

▶ **Acceptable quality level (AQL)**
The small percentage of defects that consumers are willing to accept.

▶ **Lot tolerance percent defective (LTPD)**
The upper limit of the percentage of defective items consumers are willing to tolerate.

▶ **Consumer's risk**
The chance of accepting a lot that contains a greater number of defects than the LTPD limit.

▶ **Producer's risk**
The chance that a lot containing an acceptable quality level will be rejected.

Figure 6-13

An OC curve showing producer's risk (α) and consumer's risk (β).

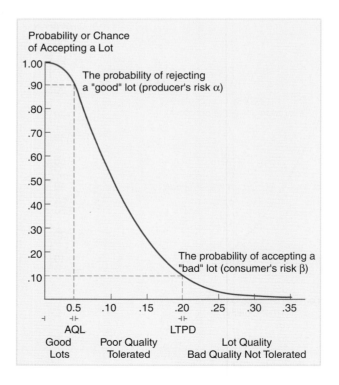

Developing OC Curves

An OC curve graphically depicts the discriminating power of a sampling plan. To draw an OC curve, we typically use a cumulative binomial distribution to obtain probabilities of accepting a lot given varying levels of lot defects.[1] The cumulative binomial table is found in Appendix C. A small part of this table is reproduced in Table 6-2. The top of the table shows values of p, which represents the percentage of defective items in a lot (5%, 10%, 20%, etc.). The left-hand column shows values of n, which represent the sample size being considered, and x represents the cumulative number of defects found. Let's use an example to illustrate how to develop an OC curve for a specific sampling plan using the information from Table 6-2.

Table 6-2 Partial Cumulative Binomial Probability Table

		\.05	.10	.15	.20	.25	.30	.35	.40	.45	.50
n	x					Percentage of Items Defective (p)					
5	0	.7738	.5905	.4437	.3277	.2373	.1681	.1160	.0778	.0503	.0313
	1	.9974	.9185	.8352	.7373	.6328	.5282	.4284	.3370	.2562	.1875
	2	.9988	.9914	.9734	.9421	.8965	.8369	.7648	.6826	.5931	.5000

[1]For $n \geq 20$ and $p \leq .05$ a Poisson distribution is generally used.

■ Example 6.8　Constructing an OC Curve

Let's say that we want to develop an OC curve for a sampling plan in which a sample of $n = 5$ items is drawn from lots of $N = 1000$ items. The accept/reject criteria are set up in such a way that we accept a lot if *no more than* one defect ($c = 1$) is found.

Solution:
Let's look at the partial binomial distribution in Table 6-2. Since our criteria require us to sample $n = 5$, we will go to the row where n equals 5 in the left-hand column. The "x" column tells us the cumulative number of defects found at which we reject the lot. Since we are not allowing more than one defect, we look for an x value that corresponds to 1. The row corresponding to $n = 5$ and $x = 1$ tells us our chance or probability of accepting lots with various proportions of defects using this sampling plan. For example, with this sampling plan we have a 99.74% chance of accepting a lot with 5% defects. If we move down the row, we can see that we have a 91.85% chance of accepting a lot with 10% defects, a 83.52% chance of accepting a lot with 15% defects, and a 73.73% chance of accepting a lot with 20% defects. Using these values and those remaining in the row, we can construct an OC chart for $n = 5$ and $c = 1$. This is shown in Figure 6-14.

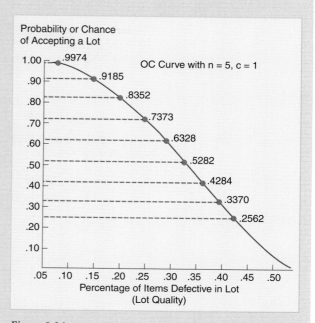

Figure 6-14

OC curve with $n = 5$ and $c = 1$.

Average Outgoing Quality

As we observed with the OC curves, the higher the quality of the lot, the higher is the chance that it will be accepted. Conversely, the lower the quality of the lot, the greater is the chance that it will be rejected. Given that some lots are accepted and some rejected, it is useful to compute the average outgoing quality (AOQ) of lots to get a sense of the overall outgoing quality of the product. Assuming that all lots have the same proportion of defective items, the average outgoing quality can be computed as follows:

$$\text{AOQ} = (P_{ac})p\left(\frac{N - n}{N}\right)$$

where P_{ac} = probability of accepting a given lot
p = proportion of defective items in a lot
N = the size of the lot
n = the sample size chosen for inspection

Usually we assume the fraction in the above equation to equal 1 and simplify the equation to the following form:

$$\text{AOQ} = (P_{ac})p$$

We can then use the information from Figure 6-14 to construct an AOQ curve for different levels of probabilities of acceptance and different proportions of defects in a lot. As we will see, an AOQ curve is similar to an OC curve.

■ Example 6.9 Constructing an AOQ Curve

Let's go back to our initial example, in which we sampled 5 items ($n = 5$) from a lot of 1000 ($N = 1000$) with an acceptance range of no more than 1 ($c = 1$) defect. Here we will construct an AOQ curve for this sampling plan and interpret its meaning.

Solution:
For the parameters $N = 1000$, $n = 5$, and $c = 1$, we can read the probabilities of P_{ac} from Figure 6-14. Then we can compute the value of AOQ as $\text{AOQ} = (P_{ac})\, p$.

p	.05	.10	.15	.20	.25	.30	.35	.40	.45	.50
P_{ac}	.9974	.9185	.8352	.7373	.6328	.5282	.4284	.3370	.2562	.1875
AOQ	.0499	.0919	.1253	.1475	.1582	.1585	.1499	.1348	.1153	.0938

Figure 6-15 shows a graphical representation of the AOQ values. The AOQ varies, depending on the proportion of defective items in the lot. The largest value of AOQ, called the av-

Figure 6-15

The AOQ for n = 5 and c = 1.

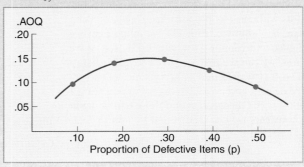

erage outgoing quality limit (AOQL), is around 15.85%. You can see from Figure 6-15 that the average outgoing quality will be high for lots that are either very good or very bad. For lots that have close to 30% of defective items, the AOQ is the highest. Managers can use this information to compute the worst possible value of their average outgoing quality given the proportion of defective items (p). Then this information can be used to develop a sampling plan with appropriate levels of discrimination.

IMPLICATIONS FOR MANAGERS ∎

In this chapter we have learned about a variety of different statistical quality control (SQC) tools that help managers make decisions about product and process quality. However, to use these tools properly managers must make a number of decisions. In this section we discuss some of the most important decisions that must be made when implementing SPC.

How Much and How Often to Inspect

Consider Product Cost and Product Volume As you know, 100% inspection is rarely possible. The question then becomes one of how often to inspect in order to minimize the chances of passing on defects and still keep inspection costs manageable. This decision should be related to the *product cost* and *product volume* of what is being produced. At one extreme are high-volume, low-cost items, such as paper, pencils, nuts and bolts, for which 100% inspection would not be cost justified. Also, with such a large volume 100% inspection would not be possible because worker fatigue sets in and defects are often passed on. At the other extreme are low-volume, high-cost items, such as parts that will go into a space shuttle or be used in a medical procedure, that require 100% inspection.

Most items fall somewhere between the two extremes just described. For these items, frequency of inspection should be designed to consider the trade-off between the cost of inspection and the cost of passing on a defective item. Historically, inspections were set up to minimize these two costs. Today, it is believed that defects of any type should not be tolerated and that eliminating them helps reduce organizational costs. Still, the inspection process should be set up to consider issues of product cost and volume. For example, one company will probably have different frequencies of inspection for different products.

Consider Process Stability Another issue to consider when deciding how much to inspect is the stability of the process. Stable processes that do not change frequently do not need to be inspected often. On the other hand, processes that are unstable and change often should be inspected frequently. For example, if it has been observed that a particular type of drilling machine in a machine shop often goes out of tolerance, that machine should be inspected frequently. Obviously, such decisions cannot be made without historical data on process stability.

Consider Lot Size The size of the lot or batch being produced is another factor to consider in determining the amount of inspection. A company that produces a small number of large lots will have a smaller number of inspections than a company that produces a large number of small lots. The reason is that every lot should have some inspection, and when lots are large, there are fewer lots to inspect.

Where to Inspect

Since we cannot inspect every aspect of a process all the time, another important decision is to decide where to inspect. Some areas are less critical than others. Following are some points that are typically considered most important for inspection.

Inbound Materials Materials that are coming into a facility from a supplier or distribution center should be inspected before they enter the production process. It is important to check the quality of materials before labor is added to it. For example, it would be wasteful for a seafood restaurant not to inspect the quality of incoming lobsters only to later uncover that its lobster bisque is bad. Another reason for checking inbound materials is to check the quality of sources of supply. Consistently poor quality in materials from a particular supplier indicates a problem that needs to be addressed.

Finished Products Products that have been completed and are ready for shipment to customers should also be inspected. This is the last point at which the product is in the production facility. The quality of the product represents the company's overall quality. The final quality level is what will be experienced by the customer and an inspection at this point is necessary to ensure high quality in such aspects as fitness for use, packaging, and presentation.

Prior to Costly Processing During the production process it makes sense to check quality before performing a costly process on the product. If quality is poor at that point and the product will ultimately be discarded, adding a costly process will simply lead to waste. For example, in the production of leather armchairs in a furniture factory, chair frames should be inspected for cracks before the leather covering is added. Otherwise, if the frame is defective the cost of the leather upholstery and workmanship may be wasted.

Which Tools to Use

In addition to where and how much to inspect, managers must decide which tools to use in the process of inspection. As we have seen, tools such as control charts are best used at various points in the production process. Acceptance sampling is best used for inbound and outbound materials. It is also the easiest method to use for attribute measures, whereas control charts are easier to use for variable measures. Surveys of industry practices show that most companies use control charts, especially x- and R-charts, because they require less data collection than p-charts.

■ STATISTICAL QUALITY CONTROL IN SERVICES

Statistical quality control (SQC) tools have been widely used in manufacturing organizations for quite some time. Manufacturers such as Motorola, General Electric, Toyota Motor Company, and others have shown leadership in statistical quality control for many years. Unfortunately, service organizations have lagged behind manufacturing firms in their use of statistical quality control. The primary reason for this is that statistical quality control requires measurement, and it is difficult to measure the quality of a service. Remember that services often provide an intangible product and that perceptions of quality are often highly subjective. For example, the quality of a service is often judged by such factors as friendliness and courtesy of the staff and promptness in resolving complaints.

A way to measure the quality of services is to devise quantifiable measurements of the important dimensions of a particular service. For example, the number of complaints received per month, the number of telephone rings after which a response is received, or customer waiting time can be quantified. These types of measurements are not subjective or subject to interpretation. Rather, they can be measured and recorded. As in manufacturing, acceptable control limits should be developed and the variable in question should be measured periodically.

Another issue that complicates quality control in service organizations is that the service is often consumed during the production process. The customer is often present during service delivery, and there is little time to improve quality. The workforce that interfaces with customers is part of the service delivery. The way to manage this issue is to provide a high level of workforce training and to empower workers to make decisions that will satisfy customers.

One service organization that has demonstrated quality leadership is The Ritz-Carlton Hotel Company. This luxury hotel chain caters to travelers who seek high levels of customer service. The goal of the chain is to be recognized for outstanding service quality. To this end, computer records are kept of regular clients' preferences. To keep customers happy, employees are empowered to spend up to $2,000 on the spot to correct any customer complaint. Consequently, Ritz-Carlton has received a number of quality awards including winning the Malcolm Baldrige National Quality Award twice. They are the only company in the service category to do so.

Another leader in service quality that uses the strategy of high levels of employee training and empowerment is Nordstrom Department Stores. Outstanding customer service is the goal of this department store chain. Its organizational chart places the customer at the head of the organization. Records are kept of regular clients' preference and employees are empowered to make decisions on the spot to satisfy customer wants. The customer is considered to always be right.

LINKS TO PRACTICE
The Ritz-Carlton Hotel Company, L.L.C.
www.ritzcarlton.com
Nordstrom Inc.
www.nordstrom.com

OM ACROSS THE ORGANIZATION

It is easy to see how operations managers can use the tools of statistical quality control to monitor product and process quality. However, you may not readily see how these statistical techniques affect other functions of the organization. In fact, statistical quality control tools require input from other functions, influence their success, and are actually used by other organizational functions in designing and evaluating their tasks.

Marketing plays a critical role in setting up product and service quality standards. It is up to marketing to provide information on current and future quality standards required by customers and those being offered by competitors. Operations managers can incorporate this information into product and process design. Consultation with marketing managers is essential to ensure that quality standards are being met. At the same time, meeting quality standards is essential to the marketing department, since sales of products are dependent on the standards being met.

Finance is an integral part of the statistical quality control process, because it is responsible for placing financial values on statistical quality control efforts. For example, the finance department evaluates the dollar costs of defects, measures financial improvements that result from tightening of quality standards, and is actively involved in approving investments in quality improvement efforts.

Human resources becomes even more important with the implementation of TQM and SQC methods, as the role of workers changes. To understand and utilize SQC tools, workers need ongoing training and the ability to work in teams, take pride in their work, and assume higher levels of responsibility. The human resources department is responsible for hiring workers with the right skills and setting proper compensation levels.

Information systems is a function that makes much of the information needed for statistical quality control accessible to all who need it. Information systems managers need to work closely with other functions during the implementation of SQC so that they understand exactly what types of information are needed and in what form. As we have seen, SQC tools are dependent on information, and it is up to information systems managers to make that information available. As a company develops ways of using TQM and SQC tools, information systems managers must be part of this ongoing evolution to ensure that the company's information needs are being met.

All functions need to work closely together in the implementation of statistical process control. Everyone benefits from this collaborative relationship. Operations is able to produce the right product efficiently, marketing has the exact product customers are looking for, and finance can boast of an improved financial picture for the organization.

Statistical quality control also affects various organizational functions through its direct application in evaluating quality performance in all areas of the organization. Statistical quality control tools are not used only to monitor the production process and ensure that the product being produced is within specifications. As we have seen in the Motorola six-sigma example, these tools can be used to monitor quality levels and defects in accounting procedures, financial record keeping, sales and marketing, office administration, and other functions. Having high quality standards in operations does not guarantee high quality in the organization as a whole. The same stringent standards and quality evaluation procedures should be used in setting standards and evaluating performance of all organizational functions.

OM IS EVERYWHERE ■

The quality standards set by companies for their products and services directly affect your everyday life. You are affected by poor product and service quality, whether it be defective lightbulbs, damaged computer disks, a university bookstore that is out of stock of a text you need, or poor delivery by the local pizzeria. The extent to which a company measures and monitors quality directly affects the quality of the products and services you purchase. However, talking about improving quality will not do the job. What is needed are specific product and service measurements that can be taken over time using the tools of statistical quality control.

The tools and concepts described in this chapter can be used to monitor many facets of your life, such as your own performance in classes you are taking, in sport activities, or when playing a musical instrument. These tools can also help you objectively monitor the quality of services that you encounter, such as evaluating the quality of airlines you use, university services provided, or even your doctor's office. You could even develop a control chart to monitor the batting average of your favorite baseball player! You now understand the differences between common and assignable causes of variation. You also know how to use control charts. These tools can provide valuable information to use in objectively evaluating quality performance in every aspect of your life.

CHAPTER HIGHLIGHTS

1 Statistical quality control (SQC) refers to statistical tools that can be used by quality professionals. Statistical quality control can be divided into three broad categories: traditional statistical tools, acceptance sampling, and statistical process control (SPC).

2 Traditional statistical tools are used to describe quality characteristics, such as the mean, range, and variance. Acceptance sampling is the process of randomly inspecting a sample of goods and deciding whether to accept or reject the entire lot. Statistical process control (SPC) involves inspecting a random sample of output from a process and deciding whether the process is producing products with characteristics that fall within preset specifications.

3 There are two causes of variation in the quality of a product or process: common causes and assignable causes. Common causes of variation are random causes that we cannot identify. Assignable causes of variation are those that can be identified and eliminated.

4 A control chart is a graph used in statistical process control that shows whether a sample of data falls within the normal range of variation. A control chart has upper and lower control limits that separate common from assignable causes of variation. Control charts for variables monitor characteristics that can be measured and have a continuum of values, such as height, weight, or volume.

Control charts for attributes are used to monitor characteristics that have discrete values and can be counted.

5 Control charts for variables include x-bar charts and R-charts. X-bar charts monitor the mean or average value of a product characteristic. R-charts monitor the range or dispersion of the values of a product characteristic. Control charts for attributes include p-charts and c-charts. P-charts are used to monitor the proportion of defects in a sample. C-charts are used to monitor the actual number of defects in a sample.

6 Process capability is the ability of the production process to meet or exceed preset specifications. It is measured by the process capability index, C_p, which is computed as the ratio of the specification width to the width of the process variability.

7 The term *six-sigma* indicates a level of quality in which the number of defects is no more than 3.4 parts per million.

8 The goal of acceptance sampling is to determine criteria for acceptance or rejection based on lot size, sample size, and the desired level of confidence. Operating characteristic (OC) curves are graphs that show the discriminating power of a sampling plan.

9 It is more difficult to measure quality in services than in manufacturing. The key is to devise quantifiable measurements for important service dimensions.

KEY TERMS

statistical quality control (SQC) 137
traditional statistical tools 137
acceptance sampling 137
statistical process control (SPC) 137
common causes of variation 138
assignable causes of variation 139
mean 139
range 140
standard deviation 140
control chart 141

out of control 141
variable 142
attribute 142
x-bar chart 143
R-chart 144
p-chart 147
c-chart 148
process capability 149
product specifications 149
process capability index 150

six-sigma quality 153
sampling plan 156
operating characteristic (OC) curve 157
acceptable quality level (AQL) 158
lot tolerance percent defective (LTPD) 158
consumer's risk 158
producer's risk 158
average outgoing quality (AOQ) 160

FORMULA REVIEW

1. Mean

$$\overline{X} = \frac{\sum\limits_{i=1}^{n} X_i}{n}$$

2. Standard Deviation

$$\sigma = \sqrt{\frac{\sum\limits_{i=1}^{n} (x_i - \overline{x})^2}{n-1}}$$

3. Control Limits for X-Bar Charts

Upper control limit
$$(UCL) = \overline{\overline{x}} + z\sigma_{\overline{x}}$$

Lower control limit
$$(LCL) = \overline{\overline{x}} - z\sigma_{\overline{x}}$$

4. Control Limits for X-Bar Charts Using Sample Range as an Estimate of Variability

Upper control limit
$$(UCL) = \overline{\overline{x}} + A_2\overline{R}$$

Lower control limit
$$(LCL) = \overline{\overline{x}} - A_2\overline{R}$$

5. Control Limits for R-Charts

$$UCL = D_4\overline{R}$$
$$LCL = D_3\overline{R}$$

6. Control Limits for p-Charts

$$UCL = \overline{p} + z(\sigma_p)$$
$$LCL = \overline{p} - z(\sigma_p)$$

7. Control Limits for c-Charts

$$UCL_c = \overline{c} + z\sqrt{\overline{c}}$$
$$LCL_c = \overline{c} - z\sqrt{\overline{c}}$$

8. Measures for Process Capability

$$C_p = \frac{\text{specification width}}{\text{process width}} = \frac{USL - LSL}{6\sigma}$$

$$C_{pk} = \min\left(\frac{USL - \mu}{3\sigma}, \frac{\mu - LSL}{3\sigma}\right)$$

9. Average Outgoing Quality

$$AOQ = (P_{ac})p$$

SOLVED PROBLEMS

■ Problem 1

A quality control inspector at the Crunchy Potato Chips Company has taken 3 samples with 4 observations each of the volume of bags filled. The data and the computed means are shown below:

Samples of Potato Chip Bag Volume in Ounces

Observation	1	2	3
1	12.5	12.8	12.6
2	12.8	12.4	12.4
3	12.1	12.6	12.5
4	12.2	12.6	12.5
Mean ($\bar{x}$)	12.4	12.6	12.5

If the standard deviation of the bagging operation is .2 ounces, use the above information to develop control limits of 3 standard deviations for the bottling operation.

Solution 1

The center line of the control data is the average of the samples:

$$\bar{\bar{x}} = \frac{12.4 + 12.6 + 12.5}{3} = 12.5 \text{ ounces}$$

The control limits are:

$$UCL = \bar{\bar{x}} + z\sigma_{\bar{x}} = 12.5 + 3\left(\frac{.2}{\sqrt{4}}\right) = 12.80$$

$$LCL - \bar{\bar{x}} - z\sigma_{\bar{x}} = 12.5 - 3\left(\frac{.2}{\sqrt{4}}\right) = 12.20$$

Following is the associated control chart:

UCL = (12.80) _____

CL = (12.5) _____

LCL = (12.20) _____

This problem can also be solved using a spreadsheet. This is shown in Spreadsheet 6-1.

Spreadsheet 6.1

# of std. deviations	3
std. dev. =	0.2
# observations/sample	4
sample std. dev.	0.1

Sample	Observation				Sample Mean	Overall Mean	UCL	LCL
	1	2	3	4				
1	12.5	12.8	12.3	12.2	12.4	12.5	12.8	12.2
2	12.8	12.4	12.6	12.6	12.6	12.5	12.8	12.2
3	12.6	12.4	12.5	12.5	12.5	12.5	12.8	12.2

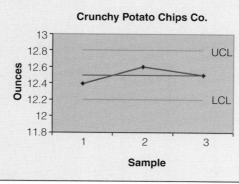

Crunchy Potato Chips Co.

SOLVED PROBLEMS

■ Problem 2

Use of the sample range to estimate variability can also be applied to the Crunchy Potato Chip operation. A quality control inspector has taken four samples with five observations each, measuring the volume of chips per bag. If the average range for the four samples is .2 ounces and the average mean of the observations is 12.5 ounces, develop three-sigma control limits for the bottling operation.

Solution 2

$$\bar{\bar{x}} = 12.5 \text{ ounces}$$
$$\bar{R} = .2$$

The value of A_2 is obtained from Table 6-1. For $n = 5$, $A_2 = .58$. This leads to the following limits:

The center of the control chart is CL = 12.5 ounces

$$\text{UCL} = \bar{\bar{x}} + A_2\bar{R} = 12.5 + (.58)(.2) = 12.62$$
$$\text{LCL} = \bar{\bar{x}} + A_2\bar{R} = 12.5 - (.58)(.2) = 12.38$$

■ Problem 3

Ten samples with five observations each have been taken from the Crunchy Potato Chip Company plant in order to test for volume dispersion in the bagging process. The average sample range was found to be .3 ounces. Develop control limits for the sample range.

Solution 3

$$\bar{R} = .3 \text{ ounces}$$
$$n = 5$$

From Table 6-1 for $n = 5$:

$$D_4 = 2.11$$
$$D_3 = 0$$

Therefore,

$$\text{UCL} = D_4\bar{R} = 2.11(.3) = .633$$
$$\text{LCL} = D_3\bar{R} = 0(.3) = 0$$

■ Problem 4

A production manager at a lightbulb plant has inspected the number of defective lightbulbs in five random samples with 30 observations each. Following are the numbers of defective lightbulbs found:

Sample	Number of Defects	Number of Observations in Sample
1	1	30
2	3	30
3	3	30
4	1	30
5	0	30
Total	8	150

Construct a three-sigma control chart ($z = 3$) with this information.

Solution 4

The center line of the chart is:

$$\text{CL} = \bar{p} = \frac{\text{number of defects}}{\text{number of observations}} = \frac{8}{150} = .053$$

$$\sigma_p = \sqrt{\frac{\bar{p}(1-\bar{p})}{n}} = \sqrt{\frac{(0.53)(.947)}{30}} = .040$$

$$\text{UCL} = \bar{p} + z(\sigma_p) = .053 + 3(.040) = .173$$
$$\text{LCL} = \bar{p} - z(\sigma_p) = .053 - 3(.040) = -.067$$

SOLVED PROBLEMS

◼ Problem 5

Kinder Land Child Care uses a c-chart to monitor the number of customer complaints per week. Complaints have been recorded over the past 10 weeks. Develop three-sigma control limits using the following data:

Week	Number of Complaints
1	0
2	3
3	4
4	1
5	0
6	0
7	3
8	1
9	1
10	0
	13

Solution 5

The average weekly number of complaints is $13/10 = 1.3$. Therefore, $\bar{c} = 1.3$.

$$UCL_c = \bar{c} + 3\sqrt{\bar{c}} = 1.3 + 3\sqrt{(1.3)} = 4.72$$

$$LCL_c = \bar{c} - 3\sqrt{\bar{c}} = 1.3 - 3\sqrt{(1.3)} = -2.12 \rightarrow 0$$

Following is the control chart for this example:

UCL = (4.72) _____

CL = (1.3) _____

LCL = (0) _____

◼ Problem 6

Three bagging machines at the Crunchy Potato Chip Company are being evaluated for their capability. The following data are recorded:

Bagging Machine	Standard Deviation
A	.2
B	.3
C	.05

If specifications are set between 12.35 and 12.65 ounces, determine which of the machines are capable of producing within specifications.

Solution 6

To determine the capability of each machine we need to divide the specification width (USL − LSL = 12.65 − 12.35 = .3) by 6σ for each machine:

Bagging Machine	σ	USL − LSL	6σ	$C_p = \dfrac{USL - LSL}{6\sigma}$
A	.2	.3	1.2	0.25
B	.3	.3	1.8	0.1666
C	.05	.3	.3	1

Looking at the C_p values, only machine C is capable of bagging the potato chips within specifications, because it is the only machine that has a C_p value at or above 1.

◼ Problem 7

Compute the C_{pk} measure of process capability for the following machine and interpret the findings. What value would you have obtained with the C_p measure?

Machine Data: USL = 80
LSL = 50
Process σ = 5
Process μ = 60

Solution 7

To compute the C_{pk} measure of process capability:

$$C_{pk} = \min\left(\frac{USL - \mu}{3\sigma}, \frac{\mu - LSL}{3\sigma}\right)$$

$$= \min\left(\frac{80 - 60}{3(5)}, \frac{60 - 50}{3(5)}\right)$$

$$= .66$$

This means that the process is not capable. The C_p measure of process capability gives us the following measure:

$$C_p = \frac{30}{6(5)} = 1$$

which leads us to believe that the process is capable.

DISCUSSION QUESTIONS

1. Explain the three categories of statistical quality control (SQC). How are they different, what different information do they provide, and how can they be used together?

2. Describe three recent situations in which you were directly affected by poor product or service quality.

3. Discuss the key differences between common and assignable causes of variation. Give examples.

4. Describe a quality control chart and how it can be used. What are upper and lower control limits? What does it mean if an observation falls outside the control limits?

5. Explain the differences between x-bar and R-charts. How can they be used together and why would it be important to use them together?

6. Explain the use of p-charts and c-charts. When would you use one rather than the other? Give examples of measurements for both p-charts and c-charts.

7. Explain what is meant by process capability. Why is it important? What does it tell us? How can it be measured?

8. Describe the process of acceptance sampling. What types of sampling plans are there? What is acceptance sampling used for?

9. Describe the concept of six-sigma quality. Why is such a high quality level important?

PROBLEMS

1. A quality control manager at a manufacturing facility has taken four samples with four observations each of the diameter of a part.
   (a) Compute the mean of each sample.
   (b) Compute an estimate of the mean and standard deviation of the sampling distribution.
   (c) Develop control limits for 3 standard deviations of the product diameter.

Samples of Part Diameter in Inches

1	2	3	4
5.8	6.2	6.1	6.0
5.9	6.0	5.9	5.9
6.0	5.9	6.0	5.9
6.1	5.9	5.8	6.1

2. A quality control inspector at the Beautiful Shampoo Company has taken three samples with four observations each of the volume of shampoo bottles filled. The data collected by the inspector and the computed means are shown here:

Samples of Shampoo Bottle Volume in Ounces

Observation	1	2	3
1	19.7	19.7	19.7
2	20.6	20.2	18.7
3	18.9	18.9	21.6
4	20.8	20.7	20.0
Mean (x)	20.0	19.875	20.0

If the standard deviation of the shampoo bottle filling operation is .2 ounces, use the information in the table to develop control limits of 3 standard deviations for the operation.

3. A quality control inspector has taken four samples with five observations each at the Beautiful Shampoo Company, measuring the volume of shampoo per bottle. If the average range for the four samples is .4 ounces and the average mean of the observations is 19.8 ounces, develop three-sigma control limits for the bottling operation.

4. A production manager at Ultra Clean Dishwashing company is monitoring the quality of the company's production process. There has been concern relative to the quality of the operation to accurately fill the 16 ounces of dishwashing liquid. The product is designed for a fill level of 16.00 ±0.30. The company collected the following sample data on the production process:

Sample	Observations			
	1	2	3	4
1	16.40	16.11	15.90	15.78
2	15.97	16.10	16.20	15.81
3	15.91	16.00	16.04	15.92
4	16.20	16.21	15.93	15.95
5	15.87	16.21	16.34	16.43
6	15.43	15.49	15.55	15.92
7	16.43	16.21	15.99	16.00
8	15.50	15.92	16.12	16.02
9	16.13	16.21	16.05	16.01
10	15.68	16.43	16.20	15.97

(a) Are the process mean and range in statistical control?

(b) Do you think this process is capable of meeting the design standard?

5. Ten samples with five observations each have been taken from the Beautiful Shampoo Company plant in order to test for volume dispersion in the shampoo bottle filling process. The average sample range was found to be .3 ounces. Develop control limits for the sample range.

6. The Awake Coffee Company produces gourmet instant coffee. The company wants to be sure that the average fill of coffee containers is 12.0 ounces. To make sure the process is in control, a worker periodically selects at random a box containing six containers of coffee and measures their weight. When the process is in control the range of the weight of coffee samples has averages .6 ounces.

(a) Develop an R-chart and an $\bar{x}$-chart for this process.

(b) The measurements of weight from the last five samples taken of the six containers are shown below:

Is the process in control? Explain your answer.

Sample	x	R
1	12.1	.7
2	11.8	.4
3	12.3	.6
4	11.5	.4
5	11.6	.9

7. A production manager at a Contour Manufacturing plant has inspected the number of defective plastic molds in 5 random samples of 20 observations each. Following are the number of defective molds found in each sample:

Sample	Number of Defects	Number of Observations in Sample
1	1	20
2	2	20
3	2	20
4	1	20
5	0	20
Total	6	100

Construct a three-sigma control chart ($z = 3$) with this information.

8. A tire manufacturer has been concerned about the number of defective tires found recently. In order to evaluate the true magnitude of the problem, a production manager selected ten random samples of 20 units each for inspection. The number of defective tires found in each sample are as follows:

(a) Develop a p-chart with a $z = 3$.

(b) Suppose that the next four samples selected had 6, 3, 3, and 4 defects. What conclusion can you make?

Sample	Number Defective
1	1
2	3
3	2
4	1
5	4
6	1
7	2
8	0
9	3
10	1

9. U-Learn University uses a c-chart to monitor student complaints per week. Complaints have been recorded over the past 10 weeks. Develop three-sigma control limits using the following data:

Week	Number of Complaints
1	0
2	3
3	1
4	1
5	0
6	0
7	3
8	1
9	1
10	

10. University Hospital has been concerned with the number of errors found in its billing statement to patients. An audit of 100 bills per week over the past 12 weeks revealed the following number of errors:

Week	Number of Errors
1	4
2	5
3	6
4	6
5	3
6	2
7	6
8	7
9	3
10	4
12	4

(a) Develop control charts with $z = 3$.

(b) Is the process in control?

11. Three ice cream packing machines at the Creamy Treat Company are being evaluated for their capability. The following data are recorded:

Packing Machine	Standard Deviation
A	.2
B	.3
C	.05

If specifications are set between 15.8 and 16.2 ounces, determine which of the machines are capable of producing within specifications.

12. Compute the Cpk measure of process capability for the following machine and interpret the findings. What value would you have obtained with the Cp measure?

Machine Data: USL $= 100$
LSL $= 70$
Process $\sigma = 5$
Process $\mu = 80$

13. Develop an OC curve for a sampling plan in which a sample of $n = 5$ items is drawn from lots of $N = 1000$ items. The accept/reject criteria are set up in such a way that we accept a lot if no more than one defect ($c = 1$) is found.

14. Quality Style manufactures self-assembling furniture. To reduce the cost of returned orders, the manager of its quality control department inspects the final packages each day using randomly selected samples. The defects include wrong parts, missing connection parts, parts with apparent painting problems, and parts with rough surfaces. The average defect rate is three per day.

(a) Which type of control chart should be used? Construct a control chart with three-sigma control limits.

(b) Today the manager discovered nine defects. What does this mean?

15. Develop an OC curve for a sampling plan in which a sample of $n = 10$ items is drawn from lots of $N = 1,000$. The accept/reject criteria is set up in such a way that we accept a lot if no more than one defect ($c = 1$) is found.

16. The Fresh Pie Company purchases apples from a local farm to be used in preparing the filling for their apple pies. Sometimes the apples are fresh and ripe. Other times they can be spoiled or not ripe enough. The company has decided that they need an acceptance sampling plan for the purchased apples. Fresh Pie has decided that the acceptable quality level is 5 defective apples per 100, and the lot tolerance proportion defective is 5 percent. Producer's risk should be no more than 5 percent and consumer's risk 10 percent or less.

(a) Develop a plan that satisfies the above requirements.

(b) Determine the AOQL for your plan, assuming that the lot size is 1000 apples.

17. A computer manufacturer purchases microchips from a world class supplier. The buyer has a lot tolerance proportion defective of 10 parts in 5000, with a consumer's risk of 15 percent. If the computer manufacturer decides to sample 2000 of the microchips received in each shipment, what acceptance number c, would they want? What is the producer's risk if the AQL is 20 parts per 5000?

18. Joshua Simms has recently been placed in charge of purchasing at the Med-Tech Corporation, a medical testing laboratory. His job is to purchase testing equipment and supplies. Med-Tech currently has a contract with a reputable supplier in the industry. Joshua's job is to design an appropriate acceptance sampling plan for Med-Tech. The contract with the supplier states that the acceptable quality level is 1 percent defective. Also, the lot tolerance proportion defective is 4 percent, the producer's risk is 5 percent, and consumer's risk is 10 percent.

(a) Develop an acceptance sampling plan for Joshua that meets the stated criteria.

(b) Draw the OC curve for the plan you developed.

(c) What is the AOQL of your plan, assuming a lot size of 1000?

CASE: *Scharadin Hotels*

Scharadin Hotels are a national hotel chain started in 1957 by Milo Scharadin. What started as one upscale hotel in New York City turned into a highly reputable national hotel chain. Today Scharadin Hotels serve over 100 locations and are recognized for their customer service and quality. Scharadin Hotels are typically located in large metropolitan areas close to convention centers and centers of commerce. They cater to both business and non-business customers and offer a wide array of services. Maintaining high customer service has been considered a priority for the hotel chain.

A Problem with Quality

The Scharadin Hotel in San Antonio, Texas had recently been experiencing a large number of guest complaints due to billing errors. The complaints seem to center around guests disputing charges on their final hotel bill. Guest complaints ranged from extra charges, such as meals or services that were not purchased, to confusion for not being charged at all. Most hotel guests use express checkout on their day of departure. With express checkout the hotel bill is left under the guest's door in the early morning hours and, if all is in order, does not require any additional action on the guest's part. Express checkout is a welcome service by busy travelers who are free to depart the hotel at their convenience. However, the increased number of billing errors began creating unnecessary delays and frustration for the guests who unexpectedly needed to settle their bill with the front desk. The hotel staff often had to calm frustrated guests who were rushing to the airport and were aggravated that they were getting charged for items they had not purchased.

Identifying the Source of the Problem

Larraine Scharadin, Milo Scharadin's niece, had recently been appointed to run the San Antonio hotel. A recent business school graduate, Larraine had grown up in the hotel business. She was poised and confident, and understood the importance of high quality for the hotel. As soon as she became aware of the billing problem, she immediately called a staff meeting to uncover the source of the problem.

During the staff meeting discussion quickly turned to problems with the new computer system and software that had been put in place. Tim Coleman, head of MIS, defended the system stating that the system was sound and the problems were exaggerated. Tim claimed that a few hotel guests made an issue of a few random problems. Scott Schultz, head of operations was not so sure. Scott said that he noticed that the number of complaints seem to have significantly in-

creased since the new system was installed. He said that he had asked his team to perform an audit of 50 random bills per day over the past 30 days. Scott showed the following numbers to Larraine, Tim, and the other staff members.

Day	Number of Incorrect Bills	Day	Number of Incorrect Bills	Day	Number of Incorrect Bills
1	2	11	1	21	3
2	2	12	2	22	3
3	1	13	3	23	3
4	2	14	3	24	4
5	2	15	2	25	5
6	3	16	3	26	5
7	2	17	2	27	6
8	2	18	2	28	5
9	1	19	1	29	5
10	2	20	3	30	5

Everyone looked at the data that had been presented. Then Tim exclaimed: "Notice that the number of errors increases in the last third of the month. The computer system had been in place for the entire month so that can't be the problem. Scott, it is probably the new employees you have on staff that are not entering the data properly." Scott quickly retaliated: "The employees are trained properly! Everyone knows the problem is the computer system!"

The argument between Tim and Scott become heated and Larraine decided to step in. She said, "Scott, I think it is best if you perform some statistical analysis of that data and send us your findings. You know that we want a high quality standard. We can't be Motorola with six-sigma quality, but let's try for three-sigma. Would you develop some control charts with the data and let us know if you think the process is in control?"

Case Questions:

1. Set up three-sigma control limits with the given data.
2. Is the process in control? Why?
3. Based on your analysis do you think the problem is the new computer system or something else?
4. What advice would you give to Larraine based on the information that you have?

INTERACTIVE LEARNING

Enhance and test your knowledge of Chapter 6 using the interactive CD.

1. **Spreadsheets** *Solved Problems 4, 5, and 6*

   Visit our dynamic Web site, www.wiley.com/college/reid, for more cases, web links, and additional information.

2. **Company Tour**
   Rickenbacker International Corporation
   Genesis Technologies, Inc.
   Canadian Springs Water Company

3. **Additional Web Resources**
   American Society for Quality, www.asqc.org
   Australian Quality Council, www.aqc.org.au

4. **Virtual Company Consulting Case**

5. **INTERNET CHALLENGE** *Safe-Air*

To gain business experience, you have volunteered to work at Safe-Air, a nonprofit agency that monitors airline safety records and customer service. Your first assignment is to compare three airlines based on their on-time arrivals and departures. Your manager has asked you to get your information from the Internet. Select any three airlines. For an entire week check the daily arrival and departure schedules of the three airlines from your city or closest airport. Remember that it is important to compare the arrivals and departures from the same location and during the same time period to account for factors such as the weather. Record the data that you collect for each airline. Then decide which types of statistical quality control tools you are going to use to evaluate the airlines' performance. Based on your findings, draw a conclusion regarding the on-time arrivals and departures of each of the airlines. Which is best and which is worst? Are there large differences in performance among the airlines? Also describe the statistical quality control tools you have decided to use to monitor performance. If you have chosen to use more than one tool, are you finding the tools equally useful or is one better at capturing differences in performance? Finally, based on what you have learned so far, how would you perform this analysis differently in the future?

BIBLIOGRAPHY

Duncan, A. J. *Quality Control and Industrial Statistics*, 5th ed., Homewood, Ill.: Irwin, 1986.

Evans, James R., and William M. Lindsay. *The Management and Control of Quality*, 4th ed. Cincinnati: South-Western, 1999.

Feigenbaum, A. V. *Total Quality Control*. New York: McGraw-Hill, 1991.

Grant, E. L., and R. S. Leavenworth. *Statistical Quality Control*, 6th ed. New York: McGraw-Hill, 1998.

Hoyer, R. W., and C. E. Wayne. "A Graphical Exploration of SPC, Part 1," *Quality Progress*, 29, no. 5 (May 1996), 65–73.

Juran, J. M., and F. M. Gryna. *Quality Planning and Analysis*, 2nd ed. New York: McGraw-Hill, 1980.

Wadsworth, H. M., K. S. Stephens, and A. B. Godfrey. *Modern Methods for Quality Control and Improvement*. New York: Wiley, 1986.

Just-in-Time Systems

Before studying this chapter you should know or, if necessary, review

1. JIT as a trend in OM, Chapter 1, page 13.
2. JIT as a competitive priority, Chapter 2, pages 30–31.
3. Total quality management concepts, Chapter 5, pages 111–114.

LEARNING OBJECTIVES

After studying this chapter you should be able to

1. Explain the core beliefs of the just-in-time (JIT) philosophy.

2. Describe the meaning of waste in JIT.

3. Explain the differences between "push" and "pull" production systems.

4. Explain the key elements of JIT manufacturing.

5. Explain the elements of total quality management (TQM) and their role in JIT.

6. Describe the role of people in JIT and why respect for people is so important.

7. Understand the impact of JIT on service and manufacturing organizations.

8. Understand the impact of JIT on all functional areas of the company.

CHAPTER OUTLINE

How many times have you looked frantically for a school paper or notebook, only to find it much later in the most unexpected place? Have you ever wasted time looking for a personal item—say, a particular shirt or shoes, or maybe a bill you needed to pay—and wondered how much easier life would be if everything was in its place? Have you ever purchased extra amounts of an item, maybe paper towels or laundry detergent, and then found that they were taking up space and getting in the way? Wouldn't life be much simpler if you could somehow receive the items that you need exactly when you need them, without having to keep extra quantities in storage?

We have all experienced these situations. They illustrate the problem of waste: wasted time looking for things we misplaced, wasted space and cost of keeping extra items, and wasted energy because of frustration of not finding things when we need them. These are the types of problems that just-in-time systems (JIT) seek to eliminate.

▶ **Waste**
Anything that does not add value.

▶ **A simplistic view of JIT**
Getting the right quantity of goods at the right place at the right time.

▶ **A broad view of JIT**
A philosophy that encompasses the entire organization.

The term **just-in-time (JIT)** in the simplest form means getting the right quantity of goods at the right place and the right time. The goods arrive just-in time, which is where the term JIT comes from. Although many people think that JIT is an inventory reduction program or another type of manufacturing process, it is far more than that. JIT is an all-encompassing philosophy that is founded on the concept of eliminating waste. The word *waste* might make you think of garbage, or paper, or inventory. But JIT considers **waste** anything that does not add value—*anything*.

JIT has contributed to the success of many organizations and is used by companies worldwide. The benefits that can be attained through JIT are so impressive that JIT has become a standard of operations in many industries, including the auto and computer industries. However, JIT is applicable to service organizations as well as to manufacturing, and can even be used in your everyday life. JIT is not about any one factor, such as quality or inventory or efficiency. It is an entirely different way of looking at things. As we will see, JIT is a philosophy that overrides all aspects of the organization, from administrative issues to manufacturing, worker management, supplier management, and even housekeeping. It has contributed to the great success of companies like General Motors and Honda, and it can even contribute to success in your own life.

■ THE PHILOSOPHY OF JIT

The philosophy of JIT originated in Japan. After World War II the Japanese set themselves the goal of strengthening their industrial base, which included full employment and a healthy trade balance. Just-in-time (JIT) developed out of the nation's need to survive after the devastation caused by the war. Although many authors say that the origins of JIT can be traced back to the 1900s, no one can argue that the philosophy

Boeing production line

gained worldwide prominence in the 1970s. It was developed at the Toyota Motor Company and the person most often credited with its development is Taiichi Ohno, a vice president of the company. JIT helped propel Toyota into a leadership position in the areas of quality and delivery. Since then, JIT has been widely adopted in all types of industries and has been credited with impressive benefits, including significant reductions in operating costs, improved quality, and increased customer responsiveness. Companies such as Honda, General Motors, GE, Ford, Boeing, Hewlett-Packard, and IBM are among those that have made JIT part of their operations.

The central belief of the JIT philosophy is *elimination of waste,* but there are other beliefs that help define this philosophy. These include a **broad view of operations, simplicity, continuous improvement, visibility,** and **flexibility.** Next we look more closely at each of these beliefs.

▶ Beliefs that define the JIT philosophy: broad view of operations, simplicity, continuous improvement, visibility, and flexibility.

Eliminate Waste

The underlying premise of JIT is that all waste must be eliminated. Many think that the roots of the philosophy can be traced to the Japanese environment, which lacks space and natural resources. Because of this, the Japanese have been forced to learn to use all their resources very efficiently, and waste of any kind is not tolerated. In JIT *waste* is anything that does not add value. There are many types of waste. Waste can be material, such as excess inventory to protect against uncertain deliveries by suppliers or poor quality. Waste can be equipment that is used as a backup because regular equipment is not maintained properly. Other types of waste include time, energy, space, or human activity that does not contribute to the value of the product or service being produced.

▶ Types of wastes: material, energy, time, and space.

The concept of waste addresses every aspect of the organization and has a far-reaching impact. For example, waste can be found in the production process itself, and JIT requires perfect synchronization in order to eliminate waiting and excess stock. Waste is also found in improper layout that necessitates the transportation of goods from one part of the facility to another. JIT requires a streamlined layout design so that resources are in close proximity to one another and material handling is kept to a minimum. Also, JIT requires compact layouts and increased visibility so that everyone can see what everyone else is doing. Waste can also take the form of poor quality, as scrap and rework cost money and add no value. Total quality management (TQM) programs thus are an integral part of JIT. Waste is also found in unnecessary motion, and JIT requires studying processes to eliminate unnecessary steps.

A Broad View of Operations

▶ In JIT all employees have a broad view of the operation.

Part of the philosophy of JIT is that everyone in the organization should have a broad view of the organization and work toward the same goal, which is serving the customer. In traditional organizations it is very easy for employees to focus exclusively on their own jobs and have a narrow view of the organization that includes only their assigned tasks. Companies whose employees have a narrow view become production-oriented, forgetting that individual tasks and procedures are important only if they meet the overall goals of the company. One example is an employee who will not help a customer with a problem, saying "it's not my job." This might occur at a grocery store when a customer asks for the location of an item from an employee who is "only responsible for stocking shelves." A broad view of operations involves understanding that all employees are ultimately responsible for serving the customer.

Simplicity

▶ JIT focuses on simple solutions to problems.

JIT is built on **simplicity**—the simpler the better. JIT encourages employees to think about problems and come up with simple solutions. Although this may seem easy and crude, it is actually quite difficult. It is often tempting to solve an organizational problem using a complex and perhaps expensive method. It is far more difficult to think of a simple solution that goes directly to the root of the problem. The value of simple solutions is demonstrated by a company whose delivery truck was lodged in a passageway because it was too high to pass through. Many costly and complex solutions were being considered, such as getting a smaller truck or expanding the height of the doorway. After a bit of thought, an employee came up with a simple solution: Reduce the air in the tires to bring down the height of the truck. The solution worked.

Continuous Improvement

▶ Continuous improvement is the cornerstone of JIT.

A major aspect of the JIT philosophy is an emphasis on quality. **Continuous improvement** in every aspect of the operation is a cornerstone of this philosophy. Continuous improvement applies to everything from reducing costs to improving quality, to eliminating waste.

To understand the full impact of continuous improvement, try answering this question: When has JIT been implemented fully? The answer: Never. The reason is that an organization is never perfect and can always be improved in some way.

Visibility

▶ Problems must be visible to be identified and solved.

Part of the JIT philosophy is to make all waste **visible**. Waste can be eliminated only when it is seen and identified. Also, if we see waste we can come up with simple solutions to eliminate it. When waste is hidden we forget about it, which creates problems.

Think about the closets in your home. Because the closet doors are closed, we often forget the clutter and junk we have inside. Now imagine that the closet doors were open and the inside was visible to us and everyone else. Certainly it would remind us that we need to eliminate the clutter.

JIT facilities are open and clean, with plenty of floor space. There is no clutter, and everyone can see what everyone else is doing. No one can hide extra inventory in a corner of his or her office or take a short nap in the afternoon. Also, part of the JIT philosophy is that a cluttered environment creates confusion and disrespect toward the workplace. By contrast, a clean and orderly environment creates calm and clear thoughts. Just because space is available, it should not automatically be filled. Visibility allows us to readily see waste. We can then eliminate it.

Flexibility

Remember that JIT was based on the need for survival, and survival means being **flexible** in order to adapt to changes in the environment. A company can be flexible in many ways. First, flexibility can mean being able to make changes in the volume of a product produced. JIT accomplishes this by keeping the costs of facilities, equipment, and operations at such a low level that breaking even typically is not a problem.

▶ **Flexibility** means a company can quickly adapt to the changing needs of its customers.

A second way in which a company can be flexible is by being able to produce a wide variety of products. Although this is difficult to achieve, JIT systems are designed to be able to produce different product models with different features, through a manufacturing process that can easily switch from one product type to another, by flexible workers who can perform many different tasks. Part of the JIT philosophy is to design operations that are highly efficient but flexible in order to accommodate changing customer demands.

ELEMENTS OF JIT ◼

Now that you understand the core beliefs that define the philosophy of JIT, let's look at the major elements that make up a JIT system. Three basic elements work together to complete a JIT system: *just-in-time manufacturing, total quality management,* and *respect for people.* These are shown in Figure 7-1 as overlapping circles. Often, it is assumed that JIT refers only to just-in-time manufacturing. However, this is only one element of JIT. Each of the three elements is dependent on the others to create a true JIT system.

▶ Three elements of a JIT system are just-in-time manufacturing, total quality management, and respect for people.

Just-in-Time Manufacturing

JIT is a philosophy based on elimination of waste. Another way to view JIT is to think of it as a philosophy of *value-added manufacturing.* By focusing on value-added processes, JIT is able to achieve high-volume production of high-quality, low-cost products while meeting precise customer needs. **Just-in-time manufacturing** is the element of JIT that focuses directly on the production system to make this possible. Many aspects of JIT manufacturing combine to provide a performance advantage. Later in the chapter we will look at some aspects of JIT manufacturing in more detail. First, let's take an overall view.

The manufacturing process in JIT starts with the final assembly schedule, often called the *master production schedule,* a statement of which products and quantities will be made in specific time periods. The master production schedule is usually fixed

Figure 7-1

The Three Elements of JIT

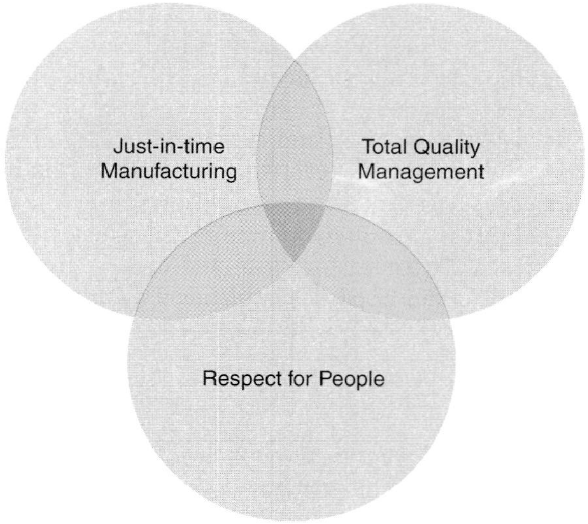

for a few months into the future to allow all work centers and suppliers to plan their schedule. For the current month, the schedule is "leveled," or developed so that the same amount of each product is produced in the same order every day. Note that with this arrangement there is repetition in the schedule from day to day, which places a constant demand on suppliers and work centers. Also, some quantity of every item is produced every day in accordance with what is needed. This is very different from traditional operations, which typically produce a large quantity of one product on one day. Since this quantity is usually more than what is immediately needed, the goods are stored in inventory. On a second day a large quantity of another product is produced and it too is stored in inventory, resulting in high inventory costs.

JIT relies on a coordination system that withdraws parts from a previous work center and moves them to the next. The system typically relies on cards, called *kanban,* to *pull* the needed products through the production system. For this reason, JIT is often referred to as a *pull system*. The kanban specifies what is needed. There is no excess production because the only products and quantities produced are those specified by the kanban. Traditional manufacturing systems, in contrast, are *push* systems: They push products through the production system by producing an amount that has been set by a forecast of future demand. This type of production results in a higher level of inventory, which is stored for future consumption. Later in the chapter we will look in detail at how the kanban system works.

The reason traditional systems produce large quantities of one type of product before switching to production of another is high **setup cost**. This is the cost incurred when equipment is set up for a new production run. Setup includes activities such as recalibrating and cleaning equipment, changing blades, and readjusting equipment settings. Because setup costs are high in traditional systems, the objective is to produce as many units of a product as possible before having to incur the setup cost again. Of course, that means incurring a high inventory cost because of the extra goods that are kept in storage. JIT systems have been very efficient at reducing setup costs, which is a key to the success of JIT manufacturing. Setup times have been reduced from hours to mere seconds and the goal is to reduce them to zero. Low setup times mean that small lot sizes of products can be produced as needed and produc-

▶ **Setup cost**
Cost incurred when setting up equipment for a production run.

tion lead times will be shorter. The ultimate goal of JIT is to produce products in a lot size of one.

A major aspect of JIT manufacturing is its view of inventory. JIT manufacturing views inventory as a waste that needs to be eliminated. According to JIT, inventory is carried to cover up a wide variety of problems such as poor quality, slow delivery, inefficiency, lack of coordination, and demand uncertainty. Inventory costs money and provides no value. Inventory also hurts the organization in another way: It does not allow us to see problems. According to JIT, by eliminating inventory we can clearly identify problems and work to eliminate them. An analogy that is often used to describe JIT's view of inventory is that of a stream, as shown in Figure 7-2. The rocks in the stream represent problems. The water in the stream covers the rocks and we cannot see what they are. By reducing the amount of water in the stream, we can finally identify the problems. However, identifying the problems is not enough—we have to solve them.

In sum, JIT manufacturing is an efficiently coordinated production system that makes it possible to deliver the right quantities of products to the place they are needed just in time.

Total Quality Management

The second major element of JIT is *total quality management,* which is integrated into all functions and levels of the organization. The foundation of JIT is to produce the exact product that the customer wants. Quality is defined by the customer, and an effort is made by the whole company to meet the customer's expectations.

Quality is an integral part of the organization; it permeates every activity and function. The benefits of JIT cannot occur if the company is not working toward eliminating scrap and rework. Traditional quality control systems use the concept of *acceptable quality level (AQL)* to indicate the acceptable number of defective parts. In JIT there is no such measure—no level of defects other than zero is acceptable.

Poor quality is considered a waste in JIT. Quality defects lead to scrap, rework, servicing returned parts, and customer dissatisfaction. Quality defects cost money and can lead to lost customers. In JIT the entire organization is responsible for quality. Rather than hide poor quality or blame it on others, it is everyone's goal to uncover and correct quality problems.

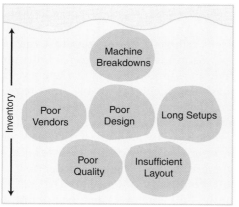

(a) Inventory Hides Problems

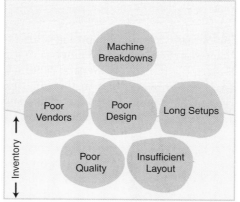

(b) Reducing Inventory Exposes Problems

Figure 7-2

Inventory hides problems.

▶ **Quality at the source**
A concept of uncovering the root cause of a quality problem.

The concept of **quality at the source** is part of JIT. The objective is not only to identify a quality problem but to uncover its root cause. Simply identifying and removing a defective product does not solve the problem. If the cause of the problem is not identified, the problem will keep repeating itself. For example, a quality control check in a bakery might reveal that pies are overcooked and burned. Quality at the source tells us to identify the cause of the problem such as an incorrect temperature setting or too long a baking time. Simply removing the burned pies does not eliminate the cause of the problem; overcooking will continue to occur.

The concept of continuous improvement is embedded in quality, which means that the company must continuously and actively work to improve. In JIT continuous improvement governs everything, from reducing the number of defects to lowering setup costs and lot sizes. For example, when implementing a JIT program we cannot expect to eliminate inventories immediately. Continuous improvement tells us that we must do it gradually, slowly identifying and solving problems and then reducing inventory appropriately. However, continuous improvement goes beyond JIT manufacturing. It includes improvement of worker skills, supplier quality and relationships, and even the performance of management.

Respect for People

The third element of JIT is *respect for people*. Often the study of JIT focuses exclusively on JIT manufacturing. However, the involvement of workers is central to the JIT philosophy. None of the improvements developed by JIT could be possible without respect for people. JIT requires total organizational reform and participation by everyone in the company. Everyone is equally important and equally involved. In a JIT system all functions of the company must work together to meet customer needs. Managers are not isolated in an administrative wing but spend time on the production floor.

Employees in JIT organizations are expected to be active participants in meeting customer needs, from developing improvements in the production process to making sure quality standards are met at every level. JIT also relies on workers to perform multiple tasks and to work in teams, including management, labor, staff, and even suppliers.

JIT considers people to be a company's most precious resource. The JIT philosophy believes in treating all employees with respect, providing job security, and offering significant rewards for well-performed tasks. Respect for people extends to suppliers. JIT believes in developing long-term relationships with suppliers in a partnership format.

LINKS TO PRACTICE
Saturn Corporation
www.Saturn.com

The Saturn Corporation provides an excellent example of the success that can be achieved by respecting and empowering people. Saturn is a highly successful division of General Motors Corporation, producing and marketing vehicles in the small car market segment. Saturn has been recognized for its quality and productivity. It has also become a model for successful use of self-managed teams.

Self-managed teams are groups of workers that have no supervisors, inspectors, time clocks, or union stewards. Each team is responsible for every aspect of their business, such as productivity, quality, cost, production, and people. The crux of self-managed teams is respect for employees and their ability to be in charge of their own work. At Saturn, people are empowered to make decisions, and everyone is involved in the decision making process. Workers are motivated through a system that directly rewards them for achieving their goals. Saturn views their workforce as a long-term asset, providing ongoing training, encouraging a sense of security and organizational belonging. Saturn demonstrates the success that can be attained when an organization respects its people.

Before You Go On

You should know that JIT is an all-encompassing philosophy that affects every level and function of the organization. The beliefs that make up the JIT philosophy include the following: (1) *Elimination of waste*, (2) *a broad view of operations*, (3) *simplicity*, (4) *continuous improvement*, (5) *visibility*, and (6) *flexibility*. The philosophy of JIT is founded on these beliefs, and they govern all aspects of the organization. These beliefs are embodied in three specific elements: (1) JIT manufacturing, (2) total quality management, and (3) respect for people. In the next section we look at specific features of each of these elements.

JUST-IN-TIME MANUFACTURING ◼

The Pull System

Traditional manufacturing operations are push-type systems. They are based on the assumption that it is better to anticipate future production requirements and plan for them. Traditional systems produce in advance in order to have products in place when demand occurs. Products are pushed through the system and are stored in anticipation of demand, which often results in overproduction because anticipated demand may not materialize. Also, there are costs associated with having inventories of products sitting in storage and waiting for consumption.

As noted earlier, JIT uses a **pull system** rather than a push system to move products through the facility. Communication in JIT starts either with the last workstation in the production line or with the customer, and works backward through the system. Each station requests the precise amount of products that is needed from the previous workstation. If products are not requested, they are not produced. In this manner no excess inventory is generated.

▶ JIT is based on a "pull" system rather than a "push" system.

To see the difference between a push and a pull system, suppose that you have decided to have a backyard cookout for your friends. You have invited 20 people and are anticipating that each one will eat at least one hamburger and one hot dog. When your friends arrive, you decide to cook all the meat as quickly as you can process it on your grill, given your anticipation of demand for food. Your goal is to make it available for your guests. At the end of the party, however, you find that you are left with some hamburgers and quite a few hot dogs. Some people didn't want both a hamburger and a hot dog, some people didn't like one or the other, and some were vegetarian and didn't want either one. As a result, after the party you are left with some cold, dried-out meat. This is the problem with a push system that produces large quantities in anticipation of demand that may or may not materialize.

Another way you could handle the cookout would be to grill a smaller quantity of meat—say, three hamburgers and three hot dogs, an amount that will fit on a serving tray. When the serving tray becomes empty you could fill it with the meat on the grill, again enough to fill the tray. When the meat that was on the grill is removed, you can put fresh meat on the grill, again in a small quantity. No additional meat is placed on the grill until the cooked meat on the grill is removed. In this example, consumption of the food is pulling the meat through the system in small quantities. By "producing" the food in this manner you will not end up with large amounts of "inventory" at the end of the cookout.

Kanban Production

▶ **Kanban**
A card that specifies the exact quantity of product that needs to be produced.

You can see that for the pull system to work there must be good communication between the work centers. This communication is made possible by the use of a device called a **kanban card;** *kanban* means "signal" or "card" in Japanese. Most often a kanban card has information on it such as the product name, the part number, and the quantity that needs to be produced. The kanban is attached to a container. When workers need products from a preceding workstation, they pass the kanban and the empty container to that station. The kanban authorizes the worker at the preceding station to produce the amount of goods specified on the kanban. In effect, the kanban is a production authorization record. In our cookout example, the tray size served the purpose of the container. Now imagine that you had a card attached to the tray that specified three hamburgers and three hot dogs, and that you could not produce any more or less than that amount. This procedure is similar to the way a kanban card works.

To make the system work smoothly and control the movement of empty and full containers, there are actually two types of kanban cards: *production cards* that authorize production and *withdrawal cards* that authorize withdrawal of materials. Figure 7-3 shows a diagram of how a pull system with two kanban cards works, with a description.

When a container becomes empty at a station (station B) and a worker needs more parts, the worker takes the empty container and a withdrawal kanban to the preceding workstation (station A). The worker then removes a production card from a full container of parts and replaces it with the withdrawal card authorizing the withdrawal of the parts. The production card is then placed on a kanban receiving post at

Figure 7-3

The pull system with two kanban cards

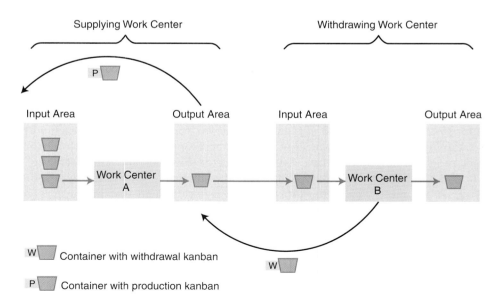

workstation B, signaling an authorization for production of another container of parts. The empty container is also left at work center B to be filled.

Now that the worker has left the empty container and production card at workstation B, he or she takes the full container of parts and the withdrawal kanban and goes back to station A. When this container becomes empty, the withdrawal kanban and the empty container go back to station B and the cycle is repeated.

When this process is used, the amount produced at any one time is the amount in one container. Production cannot take place unless a container is empty and a production card has authorized production. A full container cannot be withdrawn unless a withdrawal kanban authorizes it. It is the kanban cards that coordinate the pull production system. Without kanbans, the withdrawal and production of materials cannot take place. Another advantage of the kanban is that it is *visual*. Kanban cards and containers are all placed in clearly visible areas for everyone to see.

The system of kanbans can also be used to coordinate delivery of goods by suppliers. The suppliers bring the filled containers to the point of usage in the factory and at the same time pick up an empty container with a kanban to be filled later. Since a manufacturer may have multiple suppliers, "mailboxes" can be set up at the factory for each supplier. The suppliers can check their "mailboxes" to pick up their orders. Kanbans are usually made of plastic or metal, but there are also bar-coded kanbans and electronic kanbans that further ease communication with suppliers.

There are as many kanban cards in the system as there are containers. If there are too many kanbans in the production system, there may be too much production and too much inventory. On the other hand, if there are not enough kanbans the system may not be producing quickly enough. Sometimes the production manager may decide to add to or subtract from the number of kanbans to bring the system into balance. Remember, however, that the goal is to continually improve the efficiency of the system. This means striving to reduce the number of kanbans and the amount of inventory in the system.

The number of kanbans and, therefore, the number of containers in the system is a very important decision. The formula to compute the number of kanbans needed to control the production of a particular product is as follows:

$$N = \frac{DT}{C}$$

where : N = total number of kanbans or containers (one card per container)
D = demand rate at a using workstation
T = the time it takes to receive an order from the previous workstation (also called the lead time)
C = size of container.

Problem-Solving Tip: the demand (D) and lead time (T) have to be in the same time units. You can see from this equation that the number of containers needed at a workstation is dependent on three things: the demand rate, the size of the container, and the lead time. To control the amount of inventory, the size of containers used is typically much smaller than the demand. For example, the containers used generally do not hold more than 10% of the daily demand. The number of kanbans in the system can be reduced as efficiency improves.

Let's look at an example to see how this would work.

■ **Example 7.1 Computing the Number of Kanbans**

Jordan Tucker works for a production facility that makes aspirin. His job is to fill the bottles of aspirin, and he is expected to process 200 bottles of aspirin an hour. The facility where Jordan works uses a kanban production system in which each container holds 25 bottles. It takes 30 minutes for Jordan to receive the bottles he needs from the previous workstation. How many kanbans are needed for the filling process?

Solution:

$$D = 200 \text{ bottles per hour}$$

$$T = 30 \text{ minutes} = \tfrac{1}{2} \text{ hour}$$

$$C = 25 \text{ bottles per container}$$

$$N = \frac{DT}{C}$$

$$= \frac{(200 \text{ bottles/hour})(\tfrac{1}{2} \text{ hour})}{25 \text{ bottles}} = 4 \text{ kanbans and containers}$$

Small Lot Sizes and Quick Setups

▶ **Small-lot production**
The ability to produce small quantities of products.

A principal way of eliminating inventory and excess processing while increasing flexibility is through **small-lot production,** which means that the amount of products produced at any one time is small—say, 10 versus 1000. This allows the manufacturer to produce many lots of different types of products. It also shortens the *manufacturing lead time,* the actual time it takes to produce a product, since it takes less time to produce 10 units than to produce 1000. Shorter lead time means that customers receives the specific products they want faster. The ultimate goal of JIT is to be able to economically produce one item at a time as the customer wants it.

Small-lot production gives a company a tremendous amount of flexibility and allows it to respond to customer demands more quickly. However, to be able to achieve small-lot production companies have to reduce setup time. Recall that setup time is the time it takes to set up equipment for a production run. This includes cleaning and recalibrating equipment, changing blades and other tools, and all other activities necessary to switch production from one product to another.

To see the impact of setup time, let's pretend that we are a producer of ice cream and that we make two different flavors—say, chocolate and vanilla—on the same production line. The system works by first producing a certain amount of chocolate ice cream. The equipment is then cleaned and the machines are reset for the proper ingredients (this is setup time) in order to switch production to vanilla ice cream. A traditional manufacturing approach would be to produce as much chocolate ice cream as possible, since everything is already set up for this product. Then we would set up the machines for production of vanilla ice cream and make as much of it as possible before we have to clean the equipment again. The problem with this approach is that we end up producing extra amounts of ice cream. The extra ice cream is inventory. It costs money and requires storage space, and some of it will probably go to waste.

A more effective approach would be to lower the time it takes to change from production of one flavor of ice cream to another. Then we can produce only what we need and no more. We would not have the cost of extra inventory. This approach would also allow us to respond quickly to changes in demand. For example, if a customer needed extra chocolate ice cream, producing it would not be a problem. This has been the approach used by JIT. Many large manufacturers, such as General Motors, have been able to reduce setup times from many hours to only a few minutes, which has resulted in tremendous flexibility.

To produce economically in small lot sizes, JIT has found ways to reduce setup times. The goal is to achieve *single setups*, or setup times in single digits of minutes. There are a number of ways to achieve these low setup times. One approach is to separate setup into two components: *internal setups* and *external setups*. **Internal setups** require the machine to be stopped for the setup to be performed. **External setups** can be performed while the machine is still running. Almost all setups in traditional manufacturing systems were internal. With JIT, much of the setup process has been converted to external setups. This requires engineering ingenuity and cleverly designed fixtures and tools. In a number of companies the workers even practice the setup process and try to increase their speed.

▶ **Internal setup**
Requires the machine to be stopped in order to be performed.

▶ **External setup**
Can be performed while the machine is still running.

Uniform Plant Loading

Demand for a product can show sudden increases or decreases, which can mean disruptive changes in production schedules. These demand changes are typically magnified throughout the production line and the supply chain. They contribute to inefficiency and create waste. The JIT philosophy is to eliminate the problem by making adjustments as small as possible and setting a production plan that is frozen for the month. This is called **uniform plant loading** or "leveling" of the production schedule. The term *leveling* comes from the fact that the schedule is uniform or constant throughout the planning horizon.

To meet demand and keep inventories low, a "level" schedule is developed so that the same mix of products is made every day in small quantities. This is in contrast to traditional systems, which produce large quantities of one product on one day and of another product on the next day, causing large buildups of inventory. Table 7-1

▶ **Uniform plant loading**
A constant production plan for a facility with a given planning horizon.

Table 7-1: Contrasting Level versus Traditional Production

Weekly Production Requirements by Product:

A:	10 units/week
B:	20 units/week
C:	5 units/week
D:	5 units/week
E:	10 units/week

Traditional Production Plan

Monday	Tuesday	Wednesday	Thursday	Friday
A A A A A	B B B B B	B B B B B	D D D D D	E E E E E
A A A A A	B B B B B	B B B B B	C C C C C	E E E E E

JIT Production with Level Scheduling

Monday	Tuesday	Wednesday	Thursday	Friday
A A B B B	A A B B B	A A B B B	A A B B B	A A B B B
C D E E	C D E E	C D E E	C D E E	C D E E

shows how a level production system works in contrast to a traditional production system. In the table, a company produces five products: A, B, C, D, and E. The weekly production requirements for all products are met with both types of system. However, with the JIT system there is day-to-day repetition in the schedule, which prevents the company from having to carry large amounts of inventory and places predictable demands on all work centers and suppliers.

Flexible Resources

A key element of JIT is having flexible resources in order to meet customer demands and produce small lots. One aspect of flexibility is relying on general-purpose equipment, equipment capable of performing a number of different functions. For example, a general-purpose drilling machine may be able to drill holes in an engine block and also perform some milling and threading operations. This is very different from having specialized equipment that can perform only one task. General-purpose equipment provides flexibility of operations and eliminates waste of space, movement from one machine to another, and setup of other machines. You can see how this concept works in your own life. Isn't it easier to have one machine that is a printer, copier, and fax machine all in one, rather than have three different machines? With the press of a button you can print a copy and then fax it, rather than walk from one machine to the other, setting up each machine, not to mention the space requirements of three machines.

▶ **Multifunction workers** Capable of performing more than one job.

Another element of flexibility is the use of **multifunction workers**, who can perform more than one job—an essential aspect of JIT. To meet changing production requirements, workers in JIT are trained to operate and set up different machines. This provides flexibility in the schedule because workers can be moved around as needed. Also, workers in JIT are responsible for performing simple maintenance on their machines and are trained to perform quality control procedures. As we will see later in the chapter, workers in JIT have considerable responsibility and perform many duties. Their many abilities give a tremendous amount of flexibility to JIT.

The flexibility of workers and machines combine to produce great advantages. Note that the operating time of a machine is usually different from that of a worker, because there is a period of time while the machine is running and the worker has nothing to do. A multifunction worker can operate more than one machine at a time.

Facility Layout

Proper arrangement and layout of work centers and equipment is critical to JIT manufacturing. Physical proximity and easy access contribute to the efficiency of the production process. Because streamlined production is an important part of JIT, JIT relies heavily on dedicated assembly lines, which are dedicated to the production of a family of products.

▶ **Cell manufacturing** Placement of dissimilar machines and equipment together to produce a family of products with similar processing requirements.

JIT also relies on **cell manufacturing,** the placement of dissimilar machines and equipment together in order to produce a family of products with similar processing requirements. These machines create a small assembly line, and their grouping is usually called a cell. The machines in one grouping can be those needed to manufacture a set of parts belonging to the same family of products. The equipment in a work cell is usually arranged in a U shape, with the worker placed in the center of the U. This arrangement has a number of advantages. First, the use of cells provides production efficiency with the flexibility to produce a variety of different products. Second, the U shape allows workers to have easy reach and flexibility. No special material handling is needed because everything is within reach. Finally, worker satisfaction is higher because of the ability to perform a variety of tasks.

(a) Traditional Layout

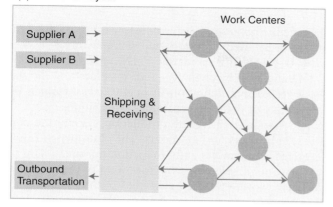

(b) JIT with Cell Manufacturing

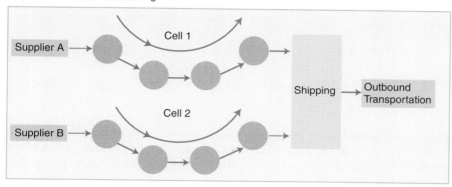

Figure 7-4

Traditional versus cell manufacturing

Each cell produces similar items, so, setup times within cells are low and lot sizes and inventories can be kept small. Figure 7-4 compares traditional production with cell manufacturing.

Companies such as Whirlpool, Xerox, Target Stores, and Saturn of General Motors have adopted JIT as a way of doing business. To achieve their goals, these companies need just-in-time deliveries. For this they use Ryder Integrated Logistics, a global and domestic provider of transportation and distribution management services, which offers just-in-time pickup and delivery of goods from suppliers. Ryder ensures that materials flow smoothly into assembly or manufacturing plants with deliveries properly sequenced. It uses a dedicated fleet of vehicles, onboard computers, and satellite/cellular communications, as well as a sophisticated distribution system that enables it to support multiple suppliers. Also, to reduce cycle time, Ryder uses bar code technology, EDI, and special software to enable the consolidation and distribution of goods in and out of facilities. All this adds up to an organization dedicated to meeting the challenge of JIT.

LINKS TO PRACTICE
Ryder Integrated Logistics
www.ryder.com

■ TOTAL QUALITY MANAGEMENT

Quality is a difficult term to define because it means different things to different people. A narrow viewpoint, typically used by traditional manufacturers, is to define quality as meeting specified target quality standards. This would mean producing a product within specified tolerances set by engineers and not exceeding the specified acceptable defect rate. However, today's definition of quality takes a much broader view: Quality is defined as meeting or exceeding customer expectations.

As customer needs and standards drive the production system, the company muse define quality as it is seen by users of the product. The customer's definition of quality then must be interpreted by engineers and production managers. This process is not always easy; customers are not always sure what they want or may not be able to articulate their needs effectively. However, once quality has been defined in measurable terms, it needs to be monitored on an ongoing basis. Targets for improvement need to be set and systematic methods for improvement developed. These methods include continual training of workers so they can identify and correct quality problems. Together, this process outlines a strategy for quality improvement in JIT, as shown in Table 7-2.

Note that the steps in Table 7-2 show an ongoing, dynamic process. Customers' quality definitions must be monitored continuously as customers' expectations and needs change over time.

Product versus Process

The costs of poor quality can be quite high when one includes product redesign, rework, scrap, servicing returned products, or even losing customers. All this represents waste. Phil Crosby, a leading quality "guru," pointed out that "quality is free." It is poor quality that is costly. For these reasons, JIT does not tolerate poor quality.

In JIT the quality of the product is distinguished from the quality of the process used to produce the product. The idea is that a faulty product is a result of a faulty process. We may be able to repair a faulty product, but if we do not correct the process we are not addressing the root cause of the problem and will continue to produce faulty products. Quality in JIT is centered on building quality into the process. A production process that is well within the set quality control limits should not produce a defective product.

Quality at the Source

The notion of *quality at the source* means that the root cause of quality problems needs to be identified. This could be a problem with the design, suppliers, the process, or any other source. We know that it is much easier and less costly to build quality into a process than to try to correct problems after they occur.

Table 7-2 Strategy for Quality Improvement
Step 1: Define quality as seen by the customer.
Step 2: Translate customer needs into measurable terms.
Step 3: Measure quality on an ongoing basis.
Step 4: Set improvement targets and deadlines.
Step 5: Develop a systematic method for improvement.

Quality problems can come from many sources. Some examples of sources of quality problems are the following:

Product design. In the design process, customer needs may be misunderstood and not incorporated into the product design.

Process design. Management and equipment problems may stem from the design of the production process. Operator error actually contributes to only about 15% of quality problems.

Suppliers. Quality problems caused by suppliers include low-quality materials and are often due to misunderstandings between manufacturer and supplier.

Monitoring quality is the responsibility of everyone in the organization. Workers are given the authority to stop the production line if quality problems are encountered; this is called **jidoka**. To perform jidoka, each worker can use a switch above his or her workstation to turn on a call light or stop production. The call lights are located above the workstations. A green light means that production is flowing normally; a yellow light is a signal for help; and a red light means that the line is stopped. When a red light goes on, all personnel rush to the troubled spot to determine what the problem is. In JIT environments stopping the line is not only allowed, but expected. At JIT facilities, if a certain amount of time has passed without a line stoppage, personnel become concerned that quality problems are passing undetected.

> ▶ **Jidoka**
> Authority given to workers to stop the production line if a quality problem is detected.

You can see that workers have much responsibility in a JIT system. Analyzing production problems is considered a serious business and is performed as part of the regular workday, not in spare time. For this reason, JIT systems usually operate with seven hours of production and one hour of problem solving and working with teams. Called *undercapacity scheduling*, it is necessary in order to leave ample time for problem-solving activities.

To help workers identify quality problems, JIT relies on visual signals. One such signal is kanban control. Other include color coding, bulletin boards, lights, process control charts, and other visual displays. For example, color-coding tools and bins helps workers know which tools belong in which bins. Color-coding different sections of the work area helps workers identify stocking points and different processing sections. Material handling routes are clearly marked in different colors. Instructional photographs located near equipment provide visual explanations of machine usage. Another type of visual signal is **poka-yoke**. The term means "foolproof," and refers to a device or mechanism that prevents defects from occurring. The device could be a clamp that can be placed only in a certain way or a lid that can be turned in only one direction.

> ▶ **Poka-yoke**
> Foolproof devices or mechanisms that prevent defects from occurring.

Preventive Maintenance

An important aspect of quality management in JIT is preventive maintenance. Not only do machines rarely break down at convenient times, but breakdowns are costly in terms of lost production, unmet deadlines, disruption of work schedules, and unhappy customers–all considered wastes in JIT. To avoid unexpected machine stoppages, a company invests in *preventive maintenance*, which is regular inspections and maintenance designed to keep machines operational. Although preventive maintenance is costly, the costs are significantly smaller than the cost of an unexpected machine breakdown. You know from your own experience how important preventive maintenance is, such as taking your car for a tune-up and oil change, or going to the dentist for regular cleaning and checkups. Neither is fun and both are costly, but we do these things because we know that the alternatives could be much costlier.

According to JIT, workers should perform routine preventive maintenance activities including cleaning, lubricating, recalibrating, and making other adjustments to equipment. These duties are viewed as part of the worker's job. JIT also places a great deal of importance on care of equipment, and in training workers to operate and maintain machines properly. Included are designing products so they can be easily produced on current machines and can be easily operated and maintained.

Work Environment

Another important element of quality management is the overall work environment. Order and simplicity are considered highly important. According to JIT, an orderly environment creates a calm, clear mind, whereas a disorganized environment creates disorganized thoughts. Also, an orderly environment encourages respect for the workplace. It is much easier to hide waste in a cluttered room. When there is plenty of empty space and everything is in its place, it is easy to see if something is out of order. When one enters a JIT facility the first thing one notices is that it is very clean and orderly, with ample space and no clutter. Keeping the facility clean is the workers' responsibility. Every worker is responsible for cleaning equipment and tools after using them and putting them back in their place. Everyone is responsible, so no one can blame anyone else if something is misplaced. All this creates a positive work environment, which is considered essential to the quality of work life and contributes to employee satisfaction.

■ RESPECT FOR PEOPLE

Respect for people is considered central to the JIT philosophy. Of all the issues discussed in this chapter, none departs more from traditional systems than the role of employees in a firm. According to JIT, *genuine* and *meaningful respect for employees* must exist for a company to get the best from its workers. Employees perform a great many functions in JIT, and for true JIT to exist they must be genuinely respected and appreciated. Their inputs must be valued, and they must feel secure. The key words here are *genuine* and *meaningful*. Achieving this state is sometimes difficult in environments with a history of adversarial relationships, particularly between labor and management. Managers cannot mandate genuine and meaningful respect. They cannot send out a memo on a Friday saying, "On Monday there will be genuine and meaningful respect for people!" This is something that requires a complete change in organizational culture. Often it takes much effort and time.

JIT organizations rely on all employees to work together, including management and labor. The organizational hierarchy is generally flatter in JIT than in traditional organizations, and organizational layers are not strictly defined. Great responsibility and autonomy is given to ordinary workers. All levels of employees often work in teams, and in many JIT organizations all dress the same way regardless of level, which helps break down traditional barriers and makes it easier for people to work together. In this section we look at some specific issues that relate to respect for people in JIT.

The Role of Production Employees

In traditional systems, production employees often perform their jobs in an automatic fashion. In JIT, the role of production employees is just the opposite: Workers are actively engaged in pursuing the goals of the company. JIT relies on *cross-functional worker skills*, meaning the ability of workers to perform many different tasks on many different machines. Part of worker's duties is to be actively engaged in improving the production process, monitoring quality, and correcting quality problems. Continuous improvement relies heavily on the knowledge and skills of the workers closest to the operation. They are the ones best suited to make improvements in their jobs.

Production workers are required to continually check and monitor the quality of the production process. This includes inspecting their own work as well as the materials received from previous operations. This is necessary in order to detect quality problems before a defective part can proceed to additional processing. For this system to succeed, workers need to have a very different attitude toward poor quality than in traditional systems. In JIT, discovering quality problems is a goal, not something that should be covered up or blamed on someone else. As we have learned, quality at the source means that all employees are responsible for getting to the root cause of quality problems.

Another part of a worker's responsibility is recording data, such as the number of setups completed, the number of units produced, the number of defects and scrap, quality process control data, equipment malfunctions, and hours worked. It is up to the worker to understand how to use the data. One way to motivate workers is to use visible displays of data, such as performance measures, on a flip chart or chalk board near each workstation. Information such as quality problems or stoppages can be recorded on the chart for everyone to see.

However, merely recording data is not enough. Record keeping and posting results also serve to remind workers that they need to act on the information. The real task of production employees is to search for causes of problems in quality and production. Time needs to be set aside at the end of a shift for data analysis. Once data have been analyzed, problem-solving activities usually take place, using the team approach in group meetings. When workers become used to their new level of responsibility and respect, they develop the initiative to solve many problems on their own. The key in problem solving is to give workers the authority and incentive to solve problems rather than view problem solving as someone else's responsibility.

Participation by all employees is vital to the success of JIT. For this reason, JIT uses a style of management called *bottom-round management*, which means consensus management by committees or teams. When a decision needs to be made, it is discussed at all levels, starting at the bottom, so that everyone in the company contributes to the decision. This decision-making process is very slow, but it achieves consensus among all involved. In JIT, top management is usually concerned with strategic issues and leaves other decisions to employees.

Because everyone needs to work together, teams are an integral part of JIT. One of the most popular types of teams is the **quality circles**. Quality circles are groups of about 5 to 12 employees who volunteer to solve quality problems in their area. Although participation is usually voluntary, the meetings take place during regular work hours. Quality circles usually meet weekly and attempt to develop solutions to problems and share them with management. Usually these work groups are lead by a supervisor or a production employee and are made up of employees from the particular areas involved.

▶ **Quality circles**
Small teams of employees that volunteer to solve quality problems.

You can see that in JIT the role of production employees is very different from their role in traditional organizations. Employees have much more responsibility and autonomy. Some of the key elements of the role of production employees in JIT are summarized in Table 7-3.

Table 7–3 Role of Production Employees in JIT
◆ Workers have cross-functional skills.
◆ Workers are actively engaged in solving production and quality problems.
◆ Workers are empowered to make production and quality decisions.
◆ Quality is everyone's responsibility.
◆ Workers are responsible for recording and visually displaying performance data.
◆ Workers work in teams to solve problems.
◆ Decisions are made through bottom-round management.
◆ Workers are responsible for preventive maintenance.

Lifetime Employment

Japanese companies have traditionally provided lifetime employment for most of their permanent employees. Employees must feel secure if they are to work in teams, feel free to say what they think, and act on their ideas. Today lifetime employment comprises a relatively small percentage of the total workforce. Even though lifetime employment is rarely possible, a company must do certain things to reduce employee insecurity and encourage trust and openness. One answer is to commit to a policy of making no layoffs as a result of productivity improvements. This helps alleviate fears that productivity improvements made by employees will result in job loss.

Most JIT facilities have company unions that work to build cooperative relationships between management and labor. It is understood that if the company performs well, the workers will share in the rewards through bonuses. This policy encourages workers to work harder.

The Role of Management

Just as the role of production employees is different under JIT, so is the role of management. Actually, it can often be difficult for management to truly accept the new role of production employees as being responsible for duties that traditionally were performed exclusively by management. However, in successful JIT environments managers realize that all employees are on the same team and that a higher level of worker responsibility means more success for the firm as a whole.

A team of employees working to solve a problem

The role of management is to create the cultural change necessary for JIT to succeed. This is one of the most difficult tasks of JIT. It involves creating an organizational culture that provides an atmosphere of close cooperation and mutual trust. Remember that JIT relies on ordinary workers to independently solve production problems and take on many tasks. To be able to do this, employees must be problem solvers and be empowered to take action based on their ideas. Workers must feel secure in their jobs and know that they will not be reprimanded or lose their jobs for being proactive. Workers must also feel comfortable enough to discuss their ideas openly. It is up to management to develop an incentive system for employees that rewards this type of behavior.

In the JIT environment, the role of managers becomes more of a supporting function. Managers are seen as facilitators and coaches rather than "bosses." Their job is to help develop the capabilities of employees, to teach, make corrections, help individuals develop their skills, and serve as motivators. They assist with team work and problem solving. Managers are also responsible for providing motivation and necessary recognition to employees. Their job also includes sharing information such as profitability and performance results, as well as making sure ample time is scheduled for all the activities employees must perform. Remember that the additional activities, such as quality control charting, maintenance, and working in teams, are not done during "free time" but during regular work hours.

The role of management is highly important for JIT to succeed. The role of management in JIT is summarized in Table 7-4.

Supplier Relationships

JIT's respect for people also extends to suppliers. With JIT a company respects suppliers and focuses on building long-term supplier relationships. The traditional approach of competitive bidding and buying parts from the cheapest supplier runs counter to the JIT philosophy. JIT companies understand that they are in a partnership with their suppliers, who are viewed as the *external factory*. The number of suppliers is typically much smaller than in traditional systems, and the goal is to shift to **single-source suppliers**, suppliers that provide an entire family of parts for one manufacturer

The benefits of long-term relationship with a small number of suppliers are many. Together the supplier and manufacturer focus on improving process quality controls. There are fewer contacts by buyers, and there is a focused effort to develop a personal relationship. There is also greater accountability for quality, delivery, or service problems. Having few suppliers makes it easier to develop stable and repetitive delivery schedules and eliminate paperwork.

With a long-term relationship a supplier can act as a service provider rather than a one-time seller. Part of such a relationship is cost and information sharing. The

Table 7–4 Role of Management in JIT

- ◆ Responsible for creating a JIT culture
- ◆ Serve as coaches and facilitators, not "bosses"
- ◆ Develop an incentive system that rewards workers for their efforts
- ◆ Develop employee skills necessary to function in a JIT environment
- ◆ Ensure that workers receive multifunctional training
- ◆ Facilitate teamwork

Table 7–5 Key Elements of JIT Supplier Relationships
◆ Suppliers viewed as external factory
◆ Use of single-source suppliers
◆ Long-term supplier relationships developed
◆ Suppliers locate near customer
◆ Stable delivery schedules
◆ Cost and information sharing

manufacturer shares information about forecasts and production schedules, allowing the supplier to "see" what is going to be ordered. The supplier, in turn, shares cost information and cost-cutting efforts with the manufacturer. Both parties help each other and together reap the benefits. Also, long-term relationships provide greater incentive for continuous quality improvement. Finally, with a long-term relationship suppliers are better able to plan capacity and production mix requirements, resulting in lower costs.

To provide JIT service to manufacturers, suppliers often locate near their customers. Good examples are the Nissan and Saturn plants in the Tennessee valley, as well as the Honda plant in Marysville, Ohio. These plants are surrounded by their suppliers. If close proximity is not possible, many suppliers have small warehouses near the manufacturing plant. These warehouses can be used for housing frequently delivered items. Because JIT suppliers are extensions of the manufacturing facility, the "pull system" concept applies to them as well. JIT suppliers use standardized containers and make deliveries according to a preset schedule. As companies advance in JIT, they expect progressively shorter delivery cycles from their suppliers, and will often fine them for not meeting the schedule. Often a few suppliers will join together to help each other make small deliveries.

Many suppliers have become JIT certified, which means that they have received one or more designations that indicate they meet certain high quality standards. Once a supplier has been certified, fewer quality checks are needed as quality standards are built into the certification process. A certified JIT supplier with a long-term agreement also has the advantage of receiving payment at regular intervals rather than on delivery of goods. Paperwork is eliminated, and electronic linkages can be set up between manufacturer and supplier. These results in direct savings for both the supplier and the manufacturer.

As you can see, supplier relationships in JIT are another fundamental departure from traditional systems. Companies have learned much from JIT, and the new way of dealing with suppliers is the wave of the future, even for firms that do not fully implement JIT. Table 7-5 shows some of the key aspects of JIT supplier relationships.

■ BENEFITS OF JIT

The benefits of JIT are very impressive. For this reason, many companies rush to adopt JIT without realizing all that is involved. Many of these companies do not reap the benefits because they do not take the time to implement the culture necessary for JIT to succeed. A recent study of JIT benefits has found that over a five-year period companies using JIT have experienced an 80–90% reduction in inventory investment, an 80–90% reduction in lead time, a 75% reduction in rework and setup, a

50% reduction in space requirements, and a 50% reduction in material-handling equipment.

The first implementation of JIT took place at the Toyota Motor Company in Japan in the early 1980s. Thus, much of what we have learned about JIT comes from Toyota's experience. Since then, hundreds of companies have successfully implemented JIT, including General Motors, Ford, General Electric, IBM, 3M, Nissan, Saturn, and many others. Even for companies that do not achieve the dramatic benefits of a full JIT implementation, JIT provides many benefits. Table 7-6 lists key benefits of JIT.

One of the greatest benefits of JIT is that it has changed the attitude of many firms toward eliminating waste, improving responsiveness, and competing based on time. Time-based competition is one of the primary ways in which companies compete today, and JIT is what makes it possible. Even companies that have not implemented JIT have had to make some changes in order to compete in a world that has left behind many traditional ways of doing business.

Table 7–6
Benefits of JIT
◆ Reduction in inventory
◆ Improved quality
◆ Reduced space requirements
◆ Shorter lead times
◆ Lower production costs
◆ Increased productivity
◆ Increased machine utilization
◆ Greater flexibility

The large benefits JIT can bring to a company are demonstrated by the success achieved by Alcoa, a leader in the aluminum industry. Alcoa's accomplishment included reducing inventories by more than a quarter of a billion dollars in 1999, while increasing sales by almost $1 billion. This is a direct benefit of implementing Toyota's JIT system just a year earlier. In 1998, Alcoa found itself ill prepared to meet customer needs. It was piling up inventory, yet not providing what the customer wanted. Alcoa turned to a full JIT, "pull" manufacturing system. Benefits quickly began to appear at facilities all over the country. For example, an extrusion plant in Mississippi lost money in 1998 but within a year was capable of delivering customer orders in two days.

LINKS TO PRACTICE
Alcoa, Inc.
www.alcoa.com

IMPLEMENTING JIT ■

We have seen that JIT affects every aspect of the organization. Therefore, the implementation of a true JIT system requires a complete cultural change for the organization. To implement JIT successfully a company does not need sophisticated systems. What is needed are the correct attitude, employee involvement, and continuous improvement. A change of such profound magnitude needs to be driven by top management. JIT implementation cannot succeed if it is done only by middle or lower management.

Implementation needs to start with a shared vision of where the company is and where it wants to go. This vision needs to consider everyone who has a stake in the company, including customers, employees, suppliers, stockholders, and even the community in which the company is located.

Once the vision has been developed, it is up to top management to create the right atmosphere. Managers need to involve workers in a meaningful way and not merely give lip service to the concept. Part of the change in atmosphere should consist of breaking down the barriers between departments and instilling "we" thinking rather than an "us versus them" attitude. Reward systems should be put in place to reward ideas and team cooperation.

A "champion" for JIT implementation must be designated, whether it is a plant manager, the CEO, or a steering committee. The purpose is to have a person or group to oversee all the steps necessary in implementing such a large change. This person or group will be responsible for reviewing progress, addressing any problems that may develop, making sure ample resources are available, and ensuring that a proper reward system is in place. Another job of the JIT champion is sharing results with everyone in the company. Such information is not shared with production workers in traditional systems. However, in JIT sharing of this type of information with everyone in the company is considered a key to success, and is done frequently and regularly. Financial information cannot be kept secret if everyone is to work together and share in the benefits.

In making specific changes in JIT manufacturing, some changes need to be implemented before others. Not all things can or should be changed at once. Following is a sequence of steps that should be followed in the implementation process:

1. **Make quality improvements.** Usually it is best to start the implementation process by improving quality. The reason is that quality is so pervasive and all the JIT objectives are dependent on quality improvement.

2. **Reorganize workplace.** Reorganizing the workplace is the next step. This means proper facility layout, cleaning and organizing the work environment, designating storage spaces for everything, and removing clutter.

3. **Reduce setup times.** The next step is to focus on reducing setup times, which will involve manufacturing and industrial engineering. It will require analysis of current setup procedures, elimination of unneeded steps, and streamlining of motions. Workers will need to be trained in the proper setup procedures.

4. **Reduce lot sizes and lead times**. Once setup times have been reduced, we can focus on reducing lot sizes and lead times. This in turn will reduce the inventory between workstations and free up space. The empty space will contribute to visibility.

5. **Implement layout changes.** The next step is to arrange equipment and workstations in close proximity to one another, and to form work cells.

6. **Switch to pull production**. After the preceding changes have been implemented, it is time to switch to pull production. Changing from a push system to a pull system, including worker training, needs to be planned very carefully. However, the change needs to be made at once because a production facility cannot use a push system and a pull at the same time.

7. **Develop relationship with suppliers.** Changes in relationships with suppliers should be among the last steps implemented. Demands for smaller and more frequent deliveries should be instituted gradually.

By now you should understand that JIT is made up of many ideas that define its philosophy. Because of that, implementation of JIT is complicated. Most companies are so eager to receive the benefits of JIT that they jump in and begin making changes without thinking them through. Often company executives will learn that for JIT implementation to succeed inventory needs to be eliminated, so they begin ordering reductions in inventory. This unplanned approach can have disastrous effects. Inventory is there to cover up problems. Unless the problems are solved first, simply reducing inventory can completely halt production.

Finally, when it comes to implementation, remember that the concept of continuous improvement is an integral part of JIT. This means that the implementation process will not start and end in definite time periods. Rather, it will be a gradual process. Reductions in inventory have to be preceded by improvements in quality, changes in layout, reductions in setup times, and worker training. As improvements are made, inventory can be reduced. As new problems become visible, they must be solved before further reductions in inventory are made. This is an ongoing, gradual process. Implementation is never complete, because improving performance is a never-ending task.

JIT IN SERVICES ■

People who think of JIT as applying only to manufacturing may not see how JIT could be applicable to service organizations. However, we have seen in this chapter that JIT is an all-encompassing philosophy that includes eliminating waste, improving quality, continuous improvement, increased responsiveness to customers, and increased speed of delivery. That philosophy is equally applicable to any organization, service or manufacturing.

Following are examples of JIT concepts seen in service firms:

Use of multifunction workers. The use of multifunction workers in service organizations helps improve quality and customer responsiveness. An example of this is seen in department stores, where workers make sales, clean sales areas, and arrange displays.

Reductions in cycle time. Competition based on speed is common in services, as can be seen in such companies as McDonald's, Wendy's, Federal Express, and Lens Crafters.

Minimizing setup times and parallel processing. The concept of setup time minimization and parallel processing can be seen in cleaning companies. Merry Maids is a cleaning company that uses teams of workers to clean homes. Each member of the team is designated to carry out specific category of cleaning tasks. For example, one worker may be responsible for all the dusting, another for all the bathrooms, and another for the vacuuming. This minimizes setup time, and parallel processing reduces the cycle time.

Workplace organization. Improved housekeeping has become a priority for many service organizations, particularly since the customer is present during part of the production process. Service companies like Disney and McDonald's pride themselves on the cleanliness of their facilities.

OM ACROSS THE ORGANIZATION

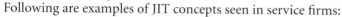

Implementing a philosophy such as JIT will inevitably have consequences for every aspect of the organization. The entire organization is affected by JIT, primarily because organizational barriers are eliminated. Functions that have not had much communication with each other in the past must now work together. Included are functions such as marketing, manufacturing, and engineering, which in traditional systems have separate agendas but now need to work together to achieve the goals of the organization as a whole. Let's see how some of these functions are affected.

Accounting is strongly affected by JIT. Traditional accounting systems generally allocate overhead on the basis of direct labor hours. The problem with this method is that it does not accurately describe the actual use of overhead by different jobs. For example, jobs that are labor intensive in nature may be assigned a disproportionately high share of overhead.

These numbers may lead management to make inappropriate decisions. JIT relies on *activity-based costing* to allocate overhead. In activity-based costing, specific costs are identified and then assigned to various types of activities, such as inspection, movement of goods, and machine processing. Overhead costs are then assigned to jobs depending on how many activities a particular job takes up.

Marketing plays a large role in JIT as the interface with customers becomes more important. JIT focuses on customer-driven quality, not quality as defined by the producer. Marketing managers must understand customer needs and ensure that this information is passed on to operations managers for proper design, production, and delivery of the product or service.

Finance is responsible for approving and evaluating financial investments. Switching to a JIT system proves financially beneficial in the long run but generally requires an investment in resources. Included are hiring consultants, training workers, purchasing or modifying equipment, more record keeping, and rearrangement of facilities. Finance must evaluate these investments and measure their performance, which requires an understanding of JIT.

Engineering plays a major role in JIT. As we have seen in this chapter, reduction of setup time is critical to the success of JIT. It is up to engineering to design machines so as to reduce setup time and to design poka-yoke, or foolproof devices, that prevent defects from occurring. Engineering is largely responsible for designing the mechanisms that enable JIT to function as desired. Without engineering, true JIT could not exist.

Information systems (IS) create the network of information necessary for JIT to function. JIT is based on the assumption that information about quality, inventory levels, order status, and product returns is available to everyone in the organization. This type of information needs to be readily available and up to date. Otherwise, a JIT system would come to a halt. Communication with suppliers is another prerequisite of JIT that requires a high-level information system. JIT cannot function without the ongoing involvement of IS. In turn, IS needs to understand JIT functioning and information requirements.

■ OM IS EVERYWHERE

As you can see, JIT is not only about manufacturing. It is about eliminating waste of every kind in order to be more efficient. You can easily apply the elements of JIT in your everyday life. You can start by organizing your work environment or home so as to have "everything in its place and a place for everything." You would also eliminate things you do not need, organize things by type and category, and use clearly visible storage areas. Files and notebooks could be clearly labeled so that you do not waste time and energy searching for school papers. Respecting your environment requires that you put things away after using them.

Other types of waste that you could eliminate are unnecessary time and effort. You could plan your activities to minimize "setup time," such as buying groceries and picking up the dry cleaning in one trip rather than two separate trips. You could also arrange the layout of the things you use on a regular basis so that they are within easy reach. For example, if you make coffee every morning it might make sense to have the coffee next to the coffee pot to eliminate extra steps.

JIT concepts apply to every environment and are based on simple principles. They have been successful in turning many corporations around, and these simple principles can easily improve the efficiency of your life as well.

CHAPTER HIGHLIGHTS

1 JIT is a philosophy that was developed by the Toyota Motor Company in the mid 1970s. It has since become the standard of operation for many industries. It focuses on eliminating waste, simplicity, taking a broad view of operations, visibility, and flexibility. Three key elements of this philosophy are JIT manufacturing, total quality management, and respect for people.

2 JIT views waste as anything that does not add value, such as unnecessary space, energy, time, or motion.

3 Traditional manufacturing systems use "push" production, whereas JIT uses "pull" production. Push systems anticipate future demand and produce in advance in order to have products in place when demand occurs. This system usually results in excess inventory. Pull systems work backwards. The last workstation in the production line (or the customer) requests the precise amounts of materials.

4 JIT manufacturing is a coordinated production system that enables the right quantities of parts to arrive when they are needed precisely where they are needed. Key elements of JIT manufacturing are the pull system and kanban production, small lot sizes and quick setups, uniform plant loading, flexible resources, and streamlined layout.

5 Total quality management (TQM) creates an organizational culture that defines quality as seen by the customer. The concepts of continuous improvement and quality at the source are integral parts that allow for continual growth and the goal of identifying the causes of quality problems.

6 JIT considers people to be the organization's most important resource. All employees are highly valued members of the organization. Workers are empowered to make decisions and are rewarded for their efforts. Team efforts make possible cross-functional and multilayer coordination.

7 JIT is equally applicable in service organizations, particularly with the push toward time-based competition and the need to cut costs.

8 JIT success is dependent on interfunctional coordination and effort. Marketing must work closely with customers to define customer-driven quality. IS must design a powerful information system. Engineering must develop equipment with low setups and design jobs with foolproof devices. Finance must monitor financial improvements with realistic expectations. Accounting must develop appropriate costing mechanisms.

KEY TERMS

waste 176
JIT philosophy 176
continuous improvement 178
visibility 178
flexibility 179
value-added manufacturing 179

total quality management 179
quality at the source 182
pull system 183
kanban 184
production card 184
withdrawal card 184

single setup 187
jidoka 191
poka-yoke 191
respect for people 192
bottom-round management 193
single-source supplier 195

FORMULA REVIEW

$$N = \frac{DT}{C}$$

SOLVED PROBLEMS

■ Solved Problem 1

Suzie Sizewick works for a manufacturer of ballpoint pens, which come in packages of 5 pens each. Her job is to fill the packages with pens, and she is expected to process 100 packages an hour. The facility where Suzie works uses a kanban production system in which each container holds 20 pen packages. It takes 15 minutes to receive the packages she needs from the previous workstation. How many kanbans are needed for the filling process?

Solution:

$D = 100$ packages per hour

$T = 15$ minutes $= 1/4$ hour

$C = 10$ packages per container

STEP 1

$$N = \frac{DT}{C}$$

STEP 2

$$N = \frac{(100 \text{ packages/hour}) \left(\frac{1}{4} \text{ hour}\right)}{10 \text{ packages}}$$
$$= 2.5 \text{ kanbans and containers}$$

DISCUSSION QUESTIONS

1. Describe the core beliefs of the JIT philosophy.
2. Identify the three major elements of JIT.
3. Explain how JIT manufacturing works and its key elements.
4. Find an example of successful JIT manufacturing.
5. Explain the importance of total quality management in JIT.
6. Find an example of successful TQM implementation.
7. Explain the importance of respect for people in JIT.

8. Find an example of a company that has high respect for people.
9. Describe the JIT implementation process. Why should some things be changed before others?
10. Find examples of JIT in services. Which aspects of JIT are easiest to apply in services?
11. Explain how you could use JIT to make your life more efficient.

PROBLEMS

1. Jason Carter works for a producer of soaps that come in packages of 6 each. His job is to fill the packages with soap, and he is expected to process 30 packages an hour. The facility where Jason works uses a kanban production system in which each container holds 5 packages of soap. It takes 20 minutes to receive the packages he needs from the previous workstation. How many kanbans are needed for the filling process?

2. A manufacturer of thermostats uses a kanban system to control the flow of materials. The packaging center processes 10 thermostats an hour and receives completed thermostats every 30 minutes. Containers hold 5 thermostats each.
   (a) How many kanbans are needed for the packaging center?
   (b) If management decides to keep 2 thermostats as safety stock, how many kanbans will be needed?

3. A production cell at Canderberry Candle facility uses a pull method to supply wicks to the assembly line. The wicks are used at a rate of 300 per day. Each container holds 20 wicks, and usually waits 20 minutes in the production cell. How many containers should be used at the Canderberry Candle facility for purposes of pull production?

4. Carlos Gonzales in production manager at an assembly plant that manufactures cordless telephones. The company is planning to install a pull system. The process is being planned to have a usage rate of 50 pieces per hour. Each container is designed to hold 10 pieces. It takes an average of 30 minutes to complete a cycle.
   (a) How many containers will be needed?
   (b) How will the number of containers needed change as the system improves?

5. A dye cell at the Acme Clothing Factory uses 100 pounds of dye each day. The dye is moved in vats at a rate of approximately 1 per hour. Each vat holds 10 pounds of dye. The facility operates 8 hours per day. How many vats should be used?

CASE: *Katz Carpeting*

Josh Wallace, President of Katz Carpeting, had much on his mind. The end-of-year performance numbers for the carpet manufacturer were below expectations. Inventories of carpets were high, yet they had frequently been out of stock of items customers wanted. It seemed that the plant was producing a lot of what they already had, yet not enough of what was needed. Quality was also becoming a problem, with customers frequently returning carpeting for rips or incorrect dye color. It seemed to Josh that operations was not doing their job. Something had to be done.

Background

Katz Carpeting is a manufacturer of high-end commercial and residential carpeting. Katz produces two product lines of carpeting. The first line, a group of standardized products called "standards," is sold through catalogs and samples available at retail sites. The second line is "specials," carpet products made to customer specifications of color and pattern. Currently, the volume of business is approximately evenly divided between standards and specials.

At Katz, standards and specials are made using a line operation and sharing the same facilities. Production of standards is made in a predictable and easily timed manner. The process begins with making the dye in large vats and dying the yarn. The yarn is then rolled, bonded, and added to a backing. The product is then cut and sent to shipping.

Production of specials is not as simple. The dying and weaving processes of specials are considerably more difficult due to the time necessary to ensure the dyes are correct. Also, patterns are frequently requested in special orders and each pattern is typically unique. Because of the customized nature of producing specials the time required for production is much longer, as is the cost involved.

At Katz, the marketing department is responsible for generating forecasts, taking orders, and establishing due dates. This information is passed on to operations on a weekly basis, and a production schedule is made. Information on special "rush" orders is passed on daily and requests are frequent. Operations tries to meet all the orders and produce extra inventories of standards to be prepared for unexpected demand.

Considering JIT

Josh Wallace called a meeting with Evelyn Jones, newly hired head of operations. He explained the problems Katz was facing. Evelyn agreed that there were problems with inventory and customer service, but noted that these ware just symptoms of a problem. "One big problem is the setup and changeover time between the two product lines," she explained. "The changeover from one standard product to another is approximately 15 minutes, enough time for the new dye color to be loaded on to the machine. However, the changeover from one standard product to a special can be as much as $2\frac{1}{2}$ hours. As both products are made on the same line, production of the specials holds up production of the standards. Also, operations frequently stops planned production to meet special rush orders."

Evelyn then explained that the facility needed to move toward just-in-time production. "Yes, I have heard of that. That is a manufacturing process based on zero inventory," said Josh. "I have even heard that workers are paid to sit around and discuss quality problems. Well, not here. Here they need to get rid of that inventory!"

Under the circumstances, Evelyn suggested that a consultant be brought in to guide Katz through the process of switching to JIT production. Josh reluctantly agreed.

Case Questions:

1. What suggestions do you have for implementing JIT at Katz? Should specials and standards be produced on the same line? (Hint: Do they require the same type of operation?)

2. If production of standards and specials is separated, how different will JIT implementation be for production of the different products? Explain what would be needed in JIT implementation for both products.

3. What suggestions do you have for improving the way the production schedule is currently made?

4. How would you characterize Josh's view of JIT? What challenges do you think a consultant will face in implementing JIT at Katz? If you were a consultant how would you approach these problems?

INTERACTIVE LEARNING

Enhance and test your knowledge of Chapter 7 using the interactive CD.

1. **Video**   *Roadway Express, Inc.*

   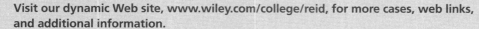

   Visit our dynamic Web site, www.wiley.com/college/reid, for more cases, web links, and additional information.

2. **Company Tour**   *Toyota Motor Corporation*

3. **Additional Web Resources**
   Association for Manufacturing Excellence, www.ame.org
   APICS, www.apics.org

4. **INTERNET CHALLENGE**   *Truck-Fleet Inc.*

Truck-Fleet Inc. is a small company that offers domestic logistics services such as distribution management and transportation management. Truck-Fleet owns a small fleet of trucks and offers movement, tracking, and handling of inventory for clients. Although Truck-Fleet is relatively small, with revenues of $500 million annually, it is growing rapidly as companies place greater emphasis on fast transportation. Truck-Fleet utilizes technology such as bar coding to facilitate consolidation and distribution of products. Its strength lies in its dedicated employees, such as drivers with excellent driving and safety records and a good management staff.

Truck-Fleet needs to become a JIT service provider to remain competitive. You have just been hired by help direct its growth. Use the Internet to identify Truck-Fleet's main competitors and their capabilities. Identify specific companies that offer just-in-time pickup and delivery against which Truck-Fleet can benchmark. Then, identify characteristics of main competitors that enable them to provide just-in-time services. Finally, establish specific guidelines for Truck-Fleet to follow in becoming a JIT service provider.

Problem-Solving Tip: One potential competitor is Ryder (www.ryder.com).

BIBLIOGRAPHY

Garg, D., Kaul, O.N., and Deshmukh, S.G. "JIT Implementation: A Case Study," *Production and Inventory Management Journal*, Third Quarter, 1998, pp. 26–31.

Hall, R.W. *Attaining Manufacturing Excellence*, Burr Ridge, Ill: Irwin Professional Publishing, 1987.

Hanna, M.D., Newman, W.R., and Johnson, P. "Linking Operational and Environmental Improvement Through Employee Involvement," *International Journal of Operations and Production Management*, 20, 2, 2000, 148–165.

Koste, L.L. and Malhotra, M.K., "Trade-offs Among the Elements of Flexibility: A Comparison From the Automotive Industry," *Omega*, 28, 2000, 693–710.

Monden, Yasuchiro. *The Toyota Management System: Linking the Seven Key Functional Areas*. Cambridge, Mass: Productivity Press, 1993.

Pun, K. and Wong, K.H., "Implementing JIT/MRP in a PCB Manufacturer," *Production and Inventory Management Journal*, First Quarter, 1998, pp. 10–16.

Shingo, Shigeo. *Modern Approaches to Manufacturing Improvement*. Cambridge, Mass.: Productivity Press, 1990.

Vergin, R.C. "An Examination of Inventory Turnover in the Fortune 500 Industrial Companies," *Production and Inventory Management Journal*, First Quarter, 1998, pp 51–56.

Womack, J.P., Jones, D.T., and D. Roos. *The Machine That Changed the World*. New York: Macmillan, 1990.

Forecasting

Before studying this chapter you should know or, if necessary, review

The role of forecasting in operations management decisions, Chapter 1, page 7.

LEARNING OBJECTIVES

After studying this chapter you should be able to

1. Identify principles of forecasting.
2. Explain the steps involved in the forecasting process.
3. Identify types of forecasting methods and their characteristics.
4. Describe time series models and causal models.
5. Generate forecasts for data with different patterns, such as level, trend, and seasonality and cycles.

6. Describe causal modeling using linear regression.
7. Compute forecast accuracy.
8. Explain the factors that should be considered when selecting a forecasting model.

CHAPTER OUTLINE

Have you ever gone to a restaurant and been told that they are sold out of their "specials," or gone to the university bookstore and found that the texts for your course are on backorder? Have you ever had a party at your home only to realize that you don't have enough food for everyone invited? Just like getting caught unprepared in the rain, these situations show the consequences of poor forecasting. Planning for any event, be it a party or sales of goods in a company, requires a forecast of the future. Whether in business or in our own lives, we make forecasts of future events. Based on those forecasts we make plans and take action.

Forecasting is one of the most important business functions because all other business decisions are based on a forecast of the future. Decisions such as which markets to pursue, which products to produce, how much inventory to carry, and how many people to hire all require a forecast. Forecasts are made at many different levels of the organization, for different purposes and different time periods. For example, strategic forecasts are made at the top level of the firm and usually look a year or more into the future. On the other hand, forecasts of weekly sales are made at a lower level and consider a much shorter time interval. In this chapter you will learn about forecasting and the different types of forecasting methods available, and how to select and use the proper techniques for your needs.

▶ **Forecasting**
Predicting future events.

■ PRINCIPLES OF FORECASTING

There are many types of forecasting models. They differ in their degree of complexity, the amount of data they use, and the way they generate the forecast. However, some features are common to all forecasting models. They include the following:

1. *Forecasts are rarely perfect.* Forecasting the future involves uncertainty. Therefore, it is almost impossible to make a perfect prediction. Forecasters know that they have to live with a certain amount of error, which is the difference between what is forecast and what actually happens. The goal of forecasting is to generate good forecasts *on the average* over time and to keep forecast errors as low as possible.

2. *Forecasts are more accurate for groups or families of items rather than for individual items.* When items are grouped together, their individual high and low values can cancel each other out. The data for a group of items can be stable even when individual items in the group are very unstable. Consequently, one can obtain a higher degree of accuracy when forecasting for a group of items rather than for individual items. For example, you cannot expect the same degree of accuracy if you are forecasting sales of long-sleeved hunter green polo shirts that you can expect when forecasting sales of all polo shirts.

3. *Forecasts are more accurate for shorter than longer time horizons.* The shorter the time horizon of the forecast, the lower the degree of uncertainty. Data do not change very much in the short run. As the time horizon increases, however, there is a much greater likelihood that changes in established patterns and relationships will occur. Because of that, forecasters cannot expect the same degree of forecast accuracy for a long-range forecast as for a short-range forecast. For example, it is much harder to predict sales of a product two years from now than to predict sales two weeks from now.

STEPS IN THE FORECASTING PROCESS ■

Regardless of what forecasting method is used, there are some basic steps that should be followed when making a forecast:

1. *Decide what to forecast.* Remember that forecasts are made in order to plan for the future. To do so, we have to decide what forecasts are actually needed. This is not as simple as it sounds. For example, do we need to forecast sales or demand? These are two different things, and sales do not necessarily equal the total amount of demand for the product. Both pieces of information are usually valuable.

   An important part of this decision is the level of detail required for the forecast (e.g., by product or product group), the units of the forecast (e.g., product units, boxes, or dollars), and the time horizon (e.g., monthly or quarterly).

2. *Evaluate and analyze appropriate data.* This step involves identifying what data are needed and what data are available. This will have a big impact on the selection of a forecasting model. For example, if you are predicting sales for a new product you may not have historical sales information, which would limit your use of forecasting models that require quantitative data.

   We will also see later in the chapter that different types of patterns can be observed in the data. It is important to identify these patterns in order to select the correct forecasting model. For example, if a company was experiencing a high increase in product sales for the past year, it would be important to identify this growth in order to forecast correctly.

3. *Select and test the forecasting model.* Once the data have been evaluated, the next step is to select an appropriate forecasting model. As we will see, there are many models to choose from. Usually we consider factors like *cost* and *ease of use* in selecting a model. Another very important factor is *accuracy*. A common procedure is to narrow the choices to two or three different models and then test them on historical data to see which one is most accurate.

4. *Generate the forecast.* Once we have selected a model we use it to generate the forecast. But we are not finished, as you will see in the next step.

5. *Monitor forecast accuracy.* Forecasting is an ongoing process. After we have made a forecast, we should record what actually happened. We can then use that information to monitor our forecast accuracy. This process should be carried out continuously, because environments and conditions often change. What was a good forecasting model in the past might not provide good results for the future. We have to constantly be prepared to revise our forecasting model as our data changes.

The rapid growth of information technology (IT) has created a forecasting challenge for manufacturers of industry components such as microchips and semiconductors. Companies like Intel have had difficulty in forecasting demand for information technology used in internal applications. Forecasts are critical in order to plan production and have enough product to meet demand. However, overforecasting means having too much of an expensive product that will quickly become obsolete. The exponential growth in requirements and a short product life cycle have added much uncertainty to the forecasting process. Intel has had to consider many factors when generating their forecasts, such as key technology trends that are driving the information revolution and future directions in the use of IT.

■ TYPES OF FORECASTING METHODS

Forecasting methods can be classified into two groups: *qualitative* and *quantitative*. Table 8-1 shows these two categories and their characteristics.

▶ **Qualitative forecasting methods**
Forecast is made subjectively by the forecaster.

Qualitative methods, often called judgmental methods, are methods in which the forecast is made subjectively by the forecaster. They are educated guesses by forecasters or experts based on intuition, knowledge, and experience. When you decide, based on your intuition, that a particular team is going to win a baseball game, you are making a qualitative forecast. Because qualitative methods are made by people, they are often biased. These biases can be related to personal motivation ("They are going to set my budget based on my forecast, so I'd better predict high."), mood ("I feel lucky today!"), or conviction ("That pitcher can strike anybody out!").

▶ **Quantitative forecasting methods**
Forecast is based on mathematical modeling.

Quantitative methods, on the other hand, are based on mathematical modeling. Because they are mathematical, these methods are consistent. The same model will generate the exact same forecast from the same set of data every time. These methods are also objective. They do not suffer from the biases found in qualitative forecasting. Finally, these methods can consider a lot of information at one time. Because people have limited information-processing abilities and can easily experience

Table 8-1 Types of Forecasting Methods	
Qualitative Methods	**Quantitative Methods**
Characteristics: Based on human judgment, opinions; subjective and nonmathematical.	Characteristics: Based on mathematics; quantitative in nature.
Strengths: Can incorporate latest changes in the environment and "inside information."	Strengths: Consistent and objective; able to consider much information and data at one time.
Weaknesses: Can bias the forecast and reduce forecast accuracy.	Weaknesses: Often quantifiable data are not available. Only as good as the data on which it is based.

information overload, they cannot compete with mathematically generated forecasts in this area.

Both qualitative and quantitative forecasting methods have strengths and weaknesses. Although quantitative methods are objective and consistent, they require data in quantifiable form in order to generate a forecast. Often we do not have such data—for example, if we are making a strategic forecast or if we are forecasting sales of a new product. Also, quantitative methods are only as good as the data on which they are based. Qualitative methods, on the other hand, have the advantage of being able to incorporate last-minute "inside information" in the forecast, such as an advertising campaign by a competitor, a snowstorm delaying a shipment, or a heat wave increasing sales of ice cream. Each method has its place and a good forecaster learns to rely on both.

The idea of relying on different types of forecasting methods and combining their results to get a final forecast is used in practice. It has even been used by weather forecasters. Weather forecasting can be challenging and many factors need to be considered, such as long-range trends and current weather fronts. Weather forecasters have been able to improve their forecast accuracy by combining the results of forecasts made at different time intervals. For example, a weather forecast for the upcoming weekend may be formulated by *combining* computer-generated forecasts made on the preceding Monday, Tuesday, and Wednesday. This method is called "ensemble forecasting" and has proven to be very successful.

LINKS TO PRACTICE
Improving Weather Forecasting

Qualitative Methods

There are many types of qualitative forecasting methods, some informal and some structured. Regardless of how structured the process is, however, remember that these models are based on subjective opinion and are not mathematical in nature. Some common qualitative methods are shown in Table 8-2 and are described in this section.

Table 8-2 Qualitative Forecasting Methods			
Type	**Characteristics**	**Strengths**	**Weaknesses**
Executive opinion	A group of managers meet and come up with a forecast.	Good for strategic or new-product forecasting.	One person's opinion can dominate the forecast.
Market research	Uses surveys and interviews to identify customer preferences.	Good determinant of customer preferences.	It can be difficult to develop a good questionnaire.
Delphi method	Seeks to develop a consensus among a group of experts.	Excellent for forecasting long-term product demand, technological changes, and scientific advances.	Time consuming to develop.

CROSS FUNCTIONAL

▶ **Executive opinion**
Forecasting method in which a group of managers collectively develop a forecast.

Executive Opinion **Executive opinion** is a forecasting method in which a group of managers meet and collectively come up with a forecast. This method is often used for strategic forecasting or forecasting the success of a new product or service. Sometimes it can be used to change an existing forecast to account for unusual events, such as an unusual business cycle or unexpected competition.

Although managers can bring good insights to the forecast, this method has a number of disadvantages. Often the opinion of one person can dominate the forecast if that person has more power than the other members of the group or is very domineering. Think about times when you were part of a group for a course or for your job. Chances are that you experienced situations in which one person's views dominated.

▶ **Market research**
Approach to forecasting that relies on surveys and interviews to determine customer preferences.

Market Research **Market research** is an approach that uses surveys and interviews to determine customer likes, dislikes, and preferences and to identify new product ideas. Usually the company hires an outside marketing firm to conduct a market research study. There is a good chance that you were a participant in such a study if someone called you and asked about your product preferences.

Market research can be a good determinant of customer preferences. However, it has a number of shortcomings. One of the most common has to do with how the survey questions are designed. For example, a market research firm may call and ask you to identify which of the following is your favorite hobby: gardening, working on cars, cooking, or playing sports. But maybe none of these is your favorite because you prefer playing the piano or fishing, and these options are not included. This question is poorly designed because it forces you to pick a category that you really don't fit in, which can lead to misinterpretation of the survey results.

Market research being conducted in a shopping mall.

Computers have made the use of quantitative models much easier.

The Delphi Method   The **Delphi method** is a forecasting method in which the objective is to reach a consensus among a group of experts while maintaining their anonymity. The researcher puts together a panel of experts in the chosen field. These experts do not have to be in the same facility or even in the same country. They do not know who the other panelists are. The process involves sending questionnaires to the panelists, then summarizing the findings and sending them an updated questionnaire incorporating the findings. This process continues until a consensus is reached.

▶ **Delphi method**
Approach to forecasting in which a forecast is the product of a consensus among a group of experts.

The idea behind the Delphi method is that a panel of experts in a particular field might not agree on certain things, but what they do agree on will probably happen. The researcher's job is to identify what they agree on and use that as the forecast. This method has the advantage of not allowing anyone to dominate the consensus, and it has been shown to work very well. Although it takes a large amount of time, it has been shown to be an excellent method for forecasting long-range product demand, technological change, and scientific advances in medicine. For example, if you wished to predict the timing for an AIDS vaccine or a cure for cancer, you would probably use this technique.

Quantitative Methods

Quantitative methods are different from qualitative ones because they are based on mathematics. Quantitative methods can also be divided into two categories: *time series models* and *causal models*. Although both are mathematical, the two categories differ in their assumptions and in the manner in which a forecast is generated. In this section we will study some common quantitative models. These are summarized in Table 8-3.

Time series models assume that all the information needed to generate a forecast is contained in the *time series* of data. A **time series** is a series of observations taken at regular intervals over a specified period of time. For example, if you were forecasting quarterly corporate sales and had collected five years of quarterly sales data, you would have a time series. Time series analysis assumes that we can generate a forecast based on patterns in the data. As a forecaster, you would look for patterns such as trend, seasonality, and cycle, and use that information to generate a forecast.

▶ **Time series models**
Based on the assumption that a forecast can be generated from the information contained in a time series of data.

Causal models use a very different logic to generate a forecast. They assume that the variable we wish to forecast is somehow related to other variables in the environment. The forecaster's job is to discover how these variables are related in mathematical terms and use that information to forecast the future. For example, we might decide that sales are related to advertising dollars and GNP. From historical data we would build a model that explains the relationship of these variables and use it to forecast corporate sales.

▶ **Causal models**
Based on the assumption that the variable being forecast is related to other variables in the environment.

Time series models are generally easier to use than causal models. Causal models can be very complex, especially if they consider relationships among many variables. However, time series models can often be just as accurate and have the advantage of simplicity. They are easy to use and can generate a forecast more quickly than causal models, which require model building. Each of these models is used for forecasting in operations management and will be described in the next section.

Table 8-3 Quantitative Forecasting Methods

Type	Formula	Strengths	Weaknesses
Naive	$F_{t+1} = A_t$	Simple and easy to use.	Only good if data change little from period to period.
Simple Mean	$F_{t+1} = \dfrac{\Sigma A_t}{n}$	Good for level pattern.	Requires carrying a lot of data.
Moving Average	$F_{t+1} = \dfrac{\Sigma A_t}{n}$	Only good for level pattern.	Important to select the proper moving average.
Weighted Moving Average	$F_{t+1} = \Sigma C_t A_t$	Good for level pattern; allows placing different weights on past demands.	Selection of weights requires good judgment.
Exponential Smoothing	$F_{t+1} = \alpha A_t + (1 - \alpha)F_t$	Provides excellent forecast results for short to medium-length forecasts.	Choice of alpha is critical.
Trend Adjusted Exponential Smoothing	**Step 1:** Smoothing the level of the series: $S_t = \alpha A_t + (1 - \alpha)(S_{t-1} + T_{t-1})$ **Step 2:** Smoothing the trend: $T_t = \beta(S_t - S_{t-1}) + (1 - \beta)T_{t-1}$ **Step 3:** Forecast including trend: $FIT_{t+1} = S_t + T_t$	Provides good results for trend data.	Should only be used for data with a trend.
Seasonality	**Step 1:** Calculate the average demand for each season. **Step 2:** Compute a seasonal index for every season of every year you have data.	Simple and logical procedure for computing seasonality.	Make sure seasonality is actually present.
Linear Regression	**Step 1:** Compute parameter b: $b = \dfrac{\Sigma XY - n\bar{X}\,\bar{Y}}{\Sigma X^2 - n\bar{X}^2}$ **Step 2:** Compute parameter a: $a = \bar{Y} - b\bar{X}$ **Step 3:** Obtain equation: $Y = a + bX$	Easy to understand; provides good forecast accuracy.	Make sure a linear relationship is present.

■ TIME SERIES MODELS

Remember that time series analysis assumes that all the information needed to generate a forecast is contained in the time series of the data. The forecaster looks for patterns in the data and tries to obtain a forecast by projecting that pattern into the future. The easiest way to identify patterns is to plot the data and examine the resulting graphs. If we did that, what could we observe? There are four basic patterns, which are shown in Figure 8-1. Any of these patterns, or a combination of them, can be present in a time series of data:

1. *Level or horizontal.* A **level or horizontal pattern** exists when data values fluctuate around a constant mean. This is the simplest pattern and the easiest to predict. An example is sales of a product that do not increase or decrease over time. This type of pattern is common for products in the mature stage of their life cycle, in which demand is steady and predictable.

2. *Trend.* When data exhibit an increasing or decreasing pattern over time, we say that they exhibit a **trend.** The trend can be upward or downward. The simplest type of trend is a straight line, or linear trend.

3. *Seasonality.* A **seasonal pattern** is any pattern that regularly repeats itself and is of a constant length. Such a pattern exists when the variable we are trying to forecast is influenced by seasonal factors such as the quarter or month of the year or day of the week. An example is a retail operation with high sales during November and December, or a restaurant with peak sales on Fridays and Saturdays.

▶ **Level or horizontal pattern**
Pattern in which data values fluctuate around a constant mean.

▶ **Trend pattern**
Pattern in which data exhibit increasing or decreasing values over time.

▶ **Seasonality**
Any pattern that regularly repeats itself and is constant in length.

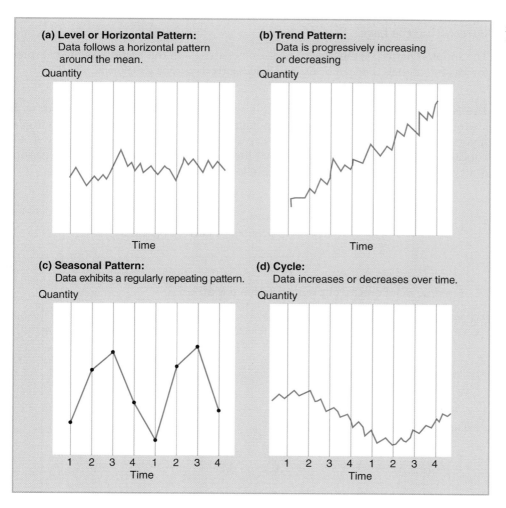

Figure 8-1

Types of data patterns

▶ **Cycles**
Data patterns created by economic fluctuations.

4. *Cycles.* Patterns that are created by economic fluctuations such as those associated with the business cycle are called **cycles.** These could be recessions, inflation, or even the life cycle of a product. The major distinction between a seasonal pattern and a cyclical pattern is that a cyclical pattern varies in length and magnitude and therefore is much more difficult to forecast than other patterns.

▶ **Random variation**
Unexplained variation that cannot be predicted.

Random variation is unexplained variation that cannot be predicted. So if we look at any time series we can see that it is composed of the following:

$$\text{Data} = \underbrace{\text{level} + \text{trend} + \text{seasonality} + \text{cycles}}_{} + \text{random variation}$$

$$\text{Data} = \qquad\qquad \text{pattern} \qquad\qquad + \text{random variation}$$

The first four components of the data are part of a pattern that we try to forecast. Random variation cannot be predicted. Some data have a lot of random variation and some have little. The more random variation a data set has, the harder it is to forecast accurately. As we will see, many forecasting models try to eliminate as much of the random variation as possible.

Forecasting the Level

The simplest pattern is the level or horizontal pattern. In this section we look at some forecasting models that can be used to forecast the level of a time series.

▶ **Naive method**
Forecasting method that assumes next period's forecast is equal to last period's actual value.

The Naive Method The naive method is one of the simplest forecasting models. It assumes that the next period's forecast is equal to the last period's actual. For example, if you sold 500 cupcakes in January the naive method would give you a forecast of 500 cupcakes for February. It is assumed that there is little change from period to period. Mathematically, we could put this in the following form:

$$F_{t+1} = A_t$$

where F_{t+1} = forecast for next period, $t + 1$
A_t = actual value for current period, t

■ **Example 8.1 Forecasting with the Naive Method**

A restaurant is forecasting sales of chicken dinners for the month of April. Total sales of chicken dinners for March were 320. If management uses the naive method to forecast, what is their forecast of chicken dinners for the month of April?

Solution:
Our equation is

$$F_{t+1} = A_t$$

Adding the appropriate time period:

$$F_{\text{April}} = A_{\text{March}}$$
$$F_{\text{April}} = 320 \text{ dinners}$$

The naive method can be modified to take trend into account. If we see that our trend is increasing by 10% and last period's sales were 100 units, a naive method with trend would give us last period's sales plus 10%, which is a forecast of 110 units for the next period. The naive method can also be used for seasonal data. For example, suppose that we have monthly seasonality and sales for last January were 230 units. Using the naive method we would forecast sales of 230 units for next January.

One advantage of the naive method is that it is very simple. It works well when there is little variation from one period to the next. Most of the time we use this method to evaluate the forecast performance of other, more complicated, forecasting models. Because naive is simple and effortless, we expect the forecasting model that we are using to perform better than naive.

Simple Mean or Average One of the simplest averaging models is the **simple average or mean.** Here the forecast is made by simply taking an average of all data:

▶ **Simple mean or average**
The average of a set of data.

$$F_{t+1} = \frac{\Sigma A_t}{n}$$

where F_{t+1} = forecast of demand for next period, $t + 1$
A_t = actual value for current period, t
n = number of periods or data points
t = the most recent period

■ **Example 8.2 Forecasting with the Mean**

New Tools Corporation is forecasting sales for its classic product, Handy-Wrench. Handy-Wrench sales have been steady, and the company uses a simple mean to forecast. Weekly sales over the past five weeks are available. Use the mean to make a forecast for week 6.

Time Period (in weeks)	Actual Sales	Forecast
1	51	
2	53	
3	48	
4	52	
5	50	
6	—	50.8

Solution:
The basic equation for the mean is

$$F_{t+1} = \frac{\Sigma A_t}{n}$$

$$F_6 = \frac{51 + 53 + 48 + 52 + 50}{5}$$

$$F_6 = 50.8$$

This model is only good for a level data pattern. As the average becomes based on a larger and larger data set, the random variation and the forecasts become more stable. One of the advantages of this model is that only two historical pieces of information need to be carried, the mean itself and the number of observations the mean was based on.

▶ **Simple moving average**
A forecasting method in which only *n* of the most recent observations are averaged.

Simple Moving Average   The **simple moving average** is similar to the simple average except that we are not taking an average of all the data, but are including only *n* of the most recent periods in the average. As new data become available, the oldest are dropped; the number of observations used to compute the average is kept constant. In this manner the simple moving average "moves" through time. Like the simple mean, this model is good only for forecasting level data. The formula is as follows:

$$F_{t+1} = \frac{\Sigma A_t}{n}$$

where F_{t+1} = forecast of demand for the next period, $t + 1$
A_t = actual value for period, t
n = number of periods or data points used in the moving average
t = the most recent period

The formula for the moving average is the same as that for the simple average, except that we use only a small portion of the data to compute the average. For example, if we used a moving average of $n = 3$, we would be averaging only the latest three periods. If we were using a moving average of $n = 5$, we would be averaging only the latest five periods.

■ **Example 8.3 Forecasting with the Simple Moving Average**

Sales forecasts for Bright-White Toothpaste are made using a three-period moving average. Given the following sales figures for January, February, and March, make a forecast for April.

Month	Actual Sales
January	200
February	300
March	200

Solution:
To find the forecast for April we take an average of the last three observations:

$$F_{t+1} = \frac{\Sigma A_t}{n}$$

$$F_{\text{April}} = \frac{A_{\text{January}} + A_{\text{February}} + A_{\text{March}}}{3} = \frac{200 + 300 + 200}{3} = 233.3$$

If the actual figure for April turns out to be 400, let's make a forecast for May. To use a three-period moving average, we average the latest three observations. Since we are adding sales for April we will drop the sales for January:

$$F_{\text{May}} = \frac{A_{\text{February}} + A_{\text{March}} + A_{\text{April}}}{3} = \frac{300 + 200 + 400}{3} = 300$$

Similarly, if the actual sales for May turn out to be 500, we can make a forecast for June:

$$F_{June} = \frac{A_{March} + A_{April} + A_{May}}{3} = \frac{200 + 400 + 500}{3} = 366.7$$

Here is a summary of the forecasts we have made and the actual values:

Month	Actual Sales	Forecast
January	200	
February	300	
March	200	
April	400	234
May	500	300
June	600	367

Just like the mean, the moving average is good only for a level pattern. You can see this in Example 8.3. The data shown in the example are level in the first three periods. However, after the third period the data begin to show a trend. You can see that the forecasts made with the moving average also begin to show a trend. Do you see a problem with the forecasts?

The problem is that the forecasts are trailing behind the actual data. We say that they are "lagging" the data. This is what happens when you apply a model that is good only for a level pattern to data that have a trend. You will not obtain a good forecast.

Weighted Moving Average In the simple moving average each observation is weighted equally. For example, in a three-period moving average each observation is weighted one-third. In a five-period moving average each observation is weighted one-fifth. Sometimes a manager wants to use a moving average but gives higher or lower weights to some observations based on knowledge of the industry. This is called a **weighted moving average.** In a weighted moving average, each observation can be weighted differently provided that all the weights add up to 1.

▶ **Weighted moving average** A forecasting method in which *n* of the most recent observations are averaged and past observations may be weighted differently.

$$F_{t+1} = \Sigma C_t A_t$$

where F_{t+1} = next period's forecast
  C_t = weight placed on the actual value in period t
  A_t = actual value in period t

■ Example 8.4 Forecasting with a Weighted Moving Average

A manager at Fit Well department store wants to forecast sales of swimsuits for August using a three-period weighted moving average. Sales for May, June, and July are as follows:

Month	Actual Sales	Forecast
May	400	
June	500	
July	600	

The manager has decided to weight May (.25), June (.25), and July (.50).

Solution:
The forecast for August is computed as follows:

$$F_{t+1} = \Sigma C_t A_t$$

$$F_{August} = (.25)\, A_{May} + (.25)\, A_{June} + (.50)\, A_{July}$$

$$= (.25)\, 400 + (.25)\, 500 + (.50)\, 600$$

$$= 525$$

▶ **Exponential smoothing model**
Uses a sophisticated weighting average procedure to generate a forecast.

Exponential Smoothing **Exponential smoothing** is a forecasting model that uses a sophisticated weighted-average procedure to obtain a forecast. Even though it is sophisticated in the way it works, it is easy to use and understand. To make a forecast for the next time period you need three pieces of information:

1. the last period's forecast
2. the last period's actual value
3. the value of a smoothing coefficient, α, which varies between 0 and 1.

The equation for the forecast is quite simple:

Next period's forecast = α (last period's actual) + $(1 - \alpha)$(last period's forecast)

In mathematical terms it looks as follows:

$$F_{t+1} = \alpha A_t + (1 - \alpha)\, F_t$$

where F_{t+1} = forecast of demand for period $t + 1$ (next period)
A_t = actual value for period t
F_t = forecast for period t
α = smoothing coefficient

Exponential smoothing models are the most frequently used forecasting techniques and are available on almost all computerized forecasting software. These models are widely used, particularly in operations management. They have been shown to produce accurate forecasts under many conditions, yet are relatively easy to use and understand.

■ **Example 8.5 Forecasting with Exponential Smoothing**

The Hot Tamale Mexican restaurant uses exponential smoothing to forecast monthly usage of tabasco sauce. Its forecast for September was 200 bottles, whereas actual usage in September was 300 bottles. If the restaurant's managers use an α of 0.70, what is their forecast for October?

Solution:
The general equation for exponential smoothing is

$$F_{t+1} = \alpha A_t + (1 - \alpha)\, F_t$$

$$F_{October} = \alpha A_{September} + (1 - \alpha)\, F_{September}$$

$$= (0.70)\,(300) + (0.30)\, 200$$

$$= 270 \text{ bottles}$$

Selecting α Note that depending on which value you select for α, you can place more weight on either the last period's actual or the last period's forecast. In this manner the forecast can either depend more heavily on what happened most recently or on the last period's forecast. Values of α that are low—say, .1 or .2—generate forecasts that are very stable because the model does not place much weight on one observation. Values of α that are high, such as .7 or .8, place a lot of weight on the last period's actual demand and can be influenced by random variations in the data. Thus, how α is selected is very important in getting a good forecast.

Starting the Forecasting Process with Exponential Smoothing One thing you may notice with exponential smoothing is that you need the last period's actual and last period's forecast to make a forecast for the next period. However, what if you are just starting the forecasting process and do not have a value for the last period's forecast? There are many ways to handle this, but the most common is to use the naive method to generate an initial forecast. Another option is to average the last few periods—say, the last three or four—just to get a starting point.

Before You Go On

We have discussed the principles of forecasting, how to forecast, and different types of qualitative and quantitative forecasting models. We have also learned about different types of patterns present in the data. You should understand that to obtain a good forecast the forecasting model should be matched to the patterns in the available data. Our example of the moving average shows what happens when the data show a trend but the model selected is useful only for forecasting a level pattern.

All the quantitative models discussed so far are meant only for level data patterns. In the next section we turn to quantitative models that can be used for other data patterns, such as trend and seasonality. However, remember that the models already discussed are the foundation of forecasting.

Forecasting Trend

There are many ways to forecast trend patterns in data. Some of these models appear complicated, but they really are not. Most of the models used for forecasting trend are the same models used to forecast the level, with one additional feature. This feature is added to the basic models to compensate for the lagging that would otherwise occur. Here we will focus on one trend model, **trend-adjusted exponential smoothing.**

The forecast for trend-adjusted exponential smoothing has three equations. The first smooths out the level of the series, the second smooths out the trend, and the third generates a forecast by adding up the findings from the first two equations. Because we are using a second exponential smoothing equation to compute trend, we have two smoothing coefficients. In addition to α, which is used to smooth out the level of the series, we have a second coefficient, β, which is used to smooth out the trend of the series. Like α, β can theoretically vary between 0 and 1, though we tend to keep the value conservatively low, around 0.1 or 0.2.

▶ **Trend-adjusted exponential smoothing** Exponential smoothing model that is suited to data that exhibit a trend.

Three steps must be followed to generate a forecast with trend:

STEP 1   SMOOTHING THE LEVEL OF THE SERIES

$$S_t = \alpha A_t + (1 - \alpha)(S_{t-1} + T_{t-1})$$

STEP 2   SMOOTHING THE TREND

$$T_t = \beta(S_t - S_{t-1}) + (1 - \beta)T_{t-1}$$

STEP 3   FORECAST INCLUDING TREND

$$FIT_{t+1} = S_t + T_t$$

where FIT_{t+1} = forecast including trend for next period (period $t + 1$)
S_t = exponentially smoothed average of the time series in period t
T_t = exponentially smoothed trend of the time series in period t
α = smoothing coefficient of the level
β = smoothing coefficient of the trend

Note that the last step simply adds up the findings from the first two steps. Next we will look at an example of how this works.

■ **Example 8.6 Forecasting with Trend-Adjusted Exponential Smoothing**

Green Grow is a lawn care company that uses exponential smoothing with trend to forecast monthly usage of its lawn care products. At the end of July the company wishes to forecast sales for August. The trend through June has been 15 additional gallons of product sold per month. Average sales have been 57 gallons per month. The demand for July was 62 gallons. The company uses $\alpha = 0.20$ and $\beta = 0.10$. Make a forecast including trend for the month of August.

Solution:
The information we have is

$$S_{\text{June}} = 57 \text{ gallons/month}$$

$$T_{\text{June}} = 15 \text{ gallons/month}$$

$$A_{\text{July}} = 62 \text{ gallons}$$

$$\alpha = 0.20$$

$$\beta = 0.10$$

Three equations must be used to generate a forecast including trend. For each equation we will substitute the appropriate values:

STEP 1   SMOOTHING THE LEVEL OF THE SERIES,

$$S_t = \alpha A_t + (1 - \alpha)(S_{t-1} + T_{t-1})$$

$$S_{\text{July}} = \alpha A_{\text{July}} + (1 - \alpha)(S_{\text{June}} + T_{\text{June}})$$

$$= (0.20)(62) + (0.80)(57 + 15)$$

$$= 70$$

STEP 2 SMOOTHING THE TREND,

$$T_t = \beta(S_t - S_{t-1}) + (1 - \beta)T_{t-1}$$

$$T_{July} = \beta(S_{July} - S_{June}) + (1 - \beta)T_{June}$$

$$= (0.1)(70 - 57) + (0.90)15$$

$$= 14.8$$

STEP 3 FORECAST INCLUDING TREND,

$$FIT_{t+1} = S_t + T_t$$

$$FIT_{August} = S_{July} + T_{July}$$

$$= 70 + 14.8$$

$$= 84.8 \text{ gallons}$$

Forecasting Seasonality

Recall that any regularly repeating pattern is a seasonal pattern. We are all familiar with quarterly and monthly seasonal patterns. Whether your university is on a quarter or semester plan, you can see that enrollment varies between quarters or semesters in a fairly predictable way. For example, enrollment is usually much higher in the fall than in the summer. Other examples of seasonality include sales of turkeys before Thanksgiving or ham before Easter, sales of greeting cards, hotel registrations, and sales of gardening tools.

The amount of seasonality is the extent to which actual values deviate from the average or mean of the data. Here we will consider only *multiplicative seasonality,* in which the seasonality is expressed as a percentage of the average. The percentage by which the value for each season is above or below the mean is a **seasonal index.** For example, if enrollment for the fall semester at your university is 1.30 of the mean, then fall enrollment is 30% above the average. Similarly, if enrollment for the summer semester is .70 of the mean, then summer enrollment is 70% of the average.

▶ **Seasonal index**
Percentage amount by which data for each season are above or below the mean.

Here we will show only the procedure for computing quarterly seasonality that lasts a year, though the same procedure can be used for any other type of seasonality. The procedure consists of the following steps:

STEP 1 CALCULATE THE AVERAGE DEMAND FOR EACH QUARTER OR "SEASON." This is done by dividing the total annual demand by 4 (the number of seasons per year).

STEP 2 COMPUTE A SEASONAL INDEX FOR EVERY SEASON OF EVERY YEAR FOR WHICH YOU HAVE DATA. This is done by *dividing* the actual demand for each season by the average demand per season (computed in Step 1).

STEP 3 CALCULATE THE AVERAGE SEASONAL INDEX FOR EACH SEASON. For each season, compute the average seasonal index by adding up the seasonal index values for that season and dividing by the number of years.

STEP 4 CALCULATE THE AVERAGE DEMAND PER SEASON FOR NEXT YEAR. This could be done by using any of the methods used to compute annual demand. Then we would divide that by the number of seasons to determine the average demand per season for next year.

STEP 5 MULTIPLY NEXT YEAR'S AVERAGE SEASONAL DEMAND BY EACH SEASONAL INDEX. This will produce a forecast for each season of next year.

■ Example 8.7 Forecasting Seasonality

U-R-Smart University wants to develop forecasts for next year's quarterly enrollment. It has collected quarterly enrollments for the past two years. It has also forecasted total annual enrollment for next year to be 90,000 students. What is the forecast for each quarter of next year?

Enrollment (in thousands)

Quarter	Year 1	Year 2
Fall	24	26
Winter	23	22
Spring	19	19
Summer	14	17
Total	80	84

Solution:

STEP 1   CALCULATE THE AVERAGE DEMAND FOR EACH QUARTER OR "SEASON."

We do this by dividing the total annual demand for each year by 4:

Year 1: 80/4 = 20
Year 2 : 84/4 = 21

STEP 2   COMPUTE A SEASONAL INDEX FOR EVERY SEASON OF EVERY YEAR YOU HAVE DATA.

To do this we divide the actual demand for each season by the average demand per season.

Enrollment (in thousands)

Quarter	Year 1	Year 2
Fall	24/20 = 1.2	26/21 = 1.238
Winter	23/20 = 1.15	22/21 = 1.048
Spring	19/20 = 0.95	19/21 = 0.905
Summer	14/20 = 0.70	17/21 = 0.810

STEP 3   CALCULATE THE AVERAGE SEASONAL INDEX FOR EACH SEASON.

You can see that the seasonal indexes vary from year to year for the same season. The simplest way to handle this is to compute an average index, as follows:

Quarter	Average Seasonal Index
Fall	(1.2 + 1.238)/2 = 1.22
Winter	(1.15 + 1.048)/2 = 1.10
Spring	(0.95 + 0.905)/2 = 0.928
Summer	(0.70 + 0.810)/2 = 0.775

STEP 4   CALCULATE THE AVERAGE DEMAND PER SEASON FOR NEXT YEAR.

We are told that the university forecast annual enrollment for the next year to be 90,000 students. The average demand per season, or quarter, is

90,000/4 = 22,500

STEP 5 MULTIPLY NEXT YEAR'S AVERAGE SEASONAL DEMAND BY EACH SEASONAL INDEX.

This last step will give us the forecast for each quarter of next year:

Quarter	Forecast
Fall	22,500 (1.22) = 27,450 students
Winter	22,500 (1.10) = 24,750 students
Spring	22,500 (0.928) = 20,880 students
Summer	22,500 (0.755) = 16,988 students

Forecasting demand at ski resorts such as Snow Shoe, Holiday Valley, and Seven Springs can be very challenging because data are highly seasonal. Multiple seasonal factors need to be considered, including the month of the year, day of the week, holidays and long weekends, in addition to considering the weather forecast. Historical data are used to develop the indexes for these seasons. In addition, the ski industry has been experiencing an upward trend over the past years, particularly with the growth of snowboarding. A simple way to make forecasts in this industry is to forecast the trend, then make adjustments based on developed seasonal indexes.

LINKS TO PRACTICE
The Ski Industry Forecast

CAUSAL MODELS ■

Recall that causal models assume that the variable we are trying to forecast is somehow related to other variables in the environment. The forecasting challenge is to discover the relationships between the variable of interest and these other variables. These relationships, which can be very complex, take the form of a mathematical model, which is used to forecast future values of the variable of interest. One of the best known and simplest causal models is linear regression. In this section we look at linear regression and how it is used in forecasting.

Linear Regression

In **linear regression** the variable being forecast, called the dependent variable, is related to some other variable, called the independent variable, in a linear (or straight line) way. Figure 8-2 shows how a linear regression line relates to the data. You can see that the dependent variable is linearly related to the independent variable. The relationship between the two variables is the equation of a straight line:

$$Y = a + bX$$

where Y = dependent variable
X = independent variable
a = Y-intercept of the line
b = slope of the line

▶ **Linear regression**
Procedure that models a straight-line relationship between two variables.

Figure 8-2

Linear regression line fit to historical data

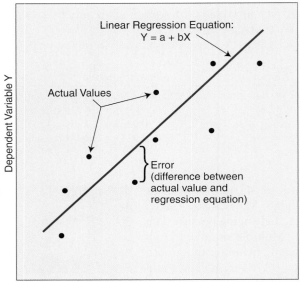

There are many straight lines that could be drawn through the data. Linear regression selects parameters *a* and *b*, which define a straight line that minimizes the sum of the squared errors, or deviations from the line. This is called the *least squares straight line*. Developing the values for *a* and *b* can be complicated, so we simply give their computation here. You can assume that computing *a* and *b* in this way will produce a straight line through the data that minimizes the sum of the squared errors. The steps in computing the linear regression equation are as follows:

STEP 1   Compute parameter *b*

$$b = \frac{\Sigma XY - n\overline{X}\,\overline{Y}}{\Sigma X^2 - n\overline{X}^2}$$

We compute parameter *b* first because that calculation is needed to compute parameter *a*.

STEP 2   Compute parameter *a*:

$$a = \overline{Y} - b\overline{X}$$

STEP 3   Substitute these values to obtain the linear regression equation:

$$Y = a + bX$$

where a = estimate of the *Y*-intercept
b = estimate of the slope of the line
$\overline{Y}$ = average of the *Y*-values
$\overline{X}$ = average of the *X*-values
n = number of data points

The linear regression equation can then be used to calculate a value of *Y* given any value of *X*.

STEP 4 To make a forecast for the dependent variable (Y), substitute the appropriate value for the independent variable (X).

■ Example 8.8 Forecasting with Linear Regression

A maker of personalized golf shirts has been tracking the relationship between sales and advertising dollars over the past four years. The results are as follows:

Sales (in thousands)	Advertising Dollars (in thousands)
130	48
151	52
150	50
158	55

Use linear regression to find out what sales would be if the company invested $53,000 in advertising for next year.

Solution:
In this example sales are the *dependent variable* (Y) and advertising dollars are the *independent variable* (X). We assume that there is a relationship between these two variables. To compute the linear regression equation, we set up the following table of information:

	Y	X	XY	X^2	Y^2
	130	48	6240	2304	16,900
	151	52	7852	2704	22,801
	150	50	7500	2500	22,500
	158	55	8690	3025	24,964
Total	**589**	**205**	**30,282**	**10,533**	**87,165**

$$\overline{X} = 51.25 \qquad \overline{Y} = 147.25$$

Now let's follow the steps necessary for computing a linear regression equation:

STEP 1 Compute parameter b:

$$b = \frac{\Sigma XY - n\overline{X}\,\overline{Y}}{\Sigma X^2 - n\overline{X}^2} = \frac{30,282 - 4\,(51.25)(147.25)}{10,533 - 4\,(51.25)^2} = \frac{95.75}{26.75} = 3.6$$

STEP 2 Compute parameter a:

$$a = \overline{Y} - b\overline{X} = 147.25 - (3.6)\,(51.25) = -37.25$$

STEP 3 Compute the linear regression equation

$$Y = a + bX$$
$$= -37.25 + 3.6X$$

STEP 4 Now that we have the equation, we can compute the value of Y for any value of X. To compute the value of sales when advertising dollars are $53,000, we can substitute that number for X:

$$Y = -37.25 + 3.6(53) = \$153.55 \text{ (in thousands)}$$

Correlation Coefficient

▶ **Correlation coefficient**
Statistic that measures the
direction and strength of the
linear relationship between
two variables.

When performing linear regression it is helpful to compute the **correlation coefficient,** which measures the direction and strength of the linear relationship between the independent and dependent variables. The correlation coefficient is computed using the following equation:

$$r = \frac{n(\Sigma XY) - (\Sigma X)(\Sigma Y)}{\sqrt{[n(\Sigma X^2) - (\Sigma X)^2]}\sqrt{[n(\Sigma Y^2) - (\Sigma Y)^2]}}$$

Although the equation seems complicated, it is easy to compute and the values of r can be easily interpreted. Values of r range between -1 and $+1$ and have the following meanings:

> $r = +1$: There is a perfect positive linear relationship between the two variables. For every one-unit increase in the independent variable there is a one-unit increase in the dependent variable.
>
> $r = -1$: There is a perfect negative linear relationship between the two variables. Just because the relationship is negative does not mean that there is no relationship. It is still a linear relationship except that it is negative; the two variables move in opposite directions. A unit increase in the independent variable is accompanied by a unit decrease in the dependent variable.
>
> $r = 0$: There is no relationship between the variables.

Obviously, the closer the value of r is to 1.00, the stronger is the linear relationship between the two variables. If we square the correlation coefficient, r^2, we can determine how well the independent variable explains changes in the dependent variable. This statistic shows how well the regression line "fits" the data. The higher the r, the better. A high r^2—say, .80 or higher—would indicate that the independent variable can be used effectively as a predictor of the dependent variable.

■ Example 8.9 Computing the Correlation Coefficient

Using the information from Example 8-8, compute the correlation coefficient and evaluate the strength of the linear relationship between sales and advertising dollars.

Solution:
Given our information, we can compute the correlation coefficient as follows:

$$r = \frac{n(\Sigma XY) - (\Sigma X)(\Sigma Y)}{\sqrt{[n(\Sigma X^2) - (\Sigma X)^2]} \cdot \sqrt{[n(\Sigma Y^2) - (\Sigma Y)^2]}}$$

$$= \frac{4(30,282) - (205)(589)}{\sqrt{[4(10,533) - (205)^2]} \cdot \sqrt{[4(87,165) - (589)^2]}} = .887$$

The computed correlation coefficient is close to 1, which means that there is a strong linear relationship between the two variables. Also, if we compute r^2 we get .786, which means that 78.6% of the variability in sales is explained by advertising dollars.

Using Time as an Independent Variable

Time is frequently used as an independent variable of demand. This approach can be very useful for computing trend for a time series. It is simple, easy to use, and easy to understand, as we can see in the next example.

■ Example 8.10 Linear Regression with Time as an Independent Variable

A cookie manufacturer has plotted sales of cookies over the past four weeks. Use a linear regression equation to compute sales of cookies for week 5.

Solution:

Weeks X	Sales Y	Weeks X^2	Sales XY
1	2,300	1	2,300
2	2,400	4	4,800
3	2,300	9	6,900
4	2,500	16	10,000
Totals **10**	**9,500**	**30**	**24,000**

$\overline{Y} = 2375 \qquad \overline{X} = 2.5$

STEP 1   Compute parameter b:

$$b = \frac{\Sigma XY - n\overline{X}\,\overline{Y}}{\Sigma X^2 - n\overline{X}^2} = \frac{24{,}000 - 4(2.5)(2375)}{30 - 4(2.5)^2} = \frac{250}{5} = 50$$

STEP 2   Compute parameter a:

$$a = \overline{Y} - b\overline{X} = 2375 - (50)(2.5) = 2250$$

STEP 3   Compute the linear regression equation:

$$Y = a + bX$$
$$= 2250 + 50X$$

STEP 4   For the fifth week, the value of sales would be

$$Y = 2250 + 50(5) = 2500$$

MEASURING FORECAST ACCURACY ■

One of the basic principles of forecasting is that forecasts are rarely perfect. However, how does a manager know how much a forecast can be off the mark and still be reasonable? One of the most important criteria for choosing a forecasting model is its accuracy. Also, data can change over time, and a model that once provided good results may no longer be adequate. The model's accuracy can be assessed only if forecast performance is measured over time. For all these reasons it is important to track model performance over time, which involves monitoring forecast errors.

Forecast Accuracy Measures

Forecast error is the difference between the forecast and actual value for a given period, or

$$E_t = A_t - F_t$$

where E_t = forecast error for period t
A_t = actual value for period t
F_t = forecast for period t

▶ **Forecast error**
Difference between forecast and actual value for a given period.

However, error for one time period does not tell us very much. We need to measure forecast accuracy over time. Two of the most commonly used error measures are the **mean absolute deviation (MAD)** and the **mean squared error (MSE)**. *MAD* is the average of the sum of the absolute errors:

▶ **Mean absolute deviation** *(MAD)* Measure of forecast error that computes error as the average of the sum of the absolute errors.

$$MAD = \frac{\Sigma|\text{actual} - \text{forecast}|}{n}$$

MSE is the sum of the squared errors divided by $n - 1$:

▶ **Mean squared error** *(MSE)* Measure of forecast error that computes error as the sum of the squared errors divided by $n - 1$.

$$MSE = \frac{\Sigma(\text{actual} - \text{forecast})^2}{n - 1}$$

One of the advantages of *MAD* is that it is based on absolute values. Consequently, the errors of opposite signs do not cancel each other out when they are added. We sum the errors regardless of sign and obtain a measure of average error. If we are comparing different forecasting methods, we can then select the method with the lowest *MAD*.

MSE has another advantage: Due to the squaring of the error term, large errors tend to be magnified. Consequently, *MSE* places a higher penalty on large errors. This can be a useful error measure in environments in which large errors are particularly destructive. For example, a blood bank forecasts the demand for blood. Because forecasts are rarely perfect, there will be errors. However, in this environment a large error could be very damaging. Using *MSE* as an error measure would highlight any large errors in the blood bank's forecast. As with *MAD*, when comparing the forecast performance of different methods we would select the method with the lowest *MSE*.

To evaluate forecast performance, you need to use only one forecast error measure. However, a good forecaster learns to rely on multiple methods to evaluate forecast performance. Example 8.11 illustrates the use of *MAD* and *MSE*.

■ Example 8.11 Measuring Forecast Accuracy

Standard Parts Corporation is comparing the accuracy of two methods that it has used to forecast sales of its popular valve. Forecasts using method A and method B are shown against the actual values for January through May. Which method provided better forecast accuracy?

Solution

Month	Actual Sales	Method A			Method B		
		Forecast	Error	Error	Error²	Forecast	Error	Error	Error²
January	30	28	2	2	4	30	0	0	0
February	26	25	1	1	1	28	−2	2	4
March	32	32	0	0	0	36	−4	4	16
April	29	30	−1	1	1	30	−1	1	1
May	31	30	1	1	1	28	3	3	9
Total			3	5	7		−4	10	30

Accuracy for method A:

$$MAD = \frac{\Sigma|actual - forecast|}{n} = \frac{5}{5} = 1$$

$$MSE = \frac{\Sigma(actual - forecast)^2}{n - 1} = \frac{7}{4} = 1.75$$

Accuracy for Method B:

$$MAD = \frac{\Sigma|actual - forecast|}{n} = \frac{10}{5} = 2$$

$$MSE = \frac{\Sigma(actual - forecast)^2}{n - 1} = \frac{30}{4} = 7.5$$

Of the two methods, method B produced a lower *MAD* and a lower *MSE*, which means that it provides better forecast accuracy. Note that the magnitude of difference in values is greater for *MSE* than for *MAD*. Recall that *MSE* magnifies large errors through the squaring process. For the month of March, method B had a magnitude of error that was much larger than for other periods, causing *MSE* to be high.

Tracking Signal

When there is a difference between forecast and actual values, one problem is to identify whether the difference is caused by random variation or is due to a *bias* in the forecast. **Forecast bias** is a persistent tendency for a forecast to be over or under the actual value of the data. We cannot do anything about random variation, but bias can be corrected.

▶ **Forecast bias**
A persistent tendency for a forecast to be over or under the actual value of the data.

One way to control for forecast bias is to use a *tracking signal*. A **tracking signal** is a tool used to monitor the quality of the forecast. It is computed as the ratio of the algebraic sum of the forecast errors divided by *MAD*:

▶ **Tracking signal**
Tool used to monitor the quality of a forecast.

$$\text{Tracking signal} = \frac{\text{algebraic sum of forecast errors}}{MAD}$$

or

$$\text{Tracking signal} = \frac{\Sigma(actual - forecast)}{MAD}$$

As the forecast errors are summed over time, they can indicate whether there is a bias in the forecast. To monitor forecast accuracy, the values of the tracking signal are compared against predetermined limits. These limits are usually based on judgment and experience and can range from ± 3 to ± 8. In this chapter we will use the limits of ± 4, which compare to limits of 3 standard deviations. If errors fall outside these limits, the forecast should be reviewed.

■ **Example 8.12 Developing a Tracking Signal**

A company uses a tracking signal with limits of ±4 to decide whether a forecast should be reviewed. Compute the tracking signal given the following historical information and decide when the forecast should be reviewed. The *MAD* for this item was computed as 2.

Weeks	Actual	Forecast	Deviation	Cumulative Deviation	Tracking Signal
				4	2
1	8	10			
2	11	10			
3	12	10			
4	14	10			

Solution:

Weeks	Actual	Forecast	Deviation	Cumulative Deviation	Tracking Signal
				4	2
1	8	10	−2	2	1
2	11	10	1	3	1.5
3	12	10	2	5	2.5
4	14	10	4	9	4.5

The forecast should be reviewed in week 4 because the tracking signal has exceeded +4.

■ FOCUS FORECASTING

Focus forecasting is a forecasting approach that has gained some popularity in business. It was developed by Bernie Smith,[1] who argues that statistical methods do not work well for forecasting. He believes simple rules that have worked well in the past are best used to forecast the future. The idea behind focus forecasting is to test these rules on past data and evaluate how they perform. New rules can be added at any time, and old ones that have not performed well can be eliminated.

Focus forecasting uses a computer simulation program that evaluates the forecast performance of a number of rules on past data. The program keeps track of the rules and evaluates how well they perform. Following are some examples of rules:

1. We will sell over the next three months what we sold over the last three months.
2. What we sold in a three-month period last year, we will sell in the same three-month period this year.
3. We will sell over the next three months 5% of what we sold over the last three months.
4. We will sell over the next three months 15% of what we sold over the same three-month period last year.

[1]Bernard T. Smith, *Focus Forecasting: Computer Techniques for Inventory Control* (Boston: CBI, 1984).

You can see that these rules use commonsense concepts. In focus forecasting, managers can come up with any new rules that they believe reflect accurate forecasts in their business and then test their value on historical data.

Smith claims to have achieved great success with focus forecasting. He states that he has compared its accuracy to that of conventional methods, such as exponential smoothing, and that focus forecasting consistently provides superior results.

SELECTING THE RIGHT FORECASTING MODEL ▪

A number of factors influence the selection of a forecasting model. They include the following:

1. *Amount and type of available data.* Quantitative forecasting models require certain types of data. If there are not enough data in quantifiable form, it may be necessary to use a qualitive forecasting model. Also, different quantitative models require different amounts of data. Exponential smoothing requires a small amount of historical data, whereas linear regression requires considerably more. The amount and type of data available play a large role in the type of model that can be considered.

2. *Degree of accuracy required.* The type of model selected is related to the degree of accuracy required. Some situations require only rough forecast estimates, whereas others require precise accuracy. Often, the greater the degree of accuracy required, the higher is the cost of the forecasting process. This is because increasing accuracy means increasing the costs of collecting and processing data, as well as the computer software required. A simpler and less costly forecasting model may be better overall than one that is very sophisticated but expensive.

3. *Length of forecast horizon.* Some forecasting models are better suited to short forecast horizons, whereas others are better for long horizons. It is very important to select the correct model for the forecast horizon being used. For example, a manufacturer that wishes to forecast sales of a product for the next 3 months will use a very different forecasting model than an electric utility that wishes to forecast demand for electricity over the next 25 years.

4. *Data patterns present.* It is very important to identify the patterns in the data and select the appropriate model. For example, lagging can occur when a forecasting model meant for a level pattern is applied to data with trend.

FORECASTING SOFTWARE ▪

Today much commercial forecasting is performed using computer software. There are many software packages that can be used for forecasting. Some can handle thousands of variables and manipulate huge databases. Others specialize in one forecasting model. Consequently, it may be difficult to select the right forecasting software. Most forecasting software packages fall into one of three categories: (1) spreadsheets, (2) statistics packages, and (3) specialty forecasting packages. In this section we look at the differences among these categories. Then we present some guidelines for selecting a software package for forecasting.

Spreadsheets

Spreadsheets are computer packages such as Microsoft Excel®, Quattro Pro®, and Lotus 1-2-3®. They are prevalent in business, and most people are familiar with at least one of them. These packages provide basic forecast capability, such as simple exponential smoothing, and regression. Also, simple forecasting programs can be written very quickly on most spreadsheet programs. However, the disadvantage of using spreadsheets for forecasting is that they do not have the capability for statistical analysis of forecast data. As we have seen, proper forecasting requires much data analysis. This involves analyzing the data for patterns, studying relationships among variables, monitoring forecast errors, and evaluating the performance of different forecasting models. Unfortunately, spreadsheets do not offer this capability as readily as packages designed specifically for forecasting.

Statistical Packages

Statistical software includes packages designed primarily for statistical analysis, such as SPSS, SAS, NCSS, and Minitab. Almost all of these packages also offer forecasting capabilities, as well as extensive data analysis capability. There are large differences among statistical packages, particularly between those for mainframe versions versus those for microcomputers. Overall, these packages offer large capability and a variety of options. However, their many features can be overwhelming for someone interested only in forecasting. Statistical software packages are best for a user who seeks many statistical and graphical capabilities in addition to forecasting features.

Specialty Forecasting Packages

Specialized forecasting software is specifically intended for forecasting use. These packages often provide an extensive range of forecasting capability, though they may not offer large statistical analysis capability. Popular packages include Forecast Master, Forecast Pro, SIBYL/Runner, Autobox, and SCA. Some of these packages offer a wide range of forecasting models, whereas others specialize in a particular model category. Forecasters who need extensive statistical analysis capability may need to use a statistical package in addition to the forecasting package.

Guidelines for Selecting Forecasting Software

There are many forecasting software packages to choose from, and the process can be overwhelming. Following are some guidelines for selecting the right package:[2]

1. *Does the package have the facilities you want?* The first question to ask is whether the forecasting methods you are considering using are available in

[2]S. Makridakis, S. Wheelwright, and R. Hyndman, *Forecasting Methods and Applications,* 3rd edition (New York: John Wiley, 1998).

the package. Other issues to consider are the software's graphics capabilities and data management and reporting facilities. You need to consider how important these are given the purpose of the forecasts you will be generating.

2. *What platform is the package available for?* You obviously need to make sure that the software is available for the platform you are using. Also, it may be necessary to consider the availability for multiple platforms, depending on who will use the software and whether there will be transferring of files.

3. *How easy is the package to learn and use?* Some packages offer many capabilities but may be hard to use. Generally, the more comprehensive the array of capabilities, the more difficult the package is to use. Make sure that you can master the software. Also check the ease of importing and exporting data.

4. *Is it possible to implement new methods?* Often forecasters prefer to modify existing methods to fit their particular needs. Many forecasting packages allow the addition of new models or the modification of existing ones through a programming language.

5. *Do you require interactive or repetitive forecasting?* In many operations management situations we need to make forecasts for hundreds of items on a regular basis, such as monthly or quarterly. For these situations it is very useful to have a "batch" forecasting capability. This is not necessary, however, for forecasts that are generated interactively with the forecaster.

6. *Do you have very large data sets?* Almost all packages have a limit on how many variables and how many observations can be processed. Sometimes very powerful forecasting packages can handle only relatively small data sets. Make sure the package you purchase is capable of processing the data you need.

7. *Is there any local support?* Make sure there is ample documentation and good technical support, and check for any other local support that may be available. Remember that all packages can encounter glitches. A number of forecasting vendors offer seminars, and there are often courses that can be taken for the more popular methods, such as SAS and SPSS.

8. *Does the package give the right answers?* Most people assume that a computer package will generate correct results. However, this is not always the case. There are small differences in output between different packages due to differences in the algorithms used for computing. Some differences can result from actual errors in the programs, especially when large data sets are used. One recommendation is to compare output from the software against published results or against output from another package.

Another factor to consider is the *cost of the package* relative to the importance of its use. Some packages are very expensive and comprehensive, while others are less expensive. Evaluate the use of the forecasts generated and their importance in the managerial situation before purchasing a highly expensive package. Finally, you need to consider *compatibility with existing software,* especially for other operations management applications such as scheduling and inventory control. The output from forecasting usually feeds into these systems, so you need to make sure these systems can communicate with one another.

CROSS FUNCTIONAL

OM ACROSS THE ORGANIZATION

Forecasting is an excellent example of an activity that is critical to the management of all functional areas within a company. In business organizations, forecasts are made in virtually every function and at every organizational level. Budgets are set, resources allocated, and schedules made based on forecasts. Without a forecast of the future, a company would not be able to make any plans, including day-to-day and long-range plans. In this section we look at how forecasting affects some of the other functions of an organization.

Operations managers make all kinds of forecasts that affect the functioning of the operation. Included are forecasting the demand for products and services, forecasting the number of person-hours required to meet a given production schedule, forecasting the demand for supplies and materials, and forecasting future needs for space and capacity.

Marketing relies heavily on forecasting tools to generate forecasts of demand and future sales. However, the marketing department also needs to forecast sizes of markets, new competition, future trends, and changes in consumer preferences. Most of the forecasting methods discussed in this chapter are used by marketing. Marketing often works in conjunction with operations to assess future demands.

Finance uses the tools of forecasting to predict stock prices, financial performance, capital invest-

ment needs, and investment portfolio returns. The accuracy of demand forecasts, in turn, affects the ability of finance to plan future cash flow and financial needs.

Information systems plays an important role in the forecasting process. Today's forecasting requires sharing of information and databases not only within a business but also between business entities. Often companies share their forecasts or demand information with their suppliers. These capabilities would not be possible without an up-to-date information system.

Human resources relies on forecasting to determine future hiring requirements. In addition, forecasts are made of the job market, labor skill availability, future wages and compensation, hiring and layoff costs, and training costs. In order to recruit proper talent, it is necessary to forecast labor needs and availability.

Economics relies on forecasting to predict the duration of business cycles, economic turning points, and general economic conditions that affect business. Whenever a plan of action is required, that plan is based on some anticipation of the future—a forecast. Whether in business, industry, government, or in other fields such as medicine, engineering, and science, proper planning for the future starts with a good forecast.

■ OM IS EVERYWHERE

Just as a business cannot make plans without a forecast of the future, neither can you. You make forecasts every day. They range from predicting the weather and planning what you will wear to forecasting the job market for your major when you graduate from college. Some of the techniques discussed in this chapter can help you in your daily forecasting. For example, you can look for patterns in data every time you forecast, and you can forecast separately for trend, seasonality, or any other pattern. Also, be cautious when using qualitative forecasting because of the biases that can reduce forecast accuracy. Since you now understand these biases, you can guard against them. You can also evaluate qualitative forecasts made by others, be they friends, weather forecasters, or economists, with greater understanding. Finally, regardless of what and how you forecast, you should always measure how you are doing, so you can learn from the past and decide whether to change your procedure in the future.

CHAPTER HIGHLIGHTS

1 Three basic principles of forecasting are: forecasts are rarely perfect; forecasts are more accurate for groups or families of items rather than for individual items; and forecasts are more accurate for shorter than longer time horizons.

2 The forecasting process involves five steps: decide what to forecast; evaluate and analyze appropriate data; select and test a forecasting model; generate the forecast; and monitor forecast accuracy.

3 Forecasting methods can be classified into two groups: *qualitative* and *quantitative*. Qualitative forecasting methods generate a forecast based on the subjective opinion of the forecaster. Some examples of qualitative methods include *executive opinion, market research,* and the *Delphi method*. Quantitative forecasting methods are based on mathematical modeling. They can be divided into two categories: *time series models* and *causal models*.

4 Time series models are based on the assumption that all the information needed for forecasting is contained in the time series of data. Causal models assume that the variable being forecast is related to other variables in the environment.

5 There are four basic patterns of data: *level* or *horizontal, trend, seasonality,* and *cycles*. In addition, data usually contain *random variation*. Some forecasting models that can be used to forecast the level of a time series are *naive, simple mean, simple moving average, weighted moving average,* and *exponential smoothing*. Separate models are used to forecast trend, such as *trend-adjusted exponential smoothing*. Forecasting seasonality requires a procedure in which we compute a *seasonal index*, the percentage by which each season is above or below the mean.

6 A simple causal model is linear regression, in which a straight-line relationship is modeled between the variable we are forecasting and another variable in the environment. The correlation coefficient is used to measure the strength of the linear relationship between these two variables.

7 Three useful measures of forecast accuracy are mean absolute deviation (*MAD*), mean square error (*MSE*), and a tracking signal.

8 There are four factors to consider when selecting a forecasting model: the amount and type of data available, the degree of accuracy required, the length of forecast horizon, and patterns present in the data.

KEY TERMS

forecasting 206
qualitative forecasting methods 208
quantitative forecasting methods 208
time series models 211
causal forecasting models 211

data patterns 212
level data 213
trend 213
seasonality 213
cycle 214

randomness 214
forecast accuracy 227
tracking signal 229

FORMULA REVIEW

1. $F_{t+1} = A_t$

2. $F_{t+1} = \dfrac{\Sigma A_t}{n}$

3. $F_{t+1} = \Sigma C_t A_t$

4. $F_{t+1} = \alpha A_t + (1 - \alpha)F_t$

5. $S_t = \alpha A_t + (1 - \alpha)(S_{t-1} + T_{t-1})$

6. $T_t = \beta(S_t - S_{t-1}) + (1 - \beta)T_{t-1}$

7. $FIT_{t+1} = S_t + T_t$

8. $Y = a + bX$

9. $b = \dfrac{(\Sigma XY) - n\overline{XY}}{\Sigma X^2 - n\overline{X}^2}$

10. $a = \overline{Y} - b\overline{X}$

11. $r = \dfrac{n(\Sigma XY) - (\Sigma X)(\Sigma Y)}{\sqrt{[n(\Sigma X^2) - (\Sigma X^2)]} \ \sqrt{[n(\Sigma Y^2) - (\Sigma Y)^2]}}$

12. $E_t = A_t - F_t$

13. $MAD = \dfrac{\Sigma |\text{actual} - \text{forecast}|}{n}$

14. $MSE = \dfrac{\Sigma(\text{actual} - \text{forecast})^2}{n - 1}$

15. $\text{Tracking signal} = \dfrac{\Sigma(\text{actual} - \text{forecast})}{MAD}$

SOLVED PROBLEMS

■ Solved Problem 1

Given the following data, calculate forecasts for months 4, 5, 6, and 7 using a three-month moving average and an exponential smoothing forecast with an alpha of 0.3. Assume a forecast of 61 for month 3:

Month	Actual Sales	Forecast Three-Month Moving Average	Forecast Exponential Smoothing
1	56		
2	76		
3	58		
4	67		
5	75		
6	76		
7			

Solution:

Month	Actual Sales	Forecast Three-Month Moving Average	Forecast Exponential Smoothing
1	56		
2	76		
3	58		
4	67	63.33	60.1
5	75	67	62.17
6	76	66.66	66.02
7		72.66	69.01

To compute the moving average forecasts:

$$F_{t+1} = \frac{\Sigma A_t}{n}$$

$$F_4 = \frac{A_1 + A_2 + A_3}{3} = \frac{56 + 76 + 58}{3} = 63.33$$

$$F_5 = \frac{A_2 + A_3 + A_4}{3} = \frac{76 + 58 + 67}{3} = 67$$

$$F_6 = \frac{A_3 + A_4 + A_5}{3} = \frac{58 + 67 + 75}{3} = 66.66$$

$$F_7 = \frac{A_4 + A_5 + A_6}{3} = \frac{67 + 75 + 76}{3} = 72.66$$

To compute the exponential smoothing forecasts:

$$F_{t+1} = \alpha A_t + (1 - \alpha)F_t$$
$$F_4 = \alpha A_3 + (1 - \alpha)F_3$$
$$F_4 = (0.30)(58) + (0.70)\,61 = 60.1$$
$$F_5 = (0.30)(67) + (0.70)\,60.1 = 62.17$$
$$F_6 = (0.30)(75) + (0.70)\,62.17 = 66.02$$
$$F_7 = (0.30)(76) + (0.70)\,66.02 = 69.01$$

This problem can also be solved using a spreadsheet. This is shown in Spreadsheet 8-1.

Spreadsheet 8.1

Alpha =   0.3

Month	Actual Sales	3 Month Forecast	Exp. Smoothing Forecast
1	56		56.00
2	76		56.00
3	58		62.00
4	67	63.33	60.80
5	75	67.00	62.66
6	76	66.67	66.36
7		72.67	69.25

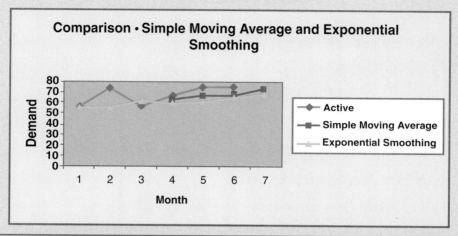

Comparison • Simple Moving Average and Exponential Smoothing

■ Solved Problem 2

True Beauty is a cosmetics company that uses exponential smoothing with trend to forecast monthly sales of its special face cream. At the end of November the company wants to forecast sales for December. The trend through October has been 10 additional boxes sold per month. Average sales have been 60 boxes per month. The demand for November was 68 boxes. The company uses $\alpha = 0.20$ and $\beta = 0.10$. Make a forecast including trend for the month of December.

Solution:

The information we have is:

$$S_{\text{October}} = 60 \text{ boxes/month}$$
$$T_{\text{October}} = 10 \text{ boxes/month}$$
$$A_{\text{November}} = 68 \text{ boxes}$$
$$\alpha = 0.20$$
$$\beta = 0.10$$

We need to use three equations to generate a forecast including trend. For each equation we substitute the appropriate values:

STEP 1   Smoothing the level of the series:

$$S_t = \alpha A_t + (1 - \alpha)(S_{t-1} + T_{t-1})$$
$$S_{\text{November}} = \alpha A_{\text{November}} + (1 - \alpha)(S_{\text{Oct}} + T_{\text{Oct}})$$
$$= (0.20)(68) + (0.80)(60 + 10)$$
$$= 69.6$$

STEP 2   Smoothing the trend:

$$T_t = \beta (S_t - S_{t-1}) + (1 - \beta)T_{t-1}$$
$$T_{\text{November}} = \beta (S_{\text{Nov}} - S_{\text{Oct}}) + (1 - \beta)T_{\text{Oct}}$$
$$= (0.1)(69 - 60) + (0.90) 10$$
$$= 9.9$$

STEP 3   Forecast including trend:

$$FIT_{t+1} = S_t + T_t$$
$$FIT_{\text{December}} = S_{\text{Nov}} + T_{\text{Nov}}$$
$$= 69 + 9.9$$
$$= 78.9 \text{ boxes}$$

■ Solved Problem 3

A gardener wants to develop a forecast for next year's quarterly sales of cactus trees. He has collected quarterly sales for the past two years and expects total sales for next year to be 500 cactus trees. How much can he expect to sell during each quarter of next year?

	Cactus Trees Sold	
Season	Year 1	Year 2
Fall	100	110
Winter	82	95
Spring	180	173
Summer	110	110
Total	**472**	**488**

Solution:

We follow the steps used in developing seasonal indexes:

STEP 1   *Calculate the average demand for each season.*

Year 1: 472/4 = 118
Year 2 : 488/4 = 122

STEP 2   *Compute a seasonal index for every season of every year for which we have data.*

	Cactus Trees Sold	
Season	Year 1	Year 2
Fall	100/118 = .847	110/122 = .902
Winter	82/118 = .695	95/122 = .778
Spring	180/118 = 1.53	173/122 = 1.42
Summer	110/118 = .932	110/122 = 0.902

STEP 3   *Calculate the average seasonal index for each season.*

Season	Average Seasonal Index
Fall	(.847 + .902)/2 = .875
Winter	(.695 + .778)/2 = .737
Spring	(1.53 + 1.42)/2 = 1.48
Summer	(.932 + .902)/2 = .917

STEP 4   *Calculate the average demand per season for next year.*

We are told that the sales forecast for next year is 500 cactus trees. The average demand per season, or quarter, is

500/4 = 125

STEP 5   *Multiply next year's average seasonal demand by each seasonal index.*

Season	Forecast
Fall	125 (.875) = 109.4 cactus trees
Winter	125 (.737) = 92.13 cactus trees
Spring	125 (1.48) = 185 cactus trees
Summer	125(.917) = 114.6 cactus trees

■ Solved Problem 4

A sneaker manufacturer has plotted sales of its most popular brand of sneakers over the past four months. Use a linear regression equation to compute sales of sneakers for month 5.

Solution:

Month X	Sales Y	X^2	XY
1	100	1	100
2	120	4	240
3	118	9	354
4	125	16	500
Total	**10**	**463**	**30**	**1194**

$\overline{Y} = 115.75$ $\overline{X} = 2.5$

STEP 1   *Compute parameter b:*

$$b = \frac{(\Sigma XY) - n\overline{XY}}{\Sigma X^2 - n\overline{X}^2}$$

$$= \frac{1194 - 4(2.5)(115.75)}{30 - 4(2.5)^2} = \frac{36.5}{5} = 7.3$$

STEP 2   *Compute parameter a:*

$a = \overline{Y} - b\overline{X} = 115.75 - (7.3)(2.5) = 97.5$

STEP 3   *Compute the linear regression equation*

$Y = a + bX$
$Y = 97.5 + 7.3X$

STEP 4   *For the fifth month, the value of sales would be*

$Y = 97.5 + 7.3(5) = 134$ sneakers

■ Solved Problem 5

A company is comparing the accuracy of two different forecasting methods. Use *MAD* to compare the accuracies of these methods on the past five weeks of sales. Which method provides greater forecast accuracy?

Solution:

Week	Actual Sales	Method A			Method B		
		Forecast	Error	|Error|	Forecast	Error	|Error|
1	25	30	−5	5	30	−5	5
2	18	20	−2	2	16	2	2
3	26	23	3	3	25	1	1
4	28	29	−1	1	30	−2	2
5	30	25	5	5	28	2	2
Total			**0**	**16**		**−2**	**12**

Accuracy for method A: $MAD = \dfrac{\Sigma|\text{actual} - \text{forecast}|}{n} = \dfrac{16}{5} = 3.2$

Accuracy for method B: $MAD = \dfrac{\Sigma|\text{actual} - \text{forecast}|}{n} = \dfrac{12}{5} = 2.4$

Of the two methods, method B produced a lower *MAD*, which means that it provides greater forecast accuracy. Note, however, that the sum of the errors was actually 0 for method A, which shows how this error measure can be misleading.

DISCUSSION QUESTIONS

1. Give three examples showing why a business needs to forecast.

2. Give three examples from your life in which you make forecast the future.

3. Describe the steps involved in forecasting.

4. Identify the key differences between qualitative and quantitative forecasting methods. Which is better in your opinion and why?

5. What are the main types of data patterns? Give examples of each type.

6. Describe the different assumptions of time series and causal models.

7. What are the differences among models that forecast the level, trend, and seasonality?

8. Explain why it is important to monitor forecast errors.

9. Explain some of the factors to be considered in selecting a forecasting model.

PROBLEMS

1. Sales for a product for the past three months have been 200, 350, and 287. Use a three-month moving average to calculate a forecast for the fourth month. If the actual demand for month 4 turns out to be 300, calculate the forecast for month 5.

2. Lauren's Beauty Boutique has experienced the following weekly sales:

Week	Sales
1	432
2	396
3	415
4	458
5	460

Forecast sales for week 6 using the naive method, a simple average, and a three-period moving average.

3. Hospitality Hotels forecasts monthly labor needs.

(a) Given the following monthly labor figures, make a forecast for June using a three-period moving average and a five-period moving average.

Month	Actual Values
January	32
February	41
March	38
April	39
May	43

(b) What would be the forecast for June using the naive method?

(c) If the actual labor figure for June turns out to be 41, what would be the forecast for July using each of these models?

(d) Compare the accuracy of these models using the mean absolute deviation (MAD).

(e) Compare the accuracy of these models using the mean squared error (MSE).

4. Following are monthly sales of jeans at a local department store. The buyer would like to forecast sales of jeans for the next month, July.

(a) Forecast sales of jeans for March through June using the naive method, a two-period moving average, and exponential smoothing with an $\alpha = 0.2$ (Hint: use naive to start the exponential smoothing process).

(b) Compare the forecasts using MAD and decide which is best.

(c) Using your method of choice, make a forecast for the month of July.

Month	Sales
January	45
February	30
March	40
April	50
May	55
June	47

5. The manager of a small health clinic would like to use exponential smoothing to forecast demand for laboratory services in their facility. However, she is not sure whether to use a high or low value of α. To make her decision, she would like to compare the forecast accuracy of a high and low α on historical data. She has decided to use an $\alpha = .7$ for the high value and $\alpha = .1$ for the low value. Given the following historical data, which do you think would be better to use?

Week	Demand (lab requirements)
1	330
2	350
3	320
4	370
5	368
6	343

6. The manager of the health clinic in problem #5 would also like to use exponential smoothing to forecast demand for emergency services in their facility. As in problem #5, she is not sure whether to use a high or low value of α. To make her decision, she would like to compare the forecast accuracy of a high and low α on historical data. Again, she has decided to use an $\alpha = .7$ for the high value and $\alpha = .1$ for the low value.

(a) Given the following historical data, which value of α do you think would be better to use?

(b) Is your answer the same as in problem #5? Why or why not?

Week	Demand (in patients serviced)
1	430
2	289
3	367
4	470
5	468
6	365

7. The following historical data has been collected representing sales of a product. Compare forecasts using a 3-period moving average, exponential smoothing with a $\alpha = .2$, and linear regression using MAD and MSE. Which forecast-

ing model is best? Are your results the same using the two error measures?

Week	Demand
1	20
2	31
3	36
4	38
5	42
6	40

8. A manufacturer of printed circuit boards uses exponential smoothing with trend to forecast monthly demand of its product. At the end of December the company wishes to forecast sales for January. The estimate of trend through November has been 200 additional boards sold per month. Average sales have been around 1000 units per month. The demand for December was 1100 units. The company uses $\alpha = 0.20$ and $\beta = 0.10$. Make a forecast including trend for the month of January.

9. Demand at Nature Trails Ski Resort has a seasonal pattern. Demand is highest during the winter, as this is the peak ski season. However, there is some ski demand in the spring and even fall months. The summer months can also be busy as visitors often come for summer vacation to go hiking on the mountain trails. The owner of Nature Trails would like to make a forecast for each season of the next year. Total annual demand has been estimated at 4,000 visitors. Given the last two years of historical data, what is the forecast for each season of the next year?

Season	Visitors Year 1	Year 2
Fall	200	230
Winter	1,400	1,600
Spring	520	580
Summer	720	831

10. Rosa's Italian restaurant wants to develop forecasts of daily demand for the next week. The restaurant is closed on Mondays, and experiences a seasonal pattern for the other six days of the week. Mario, the manager, has collected information on the number of customers served each day for the past two weeks. If Mario expects total demand for next week to be around 350, what is the forecast for each day of next week?

Day	Number of Customers Week 1	Week 2
Tuesday	52	48
Wednesday	36	32
Thursday	35	30
Friday	89	97
Saturday	98	99
Sunday	65	69

11. The president of a company was interested to determine whether there is a correlation between sales made by different sales teams and hours spent on employee training. These figures are shown below.

Sales (In thousands)	Training Hours
25	10
40	12
36	12
50	15
11	6

(a) Compute the correlation coefficient for the above data. What is your interpretation of this value?

(b) Using the above data, what would you expect sales to be if training was increased to 18 hours?

12. The number of students enrolled at Spring Valley Elementary has been steadily increasing over the past 5 years. The School Board would like to forecast enrollment for years 6 and 7 in order to better plan capacity. Use a linear regression model to forecast enrollment for years 6 and 7.

Year	Enrollment
1	220
2	245
3	256
4	289
5	310

13. Happy Lodge Ski Resorts tries to forecast monthly attendance. The management has noticed a direct relationship between the average monthly temperature and attendance.

(a) Given five months of average monthly temperatures and corresponding monthly attendance, compute a linear regression equation of the relationship between the two. If next month's average temperature is forecast to be 45 degrees, use your linear regression equation to develop a forecast.

Month	Average Temperature	Resort Attendance (in thousands)
1	24	43
2	41	31
3	32	39
4	30	38
5	38	35

(b) Compute a correlation coefficient for the above data and determine the strength of the linear relationship between average temperature and attendance. How good a predictor is temperature for attendance?

14. Small Wonder, an amusement park, experiences seasonal attendance. It has collected two years of quarterly at-

tendance data and made a forecast of annual attendance for the coming year. Compute the seasonal indexes for the four quarters and generate quarterly forecasts for the coming year, assuming annual attendance for the coming year to be 1525.

Park Attendance (in thousands)

Quarter	Year 1	Year 2
Fall	352	391
Winter	156	212
Spring	489	518
Summer	314	352

15. Burger Lover Restaurant forecasts weekly sales of cheeseburgers. Based on historical observations over the past five weeks, make a forecast for the next period using the following methods: simple average, three-period moving average, and exponential smoothing with $\alpha = .3$, given a forecast of 328 cheeseburgers for the fifth week.

Week	Cheeseburger Sales
1	354
2	345
3	367
4	322
5	356

If actual sales for week 6 turn out to be 368, compare the three forecasts using *MAD*. Which method performed best?

16. A company uses exponential smoothing with trend to forecast monthly sales of its product, which show a trend pattern. At the end of week 5, the company wants to forecast sales for week 6. The trend through week 4 has been 20 additional cases sold per week. Average sales have been 85 cases per week. The demand for week 5 was 90 cases. The company uses $\alpha = 0.20$ and $\beta = 0.10$. Make a forecast including trend for week 6.

17. The number of patients coming to the Healthy Start maternity clinic has been increasing steadily over the past eight months. Given the following data, use a linear regression equation to forecast attendance for months 9 and 10.

Month	Clinic Attendance (in thousands)
1	3.4
2	3.9
3	4.5
4	5.0
5	5.8
6	5.9
7	6.5
8	6.7

18. Given the following data, use exponential smoothing with $\alpha = .2$ and $\alpha = .5$ to generate forecasts for periods 2 through 6. Use *MAD* and *MSE* to decide which of the two models produced a better forecast.

Period	Actual	Forecast
1	15	17
2	18	
3	14	
4	16	
5	13	
6	16	

19. Pumpkin Pies Galore is trying to forecast sales of pies for the month of December. Demand for pies in September, October, and November has been 230, 304 and 415, respectively. Edith, the company's owner, uses a three-period weighted moving average to forecast sales. Based on her experience, she chooses to weight September as 0.1, October as 0.3, and November as 0.6.

(a) What would Edith's forecast for December be?
(b) What would her forecast be using the naive method?
(c) If actual sales for December turned out to be 420 pies, which method was best (use *MAD*)?

20. A company has used three different methods to forecast sales for the past five months. Use *MAD* and *MSE* to evaluate the performance of the three methods.

(a) Which forecasting method performed best? Do *MAD* and *MSE* give the same results?

Period	Actual	Method A	Method B	Method C
1	10	10	9	8
2	8	11	10	11
3	12	12	8	10
4	11	13	12	11
5	12	14	11	12

(b) Which of these is actually the naive method?

21. Two different forecasting models were used to forecast sales of a popular soda on a college campus. Actual demand and the two sets of forecasts are shown. Use *MAD* to explain which method provided a better forecast.

Period	Actual Demand	Forecast #1	Forecast #2
1	90	78	87
2	87	85	88
3	92	84	90
4	95	92	97
5	98	100	102
6	98	102	101

22. A producer of picture frames uses a tracking signal with limits of ± 4 to decide whether a forecast should be reviewed. Given historical information for the past 4 weeks, compute the tracking signal and decide whether the forecast should be reviewed. The MAD for this item was computed as 2.

Weeks	Actual Sales	Fore-cast	Devia-tion	Cumulative Deviation	Tracking Signal
				6	3
1	12	11			
2	14	13			
3	14	14			
4	16	14			

CASE: *Bram-Wear*

Lenny Bram, owner and manager of Bram-Wear, was analyzing performance data for the men's clothing retailer. He was concerned that inventories were high for certain clothing items, meaning that the company would potentially incur losses due to the need for significant markdowns. At the same time, they had run out of stock for other items early in the season. Some customers appeared frustrated by not finding the items they were looking for and needed to go elsewhere. Lenny knew that the problem, though not yet serious, needed to be addressed immediately.

Background

Bram-Wear was a retailer that sold clothing catering to young, urban, professional men. They primarily carried upscale, casual attire, as well as a small quantity of outerwear and footwear. Their success did not come from carrying a large product variety, but from a very focused style with an abundance of sizes and colors.

Bram-Wear had extremely good financial performance over the past 5 years. Lenny had attributed the success for the company to a group of excellent buyers. The buyers seemed able to accurately target the style preferences of their customers and correctly forecast product quantities. One challenge was keeping up with customer buying patterns and trends.

The Data

To determine the source of the problem Lenny had requested forecast and sales data by product category. Looking at the

sheets of data, it appeared that the problem was not with the specific styles or items carried in stock; rather, the problem appeared to be with the quantities ordered by the buyers. Specifically, the problem centered on two items: an athletic shoe called Urban Run and the 5-pocket cargo jeans.

Urban Run was a popular athletic shoe that had been carried by Bram-Wear for the past 4 years. Quarterly data for the past 4 years are shown below. The company seemed to always be out of stock of this athletic shoe. The model used by buyers to forecast sales for this item had been seasonal exponential smoothing. Looking at the data, Lenny wondered if this was the best method to use. It seemed to work well in the beginning, but now he was not so sure.

The data for the 5-pocket cargo jean seemed to also point to a forecasting problem. When the product was introduced last year it was expected to have a large upward trend. The buyers believed the trend would continue and used an exponential smoothing model with trend to forecast sales. However, they seemed to have too much inventory of this product. As with the Urban Run athletic wear, Lenny wondered if the right forecasting model was being applied to the data. It seemed he would have to dig out his old operations management text to solve this problem.

Demand for 5-Pocket Cargo Jeans

Month	Year 1 Demand	Year 2 Demand
January	36	98
February	42	101
March	56	97
April	75	99
May	85	100
June	94	95
July	101	107
August	108	104
September	105	98
October	114	104
November	111	100
December	110	102

Demand for Urban Run Athletic Wear

Quarter	Year 1 Demand	Year 2 Demand	Year 3 Demand	Year 4 Demand
I	10	14	20	30
II	29	31	26	31
III	26	29	28	33
IV	15	18	30	35

Case Questions:

1. Is seasonal exponential smoothing the best model for forecasting Urban Run athletic wear? Why?

2. Explain what has happened to the data for Urban Run. What are the consequences of continuing to use seasonal exponential smoothing? What model would you use? Generate a forecast for the 4 quarters of the 4th year using your model. Determine your forecast error and the inventory consequences.

3. Is exponential smoothing with trend the best model for forecasting 5-pocket cargo jeans? Why?

4. What method would you use to forecast monthly cargo jean demand for the second year given the previous year's monthly demand? Explain why you selected your approach. Generate the forecasts for each month of the second year with your method. Determine your forecast error and the inventory consequences.

INTERACTIVE LEARNING

Enhance and test your knowledge of Chapter 8 using the interactive CD.

1. **Spreadsheet** *Solved Problems 2 and 3*

Visit our dynamic Web site, www.wiley.com/college/reid, for more cases, web links, and additional information.

2. **Company Tour**
   Artesyn Communication Products, LLC
   Baja Spas

3. **Additional Web Resources**
   Institute of Business Forecasters, www.ibf.org
   International Institute of Forecasting, www.iif.org

4. **Virtual Company Consulting Case**

5. **INTERNET CHALLENGE** *On-line Data Access*

You have been hired by a government agency to collect and analyze economic data and generate economic forecasts. Since you do not have much experience in this area, your manager, Ms. Hernandez, has decided to give you a chance to practice your skills. Ms. Hernandez believes that it would be a good idea for you to use the Internet to collect and monitor a sample of economic data. She has given you a list of Web sites to access. Your first assignment is to collect a sample of local, national, or international economic data from one of these sites. Next, try to analyze the data you have collected and identify any patterns. Then, using one of the techniques discussed in the chapter, generate a forecast for the future. Finally, as new data are posted, evaluate your performance using the error measures discussed in the chapter. How did you do, and what have you learned about the data you collected?

Web sites:

1. Census Bureau—provides economic and demographic information from the U.S. economy
   (http://www.census.gov/)
2. Penn World Tables—provides international economic data
   (http://cansim.epas.utoronto.ca:5680/pwt/pwt.html)
3. Regional Economic Information System—provides regional, state, and local data
   (http://ptolemy.gis.virginia.edu:1080/reisl.html)
4. Resources for Economists on the Internet—provides business and economic data.
   (http://econwpa.wust1.edu/EconFAQ/EconFAQ.html)

BIBLIOGRAPHY

Armstrong, J. Scott. "Evaluating and Selecting Forecasting Methods." In J. Scott Armstrong (ed.), *Principles of Forecasting: A Handbook for Researchers and Practitioners.* Norwell, Ma: Kluwer Academic Publishers, 2001.

Armstrong, J. Scott, *Long-Range Forecasting from Crystal Ball to Computer,* 2nd ed., 1985, John Wiley & Sons.

Cattani, K. and Hauseman, W., "Why are Forecast Updates Often Disappointing?" *Manufacturing & Service Operations Management,* Vol. 2, No. 2, spring 2000, 119–127.

Clements, M. P. and Hendry, D. F. *Forecasting Economic Time Series,* Cambridge University Press, Cambridge, England, 1998.

Fischer, I. and Harvey, N. "Combining Forecasts: What Information do Judges Need to Outperform the Simple Average?" *International Journal of Forecasting,* Vol. 15, No. 3, 1999, 227–246.

Lawrence, M. and O'Connor, M. "Sales Forecasting Updates: How Good Are They in Practice?" *International Journal of Forecasting,* Vol. 16, No. 3, 2000, 369–383.

Makridakis, S., Wheelwright, S., and Hyndman, R. *Forecasting Methods and Applications,* 3rd ed., 1998, John Wiley & Sons.

McCullough, B.D. "Is It Safe to Assume That Software Is Accurate?" *International Journal of Forecasting,* Vol. 16, No. 3, 2000, 349–358.

Smith, B. *Focus Forecasting: Computer Techniques for Inventory Control* Boston: CBI, 1984.

Capacity Planning and Facility Location

Before studying this chapter you should know or, if necessary, review:

1. Globalization, Chapter 1, page 14.
2. Differences between strategic and tactical decisions, Chapter 1, pages 6–8.
3. Break-even analysis, Chapter 3, pages 46–48.
4. Qualitative forecasting methods, Chapter 8, pages 3–5.

LEARNING OBJECTIVES

After studying this chapter you should be able to:

1. Define capacity planning.
2. Define location analysis.
3. Describe the relationship between capacity planning and location, and their importance to the organization.
4. Explain the steps involved in capacity planning and location analysis.
5. Describe the decision support tools used in capacity planning.
6. Identify key factors in location analysis.
7. Describe the decision support tools used in location analysis.

CHAPTER OUTLINE

Have you ever signed up for a course at your college or university only to find out that it is closed? Have you ever attended a class that was held in a remote location and found that the room was overcrowded? Most of us have had these experiences as students. These examples illustrate problems of poor capacity planning and location—problems that can greatly affect the success of a business. Students have been known to drop out of a course that is difficult to get to or even to leave a program in which courses are frequently closed. Similarly, businesses can lose customers by not being able to produce enough goods or by being in an inconvenient location.

Capacity planning and location analysis are actually two separate decisions. Capacity planning deals with the maximum output rate that a facility can have, determined by the size of facilities and equipment. Location analysis, on the other hand, deals with the best location for a facility. You can probably see why these two decisions are usually made simultaneously. When a company decides to open a new facility, it must also decide on both the size of the facility and its location. The size of the facility may also affect the location.

In this chapter we will learn about both capacity planning and location analysis. We will see how companies make both kinds of decisions. We will also see how both of these issues can affect not only the success of a company but your everyday life as well.

CAPACITY PLANNING ■

Capacity can be defined as the maximum output rate that can be achieved by a facility. The facility may be an entire organization, a division, or only one machine. Planning for capacity in a company is usually performed at two levels, each corresponding to either strategic or tactical decisions, discussed in Chapter 2. The first level of capacity decisions is strategic and long-term in nature. This is where a company decides what investments in new facilities and equipment it should make. These decisions are strategic in nature and the company will have to live with them for a long time. Also, they require large capital expenditures and will have a great impact on the company's ability to conduct business. The second level of capacity decisions is more tactical in nature, focusing on short-term issues that include planning of workforce, inventories, and day-to-day use of machines. In this chapter we focus on the long-term, strategic capacity decisions. Short-term capacity decisions are discussed in Chapter 14.

▶ **Capacity**
The maximum output rate that can be achieved by a facility.

Why Is Capacity Planning Important?

Capacity planning is the process of establishing the output rate that can be achieved by a facility. If a company does not plan its capacity correctly, it may find that it either

▶ **Capacity planning**
The process of establishing the output rate that can be achieved by a facility.

does not have enough output capability to meet customer demands or has too much capacity sitting idle. In our university example, that would mean either not being able to offer enough courses to accommodate all students or, on the other hand, having unutilized classrooms. Both cases are costly to the university. Another example is a bakery. Not having enough capacity would mean not being able to produce enough baked goods to meet sales. The bakery would often run out of stock, and customers might start going somewhere else. Also, the bakery would not be able to take advantage of the true demand available. On the other hand, if there is too much capacity, the bakery would incur the cost of an unnecessarily large facility that is not being used, as well as much higher operating costs than necessary.

Planning for capacity is important if a company wants to grow and take full advantage of demand. At the same time, capacity decisions are complicated because they require long-term commitments of expensive resources, such as large facilities. Once these commitments have been made, it is costly to change them. Think about a business that purchases a larger facility in anticipation of an increase in demand, only to find that the demand does not occur. It is then left with a huge expense, no return on its investment, and the need to decide how to use a partially empty facility. Recall from Chapter 8 that forecasting future demands entails a great deal of uncertainty and risk—this makes long-term facility purchases inherently risky.

Another issue that complicates capacity planning is the fact that capacity is usually purchased in "chunks" rather than smooth increments. Facilities such as buildings and equipment are acquired in larger sizes and it is virtually impossible to achieve an exact match between current needs and needs based on future demand. You can see this in the classroom example. If a university anticipates a large demand for a particular course, it may offer multiple sections. Each additional section opened adds capacity in chunks equal to one class size. If one class can hold a maximum of 45 students, opening up another class means adding capacity for up to an additional 45 students. The university must consider its forecast of the additional demand for the course. If the forecast for additional demand is only 4 additional students, the university will probably not open up another section. The reason is that the cost for each section takes the form of chunks that include the room, the instructor, and supplies. This cost is the same whether 1 student or 45 students attend.

Because of the uncertainty of future demand, the overriding capacity planning decision becomes one of whether to purchase a larger facility in anticipation of greater demand or to expand in slightly smaller but less efficient increments. Each strategy has its advantages and disadvantages. Think about a young married couple who want to purchase a home. They can purchase a very small home that would be more affordable, knowing that if they have children they eventually will need to face the disruption and cost of moving. On the other hand, if they purchase a larger home now they will be better prepared for the future but will be paying for additional space that they currently do not need.

Measuring Capacity

Although our definition of capacity seems simple, there is no one way to measure capacity. Different people have different interpretations of what capacity means, and the units of measurement are often very different. Table 9-1 shows some examples of how capacity might be measured by different organizations.

Note that each business can measure capacity in different ways and that capacity can be measured using either inputs or outputs. Output measures, such as number of cars per shift, are easier to understand. However, they do not work well when a com-

Table 9-1 Examples of Different Capacity Measures

Type of Business	Input Measures of Capacity	Output Measures of Capacity
Car manufacturer	Labor hours	Cars per shift
Hospital	Available beds per month	Number of patients per month
Pizza parlor	Worker hours per day	Number of pizzas per day
Ice cream manufacturer	Operational hours per day	Gallons of ice cream per day
Retail store	Floor space in square feet	Revenues per day

pany produces many different kinds of products. For example, if we operate a bakery that bakes only pumpkin pies, then a measure such as pies per day would work well. However, if we made many different kinds of pies and varied the combination from one day to the next, then simply using pies per day as our measure would not work as well, especially if some pies took longer to make than others. Suppose that pecan pies take twice as long to make as pumpkin pies. If one day we made 20 pumpkin pies and the next day we made 10 pecan pies, using *pies per day* as our measure would make it seem as if our capacity was underutilized on the second day. When a company produces many different kinds of products, input measures work better.

When discussing the capacity of a facility, we need two types of information. The first is the *amount of available capacity*, which will help us understand how much capacity our facility has. The second is *effectiveness of capacity use*, which will tell us how effectively we are using our available capacity. Next we look at how to quantify and interpret this information.

Measuring Available Capacity Let's return to our bakery example for a moment. Suppose that on the average we can make 20 pies per day. However, if we are really pushed, such as during holidays, maybe we can make 30 pies per day. Which of these is our true capacity? We can make 30 pies per day at a maximum, but we cannot keep up that pace for long. Saying that 30 per day is our capacity would be misleading. On the other hand, saying that 20 pies per day is our capacity does not reflect the fact that we can, if necessary, push our production to 30 pies.

Having enough capacity is an important issue.

Through this example you can see that different measures of capacity are useful because they provide different kinds of information. Following are two of the most common measures of capacity:

▶ **Design capacity**
The maximum output rate that can be achieved by a facility under ideal conditions.

Design capacity is the maximum output rate that can be achieved by a facility under ideal conditions. In our example, this is 30 pies per day. Design capacity can be sustained only for a relatively short period of time. A company achieves this output rate by using many temporary measures, such as overtime, overstaffing, using equipment to the maximum, and subcontracting.

▶ **Effective capacity**
The maximum output rate that can be sustained under normal conditions.

Effective capacity is the maximum output rate that can be sustained under normal conditions. These conditions include realistic work schedules and breaks, regular staff levels, scheduled machine maintenance, and none of the temporary measures that are used to achieve design capacity. Note that effective capacity is usually lower than design capacity. In our example, effective capacity is 20 pies per day.

Measuring Effectiveness of Capacity Use Regardless of how much capacity we have, we also need to measure how effectively we are utilizing that capacity. **Utilization** simply tells us how much of our capacity we are actually using. Certainly there would be a big difference if we were using 50% of our capacity, meaning our facilities, space, labor and equipment, rather than 90%. Capacity utilization can simply be computed as the ratio of actual output over capacity:

▶ **Capacity utilization**
Percentage measure of how effectively available capacity is being used.

$$\text{Utilization} = \frac{\text{actual output rate}}{\text{capacity}} \, (100\%).$$

However, since we have two capacity measures, we can measure utilization relative to either design or effective capacity:

$$\text{Utilization}_{\text{effective}} = \frac{\text{actual output}}{\text{effective capacity}} \, (100\%)$$

$$\text{Utilization}_{\text{design}} = \frac{\text{actual output}}{\text{design capacity}} \, (100\%)$$

■ **Example 9.1 Computing Capacity Utilization**

In the bakery example, we have established that design capacity is 30 pies per day and effective capacity is 20 pies per day. Currently the bakery is producing 27 pies per day. What is the bakery's capacity utilization relative to both design and effective capacity?

Solution

$$\text{Utilization}_{\text{effective}} = \frac{\text{actual output}}{\text{effective capacity}} \, (100\%) = \frac{27}{20} \, (100\%) = 135\%$$

$$\text{Utilization}_{\text{design}} = \frac{\text{actual output}}{\text{design capacity}} \, (100\%) = \frac{27}{30} \, (100\%) = 90\%$$

The utilization rates show that the bakery's current output is only slightly below its design capacity and is considerably higher than its effective capacity. The bakery can probably operate at this level for only a short time.

Capacity Considerations

We have seen that changing capacity is not as simple as acquiring the right amount of capacity to exactly match our needs. The reason is that capacity is purchased in discrete chunks. Also, capacity decisions are long-term and strategic in nature. Acquiring anticipated capacity ahead of time can save cost and disruption in the long run. Later, when demand increases, output can be increased without incurring additional fixed cost. Extra capacity can also serve to intimidate and preempt competitors from entering the market. Other important implications of capacity that a company needs to consider when changing its capacity are discussed in this section.

Economies of Scale Every production facility has a volume of output that results in the lowest average unit cost. This is called the facility's **best operating level.** Figure 9-1 illustrates how the average unit cost of output is affected by the volume produced. You can see that as the number of units produced is increased, the average cost per unit drops. The reason is that when a large amount of goods is produced, the costs of production are spread over that large volume. These costs include the fixed costs of buildings and facilities, the costs of materials, and processing costs. The more units are produced, the larger the number of units over which costs can be spread—that is, the greater the **economies of scale.** The concept of economies of scale is very well known. It basically states that average cost of a unit produced is reduced when the amount of output is increased.

   You use the concept of economies of scale in your daily life, whether you are aware of it or not. Suppose you decide to make cookies in your kitchen. Think about the cost per cookie if you make only 5 cookies. There would be a great deal of effort—getting the ingredients, mixing the dough, shaping the cookies—all for only 5 cookies. If you had everything set up, making 5 additional cookies would not cost much more. Perhaps making even 10 more cookies would cost only slightly more because you had already set up all the materials. This lower cost is due to economies of scale.

Diseconomies of Scale What if you continued to increase the number of cookies you chose to produce. For a while, making a few more cookies would not require much additional effort. However, after a certain point there would be so much material that the kitchen would become congested. You might have to get someone to help because there was more work than one person could handle. You might have to make cookies longer than expected, and the cleanup job might be much more difficult. You would be experiencing **diseconomies of scale.** Diseconomies of scale occur at a point beyond the best operating level, when the cost of each additional unit made increases. Diseconomies of scale are also illustrated in Figure 9-1.

► **Best operating level**
The volume of output that results in the lowest average unit cost.

► **Economies of scale**
A condition in which the average cost of a unit produced is reduced as the amount of output is increased.

► **Diseconomies of scale**
A condition in which the cost of each additional unit made increases.

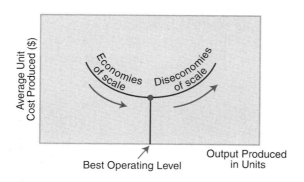

Figure 9-1

Different operating levels of a facility

Operating a facility close to its best operating level is clearly important because of the impact on costs. However, we have to keep in mind that different sizes of facilities have different best operating levels. In our cookie example, we can see that the number of cookies comfortably produced by one person in a small kitchen would be much lower than the number produced by three friends in a large kitchen. Figure 9-2 shows how best operating level varies between facilities of different sizes.

You can see that each facility experiences both economies and diseconomies of scale. However, their best operating levels are different. This is a very important consideration when changing capacity levels. The capacity of a business can be changed by either expanding or reducing the amount of capacity. Although both decisions are important, expansion is typically a costlier and more critical event.

When expanding capacity, management has to choose between one of the following two alternatives:

Alternative 1: Purchase one large facility, requiring one large initial investment.

Alternative 2: Add capacity incrementally in smaller chunks as needed.

The first alternative means that we would have a large amount of excess capacity in the beginning and that our initial costs would be high. We would also run the risk that demand might not materialize and we would be left with unused overcapacity. On the other hand, this alternative allows us to be prepared for higher demand in the future. Our best operating level is much higher with this alternative, enabling us to operate more efficiently when meeting higher demand. Our costs would be lower in the long run, as one large construction project typically costs more than many smaller construction projects due to startup costs. Thus, alternative 1 provides greater rewards but is more risky. Alternative 2 is less risky but does not offer the same opportunities and flexibility. It is up to management to weigh the risks versus the rewards in selecting an alternative.

Focused Factories   Facilities can respond more efficiently to demand if they are small, specialized, and focused on a narrow set of objectives; this concept is referred to as **focused factories.** We encountered this concept in Chapter 7 when we studied just-in-time (JIT) systems. Focused factories are only one of many factors that contribute to the success of JIT, but the concept is applicable to any facility.

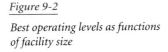
▶ **Focused factories**
Facilities that are small, specialized, and focused on a narrow set of objectives.

Figure 9-2

Best operating levels as functions of facility size

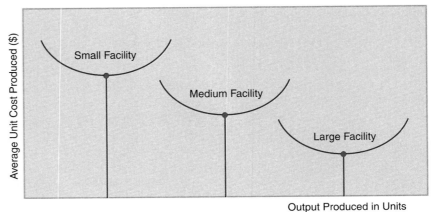

The idea that large facilities are necessary for success because they bring economies of scale is rather dated. Today's facilities must succeed in a business environment that has short product and technology life cycles and in which flexibility is more important than ever before. Large facilities tend to be less flexible because they generally contain many layers of management, procedures, and bureaucracy. Many companies have realized that to be more agile they need to be focused. A smaller, specialized facility will be more efficient because it can focus on a smaller number of tasks and fewer goals.

Even a large facility can benefit from the concept of focused factory by creating what is known as a *plant within a plant,* or *PWP.* A PWP is a large facility divided into smaller, more specialized facilities that have separate operations, competitive priorities, technology, and work force. They can be physically separated with a wall or barrier and kept independent from one another. In this manner, unnecessary layers of bureaucracy are eliminated and each "plant" is free to focus on its own objectives.

LINKS TO PRACTICE
Focus in the Retail Industry

Recent trends in the retail industry provide an excellent example of factory focus. In the 1980s retail sales were dominated by large department stores such as Sears, J.C. Penney's, and Federated. However, in the 1990s gains in sales were made by specialty stores such as The Gap, The Limited, and Ann Taylor, while large department stores faltered. The reason is that consumer preferences change very rapidly, and each small specialty store can focus precisely on the needs of its customer group. Specialty stores are able to focus on a specific set of customers and respond to their unique needs. The Limited and The Gap are excellent examples of factory focus, with specialty stores such as Limited Too, Baby Gap, and Gap Kids.

Subcontractor Networks

Another alternative to having a large production facility is to develop a large network of subcontractors and suppliers who perform a number of tasks for one client. This is one of the fastest-growing trends today. Companies are realizing that to be successful in today's market they need to focus on their core capabilities—for example, by hiring third parties or subcontractors to take over tasks that the company does not need to perform itself. Companies such as American Airlines and Procter & Gamble have hired outside firms to manage noncritical inventories. Also, many companies are contracting with suppliers to perform tasks that they used to perform themselves. A good example is in the area of quality management. Historically, companies performed quality checks on goods received from suppliers. Today, suppliers and manufacturers work together to achieve the same quality standards, and much of the quality checking of incoming materials is performed at the supplier's site. Another example can be seen in the auto industry, where manufacturers are placing more responsibility on suppliers to perform tasks such as design of packaging and transportation of goods. By placing more responsibility on subcontractors and suppliers, a manufacturer can focus on tasks that are critical to its success, such as product development and design.

■ MAKING CAPACITY PLANNING DECISIONS

The three-step procedure for making capacity planning decisions is as follows:

STEP 1 IDENTIFY CAPACITY REQUIREMENTS

The first step is to identify the levels of capacity needed by the company now, as well as in the future. A company cannot decide whether to purchase a new facility without knowing exactly how much capacity it will need in the future. It also needs to identify the gap between available capacity and future requirements.

STEP 2 DEVELOP CAPACITY ALTERNATIVES

Once capacity requirements have been identified, the company needs to develop a set of alternatives that would enable it to meet future capacity needs.

STEP 3 EVALUATE CAPACITY ALTERNATIVES

The last step in the procedure is to evaluate the capacity alternatives and select the one alternative that will best meet the company's requirements.

Let's look at these steps in a little more detail.

Identify Capacity Requirements

Long-term capacity requirements are identified on the basis of forecasts of future demand. Certainly, companies look for long-term patterns such as trends when making forecasts. However, long-term patterns are not enough at this stage. Planning, building, and starting up a new facility can take well over five years. Much can happen during that time. When the facilities are operational, they are expected to be utilized for many years into the future. During this time frame numerous changes can occur in the economy, consumer base, competition, technology, and demographic factors, as well as in government regulation and political events.

Forecasting Capacity Capacity requirements are identified on the basis of forecasts of future demand. Forecasting at this level is performed using qualitative forecasting methods, some of which we discussed in Chapter 8. Qualitative forecasting methods, such as *executive opinion* and the *Delphi method*, use subjective opinions of experts in the business. These experts may consider inputs from quantitative forecasting models that can numerically compute patterns such as trends. However, because so many variables can influence demand at this level, the experts use their judgment to validate the quantitative forecast or modify it based on their own knowledge.

One way to proceed with long-range demand forecasting at this stage is to first forecast overall market demand. For example, experts might forecast the total market for overnight delivery to be $30 billion in five years. Then the company can estimate its market share as a percentage of the total. For example, our market share may be 15%. From that we can compute an estimate of demand for our company in five years by multiplying the overall market demand with the percentage held by our company ($.15 \times \$30$ billion $= \$4.5$ billion). That forecast of demand can then be translated into specific facility requirements.

▶ **Capacity cushion**
Additional capacity added to regular capacity requirements to provide greater flexibility.

Capacity Cushions Companies often add **capacity cushions** to their regular capacity requirements. A capacity cushion is an amount of capacity added to the needed capacity in order to provide greater flexibility. Capacity cushions can be helpful if demand is greater than expected. Also, cushions can help to meet the ability of a business to respond to customer needs for different products or different volumes. Finally, businesses that operate too close to their maximum capacity experience many costs due to diseconomies of scale and may also experience deteriorating quality.

Strategic Implications   Finally, a company needs to consider how much capacity its competitors are likely to have. Capacity is a strategic decision, and the position of a company in the market relative to its competitors is very much determined by its capacity. At the same time, plans by all major competitors to increase capacity may signal the potential for overcapacity in the industry. Therefore, the decision as to how much capacity to add should be made carefully.

Develop Capacity Alternatives

Once a company has identified its capacity requirements for the future, the next step is to develop alternative ways to modify its capacity. One alternative is to do nothing and reevaluate the situation in the future. With this alternative, the company would not be able to meet any demands that exceed current capacity levels. Choosing this alternative and the time to reevaluate its needs is a strategic decision. The other alternatives require deciding whether to purchase one large facility now or add capacity incrementally, as discussed earlier in the chapter.

Capacity Alternatives: 1.   Do nothing
2.   Expand large now
3.   Expand small now, with option to add later

Evaluate Capacity Alternatives

There are a number of tools that we can use to evaluate our capacity alternatives. Recall that these tools are only decision support aids. Ultimately, managers have to use many different inputs, as well as their judgment, in making the final decision. One of the most popular of these tools is the decision tree. In the rest of this section we look more closely at how decision trees can be helpful to managers at this stage.

Decision Trees

Decision trees are useful whenever we have to evaluate interdependent decisions that must be made in sequence and when there is uncertainty of events. For that reason,

Large expansion alternatives often involve construction of new facilities.

they are especially useful for evaluating capacity expansion alternatives given that future demand is uncertain. Remember that our main decision is whether to purchase a large facility or a small one with the possibility of expansion later. You can see that the decision to expand later is dependent on choosing a small facility now. Which alternative ends up being best will depend on whether demand turns out to be high or low. Unfortunately, we can only forecast future demand and have to incur some risks.

▶ **Decision tree**
Modeling tool used to evaluate independent decisions that must be made in sequence.

A **decision tree** is a diagram that models the alternatives being considered and the possible outcomes. Decision trees help by giving structure to a series of decisions and providing an objective way of evaluating alternatives. Decision trees contain the following information:

- ◆ Decision points. These are the points in time when decisions, such as whether to expand or not, are made. They are represented by squares, called "nodes."
- ◆ Decision alternatives. Buying a large facility and buying a small facility are two decision alternatives. They are represented by "branches" or arrows leaving a decision point.
- ◆ Chance events. These are events that could affect the value of a decision. For example, demand could be high or low. Each chance event has a probability or likelihood of occurring. For example, there may be a 60% chance of high demand and a 40% chance of low demand. Remember that the sum of the probabilities of all chances must add up to 1.0. Chance events are "branches" or arrows leaving circular nodes.
- ◆ Outcomes. For each possible alternative an outcome is listed. In our example that may be expected profit for each alternative (say, expand now or later) given each chance event (say, high demand or low demand).

These diagrams are called decision trees because the diagram of the decisions resembles a tree. Simple decision trees are not hard to understand. Next we look at an example to see how a decision tree might be used to solve a capacity alternative problem.

■ **Example 9.2 Using Decision Trees**

Anna, the owner of Anna's Greek Restaurant, has determined that she needs to expand her facility. The decision is whether to expand now with a large facility, incurring additional costs and taking the risk that demand will not materialize, or expand on a smaller scale, knowing that she will have to consider expanding again in three years. She has estimated the following chances for demand:

- ◆ The likelihood of demand being high is .70.
- ◆ The likelihood of demand being low is .30.

She has also estimated profits for each alternative:

- ◆ Large expansion has an estimated profitability of either $300,000 or $50,000, depending on whether demand turns out to be high or low.
- ◆ Small expansion has a profitability of $80,000, assuming that demand is low.
- ◆ Small expansion with an occurrence of high demand would require considering whether to expand further. If she expands at that point, her profitability is expected to be $200,000. If she does not expand further, profitability is expected to be $150,000.

Next we develop a decision tree to solve Anna's problem.

Solution:
To solve this problem we first need to draw the decision tree. Table 9-2 shows steps in drawing a decision tree.

Table 9-2 Procedure for Drawing a Decision Tree
1. Draw a decision tree from left to right. Use squares to indicate decisions and circles to indicate chance events.
2. Write the probability of each chance event in parentheses.
3. Write out the outcome for each alternative in the right margin.

A decision tree is shown in Figure 9-3. We read the diagram from left to right, with node 1 representing the first decision point. The two alternatives at that decision point are presented as branches. They are labeled with the two alternatives, "Expand Small" and "Expand Large." Regardless of which alternative is followed, some chance events will take place. In our example, the chance events are the occurrence of either high or low demand. The circular node represents the chance events, with the branches providing the label and the probability of the event. For example, the chance of high demand is .70 and the chance of low demand is .30.

If we start with a small expansion and high demand occurs, we will have to decide whether to expand further or not. This second decision point is represented by node 2. The dollar amounts at the end of each alternative are the estimated profits. Now that we have drawn the decision tree, let's see how we can solve it. The procedure for solving a decision tree is outlined in Table 9-3.

Table 9-3 Procedure for Solving a Decision Tree
1. To solve a decision tree, work from right to left. At each circle representing chance events, compute the expected value (EV).
2. Write the EVs below each circle in parentheses.
3. Select the alternative with the highest EV.

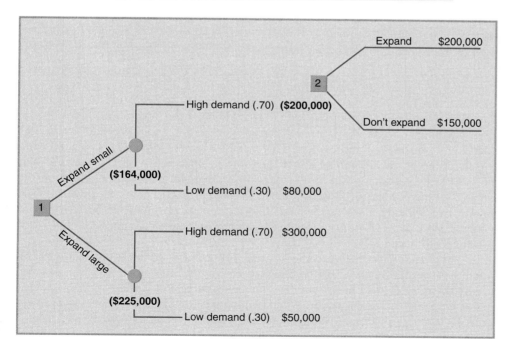

Figure 9-3

Decision tree for Anna's restaurant

We drew the decision tree from left to right. To evaluate it we work backward, from right to left. We start with the profitability of each alternative, working backward and selecting the most profitable alternative. For example, at node 2 we should decide to expand further, because the profits from that decision are higher ($200,000 versus $150,000). If we come to that point, that is the decision we should make. The expected value (EV) of profits at that point is written below node 2 in brackets. This is the expected value if we decide on a small expansion and high demand occurs.

To compute the expected value (EV) of the small expansion, we evaluate it as a weighted average of estimated profits given the probability of occurrence of each chance event:

$$EV_{\text{small expansion}} = 0.30\ (\$80,000) + 0.70\ (\$200,000) = \$164,000$$

$$EV_{\text{large expansion}} = 0.30\ (\$50,000) + 0.70\ (\$300,000) = \$225,000$$

The large expansion gives the higher expected value. This means that Anna should pursue a large expansion now.

Before You Go On

Up to this point we have focused exclusively on capacity planning. By now you should understand that capacity is the maximum output rate of a facility. Capacity is defined in different ways, depending on the nature of the business. You should understand the basic trade-off made in choosing between capacity planning alternatives and the procedure used to evaluate alternatives. Finally, make sure you understand the relationship between capacity planning and location analysis. In the next section we discuss location analysis, another decision area for operations managers. Note, however, that location analysis is usually made in conjunction with capacity planning. Because the size of a facility is typically tied to its location, these decisions are made together. Make sure you understand the relationship between these decisions and their strategic implications for the firm.

■ LOCATION ANALYSIS

You might have heard the old real estate adage: The three most important factors in the value of a property are location, location, location. Have you ever left a service provider that you liked—say, a doctor, barber, or tailor—because they were in a location that was difficult to get to or too far away? Look at the business locations in your own neighborhood. We have all seen facilities in certain locations that have a high turnover of businesses and owners. The type of business and owners may be completely different, yet something about the location does not make it successful. Why do most fast-food restaurants locate near one another? In order to draw customers to one location. Why are the large automakers centered in Michigan? To draw suppliers to one area. Why do many medical facilities locate near hospitals? To be accessible to patients. Why do retail stores typically locate near each other? To attract a higher volume of customers.

These examples illustrate the strategic importance of location decisions. All other aspects of a business can be designed efficiently, but if the location is selected poorly the business will have a harder time being successful. Different types of businesses emphasize different factors when making location decisions. Service organizations such as restaurants, movie theaters, and banks focus on locating near their customers. Manufacturing organizations seek to be close to sources of transportation, suppliers, and abundant resources such as labor. However, many other factors need to be considered.

What Is Facility Location?

Facility location is determining the best geographic location for a company's facility. Facility location decisions are particularly important for two reasons. First, they require long-term commitments in buildings and facilities, which means that mistakes can be difficult to correct. Second, these decisions require sizable financial investment and can have a large impact on operating costs and revenues. Poor location can result in high transportation costs, inadequate supplies of raw materials and labor, loss of competitive advantage, and financial loss. Businesses therefore have to think long and hard about where to locate a new facility.

In most cases there is no one best location for a facility. Rather, there are a number of acceptable locations. One location may satisfy some factors whereas another location may be better for others. If a new location is being considered in order to provide more capacity, the company needs to consider options such as expanding the current facility if the current location is satisfactory. Another option might be to add a new facility but also keep the current one. As you can see, there is a lot to consider.

Factors Affecting Location Decisions

Many factors can affect location decisions, including proximity to customers, transportation, source of labor, community attitude, proximity to suppliers, and many other factors. The nature of the firm's business will determine which factors should dominate the location decision. As mentioned earlier, service and manufacturing firms will focus on different factors. Profit-making and nonprofit organizations will also focus on different factors. Profit-making firms tend to locate near the markets they serve, whereas nonprofit organizations generally focus on other criteria.

It is important to identify factors that have a critical impact on the company's strategic goals. For example, even though proximity to customers is typically a critical factor for service firms, if the firm provides an in-home service (say, carpet cleaning) this may not be a critical issue. Also, managers should eliminate factors that are satisfied by every location alternative. Next we look more closely at some factors that affect location decisions.

Proximity to Sources of Supply Many firms need to locate close to sources of supply. The reasons for this can vary. In some cases the firm has no choice, such as in farming, forestry, or mining operations, where proximity to natural resources is necessary. In other cases the location may be determined by the perishable nature of goods, such as in preparing and processing perishable food items. Dole Pineapple has its pineapple farm and plant in Hawaii for both these purposes. Similarly, Tropicana has its processing plant in Florida.

Another reason to locate close to sources of supply is high transportation costs—for example, when a firm's raw materials are much bulkier and costlier to move than the finished product. Transporting the finished product outbound is less costly than transporting the raw materials inbound, and the firm should locate closer to the source of supply. A paper mill is an example. Transporting lumber would be much more costly than transporting produced paper.

The importance of location decisions can be seen in the case of new Internet companies. Locating in Silicon Valley or San Francisco has become a major priority. Dot-coms are seeking over four million square feet of space in San Francisco, where only one million square feet are available. Consequently, the cost of locating there, including rent and leasing requirements, has become increasingly expensive. Tenants are currently paying $60 per square foot, an increase from the $40 per square foot paid just six months earlier. Landlords have also become picky about their tenants, and some are making unusual demands. Many are requiring as much as two years rent in advance. Others are even asking for equity in the company.

Proximity to Customers Locating near the market they serve is often critical for many organizations, particularly service firms. To capture their share of the business, service firms need to be accessible to their customers. For this reason, service firms typically locate in high-population areas that offer convenient access. Examples include retail stores, fast-food restaurants, gas stations, grocery stores, dry cleaners, and flower shops. Large retail firms often locate in a central area of the market they serve. Smaller service firms usually follow the larger retailers because of the large number of customers they attract. The smaller firms can usually count on getting some of the business.

Other reasons for locating close to customers may include the perishable nature of the company's products or high costs of transportation to the customer site. Food items such as groceries and baked goods, fresh flowers, and medications are perishable and need to be offered close to the market. Also, items such as heavy metal sheets, pipes, and cement need to be produced close to the market because the costs of transporting these materials are high.

Proximity to Source of Labor Proximity to an ample supply of qualified labor is important in many businesses, especially those that are labor intensive. The company needs to consider the availability of a particular type of labor and whether special skills are required. Some companies, such as those looking for assembly line workers, want to be near a supply of blue-collar labor. Other companies may be looking for computer or technical skills and should consider locating in areas with a concentration of those types of workers.

Other factors that should be considered are local wage rates, the presence of local unions, and attitudes of local workers. Work ethics and attitudes toward work can vary greatly in different parts of the country and between urban and rural workers. Attitudes toward factors such as absenteeism, tardiness, and turnover can greatly affect a company's productivity.

Community Considerations The success of a company at a particular location can be affected by the extent to which it is accepted by the local community. Many communities welcome new businesses, viewing them as sources of tax revenues, opportunities for jobs, as well as contributing to the overall well-being of the community. However, communities do not want businesses that bring pollution, noise, and traffic, and lower the quality of life. Extreme examples are a nuclear facility, a trash dump site, and an airport. Less extreme examples are companies like Wal-Mart, which often are not accepted by smaller communities, which may view such large merchants as a threat to their way of life and actively work to discourage them from locating there.

Site Considerations Site considerations for a particular location include factors such as utility costs, taxes, zoning restrictions, soil conditions, and even climate. These factors are not too different from those one would consider when purchasing a home or a lot to build on. Just as most homeowners consider their purchase an investment, so does a business. Inspectors should be hired to perform a thorough evaluation of the grounds, such a check for adequate drainage. Site-related factors can also limit access roads for trucks and make it difficult for customers to reach the site.

Quality-of-Life Issues Another important factor in location decisions is the quality of life a particular location offers the company's employees. This factor can also become important in the future when the business is recruiting high-caliber employees. Quality of life includes factors such as climate, a desirable lifestyle, good schools, and a low crime rate. Certainly quality of life would not be considered the most critical factor in selecting a location. However, when other factors do not differ much from one location to another, quality of life can be the decisive factor.

Other Considerations In addition to the factors discussed so far, there are others that companies need to consider. They include room for customer parking, visibility, customer and transportation access, as well as room for expansion. Room for expansion may be particularly important if the company has decided to expand now and possibly expand further at a later date. Other factors include construction costs, insurance, local competition, local traffic and road congestion, and local ordinances.

Globalization

In addition to considering the specific factors affecting site location in the United States, companies need to consider how they will be affected by a major trend in business today: globalization. **Globalization** is the process of locating facilities around the world. Over the past decade it has become not only a trend but a matter-of-fact way of conducting business. Technology such as faxes, e-mails, video conferencing, and overnight delivery have made distance less relevant than ever before. Markets and competition are increasingly global. To compete effectively based on cost, many companies have had to expand their operations to include global sources of supply. Factors other than mere distance have become critical in selecting a geographic location.

Deciding to expand an operation globally is not a simple decision. There are many things to consider, and the problems must be weighed along with the benefits. In this section we look at both advantages and disadvantages of global operations. We also look at some additional implications of global operations that managers need to consider.

▶ **Globalization**
The process of locating facilities around the world.

Advantages of Globalization There are many reasons why companies choose to expand their operations globally. The main one, however, is to take advantage of foreign markets. The demand for imported goods has grown tremendously and these markets offer a new arena for competition. Also, locating production facilities in foreign countries reduces the stigma associated with buying imports. This concept works not only for U.S. companies abroad but for foreign companies in the United States as well. For example, Japanese automobile manufacturers have located in the United States and employed American workers, which has gone a long way toward eliminating negative attitudes about buying Japanese cars.

Another advantage of global locations is reduction of trade barriers. By producing goods in the country where customers are located, a company can avoid import quotas. Trade barriers have also been reduced through the creation of trading blocs such as the European Union, and trade agreements such as NAFTA (North American Free Trade Agreement) and GATT (General Agreement on Tariffs and Trade). We discussed the contribution of these agreements to globalization in Chapter 1.

Cheap labor in countries such as Korea, Taiwan, and China has also attracted firms to locate there. Often it is cheaper to send raw materials to these countries for fabrication and assembly and then ship them elsewhere for final consumption. The cost of labor can be so low that it more than offsets the additional transportation costs.

An area that has further encouraged globalization is the growth of just-in-time manufacturing, which encourages suppliers and manufacturers to be in close proximity to one another. Many suppliers have moved closer to the manufacturers they supply, and some manufacturers have moved closer to their suppliers.

Disadvantages of Globalization Although there are advantages to globalization, there are also a number of disadvantages that companies should consider. Political risks can be large, particularly in countries with unstable governments. For example, during a period of political unrest a company may have its technology confiscated. There may also be restrictions imposed by foreign governments, tariffs on particular industries, and local ordinances that must be obeyed.

Using offshore suppliers might mean that a company may need to share some of its proprietary technology. Today's age of total quality management encourages sharing this type of information between manufacturers and suppliers to the advantage of both parties. A manufacturer may want to think closely before sharing this information, however.

Another issue is whether to use local employee skills. Companies are often attracted to cheap foreign labor. However, the company might find that worker attitudes toward tardiness and absenteeism are completely different from what it is used to. Also, worker skills and productivity may be considerably lower, offsetting the benefits of lower wages.

The local infrastructure is another important issue. Many foreign countries do not have the developed infrastructure necessary for companies to operate in the manner they are used to. Infrastructure includes everything from roads to utilities as well as other support services.

Issues to Consider in Locating Globally Firms are attracted to foreign locations in order to take advantage of foreign markets, cheaper suppliers or labor, and natural resources such as copper, aluminum, and timber. However, there are many issues to consider when locating globally. One such issue is the effect of a *different culture*. Each culture has a different set of values, norms, ethics, and standards. For example, in France it is considered polite to be slightly late for an appointment, and such lateness is quite customary. The British, on the other hand, consider punctuality highly important and tardiness very rude. You can see how misunderstandings can develop even through simple differences like this one.

Language barriers are another potential problem. Employees need to be able to communicate easily in their work environment. Engaging in discussions, following instructions, and understanding exactly what is being said can become difficult when employees speak different languages.

Different laws and regulations—including everything from pollution regulations to labor laws—may require changes in business practices. Also, what is acceptable in one culture may be completely unacceptable or even illegal in another. For example, in some countries offering a bribe may be an acceptable part of doing business, whereas in others it may land you in jail.

Procedure for Making Location Decisions

As with capacity planning, managers need to follow a three-step procedure when making facility location decisions. These steps are as follows:

STEP 1 IDENTIFY DOMINANT LOCATION FACTORS
In this step managers identify the location factors that are dominant for the business. This requires managerial judgment and knowledge.

STEP 2 DEVELOP LOCATION ALTERNATIVES
Once managers know what factors are dominant, they can identify location alternatives that satisfy the selected factors.

STEP 3 EVALUATE LOCATION ALTERNATIVES
After a set of location alternatives have been identified, managers evaluate them and make a final selection. This is not easy, because one location may be preferred based on one set of factors, whereas another may be better based on a second set of factors.

Procedures for Evaluating Location Alternatives

There are a number of procedures that can help in evaluating location alternatives. These are decision support tools that help structure the decision-making process. Some of them help with qualitative factors that are subjective, such as quality of life. Others help with quantitative factors that can be measured, such as distance. A manager may choose to use multiple procedures to evaluate alternatives and come up with a final decision. Remember that the location decision is one that a company will have to live with for a long time. It is highly important that managers make the right decision.

Factor Rating You have seen by now that many of the factors that managers need to consider when evaluating location alternatives are qualitative in nature. Their importance is also highly subjective, based on the opinion of who is evaluating them. An excellent procedure that can be used to give structure to this process is called factor rating. **Factor rating** is a procedure that can be used to evaluate multiple alternatives based on a number of selected factors. It is valuable because it helps decision makers

▶ **Factor rating**
A procedure that can be used to evaluate multiple alternative locations based on a number of selected factors.

structure their opinions relative to the factors identified as important. The following steps are used to develop a factor rating:

STEP 1 Identify dominant factors (e.g., proximity to market, access, competition, quality of life).

STEP 2 Assign weights to factors reflecting the importance of each factor relative to the other factors. The sum of these factors must be 100.

STEP 3 Select a scale by which to evaluate each location relative to each factor. The most commonly used scale is a 5-point scale, with 1 being poor and 5 excellent.

STEP 4 Evaluate each alternative relative to each factor, using the scale selected in Step 3. For example, if you chose to use a 5-point scale, a location that was excellent based on quality of life might get a 5 for that factor.

STEP 5 For each factor and each location, multiply the weight of the factor by the score for that factor and sum the results for each alternative. This will give you a score for each alternative based on how you have rated the factors and how you have weighted each of the factors at each location.

STEP 6 Select the alternative with the highest score.

Let's look at an example to see how this procedure is used.

■ Example 9.3 Using Factor Rating

Antonio is evaluating three different locations for his new Italian restaurant. Costs are comparable at all three locations. He has identified seven factors that he considers important. He has decided to use factor rating to evaluate his three location alternatives based on a 5-point scale, with 1 being poor and 5 excellent. Table 9-4 shows Antonio's factors, the weights he has assigned to each factor, as well the factor score for each factor at each location.

Table 9-4 Factor Rating for Antonio's Italian Restaurant

| Factor | Factor Weight | Factor Score at Each Location | | | Weighted Score for Each Location (Factor Weight × Factor Score) | | |
		Location 1	Location 2	Location 3	Location 1	Location 2	Location 3
Appearance	20	5	3	2	100	60	40
Ease of expansion	10	4	4	2	40	40	20
Proximity to market	20	2	3	5	40	60	100
Customer parking	15	5	3	3	75	45	45
Access	15	5	2	3	75	30	45
Competition	10	2	4	5	20	40	50
Labor supply	10	3	3	4	30	30	40
Total	**100**				**380**	**305**	**340**

From Table 9-4 it is clear that Antonio considers facility appearance and proximity to market the two most important factors, because he has rated each of these with a 20. Other factors are slightly less important. Note that Antonio selected the factors first. Then he decided to weight them based on his perception of their importance. He then computed a factor score for each factor at each location. Looking at the factor scores he selected, it appears that location 1 is excellent based on appearance, parking, and visibility, but poor based on closeness to the market. Location 3 is just the opposite, being excellent based on closeness to the market but poor based on facility appearance. Location 2 appears to be somewhere in the middle. To evaluate which location alternative is best, Antonio needed to multiply the factor weight times the factor score for each factor at each location and then sum them. The best location alternative is that with the highest factor rating score. In Antonio's case it is location alternative 1.

The Load–Distance Model   The **load–distance model** is a procedure for evaluating location alternatives based on distance. The distance to be measured could be proximity to markets, proximity to suppliers or other resources, or proximity to any other facility that is considered important. The objective of the model is to select a location that minimizes the total amount of loads moved weighted by the distance traveled. What is a load? A load represents the goods moved in or out of a facility or the number of movements between facilities. For example, if 200 boxes of Kellogg's cereal are shipped between the local warehouse and a grocery store, that is the load between the warehouse and grocery store. The idea is to reduce the amount of distance between facilities that have a high load between them.

▶ **Load–distance model**
A procedure for evaluating location alternatives based on distance.

The model is shown in Table 9-5. Relative locations are compared by computing the load–distance or *ld* score for each location. The *ld* score for a particular location is obtained by multiplying the load (denoted by *l*) for each location by the distance traveled (denoted by *d*) and then summing over all the locations. This will give us an *ld* score, which is a surrogate measure for movement of goods, material handling, or even communication. Our goal is to make the *ld* score as low as possible by reducing the distance that large loads have to travel.

Next we look at the steps in developing the load–distance model.

STEP 1   IDENTIFY DISTANCES
The first step is to identify the distances between location sites. It is certainly possible to use the actual mileage between locations. However, it is much quicker, and just as effective, to use simpler measures of distance. A frequently used measure of distance is **rectilinear distance**. Rectilinear distance is the shortest distance between two points measured by using only north–south and east–west movements. To measure rectilinear distance we place grid coordinates on a map and use them to measure the distance between two locations. Figure 9-4 presents an example of how the distance between locations A and B could be measured using rectilinear distance.

▶ **Rectilinear distance**
The shortest distance between two points measured by using only north–south and east–west movements.

The rectilinear distance between two locations, A and B, is computed by summing the absolute differences between the *x* coordinates and the absolute differences between the *y* coordinates. The equation is as follows:

$$d_{AB} = |x_A - x_B| + |y_A - y_B|$$

Table 9-5 The Load–Distance Model
ld score for a location $= \Sigma\, l_{ij}d_{ij}$
where l_{ij} = load between locations *i* and *j*
d_{ij} = distance between locations *i* and *j*

Figure 9-4

Rectilinear distance between points A and B

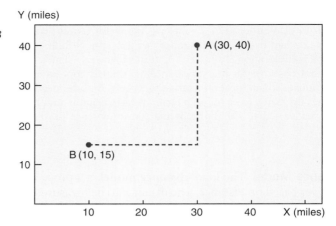

In our example, the coordinates for location A are (30, 40). The coordinates for location B are (10, 15). Therefore, the rectilinear distance between these two points is

$$d_{AB} = |30 - 10| + |40 - 15| = 45 \text{ miles}$$

STEP 2   IDENTIFY LOADS
The next step is to identify the loads between different locations. The notation l_{ij} is used to indicate the load between locations i and j.

STEP 3   CALCULATE THE LOAD–DISTANCE SCORE FOR EACH LOCATION
Next we calculate the load–distance score for each location by multiplying the load, l_{ij}, by the distance, d_{ij}. We then compute the sum of $l_{ij}\, d_{ij}$ to get the *ld* score. Finally, we then select the site with the lowest load–distance score.

Next we look at an example to see how to use the model.

■ Example 9.4 Using the Load–Distance Model

Matrix Manufacturing Corporation is considering where to locate its warehouse in order to service its four stores located in four Ohio cities: Cleveland, Columbus, Cincinnati, and Dayton. Two possible sites for the warehouse are being considered. One is in Mansfield, Ohio, and the other is in Springfield, Ohio. Let's follow the steps of the load–distance model to select the best location for the warehouse.

Solution
Step 1: Identify distances. The distances between the locations can be seen in Figure 9-5, which shows a map of the cities with grid coordinates. The coordinates allow us to compute the distances between the cities. To compute the specific distances we use the rectilinear distance measure.

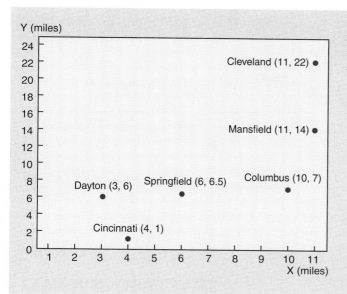

Figure 9-5

Location map for Matrix Manufacturing

From Figure 9-5 we can compute the distances between the four cities and the Springfield site as follows:

City	Distance to Springfield
Cleveland	20.5
Columbus	4.5
Cincinnati	7.5
Dayton	3.5

Similarly, we can compute the distance between the four cities and the Mansfield site as follows:

City	Distance to Mansfield
Cleveland	8
Columbus	8
Cincinnati	20
Dayton	16

Step 2: Identify loads. The next step is to identify the loads between the four cities and the warehouse. Remember that these loads will be the same regardless of where the warehouse is located. For this reason, we want to locate the warehouse at a place that will minimize the amount of distance large loads have to travel.

City	Load between City and Warehouse
Cleveland	15
Columbus	10
Cincinnati	12
Dayton	4

Step 3: Calculate the load–distance score for each location. The final step is to calculate the load–distance score for each location. The computation for Springfield is shown in Table 9-6.

Table 9-6 Computing the Load–Distance Score for Springfield

City	Load (l_{ij})	Distance (d_{ij})	$l_{ij}d_{ij}$
Cleveland	15	20.5	307.5
Columbus	10	4.5	45
Cincinnati	12	7.5	90
Dayton	4	3.5	14
Total		Load–Distance Score: (456.5)	

The load–distance score computed for Springfield does not tell us very much by itself. This number is useful only when comparing relative locations—that is, when we compare it to another load–distance score. The load–distance score for Mansfield is shown in Table 9-7.

Table 9-7 Computing the Load–Distance Score for Mansfield

City	Load (l_{ij})	Distance (d_{ij})	$l_{ij}d_{ij}$
Cleveland	15	8	120
Columbus	10	8	80
Cincinnati	12	20	240
Dayton	4	16	64
Total		Load–Distance Score: (504)	

The load–distance score for Mansfield is higher than the score for Springfield. Therefore, Matrix Manufacturing should locate its warehouse in Springfield. Note in the computation for the load–distance score for Mansfield that the load between the city and the warehouse did not change. What changed was the distance. Through the load–distance model we select a location that will minimize the distance large loads travel.

The Center of Gravity Approach When we used the load–distance model we compared only two location alternatives. The load–distance was lower for Springfield than for Mansfield. However, we can also use the model to find other locations that may give an even lower load–distance score than Springfield. An easy way to do this is to start by testing the location at the center of gravity of the target area. The X and Y coordinates that give us the center of gravity for a particular area are computed in the following way:

$$X_{c.g.} = \frac{\sum l_i x_i}{\sum l_i}$$

$$Y_{c.g.} = \frac{\sum l_i y_i}{\sum l_i}$$

The X coordinate for the center of gravity is computed by taking the X coordinate for each point and multiplying it by its load. These are then summed and divided by the sum of the loads. The same procedure is used to compute the Y coordinate.

The location identified with the center of gravity is usually not optimal because we are using rectilinear distance. Also, it may not be a feasible site because of geographic restrictions. For example, the center of gravity might turn out to be in the middle of a highway. However, the center of gravity provides an excellent starting point. We can use it to test the load–distance score of other locations in the area.

■ **Example 9.5 Computing the Center of Gravity**

Find the center of gravity for the Matrix Manufacturing problem.

Solution

Location	Coordinates (X, Y)	Load (l_i)	$l_i x_i$	$l_i y_i$
Cleveland	(11, 22)	15	165	330
Columbus	(10, 7)	10	100	70
Cincinnati	(4, 1)	12	48	12
Dayton	(3, 6)	4	12	24
Total		41	325	436

Now we need to find the coordinates for the center of gravity:

$$X_{c.g.} = \frac{\sum l_i x_i}{\sum l_i} = \frac{325}{41} = 7.9$$

$$Y_{c.g.} = \frac{\sum l_i y_i}{\sum l_i} = \frac{436}{41} = 10.6$$

Break-Even Analysis **Break-even analysis** is a technique used to compute the amount of goods that must be sold just to cover costs. The break-even point is precisely the quantity of goods a company needs to sell to break-even. Whatever is sold above that point will bring a profit. Below that point the company will incur a loss. We discussed break-even analysis in Chapter 3 as a technique for evaluating the success of different products. In this chapter we use break-even analysis to evaluate different location alternatives. Remember that break-even analysis works with costs, such as fixed and variable costs. It can be an excellent technique when the factors under consideration can be expressed in terms of costs. Let's briefly review the basic break-even equations:

▶ **Break-even analysis** Technique used to compute the amount of goods that must be sold just to cover costs.

$$\text{Total cost} = F + cQ,$$
$$\text{Total revenue} = pQ$$

where F = fixed cost
c = variable cost per unit
Q = number of units sold
p = price per unit

At the break-even point, total cost and total revenue are equal. We can use those equations to solve for Q, which is the break-even quantity:

$$Q = \frac{F}{p - c}$$

As we saw in Chapter 3, these quantities can be obtained graphically. Now let's look at the basic steps in using break-even analysis for location selection.

STEP 1: FOR EACH LOCATION, DETERMINE FIXED AND VARIABLE COSTS.
Recall from Chapter 3 that fixed costs are incurred regardless of how many units are produced, and include items such as overhead, taxes, and insurance. Variable costs are costs that vary directly with the number of units produced, and include items such as materials and labor. Total cost is the sum of fixed and variable costs.

STEP 2: PLOT THE TOTAL COSTS FOR EACH LOCATION ON ONE GRAPH.
To plot any straight line we need two points. One point is $Q = 0$, which is the y-intercept. Another point can be selected arbitrarily, but it is best to use the expected volume of sales in the future.

STEP 3: IDENTIFY RANGES OF OUTPUT FOR WHICH EACH LOCATION HAS THE LOWEST TOTAL COST.

STEP 4: SOLVE ALGEBRAICALLY FOR THE BREAK-EVEN POINTS OVER THE IDENTIFIED RANGES.
Select the location that gives the lowest cost for the range of output required by the new facility.

■ **Example 9.6 Using Break-Even Analysis**

Clean-Clothes Cleaners is a dry cleaning business that is considering four possible sites for its new operation. The annual fixed and variable costs for each site have been estimated as follows:

Location	Fixed Costs	Variable Costs
A	$350,000	$ 5/unit
B	$170,000	$25/unit
C	$100,000	$40/unit
D	$250,000	$20/unit

(a) Plot the total cost curves for each location on the same graph and identify the range of output for which each location provides the lowest total cost.
(b) If demand is expected to be 10,000 units per year, which is the best location?

Solution:
(a) Step 1 in the break-even procedure has already been completed; that is, we have identified the fixed and variable costs. The next step is to plot the total costs of each location on a graph. For each line that we have to plot, we need two points. The first point can be $Q = 0$. We can compute the second point using expected demand, which is $Q = 10,000$ units. For $Q = 10,000$ units we compute the following total costs for each location:

Location	Fixed Cost	Variable Cost	Total Cost
A	$350,000	$ 5 (10,000)	$400,000
B	$170,000	$25 (10,000)	$420,000
C	$100,000	$40 (10,000)	$500,000
D	$250,000	$20 (10,000)	$450,000

The plots of these graphs are shown in Figure 9-6. You can see that depending on the range of output, locations C, B, or A are best. Location D is never a best option.

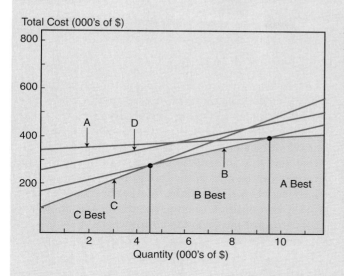

Figure 9-6

Break-even graph for Clean-Clothes Cleaners

(b) We can see the approximate ranges for each location from Figure 9-6. We can compute the exact ranges for each output level by finding the exact output level for which locations C and B are equal and for which locations B and A are equal. We can do this by computing the output levels at which the total cost equations for these locations are equal:

$$\text{Total cost equation for C} = \text{Total cost equation for B}$$

$$100{,}000 + \$40\,Q = 170{,}000 + \$25\,Q$$

$$Q = 4666.7 \text{ units}$$

Thus, the breaking point between C and B is 4666.7, or roughly 46667 units.

$$\text{Total cost equation for B} = \text{Total cost equation for A}$$

$$170{,}000 + \$25\,Q = 350{,}000 + \$5\,Q$$

$$Q = 9000 \text{ units}$$

The breaking point between B and A is 9000 units, which means that location A would provide the lowest cost if we produce 9000 units or more. If we plan to meet a demand of 10,000 units we should select location A.

The Transportation Method The transportation method of linear programming is a useful technique for solving specific location problems; it is discussed in detail in the supplement of this text. The transportation method relies on a specific algorithm to evaluate the cost impact of adding potential location sites to the network of existing facilities. For example, an existing network of facilities may consist of multiple sending and receiving sites. Our task might be to evaluate adding a new location site to this network, either a receiving site or a sending site. We might also wish to evaluate adding multiple new sites or completely redesigning the network. The transportation method can efficiently analyze all these situations and provide the lowest cost for each configuration considered.

OM ACROSS THE ORGANIZATION

By now it should be clear how capacity planning and location analysis affect operations management. However, these decisions are also important to many other functions in the company. In particular, finance and marketing have a great stake in capacity planning and location decisions.

Finance must be actively involved in the organization's capacity planning decisions. At the same time, operations managers need input from finance to finalize their capacity decisions. The reason should be clear. Capacity planning requires large financial expenditures. Building a large facility now would mean that funds would be tied up in excess capacity from which no financial return would be obtained for several years. At the same time, expanding capacity in increments could prove to be a greater financial drain due to poor planning. Location analysis, which is tied to the capacity planning decision, is basically a financial investment. Certain locations may be cheaper but may prove to be a poorer business investment. Finance needs to be an active participant in both the capacity planning and location analysis decisions.

Marketing is another function that is highly affected by capacity planning and location decisions. The amount of current and future capacity restricts the ability to meet demand. Building a large facility that enables the company to capture future demand and position itself in the marketplace could be advantageous from a marketing perspective. On the other hand, given future demands and competition this may not be a critical issue. Marketing is the function that has this information. Also, locating near customers can be critical for certain businesses, particularly service organizations. Marketing managers are in the best position to understand which location factors are most important to customers.

Capacity planning and location analysis are excellent examples of decisions that must be made by operations, finance, and marketing working together. As you can see, each of these functional areas has its domain of expertise and provides information that the others do not have. Together, they must arrive at capacity and location decisions that are best for the company in the long run.

■ OM IS EVERYWHERE

In this chapter we have discussed many issues related to capacity planning and location analysis. You may not think that much of this applies to your everyday life, but it does. Let's look first at the issue of capacity. You have a maximum output rate, whether it be studying, going to classes, going to work, or doing chores. The output rate that you are able to sustain while maintaining your normal way of life is your effective capacity. Certainly you have had periods when you worked unusually hard to keep up with the demands made on you. Maybe you have cut back on sleep and skipped meals. This would be your design capacity, and the extraordinary measures you take to achieve it are analogous to the measures taken by businesses. Remember that you cannot perform at design capacity for long periods of time. For a company it can prove very costly to perform at this level over a long period of time. Just as it would for a company, it can prove costly to your job performance or your health. Also, just as a business uses capacity cushions, so should you. You can do this by giving yourself extra time in case unexpected demands come up. Finally, you can use the concept of focused factories to be more efficient in meeting your goals. We all get distracted when we take on too many activities or projects. We can learn from the focused factory concept that we will perform much better if we focus on a small set of goals.

CHAPTER HIGHLIGHTS

1 Capacity planning is deciding on the maximum output rate of a facility.

2 Location analysis is deciding on the best location for a facility.

3 Capacity planning and location analysis decisions are often made simultaneously because the location of a facility is usually related to its capacity. When a business decides to expand, it usually also addresses the issue of where to locate. These decisions are very important because they require long-term investments in buildings and facilities, as well as a sizable financial outlay. Also, if capacity planning and location analysis are not done properly, a business will not be able to meet customer demands or may find that it is losing customers due to lack of proximity to the market.

4 In both capacity planning and location analysis, managers must follow a three-step process to make a good decision. The steps are assessing needs, developing alternatives, and evaluating alternatives.

5 To choose between capacity planning alternatives managers may use decision trees, a modeling tool used to evaluate independent decisions that must be made in sequence.

6 Key factors in location analysis include proximity to customers, transportation, source of labor, community attitude, and proximity to supplies. Service and manufacturing firms focus on different factors. Profitmaking and nonprofit organizations also focus on different factors.

7 Several tools can be used to facilitate location analysis. Factor rating is a tool that helps managers evaluate qualitative factors. The load–distance model and center of gravity approach evaluate the location decision based on distance. Break-even analysis is used to evaluate location decisions based on cost values. The transportation method is an excellent tool for evaluating the cost impact of adding sites to the network of current facilities.

KEY TERMS

capacity 247
capacity planning 247
design capacity 250
effective capacity 250
capacity utilization 250
best operating level 251

economies of scale 251
diseconomies of scale 251
focused factories 252
capacity cushion 254
decision tree 256
location analysis 258

globalization 261
factor rating 263
load–distance model 265
rectilinear distance 265
break-even analysis 269

FORMULA REVIEW

1. $ld = \Sigma \, l_{ij} d_{ij}$

2. $\text{Utilization}_{\text{effective}} = \dfrac{\text{actual output}}{\text{effective capacity}} \, (100\%)$

3. $\text{Utilization}_{\text{design}} = \dfrac{\text{actual output}}{\text{design capacity}} \, (100\%)$

4. $X_{\text{c.g.}} = \dfrac{\Sigma \, l_i x_i}{\Sigma \, l_i}$

   $Y_{\text{c.g.}} = \dfrac{\Sigma \, l_i y_i}{\Sigma \, l_i}$

5. $Q = \dfrac{F}{p - c}$

SOLVED PROBLEMS

■ Solved Problem 1

A manufacturer of ballet shoes has determined that its production facility has a design capacity of 300 shoes per week. The effective capacity, however, is 230 shoes per week. What is the manufacturer's capacity utilization relative to both design and effective capacity if output is 200 shoes per week?

Solution 1

$$Utilization_{effective} = \frac{actual\ output}{effective\ capacity}(100\%)$$

$$= \frac{200}{230}(100\%) = 86.9\%$$

$$Utilization_{design} = \frac{actual\ output}{design\ capacity}(100\%)$$

$$= \frac{200}{300}(100\%) = 66.7\%$$

The utilization rates computed show that the facility's current output is comfortably below its design capacity. It is also slightly below effective utilization, which means that the manufacturer is not using capacity to its fullest extent.

■ Solved Problem 2

EKG Software Development Corporation has determined that it needs to expand its current capacity. The decision has come down to whether to expand now with a large facility, incurring additional costs and taking the risk that the demand will not materialize, or to undertake a small expansion, knowing that the decision will have to be reconsidered in five years. Management has estimated the following chances for demand:

◆ The likelihood of demand being high is .60.
◆ The likelihood of demand being low is .40.

Profits for each alternative have been estimated:

◆ Large expansion has an estimated profitability of either $1,000,000 or $600,000, depending on whether demand turns out to be high or low.
◆ Small expansion has a profitability of $500,000, assuming that demand is low.
◆ Small expansion with an occurrence of high demand would require considering whether to expand further. If the company expands at that point, the profitability is expected to be $700,000. If it does not expand further, the profitability is expected to be $500,000.

Solution 2

To solve this problem we need to draw the decision tree and evaluate it. A decision tree for this problem is shown in Figure 9-7. We read the diagram from left to right, with node 1 representing the first decision point: expanding with a large facility or expanding small. Following each decision are chance events, which are the occurrence of either high or low demand. The probabilities for each event are shown on each branch. Notice that decision point 2 is where we may have to make our second decision, but only if we expand small now and demand turns out to be high. Then in five years we would decide whether to expand further. The estimated profits are shown in the right margins. We can see that at node 2 we should decide to expand further because the profits from that decision are higher ($700,000 versus $500,000). The expected value (EV) of profits at that point is written below node 2. The dollar amounts at the end of each alternative are the estimated profits.

Now that we have drawn the decision tree, let's see how we can solve it. We do this by computing the expected value (EV) of the small and large expansions:

$$EV_{small\ expansion} = 0.60\ (\$700,000) + 0.40\ (\$500,000)$$
$$= \$620,000$$

$$EV_{large\ expansion} = 0.60\ (\$1,000,000) + 0.40\ (\$600,000)$$
$$= \$840,000$$

A large expansion now gives us a higher expected value.

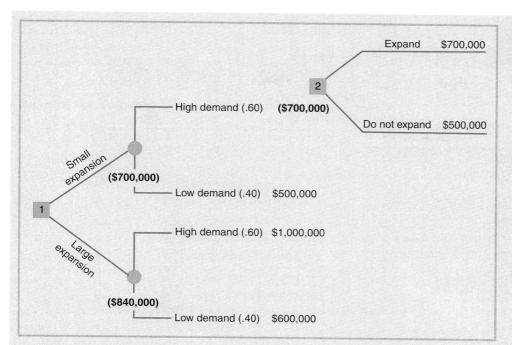

Figure 9-7

Decision tree for EKG Corporation

■ Solved Problem 3

As a recent business school graduate, you are considering two job opportunities that both require relocation. The two jobs are identical and have the same career potential. Therefore, your decision will be based on an evaluation of the two locations. You have decided to use factor rating to make your decision and have identified the most important factors. You have also placed a weight on each factor that reflects its importance, and have developed a factor score for each location based on a 5-point scale. This information is shown at right. Using the procedure for factor rating, complete the table.

Factor	Factor Weight	Factor Score at Each Location	
		Location 1	Location 2
Cost of living	10	5	2
Proximity to family	20	4	2
Climate	30	2	5
Transportation system	10	5	3
Quality of life	30	3	5

Solution 3

The completed factor rating table is shown next:

Factor	Factor Weight	Factor Score at Each Location		Weighted Score for Each Location	
		Location 1	Location 2	Location 1	Location 2
Cost of living	10	5	2	50	20
Proximity to family	20	4	2	80	40
Climate	30	2	5	60	150
Transportation system	10	5	3	50	30
Quality of life	30	3	5	90	150
Total	**100**			**330**	**390**

Based on these results, you should move to location 2.
This problem can also be solved using spreadsheets. This is
shown in Spreadsheet 9-3.

		Factor Score		Weighted Score	
Factor	Factor Weight	Location 1	Location 2	Location 1	Location 2
Cost of living	10	5	2	50	20
Proximity to family	20	4	2	80	40
Climate	30	2	5	60	150
Transportation system	10	5	3	50	30
Quality of life	30	3	5	90	150
TOTAL	100			330	390

Spreadsheet 9.3

■ Solved Problem 4

Shoeless Joe is a specialty retailer that is deciding where to
locate its new facility. The annual fixed and variable costs
for each site have been estimated as follows:

Location	Fixed Costs	Variable Costs
A	$70,000	$1/unit
B	$34,000	$5/unit
C	$20,000	$8/unit
D	$50,000	$4/unit

If demand is expected to be 2000 units, which location is
best?

Solution 4

For $Q = 2000$ units we compute the following total costs
for each location:

Location	Fixed Cost	Variable Cost	Total Cost
A	$70,000	$1 (2000)	$72,000
B	$34,000	$5 (2000)	$44,000
C	$20,000	$8 (2000)	$36,000
D	$50,000	$4 (2000)	$58,000

Shoeless Joe should locate at location C because it provides
the lowest total cost for the expected demand of 2000
units.

DISCUSSION QUESTIONS

1. Explain why capacity planning is important to a business.

2. Explain the differences between design capacity and effective capacity.

3. How is capacity utilization computed, and what does it tell us?

4. What are the steps in capacity planning?

5. What are decision trees, and how do they help us make better decisions?

6. Find and discuss business examples of overcapacity and undercapacity.

7. Explain the consequences of poor location decisions for a business.

8. Find examples of good and bad location decisions.

9. Describe three advantages and three disadvantages of globalization.

10. Describe the steps used to make location decisions.

11. Describe five factors that should be considered in the location decision.

12. Explain the differences among factor rating, the load–distance model, and break-even analysis. What criteria does each method use to make the location decision?

PROBLEMS

1. Joe's Tasty Burger has determined that its production facility has a design capacity of 400 hamburgers per day. The effective capacity, however, is 250 hamburgers per day. Lately Joe has noticed that output has been 300 hamburgers per day. Compute both design and effective capacity utilization measures. What can you conclude?

2. A manufacturer of printed circuit boards has a design capacity of 1,000 boards per day. The effective capacity, however, is 700 boards per day. Recently the production facility has been producing 950 boards per day. Compute the design and effective capacity utilization measures. What do they tell you?

3. Beth's Bakery can comfortably produce 60 brownies in one day. If Beth takes some unusual measures, such as hiring her two aunts to help in the kitchen and work overtime, she can produce up to 100 brownies in one day.

(a) What are the design and effective capacities for Beth's Bakery?

(b) If Beth is currently producing 64 brownies, compute the capacity utilization for both measures. What can you conclude?

4. The town barber shop can accommodate 35 customers per day. The manager has determined that if two additional barbers are hired, the shop can accommodate 80 customers per day. What are the design and effective capacities for the barber shop?

5. The design and effective capacities for a local paper manufacturer are 1000 and 600 pounds of paper per day, respectively. At present the manufacturer is producing 500 pounds per day. Compute capacity utilization for both measures. What can you conclude?

6. The design and effective capacities for a local emergency facility are 300 and 260 patients per day, respectively. Currently the emergency processes 250 patients per day. What can you conclude from these figures?

7. The Steiner-Wallace Corporation has determined that its needs to expand in order to accommodate growing demand for its laptop computers. The decision has come down to either expanding now with a large facility, incurring additional costs and taking the risk that the demand will not materialize, or expanding small, knowing that in three years management will need to reconsider the question.

Management has estimated the following chances for demand:

- The likelihood of demand being high is .60.
- The likelihood of demand being low is .40.

Profits for each alternative have been estimated as follows:

- Large expansion has an estimated profitability of either $100,000 or $60,000, depending on whether demand turns out to be high or low.

- Small expansion has a profitability of $50,000, assuming that demand is low.
- Small expansion with an occurrence of high demand would require considering whether to expand further. If the company expands at that point, the profitability is expected to be $70,000. If it does not expand further, the profitability is expected to be $45,000.

(a) Draw a decision tree showing the decisions, chance events, and their probabilities, as well as the profitability of outcomes.

(b) Solve the decision tree and decide what Steiner-Wallace should do.

8. The owners of Sweet-Tooth Bakery have determined that they need to expand their facility in order to meet their increased demand for baked goods. The decision is whether to expand now with a large facility or expand small with the possibility of having to expand again in 5 years.

The owners have estimated the following changes for demand:

- The likelihood of demand being high is .70
- The likelihood of demand being low is .30

Profits for each alternative have been estimated as follows:

- Large expansion has an estimated profitability of either $80,000 or $50,000, depending on whether demand turns out to be high or low.

- Small expansion has a profitability of $40,000, assuming demand is low.

- Small expansion with an occurrence of high demand would require considering whether to expand further. If the bakery expands at the point, the profitability is to be $50,000.

(a) Draw a decision tree showing the decisions, chance events, and their probabilities, as well as the profitability of outcomes.

(b) Solve the decision tree and decide what the bakery should do.

9. Demand has grown at Dairy May Farms, and it is considering expanding. One option is to expand by purchasing a very large farm that will be able to meet expected future demand. Another option is to expand the current facility by a small amount now and take a wait-and-see attitude, with the possibility of a larger expansion in two years.

Management has estimated the following chances for demand:

- The likelihood of demand being high is .70.
- The likelihood of demand being low is .30.

Profits for each alternative have been estimated as follows:

- Large expansion has an estimated profitability of either $40,000 or $20,000, depending on whether demand turns out to be high or low.
- Small expansion has a profitability of $15,000 assuming that demand is low.
- Small expansion with an occurrence of high demand would require considering whether to expand further. If the company expands at that point, the profitability is expected to be $35,000. If it does not expand further, the profitability is expected to be $12,000.

(a) Draw a decision tree diagram for Daisy May Farms.

(b) Solve the decision tree you developed. What should Daisy May Farms do?

10. Spectrum Hair Salon is considering expanding their business as they are experiencing a large growth. The question is whether they should expand with a bigger facility than needed, hoping that demand will catch up, or with a small facility, knowing that they will need to reconsider expanding in three years.

The management at Spectrum has estimated the following chances for demand:

- The likelihood of demand being high is .70.
- The likelihood of demand being low is .30.

Estimated profits for each alternative are:

- Large expansion has an estimated profitability of either $100,000 or $70,000, depending on whether demand turns out to be high or low.
- Small expansion has a profitability of $50,000 assuming that demand is low.
- Small expansion with an occurrence of high demand would require considering whether to expand further. If the business expands at the point, the profitability is expected to be $90,000. If it does not expand further, the profitability is expected to be $60,000.

Draw a decision tree and solve the problem. What should Spectrum do?

11. Jody of Jody's Custom Tailoring is considering expanding her growing business. The question is whether to expand with a bigger facility than she needs, or with a small facility, knowing that she will have to reconsider expanding in three years.

Jody has estimated the following chances for demand:

- The likelihood of demand being high is .50.
- The likelihood of demand being low is .50.

She has also estimated profits for each alternative:

- Large expansion has an estimated profitability of either $200,000 or $100,000, depending on whether demand turns out to be high or low.
- Small expansion has a profitability of $80,000 assuming that demand is low.

- Small expansion with an occurrence of high demand would require considering whether to expand further. If the business expands at that point, the profitability is expected to be $120,000. If it does not expand further, the profitability is expected to be $70,000.

Draw a decision tree and solve it. What should Jody's Custom Tailoring do?

12. Owner of Speedy Logistics, a company that provides overnight delivery of documents, is considering where to locate their new facility in the mid-west. They have narrowed their search down to two locations and have decided to use factor rating to make their decision. They have listed the factors they consider important and assigned a factor score to each location based on a 5-point scale. The information is shown here. Using the procedure for factor rating, decide on the best location.

Factor	Factor Weight	Factor Score at Each Location	
		Location 1	Location 2
Proximity to airport	40	5	3
Proximity to road access	30	4	1
Proximity to labor source	10	3	5
Size of Facility	20	2	4

13. Sue and Joe are a young married couple who are considering purchasing a new home. Their search has been reduced to two homes that they both like, at different locations. They have decided to use factor rating to help them make their decision. They have listed the factors they consider important and assigned a factor score to each location based on a 5-point scale. The information is shown here. Using the procedure for factor rating, complete the table and help Sue and Joe make their decision.

Factor	Factor Weight	Factor Score at Each Location	
		Location 1	Location 2
Proximity to work	10	5	2
Proximity to family	20	4	2
Size of home	30	2	5
Transportation system	10	5	3
Neighborhood	30	3	5

14. The Bakers Dozen Restaurant is considering opening a new location. It has considered many factors and identified the ones that are most important. Two locations are being evaluated based on these factors, using factor rating. Each location has been evaluated relative to the factors on a 5-point scale. These numbers are shown here. Use factor rating to help the restaurant decide on the best location.

Factor	Factor Weight	Factor Score at Each Location	
		Location 1	Location 2
Proximity to customers	30	5	2
Proximity to competition	10	4	2
Proximity to labor supply	30	2	5
Transportation system	20	5	3
Quality of life	10	3	5

15. Joe's Sports Supplies Corporation is considering where to locate its warehouse in order to services its four stores in four towns: A, B, C, and D. Two possible sites for the warehouse are being considered, one in Jasper and the other in Longboat. The following table shows the distances between the two locations being considered and the four store locations. Also shown are the loads between the warehouse and the four stores. Use the load–distance model to determine whether the warehouse should be located in Jasper or in Longboat.

Town	Distance to Jasper	Distance to Longboat	Load between City and Warehouse
A	30	12	15
B	6	12	10
C	10.5	30	12
D	4.5	24	8

16. Given here are the coordinates for each of the four towns to be serviced by the warehouse in Problem 9. Use the information from Problem 9 and the center of gravity method to determine the coordinates for the warehouse.

Town	Coordinates (X, Y)
A	(4, 18)
B	(12, 2)
C	(10, 8)
D	(8, 15)

17. Shoeless Joe is a specialty retailer that is deciding where to locate a new facility. The annual fixed and variable costs for each possible site have been estimated as follows:

Location	Fixed costs	Variable costs
A	$70,000	$1/unit
B	$34,000	$5/unit
C	$20,000	$8/unit
D	$50,000	$4/unit

If demand is expected to be 2000 units, which location is best?

18. The Quick Copy center for document copying is deciding where to locate a new facility. The annual fixed and variable costs for each site they are considering have been estimated as follows:

Location	Fixed costs	Variable costs
A	$85,000	$2/unit
B	$49,000	$7/unit
C	$35,000	$10/unit
D	$65,000	$6/unit

If demand is expected to be 3,000 units, which location is best?

CASE: Data Tech Inc.

Data Tech Inc. is a small but growing company started by Jeff Styles. Data Tech is a business that transfers hard copies of documents, such as invoices, bills, or mailing lists, onto CDs. As more companies move to a paperless environment, placing data on CD's is the wave of the future. Jeff had started the company in his two-car garage three years earlier by purchasing the necessary software and signing two large corporations as his first customers. Now he was about to sign on two additional corporate customers. Suddenly what was a small garage operation was turning into a major business.

The Business

The operations function of Data Tech seems deceptively simple. Every day Data Tech receives packages of mail from corporate customers containing documents they want transferred to disk. Data Tech usually receives anywhere from 10,000 to 30,000 pieces of mail per day that need to be processed. The first step requires workers to unpack and sort the mail received. Next, workers scan each item through one of two scanning machines that transfer content to disk. An accuracy check is then made to ensure that information was transferred correctly. This stage is particularly important as many of the documents contain important private information. Finally, the disks and the documents are packaged and sent back to the customer, with Data Tech keeping a backup disk for their records.

The Need for Capacity and Relocation

Running a full time business out of his two-car garage was a challenge for Jeff Styles. Jeff had spent a great deal of time ensuring that the operation of Data Tech runs smoothly without any bottlenecks. He has been successful and his two original customers had just signed long term contracts with him. In addition, he had acquired two additional customers. This meant that Data Tech needed to move to a larger facility that could accommodate the larger size of the business.

Jeff had narrowed his search to three potential locations. He identified the factors that were important to him and rated each location considering a number of criteria. Some factors were especially important, such as proximity to

Factor	Factor Weight	Factor Score at Each Location		
		#1	#2	#3
Proximity to airport	20	3	4	4
Proximity to postal service	30	4	2	5
Facility with excess capacity	?	4	5	0
Facility with potential for expansion	?	0	1	5
Close to business community	10	5	4	4
Pleasant environment	10	3	4	4

the postal service that delivered the daily packages. Another was closeness to the airport as Jeff frequently traveled to customer locations.

A factor that was particularly troubling for Jeff was the issue of capacity. Two of the locations he was considering were larger than he currently needed and offered excess capacity of growth. The third location would meet current capacity needs, but would not offer ample room for expansion. He didn't know which was a better strategy. In his list of factors Jeff made spaces for both capacity options, giving himself some time to think about the issues.

The information that Jeff had compiled is shown below.

To Expand Large or Small

Jeff was not sure how to evaluate whether he should focus on moving into a larger facility now or move into a smaller facility with potential for expansion. He estimated the following chances for demand:

- The likelihood of demand being high is .70.
- The likelihood of demand being low is .30.

He also estimated profitability for each alternative:

- Moving into a large facility had a profitability of either $1,000.000 or $600,000, depending on whether demand turned out to be high or low.
- Moving into a small facility had a profitability of $500,000 assuming that demand was low.
- Moving into a small facility would require considering expanding if demand turned high. If Data Tech decided to expand at that point, profitability would be $800,000. If it did not expand further, the profitability would be $500,000.

Case Questions:

1. Help Jeff decide whether he should put greater priority on a smaller facility with possibility for expansion, or moving into a larger facility immediately. Decide on which is the best alternative and choose weights for the two capacity factors based on your findings.

2. Once you have selected the factors for the two capacity alternatives, use factor rating to select a new location for Data Tech.

3. How would your factor analysis be different if you had selected a different capacity alternative?

INTERACTIVE LEARNING

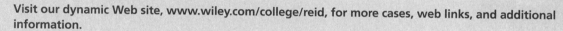

Enhance and test your knowledge of Chapter 9 using the interactive CD.

1. Spreadsheet *Solved Problem 4*

   Visit our dynamic Web site, www.wiley.com/college/reid, for more cases, web links, and additional information.

2. Company Tour
   Northeast Knitting Mills, Inc.
   Coppley Apparel Group

3. Additional Web Resources
   Association for Manufacturing Excellence, www.ame.org
   APICS, www.apics.org

4. Virtual Company Consulting Case

5. INTERNET CHALLENGE   *EDS Office Supplies, Inc.*

EDS is a national distributor of office supplies that delivers goods to department and specialty stores. It is planning to build a large distribution center in your state and is analyzing different location sites. You have been assigned the task of selecting the major city in your state that you think should be the site of the new distribution center. Here are some facts to consider. At present EDS has no other distribution center in your state. The goal is to locate in a major city that has easy access to major roadways; this will enable EDS to reach other destinations in the state. Although your decision will be subjective, be prepared to justify it. Go to the Internet to find a map of your state. Analyze roadways, distances, and access to other locations. Then use the Internet to get other information, such as traffic patterns, populations, and other geographic factors. Decide on the best location for the EDS distribution center and explain your decision.

BIBLIOGRAPHY

Berry, W. L., and Hill, T., "Linking Systems to Strategy," *International Journal of Operations and Production Management*, 12, 10, 1992, 3–15.

Florida, R., "Lean and Green: The Move to Environmentally Conscious Manufacturing," *California Management Review*, 39, 1, 1996, 80–105.

Francis, R. L., J. A. White, and L. McGinniss, *Facility Layout and Location: An Analytical Approach*, 2nd ed. Englewood Cliffs, N.J.: Prentice Hall, 1991.

Meijboom, B. and Vos, B., "International Manufacturing and Location Decisions: Balancing Configuration and Coordination Aspects," *International Journal of Operations and Production Management*, 17, 8, 1997, 790–805.

Pagell, M. and Krause, D. R., "A Multiple Method Study of Environmental Uncertainty and Manufacturing Flexibility," *Journal of Operations Management*, 17, 1999, 307–325.

Swink, M., and Hegarty, W. J., "Core Manufacturing Capabilities and Their Link to Product Differentiation," *International Journal of Operations and Production Management*, 18, 4, 1998, 374–396.

Upton, D. M., "Flexibility as Process Mobility: The Management of Plant Capabilities for Quick Response Manufacturing," *Journal of Operations Management*, 12, 1995, 205–224.

Ward, P. T., Duray, R., Leong, G. K., and Sum, C. C., "Business Environment, Operations Strategy and Performance: An Empirical Study of Singapore Manufacturers, *Journal of Operations Management*, 13, 2, 1995, 99–115.

Before studying this chapter you should know or, if necessary, review

1. The Hawthorne studies and human relations movement, Chapter 1, page 12.
2. Types of operations and their characteristics, Chapter 3, pages 52–55.
3. The load–distance model for location planning, Chapter 9, pages 265–268.
4. Measuring rectilinear distance, Chapter 9, pages 265–266.

LEARNING OBJECTIVES

After studying this chapter you should be able to

1. Define layout planning and explain its importance.
2. Identify and describe different types of layouts.
3. Compare process layouts and product layouts.
4. Describe the steps involved in designing a process layout.
5. Describe the steps involved in designing a product layout.
6. Explain the advantages of hybrid layouts.
7. Explain the meaning of group technology (cell) layouts.

CHAPTER OUTLINE

Wouldn't it be frustrating if every time you wanted to get a cup of coffee you had to go to one end of the kitchen to get a cup, then to another end to get the coffee, and then to a third end to get a spoon? What if when you wanted to study you had to go to one room to get your backpack, then to another room to get your books, and then to a third room to get your writing material? What if when you went to your college cafeteria for lunch you had to go to one area of the cafeteria for a tray, then to another area for the plates, and then to yet another area for the utensils? You would be experiencing wasted energy and time, as well as disorganization due to poor layout planning. As you can see from these examples, your experience would be frustrating. Now imagine the same kinds of problems in a company and you will appreciate the consequences of poor layout planning.

In this chapter you will learn why layout planning is important. You will also learn about different types of layouts and how to design them so as to maximize efficiency.

WHAT IS LAYOUT PLANNING? ■

Layout planning is deciding on the best physical arrangement of all resources that consume space within a facility. These resources might include a desk, a work center, a cabinet, a person, an entire office, or even a department. Decisions about the arrangement of resources in a business are not made only when a new facility is being designed; they are made any time there is a change in the arrangement of resources, such as a new worker being added, a machine being moved, or a change in procedure being implemented. Also, layout planning is performed any time there is an expansion in the facility or a space reduction.

The arrangement of resources in a facility can significantly affect the productivity of a business. As you saw in the opening examples, a lot of wasted time, energy, and confusion can result from a poor layout. There are also other reasons why layout planning is important. In many work environments, such as office settings, face-to-face interaction between workers is important. Proper layout planning can be critical in building good working relationships, increasing the flow of information, and improving communication. Similarly, in retail organizations layout can affect sales by promoting visibility of key items and contributing to customer satisfaction and convenience. As you can see, layout planning affects many areas of a business, and its importance should not be underestimated.

▶ **Layout planning**
Deciding on the best physical arrangement of all resources that consume space within a facility.

283

▶ **Intermittent processing systems**
Systems used to produce low volumes of many different products.

▶ **Continuous processing systems**
Systems used to produce high volumes of a few standardized products.

In Chapter 3 we learned about different types of operations based on degree of product standardization and volume of output. We saw that there are two broad categories of operations: intermittent and continuous processing systems. **Intermittent processing systems** are seen in organizations that produce a large variety of different products, each in low volume. An example is a typical job shop. On the other hand, **continuous processing systems** are used to produce a small variety of standardized products in high volume. An example is an assembly line. As we will see in this chapter, the nature of a company's operations is directly related to the type of layout it uses.

■ TYPES OF LAYOUTS

There are four basic layout types: *process, product, fixed position*, and *hybrid*. In this section we look at the basic characteristics of each of these types. Then we examine the details of designing some of the main types.

Process Layouts

▶ **Process layouts**
Layouts that group resources based on similar processes or functions.

Process layouts are layouts that group resources based on similar processes or functions. This type of layout is seen in companies with intermittent processing systems. You would see a process layout in environments in which a large variety of items are produced in a low volume. Since many different items are produced, each with unique processing requirements, it is not possible to dedicate an entire facility to each item. It is more efficient to group resources based on their function. The products are then moved from one resource to another, based on their unique needs.

The challenge in process layouts is to arrange resources to maximize efficiency and minimize waste of movement. If the process layout has not been designed properly, many products will have to be moved long distances, often on a daily basis. This type of movement adds nothing to the value of the product and contributes to waste. Any pair of work centers that has a large number of goods moved between them should be placed in close proximity to each other. However, this often means that some other work center will have to be moved out of the way. The process layout problem thus can become quite complex, since we are not only looking at the relationship of two resources at one time but at all our resources simultaneously.

Process layouts arrange items by type as seen in this grocery store.

A tool and die manufacturing plant is an example of a process layout.

Process layouts are very common. A hospital is an example of process layout. Departments are grouped based on their function, such as cardiology, radiology, laboratory, oncology, and pediatrics. The patient, the product in this case, is moved between departments based on his or her individual needs. A university is another example. Colleges and departments are grouped based on their function. You, the student, move between departments based on the unique program you have chosen. Another example is a metalworking shop, where resources such as drills, welding, grinding, and painting are each grouped based on the function they perform. Other examples include a printing facility that prints books, magazines, and newspapers, or a bakery that makes many different baked goods.

Recall that process layouts are designed to produce many different items, often to customer specifications. To achieve this goal they have certain unique characteristics:

1. *Resources used are general purpose.* The resources in a process layout need to be capable of producing many different products.
2. *Facilities are less capital intensive.* Process layouts have less automation, which is typically devoted to the production of one product.
3. *Facilities are more labor intensive.* Process layouts typically rely on higher-skilled workers who can perform different functions.
4. *Resources have greater flexibility.* Process layouts need to have the ability to easily add or delete products from their existing product line, depending on market demands.
5. *Processing rates are slower.* Process layouts produce many different products and there is greater movement between workstations. Consequently, it takes longer to produce a product.
6. *Material handling costs are higher.* It costs more to move goods from one process to another.
7. *Scheduling resources is more challenging.* Scheduling equipment and machines is particularly important in this environment. If it is not done properly, long

waiting lines can form in front of some work centers while others remain idle.

8. *Space requirements are higher.* This type of layout needs more space due to higher inventory storage needs.

Improper design of process layouts can result in costly inefficiencies, such as high material handling costs. A good design can help bring order to an environment that might otherwise be very chaotic.

The importance of a good process layout is illustrated by Wal-Mart, a company that has revolutionized retailing. A great deal of thought and analysis went into designing the layout of the Wal-Mart facilities. Most Wal-Mart locations have the same layout to provide predictability and comfort to customers. As in most retail operations the merchandise is grouped by category. For example, all shoes are grouped in one location, as are clothing items, stationery, and snack items. However, Wal-Mart layouts provide for maximum use of floor space. For example, the layouts are designed with multiple narrow aisles as opposed to a smaller number of wide aisles. The reason is to maximize customer exposure to merchandise. Also, Wal-Mart makes maximum use of height to store inventory and give customers visibility to products. These are some of the reasons Wal-Mart is the world's largest retailer today.

Product Layouts

▶ **Product layouts**
Layouts that arrange resources in sequence to allow for an efficient buildup of the product.

Product layouts are layouts that arrange resources in a straight-line fashion to promote efficient production. They are called product layouts because all resources are arranged to meet the production needs of the product. This type of layout is used by companies that have continuous processing systems and produce one, or a few, standardized products in large volume.

Examples of product layouts are seen on assembly lines, in cafeterias, or even at a car wash. The challenge in designing product layouts is to arrange workstations in sequence and designate the jobs that will be performed by each station in order to produce the product in the most efficient way possible. Operations managers must decide exactly what tasks will be performed by every workstation in the sequence. They need to consider the logical order in which jobs should be done. For example, at a car wash you cannot perform drying before you have performed washing. Managers also need to consider how fast production occurs and how many units can be processed through the system. The faster production occurs, the more units that can be processed through the system.

Remember that product layouts are designed to produce one, or a few, products in high volume. Product layouts have the following characteristics:

1. *Resources are specialized.* Product layouts use specialized resources designed to produce large quantities of a product.
2. *Facilities are capital intensive.* Product layouts make heavy use of automation, which is specifically designed to increase production.
3. *Processing rates are faster.* Processing rates are fast, as all resources are arranged in sequence for efficient production.

Product layouts arrange resources in a line fashion to promote efficiency. Here workers at See's Candies plant in San Francisco prepare 4-pound boxes of chocolates for Valentine's Day.

A cafeteria line is a good example of a product layout.

4. *Material handling costs are lower.* Due to the arrangement of work centers in close proximity to one another, material handling costs are significantly lower than for process layouts.
5. *Space requirements for inventory storage are lower.* Product layouts have much faster processing rates and less need for inventory storage.
6. *Flexibility is low relative to the market.* Because all facilities and resources are specialized, product layouts are locked into producing of one type of product. They cannot easily add or delete products from the existing product line.

The characteristic differences between process and product layouts are shown below in Table 10-1.

Table 10-1 Characteristics of Process and Product Layouts

Process Layouts	Product Layouts
Able to produce a large number of different products.	Able to produce a small number of products efficiently.
Resources used are general purpose.	Resources used are specialized.
Facilities are more labor intensive.	Facilities are more capital intensive.
Greater flexibility relative to the market.	Low flexibility relative to the market.
Slower processing rates.	Processing rates are faster.
High material handling costs.	Lower material handling costs.
Higher space requirements.	Lower space requirements.

The importance of an efficient product layout can be seen at the Toyota Motor Corporation, the leader of just-in-time production. Toyota had pioneered the pull production

system in the 1970s, which has been widely used in practice. The work centers are arranged in a line fashion and are in close proximity to one another, allowing easy transfer of work between stations. On the production line, a worker with any problem (e.g., a product defect or a malfunctioning machine) can pull a cord that summons a team leader to address the problem. The line has been designed so that workers can easily communicate their needs to one another. Upstream workers can respond to "pull" signals from workers downstream who require orders of goods. Also, the layout of the facility is designed so that workers can see each other as visibility of the operation is considered highly important. Toyota's system is focused on eliminating waste from every aspect of the operation, and is the factor that has contributed to Toyota's large success.

Hybrid Layouts

▶ **Hybrid layouts**
Layouts that combine characteristics of process and product layouts.

Hybrid layouts combine aspects of both process and product layouts. This is the case in facilities where part of the operation is performed using an intermittent processing system and another part is performed using a continuous processing system. For example, Winnebago, which makes mobile campers, manufactures both the vehicle itself and the curtains and bedspreads that go into the camper. The vehicles are produced on a typical assembly line, whereas the curtains and bedspreads are made in a fabrication shop that uses a process layout. Hybrid layouts are very common. Often some elements of the operation call for the production of standardized parts, which can be produced more efficiently in a product layout, whereas other parts need to be made individually in a process layout.

Hybrid layouts are often created in an attempt to bring the efficiencies of a product layout to a process layout environment. To develop a hybrid layout, we can try to identify parts of the process layout operation that can be standardized and produce them in a product layout format. One example of this is called **group technology (GT)** or **cell layouts**. First, families of products that are similar in their processing characteristics and resource requirements are identified. Managers can then create **cells**, or small product layouts, that are dedicated to the production of these families of products. This approach brings greater efficiency to the process layout environment. Later in the chapter we will learn more about group technology.

▶ **Group technology**
Hybrid layout that creates groups of products based on similar processing requirements.

Other examples of hybrid layouts can be seen in everyday life. For example, retail stores and grocery stores use hybrid layouts. In these environments, goods such as dairy items, meat, or produce are stored based on their function. From that standpoint these are process layouts. However, the layout is also designed to consider a path or sequence of purchases in a straight-line fashion, making it similar to a product layout. For example, pasta is stored immediately following spaghetti sauce.

Fixed-Position Layouts

▶ **Fixed-position layout**
A layout in which the product cannot be moved due to its size and all the resources have to come to the production site.

A **fixed-position layout** is used when the product is large and cannot be moved due to its size. All the resources for producing the product—including equipment, labor, tools, and all other resources—have to be brought to the site where the product is located. Examples of fixed-position layouts include building construction, dam or bridge construction, shipbuilding, or large aircraft manufacture. The challenge with a fixed-position layout is scheduling different work crews and jobs, and managing the project. Project management is discussed more fully in Chapter 17.

DESIGNING PROCESS LAYOUTS ■

We have mentioned that the objective in designing process layouts is to place resources close together based on the need for proximity. This need could stem from the number of trips that are made between these resources or from other factors, such as sharing of information and communication.

There are three steps in designing process layouts:

STEP 1   Gather information.

STEP 2   Develop a block plan or schematic of the layout.

STEP 3   Develop a detailed layout.

Next we look at how each of these steps is performed.

Step 1: Gather Information

The first step is to collect information that will be used to design an initial layout. Several kinds of information are needed.

Identify Space Needed The first piece of information to be collected is the amount of space needed for each of the organization's key resources. At this stage managers generally focus on larger resources, such as departments and work centers. Operations managers must identify the space requirements of each department relative to their capacity needs, such as size of equipment and number of employees, as well as circulation room such as aisles.

■ **Example 10.1 Recovery First Sports Medicine Clinic–Developing a Block Plan**

Recovery First Sports Medicine Clinic is an outpatient medical facility that provides a variety of medical services to patients suffering from sports injuries. The services include exams and x-rays, physical therapy, and outpatient surgery. The departments housed in the medical facility and their exact space requirements in square feet are shown here:

Department	Area Needed (square feet)
A. Radiology	400
B. Laboratory	300
C. Lobby and waiting area	300
D. Examining rooms	800
E. Surgery and recovery	900
F. Physical therapy	1050
Total	**3750**

▶ **Block plan**
Schematic showing the placement of resources in a facility.

Identify Available Space The available space of a facility is best seen by using a **block plan,** a schematic that shows the placement of departments in a facility. Using a block plan, we can visualize the available space and evaluate whether we can meet space needs. The current block plan for Recovery First is shown in Figure 10-1. The facility is 75 feet long by 50 feet wide, meaning that there are 3750 square feet of available space. The available space meets our total space requirements, but we will have to allocate more space to some departments. The first step in designing a process layout is to determine the best location of departments relative to one another. The easiest way to do this is to divide the available space into equal sizes to determine the departments' relative location. Much later, in the detail design stage, we can give more or less space to individual departments based on need.

Figure 10-1

Block plan for Recovery First.

A Radiology	B Laboratory	C Lobby & Waiting Area
D Examining Room	E Surgery & Recovery	F Physical Therapy

75 × 50 feet

Identify Closeness Measures Recall that the main criterion in deciding the location of departments relative to one another is the importance of proximity between them. At this stage we need a measure of the importance of having any pair of departments in close proximity to one another. There are two simple tools that can be used for this purpose: a from–to matrix and a REL chart. Both provide measures of the importance of having any pair of resources, such as work centers or departments, close together. This information can be used to design a good layout.

▶ **From–to matrix**
Table that gives the number of trips or units of product moved between any pair of departments.

A **from–to matrix** is a table that shows the number of trips or units of product moved between any pair of departments. Table 10-2 shows the from–to matrix for Recovery First, with daily trips made between each pair of departments.

The number of trips between departments can be obtained in many ways; for example, from routing slips or order forms, by performing statistical sampling to determine frequencies, or interviewing management.

Note in Table 10-2 that all entries are above the diagonal of the matrix. Remember that we are interested in the total amount of movement between any two departments, regardless of direction. Therefore, the matrix has consolidated movements

Table 10-2 From–to Matrix for Recovery First

Department	Trips between Departments					
	A	B	C	D	E	F
A. Radiology	—	—	—	45	12	25
B. Laboratory		—	—	45	14	5
C. Lobby and waiting area			—	50	20	43
D. Examining rooms				—	—	12
E. Surgery and recovery						—
F. Physical therapy						—

from both directions. For example, the total number of trips between departments A and D is 45. This could mean that 20 trips are being made from A to D and 25 trips from D to A. However, for our purpose here we are not concerned with the direction of the trips, but only with the *total number* of trips in order to measure the importance of having these departments close together.

Another tool that can be used to provide information about the importance of proximity is a REL chart, short for relationship chart. A **REL chart** is a tool that reflects opinions of managers with regard to the importance of having any two departments close together. It is a good tool to use when we need to consider the judgments of managers in deciding where to locate departments. This would be the case when other factors need to be considered in making a location decision, such as communication in an office setting, face to face contact, or customer access as in retail businesses. In these environments it is often impossible to obtain numerical values of product flow. Using a relationship chart to develop acceptable layouts is part of a classic layout technique called *systematic layout planning* (SLP). A REL chart can be used in much the same way as a from-to matrix.

A REL chart for Recovery First is shown in Table 10-3. The importance of having departments close together is determined using a predetermined scale, which is shown with the table. Values in the chart can be obtained by interviewing management and staff.

Finally, in addition to considering closeness information, a company needs to take into account other information when making layout decisions. It is very common not to be able to move certain departments due to physical constraints. For example, Recovery First has decided not to move department C, the lobby and waiting area, because it is closest to the parking lot.

Now that we have collected all the needed information, let's move to the next step in designing a process layout.

▶ **REL chart**
Table that reflects opinions of managers with regard to the importance of having any two departments close together.

CROSS FUNCTIONAL

Table 10-3 REL Chart for Recovery First

| Department | Closeness Rating between Departments | | | | | |
	A	B	C	D	E	F
A. Radiology	—	U	U	O	A(2)	O
B. Laboratory		—	U	O	I(3)	U
C. Lobby and waiting area			—	E(1)	X(4)	I(1)
D. Examining rooms				—	O	I(1)
E. Surgery and recovery						O
F. Physical therapy						—

| | Explanation of rating codes: | | |
Rating	Definition	Code	Meaning
A	Absolutely necessary	1	Patient convenience
E	Especially important	2	Sharing of medical staff
I	Important	3	Access to equipment
O	Ordinary closeness	4	Patient privacy
U	Unimportant		
X	Undesirable		

Step 2: Develop a Block Plan

The next step in the layout planning process is to develop a new block plan or a better block plan than the one already in existence. A block plan can be developed either by trial and error or by choosing from a variety of decision support tools. We will first use trial and error to develop a better block plan for Recovery First. When the layout problem is small in scope, trial and error can work well. However, when the layout problem is large it may be necessary to rely on available software. Regardless of whether you choose to use software to make your layout decisions, it is important to understand the logic behind trial and error, because decision support tools are based on heuristics that use logic similar to that used in trial and error. To understand how the decision support tools work, you need to understand the trial-and-error process.

Using Trial and Error Recall that the goal is to develop a layout that places departments close together that have been identified as needing close proximity by either the from-to matrix or the REL chart. Recovery First has decided to develop a layout that minimizes the number of trips made in order to improve efficiency. We will use information in the from-to matrix in Table 10-2 to identify critical pairings of departments.

Looking at the from-to matrix, we begin by identifying pairs of departments that need to be located close together. We look for pairs of departments with a high number of trips between them. From Table 10-2 we can identify the following pairs of departments:

> Departments C and D, which have 50 trips between them
> Departments A and D, which have 45 trips between them
> Departments B and D, which have 45 trips between them
> Departments C and F, which have 43 trips between them

These departments have a much higher number of trips between them compared to the other departments. However, note that this is an arbitrary decision, one that uses judgment. If the trips are close in numerical value, the operations manager can use information from the REL chart to decide on critical pairings of departments.

Based on these criteria, we can propose the block plan shown in Figure 10-2. This plan appears to meet set criteria, but how do we know whether it is indeed better than the current layout? We need a way to measure its effectiveness quantitatively. We can do this by using the **load–distance model** that was discussed in Chapter 9. The model is shown in Table 10-4. Recall that relative locations can be compared by computing the *ld* score. The *ld* score for a particular layout is obtained by multiplying the load for each department by the distance traveled and then summing over all the departments. The resulting score is a surrogate measure for material handling, movement, or communication. Our goal is to make the *ld* score as low as possible by reducing the distance large loads have to travel.

The load is the number obtained from the from–to matrix; it shows the number of trips between departments. But how do we determine the distance? We can obtain the distance from the block plan. Because the size of each block is the same, we do not

▶ **Load–distance model**
Model used to compare the relative effectiveness of different layouts.

Figure 10-2

Proposed block plan for Recovery First.

A Radiology	D Examining rooms	C Lobby and Waiting area
E Surgery and recovery	B Laboratory	F Physical Therapy

Table 10-4 The Load–Distance Model

ld score for a layout $= \Sigma l_{ij}\, d_{ij}$

where l_{ij} = load between departments i and j, obtained
from either the from-to matrix or the REL chart

d_{ij} = distance between departments i and j,
obtained from a block plan

need to measure the distance in feet. Rather, to keep it simple we can use one block as a measure of distance. To measure the distance between departments we typically use *rectilinear distance,* which we studied in Chapter 9. Remember that the **rectilinear distance** between any two locations is the shortest distance using only north–south and east–west movements. Therefore, from our proposed block plan we can see that the distance between departments A and D is one block unit. Between A and C the distance is two block units, and between A and F it is three block units. Using this logic, let's compute the load–distance score for the current and proposed layouts and decide which layout is better.

▶ **Rectilinear distance**
The shortest distance between two locations using north–south and east–west movements.

Table 10-5 shows computations of *ld* scores for both the current and proposed layouts for Recovery First. We can see that the proposed layout is better than the current one, as it has a lower *ld* score. In fact, the proposed layout is an almost 30% improvement over the current layout. To get the actual distance in feet, we could have multiplied the distance in the figure by 25, as each block is 25 feet long. However, multiplying both sides by 25 would not change their relative relationship.

Using Decision Support Tools Using trial and error to develop a layout plan can often lead to satisfactory results. If we continued with trial and error in our example, we could find a solution that lowered the *ld* score even further. However, when dealing

Table 10-5 *ld* Score Computations for Current and Proposed Layouts for Recovery First

Departments	Number of Trips (obtained from from-to matrix) *l*	Current Layout Distance (obtained from current block plan) *d*	Current Layout Load–Distance Score *ld*	Proposed Layout Distance (obtained from proposed block plan) *d*	Proposed Layout Load–Distance Score *ld*
A and D	45	1	45	1	45
A and E	12	2	24	1	12
A and F	25	3	75	3	75
B and D	45	2	90	1	45
B and E	14	1	14	1	14
B and F	5	2	10	1	5
C and D	50	3	150	1	50
C and E	20	2	40	3	60
C and F	43	1	43	1	43
D and F	12	2	24	2	24
		Total	515		373

with layout problems of a more realistic size we need to use decision support tools. The reason is that the layout problem is a combinatorial problem. For a block plan of six departments there are actually 6! different solutions, or 720 possible solutions. You can imagine how many layout alternatives there would be for a facility with 50 different departments.

▶ **ALDEP and CRAFT**
Computer software packages for designing process layouts.

There are a number of computer software packages that can be used as decision support tools in making the layout decision. Two of the most popular are **ALDEP** (automated layout design program) and **CRAFT** (computerized relative allocation of facilities technique). They are called decision support tools because they use different heuristics to develop a solution. They do not give an optimal solution, and they consider only one criterion at a time in designing a layout. The best way to use these software packages is to consider the software solution as a starting point in developing a final layout.

ALDEP works from a REL chart. It constructs a layout within the boundaries of the facility by trying to link together departments that have either an A or an E rating in the REL chart. Remember that an A rating stands for absolutely necessary and an E rating for especially important. ALDEP uses this logic to link these departments together. The first department is selected randomly. To evaluate a layout, the computer program computes a score that is similar to the *ld* score we computed using trial and error. Depending on the starting point selected, many different layouts can be obtained.

CRAFT works differently from ALDEP. It is also a heuristic, but it uses a different logic to find a solution. CRAFT uses a from-to matrix and an existing layout as a starting point. It proceeds by making paired exchanges of departments that lead to a reduction of the *ld* score and continues in this manner until there are no more exchanges that can reduce the *ld* score. The solution with the lowest *ld* score is the final solution.

There are many other sophisticated computer software packages for layout planning that can be used to design office buildings, warehouses, and other large facilities. They are capable of designing layouts for multiple floors, and they can consider height for assigning storage locations as in retail or warehousing. For example, SPACECRAFT is a modified version of CRAFT developed for designing multistory layouts. These software programs, including ALDEP and CRAFT, can work with a large number of departments of different sizes and shapes.

Step 3: Develop a Detailed Layout

The last step in designing a process layout is the development of a detailed layout design. At this stage the block plan is translated into a more realistic schematic. We begin to consider exact sizes and shapes of departments and work centers. We also focus on specific work elements, such as desks, cabinets, and machines, as well as aisles, stairways, and corridors. Operations managers can use a variety of tools in this final stage; they include drawings, three-dimensional models, and computer graphics software.

■ SPECIAL CASES OF PROCESS LAYOUT

A number of unique cases of process layout require special attention. In this section we look at two special cases: *warehouse layouts* and *office layouts*.

Warehouse Layouts

Warehouse layouts have the key characteristics of process layouts: Products are stored based on their function and there is movement of goods. The main difference is that movement within a warehouse is primarily between the loading/unloading dock and the areas where goods are stored. Typically there is no movement between the storage areas themselves; the primary function of a warehouse is to provide storage space, so the only movement is inbound or outbound. Think about a warehouse that stores computer equipment and supplies. Printers might be stored in one area, keyboards in another, and ink cartridges in a third. Certainly there would be no movement between the keyboard storage area and the area where ink cartridges are stored. The movement would consist of bringing items either in or out of the warehouse.

Storage Areas of Equal Sizes   The primary decision in designing warehouse layouts is to decide where to locate individual departments relative to the dock. Using the same logic we used for process layouts in general, the goal is to assign departments to locations in order to minimize the number of trips to the dock. As before, we need a from-to matrix that shows the number of trips. Since the movements are only between the departments and the dock, we simply locate the department with the highest number of trips closest to the dock. Next, we locate the department with the second highest number of trips in the next available space closest to the dock. We proceed in this manner until all the departments have been assigned. Next we look at a simple example.

■ Example 10.2 Green Grocer Makes Location Assignments

Green Grocer stores its dry goods in a nearby warehouse. The different categories of foods are stored in departments that each take up the same amount of space, shown in Figure 10-3. Given the available warehouse space and the number of trips made for each category of foods, Green Grocer needs to decide where to locate each department.

Figure 10-3

Warehouse storage areas for Green Grocer.

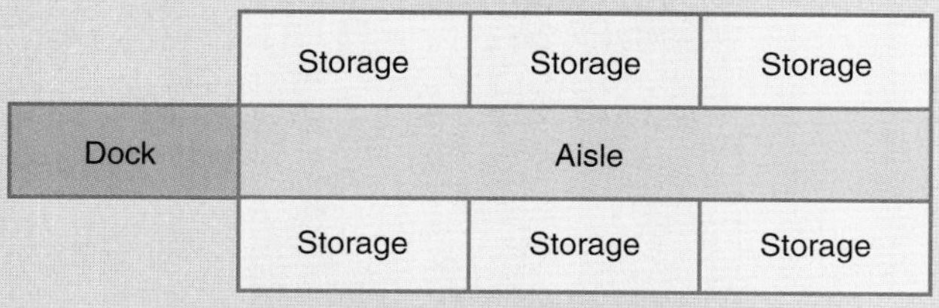

Department	Food Category	Trips to and from Dock
1	Canned goods	50
2	Cereals	63
3	Condiments	35
4	Diapers and baby products	55
5	Cookies and candies	48
6	Fruit and vegetable juices	60

Solution

To assign departments to specific storage areas we progressively assign departments with the highest number of trips closest to the dock. Department 2 is placed closest because it has the highest number of trips. Next comes department 6, and so forth. Using this logic we develop the block plan shown in Figure 10-4.

Figure 10-4

Block plan for Green Grocer Warehouse.

2		4		5
Dock		Aisle		
6		1		3

Storage Areas of Unequal Size In Example 10-2 all the departments required equal-sized storage areas. What would happen if the storage areas required were of different sizes? It is common for some departments to need more room than others based on the size of the product or volumes needed. Number of trips is not a good measure because it can be misleading. For example, if department A takes up four storage areas and makes 20 trips to the dock, it actually has fewer trips per area than department B, which takes up one storage area and makes 15 trips. The reason is that when trips per area are considered, department A only has 5 trips whereas B has 15.

To make location assignments when departments take up storage areas of unequal size we need to follow these steps:

STEP 1   Take the ratio of the number of trips relative to the storage area required.

In a warehouse distribution center, items are stored based on their function.

STEP 2   Use the ratios from Step 1 to make assignments. Assign the department with the highest ratio closest to the dock. Next, assign the department with the second highest ratio second closest to the dock. Continue in this manner until all departments have been assigned.

Next we look at another example to see how this would work.

■ Example 10.3 Looking Good Clothes Assigns Storage Areas

Looking Good Clothes is a clothing retailer for teenagers and young adults. The company is in the process of assigning storage areas in its warehouse in order to minimize the number of trips made to retrieve items needed. Following are the departments that need to be located, the number of trips made per week for each department, and the area needed by each department.

Department	Trips to and from Dock	Area Needed
1. Backpacks	160	2
2. Hiking boots	150	3
3. Jeans	100	1
4. T-shirts	120	1
5. Bomber jackets	270	3

The warehouse block plan is shown in Figure 10-5.

Figure 10-5

Warehouse storage areas for Looking Good Clothes.

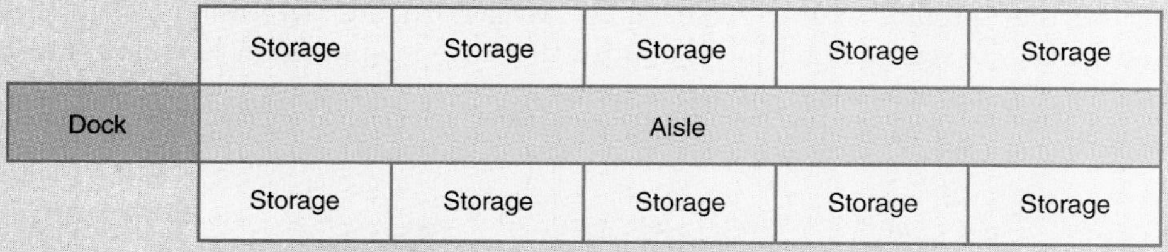

Solution:

STEP 1:   Take the ratio of trips to the number of areas taken up by the department.

Department	Trips to and from Dock	Area Needed	Ratio of Trips to Area Needed
1. Backpacks	160	2	80
2. Hiking boots	150	3	50
3. Jeans	100	1	100
4. T-shirts	120	1	120
5. Bomber jackets	270	3	90
		Total Area 10	

STEP 2: Use the ratios from Step 1 to assign departments to storage areas. These are shown in the block plan in Figure 10-6.

Figure 10-6

Block plan for Looking Good Warehouse.

3	5	5	1	2

Dock	Aisle

4	5	1	2	2

Office Layouts

Office layouts are another special case of process layouts. Merely looking at the number of trips between departments or the movement of goods is not sufficient to design a good office layout, because human interaction and communication are the primary factors that need to be considered when designing office layouts. Recall from Chapter 1 that an important lesson learned from the Hawthorne studies in the 1930s was that workers respond greatly to their physical environment and have many psychological needs. This information, coupled with the fact that almost half of the workforce in the United States works in an office environment, makes office layouts very important.

Proximity versus Privacy   One of the key trade-offs that have to be made in an office layout is between proximity and privacy. The ability for workers to communicate and interact with one another is highly important in an office environment. As companies increasingly embrace team approaches, open office environments are valued because they provide visibility and allow workers to interact easily. Studies have shown that workers that are in close proximity to one another have greater understanding, tolerance, and trust for one another.

A properly designed office layout can significantly improve productivity.

However, office layouts that enhance team interactions do not allow privacy. Often employees need privacy to think and work quietly without being interrupted. Also, it may be difficult to have confidential conversations with coworkers and clients in an open office environment. When designing an office layout, these considerations must be addressed in order to enhance productivity.

Other Factors in Designing Office Environments One important consideration in designing any layout is flexibility. **Flexible layouts** remain desirable many years into the future or can be easily modified to meet changing demands. Traditional load-bearing walls provide privacy but do not provide flexibility. Partitions, on the other hand, are very flexible but do not offer privacy.

▶ **Flexible layouts**
Layouts that remain desirable many years into the future or can be easily modified to meet changing demand.

Companies are becoming more creative in meeting the needs of their employees, enhancing productivity, and designing flexible layouts. One option is to use what is commonly called *office landscaping*. This entails using plants, decor, and indoor landscaping to provide natural looking partitions and sections that allow for privacy and flexibility and still have the feel of an open office environment. In addition, the natural look of office landscaping provides a pleasant working environment.

Before You Go On

We have described several different types of layouts. By now you should know how to design process layouts and understand the unique characteristics of warehouse and office layouts. We will now learn how to design product layouts. Since process and product layouts are very different, make sure you review these differences. Before proceeding further, also review the characteristics of product layouts.

DESIGNING PRODUCT LAYOUTS ◼

Recall that product layouts arrange resources in sequence so the product can be made as efficiently as possible. This type of layout is used in continuous processing systems that produce a large volume of one standardized product.

Product layouts are completely different from process layouts. When designing product layouts our objective is to decide exactly what tasks are to be performed by each workstation in the sequence. To accomplish this we need to consider the logical order of the tasks to be performed. Some tasks must be performed before others. Also, we need to consider the speed of the production process, which will tell us how much time there is at each workstation to perform the assigned tasks. This entire process is called **line balancing.** Next we will go through the steps that must be followed in designing product layouts.

▶ **Line balancing**
The process of assigning tasks to workstations in a product layout in order to achieve a desired output and balance the workload among stations.

Step 1: Identify Tasks and Their Immediate Predecessor

The first step in designing product layouts is to identify the tasks or work elements that must be performed in order to produce the product. We also need to determine how long each task takes to perform and which tasks must be performed in sequence. The task or tasks that must be performed immediately before another is called the task's **immediate predecessor.** We use an example to illustrate this point.

▶ **Immediate predecessor**
A task that must be performed immediately before another task.

■ **Example 10.4 Vicki's Pizzeria and the Precedence Diagram**

Vicki's Pizzeria is planning to make boxed take-out versions of its famous pepperoni, sausage, and mushroom pizza. The pizzas will be made on a small assembly line. Vicki has identified the tasks that need to be performed, the time required for each task, and each task's immediate predecessor. This information is shown here:

Work Element	Task Description	Immediate Predecessor	Task Time (seconds)
A	Roll dough	None	50
B	Place on cardboard backing	A	5
C	Spread sauce	B	25
D	Sprinkle cheese	C	15
E	Add pepperoni	D	12
F	Add sausage	D	10
G	Add mushrooms	D	15
H	Shrinkwrap pizza	E, F, G	18
I	Pack in box	H	15
		Total task time	**165**

Often it is helpful to have a visual representation of the precedence relationships between the tasks that need to be performed. This is called a *precedence diagram*. The precedence diagram for assembling Vicki's pizzas is shown in Figure 10-7. The diagram is read from left to right. The circles, or nodes, represent the tasks, and the arrows, or arcs, show the connections between them. Together, they show how the tasks are connected. To find a task's immediate predecessor, follow the arrows backward from your task. In the diagram you can see that the first task that must be performed is task A. After A has been completed, B should be done. Next comes task C and then D. After task D, however, we can do either E, F, or G. However, to be able to complete task H, we must have completed all the predecessors of H—namely, E, F, and G. Finally, after all the other tasks have been completed, task I can be performed.

Figure 10-7

Precedence diagram for Vicki's Pizzeria.

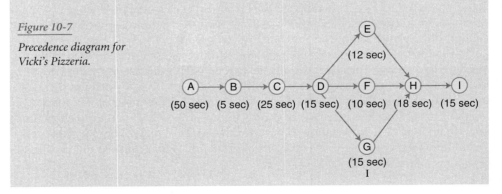

Step 2: Determine Output Rate

The next step is to determine how many units we wish to produce over a period of time, called the **output rate.** Then we can design a product layout that produces the desired number of units with as few work centers as possible, and balance the workload at each workstation. In our example, Vicki has decided that she wishes to produce 60 pizzas per hour in order to meet her growing demand.

▶ **Output rate**
The number of units we wish to produce over a specific period of time.

Step 3: Determine Cycle Time

Cycle time is the amount of time each workstation has to complete its assigned tasks. Cycle time also tells us how frequently a product is completed. Recall that in product layouts work is being performed on many workstations that are arranged in sequence. At the beginning of the line, workers are carrying out the initial stages of putting the product together. At the end of the line, the last steps of production are being completed. If you were to stop the process at any one point in time, you would find products at all stages of production, from raw materials through work in process, as well as completed products.

Cycle time is directly related to the volume that can be produced. The faster the cycle time, the lower is its numerical value. A cycle time of 50 seconds means that each workstation has 50 seconds to perform its assigned tasks and that one unit is completed every 50 seconds. By contrast, a cycle time of 100 seconds would give more time to each workstation. It also means that a product would be completed every 100 seconds. You can see that by producing a unit every 50 seconds we would have many more units at the end of the day, as opposed to producing a unit every 100 seconds. Therefore, cycle time is directly related to output.

General Cycle Time Equation Cycle time can be computed using the following equation:

$$\text{Cycle time} = C = \frac{\text{available time}}{\text{desired output}}$$

Computing Cycle Time When Output Is in Units per Hour Cycle time is generally computed in seconds per unit. Note that available time and desired output are measured over a certain period, such as per hour or per day. Remember that they need to be over the same period for the computation to work. For example,

$$\text{Cycle time (seconds/unit)} = C = \frac{\text{available time in seconds/hour}}{\text{desired output in units/hour}}$$

Note that the "per hour" in the numerator will cancel out the "per hour" in the denominator and the final measure is "seconds per unit."

Computing Cycle Time When Output Is in Units per Day The same type of computation would be performed if we were given the desired output in units per day:

$$\text{Cycle time (seconds/unit)} = C = \frac{\text{available time in seconds/day}}{\text{desired output in units/day}}$$

As before, the "per day" in the numerator cancels out the "per day" in the denominator and the final measure is "seconds per unit." The important thing is to use the same units in the denominator as in the numerator.

Now let's compute the cycle time for Vicki's assembly line. Vicki said that she wanted to produce 60 pizzas per hour. We start with the general equation for cycle time. Then we substitute the specific numerical values and perform the computations:

► **Cycle time**
The amount of time each workstation has to complete its assigned tasks.

$$\text{Cycle time (seconds/unit)} = C = \frac{\text{available time in seconds/hour}}{\text{desired output in units/hour}}$$

$$= \frac{60 \text{ minutes/hour} \times 60 \text{ seconds/minute}}{60 \text{ units/hour}}$$

$$= \frac{3600 \text{ seconds/hour}}{60 \text{ units/hour}}$$

$$= 60 \text{ seconds/unit}$$

Vicki should have a cycle time of 60 seconds per unit, which means that each workstation has 60 seconds to perform its task. Also, this means that one completed pizza will be finished every 60 seconds. After one hour, Vicki will have 60 pizzas.

Relationship between Bottleneck and Maximum Output

What if Vicki changed her mind and wanted to produce more than 60 pizzas per hour? This would mean that her cycle time would have to be faster (that is, its numerical value would be lower), and pizzas would be produced more frequently than every 60 seconds. Perhaps she could lower the cycle time to 55 seconds or even 50 seconds. But what is the possible lowest value for the cycle time?

▶ **Bottleneck task**
The longest task in a process.

Note that if Vicki lowered the cycle time below 50 seconds, there would not be enough time to do task A, which requires 50 seconds. Therefore, given the current task times, 50 seconds is the lowest cycle time Vicki's assembly line could have. Task A is the longest task and thus acts as a constraint. This is called the **bottleneck.** The bottleneck constrains the production process and determines the lowest cycle time. Sometimes it is possible to reduce the bottleneck by splitting the task into smaller ones that can be done separately. For example, maybe our bottleneck task, which is rolling dough, can be divided into smaller tasks such as placing dough on a floured board and rolling out the dough. However, there will always be a bottleneck. Once we eliminate one bottleneck, the next longest task becomes the bottleneck.

The bottleneck is important because it provides the lowest limit on the cycle time. Cycle time is related to the amount of output; therefore, this lowest cycle time determines the maximum output that can be achieved given current tasks. The relationship can be derived as follows. The general cycle time equation:

$$\text{Cycle time} = C = \frac{\text{available time}}{\text{desired output}}$$

We can algebraically change this equation to solve for output:

$$\text{Output} = \frac{\text{available time}}{\text{cycle time}}$$

We can then compute the maximum output given the lowest or minimum cycle time as defined by the bottleneck:

$$\text{Maximum output} = \frac{\text{available time}}{\text{minimum cycle time (bottleneck)}}$$

Using this equation, we can compute the maximum output Vicki can have on her assembly line given that task A takes 50 seconds:

$$\text{Maximum output} = \frac{3600 \text{ seconds/hour}}{50 \text{ units/second}} = 72 \text{ units/hour, or 72 pizzas per hour}$$

The maximum that Vicki can produce on her assembly line is 72 pizzas per hour.

Step 4: Compute the Theoretical Minimum Number of Stations

Before we decide to assign specific tasks to workstations, it is usually helpful to compute the theoretical minimum number of stations or *TM*. The **theoretical minimum number of stations** is the number of workstations that would be needed if the line was 100% efficient. Of course, we will not achieve 100% efficiency, and often we will have more stations than the theoretical minimum. However, computing this number gives us a baseline for the number of stations we should have. The computation for the theoretical minimum number of stations is as follows:

▶ **Theoretical minimum number of stations**
The number of workstations needed on a line to achieve 100% efficiency.

$$TM = \frac{\Sigma t}{C}$$

where Σt = sum of the task times needed to complete a unit
C = cycle time

For Vicki's assembly line, the theoretical minimum number of stations (*TM*) is

$$TM = \frac{165 \text{ seconds}}{60 \text{ seconds}} = 2.75, \text{ or 3 stations}$$

Theoretical minimum numbers of stations that end with a fraction are always rounded up because there can be no partial workstations.

Step 5: Assign Tasks to Workstations

Given the tasks we have to perform and their precedence relationships as well as the cycle time, we can now proceed to assign tasks to workstations. To do this, there are a number of rules that can be used at this stage. We will use the *longest task time rule*, which basically states that when selecting from a group of tasks we should pick the task that takes the longest time. However, in practice a number of other rules can be used. Following are the basis steps in this process:

Steps	Procedure for Assigning Tasks to Workstations
A	Start with the first station; make a list of tasks eligible to be performed, following precedence relationships.
B	Select from the eligible task list by picking the task that takes the longest time (*longest task time rule*). If only one task is eligible, we do not need to use the rule.
C	When the cycle time has been used up at one station or no tasks can be assigned to the remaining time, start a new station.

Let's see how these steps apply to Vicki's pizzeria. A convenient method is to make a table with columns labeled "Workstation," "Eligible Task," "Task Selected," "Task Time," and "Idle Time." We can then fill in the table following the steps we have outlined and keeping a cycle time of 60 seconds. This is shown in Table 10-6.

Table 10-6 Assignments of Tasks to Workstations for Vicki's Pizzeria				
Workstation	Eligible Task	Task Selected	Task Time	Idle Time
1	A	A	50	10
2	B	B	5	55
	C	C	25	30
	D	D	15	15
	E, F, G	G	15	0
3	E, F	E	12	48
	F	F	10	38
	H	H	18	20
	I	I	15	5

Cycle time = 60 seconds.

Step 6: Compute Efficiency, Idle Time, and Balance Delay

After tasks have been assigned to workstations we should compute the efficiency of the arrangement. **Efficiency** is the ratio of total productive time divided by total time, given as a percentage:

$$\text{Efficiency (\%)} = \frac{\Sigma t}{NC}\,(100)$$

where Σt = sum of the task times
N = number of workstations
C = cycle time

Note that in this equation the numerator is the actual work time, whereas the denominator is the time allocated for performing tasks. To improve efficiency, we try to assign as much work to the lowest number of workstations needed to produce the volume of product desired while keeping the work loads balanced.

Often it is helpful to compute the amount by which the efficiency of the line falls short of 100%. Called the *balance delay*, it is computed as follows:

$$\text{Balance delay (\%)} = 100 - \text{efficiency.}$$

■ Example 10.5 Computing Efficiency and Balance Delay

For Vicki's assembly line, we can compute the efficiency and balance delay:

$$\text{Efficiency (\%)} = \frac{165 \text{ seconds}}{3 \text{ stations} \times 60 \text{ seconds}}\,(100) = \frac{165}{180} = 91.66\%$$

$$\text{Balance delay (\%)} = 100 - 91.66 = 8.34\%$$

Other Considerations

In designing *process layouts* we went from a crude block plan to the design of a detailed layout. Similarly, there are many details of *product layout* design that need to be addressed in addition to the ones we have discussed.

Shape of the Line We know that product layouts arrange work centers in sequence to allow for efficient production. Even though this sequence is linear, the actual shape of the product layout usually is not one long, straight line. If it were, we would need an unusually long, straight building. Also, having a long, straight line may not be best from a productivity standpoint. Arranging the shape of the line so that workers can see and communicate with one another can improve productivity and worker satisfaction. The actual shape of the line can be an **S** shape, a **U** shape, an **O**, or an **L**. Much thought should go into the choice of an appropriate shape. For example, shapes such as **U** and **O** can store frequently used resources in the center, where they are accessible to everyone.

On paced lines the product being worked on automatically moves from one station to the next.

Paced versus Unpaced Lines Another issue to decide on is whether to have a paced or an unpaced line. On **paced lines** the product being worked on is physically attached to the line and automatically moved from one station to the next when cycle time elapses. The amount of time workers have to perform their tasks is identical to cycle time. Unpaced lines, on the other hand, allow the product to be physically removed from the line to be worked on. Workers can then vary the amount of time they spend working on the product. Storage areas for inventory are often placed between workstations, to be used when there is a delay in production at a station.

The work environment has a significant impact on worker satisfaction and productivity. Some studies have found that unpaced lines lead to greater productivity when they are coupled with a good incentive program. This situation provides more autonomy and freedom for workers. However, in some environments a paced line is the only option—for example, when the product is very large and cannot be moved. This would be the case when assembling large and heavy items such as a large refrigerator or an automobile.

Number of Product Models Produced Another consideration is whether to have a single-model or a mixed-model line. A **single-model line** is designed to produce only one version of a product. A **mixed-model line,** on the other hand, is designed to produce many versions of a product. For example, a single line might produce only Jeep Wranglers, whereas a mixed-model line might produce two types of Jeeps, such as the Wrangler and the Cherokee. A mixed model is more flexible, but there may be more complications with regard to scheduling and changing production from one model to the other.

▶ **Paced line**
A system in which the product being worked on is physically attached to the line and automatically moved to the next station when the cycle time has elapsed.

▶ **Single-model line**
A line designed to produce only one version of a product.

▶ **Mixed-model line**
A line designed to produce many versions of a product.

Before You Go On

Both process and product layouts have their strengths and weaknesses. Process layouts are flexible and can produce many different kinds of products. Process layouts are less efficient than product layouts because material handling costs can create much inefficiency. Product layouts, on the other hand, are less flexible because all their resources are devoted to the production of one type of product. However, they are very efficient and create little waste. Make sure you understand these differences, because in the next section we will look at ways of combining some of the strengths of process and product layouts.

■ HYBRID LAYOUTS

Hybrid layouts combine characteristics of both process and product layouts. They are created whenever possible in order to combine the strengths of each type of layout. One of the most popular types of hybrid layouts is **group technology (GT)** or cell layouts. Group technology has the advantage of bringing the efficiencies of a product layout to a process layout environment.

Group Technology (Cell) Layouts

If we look at a company that produces many different products, we may find that some products are similar to each other in the way they are made and the resources they require. For example, a company may produce 500 different products. However, if we analyze how each of the products is manufactured we may be able to create groups of products—say, one group of 150, another group of 100, and so on—that are very similar in the way they are produced. To be efficient, we could place all the resources needed for each group in a separate area, called a *cell*. The production of a group, or family, of items would be done very efficiently because all the resources required would be in close proximity. This is the goal of group technology.

Group technology is the process of creating groupings of products based on similar processing requirements. For example, Figure 10-8 shows parts that all belong to the same family. These parts are all different, but they are very similar in the way they are made. Group technology essentially creates small product layouts dedicated to the production of a group of items. Figure 10-9 shows process flows before and after the use of GT cells. The first picture is a process layout with different product routes for the many products a company produces. The second picture shows the implementation of group technology in that environment. Cells have been created for each family, and there is a much more orderly flow through the facility.

Figure 10-8

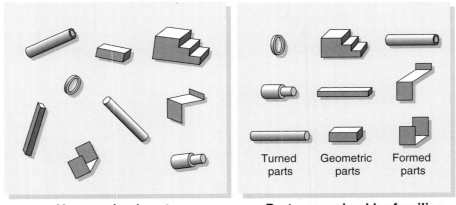

Turned   Geometric   Formed
parts   parts   parts

Unorganized parts   **Parts organized by families**

Figure 10-9

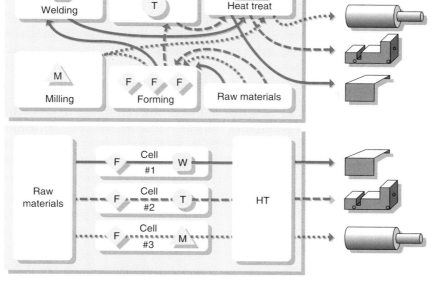

(a) Process flows before the use of GT cells

(b) Process flows after the use of GT cells

OM ACROSS THE ORGANIZATION

We have seen in this chapter why layout planning is important for operations management. The production process could not run efficiently, and there would be much waste, if we did not design a proper layout for a facility. But layout planning is also important for other functions in the organization.

Marketing is highly affected by layout planning, particularly in environments where customers and clients come to the site. This is especially true in retail environments. The location and placement of goods in the facility, their visibility, and ease of access can greatly influence sales. In these types of environments the marketing of the product takes place, in part, through the layout of a facility. For example, attractive displays and product positioning in a grocery store can promote advertising and sales. Thus, it is very important for marketing to work with operations in designing the layout.

Human resources knows how the management of people can be affected by layout planning. Studies have shown that people who work and interact together on a regular basis have better working relationships. Managers need to give much thought to which groups of people need to work closely together

and place them in close proximity to one another to facilitate teamwork and cooperation.

Finance is involved whenever large financial outlays and cost considerations are at stake. This is certainly true in layout planning. Redesign of layouts can be very costly, particularly if they are large scale, as when switching to an open office environment or a cell layout. Finance needs to measure the value of these investments and work with operations to create budgets. They must also understand the long-range implications of a good layout for the entire organization in order to evaluate them properly.

Everyone in the company is affected by the design of a facility's layout. Whatever organization you work at, you are somehow affected by its layout design, including the location of your office and department, the appearance of your office, and the degree of privacy you have. Also included are proximity to coworkers and other people you must interact with, whether you must travel long distances to get supplies or clerical assistance, and the esthetics of the layout. Regardless of what business function you are in, the degree of satisfaction with your work environment is greatly dependent on the layout.

■ OM IS EVERYWHERE

In this chapter we have seen how the layout of a facility can influence the efficiency of a business. In the same way, it can affect everyday life. Just as a business organization strives to be efficient, so do you. This means that you do not want to waste time looking for things or repeating the same steps. To avoid that, you perform layout planning. For example, you do layout planning every time you decide on the placement of items in your own home. In your kitchen, you probably group together similar items, such as plates, saucers, and cups. In your bedroom your shirts are grouped together in one area, unless you are a typical college student. In this respect your house is organized as a process layout. But you have probably also considered which items go together in a sequence, such as coffee, sugar, and cream. In this respect you have designed a product layout. Whether you are aware of it or not, layout planning is an integral part of your life.

CHAPTER HIGHLIGHTS

1 Layout planning is deciding on the best physical arrangement of all resources that consume space within a facility. Proper layout planning is highly important for the efficient running of a business. Otherwise, there can be much wasted time, and energy, as well as confusion.

2 There are four basic types of layouts: *process, product, hybrid,* and *fixed position.* Process layouts group resources based on similar processes or functions, as in a hospital or a machine job shop. Product layouts arrange resources in a straight line fashion, as on an assembly line. Hybrid layouts combine elements of both process and product layouts in their operation. Finally, fixed-position layouts occur when the product is large and cannot be moved.

3 Process layouts provide much flexibility and allow for the production of many products with differing characteristics. Product layouts, on the other hand, provide great efficiency when producing one type of product.

4 The steps in designing a process layout are: (1) gathering information about space needs, space availability, and closeness requirements of departments; (2) developing a block plan or schematic of the layout; and (3) developing a detailed layout.

5 The steps in designing a product layout are: (1) identifying tasks that need to be performed and their immediate predecessors; (2) determining output rate; (3) determining cycle time; (4) computing the theoretical minimum number of stations; (5) assigning tasks to workstations; and (6) computing efficiency, idle time, and balance delay.

6 Hybrid layouts have advantages over other layout types because they combine elements of both process and product layouts to increase efficiency.

7 An example of hybrid layouts is group technology or cell layouts. Group technology is the process of creating groupings of products based on similar processing requirements. Cells are created for each grouping of products, resulting in a more orderly flow of products through the facility.

KEY TERMS

FORMULA REVIEW

1. $ld \text{ score} = \Sigma l_{ij} d_{ij}$

2. Cycle time $= C = \dfrac{\text{available time}}{\text{desired output}}$

3. Output $= \dfrac{\text{available time}}{\text{cycle time}}$

4. Maximum output $= \dfrac{\text{available time}}{\text{minimum cycle time (bottleneck)}}$

5. $TM = \dfrac{\Sigma t}{C}$

6. Efficiency (%) $= \dfrac{\Sigma t}{NC}(100)$

7. Balance delay (%) $= 100 - \text{efficiency}$

SOLVED PROBLEMS

■ Solved Problem 1

Jeff-Co Industries is a metalworking shop that is redesign-ing its layout. The from-to matrix of the numbers of trips between departments is shown here.

Table 10-7 From-to Matrix for Jeff-Co Industries

Department	Trips between Departments					
---	A	B	C	D	E	F
A	—	10	15	—	—	50
B		—	—	20	10	20
C			—	45	—	10
D				—	—	20
E						—
F						—

The current layout is shown in Figure 10-10. Find an im-proved layout using trial and error. Which departments should you locate close together?

Figure 10-10

Current layout for Jeff-Co Industries.

A	B	C
D	E	F

Solution 1

The following departments have the highest numbers of trips between them and should be located close together:

A and F, which have 50 trips between them
C and D, which have 45 trips between them

Using this as our criterion we can construct the pro-posed layout shown in Figure 10-11.

Figure 10-11

Proposed layout for Jeff-Co Industries.

A	E	C
F	B	D

We can now compute the *ld* scores for both the current and proposed layouts in order to make an evaluation. See Table 10.8.

Based on the *ld* score, the proposed layout is an im-provement of 43% over the current layout. This problem can also be solved using a spreadsheet. This is shown in Spreadsheet 10.1.

Spreadsheet 10.1

Proposed Layout

A	E	C
F	B	D

Departments				Load-Distance
From	To	# of Trips	Distance	Score
A	B	10	2	20
A	C	15	2	30
A	D	0	3	0
A	E	0	1	0
A	F	50	1	50
B	C	0	2	0
B	D	20	1	20
B	E	10	1	10
B	F	20	1	20
C	D	45	1	45
C	E	0	1	0
C	F	10	3	30
D	E	0	2	0
D	F	20	2	40
E	F	0	2	0
				265

Table 10-8 *ld* Score Computations for Current and Proposed Layouts for Jeff-Co Industries

		Current Layout		Proposed Layout	
Departments	Number of Trips (obtained from from-to matrix) *l*	Distance (obtained from current block plan) *d*	Load–Distance Score *ld*	Distance (obtained from proposed block plan) *d*	Load–Distance Score *ld*
A and B	10	1	10	2	20
A and C	15	2	30	2	30
A and F	50	3	150	1	50
B and D	20	2	40	1	20
B and E	10	1	10	1	10
B and F	20	2	40	1	20
C and D	45	3	135	1	45
C and F	10	1	10	3	30
D and F	20	2	40	2	40
		Total	465		265

■ Solved Problem 2

Parachutes By Dave is a parachute production facility that assembles and packages parachutes. Table 10-9 shows the tasks required to perform the job, the times required by each task, and their immediate predecessors.

If Dave wants to produce 50 parachutes per hour, compute the following:

Table 10-9 Task Information for Parachutes By Dave

Work Element	Task Description	Immediate Predecessor	Task Time (seconds)
A	Cast lines	None	45
B	Attach harness	A	15
C	Sew rings	A	27
D	Attach lines B to chute	B	52
E	Perform safety check	C, D	7
F	Pack chute	E	18
		Total	164 seconds

(a) the appropriate cycle time
(b) the theoretical minimum number of stations
(c) which tasks should be assigned to which workstations (using the longest task time rule)
(d) the efficiency and balance delay of your solution

Solution 2

(a) Cycle time $= C = \dfrac{\text{available time per hour}}{\text{desired output per hour}}$

$= \dfrac{3600 \text{ seconds/hour}}{50 \text{ units/hour}} = 72 \text{ seconds/unit}$

(b) Theoretical minimum number of stations:

$$TM = \frac{\Sigma t}{C} = \frac{164 \text{ seconds}}{72 \text{ seconds/unit}}$$

$= 2.28$ stations, or 3 stations

(c) Assigning tasks to workstations with a cycle time of 72 seconds and using the longest task time rule, we obtain the following solution:

Workstation	Eligible Task	Task Selected	Task Time	Idle Time
1	A	A	45	27
	B,C	C	27	0
2	B	B	15	57
	D	D	52	5
3	E	E	7	65
	F	F	18	47

Cycle time = 72 seconds.

(d) Efficiency (%) =

$= \dfrac{\Sigma t}{N \times C}(100) = \dfrac{164}{3 \times 72}(100)$

$= 75.93\%$

Balance delay (%) $= 24.07\%$

DISCUSSION QUESTIONS

1. Explain the importance of layout planning for a business. What are the consequences of a poor layout?

2. Explain the importance of layout planning for everyday life. How has poor layout planning affected your life?

3. Identify the four types of layouts and their characteristics.

4. Identify the steps in designing a process layout.

5. Find examples of a process layout in local businesses. Draw a picture of the locations of departments.

6. Identify the steps in designing a product layout.

7. Find examples of a product layout in local businesses. Draw a picture to show the workstations and the tasks performed.

8. Explain the concept of cycle time and how it affects output. Give an example.

9. Define group technology. Why is it important?

10. Give an example of a poor layout. Find a better solution for that layout problem.

PROBLEMS

1. Fresh Foods Grocery is considering redoing its facility layout. The from–to matrix showing daily customer trips between departments is shown in Table 10-10, and their current layout is shown in Figure 10-12. Fresh Foods is considering exchanging the locations of the dry groceries department (A) and the health and beauty aids department (F). Compute the *ld* score for Fresh Foods' current and proposed layouts. Which is better?

Table 10-10 From–to Matrix for Fresh Foods

	Trips between Departments					
Department	**A**	**B**	**C**	**D**	**E**	**F**
A. Dry groceries	—	15	45	25	10	50
B. Bread		—	30	16	25	25
C. Frozen foods			—	34	15	20
D. Meats				—	40	10
E. Vegetables						20
F. Health and beauty aids						—

Figure 10-12

Current layout for Fresh Foods.

A	B	C
D	E	F

2. Use trial and error to find a better layout for Fresh Foods Grocery in Problem 1. Compute the *ld* score and compare it to the *ld* scores computed for Fresh Foods' current and proposed layouts. Which is best?

3. Mason Machine Tools is reevaluating its facility layout. The current layout is shown in Figure 10-13 and the from-to matrix is in Table 10-11. Mason has to leave department C in its current location because relocation costs are too high. It is considering exchanging departments B and D. Evaluate the proposal by computing the *ld* score for both layouts.

Figure 10-13

Current layout for Mason Machine Tools.

B	A	D
C	E	F

Table 10-11 From–to Matrix for Mason Machine Tools

	Trips between Departments					
Department	**A**	**B**	**C**	**D**	**E**	**F**
A	—	5	20	5	—	8
B		—	—	30	10	10
C			—	20	15	5
D				—	—	—
E						17
F						—

4. Use trial and error to find a better layout for Mason Machine Tools in Problem 3. Compute the *ld* score and compare it to Mason's current and proposed layouts in Problem 3.

5. Gator Office Systems is comparing two layouts for the design of its office building. It has interviewed managers in order to develop the from-to matrix shown in Table 10-12. The two layouts considered are shown in Figure 10-14. Which layout do you think is better for Gator Office Systems, using the load–distance model?

Table 10-12 From–to Matrix for Gator Office Supplies

	Trips between Departments					
Department	**A**	**B**	**C**	**D**	**E**	**F**
A	—	30	—	34	50	25
B		—	—	55	10	10
C			—	—	15	5
D				—	—	—
E						30
F						—

Figure 10-14

Current and proposed layouts for Gator Office Supplies.

Current layout

F	E	A
B	C	D

Proposed layout

C	D	A
B	E	F

6. Use trial and error to develop a better layout for Gator Office Supplies. Which departments do you think need to be in close proximity to one another?

7. T-Shirts Unlimited is a retailer that sells every kind of t-shirt imaginable. The different types of t-shirts are stored in departments that all take up the same amount of space. Given the available warehouse space (Figure 10-15) and a from-to matrix showing the number of trips to and from each department (Table 10-13), help T-Shirts Unlimited decide where to store each type of t-shirt.

Figure 10-15

Warehouse storage areas for T-Shirts Unlimited.

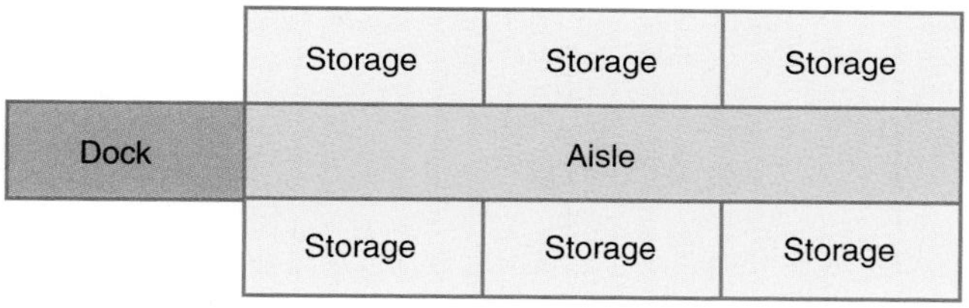

	Storage	Storage	Storage
Dock	Aisle		
	Storage	Storage	Storage

Table 10-13 From–to Matrix for T-Shirts Unlimited

Department	Category	Trips to and from Dock
1	Sports t-shirts	50
2	Men's t-shirts	63
3	Women's t-shirts	35
4	Children's t-shirts	55
5	Fashion t-shirts	48
6	Undershirts	60

8. David's Sport Supplies is a store for teenagers and young adults that sells sports equipment and gear. David's is in the process of assigning the location of storage areas in its warehouse (Figure 10-16) to minimize the number of trips made to retrieve needed items. Given here in Table 10-14 are the departments that need to be located, the number of trips made per week for each department, and the area needed by each department.

Figure 10-16

Warehouse storage areas for David's Sport Supplies.

	Storage	Storage	Storage	Storage	Storage
Dock	Aisle				
	Storage	Storage	Storage	Storage	Storage

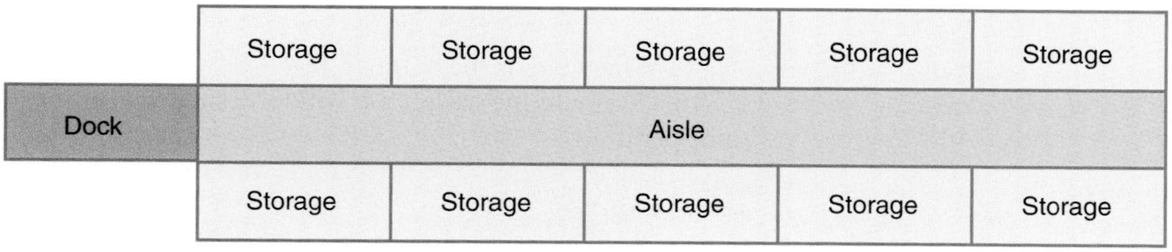

Table 10-14 Department Information for David's Sport Supplies

Department	Trips to and from Dock	Area Needed
1. Baseball equipment	160	2
2. Football gear	100	1
3. Hockey equipment	150	3
4. Basketball equipment	120	1
5. Sports clothes	270	3

9. MMS Associates is a telecommunications service provider. The company is currently redesigning its main office to accommodate six newly hired sales people. Some of the sales people expected to work in teams and office assignments are very important. Below is the from-to matrix showing the expected frequency of contacts between members of the new sales staff. The block plan in Figure 10-17 shows the assigned office locations for the six sales members. Assume equal-sized offices and rectilinear distances. How would you evaluate the developed layout? What is the *ld* score for MMS Associates?

Figure 10-17

Assigned office locations for sales staff at MMS Associates.

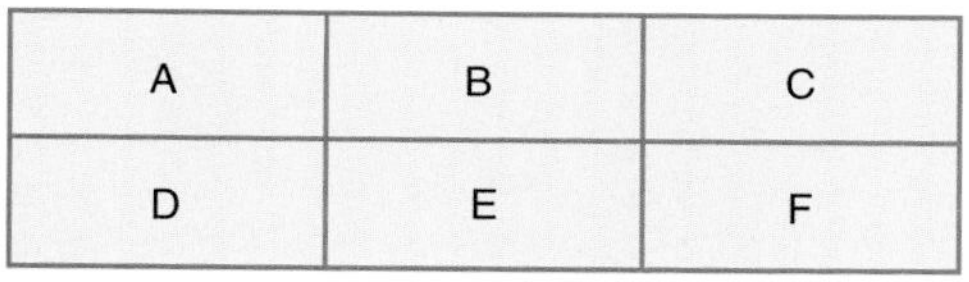

A	B	C
D	E	F

Number of Contacts Between Sales Staff

Sales Person	A	B	C	D	E	F
A	—	6	12	18	1	1
B		—	4	19	3	0
C	.		—	5	0	0
D				—	7	19
E					—	0
F						—

10. Michael Marc, the President of MMS Associates, is considering an alternative plan for the sales staff situation described in Problem 7. His alternative plan is shown in Figure 10-18. What is the *ld* score for this plan? How does it compare to the original plan considered in Problem 7?

Figure 10-18

Alternative office locations for sales staff at MMS Associates.

A	E	C
D	B	F

11. Use trial and error to find a better layout for MMS Associates. Which sales people will be your priority to keep together?

12. A manufacturing company is designing an assembly line to produce its main product. The line should be able to produce 60 units per hour. The following data give the necessary information.

Task	Immediate Predecessor	Task Time (sec)
A	None	35
B	A	50
C	A	21
D	B	38
E	C	25
F	D, E	58
G	F	15

(a) Which task is the bottleneck?
(b) Draw a precedence diagram for the above information.
(c) Compute the cycle time with a desired output of 60 units per hour.

13. An assembly line must be designed to produce 50 packages per hour. The following data give the necessary information.

Task	Immediate Predecessor	Task Time (sec)
A	None	25
B	A	60
C	B	35
D	B	45
E	B	10
F	C, D, E	50

(a) Draw a precedence diagram.
(b) Compute the cycle time (in seconds) to achieve the desired output rate.
(c) What is the theoretical minimum number of stations?
(d) Which work element should be assigned to which workstation?
(e) What are the resulting efficiency and balance delay percentages?

14. An assembly line must be designed to produce 40 containers per hour. The following data give the necessary information.

Task	Immediate Predecessor	Task Time (sec)
A	None	60
B	A	12
C	B	35
D	A	55
E	D	10
F	E	50
H	F, C	5

(a) Draw a precedence diagram.
(b) Compute the cycle time (in seconds) to achieve the desired output rate.
(c) What is the theoretical minimum number of stations?
(d) Which work element should be assigned to which workstation?
(e) What are the resulting efficiency and balance delay percentages?

15. The ABC Corporation is designing its new assembly line. The line will produce 50 units per hour. The tasks, their times, and their immediate predecessors are shown in Table 10-15:

Table 10-15 Task Information for ABC Corporation

Task	Immediate Predecessor	Task Time (Seconds)
A	None	55
B	A	30
C	A	22
D	B	35
E	B, C	50
F	C	15
G	F	5
H	G	10

(a) Which task is the bottleneck?
(b) Compute the cycle time with a desired output of 50 units per hour.
(c) Use a cycle time of 72 seconds/unit to assign tasks to workstations.

(d) Compute the theoretical minimum number of stations. Did you end up using more stations than the theoretical minimum?

(e) Compute the efficiency and balance delay of the line.

16. Kiko Teddy Bear is a manufacturer of stuffed teddy bears. Kiko would like to be able to produce 40 teddy bears per hour on its assembly line. Use the information provided in Table 10-16 to answer the following:

Table 10-16 Task Information for Kiko Teddy Bear

Work Element	Task Description	Immediate Predecessor	Task Time (seconds)
A	Cut teddy bear pattern	None	90
B	Sew teddy bear cloth	A	75
C	Stuff teddy bear	B	50
D	Glue on eyes	C	20
E	Glue on nose	C	15
F	Sew on mouth	C	35
G	Attach manufacturers label	B	15
H	Inspect and pack teddy bear	D, E, F, G	40

(a) Draw a precedence diagram.

(b) What is the cycle time?

(c) What is the theoretical minimum number of stations?

(d) Assign tasks to specific workstations using the cycle time you computed in part (b).

(e) What are the efficiency and balance delay of the line?

(f) Which task is the bottleneck?

(g) Compute the maximum output.

17. Use the longest task time rule to balance the assembly line described in Table 10-17 as the line can produce 30 units per hour.

Table 10-17 Assembly Line Task Information

Work Element	Task Time (seconds)	Immediate Predecessor
A	25	None
B	30	A
C	15	A
D	30	A
E	40	C, D
F	20	D
G	10	B
H	15	G
I	35	E, F, H
J	25	I
K	25	J

(a) What is the cycle time?

(b) What is the theoretical minimum number of stations?

(c) Which work elements are assigned to which workstations?

(d) What are the resulting efficiency and balance delay percentages?

18. A dress-making operation is being designed on an assembly line. Table 10-18 shows the tasks that need to be performed, their task times, and preceding tasks. If the goal is to produce 30 dresses per hour, answer the following questions:

Table 10-18 Dress-Making Task Information

Work Element	Task Time (seconds)	Immediate Predecessor
A. Cut dress body	30	None
B. Cut sleeves	40	None
C. Cut collar	20	None
D. Sew dress body	100	A
E. Sew sleeves to dress	25	B, D
F. Sew collar to dress	50	C, D
G. Hem dress	50	D, E, F
H. Package dress	90	G

(a) Compute the cycle time.

(b) Which task is the bottleneck?

(c) What is the maximum output for this line?

(d) Compute the theoretical minimum number of stations.

(e) Assign work elements to stations, using the longest task time rule.

(f) Compute the efficiency and balance delay of your assignment.

CASE: *Sawhill Athletic Club*

Sawhill Athletic Club was an athletic facility in suburban Scottsdale, Arizona. It was designed to provide a wide range of athletic opportunities, including racquetball courts and exercise facilities. The facilities were modern and the staff focused on providing high customer service. To provide flexibility to its members, the club had a wide range of hours of operation. The members were primarily families and young professionals who lived in the area.

Membership at the club had been steady since it opened five years ago. To monitor the club's quality, members were often asked to fill out satisfaction surveys. Most members liked the club's attention to customer satisfaction, but many complained that the facilities did not have a good layout. They complained of having to walk long distances from one location to another, citing this as a significant inconvenience. Another complaint was that all the departments were separated with high walls creating a "closed in" feeling. A new athletic facility was going to be opening in the area in the near future. The owners of Sawhill thought that they had better listen to the requests of their customers in order to remain competitive.

Improving the Layout

Lauren Nicole was hired to manage Sawhill and to offer any recommendations for changing the layout of the facility. She was told to be creative and use her knowledge of facility layout design. She was even provided with a diagram of the facility and averages of daily trips made by clients between each of the departments in the facility.

Lauren began looking at the information she received, shown below. She noticed that all the departments were of approximately equal size except the racquetball courts and exercise facilities. These were approximately twice the size of the other departments and could not be split. All the departments were eligible to be moved. She would take that into consideration. She decided to study the information and redesign the facility. Then she would think about which walls to lower between departments to create a more open environment. Decorating would come last.

Case Questions:

1. Develop an *ld* score for the current layout. What problems can you identify with the current layout?

2. Use trial and error to come up with a better layout that lowers the *ld* score. Explain the departments you thought needed to be in close proximity to one another.

3. Imagine an athletic facility such as Sawhill. What strategies would you suggest for creating an open environment?

Layout of Sawhill Athletic Club

Lobby A	Racquetball Courts B	
Exercise and Weight Room E	Food Court C	Pro Shop D
	Showers /Locker Room G	Day Care Facility F

	Number of Trips Between Departments						
Department	A	B	C	D	E	F	G
A. Lobby	—	15	34	32	14	54	76
B. Racquetball Courts		—	2	2	34	0	72
C. Food Court			—	26	0	47	3
D. Pro Shop				—	9	1	4
E. Exercise and Weight Room					—	7	74
F. Child Care Facility						—	57
G. Showers & Locker							—

INTERACTIVE LEARNING

Enhance and test your knowledge of Chapter 10 using the interactive CD.

1. **Simulation** *Designing Process and Product Layouts*

   Visit our dynamic Web site, www.wiley.com/college/reid, for more cases, web links, and additional information.

2. **Company Tour**
   Nova Cruz Products, LLC
   Thompson-Shore, Inc., http://tshore.com
   International Timers U.S.A. Corp., http://www.intima.com/manufacturing.htm

3. **Additional Web Resources**
   Association for Manufacturing Excellence, www.ame.org
   APICS, www.apics.org

4. **Virtual Company Consulting Case**

5. **INTERNET CHALLENGE** *DJ and Associates, Inc.*

The law firm of DJ and Associates has just moved into a new facility. The spacious reception area has room for three receptionists and a client waiting area. The law firm has hired you to help with the layout of the reception area. It has given you a budget of $15,000 and asked you to purchase furniture for the reception area that will fit into the layout, given certain constraints.

The reception area is 50 feet long by 20 feet wide. The client waiting area is 400 square feet, leaving 600 square feet for the three receptionists, their desks, chairs, file cabinets, and aisle room. The furniture for the client waiting area has been purchased. Your job is to purchase furniture for the receptionists. For each receptionist you are to purchase a desk with two chairs and two large file cabinets that

will fit the constraints of the room and your budget. Since appearance is an important factor, the desks must be made of a high-grade wood. Also, there must be at least 5 feet of walking space between desks.

Use the Internet to carry out your assignment. Find Web sites for commercial office furniture sellers and browse sites for the specific furniture you need, checking dimensions and prices. Finally, come up with a plan of purchase and suggestions for a layout. It may be a good idea to read up on office layouts to get suggestions. The firm is considering hiring you for future work, so you want to develop a good plan that might include additional suggestions that were not asked for.

BIBLIOGRAPHY

Binkley, C. "Sheraton Chain Gets a Makeover From Orange Shag to Pin Stripes," *The Wall Street Journal*, April 19, 2000.

Goldstein, L. "Whatever Space Works for You," *Fortune,* July 10, 2000, 269–270.

Lee, L. "Nordstrom Cleans out its Closets," *Business Week*, May 22, 2000, 105–108.

Muther, R. and McPherson, K. "Four Approaches to Computerized Layout Planning," *Industrial Engineering*, 2, (1970), 39–42.

Umble, M. M. and Srikanth, M. L. *Synchronous Manufacturing*, South-Western Publishing, Ohio, 1990.

Upton, D. M., "What Really Makes Factories Flexible," *Harvard Business Review*, July–August, 1995, 74–84.

Vokurka, R. J., O'Leary-Kelly, S. W. and Flores, B., "Approaches to Manufacturing: Use and Performance Implication," *Production and Inventory Management Journal*, Second Quarter, 1998, 42–48.

Before studying this chapter you should know or, if necessary, review

1. Competitive priorities, Chapter 2, pages 28–32.
2. Process selection, Chapter 3, pages 52–58.
3. Layout types, Chapter 10, pages 284–289.

LEARNING OBJECTIVES

After studying this chapter, you should be able to

1. Describe the elements of work system design and the objectives of each element.
2. Describe relevant job design issues.
3. Describe methods analysis.
4. Understand the importance of work measurement.
5. Describe how to do a time study.
6. Describe how to do work sampling.
7. Develop standard times.
8. Show how to use work standards.
9. Describe compensation plans.
10. Describe learning curves.

CHAPTER OUTLINE

$\mathbf{H}$ave you ever been to a restaurant, a store, or any
other place where one person seems to be doing several
different jobs? For example, is that person the maitre d',
the wine steward, the wait staff, the chef, and the dishwasher? And does that person have to switch jobs at a
moment's notice?

Productive employees are employees who know
what is expected of them and what to expect of themselves. They know what their role is in the company and
they understand the goals of their job. Designing
a work system that supports a company's objectives is essential to the company's success. Let's look at how companies design their work systems.

DESIGNING A WORK SYSTEM ■

First, a company determines its objectives, then it develops an operations strategy to
achieve those objectives. Part of the operations strategy is designing a work system,
which provides the structure for the productivity of the company. The work system includes job design, work measurement, and worker compensation. The company determines the purpose of each job, what the job consists of, and the cost of the employees
to do the job. A job must add value and enable the company to achieve its objectives.

Suppose your company is an organization with an objective to operate a fancy,
upscale restaurant. To achieve its objective, the restaurant must define a set of jobs,
the tasks each job consists of, and a system for evaluating the employee's performance
in the job. The set of jobs at your restaurant would include a chef, a trained kitchen
staff, a professional wait staff, a maitre d', a wine steward, and so forth. The chef's
tasks would include developing the food motif and menu, for example, and the performance measurement would be based on revenue.

Job design ensures that each employee's duties and responsibilities are geared
toward achieving the restaurant's mission. Methods analysis eliminates unnecessary
tasks and improves the process for completing tasks. Work measurement is a process
for evaluating employee performance and comparing alternative processes. Let's begin
with job design.

JOB DESIGN ■

Job design specifies the work activities of an individual or group in support of an
organization's objectives.

▶ **Job design**
Specifies the contents
of the job.

Designing a Job

You design a job by answering questions such as: What is your description of the job?
What is the purpose of the job? Where is the job done? Who does the job? What background, training, or skills does an employee need to do the job? For example, if one of
your company's objectives is to establish itself as a leader in customer service, jobs

must be designed to encourage and reward good customer service practices. In addition, performance measurements for each job must validate the behavior that supports the company's objective. Now let's look at three additional factors in job design: technical feasibility, economic feasibility, and behavioral feasibility.

▶ **Technical feasibility**
The job must be physically and mentally doable.

Technical Feasibility   The **technical feasibility** of a job is the degree to which an individual or group of individuals is physically and mentally able to do the job. The more demanding the job is, the smaller is the applicant pool for that job. Suppose your company requires the candidate for a job to be capable of lifting up to 250 pounds. Few people will qualify for the job. But if the company can reduce the lifting requirement to 50 pounds, many more people will qualify.

Good job design eliminates unreasonable requirements and ensures that any constraining requirements are necessary to do the job. This in turn widens the applicant pool and gives your company a chance to hire the best candidates on the market.

▶ **Economic feasibility**
Cost of the job should be less than the value it adds.

Economic Feasibility   The **economic feasibility** of a job is the degree to which the value a job adds and the cost of having the job done create profit for the company. If the job as it is designed costs more than the value it adds, then it is not economically feasible. Suppose your company can reduce a job's lifting requirement from a maximum 250 pounds to a maximum 50 pounds because the company can buy materials in smaller quantities and pack them in lighter boxes. If the materials are more expensive, however, the company has to weigh the higher material costs against the higher labor costs, choose the alternative that makes more sense economically, or even come up with a third alternative—for example, hire two workers to lift the heavy packages.

▶ **Behavioral feasibility**
Degree to which the job is intrinsically satisfying to the employee.

Behavioral Feasibility   The **behavioral feasibility** of a job is the degree to which an employee derives intrinsic satisfaction from doing the job. The challenge is to design a job so the worker feels good about doing the job *and* adds value by doing it. This presents two problems. First, what motivates one worker may not motivate another worker. Second, someone has to do the boring jobs. One solution is to provide an enjoyable work environment. Employees at companies like AES Corporation, the Men's Wearhouse, SAS, and Southwest Airlines stay with their companies because work is fun. In this case, fun means working in a place where people can use their talents and skills, and work with others in an atmosphere of mutual respect.

LINKS TO PRACTICE
The SAS Institute
www.sas.com

How does the world's largest privately held software manufacturer earn a spot in the top ten of *Fortune's* "100 Best Companies to Work for in America"? It does it by creating an infrastructure with little stress, treating employees as adults, and not having a lot of rules. SAS doesn't demand long hours from its employees; instead, it closes its facility at 6:00 P.M. Employees are not allowed to work later. SAS wants employees to have time for a life outside of work. Full-time employees at SAS work a 35-hour week and have live piano music in the cafeteria, an on-site gym, a dance studio, child-care facilities, an on-site health clinic, and an indoor lap pool. The atmosphere at SAS is part of its corporate strategy—a strategy that seeks individuals who are not ego-driven and who want to be part of something of value. The environment is designed to support those individuals.

A final concern in job design is whether or not the job can and should be automated. Let's discuss the pros and cons of machines versus people in job design.

Machines or People?

When a company considers the technical, economic, and behavioral feasibility of job design, a central question is: "Should the job or some part of it be automated?" Obviously, machines do some things better than people, whereas people do other things better than machines. For example, we use calculators to do arithmetic or when we need high levels of precision. We use a machine when a job might be dangerous. We also use machines to lift or move very heavy objects or very hot objects, or to do simple, repetitive tasks. On the other hand, people are vastly superior to machines in a number of activities. Examples are personal interactions with others, creative thinking, judgements involving multiple variables, expressions of compassion or empathy, complex operations that may not follow linear logic, and teaching.

Using machines versus people is both a tangible economic decision in job design and a decision based on intangibles such as customer acceptance. For example, automated voice messaging systems are the norm in offices today. But do these automated systems create a favorable impression on the customer? Is it worth the extra expense to provide a live receptionist so your customers can talk to a person rather than a machine? When your company makes a decision about machines versus people in job design, support of the company's objectives is the deciding factor.

If a job is designed for people rather than machines, the next question is how specialized an employee should be.

CROSS FUNCTIONAL

Machines invade the board room.

"*Please welcome R70X, our first board member from the ranks of labor.*"

Level of Labor Specialization

The higher the level of **specialization,** the narrower is the employee's scope of the expertise. The professions—medicine, law, academics—are highly specialized; some low-level assembly or service jobs are also specialized.

In the professions, worker satisfaction is one reason for specialization in a particular area of expertise. A doctor who specializes in heart disease, a lawyer who spe-

▶ **Specialization**
The breadth of the job design.

cializes in international law, or a professor who specializes in operations management may do so because of intrinsic satisfaction in the job. Without question, other factors also influence people to enter into particular professional careers.

On the other hand, an assembly or service worker whose work is highly specialized often has a monotonous job. These individuals may have narrowly focused jobs because their skill levels are limited. Yet specialized assembly and service workers contribute to organizational objectives because they yield high productivity and low unit costs. Consider the assembly worker who inserts and tightens 4 bolts into each product as it passes by on the assembly line. The work is repetitive, but the worker quickly becomes very proficient. A file clerk who spends 8 hours each day filing documents and the data entry person keying in data 8 hours each day also have highly specialized, narrowly focused jobs.

Table 11-1 highlights some of the advantages and disadvantages of using specialization in job design. The table shows that management benefits from specialization because the jobs are narrowly defined and easily learned, so less training is needed. Workers achieve high productivity and wage costs are reasonable. The table also shows that a disadvantage of specialization is worker dissatisfaction, with results such as high turnover and absenteeism, a high number of grievances filed, higher scrap rates, and worker sabotage.

From the worker's point of view, this type of job design minimizes the education and skills required, requires little mental effort, has minimal job responsibility, and provides reasonably good wages given the skill requirements. The major disadvantages of such job design are worker boredom, little room for growth or advancement, little control over the work, and minimal self-fulfillment. In an effort to reduce workers' boredom, a number of behavioral approaches have been suggested. Discussion of these approaches follows.

Eliminating Employee Boredom

Companies that choose highly specialized job design have several options for reducing worker boredom, including job enlargement, job enrichment, and job rotation.

Table 11-1 The Advantages and Disadvantages of Specialization in Job Design

Specialization from Management's Perspective	
Advantages	**Disadvantages**
Readily available labor	Worker dissatisfaction characterized by
Minimal training needed	◆ high absenteeism
Reasonable wage cost	◆ high turnover rates
High productivity	◆ high scrap rates
	◆ grievances filed

Specialization from the Employee's Perspective	
Advantages	**Disadvantages**
Minimal credentials needed	Boredom
Minimal responsibilities	Little growth opportunity
Minimal mental effort needed	Little control over work
Reasonable wages	Little room for initiative
	Little intrinsic satisfaction

Job enlargement is the horizontal expansion of a job. The job designer adds other related tasks to the job so the worker produces a portion of the final product that he or she can recognize. For example, an assembly worker gets to do additional tasks that complete a portion of the final product, which enables the worker to experience pride in the final product. The worker can then point to the final product and take pride in the portion that he or she was responsible for building. By reducing the level of specialization, however, job enlargement may result in some lost productivity over the original job design.

> ► **Job enlargement**
> A horizontal expansion of the job through increasing the scope of the work assigned.

One example of job enlargement concerns employees proofreading telephone directories. Rather than proofreading randomly assigned pages, a proofreader is responsible for specific letters in the alphabet. The proofreader can identify those portions of the directory that he/she proofread. For the assembly worker, additional operations are usually added to his or her job so that the worker can actually identify with a complete portion of the final product. Job enlargement is used to instill worker pride in the final product and give the employee some task variety.

Job enrichment is the vertical expansion of a job. The job designer adds worker responsibility for work planning and/or inspection. This allows the worker some control over the workload in terms of scheduling—although not in terms of how much work to do—and instills a sense of pride in the worker. For example, workers know they must complete 100 model As, 50 model Bs, and 150 model Cs in one week, but the sequence is up to them. They can do all of the Cs first, then the Bs followed by the As, and so forth, as long as the work is finished in one week. Or, for example, workers do their own inspection before the part or product is passed to the next workstation. This procedure instills pride in the workers' output and has the worker perform tasks usually done at a higher level in the organization.

> ► **Job enrichment**
> A vertical expansion of the job through increased worker responsibility.

Job rotation exposes a worker to other jobs in the work system. Rotation allows workers to see how the output from their previous assignment is used later in the production or service process. Workers see more of the big picture and have a better overall understanding of the work system. In addition, they acquire more skills that may increase their value to the company.

> ► **Job rotation**
> Shifts workers to different jobs to increase understanding of the total process.

Team Approaches to Job Design

Another option for job design is using teams rather than individuals for certain assignments. Problem-solving teams, special-purpose teams, and self-directed teams are three different kinds of employee teams.

Problem-solving teams are small groups of employees who meet to identify, analyze, and solve operational problems. Employees typically volunteer to participate in problem-solving teams, and team members are trained in problem-solving techniques and data collection. A team may meet once a week, during normal working hours, for one to two hours. After the team has completed its initial training, the team concentrates on a particular operational problem. The team analyzes the problem, collects data, develops alternative solutions, and then presents a proposed solution to upper management. Management then decides whether or not to use the proposed solution.

> ► **Problem-solving teams**
> Small groups of employees and supervisors trained in problem-solving techniques who meet to identify, analyze, and propose solutions to workplace problems.

The purpose of problem-solving teams is to use the employees' knowledge of operational procedures. Management cannot know as much about detailed operations as the employees who do the work daily. Problem-solving teams are useful for improving operations and as a way to improve communications between employees and management.

Special-purpose teams address issues of major significance to the company. They are often short-term, special task forces with a focused agenda. Members of

> ► **Special-purpose teams**
> Highly focused, short-term teams addressing issues important to management and labor.

special-purpose teams typically represent several functional areas for an overall view of the problem. For example, a university might use a special-purpose team to hire a new, high-level administrator. The team has a specific task and a limited time frame to do that task. Since the new administrator has many constituencies, the team may consist of representatives from each college, the operating staff, the professional/administrative staff, trustees, alumni, and students. Including each constituency in the selection process ensures that their concerns are made known.

▶ **Self-directed teams**
Integrated teams empowered to control portions of their control process.

Self-directed or self-managed teams are designed to achieve a high level of employee involvement and an integrated team approach. Their purpose is to allow the people most knowledgeable about the process to control the work flow. This approach also allows employees to develop a sense of ownership and pride in their work.

LINKS TO PRACTICE
The Santa Cruz Operation, Inc.
www.sco.com

A good example of self-directed work teams is The Santa Cruz Operation, Inc. At the Santa Cruz Operation, the initial team consisted of 12 people, including 5 assemblers and a quality control person, for both the day and evening shifts. The team subsequently added 2 material handlers, a product specialist, and a master scheduler. The team was responsible for building 65 computer operating system products on a single assembly line. Before the self-managing teams, the company had a problem with product consistency. Each shift did things its own way and blamed the other shift for any problems. The self-directed team approach greatly improved communication between shifts and allowed workers to resolve product-consistency problems. The team reduced person-minutes per unit by 22.4%, decreased defects to 1.5 or fewer per 1000 units built, cross-trained its members, and documented the procedures for what needed to be done and how it should be done. Although most workers continue to perform on-site at the company's facilities, many employees now work in alternative workplaces.

The Alternative Workplace

▶ **Alternative workplace**
Brings work to the worker rather than the worker to the workplace.

The **alternative workplace** is a combination of nontraditional work practices, settings, and locations that supplements traditional offices. The alternative workplace moves the work to the worker rather than the worker to the work.

Companies have begun using alternative workplaces for the benefits they afford in terms of cost reduction, productivity, and flexibility. The cost reduction is achieved through eliminating offices people do not need, consolidating others, and thereby reducing overhead expenses. Alternative workplaces can improve productivity because employees tend to devote more time to customers and/or meaningful work activities and less time on unproductive office routines like socializing, making up work to look busy, and attending unnecessary meetings. A survey of alternative workplace employees at IBM revealed that 87% believe their personal productivity and job effectiveness had increased significantly. The alternative workplace offers the flexibility some employees need to balance work and family, which helps companies build and keep a valuable workforce.

The alternative workplace comes in several different varieties. It can be as simple as putting some workers on different shifts or travel schedules, and letting those workers share desk and office space. Still another approach is the use of satellite offices to break up large, centralized facilities into a network of smaller workplaces that can be located closer to customers. Telecommuting—working electronically from wherever the worker chooses—is another alternative workplace idea and is typically done from home offices. Most companies use a combination of alternative workplaces customized to their individual company needs.

Disadvantages of alternative workplaces include increased logistics associated with workers in several locations as well as a lack of cohesiveness or shared focus among employees.

More and more corporations are implementing the practice of alternative work-spaces. AT&T, for example, provides flexible workstations so workers can rotate in and out as needed. At Cisco, employees choose an available workstation as they arrive for the workday (a practice known as "hot desking"). Also, Sun Microsystems gives many of its designers the option to work at home. Companies such as KPMG Peat Marwick, Ernst & Young, and Andersen Consulting practice "hotelling," in which either hotel work spaces are furnished, equipped, and supported with typical office services or corporate workspaces are reserved by an employee via the company "concierge." In both instances, the space can be booked by the hour (also referred to as "motelling"), day, or week. Today, more than 30 million employees work in alternative workspaces.

LINKS TO PRACTICE
AT&T
www.att.com

METHODS ANALYSIS ■

Methods analysis is the study of how a job is done. Whereas job design shows the structure of the job and names the tasks within the structure, methods analysis details the tasks and how to do them.

Methods analysis is used by companies when developing new products or services, and for improving the efficiency of methods currently in use. Suppose your restaurant has an accepted procedure for communicating a customer's dinner choices to the kitchen without errors. Methods analysis documents this accepted procedure, including specific notations that identify customer preferences. The result is a standard operating procedure your restaurant can use for training new employees and for evaluating the performance of existing employees.

Methods analysis consists of the following steps.

▶ **Methods analysis**
Is concerned with the detailed process for doing a particular job.

1. Identify the operation to be analyzed.
2. Gather all relevant information about the operation, including tools, materials, and procedures.
3. Talk with employees who use the operation or have used similar operations. They may have suggestions for improving it.
4. Chart the operation, whether you are analyzing an existing operation or a new operation.
5. Evaluate each step in the existing operation or proposed new operation. Does the step add value? Does it only add cost?
6. Revise the existing or new operation as needed.
7. Put the revised or new operation into effect, then follow up on the changes or new operation. Do your changes to the existing operation improve it? Does your new operation add to the company's overall operations?

Now let's look at an example of methods analysis for an established operation.

■ Example 11.1 Methods Analysis at FEAT Company

Companies typically try to identify operations that are labor intensive; are done often; are dangerous, tedious, or fatiguing; and/or are designated as problem operations. In this example, the FEAT Company, a producer of electronic consumer goods, uses a particular transformer (shown in Figure 11-1) in several of their finished products. You have the task of applying methods analysis to one of FEAT's problem operations.

Solution:
You decide to concentrate your methods analysis on the transformer wiring operation because it has been a source of quality problems in the past. After talking with the current operators, you develop a flow chart of the operation, as shown in Figure 11-2. The flow chart shows that the operator has to solder six individual wires onto six individual terminals of the transformer (Figure 11-2).

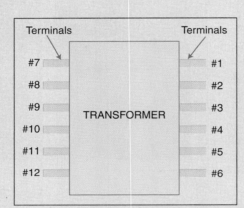

Figure 11-1

A 12-terminal transformer

Figure 11-2

Chart of the wiring activity

PROCESS FLOWCHART Job: Solder wires to transformer	Analyst: A. Maize		Page 1 of 1		
Details of method	Operation	Movement	Inspection	Delay	Storage
Transformer to work location	○		□	D	▽
Wire and solder iron to terminal #1			□	D	▽
Solder wire to terminal #1	●	⇒	□	D	▽
Solder iron to holder	○	⇒	□	●	▽
Wire and solder iron to terminal #2	○		□	D	▽
Solder wire to terminal #2	●	⇒	□	D	▽
Solder iron to holder	○	⇒	□	●	▽
Wire and solder iron to terminal #3	○		□	D	▽
Solder wire to terminal #3	●	⇒	□	D	▽
Solder iron to holder	○	⇒	□	●	▽
Wire and solder iron to terminal #4	○		□	D	▽
Solder wire to terminal #4	●	⇒	□	D	▽
Solder iron to holder	○	⇒	□	●	▽
Wire and solder iron to terminal #5	○		□	D	▽
Solder wire to terminal #5	●	⇒	□	D	▽
Solder iron to holder	○	⇒	□	●	▽
Wire and solder iron to terminal #6	○		□	D	▽
Solder wire to terminal #6	●	⇒	□	D	▽
Solder iron to holder	○	⇒	□	●	▽
Transformer to finished units	○	⇒	□	D	▼

The operator follows these steps to solder the wires onto the terminal.

1. Picks up the appropriate wire with the left hand and moves the wire to the terminal to be soldered.
2. Simultaneously picks up the solder iron in the right hand and moves it to the terminal to be soldered.
3. Solders the wire to the terminal and replaces the solder iron in its holder.
4. Solders terminal number 1, then solders terminals 2 through 6, going from right to left.

The layout of the operator's workstation is shown in Figure 11-3.

Figure 11-3

Wiring the transformer

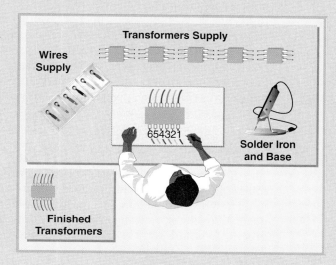

The FEAT Company is concerned about this operation—it needs significant rework because of poor solder joints and the operation is not efficient. You analyze the operation and realize that attaching the wires from right to left is problematic for a right-handed operator. You also note that when soldering the next terminal, the operator places the soldering iron directly above the recently soldered joint. This slows down the process because the operator now has to be careful not to disturb that joint.

Following your methods analysis, you make this recommendation to the FEAT Company to improve the operation:

Reverse the order in which the wires are soldered to the terminals, beginning at terminal 6 and ending at terminal 1. Now the right-handed operator does not reach directly over the recently soldered joints and can improve both the quality and efficiency of the operation.

The final step in your methods analysis is to follow up to make sure that the new operation resolves the quality problems the FEAT Company was concerned about.

THE WORK ENVIRONMENT ∎

So far we have discussed job design and methods analysis in detail. We also need to understand the effect of working conditions on worker productivity, product quality, and worker safety.

Temperature, relative humidity, ventilation, lighting, and noise level are all factors in work system design. People work well when the temperature is comfortable; typically, the more strenuous the work, the lower the temperature should be. Excess humidity is uncomfortable for most people and can be detrimental to some equipment. Too little humidity results in dry air and may create undesirable static charges. Exchanging or filtering the air can prevent the stale air caused by poor ventilation. Inadequate lighting can lead to production mistakes and/or physical discomfort such as headaches. Detailed work normally needs stronger light. Also, high noise levels can be distracting and can result in errors or accidents as well as impair hearing.

Concern for worker safety brought about the enactment in 1970 of the Occupational Safety and Health Act (OSHA), which created the Occupational Safety and Health Administration. The law was designed to ensure that all workers have healthy and safe working conditions. It mandates specific safety conditions that are inspected randomly by OSHA inspectors. Violations can result in warnings, fines and/or court-imposed shutdowns. The law requires your company to ensure a safe working environment for its employees. Therefore, worker safety is the primary concern in work system design. Workplace accidents are usually the result of worker carelessness or workplace hazards. Carelessness is defined as unsafe acts such as failing to use protective equipment, overriding safety controls, disregarding safety procedures, or improperly using tools and equipment. Workplace hazards include conditions such as unprotected equipment, poor lighting, and poor ventilation.

■ WORK MEASUREMENT

▶ **Work measurement**
Determines how long it should take to do a job.

▶ **Standard time**
The length of time it should take a qualified worker using appropriate process and tools to complete a specific job allowing time for personal, fatigue, and unavoidable delays.

The third component in work system design, **work measurement,** is a way of determining how long it should take to do a job. Work measurement techniques are used to set a standard time for a specific job. The **standard time** is the time it should take a qualified operator, working at a sustainable pace and using the appropriate tools and process, to do the job. The standard time is the sustainable time it takes to do either a whole job or a portion or element of a job. In our restaurant example, the time needed to take the customer's order and communicate that information to the kitchen staff can be calculated as the standard time.

Why should your company set the standard time for a job? Your company uses standard times for costing, evaluating, and planning.

Costing

When costing a product, your company includes labor in the total cost estimate. Instead of timing the labor to build single units, companies typically use a standard labor cost. To do this, they multiply the standard labor time by a given hourly labor cost to determine the direct labor content of a product. For example, if your company invests three standard hours of labor in building a product and its labor cost is $22.00 per hour, then the standard labor content is $66.00 per unit. This does not mean each unit has exactly three hours of labor spent on it: some units will have slightly more labor content and others will have slightly less. Thus the company estimates that it should take three hours of labor to build that product. For pricing purposes, the company charges for three labor hours of content in each unit.

Standard times allow companies to evaluate new product proposals, the use of new materials and equipment, new processes or techniques for building a product, and individual operator proficiency. The standard time provides a benchmark for companies to use when evaluating other alternatives.

■ Example 11.2 An Alternative Material for FEAT Co.

Let's return to the transformer operation in which six wires are soldered to the transformer. FEAT Company might consider buying transformers with individual wires already attached to each of the terminals, as shown in Figure 11-4. The transformer has wires attached to all 12 terminals so the operator has to remove the 6 extra wires.

Figure 11-4

A pre-wired transformer

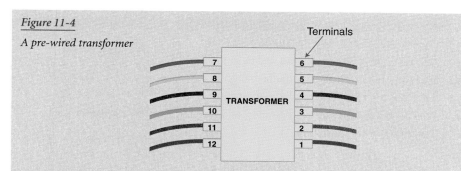

Suppose FEAT evaluates this change in material and process by determining the change in standard time and comparing that with the change in material costs. The result is a tradeoff between reduced labor costs versus higher material costs. For example, what should FEAT do if the prewired transformer costs $0.40 more than the unwired transformer, but the standard time is reduced by 45 seconds per unit and the hourly labor cost is $22.00?

Solution:
FEAT needs to determine the value of the labor saved on each unit. Then it can look at the economics of the proposed material and process change. Since 45 seconds is saved on each unit, the value of the labor saved is $0.275 or (45 seconds/60 seconds per minute times 60 minutes per hour) × (hourly labor rate of $22.00). Changing the process would increase the cost by $0.125, the difference between the increased transformer cost and the reduced labor cost. If FEAT is concerned only with the economics, they should not change processes. However, if FEAT can improve quality, this benefit must be factored in to the equation.

   We can do evaluations of this kind for any new idea. Moreover, we can use standard times to find out whether workers are producing at the expected level.

Performance

If the standard time shows that a worker should produce 96 units per 8-hour shift, a supervisor can then track the worker's performance and see whether that worker is matching the standard time. If a worker fails to match the standard time, the company should provide training to improve the worker's performance.

Planning

Standard times also help your company to plan. If you know how long it takes to do a job and how often that job is repeated, you can plan your workload from that job.

   If an operation takes 0.30 standard hours of labor and you need 1000 of these operations to complete a job, then you need 300 standard hours to complete the job (0.30 hours times 1000 operations). This information allows you to make workload forecasts, plan the labor needed, and schedule work. If you know how long a job should take, you know how long your resources will be busy with that job before you can start the next job. With this knowledge you can schedule jobs and promise viable delivery dates to your customers.

SETTING STANDARD TIMES ■

Among the commonly used processes for setting standard times are the time study, elemental time data, predetermined time data, and work sampling. The time study dates back to Frederick Winslow Taylor in the late nineteenth century.

Table 11-2 Procedure for a Time Study
Step 1. Choose the job for the time study.
Step 2. Tell the worker whose job you will be studying.
Step 3. Break the job into easily recognizable units.
Step 4. Calculate the number of cycles you must observe.
Step 5. Time each element, record the times, and rate the worker's performance.
Step 6. Compute the standard time.

How to Do a Time Study

▶ **Time study**
A technique for developing a standard time based on actual observations of the operator.

The **time study** sets a standard time based on timed observations of one employee taken over a number of cycles. A cycle includes all the elements of the job. This standard time is applied to all workers doing the job. Table 11-2 shows the steps in a time study.

Now let's look at these steps in detail.

STEP 1. As an individual, you set standards for yourself based on the tasks that are typical of your workday. The same is true for your company: you base standard times on the routine, labor-intensive jobs rather than one-of-a-kind jobs. Use this criterion for choosing your time study job in Step 1.

STEP 2. It is also important to inform the employee in advance that you will be making a time study of his or her job. Be sensitive to how the employee will feel as you time his or her performance.

STEP 3. To break a job down into easily recognizable elements, think about making a hand-tossed pizza:
1. Find the right size ball of dough (this depends on the pizza size).
2. Flatten out the dough.
3. Spin and toss the dough until it is the size you want.
4. Put the pizza on the working area.
5. Add sauce.
6. Add cheese.
7. Add additional toppings.
8. Put the pizza in the oven and bake.

Hand-tossing dough

Each of these elements has a clear starting and ending point, and you cannot break it down any further.

STEP 4. When making a time study, you need to know how many cycles, or how many times you must observe the worker, to ensure the results you want. The number of cycles is a function of the variability of observed times, the desired level of accuracy or precision, and the desired level of confidence for the estimated standard time. We often express the desired accuracy level as a percentage of the mean observed times. For example, we might want an accuracy level so that the standard time is within 10% of the true mean of the time it takes to do the job.

The formula for determining the number of observations needed is

$$n = \left[\left(\frac{z}{a} \right) \left(\frac{s}{\overline{x}} \right) \right]^2$$

where n = the number of observations of an element that are needed

z = the number of normal standard deviations needed for desired confidence

s = the standard deviation of the sample

a = the desired accuracy or precision

$\bar{x}$ = the mean of the sample observations

To compute the number of observations needed, we begin by making a small number of observations so that we can determine the sample mean and standard deviation. We also need to know the appropriate value of z to use because it determines our confidence level. Common values of z are shown in Table 11-3.

Calculating the number of observations needed will be demonstrated by Example 11.3.

Table 11-3 Common z Values	
Desired Confidence (%)	z Value
90	1.65
95	1.96
95.5	2.00
96	2.05
97	2.17
98	2.33
99	2.58

■ Example 11.3 Observing Pizza Preparation at Pat's Pizza Place

To determine the number of observations needed, we take some initial observations of the job being studied. In this case, let's observe how long it takes to prepare a large, hand-tossed pepperoni and cheese pizza.

We begin by taking ten observations of each of the seven elements. The elements, the standard deviation of the observed times for each element, and the mean observed time for each element are shown in Table 11-4. Determine the appropriate sample size if the standard time for any work element is to be within 5% of the true mean 95% of the time.

Table 11-4 Mean Observed Times

Work Unit	Standard Deviation (minutes)	Mean Observed Time (minutes)
1. Get appropriate ball of dough.	0.010	0.12
2. Flatten dough.	0.030	0.25
3. Spin and toss dough.	0.040	0.50
4. Place dough on work counter.	0.005	0.12
5. Pour sauce on formed dough.	0.035	0.30
6. Place grated cheese on top of sauce.	0.025	0.25
7. Place pepperoni on formed dough.	0.030	0.24

Solution:

We set the accuracy level a equal to 0.05 and the confidence level z equal to 1.96. Using the data from above, and the accuracy and confidence factors, we determine the number of observations needed for each of the work elements. The largest individual number of observations needed for any element becomes the number of observations used for all the work elements.

The calculations are shown here. All noninteger solutions are rounded up.

$$\text{Work element 1: } n = \left[\left(\frac{1.96}{0.05}\right)\left(\frac{0.01}{0.12}\right)\right]^2 = 11 \text{ observations}$$

$$\text{Work element 2: } n = \left[\left(\frac{1.96}{0.05}\right)\left(\frac{0.03}{0.25}\right)\right]^2 = 23 \text{ observations}$$

$$\text{Work element 3: } n = \left[\left(\frac{1.96}{0.05}\right)\left(\frac{0.04}{0.50}\right)\right]^2 = 10 \text{ observations}$$

$$\text{Work element 4: } n = \left[\left(\frac{1.96}{0.05}\right)\left(\frac{0.005}{0.12}\right)\right]^2 = 3 \text{ observations}$$

$$\text{Work element 5: } n = \left[\left(\frac{1.96}{0.05}\right)\left(\frac{0.035}{0.30}\right)\right]^2 = 21 \text{ observations}$$

$$\text{Work element 6: } n = \left[\left(\frac{1.96}{0.05}\right)\left(\frac{0.025}{0.25}\right)\right]^2 = 16 \text{ observations}$$

$$\text{Work element 7: } n = \left[\left(\frac{1.96}{0.05}\right)\left(\frac{0.03}{0.24}\right)\right]^2 = 25 \text{ observations}$$

Work element 7 requires the most observations (25) to ensure the accuracy and confidence needed. So we observe a total of 25 cycles and we take an additional 15 observations (25 less the 10 already taken). Table 11-5 shows the **mean observed times** for the seven work elements after 25 cycles of observations, following our additional observations.

▶ **Mean observed time**
The average of the observation times for each of the work elements.

Table 11-5 Revised Mean Observed Times

Work Element	Mean Observed Time (minutes)
1	0.15
2	0.25
3	0.60
4	0.15
5	0.30
6	0.28
7	0.28

After calculating the mean observed times for each work element, we can determine the normal time for the elements. The normal time is different from the observed times because we multiply it by a performance rating factor.

Performance Rating Factor   The observed work pace may be average, above average, or below average. As the time study analyst, you must make a judgment about the work pace of the observed worker in terms of how far from the average it is. This is called the **performance rating factor.** If 100% represents an average work pace, any performance rating of below 100% is a below-average work pace. A performance rating of above 100% is an above-average work pace. Performance rating is an attempt to counterbalance any unusual patterns noted in the worker's performance. For any element in which the worker performs below average, the worker may need additional training to improve efficiency.

▶ **Performance rating factor**
A subjective estimate of a worker's pace relative to a normal work pace.

It is not uncommon for workers to work faster than normal when they are observed or, in some cases, to work more slowly than normal when they are observed. The performance rating is used to develop a standard that is fair to the worker and to the company.

Frequency of Occurrence   One other factor to consider when calculating the time standard is the **frequency of occurrence** (F) for each work element. We expect most elements to be done every cycle so they would have a frequency of occurrence equal to one. However, some elements are not done each cycle so we adjust the frequency accordingly. If an element is done every other cycle, it would have a frequency equal

▶ **Frequency**
How often the work element must be done each cycle.

to .5, or on average, half of it is done each cycle. If a element is done once every 5 cycles, $F = 0.2$. We calculate the frequency of occurrence by dividing 1 by the number of cycles between occurrences (1 divided by 10 cycles between occurrences means that $F = 0.1$).

We compute the **normal time** for each work element by multiplying the mean observed time by the performance rating factor by the frequency of occurrence [$NT = (OT)(PRF)(F)$]. A 100% performance rating factor equals 1.0, a 90% rating equals 0.90, and a 110% rating equals 1.10. The normal time calculations are shown in Table 11-6. Remember that the performance rating factor scores and the frequency of occurrence must be known for you to calculate the normal time. The normal time for preparing a large cheese and pepperoni pizza is 1.966 minutes. This normal time reflects how long it may take to produce a single large cheese and pepperoni pizza. However, it does not allow for personal time, fatigue, or unavoidable delays (*PFD*) during the typical work day. Therefore, we adjust the normal time with an **allowance factor.**

▶ **Normal time**
The mean observed time multiplied by the performance rating factor.

▶ **Allowance factor**
The amount of time the analyst allows for personal, fatigue, and unavoidable delays.

Allowance Factor We use two methods to adjust for personal time, fatigue, and delays. If the allowance is based on job time, we compute the allowance factor as

$$AF_{JOB} = 1 + PFD$$

where *PFD* = percentage allowance adjustment based on job time

We use this method when jobs have different *PFD* allowances. The other method is to base the allowance on the amount of time worked. We use this method when the jobs are similar and have the same allowance factors. We compute this allowance as

$$AF_{TIME\ WORKED} = \frac{1}{1 - PFD}$$

where *PFD* = percentage allowance based on time worked

Let's look at a numerical comparison of the two methods for setting the allowance factor. If the allowance factors of *PFD* = 0.15, we compute allowance based on the job as

$$AF_{JOB} = 1 + 0.15 = 1.15\ \text{or}\ 115\%$$

Table 11-6 Calculated Normal Times				
Work Element	Mean Observed Time (minutes)	Performance Rating Factor	Frequency	Normal Time (minutes)
1	0.15	0.90	1	0.135
2	0.25	1.00	1	0.250
3	0.60	0.85	1	0.510
4	0.15	1.10	1	0.165
5	0.30	1.20	1	0.360
6	0.28	1.00	1	0.280
7	0.28	0.95	1	0.266
			Total	1.966

When computing the allowance based on time worked, the result is

$$AF_{\text{TIME WORKED}} = \frac{1}{1 - 0.15} = 1.176 \text{ or } 117.6\%$$

STEP 6. Now that we know how to calculate the allowance factor, let's continue with our pizza-making example and determine a standard time.

■ Example 11.4 Calculating Standard Time for a Hand-Tossed Cheese and Pepperoni Pizza

To determine the standard time, we multiply the normal time by the allowance factor. For the large, hand-tossed cheese and pepperoni pizza, we use an allowance factor based on time worked because all the hand-tossed pizza preparations should have a similar allowance.

Solution
We calculate the standard time for each work element as follows.

$$ST = (NT)(AF)$$

where ST = standard time
NT = normal time
AF = allowance factor

Solving for work element 1 in our example, we have

$$ST_{\text{Element 1}} = (0.135)\left(\frac{1}{1 - 0.15}\right) = 0.159 \text{ minutes}$$

The standard times for each element using a 15% allowance based on work time are shown in Table 11-7.

Table 11-7 Standard Times for Making Large Cheese and Pepperoni Pizza

Work Element	Normal Time (minutes)	Standard Time (minutes)
1. Get appropriate ball of dough.	0.135	0.159
2. Flatten dough.	0.250	0.294
3. Spin and toss dough.	0.510	0.600
4. Place dough on work counter.	0.165	0.194
5. Pour sauce on formed dough.	0.360	0.424
6. Place grated cheese on top of sauce.	0.280	0.329
7. Place pepperoni on top of cheese.	0.266	0.313
Total	1.966	2.313

The standard time for preparing a large, hand-tossed cheese and pepperoni pizza is 2.312 minutes. This means that during an 8-hour day, our worker should be able to prepare 207 (480 minutes per 8-hour shift, divided by the standard time of 2.312 minutes) large, hand-tossed cheese and pepperoni pizzas.

Before You Go On

Before you go on, let's make sure you understand how to do a time study. Remember, the first step is identifying the job you will study. Break the job into small, easily recognizable work elements, which allows you to analyze the different elements, look for ways to improve the existing operation, and identify areas where workers need additional training.

To determine the number of observations needed, you must consider the variability of observed times, the desired level of accuracy, and the desired level of confidence for the estimated standard time. Take some observations so you can determine the variability of the observed times. The degree of accuracy and level of confidence factors are managerial decisions.

After determining the number of observations needed, perform any additional observations needed. Using the observed times, calculate the mean observed time for each work element. Calculate the normal time by multiplying the mean observed time by the performance rating factor for each work element. Adjust the normal time by multiplying it by the appropriate allowance factor.

Elemental Time Data

After your company performs and validates time studies, it stores those accepted time studies in an **elemental time database** for possible future use. Many jobs consist of the same work elements. For example, in many jobs the operator has to reach for materials, position an item, or insert and tighten something. Instead of recalculating the time it should take to do a particular work element, the time study analyst checks the database for a valid time study. If the company has already done a time study for that work element, the analyst uses it in the standard time for the job. When a time study analyst uses standard elemental times, the procedure is as follows.

▶ **Elemental time data**
A technique for establishing standards based on previously completed time studies stored in an organization's database.

1. Identify the standard elements of the job.
2. Check the database for time studies done on these elements.
3. If no valid studies exist for this or a similar work element, do a time study for the new work element.
4. Adjust the database times if needed. Note that you can adjust database times if the work element is slightly different. Suppose the database has time studies on reaching 6″ for a tool and reaching 12″ for a tool, but for the job you are studying, the operator reaches 9″ for the tool. Instead of developing a new time study, you can interpolate between the two values and derive a reasonable time for reaching 9″.
5. Add the element times to determine the normal time, then multiply by the allowance factor to determine the standard time.

The advantage of using standard elemental times is that you need fewer time studies. The results of each time study go into the database and are available for setting future standard times. Also, using standard elemental times eliminates the workplace disruptions caused by making time studies. The disadvantage is that using standard elements may discourage new process development and improvements.

Predetermined Time Data

Just as elemental time databases are useful for individual companies, predetermined time data are useful for the many companies that share similar work elements. **Predetermined time data** is a larger database of valid work element times. One commonly

▶ **Predetermined time data**
Published database of elemental time data used for establishing standard times.

used system is methods-time measurement (MTM), which was developed in the 1940s. The tables used in MTM deal with basic elemental motions and associated times. An example of an MTM table is shown in Table 11-8.

Let's take a closer look at Table 11-8. The first column shows how far the operator must move the object in inches. Columns A through E explain the activity. Column A applies when the operator has to reach for an object in a fixed location or an object in the operator's other hand. Column B applies when the operator has to reach for a single object in a location that may vary slightly from cycle to cycle. Columns C and D apply when the operator has to reach for an object jumbled with other objects in a group (search and select), when the operator has to reach for a very small object, or when the operator needs an accurate grasp. Column E applies when the operator has to reach for an indefinite location to position his or her hand for the next motion. The last two columns on the right-hand side (labeled A & B) represent the time measurement units (TMUs) if the hand is already in motion.

When using predetermined time data, you split the job into basic elements (reach, grasp, move, engage, insert, turn, disengage), measure the distances involved

Table 11-8 MTM Reach Table							
Distance Moved (inches)	Time (TMUs)				Hand in Motion		Cases and Descriptions
	A	B	C or D	E	A	B	
3/4 or less	2.0	2.0	2.0	2.0	1.6	1.6	A Reach to object in fixed location, or to object in other hand or on which other hand rests
1	2.5	2.5	3.6	2.4	2.3	2.3	
2	4.0	4.0	5.9	3.8	3.5	2.7	
3	5.3	5.3	7.3	5.3	4.5	3.6	
4	6.1	6.4	8.4	6.8	4.9	4.3	B Reach to single object in location, which may vary slightly from cycle to cycle
5	6.5	7.8	9.4	7.4	5.3	5.0	
6	7.0	8.6	10.1	8.0	5.7	5.7	
7	7.4	9.3	10.8	8.7	6.1	6.5	C Reach to object jumbled with other objects in a group so that search and select occur
8	7.9	10.1	11.5	9.3	6.5	7.2	
9	8.3	10.8	12.2	9.9	6.9	7.9	
10	8.7	11.5	12.9	10.5	7.3	8.6	
12	9.6	12.9	14.2	11.8	8.1	10.1	D Reach to a very small object or where accurate grasp is required
14	10.5	14.4	15.6	13.0	8.9	11.5	
16	11.4	15.8	17.0	14.2	9.7	12.9	E Reach to indefinite location to get hand in position for body balance or next motion or out of way
18	12.3	17.2	18.4	15.5	10.5	14.4	
20	13.1	18.6	19.8	16.7	11.3	15.8	
22	14.0	20.1	21.2	18.0	12.1	17.3	
24	14.9	21.5	22.5	19.2	12.9	18.8	
26	15.8	22.9	23.9	20.4	13.7	20.2	
28	16.7	24.4	25.3	21.7	14.5	21.7	
30	17.5	25.8	26.7	22.9	15.3	23.2	

Source: Copyright by the MTM Association for Standards and Research. Reprinted with permission from the MTM Association, 1111 East Touhy Ave., Des Plaines, IL 60018.

(how far must the operator reach?), and rate the difficulty of the item (does the operator grasp a single piece of wire or does he or she have to grasp one of many wires?). For each job, you find the time for the individual elements in the appropriate data table and sum the times to get the normal time for the job. You adjust the normal time by the *PFD* allowance factor to determine the standard time. Element times are typically in time measurement units (TMUs): there are 100,000 TMUs in one hour; one TMU equals 0.0006 minutes.

To use predetermined time data, you must be skilled in the method and knowledgeable about the job being studied. You must understand how the job is done, the appropriate workplace layout, and the level of difficulty of different work elements. The advantages of using predetermined time data are that you do not have to rate individual operator performance, you do not disrupt the workplace to determine the standard time, and you can calculate standard times before the job even begins. The disadvantages are the skill level needed and the variability among analysts in assessing the level of difficulty of different work elements.

Work Sampling

Work sampling is a method used for estimating the proportion of time that an employee or machine spends on different work activities. Work sampling does not provide a standard time for an activity but instead provides an estimate of what portion of the day a worker uses for that activity. For example, a secretary may spend the day managing files, generating letters, taking phone calls, greeting visitors, and maintaining an appointment schedule. Work sampling does not specify how long it should take the secretary to generate a particular letter but does say what proportion of the day is typically spent on generating letters. For a machine, the company may use work sampling to determine what proportion of the day the machine is used for rush jobs or is idle.

▶ **Work sampling**
A technique for estimating the proportion of time a worker spends on a particular activity.

You do not time activities for work sampling. Instead, you make random observations and note the kind of activity. For example, you walk into the secretary's office and see that the secretary is composing, editing, and printing letters. You record your observations and use them to estimate the proportion of time the employee spends on different activities.

Work sampling consists of the following procedure.

1. Identify the worker or machine to be sampled.
2. Define the activities to be observed.
3. Estimate the sample size based on the desired level of accuracy and confidence.
4. Develop the random observation schedule. Make your observations over a time period that is representative of normal work conditions.
5. Make your observations and record the data. Check to see whether the estimated sample size remains valid.
6. Estimate the proportion of time spent on the given activity.

In the following example, we used work sampling to estimate the proportion of time a secretary spends scheduling appointments. You can also use work sampling to estimate the proportion of delays a worker experiences and as input when calculating the PFD (personal, fatigue, and delay) allowance factor. For example, you can observe whether a worker is working or experiencing delays. After you make enough observations, you can estimate delay time and use it as part of the PFD allowance factor.

■ Example 11.5 Determining the Proportion of Time Used to Schedule Appointments

We use work sampling to estimate the proportion of time a secretary spends doing a given activity during a normal office day. The secretary's normal activities are managing files, generating letters, taking phone calls, greeting visitors, maintaining an appointment schedule, and being idle. We want to know how much of the secretary's time is used for scheduling appointments.

Solution:
We have identified the worker and the activity. Now we determine how many observations to make. Work sampling is designed to produce a value $\hat{p}$, which estimates the true proportion p that a particular activity normally occurs, within some allowable error e. To estimate the number of observations needed for a given level of error, we use the following formula.

$$n = \left(\frac{z}{e}\right)^2 \hat{p}(1 - \hat{p})$$

where n = the number of observations that are needed
z = the number of normal standard deviations needed for desired confidence
e = the allowable error level (given as a percentage)

Let's assume that we want to estimate the proportion of time the secretary spends on scheduling appointments, with 97% confidence ($z = 2.17$), and that the resulting estimate will be within 5% of the true value. To solve the equation, we need a sample estimate. When we do not know the sample estimate of $\hat{p}$, we calculate a preliminary estimate of the sample size by setting $\hat{p} = .50$. Since we do not have an estimate for the sample proportion, we compute the preliminary sample size for our work sampling example as follows:

$$n = \left(\frac{2.17}{0.05}\right)^2 0.5(1 - 0.5) = 470.89 \text{ observations}$$

If we use a preliminary sample size, we verify that the sample size is correct after we make initial observations and compute the proportion sample. For example, we observed the secretary 30 times and he was scheduling appointments during 6 of those observations. The proportion sample is 0.2 (6 times arranging meetings/30 observations). The new estimate of the sample size is

$$n = \left(\frac{2.17}{0.05}\right)^2 0.2(1 - 0.2) = 301.37 \text{ observations}$$

Whenever the value of n is not a whole number, we round up to the next whole number. In our example, we may need to check our sample size once more after completing more observations just to be sure that we are using the right sample size. After completing the 302 observations, we see that the secretary was scheduling appointments on 60 separate occasions or 19.9% (60/302) of the time. We examine the other activities to estimate the proportion of time the secretary spends on each. The company can use these estimates to describe the job to prospective employees or in performance reviews for the current secretary.

■ COMPENSATION

Worker compensation is the third part of work system design. Companies need to develop compensation systems that reinforce the behaviors needed to meet the company's objectives.

Compensation systems are typically based either on time spent working or on output generated. Time-based systems compensate the employee according to the number of hours worked during the pay period. Compensation is not linked to employee performance but to employee presence at the workplace. Output-based or incentive systems link employee pay to performance. Employees are paid based on their output and not on the number of hours they work.

Time-Based Systems

Time-based systems are normally used when measuring output per employee is not applicable—say, for managers, administrative support staff, and some direct laborers. Consider an employee working in your company's research and development group. This employee is doing creative work, which is not easily measured in terms of output. The advantage of the time-based system is its simplicity. For the company, wages are easily calculated. For the employees, the pay is steady and they know what they will get in their regular paycheck.

▶ **Time-based compensation systems** Pay the worker based on the number of hours worked.

Output-Based Systems

Output-based (incentive) systems can be linked to Frederick Taylor's theory that man is economically motivated. These systems reward workers for their output. The more the worker produces, the more the worker earns. The assumption is that some workers are motivated by money and produce more when pay is linked to performance.

▶ **Output-based compensation systems** Pay the worker based on the number of units completed.

These incentive systems can be designed to compensate either the individual or an entire group of employees. Individual incentive plans typically provide a base salary for the employee, plus a bonus for output achieved above the standard. For example, an employee has a base salary of $250 per week regardless of how much is produced. The standard for the employee is to produce 50 units per week. The employee earns $250 per week until the employee's output exceeds the standard 50 units per week. For every unit above 50, the employee earns an additional $7. If the employee produces 55 units during the week, he or she earns $285 for that pay period—$250 base, plus a bonus of $35 (5 extra units at $7 each). An employee producing 60 units per week would earn $310.

Successful individual incentive plans are linked to quality as well as to quantity. Encouraging a worker to produce low-quality units faster does not make good business sense. The incentive plan must be clear on how output is counted.

Group Incentive Plans

Group incentive plans are designed to reward employees when the company achieves certain performance objectives. Two methods are profit sharing and gain sharing. Profit sharing rewards employees when certain profitability levels are achieved by the company.

Profit Sharing One variation of profit sharing places half the profits in excess of the minimum return on investment into a bonus pool for employees. Individual bonuses can then be based on an employee's base pay, on the percentage of time during the past year the employee worked for the company, or on similar arrangements. For example, a company may give a bonus equal to 15% of an employee's base pay. If employee Heather Jones has a base salary of $34,000, her bonus would be $5,100

($34,000 times 0.15). This may seem like a substantial bonus but if the company fails to meet its profitability levels, Heather's bonus is zero.

Gain Sharing Gain sharing emphasizes the costs of output rather than profit levels. With this plan, employees share the benefits of quality and productivity improvements made during the year. The pool of money for the bonuses comes from the cost items under the control of employees. The individual bonuses should represent an appropriate share of the gains.

A survey of the pay practices of *Fortune* 1000 firms between 1987 and 1993 reported that the percentage of companies using individual incentive plans for at least 20% of their employees increased from 38% to 50%. The same survey reported that the proportion of companies using profit sharing decreased from 45% to 43%. At the same time, companies reduced the proportion of retail salespeople paid solely on straight salary from 21% to 7%.

Incentive Plan Trends

Despite a trend toward using individual incentive systems, there are a number of disadvantages. Such systems have been shown to undermine teamwork and give employees a short-term focus. A study of 20 Social Security Administration offices showed that an individual merit pay system had no effect on worker performance. This finding tells us that individual incentive plans need significantly more data collection by management than time-based systems.

Some evidence suggests that group incentive systems suffer from the "free-rider" problem. The free-rider is the person who does not do his or her fair share but is still rewarded by the work of the group. Still, the extent of free-riding is modest, most likely because of group pressure. Overall, companies using group incentive systems tend to outperform companies that do not use such systems.

■ LEARNING CURVES

An important factor in calculating labor times is the learning effect. We all can recall a new task or job that took a long time to finish the first time we tried. However, each subsequent time we did the task, it took less time. This is the basis of learning curve theory. People learn from doing a task and get quicker each time they repeat that task. A learning curve is shown in Figure 11-5.

The major attributes of a learning curve are that it takes less time to complete the task each additional time it is done by the same employee, and the time savings decrease with each additional time that task is done by that employee. When the number of times the task is completed doubles, the decrease in time per task affects the rate of the learning curve. For example, if a learning curve has an 85% learning rate, the second time the task is done will take 85% of the time it took the first time the task was done. The fourth time the task is done will take 85% of the time it took the second time. The eighth time will take 85% of the time it took the fourth time, and so on. The formula for calculating the time the task should take is

$$T \times L^n = \text{time required for } n\text{th time the task is done}$$

$$\text{where } T = \text{time needed to complete task the first time}$$
$$L = \text{learning curve rate}$$
$$n = \text{number of times the task is doubled}$$

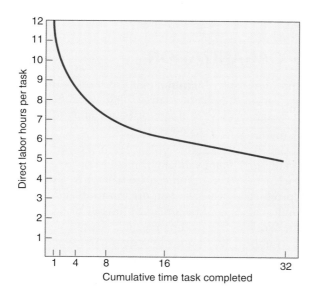

Figure 11-5

Learning curve

If the first time the task was done, the employee took 12 labor hours, and the learning rate is 85%, calculate how long the 16th time that task is done should take.

$$\text{Hours needed for 16th task} = 12 \times (.85)^4 = 6.26 \text{ hours}$$

The 16th time the task is done will be the fourth doubling of output—the 2nd time, the 4th time, the 8th time, and finally the 16th time.

Understanding learning curves is important. The amount of labor needed to finish the same task or build the same product a number of times can be calculated, which allows a company to better estimate the labor cost. The company can also better schedule its workload since it knows how much labor is needed to complete the task a specific number of times. Calculating the learning rate also is a means for evaluating productivity. The company can compare its learning rate with that of its competitors. The rate of learning is affected when there are changes in designs, personnel, or procedures. Changes mean that an employee must learn something new, which slows down the improvement rate.

An early use of the learning curve

"THERE IS A FAIRLY STEEP LEARNING CURVE. BUT ONCE YOU GET THE HANG OF IT YOU'LL WONDER HOW YOU EVER GOT ALONG WITHOUT BURNING EVERYTHING IN YOUR PATH."

CROSS FUNCTIONAL

OM ACROSS THE ORGANIZATION

Work system design affects functional areas throughout a company. Let's look at why individual functional areas are concerned with work system design.

Accounting calculates the cost of products manufactured or services provided. Labor can be a significant portion of the cost of goods sold, especially in the service industries. Accounting measures variances between planned product cost and actual product cost. Accounting also typically measures operational efficiency, which is based on work standards. Work system design is an important resource for accounting activities.

Marketing is concerned with work system design because it is the basis for determining lead time. Accurate work projections enable marketing to make viable promise dates to customers.

Information systems uses estimates of job duration and resources in the software for scheduling and tracking operations.

Purchasing handles requests for materials based on a schedule projected from the work system design. Accurate scheduling enables cost-effective materials and labor purchasing decisions. Standard time provides a benchmark for evaluation of new materials and processes.

Manufacturing responds to effective job design, process analysis, and work measurement with high levels of performance and on-time delivery of finished goods.

Human resources uses work sampling to establish and validate hiring criteria.

You can see that work system design involves all aspects of an organization and has an impact on how well the organization performs. In many manufacturing companies, job design and process analysis are both done by a manufacturing or industrial engineer. The engineer works with product blueprints and the workforce to develop job instructions. From these detailed job instructions, the company can develop time standards. Work measurement information is often provided by workers as they complete a job. Accounting may use this information to report the efficiency of manufacturing operations. In a service organization, an operations manager or operations analyst may do the job design and process analysis.

Work system design helps companies understand the total costs of making a product or providing a service. It allows companies to evaluate their product or service lines, and view the bottom line for each product or service.

■ OM IS EVERYWHERE

You may still wear different hats in your daily life but good job design can clarify your objectives. It can help you estimate the time you need for specific activities and give your day a more organized feeling. Suppose on a particular day you have several things you must do, plus some things you would like to do. You have to clean the apartment, go to the supermarket, do the laundry, prepare dinner for guests, shower and dress, spend the evening with friends, and clean up the kitchen. There's also a great one-day sale at the mall. How do you decide whether you can do the necessary activities and still have time to squeeze in that trip to the mall? You are probably not in the habit of making time studies and determining standard times for your everyday activities. However, you do use historical data to judge how long it should take for a particular activity. Based on these data, you will be able to make a schedule of when you have to start each activity to get everything done on time. You probably also use given standard times. If you are making a cake, you bake the cake according to the time given in the recipe. You typically do not experiment unless the standard time fails. You also accept standard times when you are told how long a movie will last or how long it takes to fly from one city to another. Standard times show up everywhere in your daily life. You can also use standard times to evaluate new processes. For example, maybe you can take several different routes to work. When you try a new route, you are comparing the time it takes to get to work on that route versus the route you normally take. Your historical standard time has provided you with a benchmark to use when comparing alternative processes.

CHAPTER HIGHLIGHTS

1 Work system design involves job design, methods or process analysis, and work measurement. Job design specifies the work activities of an individual or group in support of organizational objectives.

2 Relevant job design issues include design feasibility, the choice of human or machine, the use of teams, and the location where the work is to be done. Technical feasibility is the degree to which an individual or group of individuals is physically and mentally able to do the job. Economic feasibility is the degree to which the value a job adds and the cost of having the job done are profitable for the company. Behavioral feasibility is the degree to which an employee derives intrinsic satisfaction from doing the job. Another job design issue concerns whether the job should be done by people or by machines. If a person does the job, you need to decide on the level of specialization. If jobs are extremely specialized, you will probably need a way to reduce boredom. Rather than individual job design, an organization can use team approaches. These include problem-solving teams, special-purpose teams, and self-directed teams. An additional consideration is where the work is done. Many employees may work in alternative workplaces in the future.

3 Methods or process analysis is concerned with how the employee does the job and can also be used to improve the efficiency of an operation.

4 Work measurement is used to determine standard times. A standard time is how long it should take a qualified operator, using the appropriate process, material, and equipment, and working at a sustainable pace, to do a particular job. Standard times are used for product costing, process and material evaluation, and for planning workloads and staffing. Standard times are usually based on time studies. Work sampling is used to estimate the proportion of time that should be spent on an activity.

5 To do a time study, you identify the job and break the job into work elements. Then you determine the number of observations needed and perform the observations.

6 Work sampling involves random observations of a worker. Each time you observe the worker, you note what activity the worker is doing. After numerous observations, you can project the expected proportion of time the worker should spend on different activities.

7 Standard times are developed with time studies, elemental time data, and predetermined time data. You learned how to develop standard times using time studies. After conducting the time study, you compute the mean observed time for each work element. You compute the normal time for the work element by multiplying the mean observed time by the performance rating factor. You find the standard time for each work element by multiplying the normal time by the allowance factor.

8 Standards are used to compare alternative processes, evaluate new materials or components, and evaluate individual worker performance. Standards also allow you to determine when a job should be completed or how many units can be done in a period of time.

9 Worker compensation systems are either time-based or output-based. Time-based systems pay the employee for the number of hours worked. Output-based systems pay the employee for the number of units completed. Compensation schemes can be based on either individual or group performance.

10 Learning curves show the rate of learning that occurs when an employee repeats the same task. Using learning curves, you can estimate how long a particular task will take. It allows the company to schedule better and calculate costs more accurately.

KEY TERMS

FORMULA REVIEW

Calculating the number of observations for an element in a time study

$$n = \left[\left(\frac{z}{a}\right)\left(\frac{s}{\bar{x}}\right)\right]^2$$

Calculating the allowance factor based on job time

$$AF_{JOB} = 1 + PFD$$

Calculating the allowance factor based on time worked

$$AF_{TIME\ WORKED} = \frac{1}{1 - PFD}$$

Calculating standard time

$$ST = (NT)(AF)$$

Calculating the number of observations for work sampling

$$n = \left(\frac{z}{e}\right)^2 \hat{p}(1 - \hat{p})$$

Calculating the time required for the nth time the task is done

$$T \times L^n$$

SOLVED PROBLEMS

■ Solved Problem 1

Frank's BBQ Delight restaurant sells barbecued chicken sandwiches. The owner wants to set a standard time for assembling each kind of sandwich he sells. You have been asked to set a standard time for the Super Chicken sandwich—8 ounces of barbecued chicken served on a bulkie roll.

a. Determine the number of observations you need to make if the owner wants the standard time to be within 5% of the true value 90% of the time. Results from your first ten observations are shown here.

Work Element	Standard Deviation	Mean Observed Time
1. Get bulkie rolls (box of 12).	0.200	2.40
2. Prepare bulkie roll, move to prep area, open up roll.	0.005	0.08
3. Get barbecued chicken (4 lb. box).	0.550	4.00
4. Place 8 oz. chicken on roll.	0.015	0.25
5. Spread on special BBQ sauce.	0.010	0.10
6. Close bulkie roll, slice in half.	0.0125	0.10
7. Wrap sandwich, place in pickup area.	0.010	0.15

b. Determine the normal time for each of the activities. Determine the standard time if the owner decides to use a 10% allowance factor based on the time of the job.

c. If an employee works at the standard time, how many Super Chicken sandwiches can the employee prepare per hour?

d. If the owner expects demand for the Super Chicken sandwich to be 100 per hour, how many employees should be assigned to preparing the Super Chicken sandwiches?

Solution 1a

With $z = 1.65$ and $e = 0.05$, determine the number of observations needed for each work element.

Work element 1:
$$n = \left[\left(\frac{1.65}{0.05}\right)\left(\frac{0.20}{2.40}\right)\right]^2 = 7.56 \text{ or } 8 \text{ observations}$$

Work element 2:
$$n = \left[\left(\frac{1.65}{0.05}\right)\left(\frac{0.005}{0.08}\right)\right]^2 = 4.25 \text{ or } 5 \text{ observations}$$

Work element 3:
$$n = \left[\left(\frac{1.65}{0.05}\right)\left(\frac{0.55}{4.0}\right)\right]^2 = 20.59 \text{ or } 21 \text{ observations}$$

Work element 4:
$$n = \left[\left(\frac{1.65}{0.05}\right)\left(\frac{0.015}{0.25}\right)\right]^2 = 3.92 \text{ or } 4 \text{ observations}$$

Work element 5:
$$n = \left[\left(\frac{1.65}{0.05}\right)\left(\frac{0.01}{0.10}\right)\right]^2 = 10.89 \text{ or } 11 \text{ observations}$$

Work element 6:
$$n = \left[\left(\frac{1.65}{0.05}\right)\left(\frac{0.0125}{0.10}\right)\right]^2 = 17.02 \text{ or } 18 \text{ observations}$$

Work element 7:
$$n = \left[\left(\frac{1.65}{0.05}\right)\left(\frac{0.01}{0.15}\right)\right]^2 = 4.84 \text{ or } 5 \text{ observations}$$

Calculate the number of observations needed for each of the work elements. Then determine that we need a total of 21 observations for 90% confidence that we will be within 5% of the true mean. After you make the additional 11 observations, the following data are available.

Work Unit	Mean Observed Time (minutes)	Performance Rating Factor	Frequency
1	2.20	1.10	0.125
2	0.10	0.90	1
3	4.25	0.95	0.25
4	0.20	1.25	1
5	0.10	1.00	1
6	0.12	0.90	1
7	0.12	1.25	1

Spreadsheet 11.1 shows how this data could be used in a spreadsheet.

Spreadsheet 11.1

Element	Desc.	Mean	Perf. Factor	Freq.	Normal	Standard
1		2.20	1.10	0.125	0.3025	0.3328
2		0.10	0.90	1.000	0.0900	0.0990
3		4.25	0.95	0.250	1.0094	1.1103
4		0.20	1.25	1.000	0.2500	0.2750
5		0.10	1.00	1.000	0.1000	0.1100
6		0.12	0.90	1.000	0.1080	0.1188
7		0.12	1.25	1.000	0.1500	0.1650
					2.0099	2.2109

Solution 1b

The normal times are shown in spreadsheet 11.1. To calculate the normal times, multiply the mean observed time by the performance factor and the frequency factor.

To determine standard time, we multiply the normal time by the allowance factor. Since the allowance is based on job time, we use the formula 1 + allowances. The company has decided on a 10% allowance.

The standard times are shown in the far right column in spreadsheet 11.1

Solution 1c

Since the standard time is 2.2109 minutes per cycle, a worker performing at the standard should be able to produce 27.138 sandwiches per hour (60 minutes/2.2109 minutes per sandwich).

Solution 1d

If the owner plans to have staffing to prepare 100 Super Chicken sandwiches, he will need 4 employees (100 sandwiches per hour divided by 27.138 sandwiches per employee per hour).

■ Solved Problem 2

You make 20 observations of a business professor at State University. The results of the observations are as follows:

Activity	Times Observed
Professor at class	5
Professor grading	2
Meeting with students	1
Preparing for class	3
Working on research	3
Idle	2
Speaking on phone	1
Not available	3

Based on this information, how many observations do you need to estimate the proportion of the professor's time spent on classroom preparation? Assume a 95% confidence ($z = 1.96$) that the resulting estimate will be within 5% of the true value.

Solution

Based on the preliminary observations, the estimate of the proportion of time the professor spends preparing for class is 0.15 (3 observed times/20 observations taken).

$$n = \left(\frac{1.96}{0.05}\right)^2 [0.15(1 - 0.15)] = 195.92 \text{ observations}$$

We need to take a total of 196 observations to satisfy our confidence and error constraints.

DISCUSSION QUESTIONS

1. Describe the major components of work system design.

2. Visit a local business and describe the jobs to be done, the workers needed for the jobs, and how the workers help achieve the objectives of the business.

3. Describe the objectives of job design.

4. Explain why it is hard to design jobs in a business setting.

5. Explain what we mean by technical feasibility, economic feasibility, and behavioral feasibility.

6. Describe cases in which people are preferable to machines.

7. Describe cases in which machines are preferable to people.

8. Describe the advantages and disadvantages of using a high level of job specialization.

9. Describe factors affecting the work environment that must be considered in work systems design.

10. Describe the alternative workplace approach.

11. Create a process flowchart for an activity that you do daily—for example, getting ready for school each day.

12. Analyze a daily activity to see whether you can improve the process.

13. Compare and contrast the four work measurement techniques.

14. Explain the difference between time-based and output-based compensation plans.

15. Explain why it makes sense to use time-based compensation systems.

16. Explain why it makes sense to use an output-based compensation system.

PROBLEMS

1. Given the following information, determine the sample size needed if the standard time estimate is to be within 5% of the true mean 97% of the time.

Work Element	Standard Deviation (minutes)	Mean Observed Time (minutes)
1	0.20	1.10
2	0.10	0.80
3	0.15	0.90
4	0.10	1.00

2. Using the information in problem 1, determine the sample size needed if the standard time estimate is to be within 5% of the true mean 99% of the time.

3. Using the following information, determine the sample size needed if the standard time estimate is to be within 5% of the true mean 95% of the time.

Work Element	Standard Deviation (minutes)	Mean Observed Time (minutes)
1	0.60	2.40
2	0.20	1.50
3	1.10	3.85
4	0.85	2.55
5	0.40	1.60
6	0.50	2.50

4. Using the information provided in Problem 3, determine the sample size needed if the standard time estimate is to be within 5% of the true mean 99% of the time. Calculate the percentage increase in sample size for the higher precision.

Use the following information for Problems 5–10.

Work Element	Mean Observed Time (minutes)	Performance Rating Factor
1	1.20	0.95
2	1.00	0.85
3	0.80	1.10
4	0.90	1.10

5. Calculate the normal time for each of the work elements.

6. The Arkade Company a. Calculate the mean observed time for each element.has decided to use a 15% allowance factor based on job time. Calculate the standard time for each work element and for the entire job.

7. Based on the standard time calculated in problem 6, how many units should an employee performing at 100% of standard complete during an 8-hour workday?

8. The Arkade Company is considering changing to a 15% allowance factor based on time worked. Calculate the new standard time for each work element and for the entire job.

9. Based on the standard time calculated in problem 8, how many units should an employee performing at 100% of standard complete during an 8-hour workday?

10. Compare the two standards from Problem 8. What other factors should be considered in deciding on the method for determining the allowance factor?

11. Jake's Jumbo Jacks has collected the following information to develop a standard time for building jumbo jacks.

Observations	Element (in minutes)				
	1	2	3	4	5
Cycle 1	2.18	1.25	1.70	2.74	1.57
Cycle 2	2.22	1.23	1.75	2.66	1.55
Cycle 3	2.20	1.29	1.72	2.60	1.57
Cycle 4	2.18	1.30	1.80	2.56	1.57
Cycle 5	2.21	1.26	1.84	2.58	1.59
Cycle 6	2.22	1.22	1.79	2.58	1.61
Cycle 7	2.17	1.26	1.78	2.60	1.57
Cycle 8	2.21	1.26	1.75	2.58	1.61
Cycle 9	2.18	1.30	1.80	2.60	1.55
Cycle 10	2.17	1.28	1.78	2.58	1.57
Performance rating factor	0.90	0.80	1.10	1.05	0.95
Frequency	1	1	1	1	1

a. Calculate the mean observed time for each element.
b. Calculate the normal time for each element.
c. Using an allowance factor of 20% of job time, calculate the standard time for each element and for the entire job.
d. How many units should be completed each hour if the worker performs at 100% of the standard?
e. How many units should be completed each hour if the worker performs at 90% of the standard?

12. You have 25 observations of university policeman Sgt. Jack B. Nimble during his normal workday. The results are shown here.

Activity Observed	Number of Times Observed
Doing paperwork	9
On the phone	3
Eating doughnuts	3
Cleaning weapon	4
Idle	2
Not in sight	4

a. Based on your preliminary observations, how many total observations do you need to estimate the proportion of time Sgt. Nimble spends doing paperwork?
b. How many total observations do you need to estimate the proportion of time Sgt. Nimble spends on the phone?
c. How many total observations do you need to estimate the proportion of time Sgt. Nimble seems to be unavailable?

13. After taking a total of 355 observations of Sgt. Nimble, the following data are available. Interpret these data relative to Sgt. Nimble's daily activities.

Activity Observed	Number of Times Observed
Doing paperwork	135
On the phone	40
Eating doughnuts	45
Cleaning weapon	50
Idle	35
Not in sight	50

14. You are given the following information.

Observations	Element (in minutes)				
	1	2	3	4	5
Cycle 1	0.58	1.50	0.79	0.30	
Cycle 2	0.61		0.75	0.35	
Cycle 3	0.59		0.73	0.33	
Cycle 4	0.54		0.72	0.35	
Cycle 5	0.60	1.40	0.72	0.30	2.00
Cycle 6	0.57		0.71	0.32	
Cycle 7	0.53		0.80	0.30	
Cycle 8	0.59		0.78	0.28	
Cycle 9	0.63	1.54	0.77	0.35	
Cycle 10	0.58		0.79	0.33	2.20
Cycle 11	0.56		0.72	0.32	
Cycle 12	0.55		0.79	0.34	
Cycle 13	0.58	1.62	0.77	0.29	
Cycle 14	0.60		0.80	0.33	
Cycle 15	0.62		0.74	0.30	2.10
Performance Rating factor	0.95	0.90	1.00	1.10	0.90
Frequency	1	0.25	1	1	0.20

a. Develop the mean observed time for each element.
b. Calculate the normal time for each element.
c. Using an allowance factor of 15% of job time, calculate the standard time for each element and for the entire job.
d. How many units should be completed each hour if the worker performs at 100% of the standard?
e. How many units should be completed each hour if the worker performs at 110% of the standard?

15. Your 20 observations of Dr. Knowitall reveal the following information.

Activity Observed	Number of Times Observed
With patient	6
Reviewing test results	3
On phone	2
Idle	1
Away on emergency	4
Not available	4

a. Calculate the sample size needed to estimate the proportion of time Dr. Knowitall spends away on emergencies.
b. Calculate the sample size needed to estimate the proportion of time Dr. Knowitall spends reviewing test results.

16. Using the information in Problem 15, calculate the minimum number of observations which must be made to complete the work sampling analysis.

CASE: *Northeast State University*

Dr. Woodrow Bay, chairperson of the Decision Sciences Department in the College of Business Administration, sat at his desk pondering his latest predicament. For the last 45 minutes at the faculty meeting, faculty members complained about poor administrative support. Numerous examples about unavailable administrative assistants were given. As the professors left, one muttered "There are universities that provide plenty of administrative support, maybe it is time to update our resumes."

Dr. Bay knew this to be true; and that these professors could easily leave for another university given the current job market. He needed to determine whether their perceptions regarding inadequate administrative support were justified.

Background

The Decision Sciences Department houses four functional areas: operations management, quantitative methods, statistics, and information systems. The faculty have national or international reputations based on their excellent scholarship. Higher student enrollments have resulted in the department increasing its faculty from 12 to 20 full-time professors during the past three years. Unfortunately, there was no increase in the administrative support for the department.

As professors were added, the strain on the administrative staff increased. There were more classes, so more course materials needed to be prepared (syllabi, handouts, and exams). In addition, since the faculty was expected to publish research, the administrative assistants spent more time working on manuscripts. New professors required significantly more interaction with the support staff to explain what was wanted and when. Administrative assistants often ran errands for faculty members (placing items on reserve at the library, dealing with the book store, making photocopies, distributing mail, doing correspondence, providing supplies, making travel arrangements, arranging meetings, and placing meal orders). The administrative assistants seemed unable to complete all of their work in a normal 8-hour day.

The faculty on the other hand believed the primary work activity of the administrative assistants was keyboard entry: keying in manuscripts, course outlines, correspondence, and grant proposals. When faculty did not see the administrative assistants keying in information, the impression was that the staff were not doing their jobs. It seemed that too much time

was wasted talking with faculty, students, or each other, and work was not being done. Dr. Bay did not believe this was the case. He needed to gather information about how the administrative assistants spent their time and compare that with data from the faculty concerning the administrative assistants. Both the faculty and the administrative assistants believed that the solution was hiring an additional administrative assistant. For Dr. Bay this was next to impossible given the proposed budget cuts at the university, so he decided to collect data to gain insight in the problem.

For two weeks data were collected. From the faculty, Dr. Bay received estimates as to what percentage of the administrative assistant's time the faculty perceived was spent on different activities. He also did a work sample of the administrative assistants. The results are shown here.

Estimates of Administrative Assistants' Use of Time

Activity	Faculty Estimate (%)	Work Sample (%)
Working on computer	20	40
Talking on phone	25	7
Away from office	20	10
Talking with faculty	2	8
Talking with others	15	10
Filing	3	5
Photocopying	5	15
Other	10	5

Case Questions:

Your assignment is to analyze the data collected by Dr. Bay. In particular, you should

1. Describe how Dr. Bay can use the data.
2. Suggest ways in which the administrative assistants' jobs can be changed to make better use of their time and be more supportive to the faculty.
3. Suggest ways the faculty can change work habits to reduce the burden on the administrative assistants.
4. Consider other alternatives to reduce the strain on the administrative assistants.

INTERACTIVE LEARNING

Enhance and test your knowledge of Chapter 11 using the interactive CD.

1. **Video** *Lands' End Inc.*

   Visit our dynamic Web site, www.wiley.com/college/reid, for more cases, web links, and additional information.

2. **Additional Web Resources**
   The AES Corporation, www.aesc.com
   Southwest Airlines Co., www.flysouthwest.com
   Irving Paper Mill, www.ifdn.com/paper/paper.htm

3. **INTERNET CHALLENGE** *E-commerce Job Design*

You have been chosen to head up the development of an e-commerce direct retail site for your company. Since this is new to both you and your company, you need to gather some initial information. You will use this information to develop standard times for measuring your company Web site's performance. Your company is planning to start by offering between 100 and 200 popular products on-line. Of particular concern to your company is the customer's ease in using your site.

Begin by visiting at least three different Web sites and documenting your experience at the site with a process flowchart. Show the sequential steps you as the customer must follow when visiting the site to gain product information, to place an order, to arrange payment, and to track the order. For one of the sites you visit, collect data on how long it takes a customer to complete a visit to the site. Break the visit into distinct elements such as finding product information, placing an order, choosing the shipping method, making payment, and confirming your order. For one of the three sites you visit, analyze the procedures used and propose changes that you think would improve the customer effectiveness of the site.

BIBLIOGRAPHY

Barnes, Ralph M. *Motion and Time Study: Design and Measurement of Work*, 8th ed. New York: Wiley, 1980.

Hatcher, Larry, and Timothy L. Ross. "From Individual Incentives to an Organization-Wide Gainsharing Plan: Effects on Teamwork and Product Quality." *Journal of Organizational Behavior* (May 1991), p. 169.

Ledford, Jr., Gerald E., Edward E. Lawlet III, and Susan A. Mohrman. "Reward Innovations in Fortune 1000 Companies." *Compensation and Benefits Review* (April 1995), p. 76.

Marwell, Gerald. "Altruism and the Problem of Collective Action." In *Cooperation and Helping Behavior: Theories and Research*. New York: Academic Press, 1982.

Niebel, Benjamin W. *Motion and Time Study*, 9th ed. Burr Ridge, IL: Irwin, 1993.

Pace, Randy. "Santa Cruz Operation's Self Managing Work Groups, A Team Member's Story," *Target*, Vol. 8, No. 6 (November/December 1992), p. 7.

Patterson, Gregory A. "Distressed Shoppers, Disaffected Workers Prompt Stores to Alter Sales Commissions," *Wall Street Journal* (July 1, 1992), p. B1.

Pearce, Jone L., William B. Stevenson, and James L. Perry. "Managerial Compensation Based on Organizational Performance: A Time Series Analysis of the Effects of Merit Pay." *Academy of Management Journal* (June 1985), p. 261.

Pfeffer, Jeffrey. "Six Dangerous Myths About Pay," *Harvard Business Review* (May/June 1998), Vol. 76, No. 3, p. 109.

Independent Demand Inventory Management

Before studying this chapter, you should know or, if necessary, review

1. Competitive priorities, Chapter 2, pages 28–32.
2. Internal and external customers, Chapter 4, pages 79–81.
3. Advantages of small lot sizes, Chapter 7, pages 179–181.
4. Forecast error, Chapter 8, pages 227–229.

LEARNING OBJECTIVES

After studying this chapter, you should be able to

1. Describe the different types and uses of inventory.
2. Describe the objectives of inventory management.
3. Calculate inventory performance measures.
4. Understand the relevant costs associated with inventory.
5. Calculate order quantities.
6. Evaluate the total relevant costs of different inventory policies.
7. Understand the benefits of smaller order sizes.
8. Calculate appropriate safety stock inventory policies.
9. Calculate order quantities for single-period inventory.
10. Perform ABC inventory control and analysis.
11. Understand the role of cycle counting in inventory record accuracy.

CHAPTER OUTLINE

Have you ever been in a rush to get through the grocery checkout only to be stuck in line behind a person buying 24 cans of pet food, each a different flavor? You watch in dismay as the cashier scans each can separately, wondering why the cashier doesn't just scan one can and enter a quantity of 24. Although it seems easier to let the register do the work, it is critical that the cashier scan each can. The point-of-sale register collects data on each item sold and adjusts inventory records accordingly. When a cashier scans only a single flavor and enters a quantity of 24, the register records that 24 cans of that particular flavor of pet food were bought by this customer instead of one can each of 24 different flavors. Inaccurate inventory records cause stores to replenish the wrong items, resulting in shortages on the shelves.

Information collected with point-of-sale registers is the basis for making replenishment orders. When placing purchase orders, businesses decide what, when, and how much should be ordered. When a company replenishes the wrong items, the customer is not satisfied. When a company replenishes items too soon, the items can spoil or deteriorate and the company has invested money in inventory that is not needed. It is also possible that the company might not have adequate storage space.

Companies make these decisions when managing inventory. In this chapter, we look at different types of inventory and how companies use them, the costs of inventory policies, inventory management objectives and performance measures, and techniques for determining how much of an item to replenish.

■ TYPES OF INVENTORY

▶ **Raw materials**
Purchased items or extracted materials transformed into components or products.

▶ **Components** Parts or subassemblies used in final product.

▶ **Work-in-process (WIP)** Items in process throughout the plant.

▶ **Finished goods** Products sold to customers.

▶ **Distribution inventory** Finished goods in the distribution system.

▶ **MRO** Items used in support of manufacturing and maintenance.

Inventory comes in many shapes and sizes, as shown in Figure 12-1. Most manufacturing firms have the following types of inventory. **Raw materials** are the purchased items or extracted materials that are transformed into components or products. For example, gold is a raw material that is transformed in jewelry. **Components** are parts or subassemblies used in building the final product. For example, a transformer is a component in an electronic product. **Work-in-process (WIP)** refers to all items in process throughout the plant. Since products are not manufactured instantaneously, there is always some WIP inventory flowing through the plant. After the product is completed, it becomes **finished goods**—the bicycles, stereos, CDs, and automobiles that the company sells to its customers. **Distribution inventory** consists of finished goods and spare parts at various points in the distribution system—for example, stored in warehouses or in transit between warehouses and consumers. **Maintenance, repair, and operational (MRO) inventory** are supplies that are used in manufacturing but do not become part of the finished product. Examples of MRO are hand tools, lubricants, and cleaning supplies.

| Raw materials | Components | Work-in-progress | Finished goods | Distribution inventory | Maintenance, repair & operating supplies |

Figure 12-1

Types of inventory

HOW COMPANIES USE THEIR INVENTORY ■

Companies have different kinds of inventory. They also use inventory for different purposes. Let's look at six ways of using inventory.

1. Anticipation Inventory or Seasonal Inventory is built in anticipation of future demand, planned promotional programs, seasonal fluctuations, plant shutdowns, and vacations. Companies build anticipation inventory to maintain level production throughout the year. For example, the toy industry builds toys throughout the year in anticipation of high seasonal sales in December.

▶ **Anticipation inventory** Inventory built in anticipation of future demand.

2. Fluctuation Inventory or Safety Stock is carried as a cushion to protect against possible demand variation, "just in case" of unexpected demand. For example, you might keep extra food in the freezer just in case unexpected company drops in. Safety stock is also called *buffer stock* or *reserve stock*.

▶ **Fluctuation inventory** Provides a cushion against unexpected demand.

3. Lot-size Inventory or Cycle Stock results when a company buys or produces more than is immediately needed. The extra units are carried in inventory and depleted as customers place orders. Consider what happens when you buy a 24-can container of soda. You do not normally drink all 24 cans at once. Instead, what you do not need right away, you store for future consumption. You may buy more of an item than you need to take advantage of lower unit costs or quantity discounts.

▶ **Lot-size inventory** A result of the quantity ordered or produced.

4. Transportation or Pipeline Inventory is in transit between the manufacturing plant and the distribution warehouse. These items are not available for satisfying customer demand until they reach the distribution warehouse, so the company needs to decide between using slower, inexpensive transportation or faster, more expensive transportation. To calculate the average amount of inventory in transit, we use the formula

▶ **Transportation inventory** Inventory in movement between locations.

$$ATI = \frac{tD}{365}$$

where ATI = average transportation inventory (in units)
t = transit time (in days)
D = annual demand (in units)

■ Example 12.1 Calculating Average Transportation Inventory

Suppose the Nadan Company, a producer of brass sculptures, needs to ship finished goods from its manufacturing facility to its distribution warehouse. Annual demand at Nadan is 1460 units. The company has a choice of sending the finished goods regular parcel service (three days transit time) or via public carrier, which takes eight days transit time. Calculate the average annual transportation inventory for each of the alternatives. Note that the average transportation inventory does not consider shipment quantity but only transit time and annual demand. To reduce transit inventory, you reduce transit time.

Solution:
When using the regular parcel service,

$$ATI = \frac{3 \times 1460}{365} = 12 \text{ units}$$

When using the public carrier,

$$ATI = \frac{8 \times 1460}{365} = 32 \text{ units}$$

▶ **Speculative inventory**
Used to protect against some future event.

5. Speculative or Hedge Inventory is a buildup to protect against some future event such as a strike at your supplier, a price increase, or the scarcity of a product that may or may not happen. A company typically does this to ensure a continuous supply of necessary items. Think about booking an airline flight three months in advance so you can take advantage of a reduced fare. You assume that the airfare will not be reduced further and that you will still need the ticket three months from now. It is a gamble.

6. Maintenance, Repair, and Operating (MRO) Inventory includes maintenance supplies, spare parts, lubricants, cleaning compounds, and daily operating supplies such as pens, pencils, and note pads. These items support general operations and maintenance but are not part of the product the company builds.

Inventory plays multiple roles in a company's operations. For this reason, companies develop inventory management objectives and performance measures to evaluate how well they are handling their inventory investment. The six functions of inventory are summarized in Table 12.1.

Table 12-1 Functions of Inventory

Anticipation inventory	Items built in anticipation of future demand. Allows company to maintain a level production strategy.
Fluctuation inventory	Protects against unexpected demand variations. Assures customer service levels.
Lot-size inventory	Results from the actual quantity purchased. Allows for lower unit costs.
Transportation inventory	Items in movement between locations. Moves inventory from manufacturer to distribution facilities.
Speculative inventory	Extra inventory built up or purchased to protect against some future event. Allows for continuous supply.
MRO	Includes maintenance supplies, spare parts, lubricants, cleaning agents, and daily operating supplies. Facilitates day-to-day operations.

OBJECTIVES OF INVENTORY MANAGEMENT ■

The objectives of inventory management are to provide the desired level of customer service, to allow cost-efficient operations, and to minimize the inventory investment.

Customer Service

What is customer service? **Customer service** is a company's ability to satisfy the needs of its customers. When we talk about customer service in inventory management, we mean whether or not a product is available for the customer when the customer wants it. In this sense, customer service measures the effectiveness of the company's inventory management. Customers can be either external or internal: any entity in the supply chain is considered a customer.

Suppose your company, Kayaks!Incorporated, offers a line of kayaks and kayaking equipment through catalog sales and an accompanying Web site. As product manager, you need to know whether the inventory management system you introduced is effective. One way to measure its effectiveness would be to measure the level of customer service: are customers getting the kayaking equipment they request and are their orders shipped on time? To answer your questions, you can measure the percentage of orders shipped on schedule, the percentage of line items shipped on schedule, the percentage of dollar volume shipped on schedule, or manufacturing idle time due to inventory shortages.

Percentage of Orders Shipped on Schedule is a good measure for finished goods customer service, such as your kayaking equipment company, if all orders and customers have similar value and late deliveries are not excessively late. For a different kind of company, such as one that designs computer networks, some customers have much greater value. Obviously, this method does not adequately capture the value of those customers' orders.

For example, if the book publishing company John Wiley & Sons, Inc. represents 50% of your demand but is only 1 out of 20 orders on the schedule, delivering late to Wiley is certainly more harmful to your company than shipping a smaller order late. With this measure, however, all late orders are treated equally. If you have only one late shipment, the customer service level is 95% (19 of 20 shipped on schedule). But if the late order is to Wiley, you have met only 50% of your demand.

Percentage of Line Items Shipped on Schedule recognizes that not all orders are equal but fails to take into account dollar value of orders. This measure needs more information—the number of line items instead of the number of orders—than the previous measure. Therefore, this measure is more expensive to use and is most appropriate for finished goods inventory.

As an example of the percentage of line items shipped on schedule consider the following. Your sister company, White Water Rafts Inc., determines that from the 20 orders scheduled for delivery this month, customers requested 250 different line items. White Water can ship 225 of these line items on schedule. Their customer service level is 90% (225 items shipped on time divided by 250 line items requested).

Percentage of Dollar Volume Shipped on Schedule recognizes the differences in orders in terms of both line items and dollar value. Instead of measuring line items to determine the customer service level, a company totals the value of the orders. For

▶ **Customer service**
The ability to satisfy customer requirements.

Good inventory management results in satisfied customers.

▶ **Percentage of orders shipped on schedule**
A customer service measure appropriate for use when orders have similar value.

▶ **Percentage of line items shipped on schedule**
A customer service measure appropriate when customer orders vary in number of line items ordered.

▶ **Percentage of dollar volume shipped on schedule**
A customer service measure appropriate when customer orders vary in value.

Customer service of Palm-Pilots™ can be measured as a percentage of dollar volume shipped on schedule.

▶ **Setup cost**
Costs such as scrap costs, calibration costs, and down-time costs associated with preparing the equipment for the next product being produced.

example, if the 20 orders in the PalmPilot™ handheld-computer manufacturing company had a total value of $400,000 and the company shipped on schedule handheld computers valued at $380,000, the customer service level is 95% ($380,000 shipped, divided by $400,000 ordered).

Idle Time Due to Material and Component Shortages applies to internal customer service. This is an absolute measure of the manufacturing or service time lost because material or parts are not available to the workforce. Absolute measures make sense when a company has historical data to use in comparisons. For example, Kayaks!Incorporated's supplier historically has lost no more than two manufacturing days per year because of material and component shortages. This year, however, it has lost four manufacturing days for this reason. Obviously, this year's case is worse and needs management's attention.

These are only a few of the measures companies use to evaluate customer service. The desired level of customer service should be consistent with the company's overall strategy. If customer service is your company's competitive advantage, the company must achieve a very high level of customer service. Even when customer service isn't the primary focus, your company must still maintain an acceptable level of customer service.

Now let's look at how inventory helps manufacturers operate efficiently.

Cost-Efficient Operations

Companies can achieve **cost-efficient operations** by using inventory in the following ways. First, companies use work-in-process (WIP) inventory as buffer stocks between operations. Suppose one of Hewlett-Packard (HP) printed circuit board (PCB) manufacturing facilities runs two or more operations in a sequence at different rates of output. In this case, buffer inventories build up between the workstations to ensure that each of the operations runs efficiently. For example, PCBs flow from Ken's workstation (tasks take 120 seconds) to Barbara's workstation (tasks take only 90 seconds). If there are no PCBs between the two workstations, Barbara will be idle for 30 seconds out of every 120 seconds because she finishes her tasks 30 seconds before Ken finishes his. If the floor supervisor, Maria, ensures that there is buffer stock between the workstations, Barbara's idle time will be eliminated so she can produce more PCBs.

Second, inventories allow manufacturing organizations to maintain a level workforce throughout the year despite seasonal demand for production. (Level production plans are discussed in Chapter 13.) A company can do this by building inventory in advance of seasonal demands. This in turn allows the company to maintain a level workforce throughout the year and to reduce the costs of overtime, hiring and firing, training, subcontracting, and additional capacity.

Third, by building inventory in long production runs, the **setup cost** is spread over a larger number of units, decreasing the per unit setup cost. Setup costs include the cost of scrap (wasted material and labor), calibration, and downtime to prepare the equipment and materials for the next product to be manufactured. Longer runs mean that the equipment does not need as many setups so less machine time is lost preparing for production.

Fourth, a company that is willing to acquire inventory can buy in larger quantities at a discount. These larger purchases decrease the ordering cost per unit. For example, the Rustic Garden Furniture Company needs 50,000 pieces of wrought iron annually. Rustic's supplier has offered them a unit price of $1.10 if Rustic buys the wrought iron in orders of 10,000 or more pieces at a time. If Rustic chooses to buy in smaller quantities, the unit price is $1.29. Now let's look at ways to measure inventory investment.

Minimum Inventory Investment

A company can measure its **minimum inventory investment** by its **inventory turnover**—that is, by the level of customer demand satisfied by the supply on hand. We calculate the inventory turnover measure as

▶ **Inventory turnover**
A measure of inventory policy effectiveness.

$$\text{Inventory turnover} = \frac{\text{annual cost of goods sold}}{\text{average inventory in dollars}}$$

■ **Example 12.2 Calculating Inventory Turnover**

If the annual cost of goods sold at the Nadan Company is $5,200,000 and the average inventory in dollars is $1,040,000, what is the inventory turnover?

Solution:

$$\text{Inventory turnover} = \frac{\$5,200,000}{\$1,040,000} = 5 \text{ inventory turns}$$

The ratio at the Nadan Company should be compared to the inventory turnover achieved by other companies within the industry. Although there is no magic number for inventory turnover, the higher the number, the more effectively the company is using its inventory. One measure of the level of demand that can be satisfied by on-hand inventory is **weeks of supply**. Weeks of supply is calculated by dividing the average on-hand inventory by the average weekly demand.

▶ **Weeks of supply**
A measure of inventory policy effectiveness.

$$\text{Weeks of supply} = \frac{\text{average inventory on hand in dollars}}{\text{average weekly usage in dollars}}$$

■ **Example 12.3 Calculating Weeks of Supply**

Suppose that the Nadan Company wants to calculate its weeks of supply. From the previous example, we know that annual cost of goods sold is $5,200,000.

Solution:

To determine the weekly cost of goods sold, we divide the annual cost of goods sold by 52 weeks ($5,200,000/52 = $100,000). Given that Nadan maintains an average inventory of $1,040,000, we calculate the weeks of supply as follows:

$$\text{Weeks of supply} = \frac{\$1,040,000}{\$100,000} = 10.4 \text{ weeks of supply}$$

Note that there is a relationship between inventory turnover and weeks of supply. If you divide total weeks per year (52) by the weeks of supply (10.4), you see that the answer is the same as when you calculated inventory turnover. If you divide total number of weeks (52) by the inventory turnover rate (5), the answer is 10.4 weeks of supply. In some companies, inventory performance is measured in either days or hours of supply. To calculate days of supply, we use the formula

$$\text{Days of supply} = \frac{\text{average inventory on hand in dollars}}{\text{average daily use in dollars}}$$

and hours of supply is calculated as

$$\text{Hours of supply} = \frac{\text{average inventory on hand in dollars}}{\text{average hourly usage in dollars}}$$

Let's look at an example using both of these measures.

■ Example 12.4 Calculating Inventory Supply at the Jenny Company

Suppose that the Jenny Company, a specialty gift organization, wants to calculate its days of supply. The annual cost of goods sold is $1,300,000, the average inventory is $15,600, and the company operates 250 days per year.

Solution:
First, we calculate the average daily usage. We divide the annual cost of goods sold by the number of days the company operates ($1,300,000 divided by 250 days equals $5200). Second, using the formula, we divide the average inventory on hand by the average daily usage.

$$\text{Days of supply} = \frac{\$15,600}{\$5,200} = 3 \text{ days of supply}$$

Suppose the Jenny Company uses a new process that reduces the average inventory held to $3250. To calculate their current hours of supply, we first calculate the average hourly usage. Using the data provided above and assuming an eight-hour day, we divide the average daily usage ($5200) by eight hours. The average hourly usage is $650. Therefore, the hours of supply are

$$\text{Hours of supply} = \frac{\$3250}{\$650} = 5 \text{ hours of supply}$$

Table 12-2 summarizes the inventory objectives we just discussed.

Table 12-2 Inventory Objectives

Inventory Objectives	
Customer service	Measured by any of the following: ◆ Percentage of orders shipped on schedule ◆ Percentage of line items shipped on schedule ◆ Percentage of dollar volume shipped on schedule ◆ Idle time due to component and material shortages
Cost-efficient operations	Inventories help achieve cost effective operations by ◆ Using buffer stock to assure smooth production flow ◆ Maintaining a level workforce ◆ Allowing longer production runs, which spread the cost of setups ◆ Taking advantage of quantity discounts
Minimum inventory investment	Measured by any of the following: ◆ Inventory turnover ◆ Weeks of supply ◆ Days of supply

RELEVANT INVENTORY COSTS ■

Inventory management policies have cost implications. Decisions about how much inventory to hold affect item costs, holding costs, ordering costs, and stockout (shortage) costs.

Item Costs

The **item costs** of a purchased item include the price paid for the item and any other direct costs for getting the item to the plant such as inbound transportation, insurance, duty, or taxes. For an item built by the manufacturing company, the item costs include direct labor, direct materials, and factory overhead.

▶ **Item cost of a purchased item**
Includes price paid for the item plus other direct costs associated with the purchase.

Holding Costs

Holding costs include the variable expenses incurred by the firm for the volume of inventory held. As inventory increases, so do the holding costs. We can determine unit holding costs by examining three cost components: capital costs, storage costs, and risk costs. Annual holding costs are typically stated in either dollars per unit ($3.50 per unit per year) or as a percentage of the item value (25% of the unit value).

▶ **Holding costs**
Include the variable expenses incurred by the plant related to the volume of inventory held.

Capital costs are the higher of either the cost of the capital or the opportunity cost for the company. The cost of the capital is the interest rate the company pays to borrow money to invest in inventory. The opportunity cost is the rate of return the company could have earned on the money if it were used for something other than investing in inventory. The opportunity cost is at least as much as the interest the company could get at the prevailing interest rate. It may be higher if more lucrative opportunities are available. Suppose you have a startup company and need to finance your inventory with a bank loan at 8%. Or the company can invest their capital in the stock market and generate a 20% return on the investment. For its capital cost, the company would use the 20% opportunity cost rather than the 8% cost of the loan. The capital cost is typically expressed as an annual interest rate.

▶ **Capital cost**
The higher of the cost of capital or the opportunity cost for the company.

Storage costs usually include the cost of space, workers, and equipment. For our purposes, however, we are concerned only with the additional out-of-pocket expenses resulting from the size of the inventory. For example, we include the cost of storage space if it is public warehousing and varies based on the amount of inventory held. If the company already owns the storage space and incurs no additional expense for storing the inventory, we do not include it in the holding cost. The same is true for employees. If an employee works overtime because of the level of inventory, this is an out-of-pocket expense and needs to be included. However, if the employee's workload is merely higher during the normal day, the cost of the employee is not included.

▶ **Storage costs**
Include the variable expenses for space, workers, and equipment related to the volume of inventory held.

Risk costs include obsolescence, damage or deterioration, theft, insurance, and taxes. These costs vary based on industry. Companies operating in a high tech environment typically experience much greater obsolescence and theft. Companies that manufacture consumer products may find higher levels of theft.

In general, risk costs are associated with higher levels of inventory. The more inventory you have, the longer it lasts—therefore, the greater the chance of it becoming obsolete. The more inventory you have sitting around, the more likely it is to be damaged. Think of walking through an overloaded basement: you bump into something, it falls and breaks. Theft also typically increases as inventory increases. When a company has few items in inventory, it is more noticeable when an item disappears. However, if the company has a lot of inventory, it is harder to notice when only one item disappears. Insurance costs are typically based on the value of the inventory, so larger

▶ **Risk costs**
Include obsolescence, damage or deterioration, theft, insurance, and taxes associated with the volume of inventory held.

inventories have higher insurance premiums. The same is true for taxes: the more valuable the inventory, the higher the tax.

Although many textbooks use an annual holding cost of between 20% and 30%, in real life it depends on the type of business. The risk costs can vary significantly. Let's look at how annual holding costs are calculated.

■ Example 12.5 Calculating Annual Holding Cost Rate

The Nadan Company currently maintains an average inventory of $1,040,000. The company estimates its capital cost at 12%, its storage costs at 5%, and its risk costs at 8%. Calculate the annual holding costs for the Nadan Company.

Solution:
Annual holding cost per unit of inventory = 25%   (Capital cost + storage costs + risk costs)

Annual cost of holding inventory = $1,040,000 $\times$ 0.25 = $260,000

Ordering Costs

▶ **Ordering costs**
The fixed costs associated with either placing an order with a supplier or setup costs incurred for in-house production.

Ordering costs are fixed costs for either placing an order with a supplier for a purchased component or raw material, or for placing an order to the manufacturing organization for a product built in-house. When you buy an item, the ordering costs include the cost of the clerical work to prepare, release, monitor, and receive orders, and the physical handling of the goods. The ordering costs are considered constant regardless of the number of items or the quantities ordered. For example, if the cost to place an order is estimated at $100, every time you place an order with a supplier, the ordering cost is constant ($100).

When an order is released for manufacturing in-house, the ordering or setup costs are the clerical work to prepare the manufacturing order and the list of materials to be picked and delivered to the manufacturing location, plus the cost to prepare the equipment for the job (calibration, appropriate jigs and fixtures, etc.). Like the ordering costs for purchased items, the ordering or setup costs for jobs done in-house are constant.

Shortage Costs

▶ **Shortage costs**
Incurred when demand exceeds supply.

▶ **Back ordering**
Delaying delivery to the customer until the item becomes available.

▶ **Lost sale**
Occurs when the customer is not willing to wait for delivery.

CROSS FUNCTIONAL

Companies incur **shortage costs** when customer demand exceeds the available inventory for an item. Suppose a customer, Tom Martin, places an order through your kayaking equipment Web site for a high-end kayak, but that kayak is out of stock. One of two things happens. Either Tom allows you to **back order** the kayak—that is, Tom is willing to wait until the kayak is available—or Tom decides to buy the kayak from another company and the result for your company is a **lost sale.**

In both cases, your company incurs shortage costs. In the case of the back order, shortage costs result from the additional paperwork to track the order and the possible added expense of overnight shipping rather than normal delivery. There is also the lost customer goodwill, an intangible cost. Although Tom accepted the delay this time, you have no guarantee that he will buy from your company again. In the case of the lost sale, the shortage costs typically include loss of the possible profit, plus loss of the contribution to overhead costs. Your company also faces the risk that Tom will not return with future orders.

Shortage costs can also result from internal parts shortages, including the cost of downtime due to lack of materials, additional setups, premium transportation costs, and so forth.

Before You Go On

Before you continue further into the chapter, you need to be sure that you understand the relevant inventory costs. Item cost, holding cost, ordering cost, and shortage cost are summarized in Table 12-3. The next section of this chapter focuses on determining order quantities and uses inventory cost information.

Table 12-3 Relevant Inventory Costs

Item cost	Price paid per item plus any other direct costs associated with getting the item to the plant
Holding costs	Capital, storage, and risk costs
Ordering cost	Fixed, constant dollar amount incurred for each order placed
Shortage costs	Loss of customer goodwill, back order handling, and lost sales

DETERMINING ORDER QUANTITIES ■

The objectives of inventory management are to provide the desired level of customer service, enable cost-efficient operations, and minimize the inventory investment. To achieve these objectives, a company must first determine how much of an item to order at a time.

Inventory management and control are done at the level of the individual item or **stock-keeping unit (SKU)**. An SKU is a specific item at a particular geographic location. For example, a pair of jeans, size 32 × 32, in inventory at the plant and eight different warehouses, represents nine different SKUs. A pair of the same jeans held at the same locations but a different size (32 × 34) represents nine additional SKUs. The same style jeans in a different color represents additional SKUs.

▶ **Stock-keeping unit (SKU)**
An item in a particular geographic location.

Let's look at how a company determines how much of an SKU to order. We will consider some common approaches in this section, summarized in Table 12-4. In the next section, we will look at mathematical models for determining order quantity.

Table 12-4 Common Ordering Approaches

Lot-for-lot	Order exactly what is needed.
Fixed-order-quantity	Order a predetermined amount each time an order is placed.
Min-max system	When on-hand inventory falls below a predetermined minimum level, order a quantity that will take the inventory back up to its predetermined maximum level.
Order *n* periods	Order enough to satisfy demand for the next *n* periods.
Periodic review system	Review the quantity on hand at specified fixed-intervals, order up to the target inventory (*TI*) level.

▶ **Lot-for-lot**
The company orders exactly what is needed.

Lot-for-lot is ordering exactly what you need. You adjust the ordering quantity to your ordering needs, which ensures that you will not have leftover inventory. You use lot-for-lot when demand is not constant and you have information about expected needs. Ordering sandwiches for a business lunch meeting is a good example of when to use lot-for-lot. The number of persons attending the meeting can vary based on the meeting topic. Since sandwiches are perishable, you do not want to have leftover inventory. This system is also commonly used in material requirements planning systems, which we discuss in Chapter 15.

▶ **Fixed-order quantity**
Specifies the number of units to order whenever an order is placed.

Fixed-order quantity specifies the number of units to order each time you place an order for a certain SKU or item. The quantity may be arbitrary (perhaps 100 units at a time) or it may be the result of how the item is packaged or prepared (such as 144 per box or a loaf of bread). The advantage of this system is that it is easily understood; the disadvantage is that it does not minimize inventory costs.

▶ **Min-max system**
Places a replenishment order when the on-hand inventory falls below the predetermined minimum level. An order is placed to bring the inventory back up to the maximum inventory level.

The **min-max** system is to place an order when the on-hand inventory falls below a predetermined minimum level. The quantity ordered is the difference between the quantity available and the predetermined maximum inventory level. For example, if the minimum is set at 50 units, the maximum is set at 250 units, and the quantity available at the time of the order is 40 units, the order quantity is 210 units (250 − 40). With this system, both the time between orders and the quantity ordered can vary.

▶ **Order n periods**
The order quantity is determined by total demand for the item for the next *n* periods.

Order *n* periods means that you determine the order quantity by summing your company's requirements for the next *n* periods. Suppose you have to order enough each time you place an order to satisfy your company's requirements for the next three periods. If these requirements for the next three weeks are 60, 45, and 100, your order is for 205 units. A concern with this system is determining the number of periods to include in the order.

▶ **Periodic review system**
Requires periodic reviews of the on-hand quantity to determine the size of the replenishment order.

With the **periodic review** system, you determine the quantity of an item your company has on hand at specified, fixed-time intervals (such as every Friday or the last day of the month). You place an order (*Q*) for an amount equal to the **target inventory level (TI)**, minus the quantity on hand (*OH*), similar to the min-max system. The difference is that with the periodic review system, the time between orders is constant (such as every hour, every day, every week, or every month) with varying quantities ordered. The min-max system, however, varies both the time between orders and the quantities ordered.

▶ **Target inventory level**
Used in determining order quantity in the periodic review system. Target inventory less on-hand inventory equals order quantity.

An advantage of the periodic review system is that inventory is counted only at specific time intervals. You do not need to monitor the inventory level between review periods. This system also works well when you order several items from the same sup-

SKU's at a retail store

plier. If your company uses 10 different items from that supplier, you can place one order for all 10 items rather than 10 orders, 1 for each item.

The periodic review system implies a larger average inventory. When using this system, your company must carry enough inventory to protect against stockout for the replenishment lead time, plus the review period. Let's look at an example of how you determine order quantity using the periodic review system.

First, you calculate a target inventory level for the item. Calculate the target inventory as the quantity demanded during lead time, plus the average demand during the review period, plus any safety stock. The review period is given in days as the time between reviewing your inventory.

$$TI = d(RP + L) + SS$$

where TI = target inventory level (in units)
d = average daily demand (in units)
RP = review period (in days)
L = lead time (in days)
SS = safety stock (in units)

The second step is calculating the order quantity.

$$Q = TI - OH$$

where Q = order quantity
TI = target inventory
OH = on hand balance

■ Example 12.6 Target Inventory at Green's Grocery

Green's Grocery orders sour cream from a local dairy every two weeks (14 working days). Lead time is 2 days. Average demand for the sour cream is 140 sixteen-ounce containers per week (7 working days) and Green's wants to keep a safety stock equal to 3 days supply on hand. It is time to review the inventory and place an order. On-hand inventory is 100 containers. Determine the target inventory level and then determine the quantity Green's Grocers should order now.

Solution:
First step, calculate the target inventory level. Daily demand is 20 units (that is, 140 units per week, divided by 7 days). Therefore, the target inventory is

TI = 20 units per day (14 days review period + 2 days lead time) + (20 units ×
3 days)
= 380 units

The second step is to calculate the order quantity:

Q = 380 units − 100 units
= 280 units

MATHEMATICAL MODELS FOR DETERMINING ORDER QUANTITY ■

Now let's look at some mathematical models that determine order quantity and minimize inventory costs, beginning with the economic order quantity (EOQ) model.

Economic Order Quantity (EOQ)

▶ **Economic order quantity model (EOQ)**
An optimizing method used for determining order quantity and reorder points.

▶ **Continuous review systems**
Update inventory balances after each inventory transaction.

The **economic order quantity model (EOQ)** has been around since the early 1900s and remains useful for determining order quantities. EOQ is a **continuous review system,** used to keep track of the inventory on hand each time you make a withdrawal. If the withdrawal reduces the inventory level to the reorder point or below, you make a replenishment order.

Thus EOQ tells you when to place a replenishment order and determines the order quantity that minimizes annual inventory cost. Suppose you decide that your kayaking equipment company needs to place a replenishment order whenever the inventory level of item K310 reaches 100 units. Right now you have 105 units of item K310 in inventory. You withdraw 5 K310s to satisfy a customer order, resulting in an updated inventory level of 100 units. Since the inventory level has reached the reorder point, it is time to place a replenishment order for K310. A key characteristic of the continuous review system is that it keeps track of inventory as it is withdrawn.

In the following section, we look at some assumptions made by the basic EOQ model.

EOQ Assumptions

The basic EOQ model makes these assumptions:

▶ **Lead time**
The amount of time it takes from order placement until the item is received.

- Demand for the product is known and constant. This means that we know how much the demand is for every time period and that this amount never changes. For example, demand is 50 units per week every week or 10 units per day every day. This assumption is indicated by the straight line that shows the depletion of our inventory in Figure 12-2.
- **Lead time** is known and constant. Lead time is the amount of time it takes from order placement until it arrives at the manufacturing company (for example, 10 working days between order placement and receipt of merchandise).
- Because you know how long it takes for the replenishment order to arrive, you can determine when you need to place the order. By finding the reorder point (shown in Figure 12-2), you can schedule the arrival of the replenishment quantity just as your company's inventory level reaches zero. The minimum inventory level with the basic EOQ should be zero.
- Quantity discounts are not considered: the cost of all units is the same, regardless of the quantity ordered. (We discuss this in more detail later in the chapter.)
- Ordering and setup costs are fixed and constant: the dollar amount to place an order is always the same, regardless of the size of the order.
- Since the company knows demand with certainty, the assumption is that all demand is met. The basic model does not permit back orders but more advanced models are less rigid.
- The quantity ordered arrives at once, as shown in Figure 12-2. Since the order is scheduled to arrive just as the company runs out of inventory, the maximum inventory level equals the economic order quantity.

Figure 12-2 shows the basic workings of the EOQ model. The inventory replenishment process begins when the inventory reaches the reorder point. This is the point at which you place an order for Q units, which are timed to arrive just as your company's inventory level reaches zero. The inventory goes from zero to Q and then is depleted at a constant rate. Once the inventory reaches the reorder point, the process begins again.

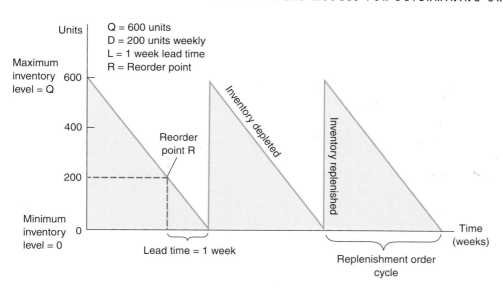

Figure 12-2

The EOQ Model

Since the basic model assumes certainty about demand and lead time, the re-order point is set equal to demand during lead time, or

$$R = dL$$

where R = reorder point
d = average daily demand
L = lead time in days

Problem-Solving Tip   When solving for R, it is possible to use other than daily demand and lead time in days. Use whatever is convenient. If lead time is given in weeks, then use average weekly demand. If lead time is given in months, then use average monthly demand.

For example, if average daily demand is 40 units and lead time is 5 days, then the re-order point is 200 (40 units times 5 days). When the inventory reaches 200, it is time to place an order.

Calculating Inventory Policy Costs   Since companies are interested in the costs associated with inventory policies, let's calculate the annual ordering or setup costs, and the annual holding costs associated with the basic EOQ model. We do not include shortage costs since all demand is satisfied with the basic EOQ model. We do not include the annual item cost either: no quantity discounts are considered in the basic EOQ model, so the annual item cost remains constant regardless of the quantity ordered each time. Given that, our total costs are

Total annual cost = annual ordering costs + annual holding costs

---

Problem-Solving Tip   When calculating total annual costs, do not round off the number of orders to whole numbers. Although it is true that a partial order cannot be placed, for purposes of comparison we leave the number of orders as a mixed number.

We calculate annual ordering costs by multiplying the number of orders placed per year by the cost to place an order. To find the number of orders placed per year, we divide the annual demand by the quantity ordered.

Suppose annual demand for motherboards at Palm Pilot hand-held computer company is 10,000 units and they currently order 500 motherboards each time. The number of orders placed per year is 20 (10,000/500). If the cost to place an order is $75, then the annual ordering cost is $1500 (20 orders × $75 ordering cost).

Problem-Solving Tip   When solving for Q, it is not necessary to always use annual demand and annual holding costs. If you have demand given in a different time frame (days, weeks, or months) you can use that as long as the holding costs are expressed in the same time frame— that is, daily demand and daily holding costs, or weekly demand and weekly holding costs.

We calculate annual holding costs by multiplying the average inventory level by the annual holding cost per unit. The average inventory is equal to the maximum inventory plus the minimum inventory divided by 2. In the EOQ model, the maximum inventory is Q and the minimum is zero. Therefore, the average inventory level is Q/2. For example, if the order quantity is 500 units, the holding cost is $6.00 per unit per year, the annual holding cost is $1500 (500 units/2 × $6.00 per unit). Sometimes the holding cost is given as a percentage, such as 20% of the item price. In this case, we multiply the item price by the percentage to determine the annual unit holding costs. For example, if the holding cost is 20% of the item price and the item price is $30, then the annual holding cost is $6 per unit ($30 item price × 20% holding cost).

The formula for calculating the total relevant annual costs for the basic EOQ model is

$$TC = \left(\frac{D}{Q}S\right) + \left(\frac{Q}{2}H\right)$$

where TC = total annual cost
D = annual demand
Q = quantity to be ordered
H = annual holding cost
S = ordering or setup cost

For our example, the total cost is

$$TC = \left(\frac{10,000}{500}\,\$75\right) + \left(\frac{500}{2}\,\$6\right)$$

or

$$TC = \$1500 + \$1500 = \$3000$$

Figure 12-3

Holding costs equal ordering costs

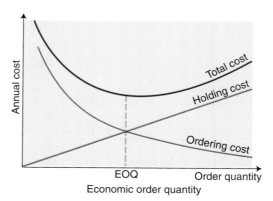

Economic order quantity

Note that the annual ordering costs equal the annual holding costs. This is true when we use the EOQ model without rounding. In addition, with the EOQ model, the minimum total cost always results when the annual ordering costs equal the annual holding costs, as shown in Figure 12-3. Note, too, in Figure 12-3 that as order quantity increases so do holding costs, and that at the same time, ordering costs decrease since fewer orders are placed. The total costs, however, are always higher when we use an order quantity other than the EOQ.

Calculating the EOQ

We calculate the economic order quantity (Q) using the following formula:

$$Q = \sqrt{\frac{2DS}{H}}$$

where Q = optimal order quantity
D = annual demand
S = ordering or setup cost
H = holding cost

■ Example 12.7 Calculating the Economic Order Quantity

Find the economic order quantity and the reorder point, given the following information:
Annual demand (D) = 10,000 units
Ordering cost (S) = $75 per order
Annual holding cost (H) = $6 per unit
Lead time (L) = 5 days
The company operates 250 days per year.

Solution:

$$Q = \sqrt{\frac{2 \times 10,000 \times \$75}{\$6}} = 500 \text{ units}$$

Daily demand is 40 units per day (10,000 units demanded annually, divided by 250 days of operation).

$$R = 40 \text{ units} \times 5 \text{ days} = 200 \text{ units}$$

The inventory policy for this item is to place a replenishment order for 500 units (Q) when the inventory reaches 200 units (R). The replenishment order will arrive just as the current inventory reaches zero. On the previous page, we calculated total annual cost for this policy ($3000). *The EOQ model always minimizes total annual costs.*

What Happens When a Non-EOQ Order Quantity is Used? To illustrate what happens to annual inventory costs when we use an order quantity other than the EOQ, let's look at an example with a non-EOQ quantity. Determine the total annual costs for your company if you choose to order 1000 units each time a replenishment order is placed.

$$TC = \left(\frac{10,000}{1000} \$75\right) + \left(\frac{1000}{2} \$6\right) = \$3750$$

The total annual cost for this non-EOQ inventory policy is $3750 compared to $3000 for the EOQ policy. Thus we can say that the *difference* between the EOQ policy and any other policy is a penalty cost incurred by your company for *not* using the EOQ policy.

Economic Production Quantity (EPQ)

▶ **Economic production quantity (EPQ)**
A model that allows for incremental product delivery.

The basic EOQ model assumes that the entire replenishment order arrives at one time, but this is not always the case. For example, if we bake 4 batches each of 1-dozen chocolate-chip cookies, our inventory will probably never reach 4-dozen cookies. Why? Because we or our friends are sure to eat some of the cookies as soon as we bake them! This means that the maximum inventory level will always be less than the total quantity we produce. If out of every batch of 1-dozen cookies, we eat 4 cookies immediately, we will end up with 32 cookies in inventory after baking the four 1-dozen batches ((12 baked − 4 used) × 4 batches).

Figure 12-4 shows the **economic production quantity (EPQ)** model. The cycle begins when we begin making the product. Each day, we use some of what we make to satisfy immediate demand; we put the remainder in inventory. We make the product until we have completed Q units. At that point, the inventory has reached its maximum level. From this point on, we satisfy demand from the on-hand inventory, depleting it daily. When we reach the reorder point, we order another batch. Our company starts producing the new batch just as we run out of the current inventory.

The EPQ model is appropriate when some of the product we make is used as soon as we make it. In manufacturing, this is typical when a single manufacturing facility produces the parts to build the end product. For example, HP builds deskjet printers using printed circuit boards (PCBs). HP's manufacturing facility builds PCBs in batches; some of these PCBs are assembled into the end product immediately, and the rest are put into inventory.

The total cost formula for the EPQ model is

$$TC = \left(\frac{D}{Q}S\right) + \left(\frac{I_{MAX}}{2}H\right)$$

Figure 12-4

The EPQ Model

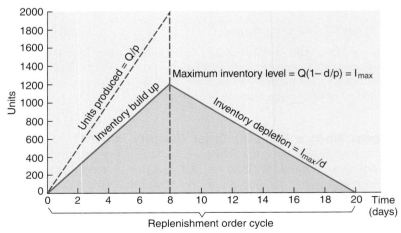

Order quantity 2000 units
Daily demand (d) = 100 units
Daily production (p) = 250 units

where TC = total annual cost
D = annual demand
Q = quantity to be ordered
H = annual holding cost
S = ordering or setup cost

$$I_{MAX} = Q\left(1 - \frac{d}{p}\right)$$

where d = average daily demand rate
p = daily production rate

■ Example 12.8 Calculating the Maximum Inventory Level

If HP uses 6 PCBs per day, can produce 20 PCBs, and produces PCBs in batches of 200 units, determine the maximum inventory buildup.

Solution:

$$I_{MAX} = 200\left(1 - \frac{6}{20}\right) = 140 \text{ units}$$

The production rate must always be greater than the demand rate. Otherwise, a company could never produce enough to satisfy demand and no inventory would be generated. Using the chocolate-chip cookie scenario as an example: it is impossible to eat more than 12 cookies after the batch is baked, because no matter how much we *want* to eat more than 12, we must wait for the next batch to be completed.

Although the formula identifies d as daily demand and p as daily production, we can use other time frames for these variables. We can use hourly demand and hourly production, weekly demand and weekly production, monthly demand and monthly production, quarterly demand and quarterly production, or even annual demand and annual production. The important thing to remember is that the time frame must be the same for both demand and production. That way, the ratio always remains the same.

Making cookies!

■ Example 12.9 Calculating Ratios

Calculate the ratio of d/p using daily, weekly, and annual demand. Annual demand is 10,000 units and annual production is 25,000 units. The company operates 50 weeks per year, 5 days per week.

Solution:
When using daily figures,

Average daily demand: d = 10,000 units/250 days = 40 units per day
Daily production: p = 25,000 units/250 = 100 units per day
Therefore, the ratio d/p = 40/100 or 0.4.

When using weekly figures,

Average weekly demand: $d = $ 10,000 units/50 weeks $= $ 200 units per week
Weekly production: $p = $ 25,000 units/50 weeks $= $ 500 units per week
Therefore, the ratio $d/p = $ 200/500 or 0.4.

When using annual figures,

Average annual demand: $d = $ 10,000 units
Annual production: $p = $ 25,000 units
Therefore, the ratio $d/p = $ 10,000/25,000 or 0.40.

Calculating EPQ The formula to calculate the economic production quantity is

$$Q = \sqrt{\frac{2DS}{H\left(1 - \dfrac{d}{p}\right)}}$$

where $D = $ annual demand in units
$S = $ setup or ordering cost
$H = $ annual holding costs per unit
$d = $ average daily demand rate
$p = $ daily production rate

■ **Example 12.10 Calculating EPQ at Ashlee's Beach Chairs**

Ashlee's Beach Chairs company produces upscale beach chairs. Annual demand for the chairs is estimated at 18,000 units. The frames are made in batches before the final assembly process. Ashlee's final assembly department needs frames at a rate of 1500 per month. Ashlee's frame department can produce 2500 frames per month. The setup cost is $800, and the annual holding cost is $18 per unit. The company operates 20 days per month. Lead time is 5 days. Determine the optimal order quantity, the total annual costs, and the reorder point.

Solution:
To determine the total cost, you must calculate the maximum inventory level. To do this you must first calculate the economic production quantity

$$Q = \sqrt{\frac{2 \times 18,000 \times \$800}{\$18\left(1 - \dfrac{1500}{2500}\right)}} = 2000 \text{ units}$$

Therefore, I_{MAX} is

$$I_{MAX} = 2000\left(1 - \frac{1500}{2500}\right) = 800 \text{ units}$$

and the total annual cost is

$$TC = \left(\frac{18,000}{2000}\$800\right) + \left(\frac{800}{2}\$18\right) = \$14,400$$

Note that the ordering cost equals the annual holding cost. The reorder point is calculated as $R = 75$ units $\times$ 5 days $= 375$ units. Therefore, the inventory policy is to order a quantity of 2000 frames when the inventory reaches 375 units. The total annual cost (excluding item cost) associated with this policy is $14,400.

Compare this policy against Ashlee's current inventory policy of producing in quantities of 1500 units. First, determine the maximum inventory level.

$$I_{MAX} = 1500\left(1 - \frac{1500}{2500}\right) = 600 \text{ units}$$

Therefore, total cost is

$$TC = \left(\frac{18,000}{1500}\$800\right) + \left(\frac{600}{2}\$18\right) = \$15,000$$

The extra cost or penalty cost associated with Ashlee's current policy is $600 ($15,000 − $14,400).

When you use the EOQ and/or the EPQ model, you need to know when the inventory level reaches the reorder point. A **perpetual inventory record** provides an up-to-date inventory balance by recording all inventory transactions—items received into inventory or items disbursed from inventory—as they happen.

An alternative to using perpetual inventory records is the **two-bin system**. In a two-bin system, a quantity equal to demand during replenishment time is held back, often in a second bin. When stock available is depleted, the held-back quantity is made available for use and a replenishment order is placed. Deciding on the right quantity replenishment order is complicated when quantity discounts are available. Let's extend the basic EOQ model to consider quantity discounts.

▶ **Perpetual inventory record**
Provides an up-to-date inventory balance.

▶ **Two-bin system**
Splits replenishment orders into two-bins, placing one bin in reserve. When the initial bin is empty, the contents of the second bin are used and a replenishment order is placed.

Quantity Discount Model

The basic EOQ model assumes that no quantity discounts are available. In real life, however, **quantity discounts** are often available, so we need to modify the basic model for these situations. Quantity discounts are price incentives to encourage your company to buy in larger quantities. For example, a supplier charges your company $7.50 per pound if your company's order is less than 500 pounds. If your order is for 500 to 999 pounds, the price per pound is $6.90. On orders of 1000 pounds or more, the supplier charges $6.20 per pound.

Whenever the price per unit is not fixed but varies based on the size of your order, the total annual cost formula for any inventory policy used must include the cost of material, as shown next.

▶ **Quantity discounts model**
Modifies the EOQ process to consider cases where quantity discounts are available.

CROSS FUNCTIONAL

$$TC = \left(\frac{D}{Q}S\right) + \left(\frac{Q}{2}H\right) + PD$$

where $D =$ annual demand in units
$Q =$ order quantity in units
$S =$ ordering or setup cost
$H =$ annual holding cost
$P =$ unit price

■ **Example 12.11 Annual Total Costs at Jeannette's Steak House**

Jeannette's Steak House currently orders 200 pounds of single-portion filet mignons at a time (a two-week supply). The annual demand for the filets is 5200 pounds. The ordering cost is estimated at $50. The annual holding cost is 30% of the unit price. Jeannette pays $7.50 per pound for the steaks. Therefore, the annual holding cost rate is $2.25, that is ($7.50 × 0.30). What are the annual total costs?

Solution:

$$TC = \left(\frac{5200}{200}\$50\right) + \left(\frac{200}{2}\$2.25\right) + (\$7.50 \times 5200) = \$40,525$$

Jeannette's supplier has offered the following price incentives. If Jeannette places an order for 500 or more pounds, the cost per pound is $6.90. For orders above 1000 pounds, the supplier will charge Jeannette $6.20 per pound. For orders of less than 500 pounds, Jeannette would continue to pay $7.50 per pound. Now there are three different prices possible based on the size of the order. Let's look at how Jeannette can determine the best policy for her.

The Quantity Discount Procedure The first step is to calculate the order quantity using the basic EOQ model and the cheapest price available. In our example, Jeannette's cheapest price is $6.20 per pound. Therefore, the annual holding cost is $1.86 (that is, $6.20 × 0.30) and the EOQ is

$$Q = \sqrt{\frac{2 \times 5200 \times \$50}{\$1.86}} = 528.74 \text{ pounds}$$

Now determine whether the order quantity is feasible. If Jeannette orders this quantity, will she be charged the price used to calculate the EOQ? If Jeannette orders 528.74 pounds, the supplier will charge her $6.90 per pound rather than the $6.20 she used in calculating the order quantity. Therefore, this is an infeasible quantity. If it were feasible, we would be done calculating Jeannette's optimal inventory policy. Since the order quantity is infeasible, we calculate the order quantity using the next higher price $6.90 per pound.

$$Q = \sqrt{\frac{2 \times 5200 \times \$50}{\$2.07}} = 501.20 \text{ pounds}$$

If Jeannette orders 501 pounds, the supplier charges her $6.90 per pound, which is the same as the price we used in calculating the order quantity. Therefore, this is a feasible order quantity. Once Jeannette finds the feasible quantity, she calculates the total annual costs for this order quantity.

$$TC = \left(\frac{5200}{501}\$50\right) + \left(\frac{501}{2}\$2.07\right) + (\$6.90 \times 5200) = \$36,917.50$$

Jeannette compares the total annual cost of this feasible order quantity with the total annual cost of the minimum order quantities necessary to qualify for any prices lower than the price at which she found the feasible solution. For example, to qualify for a price of $6.20 per pound, Jeannette must order a minimum of 1000 pounds at a time.

Table 12-5 Quantity Discount Procedure

1. Calculate the order quantity using the basic EOQ model and the cheapest price possible.

2. Determine whether the order quantity is feasible. That is, if we order this quantity will the supplier charge us the price we used to determine our order quantity? If this is a feasible order quantity, you are done. Otherwise, go to Step 3.

3. If the EOQ quantity found in step 1 was infeasible, calculate the EOQ for the next higher price.

4. Check again to determine if this quantity is feasible. If it is not feasible, repeat Step 3. If it is feasible move on to Step 5.

5. Calculate the total annual costs associated with your feasible order quantity. You must include ordering, holding, and material costs.

6. Calculate the total annual costs associated with buying the minimum quantity required to qualify for any prices that are lower than the price at which the feasible solution was found.

7. Compare the total annual costs of buying these minimum quantities to receive the cheaper price against the cost of the feasible Q.

8. Recommend whichever order policy has the lowest total annual cost.

The total annual cost of ordering 1000 pounds at a time is

$$TC = \left(\frac{5200}{1000}\$50\right) + \left(\frac{1000}{2}\$1.86\right) + (\$6.20 \times 5200) = \$33,430.00$$

In this case, Jeannette's annual cost is less if she orders 1000 pounds at a time rather than the EOQ quantity of 501 pounds at a time. The optimal inventory policy for Jeannette is to order 1000 pounds at a time.

Note that this assumes Jeannette has adequate storage capacity and can accommodate 1000 pounds at a time. The quantity discount procedure when holding costs are given as a percentage of the unit price is summarized in Table 12-5.

At times, the holding cost can remain constant regardless of the price paid for an item. When the holding cost is a constant dollar amount, there is a common Q. The Q calculated will only be feasible in one of the price ranges. If the Q is in the least expensive price range, that is the optimal order quantity. If the Q is in a higher price range, total costs must be calculated and compared to the total costs of all lower price breaks.

■ Example 12.12 Quantity Discounts with Constant Holding Costs at Valley Grand Health Clinic (VGHC)

VGHC operates its own laboratory on-site. The lab maintains an inventory of test kits for a variety of procedures. VGHC uses 780 A1C kits each year. Ordering costs are $15 and holding costs are $3 per kit per year. The new price lists indicates that orders of fewer than 73 kits will cost $60 per case, 73 through 144 kits will cost $56 per kits, larger orders will cost $53 per kit. Determine the optimal order quantity and the total cost.

Solution:
The first step is to calculate the common Q.

$$Q = \sqrt{\frac{2 \times 780 \times \$15}{\$3}} = 88.3 \text{ or } 89 \text{ kits}$$

This quantity qualifies for a price of $56 per kit. Since it is not the lowest possible price, we calculate the total cost at this price and compare it to the total cost at any lower price breaks. The total cost when ordering 89 kits is

$$TC = \left(\frac{780}{89}\$15\right) + \left(\frac{89}{2}\$3\right) + (\$56 \times 780) = \$43,944.96$$

Total cost when ordering 145 kits is

$$TC = \left(\frac{780}{145}\$15\right) + \left(\frac{145}{2}\$3\right) + (\$53 \times 780) = \$41,638.19$$

Therefore, the VGHC should order 145 kits at a time since it will save $2,306.77 each year ($43,944.96 − $41,638.19).

■ THE JUST-IN-TIME IMPACT ON ORDER QUANTITIES

One of the principles of the just-in-time philosophy, discussed in Chapter 7, is to reduce order quantities, ideally down to an order size of one unit. Smaller orders improve customer responsiveness, reduce cycle inventory, reduce work-in-process (WIP) inventory, and reduce inventories of raw materials and purchased components. Since many good things happen with smaller order quantities, we need to see how order sizes can be reduced. To economically justify smaller order quantities, a company looks at the variables used in calculating the EOQ model. Three variables to consider are annual demand, order or setup cost, and holding cost.

LINKS TO PRACTICE
Kenworth Trucks
www.kenworth.com

Kenworth Trucks, a manufacturer of one of the most elite custom-built trucks, leads the industry in operations due largely to the just-in-time effect. Turning out over 35 trucks a day, Kenworth has been able to cut production time from the industry norm

of 6 to 8 weeks down to a mere 3 weeks. Such an outstanding feat is the result of the implementation of several cutting-edge ideas. Most importantly, there is the use of electronic transmission, which allows the plant to receive specifications as soon as a buyer has placed an order and which immediately involves parts suppliers in the details of the order. This synchronization results in supplies going almost directly to the assembly line. With such a fine-tuned operation, it is no wonder Kenworth Trucks is known as the premier of its industry!

Now let's look at what happens to the economic order quantity and the total annual costs when these variables change.

Changing Annual Demand

If annual demand increases and all other variables remain constant, the economic order quantity also increases. For example, in the Palm Pilot example, annual demand is 10,000 units, ordering cost is $75, annual holding cost is $6 per unit, the economic order quantity is 500 units, and total annual cost is $3000. Now let's consider what happens if demand at Palm Pilot increases 25% from 10,000 to 12,500 units. The new Q equals

$$Q = \sqrt{\frac{2 \times 12{,}500 \times \$75}{\$6}} = 559.02 \text{ or } 559 \text{ units}$$

or an increase in lot size of 11.8 %. The total annual cost also increases 11.8%.

$$TC = \left(\frac{12{,}500}{559}\$75\right) + \left(\frac{559}{2}\$6\right) = \$3354.10$$

The only way a change in annual demand reduces lot size is if the company faces a downturn in its business. Since companies typically do not want less demand, changing the demand level is not an effective way to reduce order quantities.

Changing Annual Holding Costs

An increase in holding costs causes a company to use a smaller order quantity. Looking at the Palm Pilot example, consider what happens when the holding cost is changed from $6 per unit to $12 per unit. The new order quantity becomes

$$Q = \sqrt{\frac{2 \times 10{,}000 \times \$75}{\$12}} = 353.55 \text{ or } 354 \text{ units}$$

and total annual cost is

$$TC = \left(\frac{10{,}000}{354}\$75\right) + \left(\frac{354}{2}\$12\right) = \$4242.64$$

As you can see, an increase in holding costs does mean a smaller order quantity, but it costs a company more money and is *not* a desirable way to reduce order size. Decreasing annual holding cost per unit increases order quantity. Since the objective is to reduce order quantity this will not help us. A company obviously prefers to reduce order quantity by changing a different variable than holding cost. This example illustrates the effect of holding cost changes on order quantity.

Changing Ordering or Setup Costs

The last variable to change is the ordering or setup cost. (We discuss methods to reduce this cost in Chapter 7.) Companies can reduce transaction costs such as ordering by developing partnership relations with their major suppliers. Let's look at what happens if ordering costs are reduced from $75 per order to $25 per order. The new economic order quantity becomes

$$Q = \sqrt{\frac{2 \times 10{,}000 \times \$25}{\$6}} = 288.68 \text{ or } 289 \text{ units}$$

and total annual cost is

$$TC = \left(\frac{10{,}000}{289}\$25\right) + \left(\frac{289}{2}\$6\right) = \$1732.05$$

Reducing the ordering or setup costs achieves both of our objectives: reducing order quantity and decreasing total annual costs for the inventory policy. We have similar results with the EPQ model.

■ DETERMINING SAFETY STOCK LEVELS

CROSS FUNCTIONAL

Companies are vulnerable to shortages during replenishment lead times, so one function of inventory is to provide safety stock as a cushion for satisfying unexpected customer demand. Remember that you typically place the replenishment order when the inventory level reaches the reorder point. Remember too that your company may experience a shortage between the time you place the replenishment order and the time you receive the items you ordered.

When we have no demand uncertainty, we set the reorder point to equal-to-average demand during lead time, or

$$R = dL$$

where R = reorder point in units
d = daily demand in units
L = lead time in days

Therefore, if $d = 20$ units and $L = 10$ days, the reorder point is 200 units. Since we know demand and lead time with certainty, the replenishment order arrives just as the on-hand inventory is depleted.

Suppose your kayak suppliers cannot always keep a firm delivery date because of fluctuation in materials availability at their end. As a result, uncertainty is a condition of your kayaking equipment operation. To support your company's customer service objectives, your policy is to carry safety stock. You add the amount of safety stock carried to the reorder point, and the reorder point becomes

$$R = dL + SS$$

where SS = safety stock in units

For example, if $d = 20$ units, $L = 10$ days, and $SS = 50$ units, the reorder point is 250 units. When your company carries safety stock, it increases the reorder point, as shown in Figure 12-5. The replenishment order is now expected to arrive when the inventory on hand equals the safety stock level rather than zero. If demand is greater than expected, then your customers are satisfied from the safety stock. If demand is less than expected, the replacement inventory arrives before the on-hand inventory reaches the safety stock level. Figure 12-6 shows when the replenishment order will arrive.

How Much Safety Stock?

As safety stock increases, so does the customer service level, thus decreasing the chance of shortage. At the same time, however, holding safety stock requires additional inventory investment. Thus it is important to limit the amount of safety stock your company holds.

▶ **Order-cycle service level**
The probability that demand during lead time will not exceed on-hand inventory.

Order-cycle service level is the probability that demand during lead time does not exceed on-hand inventory—that on-hand stock is adequate to meet demand. A service level of 95% implies that demand does not exceed supply 95% of the time. If your company places 20 orders annually, a 95% service level implies that demand will not exceed the on-hand quantity in 19 of the 20 replenishment lead times. We calculate the stockout risk as (1 − the order-cycle service level) or 5% in the example above.

The amount of safety stock to hold depends on the variability of demand and lead time, and the desired order-cycle service level. The safety stock needed to achieve

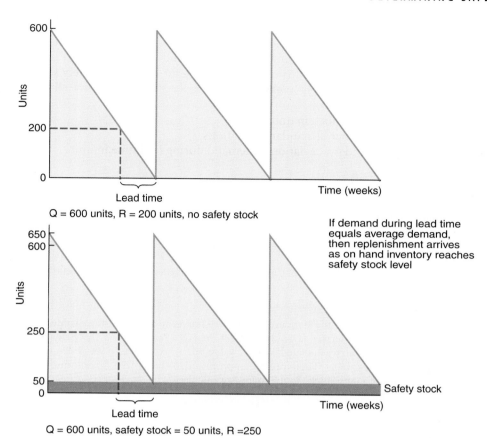

Figure 12-5

How safety stock changes the reorder point

Q = 600 units, R = 200 units, no safety stock

If demand during lead time equals average demand, then replenishment arrives as on hand inventory reaches safety stock level

Q = 600 units, safety stock = 50 units, R =250

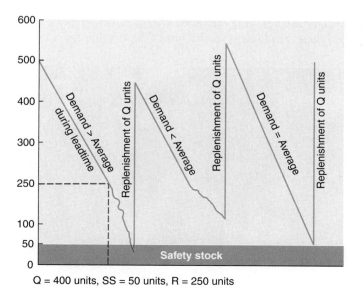

Figure 12-6

Demand uncertainty

Q = 400 units, SS = 50 units, R = 250 units

a particular order-cycle service level increases as demand and lead time variability increases. The greater the uncertainty, the more safety stock is needed.

Let's look at a case in which an estimate of demand during lead time and its standard deviation are known. In this case, the formula for calculating safety stock is

$$SS = z\sigma_{dL}$$

where SS = safety stock in units
z = number of standard deviations
σ_{dL} = standard deviation of demand during lead time in units

■ Example 12.13 Nick's Safety Stock

Suppose that the owner of the campus bar, Nick's, has determined that demand for beer during lead time averages 5000 bottles. Nick, the owner, believes the demand during lead time can be described by a normal distribution with a mean of 5000 bottles and a standard deviation of 300 bottles. Nick is willing to accept a stockout risk of approximately 4%. Determine the appropriate z value to use. Calculate how much safety stock Nick should hold. Also determine the reorder point.

Solution:
Go to Appendix B, area under the standardized normal curve, and look for the z value associated with the order-cycle service level (1 − 0.04 = 0.9600). Look for the entry closest to .9600. If you look at the entry associated with a z value of 1.75, you should see .9599, which is as close to .9600 as we can get. Therefore, the appropriate z value is 1.75. To determine the appropriate amount of safety stock, do the following calculation:

$$SS = 1.75 \times 300 \text{ bottles} = 525 \text{ bottles of safety stock}$$

The reorder point would now be

$$R = 5000 + 525 = 5525 \text{ bottles}$$

■ THE SINGLE-PERIOD INVENTORY MODEL

Some finished goods inventories have very short selling seasons. Items such as holiday decorations, Christmas trees, long-stemmed red roses, newspapers, and magazines are good examples. These products typically have a high value for a relatively short pe-

Christmas trees for sale.

riod; then the value diminishes dramatically to either zero or some minimum salvage value. For example, week-old newspapers are inexpensive compared to newspapers offering fresh news. The question is how many of these products you should order to maximize your expected profit.

The **single-period model** is designed for products that share the following characteristics:

◆ They are sold at their regular price only during a single-time period.
◆ Demand for these products is highly variable but follows a known probability distribution.
◆ Salvage value of these products is less than its original cost so you lose money when they are sold for their salvage value.

The objective is to balance the gross profit generated by the sale of a unit with the cost incurred for each unit that is not sold until after the primary selling period has elapsed. When demand follows a discrete probability distribution, we can solve the problem using an expected value matrix.

▶ **Single-period model**
Designed for use with products that are highly perishable.

CROSS FUNCTIONAL

■ Example 12.14 Walk for Diabetes

Rick Jones is chairman of this year's Walk for Diabetes event. Each year, the organizers of the event typically have commemorative tee shirts available for purchase by the entrants in the walk. Rick needs to order the shirts well in advance of the actual event. Rick must place his order in multiples of 10 (60, 70, 80, etc.). Based on past walks, the organizers have determined that the probability of selling different quantities of tee shirts in a given year is as follows:

Demand (shirts)	Probability
80	0.20
90	0.25
100	0.30
110	0.15
120	0.10

Rick plans to sell the tee shirts for $20 each. He pays his supplier $8 for each shirt and can sell any unsold shirts for rags at $2 each. Determine how many tee shirts Rick should order to maximize his expected profits.

Solution:
Based on the above information, develop a payoff table to determine expected profit with each possible order quantity. Calculate net profit for each combination of order quantity and demand as shown next.

Payoff Table

Probability of occurrence	0.20	0.25	0.30	0.15	0.10	
Customer demand (shirts)	80	90	100	110	120	
Number of shirts ordered						**Expected payoff**
80	$960	$ 960	$ 960	$ 960	$ 960	$ 960
90	$900	$1080	$1080	$1080	$1080	$1044
100	$840	$1020	$1200	$1200	$1200	$1083
110	$780	$ 960	$1140	$1320	$1320	$1068
120	$720	$ 900	$1080	$1260	$1440	$1026

The numbers in the payoff table are calculated based on what happened. The three possible outcomes are: (1) the number of shirts ordered equals the number of shirts demanded, (2) the number of shirts ordered is greater than the number of shirts demanded, and (3) the number of shirts ordered is less than the number of shirts demanded. To find the payoff when supply equals demand,

$$\text{Payoff} = \text{demand (selling price} - \text{unit cost)}$$

In our example, look at what happens when 100 tee shirts are bought and 100 tee shirts are sold.

$$\text{Payoff} = 100(\$20 - \$8) = \$1200$$

When the number of shirts ordered exceeds demand, the payoff is calculated as

$$\text{Payoff} = (\text{number of items demanded}) \times (\text{selling price} - \text{item cost}) \\ - ((\text{items ordered} - \text{items demanded}) \times (\text{item cost} - \text{item salvage value}))$$

If 100 tee shirts are ordered and demand is only for 80 shirts, the payoff is

$$\text{Payoff} = 80(\$20 - \$8) - ((100 - 80) \times (\$8 - \$2)) = \$840$$

When the number of shirts ordered is less than demand, the payoff is calculated as

$$\text{Payoff} = (\text{number of items ordered} \times (\text{selling price} - \text{item cost}))$$

Returning to the example, determine the payoff when 100 tee shirts are ordered but 120 shirts are demanded.

$$\text{Payoff} = 100(\$20 - \$8) = \$1200$$

After we calculate the payoffs for each combination, we can determine the expected profit for each order quantity. We do this by multiplying the payoff for an order quantity by the probability for each level of demand. For example, we calculate the payoff for ordering 100 shirts $1083 as

$$(\$840 \times 0.20) + (\$1020 \times 0.25) + (\$1200 \times 0.30) + (\$1200 \times 0.15) \\ + (\$1200 \times 0.10).$$

Once we generate the expected profit for each of the possible order quantities, we select the order quantity with the highest expected profit. In our case, Rick should order 100 shirts since doing so has an expected profit of $1083.

■ ABC INVENTORY CLASSIFICATION

▶ **ABC classification**
A method for determining level of control and frequency of review of inventory items.

▶ **Pareto's law**
Implies that about 20% of the inventory items will account for about 80% of the inventory value.

All items in a company's inventory are not equal and do not need the same level of control. Fortunately, we can apply **Pareto's law** to determine the level of control needed for individual items. Pareto's law implies that roughly 10% to 20% of a company's inventory items accounts for approximately 60% to 80% of its inventory costs. These relatively few high-dollar-volume items are classified as A items. Moderate dollar volume items, roughly 30% of the items, account for about 25% to 35% of the company's inventory investment. These are classified as B items. Low dollar-volume items, about 50% to 60% of the items, represent only 5% to 15% of the company's inventory investment and are classified as C items. These percentages are not absolute and are used only as guidelines.

Procedure for an ABC Inventory Analysis

The first step for an ABC inventory analysis is to determine the annual usage for each item. We calculate the total annual dollar volume by multiplying the annual usage by the item cost. We then rank items in descending order based on total dollar volume and calculate the total inventory investment.

1. Calculate the cumulative annual dollar usage.
2. List the items in descending order based on annual dollar usage.
3. Calculate the cumulative annual dollar volume.
4. Classify the items into groups.

■ Example 12.15 ABC Analysis at Auto Accessories Unlimited (AAU)

AAU is considering doing an ABC analysis of its entire inventory but has decided to test the technique on a small sample of 15 of its SKUs. The annual usage and unit cost for these items are shown in the table.

a. Calculate the annual dollar volume for each item.
b. List the items in descending order based on annual dollar usage.
c. Calculate the cumulative annual dollar volume.
d. Group the items into classes.

ABC Problem Data

Item	Unit $ Value	Annual Usage (in units)
101	12.00	80
102	50.00	10
103	15.00	50
104	50.00	40
105	40.00	80
106	75.00	220
107	4.00	250
108	1.50	400
109	2.00	250
110	25.00	500
111	5.00	450
112	7.50	80
113	3.50	250
114	1.00	1200
115	15.00	300

Solution:

a.

ABC Annual Usage Values

Item	Unit $ Value	Annual Usage (in units)	Annual Usage ($)
101	12.00	80	960
102	50.00	10	500
103	15.00	50	750
104	50.00	40	2000
105	40.00	80	3200
106	75.00	220	16,500
107	4.00	250	1000
108	1.50	400	600
109	2.00	250	500
110	25.00	500	12,500
111	5.00	450	2250
112	7.50	80	600
113	3.50	250	875
114	1.00	1200	1200
115	15.00	300	4500
		Total	$47,935

b, c, and d.

| | | ABC Solution | | |
Item	Annual Usage ($)	Percentage of Total Dollars	Cumulative Percentage of Total Dollars	Item Classification
106	16,500	34.4	34.4	A
110	12,500	26.1	60.5	A
115	4500	9.4	69.9	B
105	3200	6.7	76.6	B
111	2250	4.7	81.3	B
104	2000	4.2	85.5	B
114	1200	2.5	88.0	C
107	1000	2.1	90.1	C
101	960	2.0	92.1	C
113	875	1.8	93.9	C
103	750	1.6	95.5	C
108	600	1.3	96.8	C
112	600	1.3	98.1	C
102	500	1.0	99.1	C
109	500	1.0	100.1*	C
	47,935			

* Total exceeds 100% due to rounding.

Remember that these are not absolute rules for classifying items. Your company wants to group their more valuable items together to make sure that they get the most control.

Inventory Control Using ABC Classification

By classifying items into A, B, and C categories, we can determine the level of inventory control. For example, A items need tight control, accurate inventory records, and frequent review. B items need normal control, good inventory records, and normal review. C items need the simplest control—possibly a two-bin system or a periodic review system with infrequent reviews. For C items, companies should order large quantities and carry safety stock.

Let's compare the continuous review models with the periodic review models.

Comparison of Continuous Review Systems and Periodic Review Systems

The advantages of continuous review systems (CRs) are the disadvantages of periodic review systems (PRs). For instance, a CR system has no set review periods. This lack of specified review periods means that less inventory is needed to protect against stockouts.

With a PR system, enough inventory must be carried to cover both the lead time and the review period. So since a CR system has no review period, it has a smaller average inventory. On the other hand, a CR system needs significantly more work because the inventory balances are updated after each transaction rather than periodically. A PR system needs less work because inventory balances are only reviewed and updated periodically. So a PR system makes it easy to consolidate orders from a single supplier because you can review all items at the same time interval, whereas the CR system is designed to handle items individually.

In general, companies use CRs for items that are expensive and/or critical to the company because CRs more closely monitor these items and reduce inventory investment. Companies typically use both systems depending on the value and criticality of the items to be monitored.

INVENTORY RECORD ACCURACY ■

For effective inventory use, the inventory records must accurately reflect the quantity of materials available. Inaccurate inventory records can result in lost sales (finished good not available at time of sale), disrupted operations (not enough of a component or raw material to complete a job), poor customer service (late deliveries to customers), lower productivity (additional setups to complete a job), poor material planning (the inventory records are critical in determining MRP quantities) and excessive expediting (trying to obtain necessary items in less than normal lead time).

One exceptionally productive approach to inventory management is the automated inventory tracking system used by the very successful Cisco Systems, Inc.—a world leader in providing networking solutions for all types of businesses. This tracking system forms an intricate network of suppliers, manufacturers, and customers and provides for real-time transactions. When a customer places an order via the Internet, suppliers can instantaneously see what parts are needed and can quickly respond by shipping the needed parts and then restocking. Such a system provides accurate, timely information, which helps both Cisco and suppliers to schedule, budget, and forecast. Since most of Cisco's orders are transacted over the Web, Cisco is able to save millions of dollars annually.

LINKS TO PRACTICE
Cisco Systems, Inc.
www.cisco.com

Inventory record errors occur because of unauthorized withdrawals of material, unsecured stockrooms, inaccurate paper work, and/or human errors. Since an accurate database is needed to successfully use the information systems, it is important to detect errors in the inventory records. Two methods are available for checking inventory record accuracy: periodically counting all of the items (typically annually) and cyclically counting specified items (typically daily).

Periodic counting satisfies auditors that the inventory records accurately reflect the value of the inventory on hand. For material planners, the physical inventory is an opportunity to correct errors. The four steps in taking a physical inventory are:

1. Count the quantity of the item and record the count on a ticket attached to the item.
2. Verify by recounting.
3. After verification, collect the tickets.
4. Reconcile inventory records with actual counts. For major discrepanicies, investigate further. For minor discrepancies, adjust the inventory records.

▶ **Periodic counting**
A physical inventory is taken periodically, usually annually.

Taking physical inventories does not always improve inventory record accuracy. In many cases, companies close down manufacturing to take the physical inventory, and the job is often rushed and is typically done by employees not trained for the job. In some cases, inventory record errors are increased rather than reduced. The other alternative method is cycle counting.

Cycle counting is a method of counting inventory throughout the year. This is a series of mini-physical inventories done daily. Some prespecified items are physically counted each day. The frequency of counting a particular item depends on the importance and value of the item. Typically, A items are counted most frequently.

▶ **Cycle counting**
Prespecified items are counted daily.

The advantages of cycle counting are

◆ timely detection and correction of inventory record problems
◆ elimination of lost production time since the company does not need to shut down operations
◆ the use of employees dedicated to cycle counting

Scheduling individual item counts can be done in several ways. An item can be counted just before a replenishment order is placed. At this time, the planner has an accurate count of the item on hand and can determine whether a replenishment order is needed. At this time the quantity to be counted is relatively low. A planner also can choose to count when new orders arrive. This way the inventory is at its lowest level. Remember that most replenishment orders arrive just as the on-hand inventory is running out. Another possibility is to schedule a count after a certain number of transactions have occurred. For example, a planner can request a physical count after every 20 transactions involving a particular item. Since errors typically occur during transactions, the greater the number of transactions, the more likely an error will be introduced. One other possibility is to do a count whenever an error is detected. This allows for corrective action to be taken immediately. Regardless of the method, the intent is to improve inventory record accuracy.

OM ACROSS THE ORGANIZATION

Inventory management policies affect functional areas throughout a company. Let's consider why individual functional areas are concerned with inventory management policies.

Accounting is concerned because of the cost implications of inventory, such as the holding costs incurred, the capital needed to invest in inventory, and projected cash flow budgets. Accounting is concerned with all types of inventory.

Marketing is concerned because stocking decisions affect the level of customer service provided. Marketing's primary focus is finished goods inventory, where the goods are held within the distribution system, the response time to satisfy customers, and safety stock levels.

Information systems is involved because a system to track and control inventories is needed, especially when perpetual inventory records are used. Given the large number of SKUs and a high volume of inventory transactions, manual processing is impractical for most companies so a computerized information system is essential.

Purchasing's workload is directly affected by inventory policies. Policies regarding order frequency, order volume, acceptable suppliers, and inventory investment determine the number of purchases made. Purchasing is concerned primarily with buying raw materials, components, and subassemblies.

Manufacturing's cost efficiency can be affected by inventory decisions. If insufficient material is available, either because items are not ordered on time or not ordered in the right quantities, manufacturing efficiency decreases and unit costs increase. Unit costs can also increase when too much material is ordered or when it is ordered too soon.

As you can see, inventory decisions affect many functional areas in a company and may involve input from management in these areas. In addition, inventory decisions have a significant impact on the company's profitability.

Who makes aggregate inventory decisions? Typically it is the materials manager. This person is evaluated based on customer service levels achieved and inventory turnover. For individual finished goods products, the master scheduler makes decisions about how much of a particular item to produce and how much to keep in inventory. A master scheduler is evaluated based on customer service levels and manufacturing efficiency.

For raw materials, components, and subassemblies, inventory or material planners or controllers make decisions about when to place replenishment orders, either for in-house manufacturing or for external purchasing. Planners and controllers are typically evaluated according to customer service levels and inventory investment.

OM IS EVERYWHERE ■

Replenishing items in your household does not require a major inventory management system, but it does illustrate how we use inventory management policies in our daily lives. Inventory management systems tell us what to order, when to order, and how much to order. Maybe you keep track of your on-hand inventory by doing periodic reviews (that is, every week you check to see what items you need to replenish). Perhaps you may keep a running list of items that you've depleted from your inventory (perhaps a note on the refrigerator). You may buy a fixed quantity (a quart of milk, a dozen eggs, a 24-pack of soda, a box of crackers), or quantities may vary based on your mood or the season (we are not always sure what we want in life!). Quantity decisions are also influenced by discounts (buy two, get one free). With food purchases, we are concerned about whether an item is perishable. For perishable items, we tend to think in terms of single-period models. Like it or not, the inventory management concepts in this chapter apply to all of us!

CHAPTER HIGHLIGHTS

1 Raw materials, purchased components, work-in-process (WIP), finished goods, distribution inventory and maintenance, repair and operating supplies are all types of inventory. Inventories have several uses: anticipation inventory is built before it is needed; fluctuation stock provides a cushion against uncertain demand; cycle stock is a result of the company's ordering quantity; transportation inventory includes items in transit; speculative inventory is a buildup to protect against some future event; and MRO inventory supports daily operations.

2 The objectives of inventory management are to provide the desired level of customer service, to allow cost-efficient operations, and to minimize inventory investment. Customer service can be measured in several ways, including as a percentage of orders shipped on schedule, percentage of line items shipped on schedule, percentage of dollar volume shipped on schedule, or idle time due to material and component shortages. Cost-efficient operations are achieved by using inventory as buffer stocks, allowing a stable year round workforce, and spreading the setup cost over a larger number of units.

3 Inventory investment is measured in inventory turnover and/or level of supply. Inventory performance is calculated as inventory turnover or weeks, days, or hours of supply.

4 Relevant inventory costs include item costs, holding costs, ordering costs, and shortage costs. Holding costs include capital costs, storage costs, and risk costs. Order-

ing costs are fixed costs for placing an order or performing a setup. Shortage costs include costs related to additional paperwork, additional shipping expense, and the intangible cost of lost customer goodwill.

5 Lot-for-lot, fixed-order quantity, min-max systems, order n periods, periodic review systems, EOQ models, quantity discount models, and single-period models can be used to determine order quantities.

6 Ordering decisions can be improved by analyzing total costs of an inventory policy. Total costs include ordering cost, holding cost, and material cost.

7 Smaller lot sizes give a company flexibility and shorter response times. The key to reducing order quantities is to reduce ordering or setup costs.

8 Calculating the appropriate safety stock policy enables companies to satisfy their customer service objectives at minimum cost. The desired customer service level determines the appropriate z value.

9 Inventory decisions about perishable products (like newspapers) can be made using the single-period inventory model. The expected payoff is calculated to assist the quantity decision.

10 The ABC classification system allows a company to assign the appropriate level of control and frequency of review of an item based on its annual dollar volume.

11 Cycle counting is a method for maintaining accurate inventory records. Determining what and when to count are the major decisions.

KEY TERMS

raw materials 352
components 352
work-in-process (WIP) 352
finished goods 352
distribution inventory 352
maintenance, repair and operating
    supplies (MRO) 352
anticipation or seasonal inventory 353
fluctuation inventory or safety stock 353
lot-size inventory or cycle stock 353
transportation or pipeline inventory 353
speculative or hedge inventory 354
customer service 355
percentage of orders shipped
    on schedule 355
percentage of line items shipped
    on schedule 355

percentage of dollar volume shipped
    on schedule 355
setup cost 356
inventory turnover 357
weeks of supply 357
item cost 359
holding cost 359
capital cost 359
storage costs 359
risk costs 359
ordering costs 360
shortage costs 360
back order 360
lost sale 360
stock-keeping unit (SKU) 361
lot-for-lot 362
fixed-order quantity 362

min-max system 362
order *n* periods 362
periodic review system 362
target inventory level 362
economic order quantity (EOQ) 364
continuous review systems 364
lead time 364
economic production quantity (EPQ)
    368
perpetual inventory record 371
two-bin system 371
quantity discounts 371
order-cycle service level 376
single-period model 379
Pareto's law 380
periodic counting 383
cycle counting 383

FORMULA REVIEW

Calculating average transportation inventory (ATI):

$$ATI = \frac{tD}{365}$$

where t = transit time in days, and D = annual demand in units

Calculating inventory turnover and periods of supply:

$$Inventory\ turnover = \frac{annual\ cost\ of\ goods\ sold}{average\ inventory\ in\ dollars}$$

$$Weeks\ of\ supply = \frac{average\ inventory\ on\ hand\ in\ dollars}{average\ weekly\ usage\ in\ dollars}$$

$$Days\ of\ supply = \frac{average\ inventory\ on\ hand\ in\ dollars}{average\ daily\ usage\ in\ dollars}$$

Calculating target inventory (TI):

$$TI = d(RP + L) + SS$$

where d = average daily demand, RP = review period in days, and SS = safety stock

Calculating reorder point without safety stock:

$$R = dL$$

where d = average daily demand and L = lead time in days

Calculating the economic order quantity (EOQ):

$$Q = \sqrt{\frac{2DS}{H}}$$

where D = annual demand, S = ordering cost, and H = holding cost

Calculating total costs:

$$TC = \left(\frac{D}{Q}S\right) + \left(\frac{Q}{2}H\right)$$

Calculating the economic production quantity (EPQ):

$$Q = \sqrt{\frac{2DS}{H\left(1 - \dfrac{d}{p}\right)}}$$

Calculating total costs :

$$TC = \left(\frac{D}{Q}S\right) + \left(\frac{I_{MAX}}{2}H\right)$$

where I_{MAX} is the maximum inventory level

Calculating I_{MAX}:

$$I_{MAX} = Q\left(1 - \frac{d}{p}\right)$$

where d = daily demand, and p = daily production rate

Calculating total costs for quantity discount comparisons:

$$TC = \left(\frac{D}{Q}S\right) + \left(\frac{Q}{2}H\right) + (PD)$$

where P = price per unit

Calculating amount of safety stock:

$$SS = z\sigma_{dL}$$

where SS = safety stock, z = number of standard deviations, and σ_{dL} = standard deviation of demand during lead time in units

SOLVED PROBLEMS

■ Solved Problem 1

Tacky Souvenirs sells lovely hand-made tablecloths at its island store. These tablecloths cost Tacky $15.00 each. Customers want to buy the tablecloths at a rate of 240 per week. The company operates 52 weeks per year. Tacky, the owner, estimates his ordering cost at $50. Annual holding costs are 20% of the unit cost. Lead time is 2 weeks. Using the information given,

  a. Calculate the economic order quantity.
  b. Calculate the total annual costs using the EOQ.
  c. Determine the reorder point.

Solution:
  a. First, calculate the annual demand and the annual holding cost.

Annual demand = (52 weeks × 240 units per week) = 12,480 units

Annual holding cost = (0.20 × $15) = $3.00 per unit per year

Now calculate the economic order quantity as shown in Spreadsheet 12.1.

$$Q = \sqrt{\frac{2 \times 12480 \times \$50}{\$3}} = 644.98 \text{ or } 645 \text{ tablecloths}$$

Examine Spreadsheet 12.1 to see how you can solve EOQ problems using a spreadsheet. Note that you can use weekly demand since the lead time is given in weekly increments. Just make sure that the average demand time frame matches the time frame used with lead time.

Spreadsheet 12.1

INFORMATION

Weekly Demand (units)	240
Operating Time (# of weeks)	52
Annual Demand (units)	12,480
Ordering Cost	$ 50.00
Annual Holding Cost (%)	20%
Unit Cost	$ 15.00
Annual Holding Cost/Unit ($)	$ 3.00
Lead Time (# days, weeks)	2

SOLUTION

EOQ (units)	645
# of Orders/Year	19.35
Annual Ordering Costs	$ 967.47
Annual Holding Costs	$ 967.47
Total Costs	$1,934.94
Reorder point (units)	480

b. The total costs are

$$TC = \left(\frac{12480}{645}\$50\right) + \left(\frac{645}{2}\$3\right) = \$1,934.94$$

c. The reorder point is

$$R = 240 \text{ units} \times 2 \text{ weeks} = 480 \text{ units}$$

■ Solved Problem 2

Jack's Packs manufactures backpacks made from microfabrics. The cutting department prepares the material for use by the backpack stitching department. The cutting department can cut enough material to make 200 backpacks per day. The backpack stitching department produces 90 backpacks per day. Annual demand for the product is 22,500 units. The company operates 250 days per year. Estimated setup cost is $60. Annual holding cost is $6 per backpack.

  a. Calculate the economic production quantity for the cutting department.

  b. Calculate the total annual costs for the EPQ.

Solution:
  a. First, calculate the EPQ as follows:

$$Q = \sqrt{\frac{2 \times 22,500 \times \$60}{\$6\left(1 - \dfrac{90}{200}\right)}} = 904.53 \text{ or } 905 \text{ backpacks}$$

To calculate total costs, determine the maximum inventory level as follows.

$$I_{MAX} = 905\left(1 - \frac{90}{200}\right) = 497.75 \text{ or } 498 \text{ backpacks}$$

Now that you have determined the maximum inventory level, calculate total costs:

$$TC = \left(\frac{22,500}{905}\$60\right) + \left(\frac{498}{2}\$6\right) = \$2985.71$$

■ Solved Problem 3

Ye Olde Shoe Repair has customers requesting leather soles throughout the year. The owner, Warren, buys these soles from The Leather Company (TLC) at a price of $8 per pair. In an effort to improve profitability by selling in greater quantities, the sales rep for TLC has made the following offer to Ye Olde Shoe Repair: If Warren orders from 1 to 50 pairs at a time, the cost per pair is $8.00. If the order is between 51 and 100 pairs at a time, the cost is $7.60. On orders for more than 100 pairs at a time, the cost per pair is $7.40. The owner estimates annual demand to be 625 pairs of soles. Holding costs are 20% of unit price. The cost to place an order is $10. Determine the most cost-effective ordering policy for Ye Olde Shoe Repaire.

Solution:

a. First, we need to calculate the EOQ at the lowest price offered. The annual holding cost is 20% of the unit cost, or $1.48—that is, $7.40 times 20%.

$$Q = \sqrt{\frac{2 \times 625 \times \$10}{\$1.48}} = 91.9 \text{ or } 92 \text{ pairs}$$

Since this order quantity does not match the unit price used to calculate the EOQ, this answer is infeasible. This means if we place an order for 92 pairs, we are charged $7.60 per pair rather than the $7.40 we used in calculating the EOQ.

b. Since the first Q is infeasible, we calculate the EOQ for the next higher price. Make sure to calculate the new annual holding cost (20% of $7.60) or $1.52.

$$Q = \sqrt{\frac{2 \times 625 \times \$10}{\$1.52}} = 90.68 \text{ or } 91 \text{ pairs}$$

If we place an order for 91 pairs, we will be charged $7.60 per pair, which is the price we used to calculate this EOQ. Therefore, this is a feasible order quantity. We are ready to calculate the total annual cost for this policy.

$$TC = \left(\frac{625}{91}\$10\right) + \left(\frac{91}{2}\$1.52\right) + (\$7.60 \times 625)$$
$$= \$4887.84$$

Since the feasible solution was not at the lowest price, we must now compute the total cost of any cheaper price, assuming that we order just enough to qualify for the cheaper price. This means we need to order 101 pairs to qualify for the $7.40 price. The total cost of this policy is

$$TC = \left(\frac{625}{101}\$10\right) + \left(\frac{101}{2}\$1.48\right) + (\$7.40 \times 625)$$
$$= \$4761.62$$

Since the total annual cost of ordering 101 pairs at a time is less expensive, Ye Olde Shoe Repair should order 101 pairs each time leather soles are needed.

■ Solved Problem 4

Frank's Ribs knows that the demand during lead time for his world-famous ribs is described by a normal distribution with a mean of 1000 pounds and a standard deviation of 100 pounds. Frank is willing to accept a stockout risk of approximately 2%.

  a. Determine the appropriate z value.
  b. Calculate how much safety stock Frank should hold.

Solution:

a. Go to Appendix B, areas under the standardized normal curve, for the z value associated with the order cycle service level $(1 - 0.02 = 0.9800)$, which is for the entry closest to .9800. Looking at the entry for $z = 2.05$, you should see .9798, which is as close to .9800 as we can get. Therefore, the appropriate z value is 2.05.

b. To determine the amount of safety stock Frank should hold, multiply the z value by the standard deviation.

$$SS = 2.05 \times 100 \text{ pounds} = 205 \text{ pounds}$$

Frank should hold 205 pounds of ribs in safety stock.

■ Solved Problem 5

Peter sells programs at State University's home football games. Peter must buy the programs before the game in multiples of 100 (2000, 2100, 2200, etc.). Peter has determined that the probability of selling different quantities of programs at a given game is as follows.

Demand for programs	Probability of demand
2000	0.10
2100	0.20
2200	0.40
2300	0.20
2400	0.10

Peter plans to sell the programs for $4.00 each. He pays $2.50 for each program and there is no salvage value. Determine how many programs Peter should buy to maximize his profit.

Solution:

Based on the above information, we developed a payoff table to determine the expected profit for each possible order quantity. Net profit for each combination or order quantity and demand are calculated as shown.

The order quantity with the highest expected profit is 2200 programs. Peter should order 2200 programs.

	Probability of Occurrence					
	0.10	0.20	0.40	0.20	0.10	
Actual customer demand (programs)	2,000	2,100	2,200	2,300	2,400	
Number of programs ordered						Expected payoff
2000	$3000	$3000	$3000	$3000	$3000	$3000
2100	$2750	$3150	$3150	$3150	$3150	$3110
2200	$2500	$2900	$3300	$3300	$3300	$3140
2300	$2250	$2650	$3050	$3450	$3450	$3010
2400	$2000	$2400	$2800	$3200	$3600	$2800

DISCUSSION QUESTIONS

1. Visit a local business and identify the different types of inventory used.

2. After visiting a local business, explain the different functions of their inventory.

3. Explain the objectives of inventory management at the local business.

4. Describe how the objectives of inventory management can be measured.

5. Explain the different methods for measuring customer service.

6. Compare the two techniques, inventory turnover and weeks of supply.

7. Describe the relevant costs associated with inventory policies.

8. Explain what is included in the annual holding cost.

9. Describe what is included in ordering or setup costs.

10. Describe what is included in shortage costs.

11. Explain the assumptions of the EOQ model.

12. Describe techniques for determining order quantities other than the EOQ or EPQ.

13. Describe how changes in the demand, ordering cost, or holding cost affect the EOQ.

14. Explain how a company can justify smaller order quantities.

15. Explain what safety stock is for.

16. Explain how safety stock affects the reorder point.

17. Describe the type of products that require a single-period model.

18. Explain the basic concept of ABC analysis.

19. Explain the concept of perpetual review.

20. Explain how two-bin systems work.

PROBLEMS

1. Elyssa's Elegant Eveningwear (EEE) needs to ship finished goods from its manufacturing facility to its distribution warehouse. Annual demand for EEE is 2400 gowns. EEE can ship the gowns via regular parcel service (3 days transit time), premium parcel service (1 day transit time), or via public carrier (7 days transit time). Calculate the average annual transportation inventory for each alternative.

2. Yasuko's Art Emporium (YAE) ships art from its studio located in the Far East to its distribution center located on the West Cost of the U.S.A. YAE can send the art either via transoceanic ship freight service (15 days transit) or by air freight (2 days transit time). YAE ships 18,000 pieces of art annually.

a. Calculate average annual transportation inventory when sending the art via transoceanic ship freight service.

b. Calculate average annual transportation inventory when sending the art via air freight.

c. What additional information is needed to compare the two alternatives?

3. Joe, the owner of Genuine Reproductions (GR), a company that manufactures reproduction furniture, is interested in measuring inventory effectiveness. Last year the cost of goods sold at GR was $3,000,000. The average inventory in dollars was $250,000.

a. Calculate the inventory turnover for GR.

b. Calculate the weeks of supply. Assume 52 weeks per year.

c. Calculate the days of supply. Assume that GR operates 5 days per week.

4. Genuine Reproductions (GR) from Problem 3, plans on increasing next year's sales by 20% while maintaining its same average inventory in dollars.

  a. Calculate the expected inventory turnover for next year.

  b. Calculate the expected weeks of supply.

5. What is the inventory turnover for Genuine Reproductions from Problems 3 and 4 if sales actually increase 20% but the average inventory rises to $325,000?

6. Frederick's Farm Factory (FFF) currently maintains an average inventory valued at $3,400,000. The company estimates its capital cost at 10%, its storage cost at 4.5%, and its risk cost at 6%.

  a. Calculate the annual holding cost rate for FFF.

  b. Calculate the total annual holding costs for FFF.

7. The Federal Reserve Board has just increased the interest rate. FFF in Problem 6 now has to pay 12% for its capital. Calculate the impact on total annual holding costs for FFF.

8. A technology problem has rendered some of the inventory at FFF (Problem 6) obsolete. FFF estimates that the risk cost of their inventory is now 10%.

  a. Calculate the new annual holding cost rate.

  b. Calculate the new total annual holding costs for FFF.

9. Custom Computers, Inc. assembles custom home computer systems. The heat sinks needed are bought for $12 each and are ordered in quantities of 1300 units. Annual demand is 5200 heat sinks, the annual inventory holding cost rate is $3.00 per unit, and the cost to place an order is estimated to be $50. Calculate the following:

  a. Average inventory level.

  b. The number of orders placed per year.

  c. The total annual inventory holding cost.

  d. The total annual ordering cost.

  e. The total annual cost.

10. Custom Computers, Inc. from Problem 9 is considering a new ordering policy. The new order quantity would be 650 heat sinks. Recalculate Problem 9, parts (a) through (e), and compare results.

11. Bill Maze, recently hired by Custom Computers, Inc. has suggested using the economic order quantity for the heat sinks. Using the information in Problem 9, calculate the following:

  a. Economic order quantity.

  b. Average inventory level.

  c. The number of orders placed per year.

  d. The total annual ordering cost.

  e. The total annual holding cost.

  f. The total annual cost.

  g. Compare these results with the costs calculated in Problems 9 and 10.

12. A local nursery, Greens, uses 1560 bags of plant food annually. Greens works 52 weeks per year. It costs $10 to place an order for plant food. The annual holding cost rate is $5 per bag. Lead time is 1 week.

  a. Calculate the economic order quantity.

  b. Calculate the total annual costs.

  c. Determine the reorder point.

13. Rapid Grower, the supplier of plant food for Greens in Problem 12, has offered the following quantity discounts. If the nursery places orders of 50 bags or less, the cost per bag is $20.00. For orders greater than 50 bags but less than 100 bags, the cost per bag is $19.00. For orders of 100 bags or more, the cost is $18.00 per bag. Greens estimates their holding cost to be 25% of the unit price. Determine the most cost effective ordering policy for Greens.

14. In an effort to reduce its inventory, Rapid Grower is offering Greens, a local nursery (Problems 12 and 13), two additional price breaks to consider. If the nursery orders a 3-month supply, the cost per bag is $16. If Greens orders a 6-month supply, the cost per bag is $14.50. Should Greens change its order quantity calculated in Problem 13?

15. In a further attempt to liquidate its inventory, Rapid Grower has offered Greens, the local nursery, an option to buy the entire year's supply at one time. The cost per bag would be $12.00. Should Greens take advantage of this offer?

16. Sam's Auto Shop services and repairs a particular brand of foreign automobiles. Sam uses oil filters throughout the year. The shop operates 52 weeks per year and weekly demand is 150 filters. Sam estimates that it costs $20 to place an order and his annual holding cost rate is $3 per oil filter. Currently Sam orders in quantities of 650 filters. Calculate the total annual costs associated with Sam's current ordering policy.

17. Using the information in Problem 16, calculate the following:

  a. The economic order quantity.

  b. The total annual costs using the EOQ ordering policy.

  c. The penalty costs Sam is incurring by using his current policy.

18. The local Office of Tourism sells souvenir calendars. Sue, the head of the office, needs to order these calendars in advance of the main tourist season. Based on past seasons, Sue has determined the probability of selling different quantities of the calendars for a particular tourist season.

Demand for Calendars	Probability of Demand
75,000	0.15
80,000	0.25
85,000	0.30
90,000	0.20
95,000	0.10

The Office of Tourism sells the calendars for $12.95 each. The calendars cost Sue $5.00 each. The salvage value is estimated to be $0.50 per unsold calendar. Determine how many calendars Sue should order to maximize expected profits.

19. The Office of Tourism (see Problem 18) has decided to heavily promote local events this year and anticipate more tourists this season. Sue has changed the probability of selling different quantities of calendars as shown below. Given the new probabilities, determine how many calendars Sue should order to maximize expected profits.

Demand for Calendars	Probability of Demand
75,000	0.05
80,000	0.20
85,000	0.25
90,000	0.30
95,000	0.20

20. Given the following list of items,
   a. Calculate the annual usage cost of each item.
   b. Classify the items as A, B, or C.

Item	Annual Demand	Ordering Cost ($)	Holding Cost (%)	Unit Price ($)
101	500	10	20	0.50
102	1500	10	30	0.20
103	5000	25	30	1.00
104	250	15	25	4.50
105	1500	35	35	1.20
201	10,000	25	15	0.75
202	1000	10	20	1.35
203	1500	20	25	0.20
204	500	40	25	0.80
205	100	10	15	2.50

21. Using the information provided in Problem 20.
   a. Calculate the economic order quantity for each item. (Round to the nearest whole number).

b. Calculate the company's maximum inventory investment throughout the year.
   c. Calculate the company's average inventory level.

22. Tax Preparers Inc., works 250 days per year. The company uses adding machine tape at a rate of 8 rolls per day. Usage is believed to be normally distributed with a standard deviation of 1.5 rolls per day. The cost of ordering the tape is $10 and holding costs are $0.30 per roll per year. Lead time is 2 days.
   a. Calculate the economic order quantity.
   b. What reorder point will provide an order cycle service level of 97%?
   c. How much safety stock must the company hold to have a 97% order cycle service level?
   d. What reorder point is needed to provide an order cycle service level of 99%?
   e. How much safety stock must the company hold to have a 99% order cycle service level?

23. Healthy Plants Ltd. (HP) produces its premium plant food in 50-pound bags. Demand for the product is 100,000 pounds per week. HP operates 50 weeks per year. HP can produce 250,000 pounds per week. The setup cost is $200 and the annual holding cost rate is $0.550 per bag. Currently, HP produces its premium plant food in batches of 1,000,000 pounds.
   a. Calculate the maximum inventory level for HP.
   b. Calculate the total annual costs of this operating policy.

24. Using the data provided in Problem 23, determine what will happen if HP uses the economic production quantity model to establish the quantity produced each cycle.
   a. Calculate the economic production quantity (EPQ).
   b. Calculate the maximum inventory level using the EPQ.
   c. Calculate the total annual cost of using the EPQ.
   d. Calculate the penalty cost HP is incurring with its current policy.

CASE: *FabQual Ltd.*

FabQual Ltd. Manufactures parts and subassemblies for a number of small-volume manufacturers of specialized construction equipment, including bulldozers, graders, and cement mixers. FabQual also manufactures and distributes spare parts. The company has made a specialty of providing spare parts for equipment no longer in production; this includes wear parts that are no longer in production for any OEM.

The Materials Management Group (MMG) orders parts—both for delivery to a customer's production line and for spares—from the Fabrication Department. Spares are stocked in a Finished Goods Store. FabQual's part number 650810/ss/R9/o is a wear part made only for spares demand.

It has had demand averaging 300 units per week for more than a year and this level of demand is expected to persist for at least 4 more years. The standard deviation of weekly demand is 50 units.

The MMG has been ordering 1300 units monthly of part number 650810/ss/R9/o from the Fabrication Department to meet the forecast annual demand of 15600 units. The order is placed in the first week of each month. In order to provide Fabrication with scheduling flexibility, as well as to help with planning raw material requirements, a 3-week manufacturing lead time is allowed for parts.

In the Fabrication Department, 2 hours is now allowed for each setup for a run of part number 650810/ss/R9/o. This time includes strip-down of the previous setup; delivery of raw materials, drawings, tools and fixtures, etc.; and build-up of the new setup. The 2-hour setup time is a recent improvement over the previous 4 hours, as the result of setup reduction activities in the Fabrication Department. The Fabrication Department charges £20 per hour for setups. (If you prefer to work in dollars, you can find the current exchange rate in the *Wall Street Journal*). Part number 650810/ss/R9/o enters the Finished Goods Stores at a full manufacturing cost of £55. The Financial Office requires a 25% per item per year cost for inventory planning and control. (This is your annual holding cost rate.)

Case Questions:

1. What is the total annual cost of the present ordering policy for part number 650810/ss/R9/o?

2. What would be the lot size for part number 650810/ss/R9/o if FabQual were to use an economic order quantity (EOQ)?

3. What would be the total annual cost of using an economic order quantity for part number 650810/ss/R9/o?

4. What would be the reorder point for part number 650810/ss/R9/o if FabQual wanted a delivery performance of 95%? What would it be if the company wanted a delivery performance of 99%?

5. Under the present scheme—ordering 1300 units each month in the first week of each month—there are typically 700 to 800 units on hand when the new batch of 1300 units arrives toward the end of each month. What would be the impact on the overall inventory level of part number 650810/ss/R9/o of a change from the present order policy to an EOQ-based policy?

6. What are other implications of a change from the present scheme to one based on the economic order quantity? If this part is representative of a great many spare parts, what would be the overall impact?

Source: Copyright © by Professor L.G. Sprague, 1999. Reprinted with permission.

INTERACTIVE LEARNING

Enhance and test your knowledge of Chapter 12 using the interactive CD.

1. **Spreadsheet** *Solved Problems 2 and 5*

   Visit our dynamic Web site, www.wiley.com/college/reid, for more cases, web links, and additional information.

2. Company Tour
   Coffman—Division of Visador Company
   Folbot

3. Additional Web Resources
   Coffman Stairs,www.coffmanstairs.com/about.htm
   Folbot, wwwfolbot.com/tour1.htm
   Universal Screenprinting, www.simon.ca/simonfr.htm

4. Virtual Company Consulting Case

5. **INTERNET CHALLENGE** *Community Fund Raiser (A)*

Your nonprofit club holds a major fund raiser each year to support community improvement projects. The club sells packages of cookies throughout the community and donates the proceeds from their 2-week fund raiser. The goal of the event is to raise at least $40,000 for the community. This year you are in charge of the fund-raising event. Your first step is to search the Internet and identify at least three potential suppliers of the cookies to be sold this year. At least one of the suppliers should be in the immediate vicinity of your town or city.

From past fund raisers, the club believes that an acceptable price of the cookies to the customers does not allow for more than a $1 markup over the regular cost per package. However, if quantity discounts can be obtained then the profit per package can exceed $1. It is believed that regardless of the cookies sold, demand will be 40,000 packages. If you decide to buy more than 40,000 packages, any leftover cookies will be donated to local shelters. Since you are a nonprofit organization, no tax advantage is gained.

For each of the potential suppliers, you need to identify the total cost associated with buying the packages of cookies. Be sure to consider transportation costs as well as any quantity discounts. Remember that your objective is to raise at least $40,000 for the community. It is also important to consider the logistics of your plan. Will all of the cookies arrive at one time or will deliveries be spread over the 2-week fund raiser? Find out how far in advance you need to place your order and when payment for the cookies is due. Explain how you can be sure the cookies will arrive on time. You need to put together a report for your next meeting comparing your three suppliers and make a recommendation as to which supplier should be used, the quantity of cookies to purchase, and the expected profit to be donated and the logistics for the fund raiser.

Community Fund Raiser (B)

From historical data, the following demand distribution for the cookies is given here. Given that you are making a single-period purchase and the cookies have no salvage value, develop a report for your organization showing the expected payoff for each of the three suppliers.

Level of Demand (packages)	Probability of Demand Occurring
30,000	0.10
35,000	0.20
40,000	0.40
45,000	0.25
50,000	0.05

BIBLIOGRAPHY

Arnold, J. R. Tony. *Introduction to Materials Management,* 3rd ed. Upper Saddle River, N.J.: Prentice-Hall, 1998.

Buffa, Elwood S., and Jeffrey G. Miller. *Production-Inventory Systems: Planning and Control,* 3rd ed. Homewood, Ill.: Irwin, 1979.

Cox, James F., III, John H. Blackstone, and Michael S. Spencer, eds. *APICS Dictionary,* 9th ed. Falls Church, Va.: American Production and Inventory Control Society, Inc., 1998.

Fogarty, Donald W., John H. Blackstone, and Thomas R. Hoffman. *Production and Inventory Management,* 2nd ed. Cincinnati, Oh.: South-Western Publishing, 1991.

Inventory Management Reprints. Falls Church, Va.: American Production and Inventory Control Society, 1993.

Love, Stephen F. *Inventory Control.* New York: McGraw-Hill, 1979.

Vollmann, Thomas E., William L. Berry, and D. Clay Whybark. *Manufacturing Planning and Control Systems,* 5th ed. Burr Ridge, Ill.: Richard D. Irwin, 1997.

Before studying this chapter, you should know or, if necessary, review

1. Competitive priorities, Chapter 2, pages 28–32.
2. Work standards, Chapter 11, pages 328–329.
3. Relevant inventory costs, Chapter 12, pages 359–361.

LEARNING OBJECTIVES

After studying this chapter, you should be able to

1. Explain business planning.
2. Explain sales and operations planning.
3. Identify different kinds of aggregate planning strategies.
4. Identify options for changing demand and/or capacity in aggregate plans.
5. Develop aggregate plans, calculate associated costs, and evaluate the plans in terms of operations, marketing, finance, and human resources.
6. Describe the differences between aggregate plans for service organizations and manufacturing companies.

CHAPTER OUTLINE

As a student, you probably prepare for an exam in one of two ways. You wait until the night before the exam to cram three to five weeks of studying into one night. Or you regularly review your notes, maybe two or three times a week, and just do your normal review the night before the exam.

Companies typically take one of these two approaches to production when demand fluctuates from one period to the next. Some companies wait until the last minute and then request high output levels from their employees. Other companies maintain the same output level throughout. Your company's response to fluctuations in demand for its product or service dictates the level and timing of resources needed to generate products or services. In companies that cram, overtime is the norm in periods of heavy demand. In companies that maintain a level production output, higher inventory levels are the norm.

The level and timing of resources for production are detailed in a company's aggregate plan. Let's look at the role of aggregate planning in your company's strategic business plan.

THE ROLE OF AGGREGATE PLANNING ■

Aggregate planning is an integral part of the business planning process. This process begins when your company's top management gathers input from finance, marketing, operations, and engineering to develop a strategic business plan. The **strategic business plan,** with its long-term focus, provides your company's direction and objectives for the next 2 to 10 years. The strategic business plan is normally updated and reevaluated annually. The strategic business plan is also the starting point for sales and operations planning. It states the company's objectives for profitability, growth rate, and return on investment.

Sales and operations planning integrates the medium-range functional plans developed by marketing, operations, engineering, and finance. Sales and operations planning begins with the **marketing plan** developed by the marketing group based on information shared with operations, finance, and engineering.

Marketing Plan

The marketing plan is intended to meet the objectives of the strategic business plan. The marketing plan identifies the sales needed to achieve the profitability level, the growth rate, and the return on investment stated in the strategic business plan. Detailed in the marketing plan are the targeted market segments; necessary market share; competitive focus such as price, quality, flexibility, or time; expected profit margins; and any new products needed.

If the marketing plan does not meet the strategic business objectives, top management and marketing management revise either the objectives or the marketing plan until the marketing plan fully supports the strategic objectives.

▶ **Strategic business plan**
A statement of long-range strategy and revenue, cost and profit objectives.

▶ **Sales and operations planning**
The process that brings together all the functional business plans (marketing, operations, engineering, and finance) into one integrated plan.

▶ **Marketing plan**
Identifies the markets to be served, desired levels of customer service, product competitive advantage, profit margins, and the market share needed to achieve the objectives of the strategic business plan.

Aggregate or Production Plan

The aggregate plan, also called the *production plan*, identifies the resources needed by the operations group during the next 6 to 18 months to support the marketing plan. The **aggregate plan** details the aggregate production rate and the size of the workforce, which enables planners to determine the amount of inventory to be held; the amount of overtime or undertime authorized; any authorized subcontracting, hiring, or firing of employees; and back ordering of customer orders. The aggregate plan is usually updated and reevaluated monthly by the operations group.

Your company normally develops the aggregate plan based on a *composite* product that represents the expected product mix (to minimize the level of detail, individual products are not represented in the aggregate plan). Companies may group products into major product families to facilitate aggregate planning. For example, if your company produces several varieties of stereo equipment, you might have product families based on kinds of stereos. One product family could be home theater stereos, portable stereos, or automobile stereo systems. Each family can include different items as long as each item has similar processing needs.

Regardless of the method, the goal is to reduce the number of calculations to develop the aggregate plan. Using a composite product, or product families, reduces the level of detail but still provides the information needed for decision making at this stage. Common terms of output used in the aggregate plan are units, gallons, pounds, standard hours, and dollars.

To summarize, the purpose of the aggregate plan is to develop production rates and authorize resources that accommodate the marketing plan and allow your company to meet the objectives of the strategic business plan. Figure 13-1 summarizes the business planning flow.

▶ **Aggregate plan**
Includes the budgeted levels of finished products, inventory, backlogs, workforce size, and aggregate production rate needed to support the marketing plan.

Figure 13-1

The business planning hierarchy

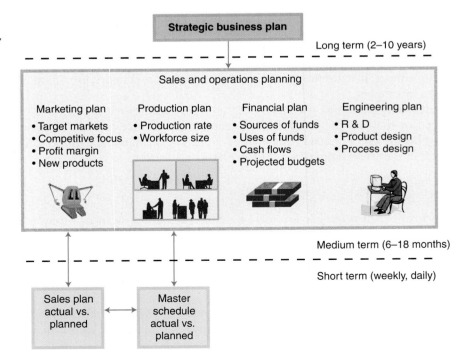

Financial and Engineering Plans

The **financial plan** indicates the sources and uses of funds, expected cash flows, anticipated profits, and projected budgets. The **engineering plan** supports the research and development for new products introduced in the marketing plan and subsequently planned for in the aggregate plan.

▶ **Financial plan**
Identifies the sources and uses of funds; projects cash flows, profits, return on investment; and provides budgets in support of the strategic business plan.

The sales and operations planning process evaluates the company's performance regularly throughout the year. The process begins in sales and marketing with comparisons of real demand against forecasted demand. The forecast is updated and the market reevaluated. Based on the updated forecast, marketing communicates to the operations, finance, and engineering groups the proposed changes to the marketing plan and makes the changes all three groups agree on. The other groups adjust their plans accordingly. If operations, finance, or engineering cannot support the proposed changes to the marketing plan, marketing again revises the marketing plan.

▶ **Engineering plan**
Identifies new products or modifications to existing products that are needed in support of the marketing plan.

Master Production Schedule

The sales and operations plan is evaluated and updated monthly. The master production schedule and the detailed sales plan are reviewed weekly or even daily. The **master production schedule** is an anticipated production schedule and is typically stated as specific finished goods. It details how operations will use available resources, and which units or models will be built in each time frame. This allows marketing to make informed commitments to their customers. (Master production scheduling and customer commitments are discussed in Chapter 14.)

▶ **Master production schedule**
The anticipated production schedule for the company expressed in specific configurations, quantities, and dates.

Aggregate planning has been important for Apple Computer Inc. The company's strategic plan focused on revolutionizing its products by making them more stylish and feature-specific. In turn, sales and operational planning streamlined operations by: (1) slashing expenses over $2 billion; (2) reducing the lineup of 15 product families to just a few that share common components; (3) outsourcing manufacturing to more efficient contractors; (4) substantially trimming the amount of inventory, the number of key suppliers, and the number of distributors; and (5) devising its own

LINKS TO PRACTICE
Apple Computer
www.apple.com

system to handle on-line purchases and shifting sales to an on-line store. Finally, the marketing plan targeted a specific audience of consumers, schools, and imaginative individuals; followed by catchy ad campaigns (including the "Think different" slogan and iMovie ads). For Apple, as for any company, strong aggregate planning has been extremely important.

Now let's look at different kinds of aggregate plans so we can see how the aggregate plan fits into the business planning hierarchy.

TYPES OF AGGREGATE PLANS ∎

Level Aggregate Plan

We usually categorize aggregate plans by the kind of resources used: level, chase, or mixed plans. A **level aggregate plan** maintains a constant workforce and produces the same amount of product in each time period.

▶ **Level aggregate plan**
A planning approach that produces the same quantity each time period. Inventory and back orders are used to absorb demand fluctuations.

■ Example 13.1 Calculating the Number of Employees

Wavetop Inc. currently has 10 employees, each producing 5 complete units per day, for a total of 50 units every workday. Figure the number of employees needed in the company's level aggregate plan if the company has an average weekly demand of 500 units.

Solution:
If average weekly demand is 500 units and employees work 5 days per week, we need to produce 100 units per day. Thus, the workforce should be 20 employees (100 units needed each day divided by 5 units completed per employee per day). If we use this method, inventory accumulates when demand is below average and depletes when demand exceeds the average level. If we do not have enough inventory on hand to satisfy demand, then back orders result.

The advantage of a level production plan is workforce stability. Your company sets labor and equipment capacity equal to average demand, rather than hire excess labor or buy additional tools and equipment just to meet peak demand. In addition, the labor force is not subjected to varying work levels during the year such as periods of layoff or undertime followed by periods of hiring and/or overtime.

The disadvantages of the level plan are the buildup of inventory and/or possible poor customer service from extensive use of back orders. The level plan is often used with make-to-stock products such as stereos, kitchen appliances, and hardware.

■ Example 13.2 Calculating Average Monthly Net Demand for Wavetop Inc.

Wavetop, Inc., a producer of water ski equipment, anticipates the following demand for its water skis. Demand for January is 12,000 units; for February, 9000; March, 12,000; April, 15,000; May, 18,000; and June, 24,000. The company has 6000 units in beginning inventory. Calculate the average monthly net demand for the company.

Solution:
Summing the monthly demands, the company needs a total of 90,000 units during the next 6 months. Since Wavetop, Inc. already has 6000 units in inventory, net demand is 84,000 units. The company has 6 months to satisfy demand, so it must build 14,000 units monthly (84,000 units divided by 6 months = 14,000 units needed per month).

By calculating the amount of production needed each month, the company can plan the appropriately sized workforce. If each employee can build 25 units per normal workday and the company operates 20 days per month, then each employee builds 500 units per month. To calculate the number of employees needed, divide the number of units needed per month by the monthly output per employee (14,000 units divided by 500 units per employee = 28 employees needed).

Chase Aggregate Plan

▶ **Chase aggregate plan**
A planning approach that varies production to meet demand each period.

A **chase aggregate plan** produces exactly what is needed to satisfy demand during each period. The production rate changes in response to demand fluctuations. Whereas the level aggregate plan sets capacity to accommodate average demand, the chase aggregate plan sets labor and equipment capacity to satisfy demand each period.

The advantage of the chase plan is that it minimizes finished-goods holding costs. This may be a better option when a company produces make-to-order products such as custom cabinets, special-purpose equipment, one-of-a-kind items, or highly perishable products. The disadvantages are constantly changing capacity needs and the need for enough equipment to meet peak demand. Many options for short-term capacity changes are expensive.

■ **Example 13.3 Chase Aggregate Plan at Wavetop Inc.**

Let's look at what would happen if Wavetop Inc. decides to adjust its capacity by hiring and firing employees each month. We calculate the number of employees needed during each period based on the net demand.

Solution:

For example, January demand is 12,000 units, but since we have 6000 units in inventory, the net demand is only 6000 units. Each employee builds 500 units per month, so Wavetop Inc. needs 12 employees (6000 units divided by 500 units per employee per month) in January. The company needs 18 employees in February, 24 employees in March, 30 employees in April, 36 employees in May, and 48 employees in June. How does this affect the space needed, the number of workstations, the sets of tools, and so forth?

When Wavetop Inc. used a level aggregate plan, it needed space and equipment to accommodate 28 employees. With the chase aggregate plan, however, the company needs space and equipment for 48 people.

Hybrid Aggregate Plan

A **hybrid aggregate plan** typically uses a combination of options. With this plan, your company might maintain a stable workforce supplemented by an inventory buildup and some overtime production to meet demand. Or the company may back order a portion of its demand. Any combination of options is possible. Because of the number of options you can combine in a hybrid plan, you need to evaluate your company's current situation and limit the options you choose from.

Next, let's look at the demand-based and capacity-based options used in aggregate plans.

▶ **Hybrid aggregate plan**
A planning approach that uses a combination of approaches while developing the aggregate plan.

AGGREGATE PLANNING OPTIONS ■

Companies can choose from two groups of options when formulating an aggregate plan. The first group, **demand-based options,** includes two reactive options and one proactive option. These are

◆ Reactive options, in which operations uses inventories and back orders to react to demand fluctuations
◆ The proactive option, in which marketing tries to shift the demand patterns to minimize demand fluctuations

An example of the proactive option is the early bird dinners offered by some restaurants. The reduced price for a specific time period encourages customers to dine earlier and spreads the demand out over a longer period of time.

The second group, **capacity-based options**, changes output capacity to meet demand through the use of overtime, undertime, subcontracting, hires, fires, and using part-timers or temps. Each of these offers relief for fluctuating demand, but each has cost and operational implications for the company. Let's look at each option individually.

▶ **Demand-based options**
A group of options that respond to demand fluctuations through the use of inventory or back orders, or by shifting the demand pattern.

CROSS FUNCTIONAL

▶ **Capacity-based options**
A group of options that allow the firm to change its current operating capacity.

Demand-Based Options

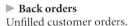
► **Finished goods inventory**
Products available for shipment to the customer.

Using **finished goods inventory** to absorb demand fluctuations allows your company to develop a stable work environment. The company produces at average demand levels throughout the year rather than change capacity from one period to the next. When demand is less than average, the extra units go into inventory. When demand exceeds production, the extra units come out of inventory. Producing at average demand levels allows your company to invest less in capacity.

As we saw earlier, when Wavetop Inc. used a level aggregate plan using inventory, the company needed space and equipment for only 28 employees. With the chase aggregate plan using hires and fires, the company needs space and equipment for 48 employees. However, this stable working environment isn't free. Your company does have increased inventory holding costs because inventory is built and warehoused in anticipation of future demand. Inventory holding costs range from 15 to 35% of the cost of the inventory. Unfortunately, some companies with highly seasonal sales may have no choice but to use this option. For example, companies that make holiday products often experience 60 to 90% of their demand over a short period of time (1 or 2 months out of the year). Producing the majority of its annual demand at the last minute could mean enormous machine and labor capacity, which would be underused or even idle the rest of the year.

► **Back orders**
Unfilled customer orders.

Back orders result when your company does not have enough production and/or inventory on hand to cover current demand, so it promises to deliver the product to the customer at a later date. Customers may wait or they may take their business elsewhere. When a customer is unwilling to wait, the back order turns into a lost sale. Your company must understand its customers and its marketplace to judge whether or not back orders are a viable option. If alternate products or sources are readily available, customers probably will not wait. They are more likely to wait for unique products.

CROSS FUNCTIONAL

Unique has different meanings. Perhaps your company is the sole producer of a certain product, the reputation of your company merits waiting, or the price may be much lower than for any substitute products. Whatever your reason for choosing back orders as an option, it must be a good one if you expect a customer to wait for your product.

In addition to possible lost sales, your company may have extra administrative costs because of the back order such as higher shipping costs for overnight delivery. (These costs are discussed in Chapter 12.) In general, the back order should be used sparingly.

► **Shifting demand**
A marketing strategy that attempts to shift demand from peak periods to non-peak periods in an attempt to smooth out the demand pattern.

Shifting demand is a proactive marketing approach to leveling demand in which your company tries to change consumer buying patterns by offering incentives. Prime examples of this are movie matinees, early bird dinners, and preseason or off-season discounts. In most cases, there is no out-of-pocket cost to the company—the profit is simply less per sale. This strategy makes sense when the company has high fixed costs and low variable costs. For example, a movie theater has a high fixed cost (the building and the projection equipment) but is empty during most of a 24-hour day. The variable cost for showing the movie is quite low. A matinee allows the theater to make better use of its capital investment.

Another way to level demand is offering preseason or off-season discounts. Shifting some of the company's demand means that less inventory is needed to satisfy demand during the prime season. Thus the inventory investment is lower, less floor space is needed, and some customers are pleased by the discount.

Capacity-Based Options

Overtime is the most common method for increasing output capacity. It is an expensive option, however, and should only be used short-term. Using overtime to increase output typically means your company pays a 50% wage premium to its workers. Unfortunately, when people work overtime their productivity does not increase proportionately, so the cost of labor per unit increases. Workers typically do not produce more during overtime.

Worker productivity—and the quality of the work—may even decrease. In fact, the more overtime a company uses, the more likely it will experience reduced productivity and quality. Reduced productivity and quality tend to increase costs even more. Therefore, overtime is at best a short-term option for increasing production capacity.

Undertime results when a company does not need an employee to produce at 100% of his or her capability. Undertime is normally the result of reduced demand and a desire not to build up inventory levels. Undertime does not cost a company a wage premium but it does increase the labor cost per unit, because fewer units are built but regular-time wages stay the same.

Why would a company keep employees around if they are not needed? The answer is straightforward: economics. It may be cost effective to carry valuable workers for a short period of time if the company expects demand to return to previous levels. If the company releases employees immediately, it may incur high replacement costs when it eventually hires new employees. The problem with undertime is that employee morale may suffer when people realize that there is not enough work to keep everyone busy. Thus undertime is also a short-term option.

Subcontracting means letting another company do some of the work for you. Subcontracting provides additional output capacity during periods of high demand. Unlike strategic outsourcing decisions that have components, subassemblies, or final products previously done in-house produced by another company, subcontracting is a tactical decision as to how to increase output in periods of high demand. For example, a publishing company may choose to outsource technical information development (a task requiring technical writing expertise) and have no in-house capability. Or a publishing company may need to subcontract additional technical information development because the in-house group has more work than it can handle. Outsourcing decisions identify the core business that the company is in. Subcontracting decisions provide extra capacity for the company.

The advantages of subcontracting are additional output without investing in additional tools, equipment, and labor. The disadvantages of subcontracting are the cost, which is substantial. The first step is to find a qualified subcontractor for the job. Then you have the additional cost of shipping parts to the subcontractor and having finished subassemblies or products shipped back to you. In addition, subcontracting means your company loses some degree of control. By contrast, work done in-house is always under your control: you know exactly where it is and how it is progressing. Since finding a good subcontractor takes time, subcontracting is a medium- to long-term option.

Hiring and firing changes the size of the workforce. Both hiring and firing can mean high costs for your company. Hiring requires the administrative work of identifying the position, communicating with potential applicants, evaluating the materials submitted by applicants, interviewing, verifying employment and references, running background checks, making decisions, verifying physical condition, making offers, and completing negotiations. After the employee is hired, your company sets up

▶ **Overtime**
Work beyond normal established operation hours that usually requires a premium be paid to the workers.

▶ **Undertime**
A condition occurring when there are more people on the payroll than are needed to produce the planned output.

▶ **Subcontracting**
Sending production work outside to another manufacturer or service provider.

CROSS FUNCTIONAL

▶ **Hiring and firing**
Long-term option for increasing or decreasing capacity.

payroll, health insurance, security ID and badge, computer log-in, phone extension, and so forth. During employee training, output is normally lower and mistakes are typically higher. Thus hiring a permanent employee is a long-term option.

Firing employees is also expensive. Excessive firing can lead to increased unemployment compensation premiums. (Unemployment compensation is like any insurance policy: when you have a lot of claims, your rates increase.) Add to that the severance pay that companies typically pay to permanently laid-off employees, and the cost mounts. Significant, too, is the expense in lost knowledge when you terminate employees. Employees may leave with individual know-how that the remaining workforce will have to learn for themselves. For example, your employee may not have documented a minor change to the job instructions that increases productivity or improves product quality. The next employee on the job will have to learn this secret of improved output.

Finally, you have the cost in morale, which may affect productivity. Deciding who will stay and who will go is not a pleasant exercise. Some companies base the decision on seniority rather than what makes sense from an operational standpoint. When senior employees remain and junior employees are forced out, the remaining employees may return to jobs that have experienced major technological change. Thus respect for seniority rewards company loyalty but often at the expense of lost productivity.

For all of these reasons, hiring and firing employees is in the category of long-term options. Table 13-1 summarizes aggregate planning options.

Table 13-1 Summary of Aggregate Planning Options	
Demand-Based Options	**Capacity-Based Options**
◆ Inventory	◆ Overtime/undertime
◆ Back orders	◆ Subcontracting
◆ Shifting demand	◆ Hiring and firing

Before You Go On

Make sure you understand the two kinds of options used in aggregate planning: demand-based options and capacity-based options.

Demand-based options stabilize capacity and react to demand fluctuations through the use of inventories and back orders, which may enable you to shift some demand to make the demand pattern smoother. Still, the longer you use either inventories or back orders, the riskier they become. Consumer preferences change over time and demand for your product may erode. Demand-based options are used primarily with level aggregate plans.

Capacity-based options are used to change capacity levels. Some capacity-based options are short-term, such as overtime and undertime; some are medium-term, such as subcontracting or using temporaries; and some are long-term, such as hiring or firing employees.

Your company should choose the option that satisfies the time frame needed (short, medium, or long) for the capacity change. Capacity-based options are used primarily with chase aggregate plans; all options can be used with hybrid aggregate plans.

Now that you understand the options and the kinds of aggregate plans, let's consider some additional factors in developing aggregate plans.

EVALUATING THE CURRENT SITUATION ■

When you are considering the different options, it is important to evaluate your company's current situation in terms of point of departure, magnitude of the change, and duration of the change.

The **point of departure** is the percentage of normal capacity your company is currently operating at. For example, if you are operating at 100% of normal capacity and need to increase capacity by 10%, you might use a relatively simple option such as overtime to achieve that 10% extra capacity. If you are already using overtime—say, you are operating at 125% of normal capacity—you might look for a different way to increase capacity. At this point, subcontracting or hiring temporary workers might be more economical. If you need to increase capacity even more, maybe it is time to hire some new permanent workers. The same is true when you need to reduce capacity. If you are making a small reduction—say, down to 90% of normal capacity—you might decide to use undertime. For even greater reduction, you might cut back hours or furlough employees. If the need to reduce is still greater, you might choose permanent layoffs. Thus point of departure affords your company perspective on the best options.

▶ **Point of departure**
The percentage of normal capacity the company is currently using.

Magnitude of the change is the size of change needed. Smaller changes may be easier to implement—as we saw when Wavetop Inc. used the chase aggregate plan and increased its workforce from 12 to 48 employees in a 6-month period. Larger capacity changes need more drastic measures, such as hiring or firing a shift, and the effects on productivity are greater.

▶ **Magnitude of the change**
The relative size of the change needed.

Duration of the change is the length of time you expect to need the different level of capacity. If the duration is a brief seasonal surge, then hiring temporary or seasonal workers makes sense. For example, many retail stores hire additional clerks during holiday seasons. Some of these employees work for several years at the same store. When you expect the increased need for capacity to be permanent, a long-term solution like subcontracting or hiring new employees is more appropriate.

▶ **Duration of the change**
The expected length of time the different capacity level is needed.

Evaluating the point of departure, magnitude of change, and duration of change allows your company to reduce the number of viable options for its aggregate plan.

When companies face highly seasonal demand, an alternative to hiring full-time permanent employees is the use of seasonal employees. UPS experiences highly seasonal demand each year, delivering approximately 300 million packages globally during the 4 weeks between Thanksgiving and Christmas. To meet this high demand, UPS hires around 90,000 part-time seasonal employees. That number includes 50,000 package handlers, who load and unload packages; 34,000 driver helpers; 2400 seasonal drivers for the delivery vans; and 850 tractor-trailer drivers. UPS hires and trains these employees each year. These trained, seasonal employees are often considered for permanent part-time jobs with UPS after the holidays. UPS has successfully implemented the use of seasonal workers to achieve its corporate strategy. As a result, UPS was recognized by *Your Money* magazine as providing the best part-time jobs in the nation.

LINKS TO PRACTICE
UPS Hires Seasonal Workers
www.ups.com

■ DEVELOPING THE AGGREGATE PLAN

Here are the steps to develop an aggregate plan:

> **STEP 1** **CHOOSE THE AGGREGATE PLAN THAT MATCHES YOUR COMPANY'S OBJECTIVES: LEVEL, CHASE, OR HYBRID.**
>
> **STEP 2** **BASED ON THE AGGREGATE PLAN, DETERMINE THE AGGREGATE PRODUCTION RATE.**

- If you use the level plan with inventories and back orders, the aggregate production rate is set equal to average demand. In addition, if you allow no back orders, the size of the workforce is changed initially so that all demand is met on time.
- If you use the chase aggregate plan, calculate how much output capacity you need each period. Calculate how many units will be produced on regular time and overtime, and how many units will be subcontracted.

> **STEP 3** **CALCULATE THE SIZE OF THE WORKFORCE.**

- If you use the level aggregate plan, calculate how many workers you need to achieve the average period demand.
- If you change capacity each period with hires and fires, calculate how many workers you need each period and make the necessary change in the workforce.
- If you change capacity through a variety of options, calculate how much of a particular option you need each period. (We will illustrate several combinations later.)

> **STEP 4** **TEST THE AGGREGATE PLAN AS FOLLOWS:**

- Using the production rate and initial workforce size, calculate your inventory levels, any shortages you face, expected hiring and firing, and when you will need overtime.
- Calculate the total costs for your plan.

> **STEP 5** **EVALUATE THE PLAN'S PERFORMANCE IN TERMS OF COST, CUSTOMER SERVICE, HUMAN RESOURCES, AND OPERATIONS.**

After you develop a plan, it is critical to evaluate each plan in terms of cost, customer service, operations, and human resources. Cost comparisons are simple if you are comparing similar ending positions—that is, plans with the same ending inventory level or producing the same number of units.

The comparisons are less clear when plans produce different quantities and leave different ending inventories. In this case, you can use a per unit cost comparison. To do this for customer service, measure how many back orders were placed during each period and throughout the duration of the plan. Decide whether this is an acceptable level of customer service to satisfy marketing's objectives. Assess the plan in terms first of operations, then of human resources. Are the workers putting in excessive overtime one month and doing little the next? How does this plan affect the workforce? Does it lower morale or does it provide stability for the workers?

When you evaluate the plan from several perspectives, you can decide how it can best satisfy your company's objectives. Table 13-2 shows you how to do this.

Table 13-2 Evaluation Perspectives and Measurements

Perspective	Measurements
Cost	Total cost
	Unit cost
	Inventory levels
Customer service	Number of back orders
Operations	Stability of schedule
	Equipment use
	Labor use
Human resources	Effect on workforce
	Employment stability

Before You Go On

Review the five steps to develop an aggregate plan:

Table 13-3 Steps to Develop an Aggregate Plan

Step 1: Choose the kind of aggregate plan: level, chase or hybrid.
Step 2: Calculate the aggregate production rate.
Step 3: Calculate the size of the workforce.
Step 4: Test the plan and calculate costs.
Step 5: Evaluate the plan in terms of cost, customer service, operations, and human resources.

AGGREGATE PLANS FOR COMPANIES WITH TANGIBLE PRODUCTS ■

Now let's develop a few plans so we can evaluate their effectiveness. We use the problem data in Table 13-4.

Table 13-4 Problem Data for Plans A, B, C, and D

Cost data	
Regular time labor cost per hour	$12.50
Overtime labor cost per hour	$18.75
Subcontracting cost per unit (labor only)	$125.00
Back order cost per unit per quarter	$25.00
Inventory holding cost per unit per quarter	$10.00
Hiring cost per employee	$800.00
Firing cost per employee	$500.00

Capacity data	
Beginning workforce	90 employees
Beginning inventory	0 units
Production standard per unit (hours)	8 hours of labor per unit
Regular time available per period (hours)	160 hours per period per employee
Overtime available per period (hours)	40 hours per period per employee

Demand data

Period 1	1,920 units	Period 5	2,040 units
Period 2	2,160 units	Period 6	2,400 units
Period 3	1,440 units	Period 7	1,740 units
Period 4	1,200 units	Period 8	1,500 units

■ Example 13.4 Plan A: Level Aggregate Plan Using Inventories and Back Orders

In this plan, you set the desired level of production output. Then you calculate the workforce needed to produce that quantity each period. You meet demand each period with current production and inventory, or with back orders.

Solution

Step 1   *Choose the kind of aggregate plan.* In this case we use a level aggregate plan.

Step 2   *Calculate the aggregate production rate.* We use the level option to calculate the average period demand rate. First, we add up the period demands and divide by the number of periods (14,400 units/8 = 1800 units per period), then we find the average production rate needed. If we have a beginning inventory, we subtract it from the total demand figure. If we have a desired ending inventory, we add that to the total demand figure. Otherwise, the 1800 units we calculated earlier is our average demand and subsequently our aggregate production rate.

Step 3   *Calculate the number of workers to produce 1800 units per period.* Since each employee works 160 hours per period and each unit takes 8 hours of labor to produce, each employee can produce 20 units per period. We need 1800 units produced, so 1800 units divided by 20 units per employee means that we need a workforce of 90. Since we have 90 workers, we do not need to hire or fire any workers.

Step 4   *Test and cost the plan.* We test the plan by using the aggregate production rate, the appropriate workforce, and the expected product demand during the planning horizon. Table 13-5 shows what happens when we produce 1800 units each month.

At the end of Period 1, we calculate whether we had excess product: did we build more than we needed for this period? If cumulative demand is greater than cumulative production, we are in a back-order situation. For example, in Period 1, cumulative demand is 1920 units, but we produced only 1800 units so we are short 120 units.

Table 13-5 Plan A: Level Aggregate Plan, Inventories and Back Orders

Period	1	2	3	4	5	6	7	8	Total
Demand (units)	1,920	2,160	1,440	1,200	2,040	2,400	1,740	1,500	14,400
Cumulative demand	1,920	4,080	5,520	6,720	8,760	11,160	12,900	14,400	
Period production	1,800	1,800	1,800	1,800	1,800	1,800	1,800	1,800	14,400
Cumulative production	1,800	3,600	5,400	7,200	9,000	10,800	12,600	14,400	
Ending inventory				480	240				720
Back orders	120	480	120			360	300		1,380

For another example, look at Quarter 4: the cumulative demand of 6720 units is less than the cumulative produced of 7200 units, which leaves us with an ending inventory of 480 units. (Note that using the cumulative columns to calculate ending inventories or shortages minimizes your calculations.)

Calculate the cost of the plan. For this plan, we use regular-time labor from 90 employees, we have some shortages (120 units in Period 1; 480 units in Period 2; 120 units in

Period 3; 360 units in Period 6; and 300 units in Period 7), and we carry some inventory (480 units for Period 4 and 240 units for Period 5). We include each of these in our total cost calculations (shown in Table 13-6).

Table 13-6 Total Cost Calculations for Plan A

Regular-time labor cost ($12.50 per hour × 160 hours per period × 8 periods × 90 employees)	$1,440,000
Carrying costs (720 units × $10 per unit)	$7,200
Back-order costs (1,380 units × $25 per unit)	$34,500
Total costs	$1,481,700

Next we evaluate Plan A based on these cost calculations.

Step 5 *Evaluate the plan for cost, customer service, operations, and human resources.* We can not really evaluate this plan from a financial standpoint because we have no alternatives for comparison. When we have developed additional plans, we will be able to do cost comparisons on those plans.

We can look at the customer service provided by this plan. Over the life of the plan, 1380 units are back ordered out of a total demand of 14,400 units, or roughly 9.6% of demand was not immediately satisfied from stock. The worst performance is in Period 2, with 480 units back ordered out of a demand of 2160 units. This means that 21% of demand for Period 2 (2160 new demand, plus 120 back orders from period 1) was not met during Period 2. Customer service performance at this level may not be sufficient to satisfy the marketing group. In terms of operations, however, this plan is workable. No employees are hired or fired, we do not need overtime or undertime, and output remains constant throughout the plan. No human resource problems are expected and morale should be good.

Now let's look at a level aggregate plan that would improve customer service with inventories but not allow back orders. All demand must be met each period.

■ Example 13.5 Plan B: Level Aggregate Plan Using Inventories but No Back Orders

Let's develop a level aggregate plan using inventories but no back orders. Demand must be met each period during the plan.

Solution

Step 1 *Choose the kind of aggregate plan.* In this case we use a level plan.

Step 2 *Calculate the aggregate production rate.* When we do not allow back orders, we do not use the average demand rate to calculate the workforce, as shown in Table 13-7. A new row, labeled "cumulative demand/number of periods," divides the cumulative demand to each point by the number of periods in which to produce that quantity. For example, by the end of Period 2, we need a total of 4080 units. Thus we plan to build 2040 units each month to satisfy all demand for the first two periods with the level aggregate plan. We calculate this value for each period. The period with the highest needed production rate determines the aggregate production rate we use in the plan. For our plan, 2040 units is the highest production rate needed, so it becomes our planned aggregate production rate.

Step 3 *Calculate how many employees we need to produce 2040 units per period.* Since each employee can produce 20 units per period during regular time, we need 102 employees for this plan. We must hire 12 employees.

Step 4 *Test and cost the plan using a production rate per period of 2040 units and a workforce of 102 employees.* Table 13.7 shows the results of the plan.

This plan creates high inventory, especially after Period 2. The inventory ranges from 0 to 1920 units, or from 0 weeks of supply to more than 4 weeks of supply.

Table 13-7 Plan B: Level Aggregate Plan, No Back Orders, All Demand Met

Period	1	2	3	4	5	6	7	8	Total
Demand (units)	1,920	2,160	1,440	1,200	2,040	2,400	1,740	1,500	14,400
Cumulative demand	1,920	4,080	5,520	6,720	8,760	11,160	12,900	14,400	
Cumulative demand/ number of periods	1,920	2,040	1,840	1,680	1,752	1,860	1,843	1,800	
Period production	2,040	2,040	2,040	2,040	2,040	2,040	2,040	2,040	16,320
Cumulative production	2,040	4,080	6,120	8,160	10,200	12,240	14,280	16,320	
Ending inventory	120	0	600	1,440	1,440	1,080	1,380	1,920	7,980

We can calculate most of the costs of the plan. However, we can not capture the true holding costs because we do not know when the ending inventory of 1920 units will be consumed. We need to remember this when we compare our plans. Table 13-8 shows the costs for this plan.

Table 13-8 Total Cost Calculations for Plan B

Hiring costs (12 employees × $800)	$9,600
Regular time labor cost ($12.50 per hour × 160 hours per period × 8 periods × 102 employees)	1,632,000
Carrying costs (7980 units × $10 per unit)	79,800
Total costs	$1,721,400

Step 5 *Evaluate the plan.* Compared with Plan A, Plan B costs at least an additional $239,700 and possibly more given the ending inventory level. This is more than a 16% increase in total cost. However, we need to make sure our comparisons are fair. In Plan A, we build 14,400 units, whereas in Plan B, we build 16,320 units. We should expect total costs of Plan B to be higher since we need more labor to build the additional units. Note that when plans require building different quantities, it may be easier to use the unit cost per plan for our comparisons. The unit cost for Plan A is $102.90 ($1,481,700 divided by 14,400 units). The unit cost for Plan B is $105.48 ($1,721,400 divided by 16,320 units). Plan B costs $2.58 more per unit or roughly 2.5% more ($2.58 divided by $102.90).

What are we getting for this extra cost? Improved customer service. Plan B provides 100% customer service because no products are back ordered. Now your company must decide whether 100% customer service is worth at least an additional 2.5% in cost or if another approach might be more cost effective.

Remember, we have understated our holding costs. From an operations standpoint this is a relatively easy plan to implement. We increase our workforce by 12 employees or just over 13%. Our output is still level and we do not need overtime or undertime. Morale should be fine.

Since the costs of Plan B are higher, let's look at a chase aggregate plan.

■ Example 13.6 Plan C: Chase Aggregate Plan Using Hiring and Firing

This plan changes capacity each period to meet demand fully. Capacity levels will change through hiring and firing. Demand must be met each period.

Solution

Step 1   *Choose the kind of aggregate plan.* In this example we use a chase plan.

Step 2   *Calculate the production rate.* For example, in Period 1, we need to build 1920 units. Since the company builds exactly what is needed to satisfy each period's demand, the production rate for each period is set equal to the demand rate. Table 13-9 shows the level of output needed in each period.

Step 3   *Calculate the size of the workforce.* The initial workforce is 90, so we hire 6 employees for Period 1. The number of employees we need to hire or fire depends on our ending workforce level in the previous period. We can see from Table 13-9 that we need 96 employees in Period 1. We calculate this by dividing the number of units needed by the number of units produced by each employee per month (1920 units divided by 20 units per employee). Since we need 108 employees in Period 2 and we ended Period 1 with 96 employees, we must hire an additional 12 employees for Period 2. We will have no ending inventories or back orders.

Step 4   *Test and cost the plan.* Table 13-9 shows the month-to-month testing of the plan. Note that this plan creates fluctuation in the size of the workforce, ranging from a high of 120 employees to a low of 60 employees. This means that your company must have enough space, tools, and equipment for up to 120 employees working simultaneously during a given time. It also means that half that space can be idle during other periods. The number of changes in the size of the workforce and the magnitude of some of these changes could cause problems. Suppose we fire a total of 48 workers during Periods 3 and 4, only to hire 42 new employees in Period 5. Your workforce has increased by 70% (42 divided by 60). Imagine the mass confusion and the loss of productivity at the beginning!

Table 13-9 Plan C: Chase Aggregate Plan Using Hires and Fires

Period	1	2	3	4	5	6	7	8	Total
Demand (units)	1,920	2,160	1,440	1,200	2,040	2,400	1,740	1,500	14,400
Employees needed	96	108	72	60	102	120	87	75	720
Number of hires	6	12			42	18			78
Number of fires			36	12			33	12	93

Table 13-10 shows the total cost calculations for Plan C.

Table 13-10 Total Cost Calculations for Plan C

Hiring costs (78 employees × $800 each)	$62,400
Firing costs (93 employees × $500 each)	$46,500
Regular time labor costs ($12.50 per hour × 160 hours per period × 720 employees)	$1,440,000
Total costs	$1,548,900

Step 5 *Evaluate Plan C.* The costs of Plan C are the highest of the three plans. The unit cost for Plan C is $107.56 ($1,548,900 divided by 14,400 units), an increase of more than $2.00 per unit from Plan B, which also provided excellent customer service.

From a customer service standpoint, Plan C is fine because no products are back-ordered. From an operations standpoint, however, this plan is not easy to implement. We need space, tools, and equipment for up to 120 individuals in Period 6, whereas we will have only 60 employees in Period 4. We need to consider the feasibility of major changes like these. Employee morale might be low because of the lack of job security. How many employees can afford to take a month or two off?

Instead, let's look at a hybrid aggregate plan that maintains a steady workforce and allows for capacity changes through the use of overtime.

■ Example 13.7 Plan D: Hybrid Aggregate Plan Using Initial Workforce and Overtime as Needed

Develop a hybrid aggregate plan using the initial workforce of 90 employees supplemented with overtime when demand exceeds regular-time production.

Solution

Step 1 *Choose the kind of aggregate plan.* In this example we use a hybrid plan.

Step 2 *Calculate the production rate.* We already know the regular-time production rate of 1800 units per period because we are using the initial workforce. This plan increases capacity when period demand exceeds the product available through that period's production and the beginning inventory for that period. For example, in Period 1, we need 1920 units to satisfy demand. The hybrid aggregate plan in Table 13-11 shows that we build 1800 units during regular-time production and produce the remaining 120 units using overtime. We do not need overtime after Period 2 because we can build up enough inventory to handle demand fluctuations.

We can see that the demand figures for Periods 4, 5, 6, 7, and 8 have changed. These changes reflect the net demand for the period after subtracting the ending inventory of the previous period. For example, in Period 4, demand is 1200 units. However, since we have 360 units in ending inventory in Period 3, we subtract those out of Period 4's demand to arrive at a net demand of 860 units.

Step 3 *Calculate the workforce size.* We know that the workforce size for this plan is 90 employees.

Step 4 *Test and cost the plan.* We test the plan using 90 employees producing 1800 units per period during regular time, and using overtime for production when regular-time production is not adequate to satisfy demand. Table 13-11 shows the plan.

Plan D uses a stable workforce of 90 employees and uses overtime in Periods 1 and 2. All other demand fluctuations are handled through inventory. Total production for this plan is 14,880 units (14,400 during regular time and 480 during overtime). Ending inventories range from 0 to 960 units. Table 13-12 shows the total costs for Plan D.

Table 13-11 Plan D: Hybrid Aggregate Plan, Initial Workforce, and Overtime as Needed

Period	1	2	3	4	5	6	7	8	Total
Demand (units)	1,920	2,160	1,440	840	1,080	1,680	1,620	1,500	14,400
Regular time units produced	1,800	1,800	1,800	1,800	1,800	1,800	1,800	1,800	14,400
Overtime units produced	120	360							480
Ending inventory	0	0	360	960	720	120	180	480	2,820

Table 13-12 Total Cost Calculations for Plan D

Regular time labor costs ($12.50 per hour × 160 hours per period × 90 employees × 8 periods)	$1,440,000
Overtime labor costs ($18.75 per hour × 8 hours per unit × 480 units)	$72,000
Holding costs (2,820 units × $10 per unit)	$28,200
Total costs	$1,540,200

Step 5 *Evaluate Plan D.* The per unit cost in Plan D is $103.51, which is only 61 cents higher than for our Plan A level aggregate plan using inventories and back orders. However, Plan D provides 100% customer service and the per unit cost differential is only about 0.6%. Plan D achieves excellent customer service at the lowest cost so far, which should satisfy both finance and marketing. In terms of operations and human resources, we are using overtime in the short term for Periods 1 and 2. We do not ask workers to put in more than 20% overtime in Period 2 (360 units on overtime in Period 2, while producing 1,800 units on regular time). Overtime in Period 1 is limited to 10% of the regular-time production. Thus we are not overusing the workers, and we keep overtime to a minimum. In addition, Plan D should not be hard to implement from an operations standpoint.

You can continue to test different aggregate plans for this example on your own. See whether you can keep customer service high and total cost low. Now let's develop some plans for a service company that provides nontangible products.

■ AGGREGATE PLANS FOR SERVICE COMPANIES WITH NONTANGIBLE PRODUCTS

In the previous examples, your company used inventory buildup as a way of leveling the aggregate plan. When your company's product is nontangible—for example, if your company offers a service as do banks, health-care providers, and hair stylists—inventory is no longer a viable option.

We use the problem data shown in Table 13-13 to develop a level aggregate plan.

Table 13-13 Problem Data for Plans E, F and G			
Cost data		**Capacity data**	
Regular time labor cost per hour	$8.00	Beginning work force	60 employees
		Service standard per call (hours)	4 hours per call
Overtime labor cost per hour	$12.00	Regular time available per period (hours)	160 hours per period period per employee
Subcontracting cost per service call (labor only)	$15.00	Overtime available per period (hours)	24 hours per period per employee
Hiring cost per employee	$250.00		
Firing cost per employee	$150.00		

Demand data (calls)					
Period 1	2400	Period 4	2040	Period 7	1320
Period 2	1560	Period 5	2760	Period 8	2400
Period 3	1200	Period 6	1680		

■ Example 13.8 Plan E: Level Aggregate Plan with No Back Orders, No Tangible Product

With this plan, your company maintains a level workforce with no back orders. Any demand not satisfied is lost to a competing service provider so the company must meet all demand.

Solution

Step 1   *Choose the kind of aggregate plan.* In this example, we use a level plan.

Step 2   *Calculate the production rate.* Since the company is not going to back order, you staff to accommodate peak demand. The aggregate production rate is set equal to the highest demand in any period during the plan. Period 5 has 2760 service calls, which means 11,040 hours of regular-time labor must be available.

Step 3   *Calculate the size of the workforce.* You need 69 employees (11,040 hours divided by 160 hours per employee per period). Each period, you have 11,040 hours of regular-time labor available.

Step 4   *Test and cost the plan.* Table 13-14 shows plan E using 69 employees and meeting demand each period. As you can see, this plan creates excess labor: only period 5 uses the total workforce. Period 3 uses a little over 43% of capacity (4,800/11,040). Over the life of the plan, your company uses just under 70% of its available regular-time workforce (61,440/88,320). Table 13-15 shows the costs of the plan. An additional calculation not shown in the table is the cost per service call, which is $46.15 ($708,810 divided by 15,360 service calls).

Table 13-14 Plan E: Level Aggregate Plan, Staffing for Peak Demand

Period	1	2	3	4	5	6	7	8	Total
Service calls	2,400	1,560	1,200	2,040	2,760	1,680	1,320	2,400	15,360
Service hours needed	9,600	6,240	4,800	8,160	11,040	6,720	5,280	9,600	61,440
Regular-time hours available	11,040	11,040	11,040	11,040	11,040	11,040	11,040	11,040	88,320
Undertime hours	1,440	4,800	6,240	2,880	0	4,320	5,760	1,440	26,880

Table 13-15 Total Cost Calculations for Plan E

Hiring costs (9 employees × $250 each)	$2,250
Regular-time labor costs ($8.00 per hour × 160 hours per period × 8 periods × 69 employees)	$706,560
Total costs	$708,810

Step 5 *Evaluate the plan.* We have no other plans for nontangible products for comparison yet, but it is likely that underuse of the regular-time workforce will make plan E cost prohibitive. It is also likely that the high undertime will lower employee morale. From an operational perspective, it might be better to keep the present workforce and supplement with overtime. (When we use overtime, we reduce undertime.) In fact, when we use the maximum amount of overtime permitted, we minimize undertime.

Let's look at a plan that uses some overtime.

■ **Example 13.9 Plan F: Hybrid Aggregate Plan Using Initial Workforce and Overtime as Needed**

Now we will develop a hybrid aggregate plan using a workforce of 60 employees working 160 regular-time hours per period. We use overtime when regular-time capacity is inadequate.

Solution

Step 1 *Choose the kind of aggregate plan.* We use a hybrid plan.

Step 2 *Calculate the production rate.* In this plan, our regular-time aggregate production rate is the same as for plan E because we are keeping the initial work force of 60 employees. Thus we have 9600 regular-time hours available each period (60 employees × 160 hours per employee per period). The overtime needed in a period depends on the number of service calls expected. For each period, we calculate the number of hours needed to satisfy the service calls. For example, in Period 4, we need 8160 hours to meet demand (2040 calls × 4 hours per call).

Step 3 *Calculate the size of the workforce.* We know that the workforce is 60 employees working 160 hours of regular time each period.

Step 4 *Test and cost the plan.* Table 13-16 shows the completed plan. We need overtime only in Period 5 the initial work force has more than enough capacity during the other periods. We calculate the overtime by subtracting the available regular-time hours (9600 hours) from the service hours needed in Period 5 (11,040), which yields 1440 hours of overtime. Table 13-17 shows the total costs of regular-time labor and overtime labor.

Table 13-16 Plan F: Hybrid Aggregate Plan, Initial Workforce and Overtime as Needed

Period	1	2	3	4	5	6	7	8	Total
Service calls	2,400	1,560	1,200	2,040	2,760	1,680	1,320	2,400	15,360
Service hours needed	9,600	6,240	4,800	8,160	11,040	6,720	5,280	9,600	61,440
Regular-time hours available	9,600	9,600	9,600	9,600	9,600	9,600	9,600	9,600	76,800
Overtime hours needed	0	0	0	0	1,440	0	0	0	1,440
Undertime hours	0	3,360	4,800	1,440	0	2,880	4,320	0	16,800

Table 13-17 Total Cost Calculations for Plan F

Regular time labor costs ($8.00 per hour × 160 hours per period × 60 employees)	$614,400
Overtime labor costs ($12.00 per hour × 1,440 hours)	$17,280
Total costs	$631,680

Step 5 *Evaluate the plan.* This plan reduces regular-time capacity from 88,320 hours in Plan E to 76,800 hours. Thus we increase regular-time labor use to 79.9%. In addition, the cost per call drops to $41.13. This is a major improvement over Plan E in terms of cost and customer service. However, it is still problematic in terms of the amount of undertime.

Next, let's see what happens when we develop a plan that eliminates undertime.

■ Example 13.10 Plan G: Chase Aggregate Plan for Nontangible Products Using Hiring and Firing

With this plan, your company reduces its undertime costs using hiring and firing.

Solution

Step 1   *Choose the kind of aggregate plan.* In this example, we use a chase plan.

Step 2   *Calculate the production rate.* We calculate the production rate based on the number of service calls each period, multiplied by the productivity rate of 4 hours per service call. Table 13-18 shows the production hours needed for each period.

Step 3   *Calculate the number of employees needed for each period.* To do this, we multiply the number of service calls for each period by the time per service call (for example, in period 2, 1,560 calls × 4 hours each call = 6240 hours needed). Divide the number of hours needed by the number of hours per employee per period (160 hours per employee) and determine that 39 employees are needed in Period 2. Table 13-18 shows the appropriate workforce for each period.

Step 4   *Test and cost the plan.* Table 13-18 shows the completed plan. We calculate the number of hires or fires by comparing the number of employees needed in the current period with the number of employees used in the previous period. For example, in Period 1, we used 60 employees and in Period 2 we need 39 employees. Thus we need to fire 21 employees at the start of Period 2. In Period 3, we need only 30 employees so we must fire an additional 9 employees.

Table 13-18 Plan G: Chase Aggregate Plan, with Hiring and Firing

Period	1	2	3	4	5	6	7	8	Total
Service calls	2,400	1,560	1,200	2,040	2,760	1,680	1,320	2,400	15,360
Service hours needed	9,600	6,240	4,800	8,160	11,040	6,720	5,280	9,600	61,440
Number of employees needed	60	39	30	51	69	42	33	60	384
Number of hires	0	0	0	21	18	0	0	27	66
Number of fires	0	21	9	0	0	27	9	0	66

In this plan, your company experiences fluctuations in the workforce with a low of 30 employees and a high of 69. The minimum change in workforce for any given period is 9 workers, which represents a substantial portion of the work force. We can easily calculate the regular time wage costs, and the cost of hiring and firing, but we cannot capture the intangible cost for such a widely fluctuating workforce. Table 13-19 evaluates the plan costs.

Table 13-19 Total Cost Calculations for Plan G

Hiring costs (66 hires × $250 each hire)	$16,500
Firing costs (66 fires × $150 each fire)	$9,900
Regular-time labor costs ($8.00 per hour × 160 hours per period × 384 employees)	$491,520
Total costs	$517,920

Step 5   *Evaluate the plan.* At $33.72, the cost per call is a good deal lower and regular-time labor utilization is 100%. Still, this plan has potential problems. Since employees interface with the customer, it is important to maintain performance level. Your company will have to train and retrain the changing workforce. This plan also needs an investment in enough space and equipment for up to 69 employees. In periods of less than high demand, this extra capacity will be severely underused.

When we compare Plans E, F, and G, it is obvious that we have not yet found the best solution. Try working with the problem data further: maybe a smaller permanent workforce and additional overtime would be a better alternative.

As you can see, the key is to look at a plan from different perspectives. Cost is important but so are customer service, operational effectiveness, and workforce morale. A successful aggregate plan considers each of these factors.

CROSS FUNCTIONAL

OM ACROSS THE ORGANIZATION

Aggregate planning affects functional areas throughout your company. Let's look at how each functional area is affected by the aggregate plan.

Accounting is affected because the aggregate plan details the resources needed by operations during the next 12 to 18 months. Accounting uses this information to project cash flows, calculate the capital needed to support operations, and project earnings. It also sets a benchmark for measuring the effectiveness of operations.

Marketing is involved because the aggregate plan supports the marketing plan. Marketing must know whether operations can provide the necessary output at a price that allows marketing to achieve its targeted profit margins. Further, the aggregate plan gives marketing insight into operations goals and activities for the year.

Information systems maintains the databases that support demand forecasts and other such information used to develop the aggregate plan.

Purchasing calculates long-term needs based on the aggregate plan. The aggregate plan gives purchasing information about the future that facilitates long-term relationships and contracts with suppliers. This information also allows purchasing to evaluate quantity discounts.

Manufacturing learns from the aggregate plan what resources are available to achieve their goals: how many workers, how much work to be subcontracted, how much inventory can be held, and so forth.

In most companies, the operations manager develops the aggregate plan. The operations manager submits an annual operations budget request based on the resources identified in the aggregate plan. The aggregate plan justifies new hiring or expected firing during the year, and planned or budgeted levels of overtime, subcontracting, and inventory. The aggregate plan identifies the resources needed for the next 6 to 18 months.

When the plan is implemented, the operations manager measures operations' performance against the plan, checking progress at least monthly. The operations manager also evaluates performance against the authorized operations budget. Variances need to be explained at all levels at and the plan updated. At that point, the past month is dropped from the aggregate plan and replaced by an additional month at the end of the aggregate plan. For example, if the aggregate plan covers January 2002 through December 2002, at the end of January 2002, we would drop January 2002 and add January 2003. In this example, the aggregate plan would always extend 12 months into the future.

The monthly review and update allows your company to monitor its performance, maintain its medium-term plan, and correct for changes since the plan was developed. It also gives the operations group a way to measure performance.

OM IS EVERYWHERE ■

Most of us probably are not in a position to have our own workforce but we still face aggregate planning problems in everyday life. Take a minute and think about how you use your study capacity each semester at school.

You can choose the level aggregate plan and study at a constant rate throughout the term, or you can use the chase aggregate plan and change your study rate each week to match the demand of that week's assignments. If you are using the level plan, you keep your study time constant by doing course work each period and spreading out the workload. Reading ahead is like building up inventory to help you through the more demanding periods. If you are using the chase plan, you do not study until you have to. You change your study capacity each week or day. You might pull an all-nighter one day and ignore your books the next.

When you think about it as an OM problem, it is obvious that life is easier when demand is stable and you can avoid large shifts in your capacity needs. A chase plan tends to create a stressful semester, especially if several projects or exams happen simultaneously (as they usually do!). You do not need to develop a full-scale level aggregate plan to handle your capacity needs during the semester. But with a little pre-planning, you can make better use of your time and reduce your stress.

CHAPTER HIGHLIGHTS

1. Planning begins with the development of the strategic business plan that provides your company's direction and objectives for the next 2 to 10 years. Marketing develops a plan that enables the company to satisfy the goals of the strategic business plan. The aggregate plan identifies the resources needed by operations to support the marketing plan.

2. Sales and operations planning integrates plans from the other functional areas and regularly evaluates the company's performance. The process begins with a comparison of actual demand and sales against planned demand. Forecasts are updated, the market reevaluated, and any changes in the marketing plan are reviewed by operations, engineering, and finance.

3. The level aggregate plan maintains the same size workforce and produces the same output each period. Inventories and back orders absorb fluctuations in demand. The chase aggregate plan changes the capacity each period to match demand.

4. Demand patterns can be smoothed through pricing incentives, reduced prices for out-of-season purchases, or nonprime service times. Capacity can be changed by using overtime or undertime, hiring or firing employees, subcontracting, using temporary employees, and so forth.

5. You develop the aggregate plan by identifying the option you want to use; calculating the production rate; calculating the size of the workforce needed to reach the production rate; calculating the cost of the plan; and evaluating the plan in terms of cost, customer service, operations, and human resources.

6. The difference in aggregate planning for companies that do not provide a tangible product is that the option to use inventories is not available.

KEY TERMS

SOLVED PROBLEMS

■ Solved Problem 1

Sophisticated Skates produces a variety of inline roller skates. Management wants you to develop an aggregate plan that covers the next 7 months.

Cost data

Regular time labor cost per hour	$15.00
Overtime labor cost per hour	$22.50
Hiring cost per employee	$500.00
Firing cost per employee	$750.00
Inventory holding cost per unit per period	$5.00
Shortage cost per unit per period	$7.50
Material cost per unit	$30.00

Capacity data

Beginning workforce (employees)	18
Beginning inventory (units)	2500
Labor standard per unit (hours)	0.64
Regular time hours available per period per employee	160
Overtime hours available per period per employee	20

Demand data

November	3000	March	4000
December	6000	April	5500
January	2000	May	8500
February	1500		

a. Develop an aggregate plan using a level production strategy, inventories, and back orders.
b. With the same problem data, develop an aggregate plan using the chase aggregate plan. Change the number of employees each period to match that period's level of demand.

Solution 1a

Step 1: *Choose the kind of aggregate plan.* We are using a level plan.

Step 2: *Find the aggregate production rate.* Remember that for this plan you calculate the aggregate production rate by taking the net cumulative demand and dividing by the number of periods in the plan (28,000 units divided by 7 periods). The aggregate production rate is 4000 units per period.

Problem-solving tip   Net cumulative demand is total cumulative demand less any beginning inventory.

Step 3: *Calculate the workforce.* The workforce is the aggregate production rate divided by the number of units per employee per period (4000 units divided by 250 units produced per employee per period). The workforce should be 16 employees, so we need to fire 2 employees to reduce the workforce from the initial 18 employees to the appropriate 16 employees.

Step 4: *Test and cost the plan.* The completed plan is shown in Spreadsheet 13.1a on next page.

Step 5: *Evaluate the plan in terms of customer service, costs, operations, and human resources.* We have no other plans to compare costs with this plan but we should question the large holding costs. Operationally, the plan is straightforward. We do the same thing every period. In terms of customer service, no products are back ordered.

Solution 1b

Step 1: *Choose the kind of aggregate plan.* In this problem we are to use a chase plan.

Step 2: *The aggregate production rate is equal to each period's net demand.* We need 500 units in November, 6000 in December, 2000 in January, 1500 in February, 4000 in March, 5500 in April, and 8500 in May as shown in Spreadsheet 13-1.

Spreadsheet 13.1a

Beginning Inventory	2500
Beginning Workforce	18
Labor Standard	0.64
Reg Hrs Available	160
OT Hrs Available	20

Period	1	2	3	4	5	6	7	Aggregate Demand	Average Aggregate Demand
Demand/period	500	6000	2000	1500	4000	5500	8500	28000.00	4000.00
Production/period	4000	4000	4000	4000	4000	4000	4000		
Cum Demand	500	6500	8500	10000	14000	19500	28000		
Cum Production	4000	8000	12000	16000	20000	24000	28000		
Excess Units	3500	1500	3500	6000	6000	4500	0	25000	
Units Short	0	0	0	0	0	0	0		

Units/Period	250
Needed Workforce	16
Hires	0
Fires	2

Cost	Per Unit	Total Cost
Materials	$30.00	$840,000.00
Labor	$9.60	$268,800.00
Overtime	$14.40	
Hiring	$500.00	$0.00
Firing	$750.00	$1,500.00
Holding	$5.00	$125,000.00
Total Costs		$1,235,300.00

Step 3: *Calculate the workforce needed each period.* The number of workers needed equals the period production rate divided by the number of units produced per employee per period. Confirm the calculations shown in Spreadsheet 13-1b.

Step 4: *Test and cost the plan.* The completed plan and costs are shown in Spreadsheet 13-1b.

Step 5: *Evaluate the plan.* On the basis of cost, this plan is cheaper than the previous plan. However, we have several areas of concern. For instance, we need enough space and equipment for up to 34 employees at a time. The first plan needed space and equipment for only 16 employees. In addition, we have no stability in the workforce. Between November and December, the workforce is increased by 1100%, only to be cut by 2/3 in January. The employees have little if any job security. We need to develop additional plans.

Spreadsheet 13.1b

Beginning Inventory	2500
Beginning Workforce	18
Labor Standard	0.64
Reg Hrs Available	160
OT Hrs Available	20

Period	1	2	3	4	5	6	7	Aggregate Demand
Demand/period	500	6000	2000	1500	4000	5500	8500	28000
Production/period	500	6000	2000	1500	4000	5500	8500	
Workers Needed	2	24	8	6	16	22	34	
Workers Hired	0	22	0	0	10	6	12	
Workers Fired	16	0	16	2	0	0	0	

Units/period per employee	250
Hires	50
Fires	34

Cost	Per Unit	Total Cost
Materials	$30.00	$840,000.00
Labor	$9.60	$268,800.00
Overtime	$14.40	
Hiring	$500.00	$25,000.00
Firing	$750.00	$25,500.00
Holding	$5.00	$0.00
Total Cost		$1,159,300.00

■ Solved Problem 2

Psychics of the World, Inc. wants an aggregate plan for their organization. Given the nature of the business, Psychics has decided that back orders are not acceptable. If a caller can not be handled immediately, the call is a lost sale.

Psychics has predicted the following number of calls: May—8000 calls, June—5000 calls, July—6000 calls, August—7000 calls, September—6000 calls, October—8000 calls, November—10,000 calls, and December—12,000 calls.

Psychics of the World pays each of their 48 employees $4000 per month. Each psychic works 160 regular-time hours per month or 40 regular-time hours per week. The regular-time labor cost of a call is $20, the overtime labor cost per call is $30. Each psychic is expected to serve 200 callers per month. The management has limited overtime to 50 calls per month per psychic. It costs $3000 to hire a new psychic and $2000 to fire a psychic.

a. Develop a level aggregate without inventory, without back orders, and without overtime.

b. Using the same problem data, develop an aggregate plan using a level workforce supplemented by overtime. Minimize the wasted capacity. No back orders are permitted.

Solution 2a

Step 1: *Choose the kind of aggregate plan.* We are using a level plan.

Step 2: *Calculate the aggregate production rate.* Since inventory and back orders are not permitted, find the period with the highest demand (December has demand of 12,000 calls). This is the aggregate production rate.

Step 3: *Calculate the workforce size given the aggregate production rate.* (12,000 calls divided by 200 calls per psychic per month). The workforce should have 60 psychics, so we need to hire 12 more psychics.

Step 4: *Test and cost the plan.* The plan is shown in Table 13-20.

We calculate wasted capacity by subtracting the capacity used (calls to be serviced) from the available regular-time capacity. We calculate the costs as follows:

Regular time costs	60 psychics @ $4,000 for 8 periods	$1,920,000
Hiring costs	12 psychics @ $3,000	$36,000
Total cost		$1,956,000

Step 5: *Evaluate the plan.* We have no other plan to compare the cost with but this plan appears to waste substantial capacity (34,000 more calls could have been handled). Total calls demanded were 62,000, whereas we had capacity for 96,000. Since management is concerned with wasting valuable psychic time, let's develop a plan that minimizes the amount of wasted capacity (minimizes undertime).

Solution 2b

Step 1: *Choose the kind of aggregate plan.* Here, we use a level workforce.

Step 2: *Calculate the aggregate production rate.* This is the same as for the previous plan (12,000 calls).

Step 3: *Calculate the appropriate workforce.* This time we divide the aggregate production rate by the maximum number of calls per psychic per period (regular time plus overtime). Each psychic can provide up to 250 calls per period. This reduces the workforce from 60 psychics in the previous plan to 48 psychics in this plan (12,000 calls divided by 250 calls per psychic). No hires or fires are needed.

Step 4: *Test and cost the plan.* The plan is shown in Table 13-21.

Table 13-20

Period	May	June	July	Aug.	Sept.	Oct.	Nov.	Dec.
Service calls	8,000	5,000	6,000	7,000	6,000	8,000	10,000	12,000
Regular time capacity (calls)	12,000	12,000	12,000	12,000	12,000	12,000	12,000	12,000
Wasted capacity (calls)	4,000	7,000	6,000	5,000	6,000	4,000	2,000	0

Table 13-21

Period	May	June	July	Aug.	Sept.	Oct.	Nov.	Dec.
Service calls	8,000	5,000	6,000	7,000	6,000	8,000	10,000	12,000
Regular time capacity (calls)	9,600	9,600	9,600	9,600	9,600	9,600	9,600	9,600
Wasted capacity (calls)	1,600	4,600	3,600	2,600	3,600	1,600	0	0
Overtime capacity needed (calls)							400	2,400

The total costs for this plan are shown here:

Regular time cost	48 psychics @ $4,000 for 8 months	$1,536,000
Overtime cost	2,800 calls @ $30	$84,000
Total cost		$1,620,000

Step 5: *Evaluate the plan.* This plan reduces the wasted regular-time capacity by 16,400 calls (34,000 − 17,600). The total cost is $300,000 less than the previous plan. Overtime is needed only in 2 periods so it should not create morale problems. This plan is an improvement but better plans are possible.

DISCUSSION QUESTIONS

1. Explain the importance of the strategic business plan. Describe sales and operations planning in terms of its purpose, components, and frequency.

3. Define the aggregate plan.

4. Explain why we use an aggregate or composite product when developing the aggregate plan.

5. Compare and contrast the level and chase aggregate plans.

6. Describe the different demand-based options used in aggregate planning and their implications for your company.

7. Describe the different capacity-based options used in aggregate planning and their implications for your company.

8. Explain what the hybrid aggregate plan is and why it is used.

9. Explain the procedure for developing an aggregate plan.

10. Describe the factors to consider before developing your aggregate plan.

11. Explain how aggregate planning is different when the company does not provide a tangible product.

12. Visit a local manufacturer and determine how it uses aggregate planning.

13. Visit a local service provider and determine how it uses aggregate planning.

14. What two items must you calculate first when developing your aggregate plan?

PROBLEMS

Use the following data in the first twelve problems.

Problem Data

Cost data	
Regular time labor cost per hour	$10.00
Overtime labor cost per hour	$15.00
Subcontracting cost per unit (labor only)	$84.00
Holding cost per unit per period	$10.00
Back order cost per unit per period	$20.00
Hiring cost per employee	$600.00
Firing cost per employee	$450.00
Capacity data	
Beginning workforce	210 employees
Beginning inventory	400 units
Labor standard per unit	6 hours
Regular time available per period	160 hours
Overtime available per period	32 hours
Subcontracting maximum per period	1000 units
Subcontracting minimum per period	500 units
Demand data	
Period 1	6000 units
Period 2	4800 units
Period 3	7840 units
Period 4	5200 units
Period 5	6560 units
Period 6	3600 units

1. The BackPack Company produces a line of backpacks. The manager, Jill Nicholas, is interested in using a level aggregate plan. Inventories and back orders will be used to handle demand fluctuations. She has asked you for some preliminary information.

   a. Calculate the aggregate production rate.
   b. Calculate the appropriate workforce given the aggregate production rate.

2. Jill Nicholas has decided that you should develop a level aggregate plan, using the aggregate production rate and workforce calculated in Problem 1.

   a. Show what would happen if this plan were implemented.
   b. Calculate the costs this plan.
   c. Evaluate the plan in terms of cost, customer service, operations, and human resources.

3. Jill has decided that the BackPack Company must have very good customer service. She has asked you to develop a level aggregate plan using inventories but not back orders. All demand must be met each period. You must calculate the:

   a. Aggregate product rate.
   b. Appropriate workforce given the aggregate production rate.

4. Continue developing a level aggregate plan using inventories and no back orders. Use the aggregated production rate and work force calculated in Problem 3.

   a. Show what would happen if this plan were implemented.
   b. Calculate the costs of this plan.
   c. Evaluate the plan in terms of cost, customer service, operations, and human resources.

5. While the BackPack Company has always used a level aggregate plan, Jill is interested in evaluating chase aggregate plans also. She has asked you to calculate how many hires and fires would be necessary to adjust capacity to meet demand exactly each period. If necessary, incur some undertime. Calculate the number of workers needed each period.

6. Now that you have calculated the number of workers needed each period in Problem 5, Jill wants to see how the plan would actually work. You need to:

   a. Show what would happen if this plan were implemented.
   b. Calculate the costs associated with this plan.
   c. Evaluate the plan in terms of cost, customer service, operations, and human resources.

7. Jill Nicholas is concerned about BackPack's corporate image and has decided against using hires and fires. Instead, she has asked you to consider a chase aggregate plan using the current workforce supplemented by overtime or undertime to change capacity as needed. She has asked for the following information from you.

   a. How many production hours would be required each period to produce the exact quantity demanded?
   b. How many regular-time production hours are available each period?
   c. How many overtime production hours would be needed each period?

8. Based on your calculations in Problem 7, Jill wants you to complete a chase aggregate plan using the current workforce supplemented by overtime or undertime.

   a. Show what would happen if this plan were implemented.
   b. Calculate the costs for this plan.
   c. Evaluate the plan with regard to cost, customer service, operations, and human resources.

9. Jill Nicholas believes there must be a better aggregate plan. She has suggested a hybrid aggregate plan, using a permanent workforce of 195 employees and subcontracting as needed. Once again, Jill has requested some preliminary calculations from you.

a. Calculate the regular-time production possible each period given a workforce of 195.

b. Calculate the number of units you must subcontract each period. Note that when you subcontract, you must buy a minimum of 500 units. You can subcontract up to 1000 units in any given period.

10. Based on your initial calculations in Problem 9, Jill has asked you to complete a hybrid aggregate plan using a permanent workforce of 195 employees supplemented by subcontracting.

a. Show what would happen if this plan were implemented.

b. Calculate the costs associated with this plan.

c. Evaluate the plan in terms of cost, customer service, operations, and human resources.

11. Jill wants you to consider a hybrid aggregate plan, using 195 permanent employees supplemented by overtime. Calculate the number of overtime hours needed each period. Do not exceed the overtime limit of 32 hours per employee per period.

12. Complete your hybrid aggregate plan, using 195 permanent employees supplemented by overtime.

a. Show what would happen if this plan were implemented.

b. Calculate the costs associated with this plan.

c. Evaluate the plan in terms of cost, customer service, operations, and human resources.

Use the information show here for Problems 13 through 22. The Draper Tax Company provides tax services to local businesses. Draper chooses to meet all demand as it occurs because customers are unwilling to accept back orders. The company has provided the following cost, capacity, and demand information.

Draper Tax Company Problem Data

Cost data	
Regular time labor cost per hour	$25.00
Overtime labor cost per hour	$37.50
Temporary worker cost per hour	$40.00
Hiring cost per permanent worker	$2000.00
Firing cost per permanent worker	$1200.00
Capacity data	
Beginning workforce	12 employees
Labor standard per service	12 hours
Regular time hours per period	40 hours
Overtime hours per period	8 hours
Demand Data	
Week 1	48 clients	Week 4	40 clients
Week 2	36 clients	Week 5	38 clients
Week 3	50 clients	Week 6	48 clients

13. Calculate the size of the workforce needed for the company to meet average weekly demand.

14. Develop a level aggregate plan for the Draper Company if back orders are permitted.

a. Show what would happen if this plan were implemented.

b. Calculate the costs associated with this plan.

c. Evaluate the plan in terms of cost, customer service, operations, and human resources.

15. Calculate the size of the workforce needed for the Draper Company if a level workforce is used and no back orders are permitted.

16. Develop a level aggregate plan for the Draper Company when no back orders are permitted and all demand must be satisfed.

a. Show what would happen if this plan were implemented.

b. Calculate the costs associated with this plan.

c. Evaluate the plan in terms of cost, customer service, operations, and human resources.

17. Calculate the number of employees needed each period if Draper Tax chooses to use a chase aggregate plan using hires and fires to adjust the capacity. All demand must be met each period.

18. Develop a chase aggregate plan using hires and fires to adjust the capacity for Draper. All demand must be met each period.

a. Show what would happen if this plan were implemented.

b. Calculate the costs of this plan.

c. Evaluate this plan in terms of cost, customer service, operations, and human resources.

19. Calculate the total number of overtime hours needed in weeks 1–6, if Draper decides to use a permanent workforce of 12 employees supplemented by overtime to satisfy all demand.

20. Develop a complete aggregate plan for Draper using a permanent workforce of 12 employees supplemented by overtime. All demand must be met each period.

a. Show what would happen if this plan were implemented.

b. Calculate the costs of this plan.

c. Evaluate this plan in terms of cost, customer service, operations, and human resources.

21. Concerned about the welfare of its workers, Draper has decided to try a strategy without any overtime. Instead of overtime, Draper has decided to supplement the permanent workforce of 12 employees with temporary workers. Any temporary worker must work the entire week. There is no hiring or firing cost associated with temporary workers.

a. Calculate the number of temporary workers Draper will need.

b. Determine which periods will require temporary workers.

22. Develop the aggregate plan for Draper that has a permanent workforce of 12 employees and is supplemented with temporary workers. A temporary worker must work the entire week.

a. Show what would happen if this plan were implemented.
b. Calculate the costs of this plan.
c. Evaluate this plan in terms of cost, customer service, operations, and human resources.

CASE: *Newmarket International Manufacturing Company (A)*

Marcia Blakely, plant manager at the Newmarket International Manufacturing Company (NIMCO), was preparing for a meeting with her management team. Joining her would be Jack Novak, the company controller; Amy Granger, regional marketing manager; and Joe Barnes, the production manager. The goal of the meeting was to develop a staffing plan for the second quarter. A quick performance review covering the past two quarters proved disappointing. Customer service was poor in spite of higher component inventory levels. Stockouts of some components were a problem and caused production inefficiencies. Nothing seemed to be working smoothly.

Company History

NIMCO was founded by Marcia Blakely, only two years out of graduate school. Marcia's knowledge of mass customization has been the driving force behind NIMCO. The company produces three major custom products. Volume on the products is quite high even though each item is customized specifically for the customer. Each of the products is processed through up to four different work centers. Although each item is unique, the processing time at each work center is constant due to the sophisticated equipment used.

NIMCO currently has 75 full time employees working in manufacturing. Each employee is scheduled to work 40 hours per week. Because mass customization is used, NIMCO carries no finished-goods inventory. The company policy is to meet all demand each period; no backorders or stock outs are permitted.

Joe Barnes, the production manager, received the following information in advance of the meeting: demand forecasts for products A, B, and C for each week of the second quarter as shown in the table, and standard labor time estimates for each product. The standard labor times are: product A—0.24 hours, product B—0.38 hours, and product C—0.29 hours.

Joe knew that it would be useful to have you, his assistant, generate additional information for this meeting. You are to convert the individual product forecasts into the total number of labor hours needed each week. For example, in week 14, 3,600 product As multiplied by 0.24 hours, 4,000 product Bs times 0.38 hours, and 2,000 product Cs times 0.29 hours. The total standard labor time associated with products demanded in period 14 is 2,964 hours. After determining the required labor hours each period, Joe wants you to develop three possible staffing plans. The first plan uses a level workforce and does not allow back orders in any period. The second plan uses the original full-time workforce (75 employees) supplemented by the use of overtime to avoid back orders. The third plan adjusts the workforce each period to satisfy all demand by hiring and firing employees. To develop these plans and calculate their associated costs, you need to know that the regular time wage rate is $14.00 per hour, overtime is $21.00 per hour, hiring costs are $500 per employee, and firing costs are $750 per employee.

Your job is to provide analyses of these three plans for Joe to use at the meeting. Make sure to include your recommendation after considering cost, customer service, and operations.

Quarter 2 Demand Forecasts			
Week	Demand for Product A	Demand for Product B	Demand for Product C
14	3600	4000	2000
15	4000	4000	2500
16	4300	4000	2800
17	4400	3800	3100
18	4500	3800	3200
19	4500	3800	3200
20	4400	3600	3200
21	4300	3600	3000
22	4000	3600	3000
23	4000	3800	2800
24	3600	3800	2800
25	3200	3800	2600
26	3000	4000	2600

INTERACTIVE LEARNING

Enhance and test your knowledge of Chapter 13 using the interactive CD.

1. **Spreadsheet** *Solved Problem 2*

2. **Video** *United Parcel Service*

   Visit our dynamic Web site, www.wiley.com/college/reid, for more cases, web links, and additional information.

3. **Additional Web Resources**
   H&R Block, www.hrblock.com
   United Parcel Service of America, Inc., www.ups.com

4. **Virtual Company** Consulting Case

5. **INTERNET CHALLENGE** *Summer Cruising*

Aggregate planning identifies the resources needed by operations during a specified time period. Once these resources have been authorized, operations has to make do or justify any deviations from the plan. With this in mind, identify the resources you'll need when you and one other person take a cruise of 10 to 14 days during the month of June.

On the Internet, investigate at least three different cruise lines. Select a cruise that you'd like to take. The destination of the cruise is up to you. In preparation for the cruise, calculate how much and what kinds of clothing you'll take, as well as what accessories (cameras, umbrellas, binoculars, snorkeling gear, etc.) and how much cash. Then check to see which items you own and which items you need to buy.

Remember to check the site to see how many formal nights, informal nights, casual nights, and theme nights there will be during your cruise. Also check the shore excursions so you can calculate adequate funding. Don't forget to check your itinerary so you have proper clothes for any ports you'll be visiting (some countries frown on tank tops and shorts).

You can put many of your expenses on a credit card but you'll also need cash for gratuities, incidental expenses at different ports, and money for the casinos. You need to consider transportation to and from the airport (or parking), and someone to water your plants and pick up your mail while you're gone.

Develop an aggregate plan detailing the resources you'll need for this cruise for two. Prepare your expected budget and justify your expenditures.

BIBLIOGRAPHY

Arnold, J. R. Tony. *Introduction to Materials Management*, 3rd ed. Upper Saddle River, N.J.: Prentice-Hall, 1998.

Cox, James F., III, John H. Blackstone, and Michael S. Spencer, eds. *APICS Dictionary*, 9th ed. Falls Church, Va.: American Production and Inventory Control Society, 1998.

Narasimhan, Sim, Dennis W. McLeavey, and Peter Billington. *Production Planning and Inventory Control*, 2nd ed. Englewood Cliffs, N.J.: Prentice-Hall, 1995.

Plossl, George W. *Production and Inventory Control: Principles and Techniques*, 2nd ed. Englewood Cliffs, N.J.: Prentice-Hall, 1985.

Vollmann, Thomas E., William L. Berry, and D. Clay Whybark. *Manufacturing Planning and Control Systems*, 4th ed. Irwin/McGraw-Hill, 1997.

Master Scheduling and Rough-Cut Capacity Planning

Before studying this chapter, you should know or, if necessary, review

1. Competitive priorities, Chapter 2, pages 28–32.
2. Capacity management concepts, Chapter 9, pages 247–255.
3. Order quantity models, Chapter 12, pages 361–371.
4. Aggregate planning strategies, Chapter 13, pages 397–402.

LEARNING OBJECTIVES

After studying this chapter, you should be able to

1. Explain the role of the master production schedule.
2. Explain the organizational links to master production scheduling.
3. Describe the objectives of master production scheduling.
4. Develop a master production schedule.
5. Calculate the capacity needed for the MPS using rough-cut capacity planning.
6. Calculate available-to-promise quantities.
7. Describe time fence policies.

CHAPTER OUTLINE

After several high-stress years of using the chase aggregate plan for studying, this term you decide that the level aggregate plan will help you take control of your life and improve your grade point. Your level aggregate plan provides for 25 hours of class prep each week. Calculate how to use those study hours: when should you work on each class and for how long?

To use your resources best, you should have the course calendar of requirements for each of your classes, your work schedule, and your social calendar. These represent the total demand placed on you. For now your concern is the 25 hours of study time. Look at the course calendars to calculate when you have specific needs to meet. Think of your faculty as customers and the course requirements as customer orders with specific due dates. Failure to meet these customer due dates can have disastrous results—a lower grade for inadequate preparation or even nonacceptance by the customer, because that professor does not accept late papers or projects.

Once you know the demands of each of your courses, develop a schedule that uses your authorized resources and enables you to meet your course requirements. How you will meet the requirements determines the level of service you can offer your customers. This is what master production scheduling and rough-cut capacity planning are about.

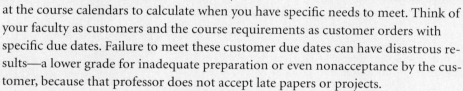

MASTER PRODUCTION SCHEDULING

Your company's **aggregate plan** specifies the resources authorized for use by the company's operations group. These resources include the size of the workforce, level of inventory held, number of planned shortages, authorized level of overtime and undertime, aggregate number of units or services to be produced in-house, and number of units or services to be subcontracted.

The **master production schedule (MPS)** is often stated in product or service specifications rather than dollars. It shows how many products or services are planned for each time period, based on the resources authorized in the aggregate plan. In manufacturing, the **master scheduler** develops the schedule based on the available capacity. In service companies, the office manager, department manager, or assistant manager might develop the schedule.

The MPS is the anticipated build schedule for manufacturing specific end products or providing specific services. The key distinction here is that the MPS is a statement of production or services and is not a statement of demand—a plan to satisfy customer demand while considering operational effectiveness and cost. Because of this, individual products can be finished ahead of time and held in inventory rather than finished as needed. In some cases, services also can be finished earlier than needed. The master scheduler or office manager balances customer service and capacity usage.

▶ **Master production schedule (MPS)**
The anticipated build schedule.

▶ **Master scheduler**
The person responsible for managing, developing, reviewing, and maintaining the master schedule.

The aggregate plan shows how many products or services are planned for each time period. The MPS identifies the specific products or services planned for a given time period. Let's look at an example of how aggregate plan is linked to the MPS.

■ **Example 14.1 Developing the MPS at Amber's Backpack Company**

Amber's Backpack Company (ABC) produces three models of backpacks: the basic backpack, the urban backpack, and the evening backpack. Each model needs the same amount of production time. ABC's aggregate production rate is 400 backpacks per week. A possible MPS for ABC is shown here.

Week	1	2	3	4	5	6	7	8
Basic backpack	400		400	400		400	400	
Urban backpack		250			250			250
Evening backpack		150			150			150
Total	400	400	400	400	400	400	400	400

The aggregate plan states that ABC should produce 400 units each week. The MPS shows the models and quantities that constitute the 400 units to be produced each week of the schedule.

Although this example involves manufacturing, think about how an MPS might look in a service operation such as a law firm. The firm knows how many hours of staff time are available (resources) and its current case load (demands). It must now decide how best to use the attorneys and law clerks each period to satisfy the corporate objectives.

■ MPS AS A BASIS OF COMMUNICATION

▶ **Demand management**
The function of recognizing all demands for goods and services to support the marketplace.

The MPS is a basis for communication between operations and other functional areas. It is stated in product or service specifications rather than dollars. Your company uses an effective MPS in making customer delivery promises, using company capacity wisely, achieving the company's objectives, and making tradeoff decisions between marketing and operations. Figure 14-1 shows the connections between the master scheduling role and other parts of the planning process. Let's examine these connections, beginning with demand management.

Demand management includes a company's forecasting, order entry, order promising, and physical distribution activities. Demand management captures all activities that use manufacturing capacity. These demands can be customer orders for products or services, a forecast of demand for products and services, interplant requirements, service parts requirements, and/or distribution requirements. If a demand is excluded, it will not be scheduled for completion. Communications between the master scheduler and demand management are ongoing.

The **production or aggregate plan** supports the marketing plan. The master scheduler must work within the authorized resources of the plan. The process for developing an MPS is as follows:

1. The master scheduler develops a proposed MPS.
2. The master scheduler uses a rough-cut capacity planning technique to calculate whether the company has the capacity to meet the proposed MPS. This is done using a rough-cut capacity planning technique.
3. If the proposed MPS is feasible, it is evaluated by the master scheduler in terms of customer service, effective use of resources, and inventory investment.
4. If the proposed MPS is accepted, it becomes the authorized MPS. If capacity is insufficient, either the MPS is modified or capacity is expanded.

The authorized MPS is a critical input into the **material requirements planning (MRP)** system. The MPS tells the MRP system what the company plans to build and when. The MRP system then calculates the materials needed to build the products in the schedule and plans for the necessary materials. (MRP systems are discussed in depth in Chapter 15.)

▶ **Material requirements planning (MRP)**
A technique using the master production schedule, bill of material data, and inventory records to calculate requirements for materials.

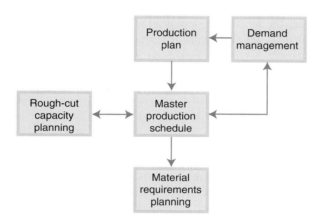

Figure 14-1

Master production schedule linkages

OBJECTIVES OF MASTER SCHEDULING ∎

The master scheduler considers the following objectives when developing the MPS:

1. Achieve the desired customer service level either by maintaining finished goods inventory or by scheduling completion of the item or service to meet the customer's delivery needs.
2. Make the best use of the company's resources: material, labor, and equipment.
3. Ensure that the inventory investment is at the appropriate level.

To meet these objectives, the master schedule must satisfy customer demand, not exceed operations's capacity, and work within the constraints of the aggregate plan. Let's look at how to develop an MPS.

DEVELOPING AN MPS ∎

The master scheduler develops a proposed MPS, checks the schedule for feasibility in terms of available capacity, modifies as needed, and authorizes the MPS. The master scheduler starts by creating, revising, and finishing an MPS record for each product. The master scheduler uses the finished MPS records to develop a proposed master production schedule, which he or she then checks for feasibility with a rough-cut capacity planning technique.

Consider the following example of an MPS record for a product built in a make-to-stock environment with inventory held. The product is built in a fixed-order quantity of 125 units and there are 110 units in inventory. Table 14-1 is an initial MPS record showing the demand forecasts for the next 12 weeks.

The top row of the record shows the time periods (weeks in our example); the forecast row shows the forecasted demand for the product. The projected available quantity row keeps track of how many units are available at the *end of each time period*. The MPS row shows when replenishment shipments need to arrive. MPS shipments arrive at the *beginning of the time period*. To calculate the projected available quantity, we use the following formula:

Projected available = beginning inventory + MPS shipment − forecasted demand

Period 1 To calculate the projected available quantity at the end of period 1, we take the beginning inventory (110 units), add any MPS shipments arriving that period (0 units), and subtract the forecasted demand for the period (50 units). This leaves the projected available quantity at the end of period 1, or (110 +0) −50 = 60 units projected available quantity.

Period 2 The beginning inventory in period 2 is 60 units, no MPS shipment is scheduled, and the forecast is 50 units. Therefore, the projected available quantity at the end of period 2 is 10 units.

Period 3 In period 3, we have 10 units beginning inventory, no MPS quantity, a forecast of 50 units, and a projected available quantity of −40 units; that is, we do not have enough of this product available to satisfy the forecasted demand in period 3. Thus we need to plan an MPS shipment to arrive at the beginning of period 3. We calculate the size of the replenishment order by the order quantity rule—in our case, a fixed-order quantity of 125 units. Table 14-2 shows the revised MPS record with an MPS quantity of 125 units scheduled to arrive in period 3.

Table 14-1 First MPS Record

Week	1	2	3	4	5	6	7	8	9	10	11	12
Forecast	50	50	50	50	75	75	75	75	50	50	50	50
Projected available	60	10	−40									
MPS												

Table 14-2 First Revised MPS Record

Week	1	2	3	4	5	6	7	8	9	10	11	12
Forecast	50	50	50	50	75	75	75	75	50	50	50	50
Projected available	60	10	85	35	−40							
MPS			125									

Table 14-3 Second Revised MPS Record												
Week	1	2	3	4	5	6	7	8	9	10	11	12
Forecast	50	50	50	50	75	75	75	75	50	50	50	50
Projected available	60	10	85	35	85	10	−65					
MPS			125		125							

Table 14-4 Completed MPS Record												
Week	1	2	3	4	5	6	7	8	9	10	11	12
Forecast	50	50	50	50	75	75	75	75	50	50	50	50
Projected available	60	10	85	35	85	10	60	110	60	10	85	35
MPS			125		125		125	125			125	

We continue to calculate the projected available quantity until we find the next period in which the projected available quantity is negative, which is period 5. Therefore, we need to schedule another MPS replenishment for delivery at the start of period 5. Table 14-3 shows the second revised MPS record. We enter the MPS quantity into the MPS record and continue calculating the projected available quantity. This continues till the next period in which the projected available becomes negative. At that point, we add another MPS shipment and continue forward. Table 14-4 shows the completed MPS record. The completed MPS record shows replenishment orders needed in periods 3, 5, 7, 8, and 11. We calculate each quantity by the given order quantity rule (125 units).

ROUGH-CUT CAPACITY PLANNING ■

Rough-cut capacity planning (RCCP) calculates a rough estimate of the workload placed on critical resources by the proposed MPS. This workload is compared against **demonstrated capacity** for each critical resource. This comparison enables the master scheduler to develop a feasible MPS. Among the several approaches to rough-cut capacity planning is capacity planning using overall planning factors (CPOPF).

Capacity planning using overall planning factors (CPOPF) is a simple, rough-cut capacity planning technique. CPOPF develops a planning factor for each critical resource based on historical data. Table 14-5 shows the procedure for using CPOPF. Next, we will work through an example using the procedure.

▶**Rough-cut capacity planning (RCCP)**
The process of converting the master production schedule into requirements for key resources such as direct labor and machine time.

▶ **Demonstrated capacity**
Proven capacity calculated from actual performance data.

▶ **Capacity planning using overall planning factors (CPOPF)**
A rough-cut capacity planning technique. MPS items are multiplied by historically determined planning factors for key resources.

Table 14-5 Procedure For CPOPF
1. Determine the appropriate planning factors using historical data.
2. Multiply the MPS quantities by the appropriate planning factor.
3. Sum capacity requirements for each resource by time period.
4. Allocate capacity requirements to individual work centers based on historical percentages.
5. Evaluate the workload at each resource to validate MPS feasibility.

■ Example 14.2 CPOPF at Heavenly Ballroom Shoes

Heavenly Ballroom Shoes, Inc. (HBS) produces two models of ballroom dance shoes. One model is for men (Model M) and the other is for women (Model W). Charles, the master scheduler, has accumulated the following historical data. During the past 3 years, HBS has produced 72,000 pairs of Model M, using 21,600 hours of direct labor and 5760 machine hours. During that same period, HBS produced 108,000 pairs of Model W, using 43,200 hours of direct labor and 12,960 hours of machine time.

STEP 1   DETERMINE THE PLANNING FACTORS.

Charles uses two resources, direct labor and machine time, for each of the products. He needs four planning factors: direct labor for Model M, machine time for Model M, direct labor for Model W, and machine time for Model W. Using the historical data, Charles computes the planning factors as follows:

$$\text{Planning factor for direct labor} = \frac{\text{total direct labor spent building model}}{\text{number of units of model built}}$$

For Model M, that is

$$\text{Planning factor for Direct Labor} = \frac{21{,}600 \text{ hours of direct labor}}{72{,}000 \text{ pairs}}$$

Direct labor for the Model M planning factor is 0.30 hours. To calculate the planning factor for machine time for Model M, Charles substitutes total machine hours spent building Model M into the numerator as shown next.

$$\text{Planning factor for machine time} = \frac{\text{total machine hours spent building model}}{\text{number of units of model built}}$$

The machine time for the Model M planning factor is 0.08 hours (5760 hours of machine time divided by 72,000 pairs of Model M). Charles continues the process to calculate the planning factors for Model W. The direct labor planning factor for the Model W is 0.40 hours and the machine time planning factor is 0.12 hours. Table 14-6 shows the four planning factors.

Table 14-6 Planning Factors	
Planning Factor	**Planning Factor Value**
Direct labor for Model M	0.30 hour
Direct labor for Model W	0.40 hour
Machine time for Model M	0.08 hour
Machine time for Model W	0.12 hour`

Given a proposed MPS, how would Charles calculate the workload for the proposed MPS? Table 14-7 shows the proposed quarterly MPS for HBS.

Table 14-7 Proposed MPS					
	Quarter 1 (pairs)	Quarter 2 (pairs)	Quarter 3 (pairs)	Quarter 4 (pairs)	Total (pairs)
Model M	6,000	5,500	9,500	6,500	27,500
Model W	10,000	12,000	7,500	10,100	39,600

STEP 2   CALCULATE THE WORKLOAD GENERATED BY THIS SCHEDULE.

Charles multiplies the MPS quantity times the appropriate planning factor. For example, Charles begins in quarter 1 and calculates how much labor is needed to build 6000 pairs of Model M and 10,000 pairs of Model W. He multiplies 6000 pairs of Model M by its labor planning factor of 0.30 hours to arrive at 1800 hours of direct labor needed. He continues for Model W, multiplying 10,000 pairs by its labor planning factor of 0.40 hours to arrive at 4000 hours of direct labor needed. The total number of direct hours needed in quarter 1 is 5800 hours (1800 for Model M and 4000 for Model W). Charles continues to do this for each time period. Table 14-8 shows all the labor needs.

To calculate the machine needs, Charles continues the process. He multiplies the quarter 1 needs for Model M by its machine time planning factor (6000 Model M's × 0.08 hours machine time = 480 hours needed). For Model W, 1,680 hours of machine time are needed (10,000 Model W's × 0.12 hours machine time = 1,200 hours needed. Table 14-9 shows the machine needs for each product in each quarter.

STEP 3   CALCULATE THE TOTAL CAPACITY NEEDS FOR EACH RESOURCE FOR EACH TIME PERIOD.

Charles does this by summing up the individual capacity needs for each of the products. Table 14-8 shows the total labor hours needed for each quarter. Table 14-9 shows the same information for machine hours needed.

STEP 4   CALCULATE INDIVIDUAL WORKCENTER CAPACITY NEEDS BASED ON HISTORICAL PERCENTAGE ALLOCATION.

Charles calculates that 60% of HBS's direct labor is used in work center 101 and 40% is used in work center 102. The same is true for its machine time. How would Charles calculate by quarters how much direct labor and machine time is needed at work centers 101 and 102? Table 14-10 shows direct labor needs by work center. To calculate the labor hours needed in work center 101 in quarter 1, Charles multiplies the total quarter 1 labor needs by 60% (5800 hours of total

Table 14-8 Direct Labor Hours Needed

Model	Direct Labor Factor	Q-1 MPS Qty.	Q-1 Hours Req'd	Q-2 MPS Qty.	Q-2 Hours Req'd	Q-3 MPS Qty.	Q-3 Hours Req'd	Q-4 MPS Qty.	Q-4 Hours Req'd	Total MPS Qty.	Total Hours Req'd
Model M	0.30	6,000	1,800	5,500	1,650	9,500	2,850	6,500	1,950	27,500	8,250
Model W	0.40	10,000	4,000	12,000	4,800	7,500	3,000	10,100	4,040	39,600	15,840
Total		16,000	5,800	17,500	6,450	17,000	5,850	16,600	5,990	67,100	24,090

Table 14-9 Machine Hours Needed

Model	Machine Hours Factor	Q-1 MPS Qty.	Q-1 Hours Req'd	Q-2 MPS Qty.	Q-2 Hours Req'd	Q-3 MPS Qty.	Q-3 Hours Req'd	Q-4 MPS Qty.	Q-4 Hours Req'd	Total MPS Qty.	Total Hours Req'd
Model M	0.08	6,000	480	5,500	440	9,500	760	6,500	520	27,500	2,200
Model W	0.12	10,000	1,200	12,000	1,440	7,500	900	10,100	1,212	39,600	4,752
Total		16,000	1,680	17,500	1,880	17,000	1,660	16,600	1,732	67,100	6,952

Table 14-10 Direct Labor Hours Needed, by Work Center

Work Center	Historical Percentage Allocation	Labor Hrs. Required Q-1	Labor Hrs. Required Q-2	Labor Hrs. Required Q-3	Labor Hrs. Required Q-4	Total Labor Required
Work center 101	60%	3,480	3,870	3,510	3,594	14,454
Work center 102	40%	2,320	2,580	2,340	2,396	9,636
Total		5,800	6,450	5,850	5,990	24,090

Table 14-11 Machine Hours Needed, by Work Center

Work Center	Historical Percentage Allocation	Labor Hrs. Required Q-1	Labor Hrs. Required Q-2	Labor Hrs. Required Q-3	Labor Hrs. Required Q-4	Total Labor Required
Work center 101	60%	1,008	1,128	996	1,039.2	4,171.2
Work center 102	40%	672	752	664	692.8	2,780.8
Total		1,680	1,880	1,660	1732	6952

labor needed by 60% equals 3480 hours of labor needed in work center 101 in quarter 1). The labor in work center 102 in quarter 1 is 2320 hours (5800 hours × 40%). Charles now has an estimate of the direct labor needs by quarter for each of the work centers. He can compare the direct labor hours needed with the available direct labors and make adjustments either to the available capacity or to the MPS.

Charles calculates machine hour needs in each department for each quarter in the same way as he calculates labor needs. Table 14-11 shows the machine hours needed by each of the work centers for each quarter. Given this information, Charles can decide whether HBS needs additional equipment or whether they have adequate machine capacity in each of the work centers. Remember that a company can increase its capacity with overtime, temporary workers, subcontracting, or by using alternative manufacturing processes. When Charles is certain that the proposed MPS is feasible, he evaluates the MPS in terms of customer service, effectiveness of resource usage, and cost.

■ EVALUATING AND ACCEPTING THE MPS

CROSS FUNCTIONAL

To evaluate the MPS in terms of customer service, the master scheduler checks that promised customer delivery dates are met. He or she also makes sure that the MPS provides enough flexibility to respond to new customer orders.

To evaluate the MPS for effective use of resources, the master scheduler checks that enough capacity is available to meet the schedule in each time period. This capacity includes short-term changes such as overtime, subcontracting, and temporary employees.

To evaluate the MPS in terms of cost, the master scheduler compares the MPS to the aggregate plan, which specifies available resources. If the MPS needs additional resources, your company may not achieve the objectives of the marketing plan and, consequently, the business plan.

When the master scheduler has evaluated and accepted the MPS, this authorized MPS is input into the MRP system, which we discuss further in Chapter 15.

Before You Go On

Be sure that you understand the sequential process of master scheduling:

1. The master scheduler uses a rough-cut capacity planning technique to calculate whether the company has the capacity to meet the proposed MPS.
2. If the proposed MPS is feasible, it is evaluated in terms of customer service, effective use of resources, and inventory investment.
3. If the proposed MPS is accepted, it becomes the authorized MPS. If capacity is insufficient, either the MPS is modified or capacity is expanded.

USING THE MPS ■

One use of the authorized MPS is order promising. When a customer places an order for a product but does not expect immediate delivery, the delivery date is negotiated. The customer typically requests delivery at a future date and the company decides whether it can promise delivery on that date. This is called **order promising**. For example, your parents order a new car custom-built for you at the factory for delivery on graduation day. The company is order promising when it decides whether it can produce the car and deliver it on that date. By extending the MPS records we began using in Table 14-2, we can do order promising. Let's look at an extended MPS record in Table 14-12.

▶ **Order promising**
The process of making order delivery commitments.

The table now has two additional rows, one for customer orders and the other for available-to-promise quantity. The customer orders row has orders promised to customers for delivery in that time period. For example, the company has promised 35 units to be delivered in period 1, 25 units for delivery in period 2, and so forth.

The **available-to-promise (ATP)** row shows how many uncommitted units the company has available for delivery at a given time. Next, we look at an example of how to calculate the ATP quantity and the projected available balances.

▶ **Available-to-promise (ATP)**
The uncommitted portion of a company's inventory and planned production, maintained in the the MPS to support order promising.

Table 14-12 Extended MPS Record

Period	1	2	3	4	5	6	7	8	9	10	11	12
Forecast	50	50	50	50	75	75	75	75	50	50	50	50
Customer orders	35	25	25	20	0	15	0	0	10	0	0	10
Projected available												
Available-to-promise												
MPS			125		125			125	115			125

■ Example 14.3 Filling in the MPS Record

Using the data shown in Table 14-13, let's look at how we get the numbers. In this case, both the forecast numbers and the customer orders are already filled in. The first calculations we need to do are in the projected available row: we take the beginning inventory, add to it any MPS shipment, and subtract the greater of the forecast quantity or the customer orders. For example, in Period 1, the beginning inventory is 110 units, there is no MPS shipment, and since the forecast of 50 is greater than the customer orders (35), we have 110 units + 0 units − 50 units = 60 units projected available at the end of Period 1.

We calculate the projected available quantity as

Projected available = Beginning inventory + MPS shipment − the greater of the period's forecast or the actual customer orders promised for delivery.

Table 14-13 shows the appropriate projected available quantities.

Table 14-13 Completed ATP MPS Record

Period	1	2	3	4	5	6	7	8	9	10	11	12
Forecast	50	50	50	50	75	75	75	75	50	50	50	50
Customer orders	35	25	25	20	0	15	0	0	10	0	0	10
Projected available [110]	60	10	85	35	85	10	60	110	60	10	85	35
Available-to-promise	50		80		110		125	115			115	
MPS			125		125		125	125			125	

▶ **Action bucket**
The current period.

We calculate the ATP quantity for the current period or, as it is called, the **action bucket**, and each time an MPS replenishment order is scheduled. In our example, that means we compute the ATP quantity in Periods 1, 3, 5, 7, 8, and 11.

We calculate the ATP quantity in the current period differently from how we calculate it in the future replenishment periods. In the current period (the action bucket), the ATP quantity equals the beginning inventory, plus any MPS quantity. These two represent the available inventory we have to work with. In Period 1, this is 110 units plus 0, or 110 total units available. From this amount, we subtract the customer orders promised for delivery between now and the next replenishment order (Period 3 in our case). The number of units already promised is 60 (35 units for delivery in Period 1 and 25 units for delivery in Period 2). After subtracting the 60 units promised from the 110 units available, we still have 50 ATP units for delivery either in Period 1, Period 2, or at some future date. We calculate ATP in the action bucket as

$$\text{ATP}_{\text{Action Bucket}} = (\text{beginning inventory} + \text{MPS shipment}) - (\text{customer orders before next replenishment})$$

As we said above, we calculate the ATP differently at future replenishment periods. In these cases, the ATP equals the MPS replenishment quantity, less any customer orders promised for delivery between the date of the replenishment received and the next replenishment scheduled. For example, a replenishment order of 125 units is arriving in Period 3. The customer orders already promised for delivery before the next replenishment order (Period 5) total 45 units (25 units in Period 3 and 20 units in Period 4). Of those 125 units arriving, we have already committed 45, leaving 80 units still available to promise. We calculate the ATP at periods other than the action bucket as

$$\text{ATP} = \text{MPS shipment} - \text{customer orders between current MPS shipment and next scheduled replenishment.}$$

In periods other than the action bucket, we do not include the beginning inventory since it is not clear what the available amount will be. Remember that we subtracted the greater of the forecast or customer orders promised for delivery each period. Thus, if the forecast is greater than the customer orders, we end up with more units in inventory than are reflected on the MPS record. Table 14-13 shows the completed ATP quantities.

■ USING THE ATP RECORDS

The ATP records show how much inventory is available to satisfy customer demand, so your company bases delivery promises to customers on these records. Using the completed ATP record in Table 14-13, let's look at whether or not your company can promise delivery of a new order.

Suppose that marketing has a customer willing to purchase 200 units if your company can deliver the units in Period 5. Using the ATP record, we need to see whether that delivery is possible. One way to do this is to adjust the ATP record as if the order had already been accepted. Table 14-14 shows a revised ATP record including the new order.

In the customer orders row, 200 units are now scheduled for customer delivery in Period 5. This changes the projected available quantities from Period 5 on and changes the ATP quantity in Period 5. The two rules to remember here are the following.

1. *A negative number in the projected available row is* **sometimes** *a problem.* We calculate the projected available quantity by subtracting the greater of the forecast or the customer orders promised for delivery each period. If the forecast is subtracted because it is larger, as in Period 1 (50 units forecast compared to 35 units of customer orders), the company may not sell any more units for delivery in Period 1. In that case, the ending inventory for Period 1 would be 75 units (110 units to start with, less 35 units delivered).

2. *A negative number in the available-to-promise row is* **always** *a problem.* This means your company does not have enough inventory to cover the delivery. In our example, the company needs an additional 90 units to cover the new order scheduled for delivery in Period 5.

"Would you like that delivered soon, pretty soon, or sometime-or-other?"

One way to handle this problem is to look at earlier ATP quantities to see whether any inventory is available from earlier shipments. Period 1 has 50 uncommitted units and Period 3 has an additional 80 available units. If we set 90 of these units aside for the Period 5 order, we can agree to the new customer order. Look at the revised ATP record in Table 14-15.

Think of it this way. We set 10 units aside in Period 1 and put the customer's name on the boxes for delivery in Period 5. In Period 3, we put names on an additional 80 boxes of units. Then in Period 5, we use the 90 boxes of units already set aside plus 110 of the new units to total the 200 units needed. In this way, we can promise delivery of 200 units in Period 5.

Table 14-14 Revised ATP MPS Record

Period	1	2	3	4	5	6	7	8	9	10	11	12
Forecast	50	50	50	50	75	75	75	75	50	50	50	50
Customer orders	35	25	25	20	200	15	0	0	10	0	0	10
Projected available 110	60	10	85	35	−40	−115	−65	−15	−65	−115	−40	−90
Available-to-promise	50		80		−90		125	115			115	
MPS			125		125		125	125			125	

Table 14-15 Second Revised ATP Record

Period	1	2	3	4	5	6	7	8	9	10	11	12
Forecast	50	50	50	50	75	75	75	75	50	50	50	50
Customer orders	45[1]	25	105[1]	20	110[1]	15	0	0	10	0	0	10
Projected available 110	60	10	30	−20	−5	−80	−30	20	−30	−80	−5	−55
Available-to-promise	40		0		0		125	115			115	
MPS			125		125		125	125			125	

[1]These quantities have changed to account for the additional 90 units needed to satisfy the order of 200 units for delivery in Period 5. We commit 80 units from the period 3 replenishment order and 10 units from the ATP quantity in Period 1.

Table 14-16 Third Revised ATP Record												
Period	1	2	3	4	5	6	7	8	9	10	11	12
Forecast	50	50	50	50	75	75	75	75	50	50	50	50
Customer orders	45[1]	25	105[1]	70	110[1]	15	0	0	10	0	0	10
Projected available 110	60	10	30	−40	−25	−100	−50	0	−50	−100	−25	−75
Available-to-promise	40		−50		0		125	115			115	
MPS			125		125		125	125			125	

Table 14-17 Final Revised ATP Record												
Period	1	2	3	4	5	6	7	8	9	10	11	12
Forecast	50	50	50	50	75	75	75	75	50	50	50	50
Customer orders	45[1]	25	105[1]	20	110[1]	15	0	50	10	0	0	40
Projected available 110	60	10	30	−20	−5	−80	−30	20	−30	−80	−5	−55
Available-to-promise	40		0		0		125	65			85	
MPS			125		125		125	125			125	

[1]These quantities have changed to account for the additional 90 units needed to satisfy the order of 200 units for delivery in Period 5. We commit 80 units from the Period 3 replenishment order and 10 units from the ATP quantity in Period 1.

After we agree to the order for 200 units for delivery in Period 5, the next order arrives requesting an additional 50 units for Period 4 delivery. We put this order into the record and see the results in Table 14-16.

The ATP quantity in Period 3 is now −50. Since a negative number in the ATP row is always a problem, we must check to see whether there is a way we can change that quantity to zero and accept the order. The only available inventory before delivery is requested is the 40 units available in Period 1. Everything else has been promised. Therefore, we cannot accept this order for delivery in Period 4. The earliest we can promise delivery is in Period 7. Unless the customer is willing to agree with this delivery date, we cannot accept the order. We delete the 50 units from the Period 4 customer orders and recalculate the other quantities. The ATP record reverts back to the numbers previously shown in Table 14-15.

Let's look at a couple of additional orders and calculate whether they can be accepted for delivery at the requested time. The first new order is for an additional 50 units to be delivered in Period 8; the second order is for 30 additional units in Period 12. When we put these orders into the customer order row, the ATP record is updated, as shown in Table 14-17. Since there are no negative values in the ATP row, we can promise both of these orders for delivery.

The key requirement for using ATP is that manufacturing delivers the MPS replenishment on the scheduled date. For your company to meet these critical dates, operations must have the capacity specified in the MPS, and therefore the MPS itself must be feasible.

■ STABILIZING THE MPS

The master scheduler tries to minimize the number of changes made to an authorized MPS because each proposed change can affect the feasibility of the MPS. To deal with MPS changes, companies sometimes use **time fence policies**. Figure 14-2 is a diagram

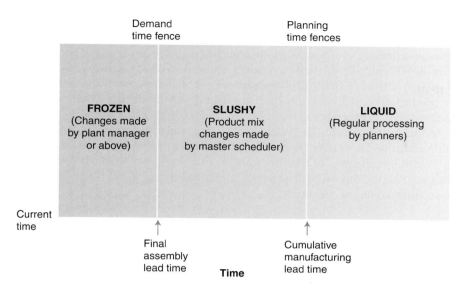

Demand
time fence

Planning
time fences

Figure 14-2

Time fences

FROZEN
(Changes made
by plant manager
or above)

SLUSHY
(Product mix
changes made
by master scheduler)

LIQUID
(Regular processing
by planners)

Current
time

Final
assembly
lead time

Cumulative
manufacturing
lead time

Time

illustrating the MPS and time fences. The figure shows the **demand time fence** and the **planning time fence**, which split the MPS into three parts. The portion of the master schedule from the current time up to the demand time fence is frozen and any changes are kept to a minimum.

Companies typically require these changes to be authorized by a person other than the master scheduler because they may need additional resources. This portion of the MPS normally uses all available capacity to produce customer orders. Adding any orders without adding resources results in a delay of the currently scheduled jobs.

▶ **Time fence policies**
Partition the MPS into areas requiring different operating procedures.

▶ **Demand time fence**
Establishes that point of time in the future inside of which changes to the MPS must be approved by a higher authority.

▶ **Planning time fence**
Establishes a point of time in the future inside of which changes must be made by the master scheduler, and changes outside of which can be changed by system planning logic

■ **Example 14.4 Time Fences at HBS**

Heavenly Ballroom Shoes (HBS) has frozen the first month of its MPS. Quarter 1 is shown in monthly time periods. The HBS marketing director, Marilee, has gotten an endorsement from this year's national ballroom champions for HBS shoes. Because of this endorsement, marketing needs two new, more upscale shoe models (Model WC and Model MC) for use in major competitions. The new models must be available by the end of January or HBS will lose market share. Marilee has asked Charles, the master scheduler, to schedule production of 500 pairs of each of these new models in January. The endorsement represents a major business opportunity for HBS, but HBS does not have the capacity to accept the order for the new shoes. HBS can accept the order only by authorizing more resources for manufacturing or by delaying the shoes that are currently scheduled.

Model	January (pairs)	February (pairs)	March (pairs)	Total Q-1 (pairs)
Model M		666	5,334	6,000
Model W	5,333	4,667		10,000
Total	5,333	5,333	5,334	16,000
Planned capacity available (pairs)	5,335	5,335	5,335	16,005

HBS has set up its MPS so that a decision to change the frozen portion has to be authorized by a manager who is also authorized to provide resources. In this way, HBS protects against jeopardizing existing orders to satisfy new ones.

The second portion of the MPS is the time between the demand time fence and the planning time fence. This is called the slushy portion of the MPS, during which it is the master scheduler's responsibility to negotiate changes in the MPS. For example, if Marilee in HBS marketing needs a product other than what is scheduled, Charles, the HBS master scheduler, first calculates whether the materials are available to make the other product. Then Charles asks Marilee which items marketing would be willing to do without. This is necessary to free up capacity so that the other product can be made.

In this portion of the MPS, changes in the product mix are possible, but changes needing additional resources are not. Thus HBS will produce 5333 pairs of shoes during a month but the mix of the shoe models may vary. A revised MPS for February might look like the following. The product mix has changed but the total number of pairs produced remains constant.

Model	Quantity
Model M	166
Model MC	500
Model W	3667
Model WC	1000
Total pairs	5333

The third portion of the MPS starts at the planning time fence and extends into the future. This portion of the MPS is considered liquid because all orders requested during this portion are accepted as long as the resources authorized by the aggregate plan are adequate. The planning time fence is typically placed far enough into the future so that there is enough time to order any necessary materials and complete the normal manufacturing process. Production planners, discussed in Chapter 15, generally place these orders.

OM ACROSS THE ORGANIZATION

Master production scheduling and rough-cut capacity planning affect functional areas throughout an organization, and the MPS is a basis for communication among those functional areas. Let's look at how this works.

Accounting learns from the MPS how and when resources will be consumed. The MPS enables revenue and cash flow management projections based on scheduled completion dates. It is also a means for measuring the effectiveness of operations in comparisons of planned performance versus real performance.

Marketing uses the MPS to make viable promises to customers because the MPS provides insight into planned production; for example, time fence policies show whether the MPS can be modified to accept orders. The MPS is also a basis for negotiation between marketing and operations.

Information systems provides and supports the databases for MPS development and rough-cut capacity planning.

Purchasing is affected by the MPS because the MRP system uses the MPS to generate the timing and quantity of material requirements. The MPS provides visibility into future needs, so purchasing can decide when long-term contracts and quantity discounts are justified.

Manufacturing is guided by the MPS in using the resources authorized by the aggregate plan. The time fence policies allow manufacturing to maintain stability in daily operations. Rough-cut capacity planning ensures the resources needed to meet the schedule.

The MPS is an important tool within an organization. The person responsible for developing the MPS is the master scheduler. To develop the MPS, the master scheduler interacts with marketing, operations, demand management, and customers. The master scheduler's job is to develop an MPS that achieves the company's desired customer service level, uses capacity effectively, and minimizes inventory investment.

OM IS EVERYWHERE ■

Businesses use the master schedule to improve customer service and make effective use of resources. Developing your own schedule can improve your on-time delivery as well. Most of us can remember having multiple demands on our time. For example, a major paper due in your psych class the same time as a big stat exam. You set the paper aside and concentrate on the exam. Later, you find out that your psych professor does not accept late papers. Even though you completed the paper, your psych grade drops down to a C. Good schedules can prevent this by giving you visibility into future demands on your time and allowing you to make rational capacity allocation decisions.

Identifying your resources is an important first step in meeting your objectives, but it is only the beginning of the planning process. Next, you need to decide how to use those resources. You do this by analyzing the demands of your courses and then allocating the resources to meet those demands. This does not mean you spend the same time studying for each class each week. It means that you develop a schedule that uses your available resources to satisfy your overall objectives.

CHAPTER HIGHLIGHTS

1 The MPS shows how the resources authorized by the aggregate plan will be used to satisfy the objectives of the organization. The MPS specifies the products and quantities to be built in each time period.

2 The MPS is a common organizational document used to facilitate communication between different functional areas. The master scheduler develops a proposed MPS based on input received from the aggregate plan and demand management. The proposed MPS takes into account customer service objectives, effective resource use, and cost. This MPS is checked for feasibility using a rough-cut capacity planning technique.

3 The objectives of master scheduling are to satisfy customer service objectives, use resources effectively, and minimize costs.

4 An MPS is developed by looking at individual MPS records and calculating when replenishment quantities are needed. The individual MPS records are summed together to show the total proposed workload.

5 The proposed MPS is then evaluated for feasibility using a rough-cut capacity planning technique. CPOPF uses historical data to determine how much of each resource is needed to complete the proposed MPS.

6 Available-to-promise logic is used when promising order delivery dates to customers. ATP logic allows the company to make viable delivery promises.

7 Time fence policies stabilize the MPS. The demand time fence and the planning time fence divide the MPS into three portions: frozen, slushy, and liquid. Changes in the frozen portion are infrequent and must be authorized by a manager with authority to release additional resources to operations. Changes to the slushy portion are negotiated between the master scheduler and marketing. Changes in product mix can occur but not changes in total volume. Changes in the liquid portion are made by planners since adequate lead time is available.

KEY TERMS

master production schedule 427
master scheduler 427
demand management 428
material requirements planning
   system (MRP) 429

rough-cut capacity planning (RCCP) 431
demonstrated capacity 431
capacity planning using overall
   planning factors (CPOPF) 431
order promising 435

available-to-promise 435
action bucket 436
time fence policies 439
demand time fence 439
planning time fence 439

FORMULA REVIEW

Calculating the projected available quantity

Projected Available = beginning inventory + MPS shipment − forecasted demand

Calculating a planning factor for direct labor

Planning factor for direct labor =
$$\frac{\text{total direct labor spent building model}}{\text{number of units of model built}}$$

Calculating a planning factor for machine time

Planning factor for machine time =
$$\frac{\text{total machine time spent building model}}{\text{number of units of model built}}$$

Calculating projected available quantity when using ATP MPS records

Projected available = beginning inventory + MPS shipment − (the greater of the period's forecast or the actual customer orders promised for delivery that period)

Calculating ATP quantity in the action bucket

$\text{ATP}_{\text{Action Bucket}}$ = (beginning inventory + MPS shipment) − (customer orders before next replenishment)

Calculating ATP quantity at future replenishment periods

ATP = (MPS shipment) − (customer orders between current MPS shipment and next scheduled replenishment)

SOLVED PROBLEMS

■ Solved Problem 1

Complete the following MPS records. The beginning inventory is 20 units and the order quantity is an *FOQ* = 50 units in part (a) and a *POQ* = 2 periods in part (b).

a. Using an *FOQ* = 50 units, complete the MPS record shown here.

Solution

Begin by calculating the projected available quantities. At the end of Period 1, the projected available should be 0 (20 units of beginning inventory less 20 units forecasted demand). If no order is received, the projected available row is negative at the end of Period 2. When this row turns negative, we need a replenishment order for that period. The replenishment order in this case is 50 units. The updated MPS record is shown next.

Period	1	2	3	4	5	6	7
Forecast	20	20	20	20	10	10	10
Projected available 20							
MPS							

Period	8	9	10	11	12	13
Forecast	10	10	10	20	20	20
Projected available						
MPS						

Period	1	2	3	4	5	6	7
Forecast	20	20	20	20	10	10	10
Projected available 20	0	30	10				
MPS		50					

Period	8	9	10	11	12	13
Forecast	10	10	10	20	20	20
Projected available						
MPS						

When spreadsheeting this problem, you can include a conditional statement to check whether the projected available quantity is negative. When the projected available is negative, an MPS quantity is then entered into the appropriate cell. The program then recalculates the projected available quantity and continues on to the next negative result.

When you are solving the problem manually, continue calculating the projected available quantities until the next negative. At the point, we need another replenishment order. The completed MPS is shown here.

Period	1	2	3	4	5	6	7
Forecast	20	20	20	20	10	10	10
Projected available	0	30	10	40	30	20	10
MPS		50		50			

Period	8	9	10	11	12	13
Forecast	10	10	10	20	20	20
Projected available	0	40	30	10	40	20
MPS		50			50	

b. Using an order quantity of *POQ* = 2 periods, complete the MPS record.

Solution

Period	1	2	3	4	5	6	7
Forecast	20	20	20	20	10	10	10
Projected available	0						
MPS							

Period	8	9	10	11	12	13
Forecast	10	10	10	20	20	20
Projected available						
MPS						

Once again, we need an MPS replenishment in Period 2. To calculate the quantity, we sum the forecasted demand for the next two periods and subtract any beginning inventory. We need 20 units in both periods 2 and 3 for a total of 40 units; we have no beginning inventory, so we order 40 units. Look at the updated MPS record that follows.

Period	1	2	3	4	5	6	7
Forecast	20	20	20	20	10	10	10
Projected available	0	20	0				
MPS		40					

Period	8	9	10	11	12	13
Forecast	10	10	10	20	20	20
Projected available						
MPS						

We need the next replenishment order in Period 4, which should be for 30 units (20 demanded in Period 4 and 10 units for period 5). The completed MPS record is shown is Spreadsheet 14.1.

Note that replenishment orders are now scheduled for Periods 2, 4, 6, 8, 10, and 12.

Spreadsheet 14.1

Beginning Inventory	20
FOQ	50

Week		1	2	3	4	5	6	7	8	9	10	11	12	13
Forecast		20	20	20	20	10	10	10	10	10	10	20	20	20
Projected Available	20	0	30	10	40	30	20	10	0	40	30	10	40	20
MPS		0	50	0	50	0	0	0	0	50	0	0	50	0

■ Solved Problem 2

Tim's Wire Shop builds two different, complicated wiring assemblies. Production of the WA-1001 model has averaged 50,000 units annually. Historically, Tim's Wire Shop has used 12,000 direct labor hours and 5000 hours of machine time annually to build the WA-1001 wiring harness. The other wiring assembly, WA-5005, has an average annual production of 40,000 units. Annual direct labor used on the WA-5005 is 26,000 hours and 2000 hours of machine time.

a. Develop the following four planning factors:
   Planning factor for direct labor for WA-1001
   Planning factor for direct labor for WA-5005
   Planning factor for machine time for WA-1001
   Planning factor for machine time for WA-5005

Solution

To calculate the planning factor for direct labor for WA-1001, divide the annual direct labor hours by the annual number of units produced.

Planning factor for direct labor for WA-1001 = 12,000 direct labor hours/50,000 units or 0.24 hours per unit

Planning factor for direct labor for WA-5005 = 26,000 direct labor hours/40,000 units or 0.65 hours per unit

Planning factor for machine time for WA-1001 = 5,000 hours of machine time/50,000 units, or 0.10 hours per unit

Planning factor for machine time for WA-5005 = 2,000 hours of machine time/40,000 units, or 0.05 hours per unit

■ Solved Problem 3

Given the proposed MPS below and the planning factors from Solved Problem 2, calculate the needed capacity for each period for direct labor and machine time.

Solution

To find the direct labor hours needed, multiply the MPS quantity for each item by its planning factor. Do this for each period.

Item	Quarter 1	Quarter 2	Quarter 3	Quarter 4
WA-1001	10,000	15,000	15,000	13,000
WA-5005	15,000	10,000	9,000	8,000
Total	25,000	25,000	24,000	21,000

Model	Direct Labor Factor	Q-1 MPS Qty.	Q-1 Hours Req'd	Q-2 MPS Qty.	Q-2 Hours Req'd	Q-3 MPS Qty.	Q-3 Hours Req'd	Q-4 MPS Qty.	Q-4 Hours Req'd	Total MPS Qty.	Total Hours Req'd
WA1001	0.24	10,000	2,400	15,000	3,600	15,000	3,600	13,000	3,120	53,000	12,720
WA5005	0.65	15,000	9,750	10,000	6,500	9,000	5,850	8,000	5,200	42,000	27,300
Total		25,000	12,150	25,500	10,100	24,000	9,450	21,000	8,320	95,000	40,020

Use the same approach to calculate machine time needs.

Model	Machine Time Factor	Q-1 MPS Qty.	Q-1 Hours Req'd	Q-2 MPS Qty.	Q-2 Hours Req'd	Q-3 MPS Qty.	Q-3 Hours Req'd	Q-4 MPS Qty.	Q-4 Hours Req'd	Total MPS Qty.	Total Hours Req'd
WA1001	0.10	10,000	1,000	15,000	1,500	15,000	1,500	13,000	1,300	53,000	5,300
WA5005	0.05	15,000	750	10,000	500	9,000	450	8,000	400	42,000	2,100
Total		25,000	1,750	25,000	2,000	24,000	1,950	21,000	1,700	95,000	7,400

■ Solved Problem 4

Tim's Wire Shop uses three different departments to produce these wire assemblies. Each of these departments uses direct labor and machine time. Historically, Department 101 uses 25% of the direct labor time and machine time for these products, Department 102 uses 35%, and Department 103 uses 40%. Calculate the direct labor and machine time needs for each department for each quarter.

Solution

To calculate the direct labor hours needed for each department, take the total direct labor needed for the quarter and multiply it by the appropriate percentage for each work center. For example, in Quarter 1, the total direct labor needed is 12,150 hours. Multiply that by 25% to allocate the appropriate amount of labor to department 101. The same approach is used for allocating machine time between departments. The completed allocations are shown here.

Labor Allocations

Department	Historical Percentage Allocation	Labor Hours Required Q-1	Labor Hours Required Q-2	Labor Hours Required Q-3	Labor Hours Required Q-4	Total Labor Required
Department 101	25%	3,037.5	2,525	2,362.5	2,080	10,005
Department 102	35%	4,252.5	3,535	3,307.5	2,912	14,007
Department 103	40%	4,860	4,040	3,780	3,328	16,008
Total		12,150	10,100	9,450	8,320	40,020

Machine Allocations

Department	Historical Percentage Allocation	Machine Hours Required Q-1	Machine Hours Required Q-2	Machine Hours Required Q-3	Machine Hours Required Q-4	Total Machine Labor Required
Department 101	25%	437.5	500	487.5	425	1,850
Department 102	35%	612.5	700	682.5	595	2,590
Department 103	40%	700	800	780	680	2,960
Total		1,750	2,000	1,950	1,700	7,400

■ Solved Problem 5

Jeannette's Cashmere Sweaters has authorized the following MPS for her exclusive line of cashmere sweaters. She wants to use the MPS record for promising future orders. Current order promises are included. The MPS order quantity is 60 units. Beginning inventory is 0. Complete the following MPS record.

Period	1	2	3	4	5	6
Forecast	15	15	15	15	20	20
Customer orders	12	10	8	5	0	0
Projected available 0						
Available-to-promise						
MPS	60				60	

Period	7	8	9	10	11	12
Forecast	20	20	25	25	25	25
Customer orders	15	0	30	0	0	0
Projected available						
Available-to-promise						
MPS		60		60		60

Solution

Projected available is calculated as

Projected available = Beginning inventory + MPS Shipment − the greater of the period's forecast or the customer orders promised for delivery

Therefore, the projected available at the end of Period 1 is 45 units (the beginning inventory of 0 plus the MPS shipment of 60, less the forecast of 15). The correct projected available quantities are shown here.

Period	1	2	3	4	5	6
Forecast	15	15	15	15	20	20
Customer orders	12	10	8	5	0	0
Projected available 0	45	30	15	0	40	20
Available-to-promise	25				45	
MPS	60				60	

Period	7	8	9	10	11	12
Forecast	20	20	25	25	25	25
Customer orders	15	0	30	0	0	0
Projected available	0	40	10	45	20	55
Available-to-promise		30		60		60
MPS		60		60		60

The ATP quantity in the action bucket is 25 units: a beginning inventory of 0 plus an MPS shipment of 60 units, less the customer orders of 35 units before the next replenishment (12 in Period 1, 10 in Period 2, 8 in Period 3, and 5 in Period 4). Use the formula for ATP at MPS replenishments to calculate the other ATP quantities.

ATP = MPS shipment − customer orders between current MPS shipment and next scheduled replenishment

Compare your answers with those shown on the previous page.

■ Solved Problem 6

Jeannette has received several additional orders to consider. Using the ATP record calculated in Solved Problem 5, calculate which of the new orders Jeannette should accept. The new orders are: (1) 20 units for delivery in Period 4, (2) 50 units for delivery in Period 8, (3) 40 units for delivery in Period 12.

Solution

The first step is to put the new orders into the MPS record and consider the implications. The updated MPS record is shown here.

Period	1	2	3	4	5	6
Forecast	15	15	15	15	20	20
Customer orders	12	10	8	25	20	0
Projected available 0	45	30	15	−10	30	10
Available-to-promise	5				45	
MPS	60				60	

Period	7	8	9	10	11	12
Forecast	20	20	25	25	25	25
Customer orders	15	50	30	0	0	40
Projected available	−10	0	−30	5	−20	0
Available-to-promise		−20		60		20
MPS		60		60		60

Period	1	2	3	4	5	6
Forecast	15	15	15	15	20	20
Customer orders	12	10	8	25	0	0
Projected available 0	45	30	15	−10	30	10
Available-to-promise	5				45	
MPS	60				60	

Period	7	8	9	10	11	12
Forecast	20	20	25	25	25	25
Customer orders	15	30	30	0	0	40
Projected available	−10	20	−10	25	0	20
Available-to-promise		0		60		20
MPS		60		60		60

Note that Jeannette can accept order 1 for delivery of 20 additional sweaters in Period 4. She can also accept order 3 for 40 units delivered in Period 12. However, Jeannette has a problem accepting order 2. The ATP quantity in Period 8 is −20, which means Jeannette must ensure that enough sweaters are available to satisfy that order. Since the ATP quantity in Period 5 is 45 sweaters, Jeannette can set aside 20 of these sweaters so that she has enough to satisfy order 2. Therefore, she can accept all three orders.

On the revised MPS record, we see that the customer order in Period 8 is reduced 20 units, which are transferred to Period 5. The 20 units transferred to Period 5 are the 20 units that were not available in Period 8. Look at the changes in the updated MPS record.

DISCUSSION QUESTIONS

1. Visit a local business and learn how it calculates its resources.
2. Describe the inputs needed to do master production scheduling.
3. Describe the different sources of demand.
4. Discuss the objectives of the master scheduler and how they influence master scheduling decisions.
5. Explain the process of developing an authorized MPS.
6. Explain the importance of rough-cut capacity planning in the MPS process.
7. Describe the role of time fence policies.
8. Explain the changes you can make in the frozen portion of the MPS and who must authorize such changes.
9. Explain the changes you can make in the slushy portion of the MPS and who authorizes such changes.
10. Discuss how the MPS might be used in a service organization.

PROBLEMS

1. David's Delightful Kites Company (DDKC) manufactures kites. The most popular is David's Daredevil model. Demand management has prepared forecast estimates for the next 6 weeks. Beginning inventory is 15 David's Daredevils. As the master scheduler for DDKC, you must prepare an MPS. Your MPS order quantity is 72 kites.

Week	1	2	3	4	5	6
Forecast	20	35	50	50	45	40
Projected Available 15						
MPS						

    a. Prepare the MPS using an order quantity of 72 kites.
    b. Calculate the ending inventory for each period.
    c. What is the maximum number of units held in inventory?
    d. How many MPS orders are needed?

2. In an effort to reduce setup frequency, DDKC has decided to use an MPS order quantity of 120 kites.

    a. Prepare the MPS using the new order quantity.
    b. Calculate the ending inventory for each period.
    c. Compare this MPS with the MPS developed in Problem 1.

3. DDKC has decided to change its replenishment policy. Instead of producing 72 or 120 kites each order, DDKC has reduced its MPS order quantity to 48 kites.

    a. Develop an MPS using 48 kites as the order quantity.
    b. Calculate the ending inventory for each period.
    c. Compare this MPS with the schedules developed in Problems 1 and 2.

4. Wine Accessories Inc. (WAI) produces two models of corkscrews, the standard model and a deluxe model. WAI follows a level aggregate plan, producing 20,000 corkscrews per month or 5,000 corkscrews per week. The MPS is developed in weekly time periods. The forecasts for each model and the projected available are shown in the next two tables. The replenishment order quantity is 2,000 units for the standard model and 1,000 units for the deluxe model. Note that you can place multiple orders if a single order is insufficient to cover the forecast (you can produce 4,000 or 6,000 units of the standard model if necessary, or 2,000 or 3,000 units of the deluxe model). Remember that total weekly production is limited to 5,000 corkscrews. Develop an MPS for each of the products.

Standard Corkscrew	1	2	3	4
Forecast	3000	3500	5000	4000
Projected Available 2000				
MPS				

Deluxe Corkscrew	1	2	3	4
Forecast	2000	1500	1000	3000
Projected Available 2000				
MPS				

5. WAI uses two resources for each product that it builds: direct labor and machine time. From historical records, WAI calculates the following planning factors:

    Direct labor for standard corkscrew is 0.20 hours
    Direct labor for deluxe corkscrew is 0.50 hours
    Machine time for standard corkscrew is 0.10 hours
    Machine time for deluxe corkscrew is 0.30 hours

Calculate the capacity needed for the MPS developed in Problem 4.

6. WAI is evaluating a new machine that reduces the machine time needed for the standard corkscrew to 0.08 hours but increases the machine time for the deluxe corkscrew to 0.40 hours.

    a. Calculate the machine capacity needed for each period if WAI uses the new machine.
    b. Will the new machine prove beneficial to WAI?

7. WAI knows from historical records that approximately 40% of its labor is used in Department 101 and 60% is used in Department 102. The reverse is true of machine time; 60% is used in Department 101 and 40% is used in Department 102.

    a. Calculate the labor and machine hours needed in Department 101 for each period of the MPS developed in Problem 4.
    b. Calculate the labor and machine hours needed in Department 102 for each period of the MPS developed in Problem 4.

8. WAI has developed the following MPS. Calculate the projected available and the available-to-promise quantities for WAI.

	1	2	3	4	5	6	7	8
Forecast	30	30	30	40	40	40	45	45
Customer Orders	35	15	20	18	12	0	15	0
Projected Available 50								
Available-to-promise								
MPS		100			100		100	

9. WAI, the company in Problem 8, has received the following additional customer orders shown here. You must determine which of the orders the company can accept. If the company must reject any orders, you must explain why.

Order Number	Order Quantity	Desired Week
1	10	3
2	25	1
3	40	5
4	20	6

10. Josh Randall, a sales representative for WAI, has convinced his customer (order number 2 in Problem 9) to reschedule. Order number 2 has agreed to accept delivery of 24 units in week 2 as along as WAI can also guarantee delivery of an additional 25 units in week 5. If WAI cannot meet both delivery requirements, the customer has threatened to withdraw its entire order. You have already promised orders 1, 3 and 4. Can you assure Josh that WAI will deliver on time? Show your calculations.

CASE: *Newmarket International Manufacturing Company (B)*

Newmarket International Manufacturing Company (NIMCO) was founded by Marcia Blakely only two years after leaving graduate school. Her knowledge of mass customization has been the driving force behind starting NIMCO. The company produces three major custom products. Volume on the products is high even though each item is customized specifically for the customer. The products are processed through up to four different work centers. Even though each item is unique, the processing time at each work center is constant due to the sophisticated equipment used.

Today's Opportunity

Joe Barnes had just left the staffing meeting. The information you provided was quite helpful and he believes he has adequate resources to accomplish the required manufacturing for the second quarter. Effective capacity levels (including regular time and planned overtime) for each work center are shown here, as is the amount of time required for each product at each work center. The demand forecasts for each product are also shown.

Effective Weekly Capacity Levels

Work Center 1	Work Center 2	Work Center 3	Work Center 4
920 hours	740 hours	920 hours	725 hours

Product Standard Time by Work Center

Product	Standard Hours at Work Center 1	Standard Hours at Work Center 2	Standard Hours at Work Center 3	Standard Hours at Work Center 4	Total Standard Time (Hours)
A	0.06		0.14	0.04	0.24
B	0.15	0.13		0.10	0.38
C	0.03	0.08	0.12	0.06	0.29

	Quarter 2 Demand Forecasts		
Week	Demand for Product A	Demand for Product B	Demand for Product C
14	3600	4000	2000
15	4000	4000	2500
16	4300	4000	2800
17	4400	3800	3100
18	4500	3800	3200
19	4500	3800	3200
20	4400	3600	3200
21	4300	3600	3000
22	4000	3600	3000
23	4000	3800	2800
24	3600	3800	2800
25	3200	3800	2600
26	3000	4000	2600

1. Joe now needs a rough cut capacity check to determine whether the capacity at each work center is adequate to support the expected demand. Using the forecasted demand as your proposed master schedule, calculate the load profile for each work center for each week of the second quarter. Highlight any weeks in which problems might occur.

2. Joe knows from past experience that he has some flexibility in his workforce. Therefore as long as the total capacity needed does not exceed the total available, the master schedule should be feasible. He also knows that he can increase his capacity total an additional 2.5% through extra overtime and still be within his budget. Given this new information, what recommendations do you have for Joe? What weeks are likely to be problems, and how should he use the capacity in those weeks? How important to NIMCO is it to have a flexible workforce?

INTERACTIVE LEARNING

Enchance and test your knowledge of Chapter 14 using the interactive CD.

1. **Spreadsheet** *Solved Problems 2 and 3*

   Visit our dynamic Web site, www.wiley.com/college.reid, for more cases, web links, and additional information.

2. **Additional Web Resources**
   APICS, www.apics.org

3. **Virtual Company Consulting Case**

4. INTERNET CHALLENGE *The Open Road*

Master production scheduling allocates resources authorized in the aggregate plan. For your Internet Challenge, plan a road trip and calculate how you will use your resources during the trip. Your resources include a new car, which averages 28 miles per gallon using regular unleaded gasoline, enough clothing for a week, and combined available cash of $2500.

Your objective is a two-week adventure on the open highway. Your trip is limited to a total of 2500 to 3000 miles. You must stay in a motel or hotel each night during your trip.

Make a schedule and draw a map showing where your trip begins and ends each day. For each day, calculate how much of your resources you will need. Decide how many miles you will drive; where you will stay each night; the cost of the lodgings (do not forget the taxes); and estimate eating expenses, and admission or sightseeing costs you expect to incur. For your expected driving time, use the driving time estimate provided with your map. You do not have to drive every day if you want to stay at a location for more than one day.

The challenge is to develop a daily schedule for your road trip using the authorized resources available to you. Happy motoring.

BIBLIOGRAPHY

Arnold, J.R. Tony. *Introduction to Materials Management*, 3rd ed. Upper Saddle River, N.J.: Prentice-Hall, 1998.

Blackstone, Jr., John H. *Capacity Management*. Cincinnati, Oh.: South-Western, 1989.

Cox, James F., III, John H. Blackstone, and Michael S. Spencer, eds. *APICS Dictionary*, 9th ed. Falls Church, Va.: American Production and Inventory Control Society, Inc., 1998.

Gessner, Robert A. *Master Production Schedule Planning*. New York: Wiley, Inc., 1986.

Vollmann, Thomas E., William L. Berry, and D. Clay Whybark. *Manufacturing Planning and Control Systems*, 5th ed. Burr Ridge, Ill.: Irwin, 1997.

Material Requirements Planning

Before studying this chapter you should know or, if necessary, review

1. Calculating available capacity, Chapter 9, pages 247–255.
2. Calculating order quantities, Chapter 12, pages 361–371.
3. Inventory record accuracy, Chapter 12, pages 383–384.
4. Developing the MPS, Chapter 14, pages 429–431.

LEARNING OBJECTIVES

After studying this chapter, you should be able to

1. Explain the difference between independent and dependent demand.
2. Provide an overview of MRP.
3. Describe the objectives of MRP.
4. Describe the inputs needed for MRP.
5. Explain MRP operating logic.
6. Describe action notices.
7. Use different lot size rules with MRP.
8. Describe the role of capacity requirements planning (CRP).
9. Calculate work loads at critical work centers using CRP.
10. Describe resource planning systems.

CHAPTER OUTLINE

$\mathbf{D}$o you remember the first time you invited your fiancée and her parents for dinner? The steaks were still cooking when the corn was hot and ready to eat. You didn't want to leave the corn in the pot because it would get overcooked, so you took it out—cold corn on the cob! Then the steaks were ready but the baked potatoes were still half raw inside. Too bad you hadn't learned the concept of **backward scheduling** in time for that dinner party!

In backward scheduling we take a desired completion time or due date, consider the activities we have to complete between that time or date and now, and then schedule the activities so that everything is ready at the appropriate time or date. Cooking a meal is a great example of backward scheduling since most foods need different amounts of cooking time. You typically don't start everything on the menu at the same time unless you are cooking a TV dinner.

The same is true for products that need processing, whether by a company building a manufactured product or a caterer preparing food for a social event. When the outcome depends on completion of many activities at a specific time, backward scheduling is the best method.

▶ **Backward scheduling**
Starts with the due date for an order and works backward to determine the start date for each activity.

▶ **Material requirements planning (MRP)**
A system that uses the MRP, inventory record data, and BOM to calculate material requirements.

▶ **Capacity requirements planning (CRP)**
Determines the labor and machine resources needed to fill the open and planned orders generated by the MRP.

Material requirements planning (MRP) is an information system that uses the concept of backward scheduling. MRP enables companies that produce items in batches to have the right materials in the right amounts available at the right time. In the case of your dinner, it means that you have the ingredients you need to have the meal ready when you want to serve it.

Although having the material is critical, you also need the capacity to process the materials on time. For a dinner party, this means having the pots and pans for cooking; the dishes for serving and eating; and the flatware, glasses, napkins, and so forth, for your table. Just having the raw materials is not enough, however; you must be able to transform the materials into the desired products. Companies use **capacity requirements planning (CRP)** to check that enough work is scheduled for operations and that the amount of work scheduled is feasible. CRP reveals potential problems, which gives operations a chance to prevent the problems from happening. For example, if you know you do not have enough dishes for your dinner party, you might borrow some dishes from a friend or consider buying more dishes. You do not wait until you start serving to find out that you are short by three soup bowls.

In this chapter, we cover material requirements planning (MRP), capacity requirements planning (CRP), and briefly discuss resource planning systems. MRP provides the schedule and CRP checks to make sure that the schedule is feasible. The next generation of planning systems now used in organizations needs an integrated, enterprise-wide information system. We begin this chapter by looking at the differences between independent and dependent demand.

TYPES OF DEMAND ■

The two types of demand are independent and dependent. **Independent demand** is the demand for finished products; it does not depend on the demand for other products. Finished products include any item sold directly to a consumer. For example, if a company builds and sells pie safes (a free-standing wooden cupboard), the demand for the pie safes is not dependent on anything else. The company could also sell decorative replacement hinges or punched tin door inserts as independent products. Figure 15-1 is a drawing of a pie safe.

▶ **Independent demand** for an item is unrelated to demand for other items.

Dependent demand is demand derived from finished products. For example, when a company makes pie safes, it needs sides, doors, knobs, insert panels, hinges, shelves, a top, a bottom, and a closure. The company can determine how many of each of these items is needed based on how many pie safes the company plans to build. If the company builds 100 pie safes, operations needs 200 sides, 200 doors, 200 knobs, 200 insert panels (2 of each of these are needed to build 1 finished product), 400 hundred hinges (4 for each pie safe), 300 shelves (3 per finished unit), 100 tops, 100 bottoms, and 100 closures (1 of each needed). The company does not forecast dependent demand but, rather, calculates the material needs based on the final products to be produced. MRP, a computerized information system, is designed to manage dependent demand inventory and to schedule necessary item replenishment orders. Let's look at a typical MRP system.

▶ **Dependent demand** for component parts is based on the number of end items being produced.

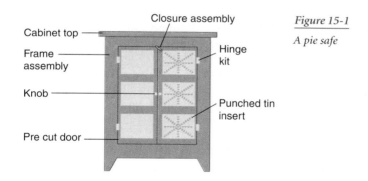

Figure 15-1

A pie safe

AN OVERVIEW OF MRP ■

Think about what it takes to prepare and host a dinner party:

1. You plan the menu.
2. You calculate the number of servings.
3. You review the recipes for each dish on the menu.
4. You assemble the raw materials for each dish on the menu.

Planning the menu and calculating the number of servings is equivalent to creating an authorized master production schedule (MPS). Reviewing the recipes to assemble the raw materials is equivalent to checking the **bill of material (BOM)** file for the needed materials. The BOM file is just like a recipe: it lists the materials needed to build a product or bake a cake. Using the BOM as an input, MRP checks the inventory records for the materials on hand and those purchasing needs to procure. For the dinner, we check our food inventory. We check the refrigerator, the cupboards, the freezer, and the pantry for the materials we have on hand and those we need to buy.

▶ **Bill of material (BOM)** Lists all the subassemblies, component parts, and raw materials that go into an end item and shows the usage quantity of each required.

Figure 15-2

Overview of the MRP process

Authorized master production schedule

Bill of material file ↔ MRP system ↔ Inventory records file

Primary Output
Schedule of replenishment orders (timing and quantity)

▶ **Time-phased**
Expressing future demand, supply, and inventories by time period.

▶ **Gross requirements**
The total-period demand for an item.

Figure 15-2 is an overview of an MRP system. The authorized MPS is the primary input to the MRP system. The MPS details the company's planned products, quantity, and the schedule used by marketing when promising deliveries. The product due dates are critical to the MRP system since they set the completion dates used to backward-schedule production. Part of the MRP system is developing a **time-phased** schedule that shows future demand, supply and inventories by time period. The time-phased schedule shows the production planner when in the production process parts and materials must be available. Not all parts and materials have to be available at the start of production but they must be available at the stage of production that they are needed. For example, when you are building a furniture cabinet, you do not need the stain before you start building the cabinet; you need it when you are ready to apply the finish. On the other hand, you must have the wood before you can begin building the cabinet.

The MRP system checks the BOM file to determine the materials needed, how much, and when. The system generates the **gross requirements** of each part and material needed to accomplish the MPS. The system inserts the gross requirements into the individual inventory records and computes the projected available quantity for each item, so that you know if there's enough inventory or if you need a replenishment order. If you need a replenishment order, the MRP system tells you when to place the order, either to a supplier or to the manufacturing floor, to ensure that the parts or material are available when needed. The MRP system generates planned replenishment order release schedules and can generate additional reports, which we discuss later in this chapter. Now let's consider the objectives of an MRP system.

■ OBJECTIVES OF MRP

The objectives of an MRP system are to determine the quantity and timing of material requirements, and to keep priorities updated and valid.

◆ *Determine the quantity and timing of material requirements.* Your company uses MRP to determine what to order (it checks the BOM), how much to order (it uses the lot size rule for the specific item), when to place the order (it looks at when the material is needed and backward-schedules to account for lead time), and when to schedule delivery (it schedules the material to arrive just as it is needed).

◆ *Maintain priorities.* Your company also uses MRP to keep priorities updated and valid. Requirements change. Customers change order quantities and/or timing. Suppliers deliver late and/or the wrong quantities. Unexpected scrap results from manufacturing. Equipment breaks down and production is delayed. In an ever-changing environment, you use an MRP system to respond to changes in the daily environment, to reorganize priorities, and to keep plans current and viable.

Next, we discuss the inputs needed to run an MRP system.

MRP INPUTS ∎

The three inputs to an MRP system are the authorized MPS, the BOM, and the individual item inventory records. Using the unfinished pie safe from Figure 15-1 as our end item, let's look at each of these inputs.

Authorized MPS

The authorized MPS is a statement of what and when your company expects to build. Table 15-1 shows the first MPS record for the pie safe. From the MPS record, we calculate when we need to have replenishment orders of pie safes. We calculate the timing of MPS orders by the projected available quantity. When we do not have enough inventory to satisfy the forecast for a particular period, we need an MPS order. The quantity of the replenishment order is based on the lot sizing rule used.

Table 15-1 Initial MPS Record for Pie Safe

Item: Pie Safe
Lot Size Rule: FOQ = 100

Week	1	2	3	4	5	6	7	8	9	10	11	12
Forecast	25	25	25	25	30	30	30	30	35	35	35	35
Projected available 80	55	30	5	−20								
MPS												

∎ Example 15.1 Calculating Replenishment Orders at Pie Safe, Inc.

In period 4, the demand is for 25 pie safes. If no MPS order arrives, we will not have enough remaining inventory at the end of period 3 (only 5 units) to satisfy period 4's demand. An MPS order is scheduled to arrive in period 4. We need to determine the quantity of the replenishment order.

Solution
The quantity of the replenishment order is determined by the lot size rule. Common lot size rules include fixed order quantity (FOQ), period order quantity (POQ), and lot-for-lot (L4L). A MPS replenishment order of 100 pie safes is scheduled to arrive in period 4. The company satisfies its demand in period 4 and has 80 units left in inventory (5 units of beginning inventory, plus 100 units arriving, minus the 25 units demanded). The quantities

from the MPS row become the gross requirements for the pie safe. Table 15-2 shows the updated MPS record with the planned replenishment orders.

Table 15-2   Updated MPS Record for Pie Safe

Item: Pie Safe
Lot Size Rule: FOQ = 100

Week	1	2	3	4	5	6	7	8	9	10	11	12
Forecast	25	25	25	25	30	30	30	30	35	35	35	35
Projected available 80	55	30	5	80	50	20	90	60	25	90	55	20
MPS				100			100			100		

Inventory Records

To determine whether enough inventory is available or whether a replenishment order is needed, the MRP system checks the inventory records of all items listed in the BOM. Table 15-3 shows the pie safe's inventory record. Let's look at the information in the record.

The top part of the record contains product or part identification information—typically either a part number, part name, or description. In our example, this is the part name, Pie Safe. The top portion also contains **planning factors**. These can include the lot size rule, **lead times**, safety stock requirements, and so forth.

In our example, the lot size rule is lot-for-lot (L4L) and the planned lead time is 1 week. This information remains relatively constant and is needed by the system to determine how much to order and when to place the replenishment order. Additional information in the records changes with each inventory transaction. These transactions include releasing new orders, receiving previously ordered materials, withdrawing inventory, canceling orders, correcting inventory record errors, and adjusting for rejected shipments. The record shows how much inventory of an item is available, projects future needs, and shows the projected inventory level in different time periods.

One problem with an MRP system is inventory record accuracy. Because the system checks the inventory record to see whether it has to generate a replenishment order, an inaccuracy in the record can cause an error in replenishment ordering. Cycle counting, discussed in Chapter 12, is a technique for improving inventory record accuracy. Let's look at the inventory record shown in Table 15-3.

► **Planning factors**
Include the lot size rule, replenishment lead times, and safety stock requirements.

► **Lead time**
The span of time needed to perform an activity or series of activities.

Problem-Solving Tip   Remember that lot for lot means that the replenishment order quantity is the exact amount needed to satisfy the requirements for that period.

Table 15-3 First Inventory Record for Pie Safe

Item: Pie Safe
Lot Size Rule: L4L
Lead Time: 1 week

	1	2	3	4	5	6	7	8	9	10	11	12
Gross requirements	0	0	0	100	0	0	100	0	0	100	0	0
Scheduled receipts												
Projected available 0	0	0	0	−100								
Planned orders												

The item is a Pie Safe and the lot size rule is lot-for-lot. The lead time is one week. Thus if we want 100 pie safes to be available in week 4, we have to begin the final assembly of the pie safes in week 3. For our purposes, gross requirements are due at the beginning of the period (Monday morning) and planned orders are started at the beginning of a time period. Final assembly is done during week 3 so we can have 100 pie safes at the beginning of week 4.

Gross requirements for finished products are taken from the authorized MPS. **Scheduled receipts** are replenishment orders that have been placed but not yet received. For example, if we placed an order last week and we know it will arrive in period 1, it would be in the scheduled receipts row.

> ▶ **Scheduled receipt**
> An open order that has an assigned due date.

The **projected available** quantity is a period-by-period projection of how much inventory should be available. The projected available quantity equals the beginning inventory, plus any replenishment order due, less the gross requirements for that period. For example, in period 4, we have no beginning inventory but we have 100 units scheduled to arrive, less our gross requirements of 100 units in period 4. Thus our projected available at the end of period four is 0. The beginning inventory for any time period is equal to the projected available quantity at the end of the previous period.

> ▶ **Projected available**
> The inventory balance projected into the future.

Planned orders result when we do not have enough inventory to cover the gross requirements for a period. For example, unless we plan an order to arrive in period 4, we will be short 100 pie safes. When we need a replenishment order, we calculate the quantity by the lot size rule and we calculate the timing by the lead time. For example, we need an order to arrive in period 4, the lot size rule L4L dictates that we order just enough to cover our requirement (100 units), and the lead time of 1 week means that we must place the order 1 week before we need it (so we have a planned order of 100 units in period 3). Table 15-4 shows the updated inventory record for the pie safe.

> ▶ **Planned orders**
> Suggested order quantities, release dates, and due dates created by an MRP system.

Bills of Material

A **bill of material (BOM)** lists the subassemblies, intermediate assemblies, component parts, raw materials, and the quantities of each needed to produce one final product. It is exactly like a recipe for baking a cake. As we would follow the recipe for the cake, the manufacturer is expected to follow the BOM precisely. No extra parts are added. No substitutions are made without appropriate paperwork. Companies that use MRP systems must have a disciplined workforce that uses only the materials authorized by the BOM. The BOMs used as input to the MRP system are **indented bills of materials**. Table 15-5 shows an indented bill of material for the pie safe. In an indented BOM, the highest-level item is closest to the left margin, with components go-

> ▶ **An indented BOM**
> Shows the highest level parents closest to the left margin and the children indented toward the right. Subsequent levels are indented farther to the right.

Table 15-4 Updated Inventory Record for Pie Safe

Item: Pie Safe
Lot Size Rule: L4L
Lead Time: 1 week

	1	2	3	4	5	6	7	8	9	10	11	12
Gross requirements	0	0	0	100	0	0	100	0	0	100	0	0
Scheduled receipts												
Projected available 0	0	0	0	0	0	0	0	0	0	0	0	0
Planned orders			100			100			100			

Table 15-5 Indented BOM		
Part Number	**Description**	**Quantity Required**
PS1001-U	Unfinished pie safe	1
PSF1001-U	Frame assembly	1
PST1001-U	Cabinet top	1
PSD1001-U	Door assembly	2
PSD1001-D	Pre-cut door	1
PSD1001-I	Punched tin insert	1
PSD1001-K	Knob	1
PSC1001-U	Closure assembly	1
PSH1001-U	Hinge kit	4

ing into that item, indented to the right. In our example, the pie safe is the highest-level item and all the components are indented. The components for the door assembly are indented even further to the right since these components go directly into the door assembly rather than the pie safe.

A **product structure tree** visually represents the BOM for a product. Although product trees are seldom used in the workplace, for our purposes they make it easier to explain the MRP process. Figure 15-3 is a product structure tree for the pie safe, with the name of the item, the part number, the usage quantity per parent item, and the replenishment lead time.

At the top of the product structure tree is the **end item**, the product sold to the customer. In this case, the end item is the unfinished pie safe, but the end item could also be a repair part such as decorative hinges or punched tin inserts.

In the MRP system, a **parent item** is any end item made from one or more **components**. In our example, the pie safe is made from these components: a frame assembly, cabinet top, two door assemblies, a closure, and four hinge assemblies. To simplify MRP processing logic, we call the end item the "parent" and its components the "children," and we show each item's parents or children in each of the inventory records. Table 15-6 shows the updated inventory record for the pie safe with this additional information. Since the pie safe is the end item, it has no parents. The components of the pie safe (the frame assembly, cabinet top, door assembly, closure assembly, and hinge kit) are its children.

▶ **Product structure tree**
The visual representation of the BOM, clearly defining the parent and child relationships.

▶ **End item**
A product sold as a completed item or repair part.

▶ A **parent item**
is produced from one or more children.

▶ **Components**
Raw materials, purchased items, or subassemblies that are part of a larger assembly.

Figure 15-3

Product structure tree

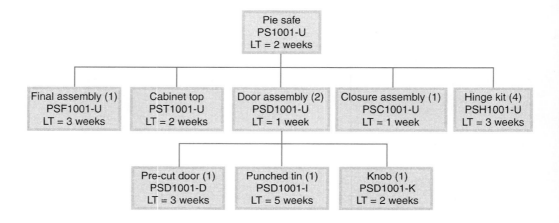

Table 15-6 Updated Inventory Record for Pie Safe												
Item : Pie Safe Lot Size Rule: L4L Lead Time : 1 week	Parent: None Children: Frame assembly, cabinet top, door assembly, closure assembly, hinge kit											
	1	2	3	4	5	6	7	8	9	10	11	12
Gross requirements	0	0	0	100	0	0	100	0	0	100	0	0
Scheduled receipts												
Projected available 0	0	0	0	0	0	0	0	0	0	0	0	0
Planned orders			100			100			100			

■ Example 15.2 Calculating Cumulative Lead Time for a Pie Safe

We need to calculate the cumulative lead time for the end item, a pie safe.

Solution

We can use the product tree to calculate the cumulative lead time for the end item. We do this by summing the individual lead times for each route from the lowest level to the end item. The first possible route includes only the frame assembly and the final assembly of the pie safe. Thus the total lead time for this route is 4 weeks (3 weeks for the frame assembly and 1 week for the pie safe assembly). The next path includes the cabinet top and the final assembly of the pie safe and takes 3 weeks. The third path starts with the precut door, and includes the door assembly and the final assembly of the pie safe and takes 5 weeks. The longest path through this product structure tree begins with the punched tin inserts and includes the door assembly and the pie safe. The *cumulative lead time*, the longest planned length of time to complete the end product, is 7 weeks. Table 15-7 shows all the paths through the product structure tree.

Table 15-7 Paths through the Product Structure Tree

Path from Bottom to Top	Cumulative Lead Time (weeks)
Frame assembly to pie safe	4
Cabinet top to pie safe	3
Pre-cut door to door assembly to pie safe	5
Punched tin insert to door assembly to pie safe	7
Knob to door assembly to pie safe	4
Closure assembly to pie safe	2
Hinge kit to pie safe	4

When your company has inventory on hand, the lead time can be less than the cumulative lead time. Suppose all the items for the door assembly are in stock. The lead time for the pie safes is only 4 weeks, calculated by the time it takes to get the frame assembly and the hinge kit (both are 3 weeks, plus the 1 week for the pie safe assembly). Thus having inventory on hand allows you to respond more quickly because of shorter lead times.

Before You Go On

Be sure that you understand the logic behind MRP. The system checks the gross requirements for each period, compares that with the inventory available (the beginning inventory for that period, plus any replenishment orders due). If the gross requirements exceed the inventory available, an order must be scheduled to arrive in that period. The system calculates the timing of the replenishment order by subtracting the lead time (in weeks) from the period the material is needed to satisfy the gross requirements. The system calculates the quantity of the replenishment order by the lot size rule for that item.

▶ The **explosion process**
Calculates the demand for the children of a parent by multiplying the parent requirements by the children's usage as specified in the BOM.

■ Example 15.3 The MRP System at Pie Safe, Inc.

This example illustrates the MRP explosion process. Using Table 15-6, we begin the MRP **explosion process**. MRP calculates the materials needed to meet the authorized MPS. *The gross requirements for end items are* always *dictated by the authorized MPS.* When we input these quantities into the proper time frame, MRP calculates the gross requirements for each component. The MRP program begins by processing the inventory records of each component of the end item.

We will work through this example starting with the frame assembly. Table 15-8 shows the first inventory record for the frame assembly. Let's look at the differences in the inventory record. First, the lot size rule is a fixed-order quantity of 144 units, which means the order quantity remains constant at 144 units. If 144 units are not enough to cover the gross requirements, we can place a double order (288 units) or triple order (432 units). The lead time is 3 weeks, so we must place the order 3 weeks before it is needed. Gross requirements for a component or child are determined by the inventory record of its parent or parents.

The planned orders of the parent item determine the timing of the gross requirements of the child. In our case the parent item (the pie safe) has planned orders in Periods 3, 6, and 9 and its children (frame assembly, cabinet top, door assembly, closure assembly, and hinge kit) will all have gross requirements in Periods 3, 6, and 9. The quantity of the gross requirement for the child is determined by the usage quantity. Since each pie safe needs one frame assembly, the gross requirement for the frame assembly is 100 pieces. This is the planned order quantity of the parent, times the usage rate of the child (100 times 1). The beginning inventory of the frame assemblies is 120 units.

We can see from the record in Table 15-8 that if no replenishment orders are planned, the projected available becomes negative in Period 6. To prevent this, we need to place a replenishment order in Period 3 for a quantity of 144 units. This order will arrive in Period 6, just as it is needed. The updated record with the planned replenishment orders is shown in Table 15-9.

Table 15-10 has the inventory records for the remaining children of the pie safe. Note that all the pie safe children have gross requirements in Periods 3, 6, and 9. This is because the timing of gross requirements for a child are derived from the planned orders of its parent. After the system sets the gross requirements, it projects the available inventory and

Table 15-8   First Inventory Record for Frame Assembly

Item: Frame Assembly Lot Size Rule: FOQ = 144 Lead Time: 3 weeks		Parent: Pie Safe Children: None											
	1	2	3	4	5	6	7	8	9	10	11	12
Gross requirements	0	0	100	0	0	100	0	0	100	0	0	0
Scheduled receipts												
Projected available 120	120	120	20	20	20	−80						
Planned orders												

back-schedules replenishment orders using the lead time needed for the order to arrive in the appropriate period. For example, the 100 cabinet tops ordered in period 1 will arrive in Period 3 to satisfy that gross requirement. The 800 hinge kits ordered in Period 3 will arrive in Period 6.

Table 15-9   Updated Inventory Record for Frame Assembly

Item: Frame Assembly   Parent: Pie Safe
Lot Size Rule: FOQ = 144   Children: None
Lead Time: 3 weeks

	1	2	3	4	5	6	7	8	9	10	11	12
Gross requirements	0	0	100	0	0	100	0	0	100	0	0	0
Scheduled receipts												
Projected available 120	120	120	20	20	20	64	64	64	108	108	108	108
Planned orders			144			144						

Table 15-10   Inventory Records for Remaining Pie Safe Components

Item: Cabinet Top   Parent: Pie Safe
Lot Size Rule: L4L   Children: None
Lead Time: 2 weeks

	1	2	3	4	5	6	7	8	9	10	11	12
Gross requirements	0	0	100	0	0	100	0	0	100	0	0	0
Scheduled receipts												
Projected available 0	0	0	0	0	0	0	0	0	0	0	0	0
Planned orders	100			100			100					

Item: Door Assembly   Parent: Pie Safe
Lot Size Rule: L4L   Children: Pre-cut door, punched tin insert, knob
Lead Time: 1 week

	1	2	3	4	5	6	7	8	9	10	11	12
Gross requirements	0	0	200	0	0	200	0	0	200	0	0	0
Scheduled receipts												
Projected available 0	0	0	0	0	0	0	0	0	0	0	0	0
Planned orders		200			200			200				

Item: Closure Assembly   Parent: Pie Safe
Lot Size Rule: FOQ = 144   Children: None
Lead Time: 1 week

	1	2	3	4	5	6	7	8	9	10	11	12
Gross requirements	0	0	100	0	0	100	0	0	100	0	0	0
Scheduled receipts												
Projected available 44	44	44	88	88	88	132	132	132	32	32	32	32
Planned orders		144			144							

Item: Hinge Kit   Parent: Pie Safe
Lot Size Rule: FOQ = 800   Children: None
Lead Time: 3 weeks

	1	2	3	4	5	6	7	8	9	10	11	12
Gross requirements	0	0	400	0	0	400	0	0	400	0	0	0
Scheduled receipts												
Projected available 700	700	700	300	300	300	700	700	700	300	300	300	300
Planned orders			800									

Now that MRP has reviewed and updated the children of the pie safe, it drops to the next lower level in the BOM and processes the inventory records at that level. In our example, those records are for the precut door, punched tin insert, and knob. The parent item for these three items is the door assembly. Table 15-11 shows the inventory records for the door assembly and its three children. The process is the same as for the children of the pie safe. The door assembly is now a parent item and we can look at each of its children to see how the system calculates the material requirements.

Table 15-11   Inventory Records for Door Assembly and Components

Item: Door Assembly   **Parent: Pie Safe**
Lot Size Rule: L4L   **Children: Pre-cut door, punched tin insert, knob**
Lead Time: 1 week

	1	2	3	4	5	6	7	8	9	10	11	12
Gross requirements	0	0	200	0	0	200	0	0	200	0	0	0
Scheduled receipts												
Projected available 0	0		0	0	0		0	0	0	0	0	0
Planned orders		200			200			200				

Item: Pre-cut Door   **Parent: Door Assembly**
Lot Size Rule: FOQ = 500 **Children: None**
Lead Time: 3 weeks

	1	2	3	4	5	6	7	8	9	10	11	12
Gross requirements	0	200	0	0	200	0	0	200	0	0	0	0
Scheduled receipts												
Projected available 300	300	100	100	100	400	400	400	200	200	200	200	200
Planned orders		500										

Item: Punched Tin Inserts **Parent: Door Assembly**
Lot Size Rule: FOQ = 500   **Children: None**
Lead Time: 5 weeks

	1	2	3	4	5	6	7	8	9	10	11	12
Gross requirements	0	200	0	0	200	0	0	200	0	0	0	0
Scheduled receipts												
Projected available 400	400	200	200	200	0	0	0	300	300	300	300	300
Planned orders			500									

Item: Knob   **Parent: Door Assembly**
Lot Size Rule: FOQ = 300 **Children: None**
Lead Time: 2 weeks

	1	2	3	4	5	6	7	8	9	10	11	12
Gross requirements	0	200	0	0	200	0	0	200	0	0	0	0
Scheduled receipts												
Projected available 250	250	50	50	50	150	150	150	250	250	250	250	250
Planned orders			300			300						

The timing and quantity of the children's gross requirements are determined by the planned orders of the parent (the door assembly). Since the door assembly has planned orders in Periods 2, 5, and 8, each of the children will have a gross requirement in Periods 2, 5, and 8. MRP calculates the replenishment orders for each of the children. Next, let's look at how MRP provides information to the production and inventory control planners.

ACTION NOTICES ■

MRP systems typically provide inventory planners with **action notices**, which indicate the items that need the planner's attention. An action notice is created when a planned order needs to be released, when dues dates of orders need to be adjusted, or when there is insufficient lead time for a planned replenishment order. Let's look at the different kinds of action notices.

A positive quantity in the current period's planned order row means that an order must be released. We call the current period the **action bucket** because that is the period in which we take actions such as releasing, rescheduling, or canceling orders.

Production and inventory control planners release orders to either an external supplier or to the shop floor. An order released to a supplier authorizes the shipment of the material so that it arrives as needed. An order released to the shop authorizes withdrawal of the needed materials and the start of production. Action notices are generated only for actions taken in the current period. Production and inventory control planners adjust the due dates of orders (both opened and planned) to make sure the material does not arrive too soon or too late but just as it is needed. If an order is scheduled to arrive before it is needed (for example, because the gross requirements changed), the planner delays receipt of the replenishment order until it is needed. If the order is not scheduled to arrive in time, the planner tries to rush or **expedite** the order. Action notices indicate that a decision must be made or an action taken. The production and inventory control planner uses the available information and makes the decision.

▶ **Action notices**
Output from an MRP system that identifies the need for an action to be taken.

▶ **Action bucket**
The current time period.

▶ **Expedite**
To rush orders that are needed in less than the normal lead time.

COMPARISON OF LOT SIZE RULES ■

Different lot size rules can be used with MRP systems, such as least unit cost, least total costs, and parts period balancing. In this book, we cover the fixed order quantity (FOQ), lot for lot (L4L), and period order quantity (POQ). Different lot size rules change the frequency of replenishment orders and determine the quantity of the order.

Let's look at an example comparing FOQ, L4L, and POQ.

■ **Example 15.4 Comparing Different Lot Size Rules at Pie Safe, Inc.**

Given the following gross requirements, let's calculate the planned replenishment orders needed, then calculate the inventory and ordering costs for the 13 weeks.

Solution
The end item has gross requirements in Periods 2 and 3 of 25 units; 40 units in Periods 4 and 5; and 60 units in Periods 7, 8, 9, 11, 12, and 13. The cost to place an order is $25 and the holding cost per unit per period is $0.10. Table 15-12 shows the completed inventory records.

Table 15-12   Inventory Records Comparing Lot Size Rules

Item: Pie Safe
Lot Size Rule: FOQ = 144
Lead Time: 1 week

	1	2	3	4	5	6	7	8	9	10	11	12	13
Gross requirements	0	25	25	40	40	0	60	60	60	0	60	60	60
Scheduled receipts													
Projected available 0	0	119	94	54	14	14	98	38	122	122	62	2	86
Planned orders	144					144		144				144	

Item: Pie Safe
Lot Size Rule: L4L
Lead Time: 1 week

	1	2	3	4	5	6	7	8	9	10	11	12	13
Gross requirements	0	25	25	40	40	0	60	60	60	0	60	60	60
Scheduled receipts													
Projected available 0	0	0	0	0	0	0	0	0	0	0	0	0	0
Planned orders	25	25	40	40		60	60	60		60	60	60	

Item: Pie Safe
Lot Size Rule: POQ = 4 periods
Lead Time: 1 week

	1	2	3	4	5	6	7	8	9	10	11	12	13
Gross requirements	0	25	25	40	40	0	60	60	60	0	60	60	60
Scheduled receipts													
Projected available 0	0	105	80	40	0	0	120	60	0	0	120	60	0
Planned orders	130					180				180			

As you can see, the planned replenishment orders vary in frequency and in quantity. Also note the different levels of inventory carried because of the lot size rule. Lot for lot always minimizes a company's inventory investment because it orders only what is needed for one period. However, L4L also maximizes a company's ordering costs.

Let's calculate the costs for each of these different lot size rules for this 13 weeks. The FOQ lot size rule has ending inventory in all but the first period. In total, 825 units are held for a carrying cost of $82.50 (825 units × $0.10 per unit per period). The ordering cost is $100 (4 orders × $25 per order). Total holding and ordering cost using FOQ is $182.50. The L4L lot size rule has no ending inventory during the 13 weeks. However, it does need a total of 10 replenishment orders. The ordering cost is $250 (10 orders × $25). The total holding and ordering cost for this lot size rule is $250. The POQ = 4 weeks lot size rule has ending inventory in Periods 2, 3, 4, 7, 8, 11, and 12. Total units held is 585, or holding costs of $58.50. This lot size rule needs three replenishment orders to be placed at an ordering cost equal to $75.00. Total holding and ordering costs for this lot size rule are $133.50. In this case, the POQ lot size rule has the lowest holding and ordering costs. To ensure that costs are minimized, we have to do the cost comparisons.

■ THE ROLE OF CAPACITY REQUIREMENTS PLANNING (CRP)

A company uses a rough-cut capacity planning technique to determine whether a proposed MPS is feasible. In Chapter 14, we saw how to evaluate the feasibility of a proposed MPS with capacity planning using overall planning factors (CPOPF). Rough-cut capacity planning techniques use data from the proposed MPS. Capacity requirements planning (CRP) uses data from MRP. We calculate workloads for critical work centers based on **open shop orders** and planned shop orders. Work begins on open shop orders while planned shop orders are scheduled to be done. We translate these orders into hours of work by work center and by time period.

▶ **Open shop orders**
Released manufacturing orders.

■ Example 15.5 Calculating Workloads

Table 15-13 shows items scheduled for Work Center 101. These items are either taken directly from MRP's planned orders or they are already open shop orders. We want to calculate workloads for Work Center 101.

Table 15-13   Workload for Work Center 101

Period	Item Number	Quantity	Setup Time (hours)	Run Time per Unit in Standard Hours	Total Item Time (hours)	Weekly Workload (hours)
4	DN100	250	3.0	0.20	53.0	
	DP100	250	5.0	0.18	50.0	
	DS119	150	2.5	0.30	47.5	
	DT136	400	3.5	0.27	111.5	262.0
5	EQ555	1000	8.0	0.08	88.0	
	ER616	500	4.0	0.22	114.0	
	ES871	100	2.0	0.35	37.0	239.0
6	FA314	250	3.0	0.30	78.0	
	FF369	100	1.5	0.12	13.5	
	FR766	50	0.5	0.15	8.0	
	FS119	200	3.0	0.35	73.0	
	FY486	500	6.0	0.27	141.0	313.5

Solution:

We calculate the total item time by summing the setup time and the total run time for the item.

$$\text{Total item time} = \text{setup time} + (\text{quantity} \times \text{run time per unit})$$

The setup time is incurred each time the machine is prepared to produce the desired quantity of an item. We calculate the total run time by multiplying the quantity to be produced by the run time per unit. In our example, for item DN100, we plan to produce 250 units with each unit needing 0.20 hours of run time. The total run time is 50.0 hours (250 units × 0.20 hours per unit). Total workload placed on the work center by item DN100 is 53.0 hours: 3.0 hours to set up the machine and 50 hours to run the quantity. We make similar calculations for each of the other items. When we have calculated the workload, we compare it to the available capacity for the work center in those time periods.

We calculate available capacity (discussed in Chapter 9) by multiplying the (number of machines available × number of shifts used × number of hours per shift × number of days per week × usage × efficiency).

$$\text{Available capacity} = \text{number of machines available} \times \text{number of shifts used} \times \text{number of hours per shift} \times \text{number of days per week} \times \text{utilization} \times \text{efficiency}$$

In our case, we have 4 machines and we use two 10-hour shifts for 5 days per week so our usage is 85% and our efficiency is 95%.

$$\text{Available capacity} = 4 \text{ machines} \times 2 \text{ shifts per shift} \times 10 \text{ hours per week} \times 5 \text{ days} \times 0.85 \text{ utilization} \times 0.95 \text{ efficiency}$$

The available capacity per week is 323.0 standard hours. Figure 15-4 shows the workload compared to available capacity.

If the available capacity is not adequate, your company has a number of options. The easiest and quickest way to increase available capacity may be to authorize overtime at the work center. Another approach is to reduce the capacity needed by doing some of the work at an alternate work center. If the gap between available and needed capacity is significant, the company can hire a subcontractor for temporary extra capacity.

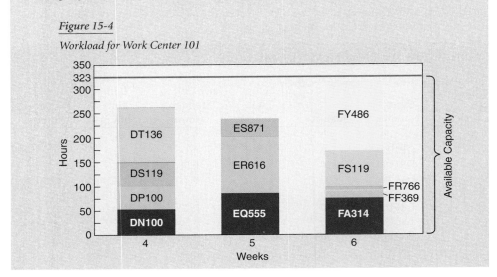

Figure 15-4

Workload for Work Center 101

CRP enables your company to evaluate both the feasibility of the MRP system and how well the company is using its critical work centers.

■ RESOURCE PLANNING SYSTEMS

▶ **Manufacturing resource planning (MRP II)**
A method for the effective planning and integration of all internal resources.

MRP systems are used to determine the timing and quantity of material requirements and to maintain priorities. The information needed for MRP is also useful in other functional areas within the company, as we see next.

Manufacturing resource planning (MRP II), the second generation of MRP, connects MRP to the company's financial system. MRP II allows managers to look at the financial implications of OM decisions. For example, a manager can see the financial impact of an MPS. The manager knows the work that is scheduled, when it is to be completed, who the customer is, how much revenue will be generated, and how much material must be bought. With this information, the manager can project cash flow and make intelligent decisions based on the financial impact of changes. MRP II is used extensively in business and enables additional use of the information generated by MRP.

▶ **Enterprise resource planning (ERP)**
An information system designed to integrate internal and external members of the supply chain.

Although MRP II synchronizes internal operations, it does not provide the information needed to manage supply chains. **Enterprise resource planning (ERP)** is defined in the APICS Dictionary, 9th edition, as "an accounting-oriented information system for identifying and planning the enterprise resources needed to take, make, ship and account for customer orders." ERP systems work from a common, central database, as shown in Figure 15-5. ERP integrates all your company's information systems so that each functional area is using the same information. Sales and marketing, service, finance, human resources management, operations, and inventory planning all use the same database.

ERP goes even further than MRP II. ERP typically allows external customers or suppliers to access your information system. For example, one of your suppliers might

Figure 15-5

Enterprise resource management

Managers

Performance reports

Sales

Finance

Customer

Central database

Operations

Supplies

Service parts & repair

Inventory planning

HRM

Employees

view the production schedule to decide when more parts will be needed and plan their parts production to accommodate that need. Your supplier might even generate the planned replenishment order and input it into your system. Then your supplier would be responsible for planning replenishment orders. With ERP, the supplier has the information needed to make intelligent decisions. External customers access a company's manufacturing schedules and inventory records using ERP to determine when the company can supply a certain product. This is typically done via electronic data interchange (EDI), but the Internet will probably be the mode of access in the near future.

CROSS FUNCTIONAL

One company that has developed various ERP software packages that enable manufacturers to enhance their overall productivity is i2 Technologies, Inc. By using this software, manufacturers can now improve supply-chain activities by monitoring, managing, and optimizing their internal and external activities. For example, manufacturers can connect immediately with suppliers and shippers in real time and can examine the supply chain. In addition, manufactur-

LINKS TO PRACTICE
i2 Technologies, Inc.
www.i2.com

ers can obtain reports that discuss efficiency and forecast potential problems. i2 Technologies Transportation Solutions help manufacturers optimize delivery schedules. Also, i2 Technologies, Inc.'s Softgoods Matrix.com helps softgoods retailers, manufacturers, and suppliers coordinate on-line business, improve response to changes in consumer trends, and attract potential customers. Some of the world's largest manufacturing firms have adopted software developed by i2 Technologies, Inc.

LINKS TO PRACTICE
SAP AG
www.sap.com

SAP AG, one of the leading developers of enterprise solutions software, provides companies with mySAP.com, a software platform for open systems. Open systems allow users to communicate with another user without being constrained by a particular organization's solution. This software includes functionality for material requirements planning, including: manufacturing and financial applications, materials management, product design management, sales and distribution, human resources, production planning, quality assurance, and plant maintenance. SAP also provides functionality that promotes the ability for collaborative planning on the web, via collaborative exchanges and public marketplaces.

While enterprise software (formerly known as ERP) is often associated with manufacturing operations, it also has applications in the service sector. SAP Public Sector and Education SAP Public Services, Inc. announced a plan to offer an offender management system that may revolutionize the corrections industry. The initial implementation will modernize the Commonwealth of Virginia's Department of Corrections. The SAP offender management system will provide web-based case management. The new system enables the Virginia Department of Corrections to enter into the e-Government world.

LINKS TO PRACTICE
Hershey Foods Corporation
www.hersheys.com

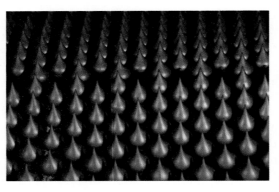

In July 1999, Hershey Foods Corporation switched to a new $112 million computer system designed to automate and modernize its information flows—from taking new candy orders to loading the trucks.

Some 3½ months later, Hershey was still working out the bugs in the new system. Hershey had plenty of candy to fill orders but the new system was not releasing candy from the warehouses. As a result Hershey was unable to satisfy some of its major customers. Poor delivery prior to major candy seasons has strained Hershey's relationships with several major customers.

In most manufacturing operations, production or inventory control planners are responsible for working with MRP. Planners are typically responsible for certain inventory items, including end items, subassemblies, and components. The planner checks the MRP output for action notices related to the items for which they are responsible. Planners schedule, reschedule, and expedite materials to support the MPS. A planning position is often an entry-level job in the materials field.

As companies continue to move toward ERP, all functional areas will work from a central database. The database gives all areas in the company access to the same information simultaneously and improves organizational effectiveness.

OM ACROSS THE ORGANIZATION

Since MRP determines the quantity and timing of materials needed, it affects several functional areas in the company. Let's look at how each functional area is affected.

Accounting calculates future material commitments based on MRP output. Accounting then develops cash flow budgets and the inventory investment to support the current MPS.

Marketing is primarily concerned with the MPS, which identifies when finished goods will be completed. However, MRP reveals potential material shortages, which directly affect marketing. Marketing can also use MRP for allocating scarce materials to maximize customer service.

Information systems maintains MRP, which is a large database that includes the BOM, the inventory records, and the MPS. Minimizing errors in the database is essential to producing useful reports.

Purchasing uses the planned orders generated by MRP to evaluate the feasibility of long-term or blanket contracts and to determine delivery need. The lead times input into MRP may come directly from purchasing.

Manufacturing uses the output generated by MRP to develop daily manufacturing schedules. MRP ensures that the right materials in the right quantity are available to support the MPS. Manufacturing also uses MRP output to allocate scarce materials.

OM IS EVERYWHERE ■

You probably do not use an authorized MPS or a formal BOM or inventory records in your daily life, but MRP concepts do apply to how you manage your time and commitments. Whether you are planning a dinner party for your fiancée and her parents or building an outdoor barbecue, backward scheduling is an essential concept. You need to schedule each activity so the final product will be ready at the expected time. You also need to know what materials you will need, their quantity, and when you will need them.

CRP takes the process one step further by making sure you have adequate capacity for your project. Having the food for your dinner party and knowing when to start cooking is not enough. For example, if you need two grills to cook steaks for four people and you have only one grill, you have a capacity problem. Next time you need to plan an event that consists of several activities, think about backward scheduling and the MRP system. Your fiancée and her parents will thank you for a good dinner.

CHAPTER HIGHLIGHTS

1. Independent demand is the demand for finished products, whereas dependent demand is demand that is derived from finished products. MRP systems use dependent demand.

2. Material requirements planning (MRP) systems are designed to calculate material requirements for items with dependent demand. MRP systems use backward scheduling to determine when each activity starts so that the finished product or service is completed on time.

3. The objectives of MRP are to determine the quantity and timing of material requirements and to keep schedule priorities updated and valid. MRP determines what to order, how much to order, when to place the order, and the schedule for the order's arrival. It maintains priorities by recognizing changes in the operations environment and making the necessary adjustments.

4. MRP needs three inputs: the authorized MPS, the BOM file, and the inventory records file. The MPS is the planned build schedule, the BOM file shows the materials needed to build an item, and the inventory records file shows the inventory on-hand.

5. Once the MPS has been input, MRP checks inventory

records to see if enough end-item inventory is on hand. If inventory is not sufficient, MRP plans the replenishment orders. MRP checks the end item's BOM to determine what materials are needed and in what quantities, then generates planned replenishment orders.

6 Action notices show when to release planned orders, reschedule orders, or adjust due dates. They allow the planner to use the MRP output information more effectively.

7 Different lot size rules are used with MRP systems to generate different order quantities and order frequencies. The lot-for-lot rule always minimizes inventory investment but maximizes ordering costs. A cost comparison of the different techniques shows which lot size rule to use.

8 Planned orders generated by MRP, plus any open shop orders, are inputs to capacity requirements planning

(CRPs). CRP checks to see if available capacity is sufficient to complete the orders scheduled in a particular work center during a particular period.

9 CRP calculates the workloads at critical work centers by using the planned orders generated by the MRP system. These planned order quantities are multiplied by the standard times to calculate individual work center loads.

10 Resource planning systems recognize the value of the information collected in MRP systems and attempt to use it even further. MRP II integrates MRP with the financial system so that managers can evaluate the impact of schedule changes. MRP II synchronizes internal functions with a common database. Enterprise resource planning (ERP) systems provide a central database for all internal and external members of the supply chain.

KEY TERMS

backward scheduling 452
material requirements planning (MRP) 452
capacity requirements planning (CRP) 452
independent demand 453
dependent demand 453
bill of material (BOM) 453
time-phased 454

gross requirements 454
planning factors 456
lead time 456
scheduled receipts 457
projected available 457
planned orders 457
indented bill of material 457
product structure tree 458
end item 458

parent item 458
components 458
explosion process 460
action notices 463
open shop orders 465
manufacturing resources planning (MRPII) 466
enterprise resource planning (ERP) 466

FORMULA REVIEW

To calculate total item time:

Total item time = setup time + (quantity × run time per unit)

To calculate available capacity:

Available capacity = number of machines available × number of shifts used × number of hours per shift × utilization × efficiency

SOLVED PROBLEMS

■ Solved Problem 1

Using the product tree shown in Figure 15-6, calculate the cumulative lead time for item 500 if you have no inventory. How long is the lead time if you have enough inventory for Parts 102, 104, 201, and 203?

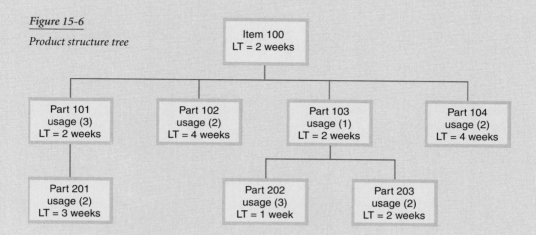

Figure 15-6

Product structure tree

Solution 1

Check all the paths through the product structure tree to find the longest path

Path through the Product Structure	Total Lead Time (weeks)
Part 201 to Part 101 to item 100	7
Part 102 to item 100	6
Part 202 to Part 103 to item 100	5
Part 203 to Part 103 to item 100	6
Part 104 to item 100	6

The path from Part 201 to Part 101 to item 100 is the longest (7 weeks), so it is the cumulative lead time.

When we have enough inventory for some parts, we can eliminate that segment of the path and all levels below that inventory. For example, if we have enough of Part 101, we do not need any more of its component Parts (201). The new paths when we have sufficient inventory for Parts 102, 104, 201, and 203 are shown here.

Path through the Product Structure	Total Lead Time (weeks)
Part 101 to item 100	4
Part 202 to Part 103 to item 100	5

Given that we have enough inventory, we are concerned with only two paths through the product tree. In this situation, the minimum time to produce this item is 5 weeks.

■ Solved Problem 2

Complete the inventory record for item 500 and do an MRP explosion of its component parts. Figure 15-7 shows the product tree for item 500.

Solution 2

Begin by completing the partially filled-in inventory record for item 500. Remember that the gross requirements for the end item come directly from the authorized MPS.

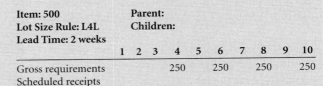

Item: 500 Lot Size Rule: L4L Lead Time: 2 weeks		Parent: Children:								
	1	2	3	4	5	6	7	8	9	10
Gross requirements				250		250		250		250
Scheduled receipts										
Projected available 0										
Planned orders										

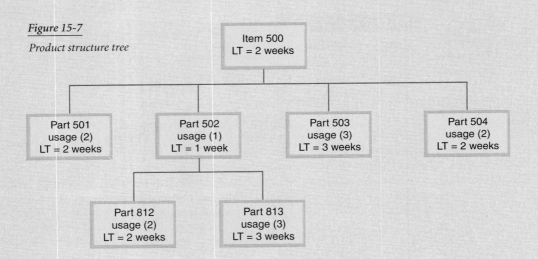

Figure 15-7

Product structure tree

Given the gross requirements, we will need planned orders for item 500 in weeks 2, 4, 6, and 8. Each of the planned orders is for 250 units. The completed record is shown here.

Item: 500 Lot Size Rule: L4L Lead Time: 2 weeks		Parent: None Children: 501, 502, 503, 504								
	1	2	3	4	5	6	7	8	9	10
Gross requirements				250		250		250		250
Scheduled receipts										
Projected available	0	0	0	0	0	0	0	0	0	0
Planned orders		250		250		250		250		

Now that we have a completed inventory record for the end item, we can do the MRP explosion for its children. Remember that each of the children will have gross require-

ments in the periods that the parent has a planned order (weeks 2, 4, 6, and 8). The completed records for the four children follow.

(continued)

Since the usage rate is (2) per parent item, the gross requirement is double the planned order quantity of the parent, or 250 × 2 = 500 units. The lot size rule is a fixed order quantity of 1000 pieces. Each time an order is placed, it is for 1000 pieces. Thus item 501 has two planned orders, one in Period 2 and one in Period 6.

Item: 501
Lot Size Rule: FOQ = 1000
Lead Time: 2 weeks
Parent: 500
Children: None

	1	2	3	4	5
Gross Requirements		500		500	
Scheduled Receipts					
Projected Available 500	500	0	0	500	500
Planned Orders		1000			

	6	7	8	9	10
Gross Requirements	500		500		500
Scheduled Receipts					
Projected Available	0	0	500	500	500
Planned Orders	1000				

Using lot for lot as our lot size rule, we need to place four orders. We have planned orders in Periods 1, 3, 5, and 7.

Item: 502
Lot Size Rule: L4L
Lead Time: 1 week
Parent: 500
Children: 812, 813

	1	2	3	4	5
Gross Requirements		250		250	
Scheduled Receipts					
Projected Available 0	0	0	0	0	0
Planned Orders	250		250		250

	6	7	8	9	10
Gross Requirements	250		250		
Scheduled Receipts					
Projected Available	0	0	0	0	0
Planned Orders		250			

Once again, we calculate the gross requirements by multiplying the parent's planned order quantity by the usage factor (3) shown in the product structure tree. This results in the gross requirements for item 503, which is triple the order quantity of the parent's planned order.

Item: 503
Lot Size Rule: FOQ = 1500
Lead Time: 3 weeks
Parent: 500
Children: None

	1	2	3	4	5
Gross Requirements		750		750	
Scheduled Receipts					
Projected Available 800	800	50	50	800	800
Planned Orders	1500				1500

	6	7	8	9	10
Gross Requirements	750		750		
Scheduled Receipts					
Projected Available	50	50	800	800	800
Planned Orders					

(continued)

Item: 504   **Parent: 500**
Lot Size Rule: FOQ = 2000   **Children: None**
Lead Time: 2 weeks

	1	2	3	4	5
Gross Requirements		500		500	
Scheduled Receipts					
Projected Available 600	600	100	100	1600	1600
Planned Orders	2000				

	6	7	8	9	10
Gross Requirements	500		500		
Scheduled Receipts					
Projected Available	1100	1100	600	600	600
Planned Orders					

Given the lot size rule for this item, we need only one planned order. Now let's look at the children of item 502.

Item: 812:   **Parent: 502**
Lot Size Rule: POQ = 4 periods   **Children: None**
Load Time: 2 weeks

	1	2	3	4	5	6	7	8	9	10
Gross requirements	500		500		500		500			
Scheduled receipts										
Projected available 500		0	0	500	500	0	0	0	0	0	0
Planned orders	1000				500					

The gross requirements for item 812 are double the quantity of its parent's planned orders. The lot size rule, POQ = 4 periods, means that the planned order quantity should be enough to cover the requirements in the period it is scheduled to arrive, plus the next three periods. For example, we need an order to arrive in Period 3. This planned order must be large enough to cover the gross requirements in Periods 3, 4, 5, and 6. The last inventory record is shown next.

Item: 813   **Parent: 502**
Lot Size Rule: FOQ = 1500   **Children: None**
Lead Time: 3 weeks

	1	2	3	4	5	6	7	8	9	10
Gross requirements	750		750		750		750			
Scheduled receipts										
Projected available 1500	750	750	0	0	750	750	0	0	0	0
Planned orders		1500								

■ Solved Problem 3

EJ Fabricators operates 6 machines, three 8-hour shifts, 5 days per week. EJ's usage rate is 82% and its efficiency rate is 90%. Calculate the available capacity. Calculate EJ's workload in Periods 7 and 8 and determine whether there is a capacity problem.

Solution

We calculate the available capacity by multiplying the number of machines by the number of shifts by the number of hours per shift by the number of days per week by the utilization rate by the efficiency rate:

6 machines × 3 shifts × 8 hours per shift × 5 days
per week × 0.82 utilization × 0.90 efficiency

which equals 531.36 hours of available capacity. To calculate the workload, we need information about the jobs scheduled in each period. We have shown you how to calculate the capacity available. Now go to Spreadsheet 15.3 on your CD to calculate the workload for each period.

DISCUSSION QUESTIONS

1. Explain what independent demand is and give examples of products with independent demand.

2. Explain what dependent demand is and give examples of how you can use dependent demand in your personal life.

3. Explain the concept of backward scheduling and give examples of how you use backward scheduling in your personal life.

4. What are the objectives of MRP?

5. Describe how MRP works.

6. Describe the inputs needed for MRP.

7. For each input needed, describe problems that might arise when you run MRP.

8. Explain what happens when you use different lot size rules in MRP.

9. Explain why companies do capacity requirements planning.

10. Describe the inputs needed for capacity requirements planning.

11. Describe how MRP II differs from MRP.

12. Describe enterprise resource planning.

PROBLEMS

Use the information given here for the next five problems.

Item	Usage per Parent	Lead Time (weeks)
Q	—	2
R	2	3
S	1	4
T	3	2
X	2	3
Y	1	2
V	1	3
Z	3	2

1. Will's Welded Widgets (WWW) makes its Q Model from components R, S, and T. Component R is made from two units of component X and one unit of component Y. Component T is made from one unit of component V and 3 units of component Z. Draw the product structure tree for the Q Model.

2. Using the given information, calculate the replenishment lead time for the Q Model assuming that you have no beginning inventories.

3. Using the given information, calculate the gross requirements for each of the components if the company plans to build 100 of its Q Model. Assume that there are no beginning inventories.

4. Using the given information, calculate the gross requirements for each of the components when the company plans to build 100 of its Q Model if you have these inventories: 150 units of component T and 200 units of component R.

5. Using the given information and the beginning inventories from Problem 4, calculate the minimum replenishment time for the 100 Q Models.

Use the following information for Problems 6 through 10.

Component	Immediate Parent	Usage per Parent	Lead Time (weeks)	Beginning Inventory
A	none	—	1	0
B	A	2	2	250
C	A	1	6	500
D	A	3	3	750
E	A	2	2	750
F	B	4	2	3000
G	B	2	4	1000
H	D	3	2	5000
I	D	2	4	5000
J	E	1	8	1000
K	E	5	1	5000
L	E	2	4	2500
M	F	3	3	250
N	F	6	3	250
O	H	2	4	0
P	K	1	2	500
Q	K	2	3	1000

6. Flora's Fabulous Fountains (FFF) top product is its Model A. Using the information given, draw the product structure tree for the Model A.

7. Using the information given, calculate the replenishment time when no beginning inventory exists.

8. Flora is preparing for her busy season and is building 2500 Model A fountains. Calculate the gross requirements for each component assuming that there is no beginning inventory.

9. Using the information given and assuming that 2500 Model A fountains are scheduled for completion, calculate the gross requirements of each component. Use the beginning inventories given.

10. Calculate the minimum replenishment for the Model A fountains given the beginning inventories.

11. Fill in the partially completed inventory record shown here.

Item: AB500
Lot Size Rule: L4L
Lead Time: 2 weeks

Parent: None
Children: AB501, AB511, AB521

	1	2	3	4	5
Gross Requirements			150	250	150
Scheduled Receipts					
Projected Available					
Planned Orders					
	6	7	8	9	10
Gross Requirements	250	150	250	150	250
Scheduled Receipts					
Projected Available					
Planned Orders					

12. Using the planned orders generated in Problem 11, complete inventory records for components AB501, AB511, and AB521. The lot size rule, lead time, and usage information is shown here.

Component	Lot Size Rule	Lead Time (weeks)	Usage Factor	Beginning Inventory
AB501	L4L	2	2	1100
AB511	FOQ = 250	3	1	550
AB521	POQ = 3	2	3	1650

13. Using the inventory records completed in Problem 12, calculate the average inventory level of AB501, AB511, AB521.

14. Use the planned orders generated in Problem 11. Calculate the average inventory records if the company decides to switch the lot size rule for AB511 and AB521 to lot-for-lot. Compare the number of replenishment orders using the new lot size rules.

15. Using the information given, fill in the partially completed inventory record shown here.

Item: AB500
Lot Size Rule: FOQ = 3 Period
Lead Time: 2 weeks

Parent: None
Children: AB501, AB511, AB521

	1	2	3	4	5
Gross Requirements			150	250	150
Scheduled Receipts					
Projected Available					
Planned Orders					
	6	7	8	9	10
Gross Requirements	250	150	250	150	250
Scheduled Receipts					
Projected Available					
Planned Orders					

16. Using the planned orders generated in Problem 15, complete inventory record for components AB501, AB511, and AB521. Use the lot size rule, lead time, and usage information given in Problem 12. Indicate any problems that occur.

17. Fill in the partially completed inventory record shown here.

Item: AB500
Lot Size Rule: POQ = 3 Period
Lead Time: 2 weeks

Parent: None
Children: AB501, AB511, AB521

	1	2	3	4	5
Gross Requirements			150	250	150
Scheduled Receipts					
Projected Available					
Planned Orders					
	6	7	8	9	10
Gross Requirements	250	150	250	150	250
Scheduled Receipts					
Projected Available					
Planned Orders					

18. Using the planned orders generated in Problem 17, complete inventory records for components AB501, AB511, and AB521. Use the lot size rule, lead time, and usage information given in Problem 12.

19. The Yankee Machine Shop has the following orders scheduled in Work Center 111 for week 12. Calculate the capacity needed.

Orders	Quantity	Setup Time (hours)	Run Time per Piece (hours)
LL110	10	2.0	1.2
LL118	25	4.0	0.4
LL131	100	6.0	0.6
LL140	50	4.0	0.2

20. The Yankee Machine Shop currently has three machines working in Work Center 111, 8 hours per day, 5 days per week, a utilization rate of 90% and an efficiency rate of 90%.

a. Calculate the available capacity.

b. Is the available capacity enough to complete the orders given in Problem 19 that are already scheduled in Work Center 111? If not, how much additional capacity is needed?

21. The Yankee Machine Shop has decided to schedule its work force to work 10 hours per day, 5 days per week. Does this new policy provide enough capacity to complete the orders shown in Problem 19?

22. Unfortunately, after extending the work day from 8 hours to 10 hours, the Yankee Machine Shop has noted that efficiency had decreased to 80%. Given this new piece of information, is there enough capacity to complete the orders given in Problem 19?

23. In week 13, the Yankee Machine Shop, has the following orders scheduled for Work Center 111. Calculate the capacity needed.

Orders	Quantity	Setup Time (hours)	Run Time per Piece (hours)
MM078	100	4.0	0.3
MM118	250	6.0	0.1
MM213	100	3.0	0.3
MM240	500	8.0	0.1

24. In an effort to increase capacity in Work Center 111 for week 13, Yankee Machine Shop has authorized overtime. The work center will be staffed 12 hours per day for 6 days. Because of the additional stress on the 3 machines, it is expected that the utilization rate will drop to 85%. The efficiency rate is expected to fall to 80%.

a. Calculate the capacity available in Work Center 111 for week 13.

b. Will this plan provide sufficient capacity to complete the orders given in Problem 23? If not, what do you recommend be done?

CASE: *Newmarket International Manufacturing Company (C)*

The Newmarket International Manufacturing Company (NIMCO) was founded by Marcia Blakely only two years after she finished graduate school. Her knowledge of mass customization has been the driving force behind starting NIMCO. The company produces three major custom products. Volume on the products is high even though each item is customized specifically for the customer. The products are processed through up to four different work centers. Even though each item is unique, the processing time at each work center is constant due to the sophisticated equipment used.

Developing a Material Requirements Plan

Joe Barnes, the production manager, reviewed your rough-cut capacity planning report and developed a new MPS that better uses capacity at each work center. Joe has given you an authorized MPS and has asked you to generate the schedule of material requirements. The authorized master production schedule is shown in Table 15-14.

a. Generate the material requirements. You need a BOM for each of the three products, beginning inventory levels, and scheduled receipts. The BOMs are shown in Figure 15-8. All items use lot for lot as the lot size rule. No beginning inventories exist. Lead time is 2 weeks for all items except items D and F which have a lead time of 3 weeks. All other information is provided for you in Table 15-15.

b. After completing the material requirements plan, develop a load profile for each work center for each week of the second quarter. Use the planned order releases and calculate the workload at each work center for weeks 14 through 20. The standard times are shown in the table. Use the load profiles to identify potential problems. Capacity at each work center is 960 hours each period.

Table 15-14

	Authorized MPS												
Period	14	15	16	17	18	19	20	21	22	23	24	25	26
Product A	7600		8700		9000		8700		8000		6800		3000
Product B	4000	4000	4000	3800	3800	3800	3600	3600	3600	3800	3800	3800	4000
Product C		5300		6300		6400		6000		5600		5200	

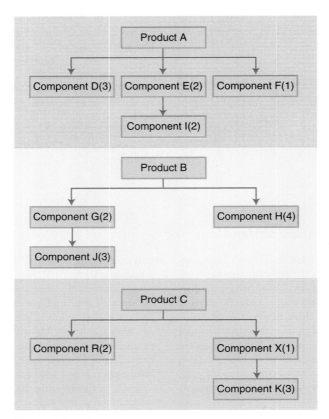

Figure 15-8

Product structure tree

Table 15-15   **Additional Information**

Item	Scheduled Receipts	Work Done at Work Center	Standard Hours per Piece
A	0	4	0.04
B	0	4	0.10
C	0	4	0.06
D	22800 in period 12	1	0.02
E	15200 in period 12	3	0.02
F	7600 in period 12	3	0.02
G	8000 in period 12	2	0.02
H	16000 in period 12	1	0.0375
I	34800 in period 12	3	0.02
J	24000 in period 11		
	24000 in period 12	2	0.015
K	15900 in period 11	3	0.03
R	none scheduled	2	0.04
X	none scheduled	3	0.04

INTERACTIVE LEARNING

Enhance and test your knowledge of Chaper 15 using the interactive CD.

1. **Spreadsheet** *Solved Problem 3*

   Visit our dynamic Web site, www.wiley.com/college/reid, for more cases, web links, and additional information.

2. **Company Tour**
   Hershey Foods Corporation
   Mars, Inc.

3. **Additional Web Resources**
   IBM, http://houns54.clearlake.ibm.com
   Hershey Foods Corporation, www. hersheys.com/tour/index.html
   Mars, Inc., www.m-ms.com/factory/tour

4. **INTERNET CHALLENGE** *The Gourmet Dinner*

Your university's Department of Hospitality Management hosts several gourmet dinners throughout the year. To show how OM concepts are useful in the service industry, the department has asked you to help manage the next gourmet dinner from the standpoint of materials planning.

The dinner is typically a five-course meal: appetizer, soup, salad, entrée, and dessert. Your Internet challenge is to develop the menu using the many cooking Web sites available and then to calculate the kinds and quantities of raw material you will need. Assume that the facility where the dinner is hosted will take care of beverages and that the kitchen and staff have enough capacity for your menu se-

lections. The gourmet dinner will have 300 attendees. If any menu items need more than 12 hours of preparation (remember you are planning for 300 guests), be sure the items arrive in time. Based on your menu, make a list of the raw materials you will need. Specify delivery dates for each item. Calculate how long each item on the menu will take to prepare for the 300 guests. Decide what time the staff needs to start preparation for the dinner to be served beginning at 8:00 P.M. Calculate the time the staff needs to start preparing each item, assuming that the appetizers will be served at 8:00, the soup at 8:20, the salad at 8:35, the entree at 8:50, and dessert at 9:15. Bon appetit!

BIBLIOGRAPHY

Arnold, J. R. Tony. *Introduction to Materials Management,* 3rd ed. Upper Saddle River, N.J.: Prentice-Hall, 1998.

Blackstone, John H. *Capacity Management.* Cincinnati, Oh.: South-Western, 1989.

James F. Cox, III, John H. Blackstone, and Michael S. Spencer, eds. *APICS Dictionary,* 9th ed. Falls Church, Va.: American Production and Inventory Control Society, Inc., 1998.

Nelson, Emily, and Evan Ramstad. "Hershey's Biggest Dud Has Turned Out to Be New Computer System." *Wall Street Journal* (October 29, 1999), p. 1.

Orlicky, J. *Material Requirements Planning.* New York: Mc-Graw-Hill, 1975.

"SAP offers supply chain optimization to help industry meet global challenge." *Chemical Market Reporter* (October 12, 1998), Vol. 254, Issue 15.

Stefanac, Rosalind. "As the picture gets bigger, the focus becomes sharper." *Computing Canada* (November 30, 1998), Vol. 24, Issue 45.

Stein, Tom. "ERP's Future Linked to E-Supply Chain." *Information Week* (October 19, 1998).

Vollmann, Thomas E., William L. Berry, and D. Clay Whybark. *Manufacturing Planning and Control Systems,* 4th ed. Burr Ridge, Ill.: Irwin, 1997.

Wight, Oliver W. *Manufacturing Resource Planning: MRP II.* Essex Junction, Vt.: Oliver Wight, 1984.

Before studying this chapter you should know or, if necessary, review

1. Operational impact of competitive priorities, Chapter 2, pages 28–32.
2. The differences between high volume and low volume operations, Chapter 10, pages 284–289.
3. Line balancing, Chapter 10, pages 299–305.
4. Techniques for reducing employee boredom, Chapter 11, pages 322–324.
5. Order promising, Chapter 14, pages 435–438.
6. Order planning, Chapter 15, pages 460–462.

LEARNING OBJECTIVES

After studying this chapter, you should be able to

1. Explain the different kinds of scheduling operations.
2. Describe different shop loading methods.
3. Develop a schedule using priority rules.
4. Calculate scheduling performance measures.
5. Develop a schedule for multiple workstations.
6. Describe the theory of constraints.
7. Describe scheduling techniques for service applications.
8. Develop a workforce schedule in which each employee has two consecutive days off.

CHAPTER OUTLINE

Are you a list-maker? Many of us are. For some people, the To Do list is a way of life. We usually make lists of things we have to do: pick up the dry cleaning, wash the dog, buy a new remote for the TV, clean out the garage, meet a friend for lunch, call Mom, and so forth. Making the list is easy: we usually add items as we think of them. Organizing the list into a schedule is more difficult; it takes a little extra effort to group and sequence operations. But without that extra effort, we can easily use up a day and run ourselves ragged in the process.

Suppose your Saturday activities include the assorted items listed above. Some are errands, some are house chores, and two are social/family obligations. You could run out and pick up the dry cleaning, come back and wash the dog, put on dry clothes, go out again to buy the remote for the TV set, come back and clean out the garage, change your clothes again to meet your friend for lunch, and call Mom when you are trying to get out the door and are already running late.

On the other hand, you could develop your To Do list into an operational schedule and sequence the activities according to priority; include start and stop times for each activity; and group the activities that need similar processing, tools, clothing, or location. In this way you would maximize your resources to meet the goal of getting everything done by the projected time. This might mean picking up the dry cleaning, buying the remote for the TV, and meeting your friend for lunch in one sequence, and washing the dog and cleaning out the garage in another. You might call Mom on your cell phone en route during the first sequence. Or you could schedule time between washing the dog and cleaning out the garage, giving yourself a break between those two activities to sit down and relax while talking on the phone.

In this chapter, we learn why the schedule is a critical document in business, especially for companies concerned with on-time delivery to their customers. We look at two kinds of scheduling operations, high-volume and low-volume; different ways of scheduling jobs; schedule effectiveness measurements; the theory of constraints; and scheduling for service organizations. Let's begin with scheduling operations.

SCHEDULING OPERATIONS ■

A company's overall strategy provides the framework for making decisions in many operational areas. Companies differentiate themselves based on product volume and product variety. This differentiation affects how the company organizes it operations.

A company providing a high-volume, standardized, consistent quality, lower-margin product or service such as a commercial bakery or a fast-food restaurant focuses on product and layout. This type of operation needs dedicated equipment, less-skilled employees, and a continuous or repetitive process flow. Companies providing low-volume, customized, higher-margin products or services such as a custom furniture maker or an upscale restaurant focus on process. The need is for general-purpose equipment, more highly skilled employees, and flexible process flows. Each kind of operation needs a different scheduling technique. Let's look at high-volume operations first.

■ HIGH-VOLUME OPERATIONS

▶ **Flow operations** are designed to handle high-volume, standard products.

A high-volume operation at the DMV.

▶ **Routing** provides information about the operations to be performed, their sequence, the work centers, and the time standards.

▶ **Bottleneck** A facility, department, or resource whose capacity is less than the demand placed on it.

High-volume operations, also called **flow operations**, can be repetitive operations for discrete products like automobiles, appliances, or bread, or services like license renewals at the Division of Motor Vehicles. Or they can be continuous operations for goods produced in a continuous flow as in a product like gasoline or a service like waste treatment. High-volume standard items, either discrete or continuous, have smaller profit margins so cost efficiency is important. Companies achieve cost efficiency in a high-volume operation through high levels of labor and equipment utilization. Design of the work environment ensures a smooth flow of products or customers through the system. One design is line balancing, which we cover in Chapter 10. Flow operations have the following characteristics.

Characteristics of Flow Operations

Flow operations use fixed **routings**—the product or service is always done the same way in the same sequence with the same workstations. The workstations are arranged sequentially according to the routing. Similar processing times are needed at each workstation to achieve a balanced line. Workstations are dedicated to a single product or a limited family of products. Workstations use special-purpose equipment and tooling. In a service operation, individuals performing a specific but limited activity are the equivalent of special-purpose equipment. For example, when you attend the theater, you go through a number of processing points. First you buy the tickets at the box office. Then you hand the ticket to the ticket taker. Next you are escorted to your seat by an usher. Each person attending the performance goes through these same processing points.

Material flows between workstations may be automated. A well-designed system minimizes work-in-process inventory and reduces the throughput time for the product or service. The design of the production line dictates the capacity of the flow system. The workstation or processing point that needs the greatest amount of time is the system's **bottleneck**, and it determines how many products or services the system can complete. Thus the goal is to sequence the operations so they need the least control possible.

A major concern with flow operations is employee boredom with repetitive tasks. Companies use techniques like job enrichment, job enlargement, and job rotation (discussed in Chapter 11) to reduce boredom and maximize line output. At the other extreme in scheduling environments is the low-volume operation, discussed next.

LOW-VOLUME OPERATIONS ■

Low-volume or job-shop operations are used for high-quality, customized products such as custom stereo systems or custom automobile paint jobs, or for services such as personal fitness, with higher profit margins. Companies with low-volume operations use highly skilled employees, general-purpose equipment, and a process layout. The objective is flexibility, both in product variation and product volume. Equipment is not dedicated to particular jobs but is available for all jobs. In low-volume operations, products are made to order. Each product or service can have its own routing through a unique sequence of workstations, processes, materials, or setups. As a result, scheduling is complex. The workload must be distributed among the work centers or service personnel. A useful tool for viewing the schedule and workload is a Gantt chart. Let's look at how a Gantt chart is used.

Personal trainer looks on

Gantt Chart

Gantt charts are named after Henry Gantt, who developed these charts in the early 1900s. A Gantt chart is a visual representation of a schedule over time. Two kinds of Gantt charts are the **load chart** and the **progress chart**.

Load Chart The load chart shows the planned workload and idle times for a group of machines or individual employees, or for a department. Figure 16-1 is an example of a load chart showing the jobs assigned to each mechanic and each mechanic's lunch break. In this example, Bob and J.J. are at lunch from 12:00 to 1:00, and Alex and Sam are at lunch from 12:30 to 1:30 P.M. All employees work from 8:00 A.M. to 5:00 P.M.

Progress Chart The progress chart monitors job progress by showing the relationship between planned performance and actual performance. In the progress chart in Figure 16-2, the brackets indicate when the activity is scheduled to be finished and the shaded area shows the progress of the activity. Note that the first activity, "Complete design specifications," begins on time and is finished as scheduled. The second and third operations are started early. Materials sourcing is finished on time but process design is not finished until mid-April. Because of the delay in the process design, the pilot run does not start as scheduled and the feedback activity has not yet begun. Both of these operations are behind schedule. The transition to manufacturing will probably also be behind schedule. Gantt charts provide a visual image of the progress of jobs through the system. Now we need to learn how to schedule work.

▶ **Gantt chart**
Planning and control chart designed to graphically show workloads or to monitor job progress.

▶ A **load chart**
visually shows the workload relative to the capacity at a resource.

▶ A **progress chart**
visually shows the planned schedule compared to actual performance.

Mechanic	8–9	9–10	10–11	11–12	12–1	1–2	2–3	3–4	4–5
Bob	JOB A			JOB G	✕	JOB I			
Sam	JOB B			JOB H		JOB J		JOB N	
Alex	JOB C		JOB E		✕	JOB K			JOB O
J.J.	JOB D		JOB F		✕	JOB L	JOB M		

Figure 16–1

Sample load chart

Figure 16–2

Sample progress chart

Activity	Jan	Feb	Mar	April	May	June	July
Complete design specs	[ ]						
Source materials		[ ]					
Design process		[	]				
Pilot run				[ ]			
Feedback				[	]		
Transition to manufacturing						[	]

[ ] = planned activity progress

⬜ = actual activity progress

Current date

■ SCHEDULING WORK

▶ **Infinite loading** calculates the capacity needed at work centers in the time period needed without regard to the capacity available to do the work.

▶ **Finite loading** loads work centers up to a predetermined amount of capacity.

Two kinds of work scheduling or work loading are **infinite loading** and **finite loading**. Infinite loading schedules work without regard to capacity limits. Infinite loading lets you know how much capacity you need to meet a schedule.

Infinite Loading

Manufacturing companies can use infinite loading according to a proposed master production schedule (MPS). A service organization like a law firm can use infinite loading to identify the resources needed to complete the proposed case load. Infinite loading identifies uneven workloads and bottlenecks. Figure 16-3 is an example of infinite loading. We can see from the chart that the shop has enough capacity in periods 4 and 7 but not enough capacity in periods 5 and 8. In this way, we identify time periods when capacity is either poorly used or inadequate, and change the schedule to level the resource requirements.

Finite Loading

Finite loading is an operational schedule with start and finish times for each activity. It does not allow you to load more work than can be done with the available capacity. The finite loading schedule shows how a company plans to use available capacity at each work center. In a manufacturing company, the schedule shows the jobs to be done at a particular work center if the work center uses a set number of production hours each day. For example, if the work center can build 50 wire assemblies per hour and the company needs 1000 wire assemblies, the job will take 20 hours of capacity at that work center. In a service organization, a doctor's office is a good example. To

Figure 16–3

Infinite loading

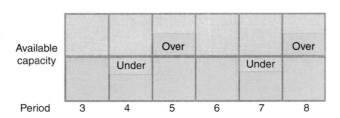

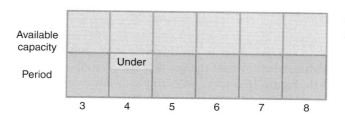

Figure 16–4

Finite loading

spend 10 minutes with each patient, the doctor can have 6 patients scheduled per hour.

Figure 16-4 is an example of finite loading. Note that no work center is assigned more work than it should be able to handle. The disadvantage of finite loading is that it tends to break down over the long term: problems arise and the schedule slips, causing jobs to be rescheduled. Finite loading is why you may have to wait at the doctor's office.

Companies benefit from both infinite and finite loading. Infinite loading identifies resource bottlenecks for a proposed schedule so that planners can find solutions proactively such as changing the schedule and increasing the resource capacity. Finite loading develops the operational schedule that uses the available capacity. Finite and infinite loading assign work to specific work centers based on a proposed schedule. Both techniques use either a schedule (infinite loading) or a prioritized list of jobs to be done (finite loading). Two additional techniques are forward scheduling and backward scheduling.

Forward Scheduling

With **forward scheduling**, processing starts immediately when a job is received, regardless of its **due date**. Each job activity is scheduled for completion as soon as possible, which allows you to determine the job's earliest possible completion date. Figure 16-5 shows an example of forward scheduling. The job is due at the end of week 10 but it can be finished as early as the end of week 7. With forward scheduling, it is not unusual for jobs to be finished before their due date. The disadvantage to finishing a job early is that it causes an inventory buildup if items are not delivered before the due date.

▶ **Forward scheduling** determines the earliest possible completion date for a job.

▶ The **due date** is when the job is supposed to be finished.

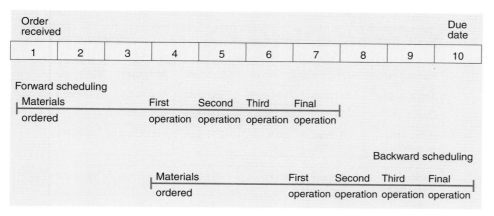

Figure 16–5

Forward and backward scheduling

Backward Scheduling

▶ **Backward scheduling**
determines when the job
must be started to be done
on the due date.

With **backward scheduling**, you begin scheduling the job's last activity so that the job is finished right on the due date. To do this, you start with the due date and work backward, calculating when to start the last activity, when to start the next-to-last activity, and so forth. Figure 16-5 gives an example of backward scheduling. Backward scheduling shows you how late the job can be started and still be finished on time. When you are using backward scheduling and forward scheduling together, a difference between the start time of the first activity indicates **slack** in the schedule. Slack means that you can start a job immediately but you do not have to do so. You can start it any time up to the start time in your backward schedule and still meet the due date.

▶ **Slack**
The amount of time a job can
be delayed and still be finished by its due date.

Monitoring Work Flow

▶ **Input/output control**
A technique for monitoring
the flow of jobs between work
centers.

Input/output control is a capacity-control technique used to monitor work flow at individual work centers. Input/output control monitors the planned inputs and outputs at a work center against the actual inputs and outputs. Planned inputs are based on the operational schedule, whereas planned outputs use capacity-planning techniques. Actual input is compared with planned input to ensure that enough work enters the measured work center. A work center cannot process items that have not yet arrived. Actual output is used to identify possible problems in the work center such as an equipment problem or unexpected absences.

■ Example 16.1 Input/Output Control at JT's Custom Storage Units

JT's produces custom wine storage units. JT is very concerned about the performance of Work Center 101, the bottleneck in the manufacturing process. He has given you the input/output report shown in Figure 16-6 and asked you to explain the numbers.

Figure 16–6

Input/output report for Work Center 101

Input information	4	5	6	7	8
Planned input	800 hours	750 hours	800 hours	820 hours	800 hours
Actual input	750 hours	780 hours	780 hours	810 hours	810 hours
Deviation	−50 hours	+30 hours	−20 hours	−10 hours	+10 hours
Cumulative deviation	−50 hours	−20 hours	−40 hours	−50 hours	−40 hours

Output Information	4	5	6	7	8
Planned output	800 hours	800 hours	800 hours	800 hours	800 hours
Actual output	800 hours	750 hours	780 hours	850 hours	825 hours
Deviation	0 hours	−50 hours	−20 hours	+50 hours	+25 hours
Cumulative deviation	0 hours	−50 hours	−70 hours	−20 hours	+5 hours

| Backlog 100 hours | 50 hours | 80 hours | 80 hours | 40 hours | 25 hours |

Solution:
The input/output report for Work Center 101 shows any deviations in input or output at the work center. The input deviation is calculated by subtracting the planned input from the actual input. The output deviation is calculated as planned output from actual output. For example, based on the input information in Period 4, the planned input was 800 standard hours of work, but the actual input was only 750 standard hours. Remember that standard hours of work are the amount of time needed to complete the work if the employee works at 100% efficiency. Subtracting the planned input from the actual input (750 standard hours minus 800 standard hours) results in a deviation of −50 standard hours. In Period 5, the actual input exceeded the planned input, resulting in a positive deviation (780 standard hours minus 750 standard hours = 30 standard hours deviation).

The cumulative deviation is a running sum of the deviations. For example, in Period 4, the deviation is −50 hours; the cumulative deviation is equal to this period's deviation plus the previous cumulative deviation total. In our case, the previous cumulative deviation is zero, so the cumulative deviation at the end of Period 4 is −50 hours. After Period 5, the cumulative deviation is −20 hours (a +30 hour deviation in Period 5, plus the previous cumulative deviation (−50 hours). We calculate the deviations and cumulative deviations in the same way for both input and output. Management uses cumulative deviation values to indicate possible input or output problems. If planned input is consistently below actual input, the feeding work center may not have enough capacity to meet the planned input. The same is true when the work center's actual output is consistently less than the planned output. The work center is not producing with the efficiency expected.

The backlog row is the amount of work waiting to be finished at the work center. In our example, Work Center 101 has 100 standard hours of work waiting. *The only time the size of the backlog changes is when actual input does not equal actual output.* When a work center receives more work than it finishes, the backlog increases. When a work center produces more output than the input received, the backlog decreases. In Period 4, Work Center 101 receives 750 standard hours of new work. Work Center 101 finishes 800 standard hours of work during Period 4; this is possible only if Work Center 101 finishes some of the 100 hours of backlog from the beginning of Period 4. The new input plus the backlog equals the maximum amount of work that can be finished at Work Center 101 (850 standard hours). Since the work center finishes 800 standard hours of work, the backlog decreases to 50 standard hours of work. In Period 5, the backlog increases because Work Center 101 receives 780 standard hours of work but only produces 750 standard hours of work. The difference between the actual input and the actual output is 30 standard hours, therefore the backlog increases by 30 standard hours. The input/output report allows a planner to monitor how well the available capacity is used at individual work centers and provides insight into process problems.

HOW TO SEQUENCE JOBS ∎

When several jobs need to be done, how do you decide which one to do first? Do you work on the job that you have to finish first? The job you enjoy doing? The job you can finish the fastest? The job that has the biggest payoff? When you decide which job to do first, you are sequencing them.

Lines are everywhere!

▶ **Operation sequencing**
A short-term plan of actual jobs to be run in each work center based on available capacity and priorities.

▶ **Queue**
Waiting line.

▶ A **priority rule**
determines the priority of jobs at a work center.

▶ A **local priority rule**
makes a priority decision based on jobs currently at that work center.

▶ A **global priority rule**
makes a priority decision based on information that includes the remaining work centers a job must pass through.

The ninth edition of the *APICS Dictionary* defines **operation sequencing** or job sequencing as a technique for short-term planning of actual jobs to be run in each work center based on capacity and priorities. We expect a work center to have several jobs waiting to be processed so we decide on the sequence for processing the jobs. Operation sequencing sets projected start and finish times, and expected **queues**. A job's priority is its position in the sequence.

Priority Rules

Job priority is often set by a **priority rule**. (See Table 16-1 for explanations of some commonly used priority rules.) Priority rules are typically classified as local or global. A **local priority rule** sets priority based only on the jobs waiting at that individual work center. For example, the highest priority might be given to the job that arrives first or the job that can be done the fastest. **Global priority rules**, like critical ratio or slack over remaining operations, set priority according to factors such as the scheduled workload at the remaining workstations that the job must be processed through.

A work center needs priority rules when multiple jobs await processing (but not if only a single job needs processing). Priority rules assume that there is no variability in either the setup time or the run time of the job. Let's look at how to use priority rules.

How to Use Priority Rules

Using priority rules is straightforward. Just follow these steps.

STEP 1 DECIDE WHICH PRIORITY RULE TO USE.
Different priority rules achieve different results. We will discuss this when we look at performance measurements.

STEP 2 LIST ALL THE JOBS WAITING TO BE PROCESSED AT THE WORK CENTER AND THEIR JOB TIME.
Job time includes setup and processing time.

Table 16-1 Commonly Used Priority Rules

First come, first served (FCFS): Jobs are processed in the order in which they arrive at a machine or work center.

Last come, first served (LCFS): The last job in to the work center or at the top of the stack is processed first.

Earliest due date (EDD): The job due the earliest has the highest priority.

Shortest processing time (SPT): The job that requires the least processing time has the highest priority.

Longest processing time (LPT): The job that requires the longest processing time has the highest priority.

Critical ratio (CR): The job with the smallest ratio of time remaining until due date to processing time remaining has the highest priority.

Slack per remaining operations (S/RO): The job with the least slack per remaining operations is given the highest priority. Calculate by dividing slack by remaining operations.

STEP 3   USING YOUR PRIORITY RULE, DETERMINE WHICH JOB HAS THE HIGHEST PRIORITY AND SHOULD BE WORKED ON FIRST, SECOND, THIRD, AND SO ON.
To illustrate the use of priority rules, let's use SPT to sequence a group of jobs waiting at Work Center 102, Jill's Machine Shop.

■ **Example 16.2 Using SPT at Jill's Machine Shop**

Using SPT as a priority rule, determine the sequence for the following jobs waiting at Work Center 102 at Jill's Machine Shop. The job information follows.

Job Number	Job Time at Work Center 102 (includes setup and run time)
AZK111	3 days
BRU872	2 days
CUF373	5 days
DBR664	4 days
EZE101	1 day
FID448	4 days

STEP 1   Choose the priority rule. You must use SPT.

STEP 2   List the jobs waiting for processing at Work Center 102 and their job times. This information is given in the table.

STEP 3   Using the priority rule, determine the sequence of jobs.

The highest priority goes to job EZE101 (1 day) since it takes the least amount of time. The second job is BRU872 (2 days). The third job is AZK111 (3 days). Job DBR664 and job FID448 are tied for fourth place because both take 4 days. Since we have no additional information, it does not matter which of these is done fourth and which one is done fifth. We will do DBR664 fourth and FID448 fifth. The last job is CUF373. Our completed sequence is:

Position in Sequence	Job Number
First	EZE101
Second	BRU872
Third	AZK111
Fourth	DBR664
Fifth	FID448
Sixth	CUF372

How well a priority rule works depends on the performance measurement the company uses. In the next section, we will cover commonly used performance measurements.

MEASURING PERFORMANCE ■

Companies measure scheduling effectiveness according to their competitive priorities. For example, if your company is concerned with customer response time, you measure scheduling effectiveness in terms of response time. Mean job flow time and the mean number of jobs in the system each measure a company's responsiveness. On the other hand, if your company competes on cost, it is concerned with efficiency. If on-time delivery is of primary concern, the company measures on-time delivery performance. Makespan measures efficiency; mean job lateness and mean job tardiness measure due-date performance. We discuss each of these measurements next.

LINKS TO PRACTICE
Airline Scheduling

Consider scheduling in the airline industry. Cheaper fares, competition factors, weather patterns, equipment and expansion difficulties, and poor scheduling are only some of the reasons why scheduling problems occur. However, various remedies can help alleviate these scheduling problems. These remedies include charging peak travel fares, requiring the FAA and weather service to work more closely for more accurate and frequent weather forecasts, "technologizing" (i.e. utilizing scheduling technology, modernizing the air traffic control system, and automating ticketing and boarding), building new runways and using abandoned military airfields, and, most important, designing realistic schedules (i.e., cutting back the number of flights, moving leisure flights to off-peak times, extending the operation day, and spreading out arrival and departure times). As long as the number of air travelers continues to boom, optimal scheduling will be an important issue to the airline industry.

Job Flow Time

Job flow time measures response time—the time a job spends in the shop, from the time it is ready to be worked on until it is finished. It includes waiting time, setup time, process time, and possible delays. We calculate job flow time as

Job flow time = time of completion − time job was first available for processing

■ **Example 16.3 Calculating Mean Flow Time**

To calculate mean job flow time, we sum the job flow times for each job and divide by the number of jobs. For example, if job A has a flow time of 10 days, job B has a flow time of 13 days, job C has a flow time of 17 days, and job D has a flow time of 20 days, then the mean flow time is 15 days (10 + 13 + 17 + 20)/4 jobs). Mean job flow time should have some similarity to your quoted lead time. The lower your mean job flow time, the faster you can respond to your customers. The SPT priority rule always minimizes the mean job flow time.

Average Number of Jobs in the System

▶ **Average number of jobs in the system**
is a measure of work-in-process.

The **average number of jobs** measures the work-in-process inventory and also affects response time. The greater the number of jobs in the system, the longer the queues and subsequently the longer the job flow times are. If quick customer response is critical to your company, the number of jobs waiting in the system should be relatively low.

■ **Example 16.4 Calculating the Average Number of Jobs in System**

To calculate the average number of jobs in the system, we need to know the individual job flow times for each job. We sum the individual job flows and divide by the total number of days it takes to finish the whole batch of jobs. If we use jobs A, B, C, and D from above, the individual job flows sum to 60 days (10 + 13 + 17 + 20). If the time it takes to finish all four jobs is 20 days, then the average number of jobs in the system is 3 jobs (60 days of total job flow time divided by 20 days to finish the batch of jobs). The higher the average number of jobs in the system, the longer is the waiting time.

Job A finishes on day 10	Job B finishes on day 13	Job C finishes on day 17	Job D ends on day 20

Figure 16–7

Makespan

Makespan

Makespan measures efficiency by telling us how long it takes to finish a batch of jobs. To calculate makespan, we subtract the starting time of the first job from the completion time of the last job in the group. Using the data from Example 16.4, a calendar showing the progress of the jobs would look like Figure 16-7. In this case, the makespan for this group of jobs is 20 days. Note that makespan has no link to customer due dates: you can have an efficient schedule in terms of finishing a batch of jobs but still have relatively poor customer service.

> ▶ **Makespan**
> is the amount of time it takes to finish a batch of jobs.

Job Lateness and Tardiness

Job lateness, a measure of customer service, is the difference between the time a job is finished and the time it is supposed to be finished (its due date). When a job is finished ahead of schedule, it has negative lateness. For example, if job X is due on day 15 and it is finished on day 12, it has a lateness value of negative 3 days. If job X is finished on day 15, its lateness value is zero. If job X is done on day 17, its lateness value is a positive 2 days.

> ▶ **Job lateness**
> is a measure of whether the job is done ahead of, on, or behind schedule.
>
> ▶ **Job tardiness**
> is a measure of how long after the due date the job is completed.

■ Example 16.5 Calculating Job Lateness

Let's calculate job lateness using the following data.

Job	Completion Date	Due Date	Lateness
A	10	15	−5
B	13	15	−2
C	17	10	7
D	20	20	0

Job A is finished 5 days ahead of its due date, and job B is finished 2 days earlier than its due date. Job C is finished 7 days tardy, and job D is finished on its due date. The performance measure we use to evaluate the schedule is mean job lateness, which sums all the individual lateness values and divides by the number of jobs processed. In our case, it is 0 divided by 4 jobs equals 0 days job lateness. On average, the jobs are finished on their due dates.

Some companies do not include negative values of lateness in the calculation because there is no perceived benefit for finishing the job early. In this case, we substitute zeroes for the negative numbers, and we sum the lateness values and then divide by the number of jobs to get the **average tardiness** of the jobs. The updated information using zeroes instead of negative lateness values is as shown in the table.

Job	Completion Date	Due Date	Tardiness
A	10	15	0
B	13	15	0
C	17	10	7
D	20	20	0

In this case, average tardiness is 1.75 days ((0 + 0 + 7 + 0)/4 jobs). If customer service is important to your company, average tardiness is probably a more relevant measurement than job lateness.

Before You Go On

Be sure you know how to use priority rules and how to measure a schedule's effectiveness. Different priority rules measure different aspects of performance, depending on your company's competitive priorities. SPT always minimizes mean job flow time, mean job lateness, and average number of jobs in the system. FCFS is considered a fair rule because everyone is treated equally. EDD and S/RO tend to perform well in terms of minimizing mean job tardiness.

Let's compare two priority rules.

■ COMPARING PRIORITY RULES

Now that we know how to use priority rules and how to measure schedule effectiveness, let's look at an example comparing different priority rules with different performance measurements. Our example compares shortest processing time (SPT) and slack per remaining operations (S/RO). The first step is to find the sequence using each of the priority rules. Using that sequence, we calculate mean job flow time, the average number of jobs in the system, mean job lateness, and mean job tardiness. Table 16-2 shows the job data for our example.

Table 16-2 Job Data				
Job	Job Time at Work Center 301 (days)	Due Date (days from now)	Remaining Job Time at Other Work Centers (days)	Remaining Number of Operations
A	3	15	6	2
B	7	20	8	4
C	6	30	5	3
D	4	20	3	2
E	2	22	7	3
F	5	20	5	3

■ Example 16.6 Using SPT

The first priority rule is SPT and the available jobs are listed, so we need to calculate only the sequence. Using SPT, we base the sequence on doing the job that needs the least amount of time at the work center first (in our case, job E). We do job E first and then we look for the next shortest job time (job A takes 3 days) to be second in our sequence. The complete sequence for SPT is job E, A, D, F, C, and then B, shown graphically here.

E done at end of day 2	A done at end of day 5	D done at end of day 9	F done at end of day 14	C done at end of day 20	B done at end of day 27

Using this information, we calculate the mean job flow time. The flow time for job E is 2 days; for job A it is 5 days; for job D it is 9 days; for job F it is 14 days; for job C it is 20 days, and for job B it is 27 days. To find the mean job flow time, we add up these individual job flow times and divide by the number of jobs: (2 + 5 + 9 + 14 + 20 + 27)/6 jobs = 12.83 days. We calculate the average number of jobs in the system by dividing total job flow time by the makespan, which is 27 days. Total job flow time is 77 days (2 + 5 + 9 + 14 + 20 + 27). The average number of jobs in the system is 2.85 jobs. To calculate the mean lateness and mean tardiness of the jobs processed, we need to know when each job leaves Work Center 301. Table 16-3 shows those results.

Problem-Solving Tip   Remember that job flow time is the amount of time the job is in the system (its completion date minus when the job was first available). Since all the jobs were available at the same time, their flow time is the same as their completion time.

To find mean job lateness, we add up the individual lateness values (−10 + 7 − 10 − 11 − 20 − 6), which equals −50 days. Dividing by the number of jobs (6), the mean job lateness is −8.33 days. On average, jobs take 8.33 fewer days to get through the shop than we expected. How is this information useful? Your company can correlate job flow time with lead times quoted to customers. If the job flow time is less than expected, marketing can consider using reduced lead times as a competitive advantage.

Table 16-3   Work Center 301 Completion Data Using SPT

Job	Completion Date	Due Date	Lateness (days)	Tardiness (days)
A	5	15	−10	0
B	27	20	7	7
C	20	30	−10	0
D	9	20	−11	0
E	2	22	−20	0
F	14	20	−6	0

Problem-Solving Tip   Negative lateness means the job is finished ahead of its due date. Zero lateness means the job finished on its due date. Positive lateness means the job finished after its due date.

Tardiness applies only to jobs finished after the due date. We treat all negative lateness values as zeroes. To find mean job tardiness, we sum the individual job tardiness values and divide by the number of jobs. In this example, only 1 job is tardy and the sum of the tardiness values is 7. The mean job tardiness is 1.17 days or 7/6 jobs. The maximum tardiness is 7 days. This information is also important for marketing because it implies the level of customer service provided. Now let's look at what happens when we use the S/RO priority rule to develop our sequence.

■ Example 16.7 Using S/RO

We calculate the S/RO by finding the amount of slack each job has and then dividing that slack by the remaining number of operations (including the current operation). We calculate slack by subtracting the total work remaining (current operation plus all other undone operations times) from the amount of time left until the due date. We calculate the values in the slack time column by adding the job time at Work Center 301 plus the remaining job time at other work centers (for job A, 3 + 6 = 9 days of remaining work) and subtracting that total from the number of days till the due date (for job A, 15 days). The difference is the slack (for job A, 6 days).

Table 16-4   Job Data with Slack Calculations

Job	Job Time at Work Center 301 (days)	Remaining Job Time at Other Work Center (days)	Due Date (days from now)	Slack Time (days)	Remaining Number of Operations after Work Center 301	S/RO
A	3	6	15	6	2	2
B	7	8	20	5	4	1
C	6	5	30	19	3	4.75
D	4	3	20	13	2	4.33
E	2	7	22	13	3	3.25
F	5	5	20	10	3	2.5

We calculate the S/RO values by dividing the slack for the job (6 days for job A) by the number of remaining operations, including the current operation (2 plus the current one, or 3 remaining operations), which equals an S/RO of 2 for job A. The lower the value of the S/RO, the higher is its priority. For our problem, job B should be done first, followed by A, F, E, D, and then C. Graphically, the sequence appears as follows.

B done at end of day 7	A done at end of day 10	F done at end of day 15	E done at end of day 17	D done at end of day 21	C done at end of day 27

Table 16-5 shows the completion dates of the jobs when we use S/RO.

Table 16-5   Work Center 301 Completion Data Using S/RO

Job Date	Completion Date	Due Date	Lateness (days)	Tardiness (days)
A	10	15	−5	0
B	7	20	−13	0
C	27	30	−3	3
D	21	20	1	1
E	17	22	−5	0
F	15	20	−5	0

Comparing SPT and S/RO

Mean job lateness using S/RO is −5 days, compared to −8.33 days using SPT. The SPT rule always minimizes mean job lateness. The mean tardiness using S/RO is 0.67 days, compared to 1.17 days using SPT. The maximum tardiness is less using S/RO (3 days), compared to SPT (7 days). Priority rules based on due date are better at reducing the maximum tardiness. Mean job flow time using S/RO is 16.67 days, compared to only 12.83 days with SPT. Note that the SPT priority rule always minimizes mean job flow time. Average number of jobs in the system using S/RO is 3.59 jobs, compared to 2.85 jobs using SPT. Since SPT sets priority on getting several jobs done as quickly as possible, we can expect less work in process or fewer average jobs in the system. Now that we have used two different priority rules to develop a sequence for a single machine or work center, let's look at a technique for developing the sequence when two different work centers are involved.

SEQUENCING JOBS THROUGH TWO WORK CENTERS ■

At times, all jobs must be processed through the same two work centers sequentially. For example, when you do laundry, clothes go through the washer before the dryer. Different kinds of clothing need different wash cycles and different drying times, but the sequence is the same. To shorten the time it takes to do your laundry, you can use Johnson's rule. **Johnson's rule** is a scheduling technique for developing a sequence when jobs are processed through two successive operations. The operations can be at machine centers, departments, or different geographical locations. The job flow must be unidirectional: the first activity for every job is the same and you must finish it before you can begin the second activity (wash the clothes before you dry the clothes). Johnson's rule is an optimizing technique and always minimizes makespan. To use Johnson's rule, follow this procedure.

▶ **Johnson's rule**
A technique for minimizing makespan in a two-stage, unidirectional process.

STEP 1   List the jobs and the processing time for each activity.

STEP 2   Find the shortest activity processing time among all the jobs not yet scheduled. If the shortest activity processing time is a first activity, put the job needing that activity in the earliest available position in the job sequence. If the shortest activity processing time is a second activity, put the job needing that activity in the last available position in the job sequence. When you schedule a job, eliminate it from further consideration.

STEP 3   Repeat Step 2 until all you have put all the activities for the job in the schedule.

■ Example 16.8 Vicki's Office Cleaners

Vicki's Office Cleaners does the annual major cleaning of university buildings. The job requires mopping and waxing the floors in five buildings at Mideast University. Each building must have the floors mopped and stripped (first activity), and then waxed and buffed (second activity). Vicki wants to minimize the time it takes her crews to finish cleaning the five buildings. Use Johnson's method to develop the sequence Vicki should follow.

STEP 1   LIST THE JOBS AND THE PROCESSING TIME.

	Activity 1 Mopping (days)	Activity 2 Waxing (days)
Adams Hall	1	2
Bryce Building	3	5
Chemistry Building	2	4
Drake Union	5	4
Evans Center	4	2

STEP 2   FIND THE SHORTEST ACTIVITY PROCESSING TIME AMONG THE JOBS.
The shortest activity processing time is 1 day for mopping Adams Hall. Since the shortest activity time is a first activity, we put mopping Adams Hall in the top available position in the sequence. The first job in our sequence is mopping Adams Hall. We eliminate Adams Hall since it has a spot in our sequence. We also eliminate the first position in our sequence. Let's look at the remaining jobs and repeat Step 2.

	Activity 1 Mopping (days)	Activity 2 Waxing (days)
Bryce Building	3	5
Chemistry Building	2	4
Drake Union	5	4
Evans Center	4	2

STEP 2   FIND THE SHORTEST ACTIVITY PROCESSING TIME AMONG THE REMAINING JOBS.
There are two activities tied this time: waxing the Evans Center and mopping the Chemistry Building each take 2 days. When a tie occurs and the shortest processing time is for the same activity, either building can be selected. In a case like this where the shortest processing times are for different activities, we schedule both. Since the shortest time for the Evans Center is the second activity, it takes the lowest available spot in our sequence. The Evans Center will be done fifth. The shortest processing time for the Chemistry Building is for its first activity so it takes the highest available spot in our sequence. The Chemistry Building will be mopped second. We update our remaining jobs, removing the Evans Center and the Chemistry Building and the fifth and second positions. Now repeat Step 2 again.

	Activity 1 Mopping (days)	Activity 2 Waxing (days)
Bryce Building	3	5
Chemistry Building	5	4

STEP 2   FIND THE SHORTEST ACTIVITY PROCESSING TIME AMONG THE REMAINING JOBS.
The shortest activity processing time is 3 days for mopping the Bryce Building. Since this is the first activity, we put mopping the Bryce Building in the earliest available spot in the sequence, which is third. Since only 1 job is left, Drake Union, we put it in the only remaining spot in the sequence, fourth.

   The sequence Vicki should use is shown here. When we have a tie for the shortest activity, it does not matter which job we put first.

Sequence Position	Job
First	Adams Hall (A)
Second	Chemistry Bldg (C)
Third	Bryce Building (B)
Fourth	Drake Union (D)
Fifth	Evans Center (E)

Now let's look at the sequence graphically.

	1	2	3	4	5	6	7	8	9	10	11	12	13	14	15	16	17	18
Mopping	A	C	C	B	B	B	D	D	D	D	D	E	E	E	E			
Waxing		A	A	C	C	C	B	B	B	B	B	D	D	D	D	E	E

   Vicki's Cleaners begins mopping Adams Hall on day 1. No waxing is done because none of the floors have been mopped yet. At the end of day 1, Vicki's Cleaners have finished mopping Adams Hall. On day 2, the mopping crew starts mopping the Chemistry Building while the waxing crew begins at Adams Hall. At the end of day 3, the mopping crew finishes the Chemistry Building and moves on to the Bryce Building to start day 4. The waxing crew finishes Adams Hall and starts the Chemistry Building on day 4. Note that this sequence has a makespan of 18 days. We can find no other sequence for these jobs that can take less time because Johnson's rule always minimizes makespan.

SCHEDULING BOTTLENECKS ■

When companies schedule a job shop, bottlenecks are common. A bottleneck is any resource whose capacity is less than the demand placed on it. For example, let's consider Akito's Flowers, a retail florist. When a customer orders flowers, three steps follow. First, the clerk takes the order and processes payment. Second, the clerk gives the order to the flower arrangers, who gather the appropriate materials and do the flower arrangement. Third, the drivers deliver the flowers. At Akito's Flowers, the clerk can process 30 telephone orders per hour. Each of the 3 flower arrangers can make 7 arrangements per hour and each of the 3 drivers can make 10 deliveries per hour. The flower arrangers are the bottleneck in this process. Regardless of the number of orders processed by the clerk, the arrangers can do a maximum of 21 arrangements per hour, and Akito's can deliver no more than 21 floral arrangements per hour. Thus the output of the process is reduced to the capacity of the bottleneck. Bottlenecks typically result when one operation in a job takes longer than the other operations.

Techniques for scheduling bottleneck systems emerged in the late 1970s with the introduction of **optimized production technology (OPT)** by Eli Goldratt. OPT classifies resources as either bottlenecks or **non-bottlenecks**, and makes bottlenecks the basis for scheduling and capacity planning. According to OPT, companies should schedule bottleneck resources to full capacity and schedule non-bottleneck resources to support the bottleneck resources. In our example, the bottleneck resource is the flower arrangers; the non-bottleneck resources are the clerks processing orders and the delivery drivers. Non-bottleneck resources can be idle and still not affect the output of the system because output is determined by the bottleneck resource, not by capacity at the non-bottleneck resources. OPT also introduces the concept of **capacity-constrained resources**—resources that have become bottlenecks because of inefficient usage. In our florist shop example, the delivery drivers could become a capacity-constrained resource if Akito's does not attend to consolidating shipments and using the drivers efficiently. Table 16-6 lists OPT principles.

Let's look at each of these principles.

> ▶ **Optimized production technology (OPT)**
> A technique used to schedule bottleneck systems.

> ▶ **Non-bottleneck**
> A work center with more capacity than demand.

> ▶ **Capacity-constrained resource**
> Bottleneck caused by inefficient usage.

> ***Balance the process rather than the flow.*** Traditionally, managers try to make the same amount of capacity available in each department or work center. This means every resource is a bottleneck. At Akito's Flowers, balanced capacity means processing 21 orders per hour or needing only 0.7 order clerks and 2.1 drivers. Although in theory this approach provides capacity for 21 floral arrangements per hour, in real life we cannot use partial employees or

---

Table 16-6 OPT Principles

◆ Balance the process rather than the flow.
◆ Use of a non-bottleneck resource is determined by some other constraint within the system.
◆ Use and activation of a resource are not the same.
◆ An hour lost at a bottleneck resource is an hour lost forever.
◆ An hour lost at a non-bottleneck resource is just a mirage.
◆ Bottlenecks determine throughput and inventory in the system.
◆ The transfer batch does not need to be equal to the process batch.
◆ The process batch should be variable.
◆ Schedules should be established by considering all constraints simultaneously. Lead times are the result of the schedule and are not predetermined.

machines so we have some excess capacity. If we have no excess capacity, we guarantee that fewer than 21 orders will be processed each hour, because real life has statistical fluctuations and dependent events. At Akito's Flowers, processing does not begin until the clerk receives an order. What happens when no orders are received for the first 20 minutes of the day? That 20 minutes is lost capacity not only for the clerk, but also for the floral arrangers and the delivery drivers. If we have some excess capacity at the non-bottleneck resources, we can operate the bottleneck at full capacity.

Non-bottleneck usage is determined by some other constraint in the system. At the floral shop, the order processing and the delivery service are non-bottlenecks. Their level of usage is determined by the flower arrangers (the bottleneck resource).

Usage and activation of a resource are not the same. Activation of a resource means the resource is used to process materials or products. Usage means that the resource activated is contributing positively to the company's performance. Thus usage means the resource is performing a needed activity.

An hour lost at a bottleneck resource is an hour lost forever. If an organization's goal is to maximize **throughput**, the bottleneck must be fully used. Suppose our floral arrangers cannot produce arrangements for an hour because the delivery of flowers to the shop is delayed. Thus the shop can only produce a maximum of 147 arrangements that day instead of 168 arrangements (7 hours $\times$ 3 arrangers $\times$ 7 arrangements per hour instead of 8 hours $\times$ 3 arrangers $\times$ 7 arrangements per hour).

An hour lost at a non-bottleneck is a mirage. Time lost at a non-bottleneck resource is critical only if the lost time causes the resource to become a bottleneck. For example, if one of the florist's drivers leaves work an hour early, it may or may not affect the output for the day. It affects the output only if more than 14 deliveries must be made during that last hour. Otherwise there is no decrease in output. If more than 14 deliveries are needed, the delivery service has become a bottleneck resource.

Bottlenecks determine throughput and system inventory. A bottleneck resource determines the throughput for the system. It also determines how much inventory is needed in the system to ensure the continuous operation of the bottleneck resource. For example, the florist can process 168 orders per day. Therefore, the flower inventory must be sufficient to produce 168 arrangements.

The transfer batch does not have to equal the process batch. The **transfer batch** is the quantity of items moved at the same time from one resource to the next. At Akito's Flowers, that is the number of orders the clerk processes before forwarding the orders to the floral arrangers. If the clerk forwards orders only once per hour, the floral arrangers' output is directly affected. If the clerk forwards each order as it arrives, the number of orders the clerk can process per hour is probably affected.

The process batch is the quantity of an item processed at a resource before that resource is changed to produce a different product. If one of the floral arrangers specializes in preparing business floral arrangements and typically produces these arrangements in batches of 14, the process batch is 14 units. The arranger could transfer these arrangements immediately to the delivery area after each one is produced. In this case, the transfer batch quantity is 1. The delivery service could begin immediately to prepare the arrangement for delivery rather than waiting until all 14 arrangements are ready.

▶ **Throughput**
The quantity of finished goods that can be sold.

▶ **Transfer batch**
The quantity of items moved at the same time from one resource to the next.

▶ **Process batch**
The quantity produced at a resource before the resource is switched over to produce another product.

The process batch should be variable. We do not always have to produce the same quantity but instead we should produce what is needed. At Akito's Flowers, one of the floral arrangers produced a batch of 14 business floral arrangements at a time, but this does not mean that the arrangers always have to produce 14. Maybe two of the business customers close for summer vacation. In this case, the arranger should make only 12 arrangements and not 14, because the additional 2 will not be sold. Thus the process batch quantity should be linked to demand.

Schedules should be established by considering all constraints simultaneously. Lead times are the result of the schedule and are not predetermined. You should develop the schedule considering all your constraints. If you do not know what your workload is, you cannot tell a customer how long it will take to do a job. Once you know how much work you need to do, you can determine how long it should take.

Instead of losing capacity because of order-processing delays, a florist can improve the order entry procedure. An approach by 1-800-FLOWERS.com, a nationwide network of 1500 independent florists, allows customers to enter a Web site, enter a private chat room, and discuss their order with a customer service representative in real time. With its on-line proprietary order-processing system designed to handle a high volume of transactions, 1-800-FLOWERS.com is positioned to provide highly personalized real-time customer service. The company has been operating on the Web since 1992.

LINKS TO PRACTICE
1-800-FLOWERS.com
www.1800flowers.com

THEORY OF CONSTRAINTS ■

The **theory of constraints (TOC)** is an extension of OPT. According to the TOC, a system's output is determined by its constraints. TOC defines three kinds of constraints and has a range of applications. The three kinds of constraints are internal resource constraint, market constraint, and policy constraint. An **internal resource constraint** is the classic bottleneck discussed in the previous section. A **market constraint** results when market demand is less than production capacity. Since companies do not want excess inventory buildup, the market determines the rate of production. **Policy constraint** means that a specific policy dictates the rate of production (for example, a policy of no overtime).

TOC tries to improve system performance by focusing on constraints. Improvement is measured financially and operationally. Financial measurements are net profit, return on investment, and cash flow. Operational measurements include throughput, inventory, and operating expenses. Throughput is the rate at which money is generated by the system through sales. Unsold product is not throughput. Inventory is the money the system has invested in buying materials to produce items it intends to sell and does not include labor or overhead. Operating expense is the

▶ **Theory of constraints**
A management philosophy that extends the concepts of OPT.

▶ **Internal resource constraint**
A regular bottleneck.

▶ **Market constraint**
The condition that results when market demand is less than production capacity.

▶ **Policy constraint**
The condition that results when a specific policy dictates the rate of production.

money spent to convert inventory into throughput, including all labor, overhead, and other expenses.

The procedure for using TOC consists of the following steps.

STEP 1   IDENTIFY THE SYSTEM'S BOTTLENECK(S).
At Akito's Flowers, identify the floral arrangers as the bottleneck.

STEP 2   EXPLOIT THE BOTTLENECK(S).
For the floral shop, take orders ahead of time to make sure there is always a buffer of orders for the arrangers to work on. This prevents idle time at the bottleneck resource.

STEP 3   SUBORDINATE ALL OTHER DECISIONS TO STEP 2.
Schedule non-bottleneck resources to support the maximum use of the bottleneck. For Akito's Flowers, have the clerk transfer orders to the arrangers every 10 minutes at the start of the day to make sure the bottleneck is fully used. You may have to arrive early or stay late to be sure the orders are processed and waiting for the arrangers first thing each day.

STEP 4   ELEVATE THE BOTTLENECK(S).
If after Steps 1 through 3 the bottleneck is still a constraint, then consider increasing the capacity of the bottleneck. At Akito's Flowers, add an additional floral arranger.

STEP 5   DO NOT LET INERTIA SET IN.
Although the floral arrangers may improve their throughput, check to see whether new constraints have developed. If so, work on increasing throughput.

■ SCHEDULING FOR SERVICE ORGANIZATIONS

In many service organizations, scheduling is complicated because service demand —quantity, type of service, and timing—is often variable and hard to forecast. In addition, inventories may not be possible and capacity is limited. For example, a movie theater cannot show the movie before the customers arrive and hope to satisfy demand. The theater is also limited as to how many people can occupy the theater at any given time. Because of these constraints, some additional techniques are available for scheduling services. These include scheduling the services demanded and scheduling the workforce.

Scheduling Services Demanded

Techniques for scheduling services demanded range from setting appointments, requiring reservations, using a public schedule, and delaying or back ordering the service. Let's look at each of these individually.

Appointments Appointment systems set a time for the customer to use the service. For example, students make appointments with professors to discuss class work. Appointments minimize customer waiting time and make good use of the service provider's capacity. Appointment systems are used by physicians, lawyers, auto repair or service shops, and hair salons. The shared component of each of these services is that no tangible inventory is usually possible. Disadvantages of an appointment system include the problem of "no shows"—people who miss appointments—and insufficient time scheduled for customers. In the case of "no shows," the service provider may be idle until the next scheduled appointment and incur a loss of revenue. In the case of insufficient time, the service provider often falls behind schedule and keeps customers waiting.

Reservations A reservation system enables the customer to take control or temporary possession of an item—for example, a hotel room, an automobile, or a banquet hall. A reservation system provides advance notice of when the item is needed and for how long. Deposits usually reduce the problem of last minute cancellations or "no-shows."

Posted Schedules Many service providers post a schedule indicating when a service is available. Movie theaters, universities, airlines, trains, buses, retail stores, museums, concerts, and sporting events are all examples of services that post schedules. The posted schedule tells the customer the event's date and time.

Delayed Services or Backlogs Another method used to schedule customer demand is delayed services or backlogs. Restaurants that do not take reservations are one example. The restaurant puts customers on a waiting list until a table becomes available. Other examples are banks, grocery stores, retail stores, repair services, and barber shops. In most of these organizations, customers are served in the order in which they arrive. These methods are aimed at better managing the service organization's capacity. An alternative method for managing capacity involves the way the workforce is scheduled.

Scheduling Employees

Since organizations may not always be able to schedule demand, the alternative is to manage capacity in the way they schedule employees. Organizations can staff for peak demand, use floating personnel, have employees on call, use temporary employees, use seasonal employees, use part-time employees, or use any combination of the above.

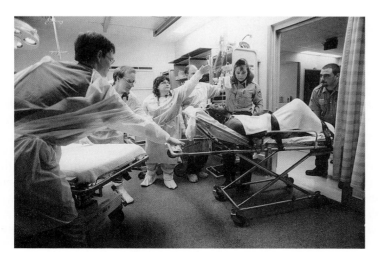

When demand occurs, service must be available.

Staffing for Peak Demand With this procedure the organization has enough service providers to accommodate the maximum level of customer demand. The obvious problem with this is cost. The workforce is fully used only during peak demand. Otherwise, a portion of the workforce is idle. Organizations typically staff for peak demand when the service providers have significant skills and the size of the workforce cannot be changed quickly. An example is your local fire or police department.

Floating Employees When customer demand for services can change daily, organizations use floating employees to advantage. Floating employees perform a number of services and are assigned where they are needed each day. Hospitals use floating employees because the number of patients and degree of care needed can change daily. A disadvantage of this approach for some employees is the uncertainty of their work location and the transient nature of short-term assignments.

Employees on Call Some organization use on-call employees during specific periods of the week. Physicians at a hospital may be on call in case of emergencies though not physically present unless needed. Maintenance employees may also be on-call in case of emergencies. Although being on call restricts an employee's normal free time, it also means the employee does not have to be physically present in the workplace during the specified period.

Temporary Employees Using temporary employees is another way for an organization to adjust workforce level. An organization can hire temporary employees with almost any skill set through a temp agency. The agency provides the employees and bills the organization.

Seasonal Employees Service organizations such as retailers with seasonal customer demand hire seasonal employees. These are short-term hires who expect their job to be terminated at the end of the season. Growers, for example, use seasonal employees to process items as they ripen. These organizations need an expanded workforce for a short period of time and cannot justify hiring additional permanent employees.

Part-Time Employees For some organizations, customer demand is higher during certain times of the day and low at other times. At a fast-food restaurant, for example, demand is high at meal times—breakfast, lunch, and dinner—and lower during the rest of the day. Instead of hiring employees for a full 8-hour shift, the organization uses its capacity more effectively by hiring part-time employees.

Organizations can combine any of these techniques to manage their service capacity effectively. Although these techniques provide the means for managing capacity, organizations still need to develop employee schedules that comply with legal requirements and contractual obligations. Legal requirements may dictate the minimum number of employees physically present and on duty at a fire station, for example. Contractual obligations are determined by labor agreements. These obligations may limit overtime and concern the number of consecutive days off each week.

Now let's look at a technique for developing a workforce schedule when each employee works full time and needs to have 2 consecutive days off each week.

DEVELOPING A WORKFORCE SCHEDULE ◼

Tibrewala, Philippe, and Brown developed a technique in 1972 that enables a company to operate 7 days a week and give each of its full-time employees 2 consecutive days off. The purpose is to find the 2 consecutive days off for each employee, satisfy staffing needs, and minimize excess capacity. For example, a swimming pool or beach needs lifeguards 7 days a week. This scheduling technique can develop the schedules to be used so that each lifeguard has 2 consecutive days off during the week. Since most companies define the starting day and ending day of their pay week, we will use Monday as the first day of the week. Thus an employee cannot be off on Sunday and Monday since those are not two consecutive days during the same pay week. We use Tibrewala, Philippe, and Brown's technique for developing the schedule by following these steps:

STEP 1   FIND OUT THE MINIMUM NUMBER OF EMPLOYEES NEEDED FOR EACH DAY OF THE WEEK.

Day of the Week	M	T	W	Th	F	Sa	Su
Number of Staff Needed	4	5	5	3	5	2	3

STEP 2   GIVEN THE MINIMUM NUMBER OF EMPLOYEES NEEDED EACH DAY, CALCULATE THE NUMBER OF EMPLOYEES NEEDED FOR EACH PAIR OF CONSECUTIVE DAYS DURING THE PAY WEEK.

For example, a total of 9 employees are needed on Monday and Tuesday. The sum for each pair of days is as shown in the table.

Pair of Consecutive Days	Total of Staff Needed
Monday and Tuesday	9 employees
Tuesday and Wednesday	10 employees
Wednesday and Thursday	8 employees
Thursday and Friday	8 employees
Friday and Saturday	7 employees
Saturday and Sunday	5 employees

STEP 3   FIND THE PAIR OF DAYS WITH THE LOWEST TOTAL NEEDED.

These are the 2 consecutive days off for 1 employee, who will work the other 5 days of the week. In our case, the lowest total is for the Saturday and Sunday pair of days. Employee number 1 works Monday, Tuesday, Wednesday, Thursday, Friday, and is off on Saturday and Sunday. When there is a tie, we can choose any of the tied pairs. We base our decision on an existing labor contract or established company procedures, or we can break the tie arbitrarily.

STEP 4   UPDATE THE NUMBER OF EMPLOYEES YOU STILL NEED TO SCHEDULE FOR EACH DAY.

We decrease our employee needs for Monday through Friday by 1 because employee number 1 is scheduled to work those days. The number of employees needed for Saturday and Sunday has not changed because no one has been scheduled yet to work those days. The updated staffing needs are shown here.

Day of the Week	M	T	W	Th	F	Sa	Su
Number of Staff Needed	3	4	4	2	4	2	3

STEP 5 USING THE UPDATED STAFFING NEEDS, REPEAT STEPS **2** THROUGH **4** UNTIL YOU HAVE SATISFIED ALL NEEDS.

Now we repeat Step 2.

STEP 2 THE NEW TOTAL NUMBER OF STAFF FOR EACH PAIR OF DAYS IS AS FOLLOWS.

Pair of Consecutive Days	Total of Staff Needed
Monday and Tuesday	7 employees
Tuesday and Wednesday	8 employees
Wednesday and Thursday	6 employees
Thursday and Friday	6 employees
Friday and Saturday	6 employees
Saturday and Sunday	5 employees

STEP 3 THE DAYS OFF FOR EMPLOYEE NUMBER **2** ARE ALSO **SATURDAY** AND **SUNDAY**.

This employee will work Monday through Friday.

STEP 4 UPDATE THE STAFFING NEEDS.

Day of the Week	M	T	W	Th	F	Sa	Su
Number of Staff Needed	2	3	3	1	3	2	3

Since there are still unsatisfied needs, we return to Step 2.

STEP 2 THE NEW TOTAL NUMBER OF STAFF FOR EACH PAIR OF DAYS IS AS FOLLOWS.

Pair of Consecutive Days	Total of Staff Needed
Monday and Tuesday	5 employees
Tuesday and Wednesday	6 employees
Wednesday and Thursday	4 employees
Thursday and Friday	4 employees
Friday and Saturday	5 employees
Saturday and Sunday	5 employees

STEP 3 THE LOWEST TOTAL STAFF IS TIED.

We can give employee number 3 either Wednesday and Thursday off, or Thursday and Friday off. We arbitrarily decide to give the employee Wednesday and Thursday off, and have the employee work Monday, Tuesday, Friday, Saturday, and Sunday.

STEP 4   UPDATE THE STAFFING NEEDS.

Day of the Week	M	T	W	Th	F	Sa	Su
Number of Staff Needed	1	2	3	1	2	1	2

There are still unsatisfied staffing needs so we return to Step 2.

STEP 2   THE NEW TOTAL NUMBER OF STAFF FOR EACH PAIR OF DAYS IS AS FOLLOWS.

Pair of Consecutive Days	Total of Staff Needed
Monday and Tuesday	3 employees
Tuesday and Wednesday	5 employees
Wednesday and Thursday	4 employees
Thursday and Friday	3 employees
Friday and Saturday	3 employees
Saturday and Sunday	3 employees

STEP 3   WE CAN GIVE EMPLOYEE NUMBER 4 MONDAY AND TUESDAY OFF, THURSDAY AND FRIDAY OFF, FRIDAY AND SATURDAY OFF, OR SATURDAY AND SUNDAY OFF.

We arbitrarily decide to give the employee Saturday and Sunday off, and have the employee work Monday through Friday.

STEP 4   UPDATE THE STAFFING NEEDS.

Day of the Week	M	T	W	Th	F	Sa	Su
Number of Staff Needed	0	1	2	0	1	1	2

We return to Step 2 because we still have unfinished staffing needs.

STEP 2   THE NEW TOTAL NUMBER OF STAFF FOR EACH PAIR OF DAYS IS AS FOLLOWS.

Pair of Consecutive Days	Total of Staff Needed
Monday and Tuesday	1 employee
Tuesday and Wednesday	3 employees
Wednesday and Thursday	2 employees
Thursday and Friday	1 employee
Friday and Saturday	2 employees
Saturday and Sunday	3 employees

STEP 3   WE ARBITRARILY DECIDE TO GIVE EMPLOYEE NUMBER FIVE MONDAY AND TUESDAY OFF.

This employee will work Wednesday through Sunday.

STEP 4   UPDATE THE STAFFING NEEDS.

Day of the Week	M	T	W	Th	F	Sa	Su
Number of Staff Needed	0	1	1	0	0	0	1

Return to Step 2.

STEP 2   THE NEW TOTAL NUMBER OF STAFF FOR EACH PAIR OF DAYS IS AS FOLLOWS.

Pair of Consecutive Days	Total of Staff Needed
Monday and Tuesday	1 employee
Tuesday and Wednesday	2 employees
Wednesday and Thursday	1 employee
Thursday and Friday	0 employees
Friday and Saturday	0 employees
Saturday and Sunday	1 employee

STEP 3   EMPLOYEE NUMBER 6 COULD HAVE EITHER THURSDAY AND FRIDAY OFF OR FRIDAY AND SATURDAY OFF.

We arbitrarily decide to give employee number 6 Friday and Saturday off. This employee will work Monday, Tuesday, Wednesday, Thursday, and Sunday.

STEP 4   UPDATE THE STAFFING NEEDS.

Day of the Week	M	T	W	Th	F	Sa	Su
Number of Staff Needed	0	0	0	0	0	0	1

Return to Step 2.

STEP 2   THE NEW TOTAL NUMBER OF EMPLOYEES FOR EACH PAIR OF DAYS IS AS FOLLOWS.

Pair of Consecutive Days	Total of Staff Needed
Monday and Tuesday	0 employees
Tuesday and Wednesday	0 employees
Wednesday and Thursday	0 employees
Thursday and Friday	0 employees
Friday and Saturday	0 employees
Saturday and Sunday	1 employee

STEP 3   EMPLOYEE NUMBER 7 CAN HAVE ANY DAY BUT SUNDAY OFF.

We arbitrarily decide to give employee number 7 Friday and Saturday off. This employee will work Monday, Tuesday, Wednesday, Thursday, and Sunday.

STEP 4   UPDATE THE STAFFING NEEDS.

Day of the Week	M	T	W	Th	F	Sa
Number of Staff Needed	0	0	0	0	0	0	0

STEP 5   WE HAVE MET THE STAFFING NEEDS: THE FINAL SCHEDULE IS SHOWN HERE.

Employee	M	T	W	Th	F	S	Su
1	X	X	X	X	X	off	off
2	X	X	X	X	X	off	off
3	X	X	off	off	X	X	X
4	X	X	X	X	X	off	off
5	off	off	X	X	X	X	X
6	X	X	X	X	off	off	X
7	X	X	X	X	off	off	X

This technique gives the manager work schedules for each employee to satisfy minimum daily staffing requirements. Although it is not a unique solution, this schedule gives each full-time employee 2 consecutive days off. The next step is to replace employee numbers with employee names. The manager can give the senior employee first choice of schedules and proceed until all the employees have been assigned a schedule.

OM ACROSS THE ORGANIZATION

Scheduling executes a company's strategic business plan so it affects functional areas throughout the company.

Accounting relies on schedule information and completion of customer orders to develop revenue projections, calculate actual job costs, and do cash flow analysis.

Marketing uses schedule effectiveness measurements to determine whether the company is using lead times for competitive advantage, whether flow time is correlated to estimated lead times, and whether deliveries are made on time. Knowing lead times allows marketing to make accurate delivery promises to customers.

Information systems maintains the scheduling database, which includes routings and processing times. Information systems also provides the software to monitor product movement through the scheduling process.

Purchasing follows items through the process to determine whether items need to be expedited when the job is ahead of schedule or de-expedited when jobs are behind schedule to ensure the materials and parts are available when needed.

Operations uses the schedule to maintain its priorities and to provide customer service by finishing jobs on time. The schedule reflects operations' workload and is used to measure performance.

In manufacturing companies, production planners typically schedule individual jobs; in service organizations, the office manager or shift supervisor does the scheduling. Both planners and managers are evaluated on the customer service levels they achieve. The production planner is concerned with the sequencing of jobs through the factory. The office manager or shift supervisor is concerned with adequate staffing. Scheduling jobs and developing work schedules should reflect the company's competitive strategy and serve as a tool to keep all the functional areas synchronized.

◀ OM IS EVERYWHERE

Effective scheduling means that you use your resources wisely while achieving your objectives. In everyday life, we can use time management techniques to do this. For example, we might plan our work day so we respond to e-mail messages twice a day—when we get to the office and again before we leave—rather than responding throughout the day. We might plan our home chores so that we consolidate dirty laundry and make one trip a week to the laundry rather than a trip every day or so. How we schedule activities sets the priorities for those activities. We put important activities at the beginning of the schedule and less important activities at the end. Thus an individual's schedule reflects personal priorities just as an organization's schedule reflects organizational priorities. In both the personal and the business world, we use the schedule to manage our resources and meet personal or organizational objectives.

CHAPTER HIGHLIGHTS

1 Different kinds of environments need different scheduling techniques. Scheduling in the high-volume environment is typically done through line design and balancing. Scheduling in a low-volume environment typically involves the use of priority rules. In this environment, Gantt charts are often used to view the workload and jobs in process.

2 Shop loading techniques include infinite and finite loading. Infinite loading loads jobs without capacity constraints. Finite loading loads jobs up to a predetermined capacity level. Loading can be done using forward or backward scheduling. Forward scheduling starts the job as soon as possible, whereas backward scheduling works back from the due date.

3 Priority rules are used to make scheduling decisions. SPT always minimizes mean job flow time, mean job lateness, and average number of jobs in system. FCFS is considered one of the fairest priority rules. Rules related to due dates tend to minimize the maximum tardiness of the jobs. Priority rules need to support organizational objectives.

4 Performance measurements reflect the priorities of the organization. Mean job flow time, mean job lateness, mean job tardiness, makespan, and the average number of jobs in the system measure the effectiveness of schedules.

5 Johnson's rule is an effective technique for minimizing makespan when 2 successive workstations are needed to complete the process.

6 When scheduling bottleneck systems, the basic principles of OPT apply. The theory of constraints expands OPT into a managerial philosophy of continuous improvement.

7 Service organizations use different scheduling techniques such as appointments, reservations, and posted schedules for effective use service capacity.

8 A method developed by Tibrewala, Phillippe, and Brown develops workforce schedules when a company uses full-time employees, operates 7 days each week, and gives its employees 2 consecutive days off.

KEY TERMS

flow operations 482
routing 482
bottleneck 482
Gantt chart 483
infinite loading 484
finite loading 484
forward scheduling 485
due date 485
backward scheduling 486
slack 486
input/output control 486

operation sequencing 488
queue 488
priority rule 488
local priority rule 488
global priority rule 488
job flow time 490
average number of jobs in system 490
makespan 491
job lateness 491
job tardiness 491
Johnson's rule 495

optimized production technology (OPT) 497
non-bottleneck 497
capacity-constrained resource 497
throughput 498
transfer batch 498
process batch 498
theory of constraints (TOC) 499
internal resource constraint 499
market constraint 499
policy constraint 499

FORMULA REVIEW

To calculate job flow time:

Job flow time = time of completion − time job was first available for processing

To calculate mean job flow time:

Mean job flow time = sum of individual flow times/ number of jobs

To calculate average number of jobs in system:

Average number of jobs in system = total flow time/ makespan

SOLVED PROBLEMS

■ Solved Problem 1

The Fargoe Forge Company has collected the following data regarding the input and output of work into Work Center 222. Complete the partially filled in input/output charts.

Input information (hours)

	4	5	6	7	8
Planned input	600	675	625	650	650
Actual input	650	700	600	575	675
Deviation					
Cumulative deviation					

Output Information (hours)

	4	5	6	7	8
Planned output	680	680	680	680	680
Actual output	680	700	650	600	680
Deviation					
Cumulative deviation					

Backlog 125 hours

Solution

STEP 1   Calculate the period-by-period deviations. Subtract the planned input from the actual input. Subtract the planned output from the actual output. The results are shown here.

STEP 2   Calculate the cumulative deviation for the input and the output. Add the deviation for the current period to the cumulative deviation of the previous period. For example, in period 5, the cumulative deviation of the input is 75 hours of work (50 hours at the end of period 4, plus 25 hours in period 5). The cumulative deviation values are shown in Spreadsheet 16.1.

STEP 3   Calculate the backlog at Work Center 222. The backlog changes only when the actual input is different than the actual output in a period. The beginning backlog is 125 hours of work. The backlog at the end of period 4 changes to 95 hours because the actual input is only 650 hours of work, whereas the actual output is 680 hours of work. Since the work center completed 30 hours more of work than it received, the backlog has to be reduced by 30 hours, or a total of 95 hours. The backlog for period 5 remains at 95 hours. Backlog in period 6 drops to 45 hours. The backlog in period 7 drops to 20 hours and then to 15 hours in period 8. This problem can also be solved using a spreadsheet. This is shown in Spreadsheet 16.1.

Spreadsheet 16.1

Input Information

	PERIOD				
	4	5	6	7	8
Planned input	600	675	625	650	650
Actual input	650	700	600	575	675
Deviation	50	25	-25	-75	25
Cumulative Deviation	50	75	50	-25	0

Output Information

	PERIOD				
	4	5	6	7	8
Planned output	680	680	680	680	680
Actual output	680	700	650	600	680
Deviation	0	20	-30	-80	0
Cumulative deviation	0	20	-10	-90	-90
Backlog 125	95	95	45	20	15

Solved Problem 2

Custom Glass, Inc. produces custom storm windows. The company has the following jobs waiting to be processed at its glass-cutting work center.

Job	Job Time (days)	Due Date (days from now)
A	8	20
B	4	15
C	6	30
D	7	24
E	9	10

a. Using earliest due date as the priority rule, determine the sequence for these jobs.
b. Using shortest processing time as the priority rule, determine the sequence for these jobs.
c. Calculate the mean job flow time, average number of jobs in the system, mean job lateness, and mean job tardiness for the schedule using earliest due date.
d. Calculate the mean job flow time, average number of jobs in the system, mean job lateness, and mean job tardiness for the schedule using the shortest processing time.

Solution

a. The sequence generated using earliest due date as the priority rule is E, B, A, D, C. Job E has the highest priority since it is due in the least amount of time. The schedule is as follows.

- Job E is done after 9 days
- Job B is done after 13 days
- Job A is done after 21 days
- Job D is done after 28 days
- Job C is done after 34 days

b. The sequence generated using shortest processing time as the priority rule is B, C, D, A, E. Job B has the highest priority since it takes the least amount of time to complete. The SPT schedule is as follows.

- Job B is done after 4 days
- Job C is done after 10 days
- Job D is done after 17 days
- Job A is done after 25 days
- Job E is done after 34 days

c. Based on the schedule generated using the EDD rule, the results are shown above.

(Solution Step 3, continued)

EDD Results

Job	Job Flow Time (days)	Due Date (days from now)	Job Lateness (days)	Job Tardiness (days)
A	21	20	1	1
B	13	15	−2	0
C	34	30	4	4
D	28	24	4	4
E	9	10	−1	0
Totals	105		6	9

Mean job flow time is 21 days (105 days divided by 5 jobs). Remember that job flow time extends from the time the job is available to work on to its completion. Since all the jobs are available at the same time, the flow time for each job is equal to its completion time. The average number of jobs in the system is 3.1 jobs (105 days of total flow time divided by the makespan of 34 days). Total lateness is 6 days (1 − 2 + 4 + 4 − 1); therefore, mean job lateness is 1.2 days (6 days divided by 5 jobs). Total tardiness is 9 days; therefore, mean job tardiness is 1.8 days.

SPT Results

Job	Job Flow Time (days)	Due Date (days from now)	Job Lateness (days)	Job Tardiness (days)
A	25	20	5	5
B	4	15	−11	0
C	10	30	−20	0
D	17	24	−7	0
E	34	10	24	24
Totals	90		−9	29

d. Based on the schedule generated using the SPT rule, the results are provided here.

Mean job flow time is 18 days (90 days divided by 5 jobs). The average number of jobs in the system is 2.65 jobs (90 days of total flow time divided by the makespan of 34 days). Total lateness is negative 9 days (5 − 11 − 20 − 7 + 24); therefore, mean job lateness is −1.8 days (−9 days divided by 5 jobs). Total tardiness is 29 days; therefore, mean job tardiness is 5.8 days.

■ Solved Problem 3

Jack's Machine Shop has the following batch of jobs that need to be scheduled so the makespan is minimized. Each job is processed first at Machine Center 1 and then at Machine Center 2. The job information is as follows:

Job	Machine Center 1 Processing Time (days)	Machine Center 2 Processing Time (days)
A	4	3
B	2	7
C	6	5
D	4	5
E	3	4
F	5	1

Using Johnson's rule, develop a sequence for Jack's Machine Shop that minimizes makespan.

Solution

The jobs and the processing times are listed so we can begin at Step 2.

STEP 2 The shortest individual activity processing time is 1 day for job F at Machine Center 2. Since this time is on the second activity, job F takes the last available spot in the sequence, which is sixth.

STEP 3 Removing the job we just sequenced, we repeat Step 2 until we have sequenced all jobs. The remaining jobs are as follows.

Job	Machine Center 1 Processing Time (days)	Machine Center 2 Processing Time (days)
A	4	3
B	2	7
C	6	5
D	4	5
E	3	4

STEP 2 The shortest individual activity processing time is from job B at Machine Center 1. Therefore, we put job B in the highest available spot in the sequence, which is first. Now we eliminate job B from consideration and repeat Step 2.

Job	Machine Center 1 Processing Time (days)	Machine Center 2 Processing Time (days)
A	4	3
C	6	5
D	4	5
E	3	4

STEP 2 The shortest activity processing time is now in two places, from job A for 3 days at Machine Center 2 and from job E for 3 days at Machine Center 1. We can put both of these jobs into our sequence. Job A goes into the last available spot, fifth, and job A goes into the highest available spot, second. We can now eliminate both jobs from consideration. The updated list of remaining jobs is shown here.

Job	Machine Center 1 Processing Time (days)	Machine Center 2 Processing Time (days)
C	6	5
D	4	5

STEP 2 The shortest activity processing time is 4 days for job D at Machine Center 1. Job D should be placed in the highest available slot, third. We put the remaining job in the only available position in the sequence, fourth.

The final sequence is B, E, D, C, A, F.

■ Solved Problem 4

The Sports Injury Clinic operates 7 days a week. Based on historical data, the manager, Joan, has determined the following daily minimum staffing requirements. She believes that she needs 3 employees on Monday and Thursday, 4 employees on Tuesday, 2 employees on Wednesday and Sunday, and 5 employees on Friday and Saturday. Joan wants a workforce schedule that allows each employee 2 consecutive days off each week and minimizes excess staffing. Develop a schedule.

Solution

STEP 1   Find out the minimum number of employees needed for each day of the week.

Day of the Week	M	T	W	Th	F	S	Su
Number of Staff Needed	3	4	2	3	5	5	2

STEP 2   Given the minimum staff needed each day, calculate the number of employees needed for each pair of consecutive days.

Pair of Consecutive Days	Total of Staff Needed
Monday and Tuesday	7
Tuesday and Wednesday	6
Wednesday and Thursday	5
Thursday and Friday	8
Friday and Saturday	10
Saturday and Sunday	7

STEP 3   Find the pair of days that has the lowest total need. Wednesday and Thursday have the lowest total need so they become the days off for the first employee.

STEP 4   Update the number of staff still needed. Reduce the staff needed by 1 employee for Monday, Tuesday, Friday, Saturday, and Sunday since the first employee will work on those days.

STEP 5   Using the updated requirements, repeat Steps 2 through 4 until all requirements have been met. If you continue to develop the workforce schedule, an alternative schedule is shown below. Given the amount of slack, several other alternatives are also possible.

Employee	M	T	W	Th	F	S	Su
1	X	X	off	off	X	X	X
2	X	X	X	X	X	off	off
3	off	off	X	X	X	X	X
4	X	X	off	off	X	X	X
5	off	off	X	X	X	X	X
6	X	X	off	off	X	X	X

DISCUSSION QUESTIONS

1. Compare and contrast high-volume and low-volume scheduling operations.
2. Describe a high-volume service operation and describe how scheduling should be done.
3. Describe a low-volume service operation and describe how scheduling should be done.
4. Visit a local service operation and describe their scheduling procedures.
5. Visit a local manufacturing operation and describe how they sequence jobs through the shop.
6. Describe infinite loading.
7. Explain how the output from infinite loading is used.
8. Explain how finite loading is done.
9. Explain the benefits of finite loading.
10. Describe forward scheduling.
11. Describe backward scheduling.
12. Visit a local service or manufacturing operation and learn how they measure schedule effectiveness.
13. Describe the principles of OPT.
14. Describe the theory of constraints.
15. Describe different methods that might be useful for scheduling service operations.

PROBLEMS

1. Jack, the owner and manager of Jack's Box Company, wants to monitor usage at Work Center 3, a bottleneck in the system. He has collected data on the planned and actual input and output.

Input information (in hours)					
	4	5	6	7	8
Planned input	40	50	50	60	60
Actual input	45	45	45	55	60
Deviation					
Cumulative deviation					
Output Information (in hours)					
	4	5	6	7	8
Planned output	70	70	70	70	70
Actual output	60	60	60	60	60
Deviation					
Cumulative deviation					
Backlog 75 hours					

a. Complete the input/output record.
b. Describe your concerns based on the results of the input/output analysis.

2. Since Jack believes that Work Center 3 is his bottleneck. He has asked you to do the following.

a. Calculate the planned efficiency level of Work Center 3 at Jack's Box Company.

b. Compare the planned efficiency with the actual efficiency.
c. Given your results, do you agree that Work Center 3 is the bottleneck?

3. Based on your concerns, Jack has gathered information for Work Center 2, the cork center that directly feeds Work Center 3. Complete the input/output analysis of Work Center 2.

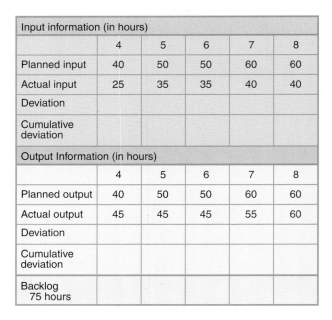

Input information (in hours)					
	4	5	6	7	8
Planned input	40	50	50	60	60
Actual input	25	35	35	40	40
Deviation					
Cumulative deviation					
Output Information (in hours)					
	4	5	6	7	8
Planned output	40	50	50	60	60
Actual output	45	45	45	55	60
Deviation					
Cumulative deviation					
Backlog 75 hours					

a. Complete the input/output record.
b. Describe your concerns based on the results of the input/output analysis.

4. Jack has asked you to do the following.

   a. Calculate the planned efficiency level Work Center 2 at Jack's Box Company.
   b. Compare the planned efficiency with the actual efficiency.
   c. What insights can you offer Jack?

5. Henri's Custom Gowns has 6 jobs waiting to be processed. Each gown is at the beading work center. The job information is shown here.

Job	Job time (in days)	Days Until Due	Job Time at Other Work Centers	Operations Remaining at Other Work Centers
A	9	30	10	3
B	5	10	2	1
C	8	24	8	2
D	10	40	18	3
E	7	26	12	1
F	6	15	6	2

   a. Determine the sequence Henri should follow if he uses the SPT (shortest processing time) priority rule.
   b. Based on the sequence developed in part (a), calculate the following performance measures: makespan, mean job flow time, average number of jobs in the system, mean job lateness, mean job tardiness, and maximum tardiness.

6. Henri has decided to try a different priority rule.

   a. Using the data in Problem 5, determine the sequence Henri should follow if he uses the EDD (earliest due date) priority rule.
   b. Based on the sequence developed in part (a), calculate the following performance measures: makespan, mean job flow time, average number of jobs in the system, mean job lateness, mean job tardiness, and maximum tardiness.

7. Henri has heard of LPT (longest processing time) priority rule and wonders how that would change the sequence of the jobs listed in Problem 5.

   a. Determine the sequence Henri should follow if he uses the LPT (longest processing time) priority rule.
   b. Based on the sequence developed in part (a), calculate the following performance measures: makespan, mean job flow time, average number of jobs in the system, mean job lateness, mean job tardiness, and maximum tardiness.

8. In an effort to be fair to his customers, Henri has decided to use the FCFS (first come, first served) priority rule. Using the job date from Problem 5, assume that the jobs arrive in order—that is , A first, then B, then C.

   a. Using the data in Problem 5, determine the sequence Henri should follow if he uses the FCFS (first come, first served) priority rule.
   b. Based on the sequence developed in part (a), calculate the following performance measures: makespan, mean job flow time, average number of jobs in the system, mean job lateness, mean job tardiness, and maximum tardiness.

9. Henri recently learned about global priority rules. He is interested in the slack over remaining operations (S/RO) rule.

   a. Using the data in Problem 5, determine the sequence Henri should follow if he uses the S/RO (slack over remaining operations) priority rule.
   b. Based on the sequence developed in part (a), calculate the following performance measures: makespan, mean job flow time, average number of jobs in the system, mean job lateness, mean job tardiness, and maximum tardiness.

10. Joe's Twenty-four Seven Laundromat has the following jobs waiting to be processed. The first step of the process includes washing and drying the clothes; the second step is pressing the clothing. Joe wants to minimize the amount of time it takes to do all the jobs. The fives jobs waiting to be processed are shown here.

Job	Wash and Dry (hours)	Press (hours)
A	6	4
B	3	5
C	2	3
D	7	5
E	4	3

   a. Using FCFS (first come, first served), assume the jobs arrive in the order shown, (A, then B, then C, etc.) Show the beginning and ending time for each job.
   b. Calculate the makespan, the mean job flow time, and the average number of jobs in the system.

11. Joe thinks that it is probably more efficient to use SPT (shortest processing time) as his priority rule.

   a. Develop a Sequence using SPT based on processing time for the wash and dry operation.
   b. Calculate the makespan, the mean job flow time, and the average number of jobs in the system.

12. Joe has asked you to develop a sequence that minimizes makespan for the sequence of jobs given in Problem 10. Compare the makespan, mean job flow time, and the average number of jobs in the system compared to your results in Problems 10 and 11.

13. Raquel's Landscaping Company has contracted for several landscaping jobs. Each job requires preparing the areas (identifying the locations and types of plants, preparing the soil, etc.) and then planting the trees, bushes, and shrubs. The expected time for each of the jobs is shown next.

Job	Preparing the area (days)	Planting (days)
R	3	2
S	1	3
T	4	5
U	8	5
V	6	4
W	4	3

   a. Using FCFS (first come, first served), assume the jobs arrive in the order shown, (R, then S, then T, etc.) Show the beginning and ending time for each job.

   b. Calculate the makespan, the mean job flow time, and the average number of jobs in the system.

14. Raquel is concerned with efficiency. She believes it is probably more efficient to use SPT (shortest processing time) as her priority rule.

   a. Develop a sequence using SPT based on processing time for preparing the area.

   b. Calculate the makespan, the mean job flow time, and the average number of jobs in the system.

15. Raquel has asked you to develop a sequence that minimizes makespan for the sequence of jobs given in Problem 13. Compare the makespan, mean job flow time, and the average number of jobs in the system compared to your results in Problems 13 and 14.

16. Barb's Beach Bar operates 7 days per week. Barb uses only full-time employees and wants each employee to have 2 consecutive days off each week. She believes that she needs a minimum of 3 employees on Monday, Tuesday, Wednesday, Thursday, and Sunday. On Friday and Saturday, she believes that she needs 6 employees. Develop a workforce schedule for Barb.

17. Next week is a 3-day weekend. Barb believes that she will need a minimum of 6 employees on Friday, Saturday and Sunday. The other days will still need a minimum of 3 workers. Remember that Barb wants each employee to have 2 consecutive days each week. Develop a workforce schedule for the holiday weekend.

18. Marvin's Beach Cleaners are responsible for keeping the beach clean. Marvin estimates that he needs a minimum of 2 people on Monday; 3 people on Tuesday and Sunday; 4 people on Wednesday and Thursday, and 5 people on Friday and Saturday. Contractually, Marvin is required to give each employee 2 consecutive days off during the week. Develop a workforce schedule for Marvin to use.

19. Marvin is preparing for the upcoming 3-day weekend. He estimates that he will need 3 additional workers on Sunday of that week. Using the requirements given in Problem 18 for the other days of the week, develop a workforce schedule for Marvin to use.

20. Cathy's Coney Islands operates 7 days per week. Demand is relatively constant during the week and tails off on the weekend. She estimates that she needs 5 employees Monday through Friday, and 2 employees on Saturday and Sunday. She is committed to giving each employee 2 consecutive days off during the week. Develop a workforce schedule for Cathy.

21. Cathy's Coney Islands has just purchased new equipment. Cathy believes the improved efficiency will reduce the number of people needed Monday through Friday down to 4. She does not believe she can ever have fewer than 2 persons working, so the weekend requirements remain the same. Develop a workforce schedule for Cathy.

22. Bill's Bar & Grill is open 7 nights a week. Business is busiest on Thursday when there is a concert in the park across the street. Bill wants a workforce schedule that allows each employee 2 consecutive days off each week. He believes that he needs 4 employees every day but Thursday. On Thursday Bill believes he needs 6 employees. Develop a workforce schedule for Bill.

23. During the winter, no concerts are given in the park. Bill believes that he needs a minimum of 4 employees every day of the week. Develop a workforce schedule for Bill that allows each employee two consecutive days off each week. Compare the number of workers he needs during the winter to the number of workers needed during the concert season.

CASE: *Air Traffic Controller School (ATCS)*

ATCS provides training for future air traffic controllers. One of the skills air traffic controllers need is the ability to sequence aircraft for landing purposes. The controller decides who lands immediately and who goes into a holding pattern. The following data are provided to you, the student, to develop an acceptable landing sequence. Any sequence that results in an aircraft not being scheduled to land before it runs out of remaining flying time is unacceptable. The following aircraft are currently awaiting your decision as to the landing sequence.

Flight Number	Minutes on Runway	Remaining Flying Time (minutes)	Cost per minute of flying time ($)
101	2.00	10	100
118	3.00	15	150
217	2.75	8	125
8076	1.50	5	80
219	3.50	12	200
894	1.75	19	150
024	2.50	16	400
616	3.25	22	300

There are many ways to sequence this group of aircraft waiting to land. Since cost is an obvious factor, consider a sequence that minimizes total cost to land the aircraft. Multiply the cost per minute of flying time by the remaining number of minutes left. This gives you the maximum cost associated with an airplane circling in a holding pattern until the last possible moment.

a. Develop a landing sequence that gives priority to those aircraft with the highest cost of slack time (excess flying time multiplied by cost per minute of flying time). For example, flight 616 has 18.75 minutes of slack time (22 − 3.25) times $300 per minute means that if flight 616 does not land until its time is all used up, it incurs an extra flying cost of $5,625. Make a Gantt chart showing the landing sequence and evaluate the sequence in terms of performance. Calculate mean flow time, mean lateness, and average number of planes in the system.

b. Develop a sequence using SPT as a priority rule. Make a Gantt chart showing the landing sequence and evaluate the sequence in terms of performance. Calculate mean flow time, mean lateness, and average number of planes in the system.

c. Develop a third sequence using EDD (earliest due date) as a priority rule. The plane with the least amount of flying time remaining has the highest priority. Make a Gantt chart showing the landing sequence and evaluate the sequence in terms of performance. Calculate mean flow time, mean lateness, and average number of planes in the system. Calculate the total cost associated with this sequence (flow time multiplied by cost per minute of flying time for each flight).

d. Try and develop an alternative sequence that lands all of the aircraft safely and reduces the total cost.

INTERACTIVE LEARNING

Enhance and test your knowledge of Chapter 16 using the interactive CD.

1. **Spreadsheet** *Solved Problem 2*

2. **Video** *Airline Scheduling*

   Visit our dynamic Web site, www.wiley.com/college/reid, for more cases, web links, and additional information.

3. **Company Tour**
   Herman Goelitz Candy Co., Inc.
   Merlin Metalworks

4. **Additional Web Resources**
   Herman Goelitz Candy Co., Inc., www.jellybelly.com
   Merlin Metalworks, www.merlinbike.com/html/technology/technology/html
   United Air Lines, Inc., www.ual.com/home default.asp
   Production-Scheduling.com, www.production-scheduling.com
   Suzy Systems, Inc., www.suzy.com

5. **Virtual Company Consulting Case**

6. **INTERNET CHALLENGE** *Batter Up*

As a world-class fan of major league baseball, you have always wanted to watch a game in person at each of the ballparks across the country. Now that you are about to graduate, you have decided it is time to achieve this goal. To do so, you must first know the location of each ballpark, when ball games are scheduled, and the driving distance between parks. The Internet can give you all this information.

Decide on a priority rule for building your schedule. You will drive between ballparks, so be sure to leave enough time to reach the next ballpark. You can average 60 miles per hour when traveling on the open road and cover up to 600 miles each day. You must visit each of the major league ballparks during the course of one season. Since you do not graduate until the end of May, you cannot start your adventure until June 1. Your objective is to minimize the total amount of time it takes to visit each ballpark and to minimize the number of miles you drive. You must include any time it takes to return home. You are constrained to driving no more than 10 hours or 600 miles per day. Use the Internet to find the locations of each ballpark, the scheduled baseball games, and the mileage between cities. Batter up!

BIBLIOGRAPHY

Abernathy, W., N. Baloff, and J. Hershey. "The Nurse Staffing Problem: Issues and Prospects." *Sloan Management Review* 13, no.1 (Fall 1971).

Blackstone Jr., John H. *Capacity Management.* Cincinnati, Oh.: South-western, 1989.

Buffa, Elwood S., and Jeffrey G. Miller. *Production-Inventory Systems: Planning and Control*, 3rd ed. Homewood, Ill.: Irwin, 1979.

Cox, James F., III, John H. Blackstone, and Michael S. Spencer, eds., *APICS Dictionary*, 9th ed. Falls Church, Va.: American Production and Inventory Control Society, Inc., 1998.

Johnson, S. M. "Optimal Two Stage and Three Stage Production Schedules with Setup Times Included." *Naval Logistics Quarterly* 1, no.1 (March 1954).

Sipper, Daniel, and Robert L. Buffin, Jr. *Production: Planning, Control and Integration.* Burr Ridge, Ill.: McGraw-Hill, 1998.

Umble, M. Michael, and M. L. Srikanth. *Synchronous Manufacturing.* Cincinnati, Oh.: South-western, 1990.

Vollmann, Thomas E., William L. Berry, and D. Clay Whybark. *Manufacturing Planning and Control,*. 4th ed Homewood, Ill.: Irwin, 1997.

Project Management

Before studying this chapter you should know or, if necessary, review

1. The implications of competitive priorities, Chapter 2, pages 28–32.
2. Time standards, Chapter 11, pages 329–331.
3. Gantt Charts, Chapter 16, pages 483–484.

LEARNING OBJECTIVES

After studying this chapter, you should be able to

1. Describe project management applications.
2. Describe the project life cycle.
3. Diagram networks of project activities.
4. Estimate the completion time of a project.
5. Compute the probability of completing a project by a specific time.
6. Determine how to reduce the length of a project effectively.
7. Describe the critical chain approach to project management.

CHAPTER OUTLINE

Think about life's major events and what it takes to make them successful. A wedding is a good example: it's a complex project with many simultaneous and sequential preparations leading up to the big day. Consider the following partial list of activities to prepare for a wedding.

1. Decide on the date of the wedding.
2. Decide on the location of the wedding.
3. Decide on the size of the wedding and the participants in the wedding.
4. Choose and order the wedding dress.
5. Choose and order gowns for the maid of honor and bridesmaids.
6. Choose and order formal wear for the groom and attendants.
7. Decide where to register for gifts.
8. Make the guest list.
9. Complete gift registration forms.
10. Choose and order the wedding invitations.
11. Choose and order the floral arrangements.
12. Choose and order the wedding cake.
13. Hire the caterer and choose food for the reception.
14. Hire the band for the reception.
15. Make reservations for the honeymoon resort.
16. Arrange and make reservations for the rehearsal dinner.
17. Buy gifts for members of wedding party.
18. Arrange the seating chart for the reception.
19. Hire the limo service.

You need to do most of these activities before the wedding. You can do several simultaneously, but you must do some activities before others. For example, you must set the wedding date before you book the facility, the band, the caterer, and the florist. You need to know about how many people you are inviting before you order the invitations, and you have to know how many people plan to attend the reception before you know the size of the wedding cake to order. Each activity in preparation for the wedding is related to other activities, and the order of these activities is clearly defined.

Project management techniques are useful when a project consists of several activities, some simultaneous and others sequential. A **project** is a unique, one-time event that is intended to achieve an objective in a given time period. The project is of some length (weeks, months, or even years) and uses resources (human, capital, materials, and equipment). For example, the project described here is to plan the wedding of two people on a particular date. Planning the wedding can easily take 6 to 12 months and cost thousands of dollars. In the business world, projects can be designing new products, installing new systems, constructing new facilities, designing an advertising campaign, designing information systems, and developing company Web sites. In politics, a project can be designing a political campaign. Projects consist of several tasks and take place in a given time period. Every project has a life cycle.

▶ **Project**
Endeavor with a specific objective, multiple activities, and defined precedence relationships, to be completed in a specified time period.

520

PROJECT LIFE CYCLE ■

Projects vary in terms of objectives but each project has a common life cycle or sequence of activities. The life cycle begins with an initial concept, followed by a feasibility study, the planning of the project, the execution of the plan, and finally the termination of the project. Let's look at each phase of a project life cycle.

Conception Identify the need for the project. In our wedding example, the concept is two individuals' decision to marry. In the business world, the concept might be the company's decision to launch a new product, implement a new information system, or become involved in e-commerce. In politics, the concept might be a candidate's decision to run for office.

Feasibility Analysis or Study Evaluate expected costs, benefits, and risks of the project. For our wedding example, a feasibility study means deciding whether the benefits of a large wedding justify the expense or if the couple would be better off using their resources in a different way such as making a down payment on a home. For the company launching a new product, a feasibility study means examining the potential market, the market share, and profits for the new product compared to the costs. In politics, a feasibility study is a candidate's assessment of the resources needed to run a successful political campaign and the benefits of elected office.

Planning Analyze the work to be done and develop time estimates for completing each of the activities. In our wedding example, the couple plans what must be done, by whom, and when. For a couple planning a wedding, a friend or family member might do the initial screening of caterers, musicians, and so forth, and the couple might make the final decisions. In business, planning consists of the activities needed to launch the new product. For example, the company must design the new product; source and order the materials, equipment, and tools; choose the process to use; design the layout; write the job instructions; do a pilot run; evaluate the process and the product design; and transition the product to manufacturing. In politics, planning might include deciding how to raise funds, schedule personal appearances and debates, handle public relations, and adopt policy positions.

Presidential candidates debate

Execution Carry out the activities that make up the project. For our couple this includes booking the facility, hiring the band, choosing the caterer, taking vows together, exchanging rings, celebrating with family and friends, and heading off on the honeymoon. In business, the execution of the project is completing the product design, obtaining the materials and equipment needed, setting up the process, writing job instructions, and making the product. For a political candidate, execution includes fund raising, making public appearances, and showcasing the political message.

Termination End the project. After this date, resources can be used for different activities. For the couple, termination is returning from the honeymoon and setting up house. In business, termination means product design engineers work on new products, purchasing agents can return to routine activities or a new project, and manufacturing engineers work on new projects. For a political candidate, termination means serving in an elected office or looking for a new job. See Table 17-1 for a summary of these project life cycle phases.

Table 17-1 Project Life-Cycle Phases	
Concept:	identify the need for the project
Feasibility analysis or study:	evaluate costs, benefits, and risks
Planning:	decide who does what, how long it should take, and what you need to do it
Execution:	do the project
Termination:	end the project

■ NETWORK PLANNING TECHNIQUES

LINKS TO PRACTICE
PERT and the Polaris Missile

Program evaluation and review technique **(PERT)** and **critical path method (CPM)** date back to the 1950s. PERT was originally developed to plan and monitor the Polaris missile, an extremely large project using over 3000 contractors and involving thousands of activities. PERT is credited with reducing the project duration by two years. Because of its success, most government contracts still require the use of PERT or a similar technique. CPM was initially developed to plan and coordinate maintenance projects in chemical plants.

The benefits of network planning techniques include the following:

◆ Graphical display of the project, including the relationships and sequence of activities.
◆ Estimate of the expected project length.
◆ Method for determining which activities are critical to the timely completion of the project and are therefore included in the critical path.
◆ Method for determining the amount of slack associated with individual project activities.

▶ **Program evaluation and review technique (PERT)**
Network planning technique used to determine a project's planned completion date and identify the project's critical path.

▶ **Critical path method (CPM)**
Network planning technique used to determine a project's planned completion date and identify the project's critical path.

▶ **Project activities**
Specific tasks that must be completed and that require resources.

▶ **Precedence relationships**
Establish the sequencing of activities to ensure that all necessary activities are completed before a subsequent activity is begun.

Both PERT and CPM portray the project as a network diagram. The **project activities** and their **precedence relationships** are illustrated in the network diagram by nodes (circles) and arrows. Project activities are actions that consume resources and/or time. For example, making the drawings for a new product is an activity—it takes time and uses resources (human and equipment). Precedent relationships structure the sequencing of activities; that is, you have to finish one before you can start the next. These are like course prerequisites: before you can enroll in an operations management class, you have to take a basic statistics course. In business, before a company can source materials for a new product, the designers have to finish the product design.

Project managers use these network planning techniques to

Identify project activities and precedent relationships. Project managers use this technique to create a document reflecting the activities, the responsible department, and the necessary resources (time, people, and equipment).

Calculate the expected completion time of the project. Project managers use this technique to plan additional projects and negotiate contracts with clients. For example, the customer may include a monetary penalty if the project is not completed by a certain date or a bonus if the project is completed ahead of schedule. The project manager can evaluate whether the probability risk of completing the project on schedule is acceptable or if additional resources are needed to assure timely completion.

> *Identify the activities critical to the timely completion of the project.* Project managers use this technique to identify activities that can be delayed without affecting the project's completion, to provide some flexibility for the project manager.

Suppose you are a project manager using network planning techniques. You would typically describe the project, diagram the network, estimate the project's completion time, and monitor the project's progression. Let's look at these four steps in detail.

Step 1   Describe the Project

Describe the project in terms that everyone involved will understand. Include the project objective and the project end date. For example, the project may be the release of a specific new product by September 15 or it may be ISO certification by the end of the calendar year. Given the project objective, define the project activities in terms of resource requirements (labor, equipment, and cash) and precedence relationships.

Step 2   Diagram the Network

Diagram the project as a network, visually displaying the interrelationships between the activities. The two kinds of network diagram are activity-on-arrow or activity-on-node. The **activity-on-arrow (AOA)** represents activities by arrows and **events** by nodes. An event is a point in time when one or more activities have been completed and one or more new activities can begin. An event consumes neither resources nor time. By convention, we usually number events sequentially from left to right in the diagram as shown in Figure 17-1. In activity-on-arrow diagrams, we must finish all activities entering into an event before we can begin any activity following the event. A good example of this is shown in Figure 17-1 (c). In this example, we must finish both activities a and b before we can begin either activity c or d.

> ▶ **Activity-on-arrow notation**
> A network diagramming approach that places activities on the arrows between events.

> ▶ **Events** signify the completion of an activity and need no resources.

> *Figure 17-1*
>
> *Network notation*

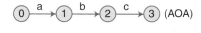

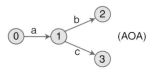

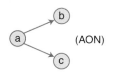

a. Activity a precedes activity b which precedes activity c

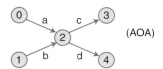

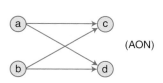

b. Activity a must be completed before activities b and c can begin.

c. Activities a and b must both be completed before activity c or d can begin.

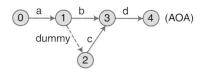

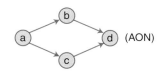

d. Activities b and c can begin once activity a has been completed, activity d cannot begin until both b and c are completed.

▶ **Activity-on-node**
Network diagramming notation that places activities in the nodes and arrows to signify precedence relationships.

The **activity-on-nodes (AON)** diagram represents activities by nodes and precedence relationships by arrows. Figure 17-1 (a) compares AOA and AON notation for the simple case in which we must do activity A before activity B, which we must do before activity C. Other examples comparing the two kinds of diagrams are shown in Figure 17-1. The diagrams in part (b) show an example in which we must finish activity A first and then begin both activities B and C. In AOA notation, activity A begins at event 0 and ends at event 1. Activity B begins at event 1 and ends at event 2, whereas activity C begins at event 1 and ends at event 3. In Figure 17-1 (c), we must finish both activities A and B before either activity C or D can begin. We must finish activities terminating at event 2 before we can begin any activities starting at event 2. The AON diagram shows that before we can begin activity C, we must finish both activities A and B. The same is true for activity D. Figure 17-1 (d) is an example in which we can begin two activities (B and C) when we finish activity A and we can begin activity D only after we finish both activities B and C. AOA notation does not allow activities to start at the same event and end at the same event. For example, activities B and C cannot both start at event 1 and both end at event 2. In these cases, we add a dummy activity to the network. As you can see, we added a dummy activity to the diagram in Figure 17-1 (d). We now have distinct routes from event 1 to event 3 for the two activities B and C. Activity B goes from event 1 to event 3, whereas activity C goes from event 1 to event 2 to event 3. Dummy activities consume neither time nor resources. We need the dummy activity to determine whether either of these activities is part of the project's **critical path**. The critical path is the longest sequential path of interrelated activities in the network and shows the minimum completion time for the project. Any delay in an activity that is on the critical path will delay the whole project. Let's diagram a sample project.

▶ **Critical path**
The longest sequential path through the network diagram.

■ **Example 17.1 AOA Diagram of the New Product Project for Cables By Us**

Two recent graduates, Michael and Elyssa, own Cables By Us, a company that produces cable assemblies. Business has been good so Michael and Elyssa have decided to expand their product line to include a new cable product. The new product will be manufactured in the current facility in an area not now in use. Michael and Elyssa have decided to use a project management approach to bring the new product on line. Let's help them through the process. Michael and Elyssa have identified 11 activities and their precedence relationships, as shown in Table 17-2. Develop an AOA diagram of the project.

Table 17-2   Project Activities and Precedence Relationships

Activity	Description	Immediate Predecessors
A	Develop product specifications	none
B	Design manufacturing process	A
C	Source and purchase materials	A
D	Source and purchase tooling and equipment	B
E	Receive and install tooling and equipment	D
F	Receive materials	C
G	Pilot production run	E, F
H	Evaluate product design	G
I	Evaluate process performance	G
J	Write documentation report	H, I
K	Transition to manufacturing	J

Solution:

In Figure 17-2, note that the project begins with event 0, which is when activity A can begin. On completion of activity A (event 1), both activities B and C can begin. Events can be arbitrarily numbered since the number is merely used to identify the event's location in the network.

Table 17-2 shows that we must finish activity A before we can begin either activity B or C. On completion of activity B, we can begin activity D. On completion of activity D, we can begin activity E. On completion of activity C, we can begin activity F. We cannot begin the pilot production run, activity G, until we finish both activities E and F. And we cannot write the documentation (activity J) until we finish both the product design evaluation and the process performance evaluation.

We add a dummy activity because both activities H and I can begin after activity G is completed, and both must be done before activity J can start. Activity G is finished at event 7, allowing activities H and I to begin. We add the dummy activity to uniquely identify each activity. Activity H goes from event 8 to event 9, whereas activity I goes from event 7 to event 9. The dummy activity links events 7 and 8.

Figure 17-2

AOA network diagram

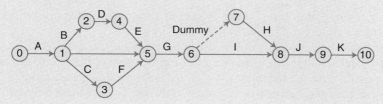

■ Example 17.2 AON Diagram of the New Product Project at Cables By Us

An alternative approach is the AON diagram. Construct the AON diagram.

Solution:

When we diagram the project placing the activities on the nodes, the diagram looks slightly different, as shown in Figure 17-3. AON notation does not use dummy activities.

Figure 17-3

Initial AON network diagram

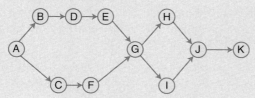

Step 3   Estimate the Project's Completion Time

To estimate the completion time of the project, the project manager evaluates the connected paths through the diagram to determine which of the routes takes the longest time. The longest connected route through the diagram is the critical path. The sum of the lengths of time of each of the activities on the critical path determines

Table 17-3 Deterministic Time Estimates		
Activity	**Description**	**Time Estimate (weeks)**
A	Develop product specifications	4
B	Design manufacturing process	6
C	Source and purchase materials	3
D	Source and purchase tooling and equipment	6
E	Receive and install tooling and equipment	14
F	Receive materials	5
G	Pilot production run	2
H	Evaluate product design	2
I	Evaluate process performance	3
J	Write documentation report	4
K	Transition to manufacturing	2

the minimum completion time for the project. If an activity on the critical path is delayed, the completion of the project is delayed.

We estimate the project completion time based on the time estimates for the project activities. Activity time estimates can be either **probabilistic** or **deterministic**. We use probabilistic time estimates when we are unsure about the duration of project activities—for example, because of technical problems, bad weather, delayed material delivery, and less than expected labor productivity. We use deterministic time estimates when we have done similar activities in the past and can make a reliable time estimate. Let's look first at estimating the project's completion date using deterministic time estimates.

> ▶ **Probabilistic time estimates** use optimistic, most likely, and pessimistic time estimates.

> ▶ **Deterministic time estimates** assume that the activity duration is known with certainty.

Step 3 (a)   Deterministic Time Estimates

With the deterministic time estimate, we make a single time estimate for each project activity. Table 17-3 shows the time estimates for each of Michael and Elyssa's project activities.

Given this information, we need to transfer the activity time requirement to the network diagram, as shown in Figure 17-4. We include the time estimate with the activity designator in the appropriate node. For example, activity A should take 4 weeks. We determine project completion time by calculating how long each of the paths through the network will take.

Figure 17-4

Identifying paths

Connected paths
1. A, B, D, E, G, H, J, K
2. A, B, D, E, G, I, J, K
3. A, C, F, G, H, J, K
4. A, C, F, G, I, J, K

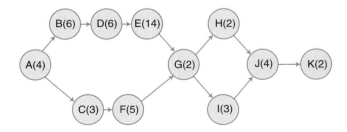

■ Example 17.3 Calculating the Path Completion Times Using Deterministic Time Estimates

Identify the four paths in the project, running from the beginning to the end, and calculate how long it takes to complete each path.

Solution:

For example, the first path includes activities A, B, D, E, G, H, J, and K. Add the time estimates for each of these activities together to find the length of time it takes to complete the path. Verify the results shown in Table 17-4.

Table 17-4   Completion Times for Each Path

Activities on Path	Completion Time (weeks)
A, B, D, E, G, H, J, K	40
A, B, D, E, G, I, J, K	41
A, C, F, G, H, J, K	22
A, C, F, G, I, J, K	23

Since the critical path is the longest connected path through the network, the critical path includes activities A, B, D, E, G, I, J, and K. Activities C, F, and H are not included on the critical path. When the project and the number of connected paths are larger, we can use another technique to estimate the project completion time and subsequently the project's critical path, discussed next.

We use *ES* (earliest start time), *EF* (earliest finish time), *LS* (latest start time), and *LF* (latest finish time) with the deterministic time estimates to find activities that have slack. Figure 17-5 shows the network diagram, and the *ES*s and *EF*s calculated. By convention, we start at time 0, which is the earliest any activity can begin. Since activity A must be done first, it has $ES = 0$. The earliest that activity A can be finished is its earliest start time plus the time it takes for the activity.

$$EF = ES + \text{activity time estimate}$$

or for activity A, it is

$$EF_A = ES_A + \text{activity A time estimate}$$

Figure 17-5

Early start, early finish network

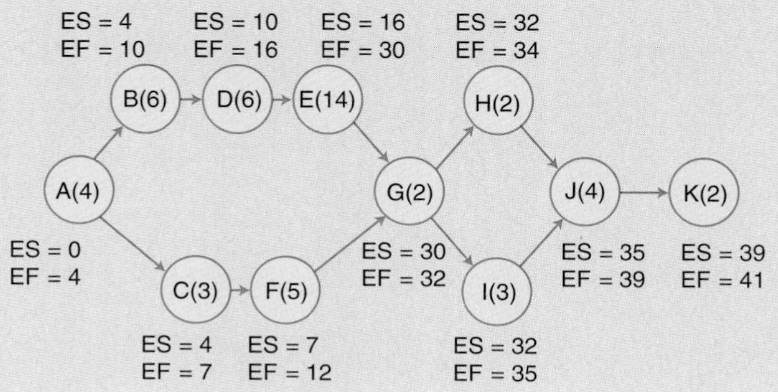

or

$$EF_A = 0 + 4 \text{ weeks, or 4 weeks}$$

The earliest that activity B can start equals the *EF* of the activity immediately preceding it (A), or 4, and the earliest activity B can be finished is time 10. Activity C can also begin at time 4 and can be done as early as time 7.

We continue calculating the *ES*s and *EF*s going from left to right through the diagram. When two activities must be completed (activities E and F) before another activity (G) can begin, we calculate the earliest finish time for both the preceding activities (E = 30 and F = 12). The activity with the larger *EF* determines the *ES* for the following activity (G in our case). Therefore, we cannot begin activity G before time 30 because that is the earliest that we can finish activity E. It does not matter that we can finish activity F by time 12: we must finish both activities before we can begin activity G. Eventually, we determine that the project should be completed in 41 weeks. After computing the *ES*s and *EF*s, we are ready to compute the *LS*s and *LF*s. Since we do not want the project to take any more time, we set the *LF* for the final activity equal to the *EF* for that activity. In our case, the final activity is K and the *EF* = 41. Figure 17-6 shows the network diagram with the *LS*s and *LF*s.

Using the *LF* for the final activity, we work from right to left through the network diagram. If time 41 is the latest that we can finish activity K without delaying the completion time of the project, then the latest we can begin activity K (2 weeks) is time 39. If we must begin activity K no later than time 39, then we must finish activity J no later than time 39. For activity J to be finished by time 39, we must begin it no later than time 35. If more than one activity (H and I) cannot be started until a preceding activity (G) is finished, we calculate the *LS* for both activities H and I. The *LS* for activity H is 33, whereas the *LS* for activity I is 32. When calculating which *LS* to use to determine the *LF* for activity G, we always use the smaller number. Remember that the latest we can begin activity I is time 32, so we must finish activity G by then. When we finish computing the *LS*s and *LF*s for the network, we can determine which activities are on the critical path. We identify activities that have no slack by comparing the *ES* value with the *LS* value. If these two values are equal, that activity has no slack.

Figure 17-6

Latest start, latest finish network

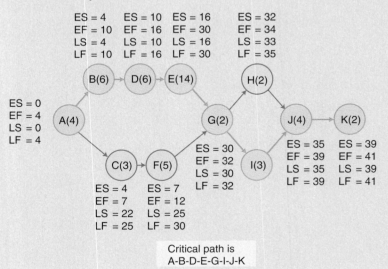

Critical path is
A-B-D-E-G-I-J-K

■ **Example 17.4 Finding the Critical Path**

Find the critical path for this project.

Solution:
To find the critical path of this project, we identify activities that have no slack. Each of these activities is on the critical path. Any activities with slack are not on the critical path. In this example, activities A, B, D, E, G, I, J, and K are on the critical path and activities C, F, and H have slack.

Step 3 (b)   Probabilistic Time Estimates

With probabilistic time estimates, we make three time estimates for each project activity: the **optimistic time**, the **most likely time**, and the **pessimistic time**. The optimistic time, denoted as (o), is the shortest time in which the activity can be completed. The most likely time, denoted as (m), is the most reasonable time estimate. The pessimistic time, denoted as (p), is the longest time in which the activity can be completed. Using Michael and Elyssa's plan for a new product, let's add some time estimates so we can determine the project's critical path. Table 17-5 shows the optimistic, most likely, and pessimistic time estimates for the project activities.

     When we calculate the expected time for an activity, we treat each activity time estimate as a random variable derived from a **beta probability distribution**. The beta distribution can have various shapes typically found in project management activities and has definite end points. These end points limit the possible completion times of the project between the optimistic and the pessimistic completion times. The most likely time completion date is the mode of the beta distribution. Figure 17-7 shows an example of a beta probability distribution.

     We use three time estimates to compute an expected time for finishing each of the activities. The expected time for each activity is a weighted average, calculated using the formula

$$\text{Expected time} = \frac{\text{optimistic time} + 4(\text{most likely time}) + \text{the pessimistic time}}{6}$$

For activity A, the expected time is 4 weeks.

$$\text{Expected time}_A = \frac{2 + 4(4) + 6}{6} = \frac{24}{6} = 4 \text{ weeks}$$

▶ **Optimistic time**
The shortest time period in which the activity can be completed.

▶ **Most likely time**
The normal time that the activity is expected to take.

▶ **Pessimistic time**
The longest time period in which the activity will be completed.

▶ **The beta probability distribution** typically represents project activities.

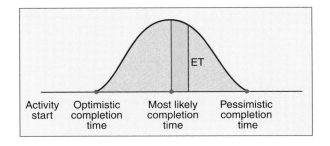

Figure 17-7

Beta distribution

■ **Example 17.5 Calculating the Expected Times**

Using the preceding formula, calculate the expected times for each of the activities in the Cable By Us project. Table 17-5 shows the expected time for each of the activities. Note that in some cases, the optimistic, most likely, and pessimistic times can be identical, as it is for activities G and K. For those activities, no uncertainty exists; we know for sure how long those activities will take. Also note that the dummy activity takes no time but that we use it to clarify the network diagram.

Table 17-5   Probabilistic Time Estimates

Activity	Description	Optimistic Time (o) (weeks)	Most Likely Time (m) (weeks)	Pessimistic Time (p) (weeks)	Expected Time (ET) (weeks)
A	Develop product specifications	2	4	6	4
B	Design manufacturing process	3	7	10	6.83
C	Source and purchase materials	2	3	5	3.17
D	Source and purchase tooling and equipment	4	7	9	6.83
E	Receive and install tooling and equipment	12	16	20	16
F	Receive materials	2	5	8	5
G	Pilot production run	2	2	2	2
H	Evaluate product design	2	3	4	3
I	Evaluate process performance	2	3	5	3.17
J	Write documentation report	2	4	6	4
K	Transition to manufacturing	2	2	2	2

The next step is to transfer the expected activity times to the network diagram, as shown in Figure 17-8. Now we determine the critical path through the project. We have two ways to find the critical path. The first, which is more practical for small network diagrams, is to calculate the expected time each path through the network takes to complete. In Figure 17-8, we can see four connected or sequential paths through the project. Table 17-6 shows these paths and the expected times to complete them.

The first connected path includes activities A, B, D, E, G, dummy, H, J, and K. The second path includes activities A, B, D, E, G, I, J, and K. The third path includes activities A, C, F, G, dummy, H, J, and K. The fourth path includes activities A, C, F, G, I, J, and K. There are no other connected paths through the project. To calculate the expected time of each path, we sum the expected times for the activities on the path. For example, we expect the first path to take 44.66 weeks (4 weeks for activity A + 6.83 weeks for activity B + 6.83 weeks for ac-

Figure 17-8

Initial AOA network diagram

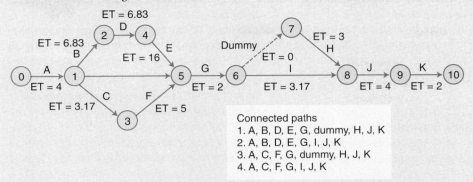

Connected paths
1. A, B, D, E, G, dummy, H, J, K
2. A, B, D, E, G, I, J, K
3. A, C, F, G, dummy, H, J, K
4. A, C, F, G, I, J, K

tivity D + 16 weeks for activity E + 2 weeks for activity G + 0 weeks for the dummy activity + 3 weeks for activity H + 4 weeks for activity J + 2 weeks for activity K). The critical path is the longest connected path through the network. Therefore, the second path A, B, D, E, G, I , J, K is the critical path and determines the expected completion time for the project.

Table 17-6   Paths Through the Network

Activities on Path	Expected Completion Time (weeks)
A, B, D, E, G, dummy, H, J, K	44.66
A, B, D, E, G, I, J, K	44.83
A, C, F, G, dummy, H, J, K	23.17
A, C, F, G, I, J, K	23.34

An alternative method for determining the expected project duration using probabilistic time estimates is to find which activities have slack time. These are the activities we can delay without affecting the project completion date.

■ Example 17.6 Calculating Earliest Start Times

Given Michael and Elyssa's project, let's determine which activities have slack. The diagram in Figure 17-9 shows the addition of *TEs*. *TE* is the earliest time we can begin an activity following another event.

Solution:
Calculate the earliest start times for each event in the network. For example, we can begin activity A as early as time 0, whereas we can begin activity B as early as time 4. We calculate these numbers going from left to right. By convention, we set the timing at 0 to begin the project. We should finish activity A between events 0 and 1. The expected time to finish activity A is 4 weeks. Therefore, the earliest we expect to be at event 1 is 4 weeks (the earliest time we could leave event 0, plus the expected time to complete activity A). We continue through the diagram. The earliest time we can reach event 2 is 10.83 weeks, which is the TE of 4 weeks at event 1, plus the 6.83 weeks expected time to finish activity B.

When we have to finish two or more activities at an event, such as activities E and F going into event 5, we calculate the *TE* associated with each activity. Figure 17-9 shows that we can begin activity F as early as time 7.17 weeks and we expect it to take 5 weeks. Therefore, we could finish it as early as time 12.17 weeks. We cannot begin activity E until time 17.66 weeks and we expect it to take 16 weeks. Therefore, we cannot finish activity E before time 33.66 weeks. Since we have to finish both activities E and F before we can begin activity G, the earliest we can begin activity G is time 33.66 weeks. (Note that whenever two or more activities go into the same event, the *TE* of the event is the larger of the incoming activities.)

Figure 17-9

Earliest start AOA network

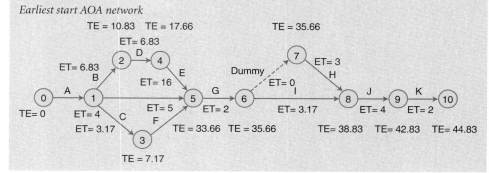

■ Example 17.7 Computing the Latest Start Times

The Gantt chart in Figure 17-10 shows the project with each activity finished at the earliest possible start date. Note that we cannot begin activity D until we finish both activities B and C. We can begin activity F as soon as we finish activity C.

Figure 17-10

Earliest start Gantt chart

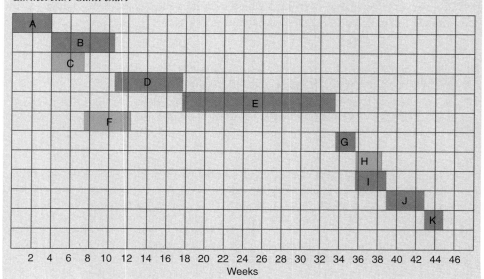

Figure 17-11

Final AOA network diagram

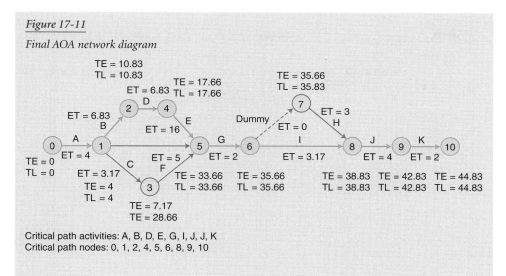

Critical path activities: A, B, D, E, G, I, J, J, K
Critical path nodes: 0, 1, 2, 4, 5, 6, 8, 9, 10

Solution

In Figure 17-11, we have added *TL*s to the network diagram. *TL* is the latest time we can begin an activity without delaying the project's completion. By convention, we set the *TL* for the final event equal to the *TE* for the final event (44.83 weeks in this example). To calculate the *TL*s for each event, we work from right to left through the diagram. For example, the *TL* for event 9 is the *TL* for event 10, minus the expected time to finish activity K (44.83 − 2). The *TL* for event 8 is the *TL* for event 9, minus the expected time to finish activity J. When we have two activities going back to a common event such as activities B and C, we calculate the *TL* for each of the activities and use the smaller one. For example, the *TL* at event 2 is 10.83 weeks and the expected time to finish activity B is 6.83 weeks, so the *TL* for event 1 is 4 weeks. However, the *TL* at event 3 is 28.66 weeks, and the expected time to complete activity C (3.17 weeks), so the *TL* for event 1 is 25.49 weeks. Activity C can be delayed without affecting the project's completion time, but activity B cannot; therefore, the smaller number must be used for the *TL* at event 1.

The Gantt chart in Figure 17-12 shows the project schedule using the latest possible start times for each of the activities if the project is to be completed in 44.83 weeks.

When we compare the earliest start schedule with the latest start schedule, we can see that three activities (C, F, and G) have different starting and ending times. We can start activity C as early as week 4 or as late as week 25.49, so activity C has slack. The same is true for activity F: we can start it as early as week 7.17 and as late as week 28.66. Activity H has less slack. We can start it as early as week 35.66 and no later than week 35.83. Since each of these activities has slack, we do not include them in the project's critical path.

When we have computed the *TE*s and *TL*s for each event, we can determine which events are on the critical path. *All events that have equal TEs and TLs are on the critical path.* From Figure 17-12, we can see that events 0, 1, 2, 4, 5, 6, 8, 9, and 10 are all on the critical path. Events 3 and 7 are not on the critical path, and activities associated with either of these events are also not on the critical path. Thus activities C and F, which are associated with event 3, are not on the critical path. The dummy activity and activity H are also not on the critical path. Any activity not on the critical path has slack time, so we can delay the completion of that activity and not delay the completion time of the project. To illustrate this, let's look at our network diagram in

Figure 17-12

Latest start Gantt chart

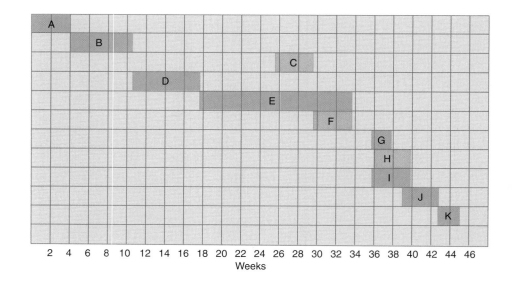

Figure 17-11. We can see that activities C and F together need only an expected time of 8.17 weeks. The other activities that we must finish before event 5—activities B, D, and E—are expected to take 29.66 weeks. The difference (21.49 weeks) represents how long we can delay activities C and F and still not affect the project's completion date. As long as we finish C and F by time 33.66, we can finish the project as planned.

Step 4   Monitor the Project's Progression

Even though you have carefully planned the project, things happen that can affect its progress. Parts or equipment may arrive later than expected, materials may not meet

Dilbert's approach to project management

quality specifications and need to be replaced, less labor than expected was available, and bad weather—all can delay the project's completion. Planning the project is necessary but monitoring its progress is even more important in meeting the scheduled completion date. You focus initially on activities in the critical path since any delay in these activities delays the whole project. You are also aware of activities not on the critical path that have little slack because a relatively short delay in these activities can affect the project's completion time.

One large-scale project to manage is the Olympic Games—a project that necessitates an exceptional amount of advance research and planning. The logistics infrastructures of the city that hosts the Olympic Games and the Organizing Committee for the Games both have to oversee hundreds of smaller projects that culminate to ensure a successful run of the Olympics. From tasks such as shipping and receiving the

LINKS TO PRACTICE
Managing the Olympic Games
www.olympics.com

tremendous amount of freight (for example, broadcast equipment) to facilitating the stay of the athletes, project managers must pay close attention to details. Of course, with such a large-scale event comes a myriad of problems, such as enough timely transportation, leadership changes, and security concerns. However, only with extensive preparation can such a large-scale event be successful.

Before You Go On

Be sure that you understand how to use network planning techniques.

1. Describe the project in terms of your objective, the project activities, and the precedence relationships.
2. Estimate the project activities. For probabilistic time estimates, make an optimistic, most likely, and pessimistic estimate and compute the expected time for each project activity. For deterministic time estimates: Make a single time estimate for each activity.
3. Diagram the project using either activity-on-arrow or activity-on-node notation to reflect the precedence relationships between activities.

ESTIMATING THE PROBABILITY OF COMPLETION DATES ■

An advantage of using probabilistic time estimates is the ability to predict the probability of project completion dates. We learned how to calculate the expected time for each activity with the three time estimates provided. Now we need to calculate the variance for each activity. The variance of the beta probability distribution for each activity is

$$\sigma^2 = \left(\frac{p - o}{6} \right)^2$$

where p = pessimistic activity time estimate
o = optimistic activity time estimate

■ Example 17.8 Calculating the Variance of Activities

Calculate the variance of each of the activities in the Cables By Us project. Begin with activity A, which has variance

$$\sigma_A^2 = \left(\frac{6-2}{6}\right)^2 = \left(\frac{4}{6}\right)^2 = 0.44$$

Verify the variances for each activity shown in Table 17-7.

Table 17-7   Project Activity Variance

Activity	Optimistic Time	Most Likely Time	Pessimistic Time	Variance
A	2	4	6	0.44
B	3	7	10	1.36
C	2	3	5	0.25
D	4	7	9	0.69
E	12	16	20	1.78
F	2	5	8	1.00
G	2	2	2	0.00
H	2	3	4	0.11
I	2	3	5	0.25
J	2	4	6	0.44
K	2	2	2	0.00

Using the variance for each activity, we can calculate the variance for paths through the network. We identified four possible paths through the network in Table 17-4. To calculate the variance for a specific path through the network, we add together the variances for each activity on the path. For example, the variance for the critical path A, B, D, E, G, I, J, K is 4.96 weeks (0.44 + 1.36 + 0.69 + 1.78 + 0.00 + 0.25 + 0.44 + 0.00). The size of the variance reflects the degree of uncertainty for the path. The greater the variance, the greater is the uncertainty. The variance for the second longest path through the network (A, B, D, E, G, dummy, H, J, K) is 4.82 weeks. Remember that a dummy activity takes up neither time nor resources. Table 17-8 shows the four specific paths and their variances.

Table 17-8   Variances of Paths through the Network

Path Number	Activities on Path	Path Variance (weeks)
1	A, B, D, E, G, dummy, H, J, K	4.82
2	A, B, D, E, G, I, J, K	4.96
3	A, C, F, G, dummy, H, J, K	2.24
4	A, C, F, G, I, J, K	2.38

When you know the expected completion time of each path and its variance, you can determine the probability of specific completion dates. For example, you may want to know the probability of completing the project in 48 weeks. We can use the following formula to determine the probability of finishing each of the paths at a specified date:

$$z = \frac{\text{specified time } - \text{ path expected completion time}}{\text{path standard deviation}}$$

or

$$z = \left(\frac{D_T - T_E}{\sqrt{\sigma_P^2}} \right)$$

where D_T = the specified completion date
T_E = the expected completion time of the path
σ_P^2 = variance of path

For a particular path through the project, the *z value* shows the path's number of standard deviations that the specified time is past the expected path completion time. A negative z-value shows that the specified time is earlier than the expected path completion time. After calculating the z-value, you can look up the z-value in Appendix B to determine the probability of finishing the path by the specified time. Note that the probability of finishing the path by the specified time equals the area under the normal curve to the left of z, as shown in Figure 17-13.

Figure 17-13

Probability of path 1 finished in 48 days

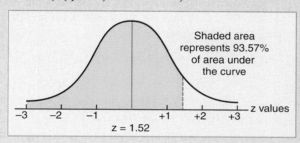

■ Example 17.9 Calculating the Probability of Finishing the Project in 48 Weeks

Michael and Elyssa want to know the probability of finishing the project in 48 weeks.

Solution:
We compute the probability of path number 1 as follows:

$$z = \frac{48 \text{ weeks } - 44.66 \text{ weeks}}{\sqrt{4.82}} = 1.52$$

The z-value of 1.52 in Appendix A shows that there is a 0.9357 probability of finishing the path in no longer than 48 weeks. Conversely, there is only a 0.0643 probability of not finishing this path by 48 weeks. Table 17-9 shows the z-value calculations and the probability of completion for the other three paths.

Table 17-9 Z-Value Calculations and Path Probabilities of Finishing in 48 Weeks

Path Number	Activities on Path	Path Variance (weeks)	z-value	Probability of Completion
1	A, B, D, E, G, dummy, H, J, K	4.82	1.5216	0.9357
2	A, B, D, E, G, I, J, K	4.96	1.4215	0.9222
3	A, C, F, G, dummy, H, J, K	2.24	16.5898	1.000
4	A, C, F, G, I, J, K	2.38	15.9847	1.000

In general, we give any activity with a z-value of 2.50 or larger a 100% probability of completion by the specified time. You may be more concerned with the probability of the critical path's completion by the specified time. Still, it is a good idea to determine the probability of other paths with similar completion times. The probability of finishing the critical path for this project in 48 weeks is 0.9222. It is true that a delay in any activity in the critical path will delay the project's completion. This does not mean, however, that we ignore what happens in the other paths. Other paths' lengths through the project are sometimes almost the same as the critical path. Thus an extended delay or delay in a combination of activities on an alternate path could ultimately delay the project's completion.

■ REDUCING PROJECT COMPLETION TIME

You may need to reduce the time you spend finishing a particular project because of deadlines, promised completion dates, penalty clauses for late completion, or the need to put resources on a new project. When you plan a project, you make time estimates based on normal procedures and resources. However, you may be able to speed up a project by making additional resources available. For example, your company could have materials shipped via premium rather than normal transportation to get the materials faster and the activity finished sooner. You could authorize overtime to speed

Night work speeds completion.

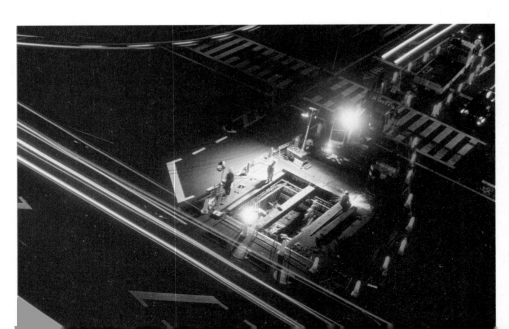

up an activity. Another possibility as is done in highway construction, is to bring in lights so workers can work through the night and minimize traffic disruptions. Whatever the method, you can often reduce the time needed to finish an activity.

Crashing Projects

At the same time that you shorten a project's duration, you also need to minimize the additional expense. We call shortening a project **crashing** the project. To crash the project and minimize expense, you need additional information about your project activities. Let's use Michael and Elyssa's project with deterministic time estimates (shown in Figure 17-6). Table 17-10 shows the new crashing information.

▶ **Crashing**
Reducing the completion time of the project.

Table 17-10 Normal and Crash Cost Estimates

Activity	Normal Time (weeks)	Normal Cost ($)	Crash Time (weeks)	Crash Cost ($)	Maximum weeks of reduction	Cost per week to reduce ($)
A	4	8,000	3	11,000	1	3,000
B	6	30,000	5	35,000	1	5,000
C	3	6,000	3	6,000	0	0
D	6	24,000	4	28,000	2	2,000
E	14	60,000	12	72,000	2	6,000
F	5	5,000	4	6,500	1	1,500
G	2	6,000	2	6,000	0	0
H	2	4,000	2	4,000	0	0
I	3	4,000	2	5,000	1	1,000
J	4	4,000	2	6,400	2	1,200
K	2	5,000	2	5,000	0	0

Note that we cannot reduce all activities, so for those activities the maximum number of weeks we reduce is set to 0. Also note that reducing the lengths of different activities costs different amounts. We can reduce activity I by one week for a cost of $1000, whereas we can reduce activity B by one week for a cost of $5000. When you need to reduce the length of a project, you first consider reducing activities on the critical path. Activities not on the critical path have slack and typically do not need to be reduced.

■ Example 17.10 Crashing the Project

Suppose you are the project manager for Cables By Us. Consider what activities you would crash if Michael and Elyssa want to finish their project in 36 weeks. A quick look at Figure 17-6 shows you that the normal project completion time is 41 weeks and the critical path includes activities A, B, D, E, G, I, J, and K. You need to consider crashing these activities to reduce the overall project length from 41 to 36 weeks. Table 17-10 shows that activities G and K cannot be crashed so you eliminate them. Table 17-11 shows the remaining activities on the critical path.

Solution:
To minimize the cost to crash the project, look in the last column for the least expensive critical path activity to crash per week. Activity I costs $1000 to crash per week and you can crash it by 1 week. If you crash activity I by 1 week, the project will take 40 weeks. You still need to cut the project by four more weeks. The next least expensive activity to crash is activity J. It costs $1200 per week to crash and you can crash it for 2 weeks. This reduces the project's length to 38 weeks. The next least expensive activity to crash is activity D at a cost of $2000 per week and you can crash it for 2 weeks. This reduces the total project duration to 36 weeks at a cost of $7400.

Crash activity I from 3 weeks to 2 weeks	$1000
Crash activity J from 4 weeks to 2 weeks	$2400
Crash activity D from 6 weeks to 4 weeks	$4000
Total Crash Cost	$7400

Table 17-11   Normal and Crash Cost Estimates for Remaining Critical Path Activities

Activity	Normal Time (weeks)	Normal Cost ($)	Crash Time (weeks)	Crash Cost ($)	Maximum Weeks of Reduction	Cost per Week to Reduce ($)
A	4	8,000	3	11,000	1	3,000
B	6	30,000	5	35,000	1	5,000
D	6	24,000	4	28,000	2	2,000
E	14	60,000	12	72,000	2	6,000
I	3	4,000	2	5,000	1	1,000
J	4	4,000	2	6,400	2	1,200

Figure 17-14 shows the revised network diagram.

Figure 17-14

Crashed project diagram

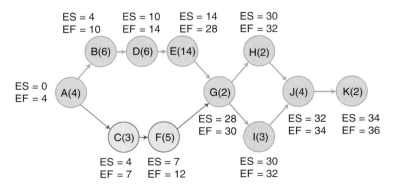

Critical path: A, B, D, E, G, H, J, K
A, B, D, E, G, I, J, K

Before You Go On

In summary, to reduce project length, you need this information:

1. Normal activity time estimate and normal activity cost
2. Crash activity time estimate and crash activity cost
3. The activities on the critical path

When you have this information, you need to do the following:

1. Determine how much the project needs to be reduced.
2. Determine which activities on the critical path can be reduced.
3. Crash critical activities on the basis of increasing cost.
   ◆ Crash the least expensive activity first, the next least expensive second, and so on, until you have shortened the project to the desired length.
   ◆ Calculate the total costs associated with crashing the project and determine whether the cost is justified.

THE CRITICAL CHAIN APPROACH ■

The **critical chain approach** is to get projects done faster and more consistently at or before the project due date. The focus is on the final due date rather than on individual activities or project milestones. The idea of the critical chain is that project activities are uncertain. Because of this uncertainty, we add safety time to project time estimates. In some cases, the safety time added exceeds 200% of the work time estimate.

▶ **The critical chain approach** is based on the theory of constraints.

Adding Safety Time

We have three ways to add safety time. First, we base time estimates on a pessimistic experience. Most time estimates include enough safety time to ensure that the project activity is completed on time 80 to 90% of the time. From statistics, we know that to cover 80 to 90% of the area under the curve, we have to add a substantial safety factor. Second, the more management levels involved, the greater the safety factor. Since no manager wants to look bad, we add more safety factors (perhaps an extra 10 to 20%). When each management level adds this safety factor, the total safety is greatly increased. Third, top management may make global reductions in project length. If we know that the total project length is likely to be reduced by 20 to 25%, we inflate our time estimate by 20 to 25%.

Wasting Safety Time

Just as we have three ways to add safety time, we have three ways to waste safety time. One is the student syndrome. If we have 6 weeks allotted for an activity that should take only 2 weeks, we do not start it until 2 weeks before it is due. Then if anything unexpected happens, we miss the due date because we wasted the safety cushion. A second way is multitasking, which uses a person or resource for more than one project. Thus we have to decide which project to work on: assigning resources to a low-priority project wastes valuable safety time. On the other hand, the amount of safety time may be the reason for using it on a lower-priority project. Suppose we have two activities. Activity A is on schedule and has plenty of safety time, whereas activity B is

Comparing Critical Paths

Activity A	Activity B	Activity C	Activity D	Activity E

Original critical path

Activity A	Activity B	Activity C	Activity D	Activity E	Project Buffer

Critical path with project buffer

Figure 17-15

Comparing critical paths

behind schedule and has little safety time. Typically we work on activity B first and waste activity A's safety time. The third way to waste safety time comes from dependencies between activities in which delays accumulate and advances are wasted. Let's look at an example. Activity A is scheduled to take 10 days. Activity B is scheduled to start on day 10 after activity A is finished. Think about what happens if we finish activity A in 8 days. Do we start activity B earlier? Typically, no: we start activity B on day 10 as originally planned and we waste the safety time. What happens if we do not finish activity A until day 12? When do we start activity B? Day 12. The delays accumulate and they are passed on.

How does the critical chain approach solve the problem of safety time? The critical chain removes safety time from the individual activities and puts the total safety time at the end of the critical path, which creates a **project buffer**. Let's compare the critical paths shown in Figure 17-15. The completion time is the same but the original critical path has safety time added to each activity. The critical path with the project buffer eliminates the individual safety times. Activities not finished on time eat into the project buffer instead of wasting activity safety time.

▶ **Project buffer**
Safety time placed at the end of the critical path.

Since the theory of constraints (discussed in Chapter 16), which is the basis of the critical chain, focuses on keeping the bottleneck busy, we can put time buffers before bottlenecks in the critical path, as shown in Figure 17-16. The feeding buffer protects the critical path from delays in noncritical paths. When the delay exceeds the feeding buffer, the project completion date is still protected by the project buffer. (For more information, see *Critical Chain* by Eliyahu M. Goldratt.)

Figure 17-16

Example with feeder buffers

Example with Feeder Buffers

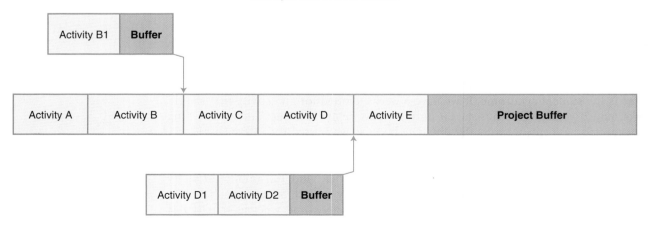

OM ACROSS THE ORGANIZATION

Since projects tend to be long term and consume a company's resources, functional areas across the company work with expected completion dates, resource requirements, and the consequences of activity delays. Let's look at how the functional areas use project management information.

Accounting uses project management information to provide a time line for major expenditures associated with the project. Accounting measures actual cost performance against planned costs to calculate profits. Accounting also calculates the cost benefit of crashing a particular project.

Marketing uses project management information to monitor the progress of a project and to provide honest and realistic updates to the customer. The project schedule allows marketing to evaluate whether or not to crash a project.

Information systems develop and maintain the software that supports project management. Choosing, installing, and training users in the appropriate software is vital to successful project management.

Purchasing uses project management information to deal with project delays by deexpediting items and rescheduling these items for later delivery. This allows the company to keep a lower inventory investment. Purchasing can also suggest when to avoid late deliveries to keep the project on schedule and how to reduce delivery time to help put a project back on schedule.

Operations uses project management information to monitor the progress of activities on and off the critical path, and to manage resource requirements in terms of the quantity and time needed for operations. Within an organization, the project manager or an assistant may develop the project schedule, typically using software for projects with many activities. Project managers can be product managers, manufacturing engineers, operations analysts, or office managers. Project management is a function not only of manufacturing companies but of service organizations too. Suppose you are planning the worldwide tour of a major art exhibit. Project scheduling techniques will help you effectively manage the many activities in this and other similar projects for your organization.

OM IS EVERYWHERE ■

You may have only a few major projects to manage in your personal life: a wedding, a political campaign, a round-the-world vacation. But for each one of these, project management techniques will make the process more efficient and the results more satisfying than if you try to "wing it." Project management techniques identify the project activities and the resources you will need. These techniques help prevent delays and eliminate last-minute emergencies. Think about the preparations for a wedding and all the interrelated activities our couple has to juggle between the day they send the invitations and the Big Day itself. Planning, scheduling, adding safety cushions, preparing for contingencies—all these project management techniques are as valuable in your personal life as they are in business.

CHAPTER HIGHLIGHTS

1 A project is a unique, one-time event of some duration (weeks, months, or even years) that consumes resources (human, capital, materials, and equipment capacity) and is designed to achieve an objective in a given time period. In business, projects can be designing new products, installing new systems, constructing new facilities, mounting advertising campaigns, designing information systems, and developing company Web pages. In politics, a project can be designing a political campaign.

2 Each project goes through a five-phase life cycle: concept, feasibility study, planning, execution, and termination. In the concept phase, we identify the need for the project. With the feasibility study, we evaluate expected costs, benefits, and risks. Planning consists of calculating the work and the time to do it; execution is doing the work; and termination is finishing the project.

3 Two network planning techniques are PERT and CPM. PERT uses probabilistic time estimates. CPM uses deterministic time estimates.

4 PERT and CPM determine the critical path of the project and the estimated completion time. On smaller projects, we determine completion time by evaluating each connected path through the network. On larger projects, software programs are available to identify the critical path.

5 PERT uses probabilistic time estimates to determine the probability that a project will be done by a specified time. We calculate a z-value and then determine the probability that the critical path and other near critical paths will be completed by a given date.

6 To reduce the length of a project, we need to know the critical path of the project and the cost of reducing individual activity times. Crashing activities that are not on the critical path typically does not reduce project completion time.

7 The critical chain approach removes excess safety time from individual activities and creates a project buffer at the end of the critical path. Feeder buffers are used on noncritical paths merged with the critical path.

KEY TERMS

project 520
PERT 522
CPM 522
project activities 522
precedence relationships 522
activity-on-arrow 523

events 523
activity-on-node 524
critical path 524
probabilistic time estimates 526
deterministic time estimates 526
optimistic time estimate 529

most likely time estimate 529
pessimistic time estimate 529
beta probability distribution 529
crashing 539
critical chain 541
project buffer 542

FORMULA REVIEW

Expected time for each activity:

$$\text{Expected time} = \frac{\text{optimistic time} + 4(\text{most likely time}) + \text{the pessimistic time}}{6}$$

Variance for each activity:

$$\sigma^2 = \left(\frac{p - o}{6}\right)^2$$

Calculating the z-value to estimate probability of completion:

$$z = \frac{\text{specified time} - \text{path expected completion time}}{\text{path standard deviation}} \quad \text{or} \quad z = \left(\frac{D_T - T_E}{\sqrt{\sigma_P^2}}\right)$$

SOLVED PROBLEMS

■ Solved Problem 1

Use the following information to diagram the project network.

Activity	Immediate Predecessors
A	none
B	A
C	A
D	B
E	C
F	D, E
G	F

a. Diagram the network using AOA notation.
b. Diagram the network using AON notation.

Solution:

a. When you diagram the project, the first activity is A. It must be done before either B or C can begin. At event 1, both activities B and C can begin. At event 2, activity B is finished and activity D can begin. At event 3, activity C is finished and activity E can begin. At event 4, both activities D and E are finished and F can begin. Figure 17-17 shows the diagrammed network.

Figure 17-17

AOA network diagram

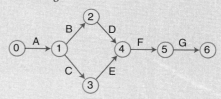

b. The AON notation is straightforward for this project. Activity A is done first, then activities B and C can begin. When B is done, activity D begins. When C is done, activity E begins. Activity F begins after both D and E are finished. Figure 17-18 shows the diagrammed network.

Figure 17-18

AON network diagram

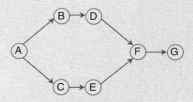

■ Solved Problem 2

Your boss gives you the following information about the new project you are leading. The information includes the activities, the three time estimates, and the precedence relationships, as shown in Figure 17-19.

Activity	Optimistic Time (wks)	Most likely Time (wks)	Pessimistic Time (wks)
A	6	10	14
B	3	6	10
C	4	8	10
D	5	6	7
E	4	6	12
F	3	3	3
G	3	4	5

a. Calculate the expected time for each of the activities.
b. Determine the expected completion time of the project.
c. Calculate the variance of each of the project activities.
d. Determine the probability that each of the connected paths through the project will be completed within 30 weeks.

Solution:

a. We calculate the expected time for an activity using the following formula:

$$\text{Expected time} = \frac{\text{optimistic time} + 4(\text{most likely time}) + \text{pessimistic time}}{6}$$

We calculate the expected time for activity A as

$$\text{Expected time}_A = \frac{6 + 4(10) + 14}{6} = 10 \text{ weeks}$$

The expected times for each of the activities are shown in Spreadsheet 17.2.

b. Using Figure 17-19, we can identify the two connected paths running through the project. The first path includes activities A, B, D, F, and G and needs 29.17 weeks to complete. The second path includes activities A, C, E, F, and G and needs 31.34 weeks to complete.

c. We calculate the variance using the formula

$$\sigma^2 = \left(\frac{p - o}{6}\right)^2$$

Spreadsheet 17.2

CALCULATION OF EXPECTED TIME

Activity	Optimistic Time	Most Likely	Pessimistic Time	Expected Time	Standard Dev	Variance
A	6	10	14	10.00	1.33	1.78
B	3	6	10	6.17	1.17	1.36
C	4	8	10	7.67	1.00	1.00
D	5	6	7	6.00	0.33	0.11
E	4	6	12	6.67	1.33	1.78
F	3	3	3	3.00	0.00	0.00
G	3	4	5	4.00	0.33	0.11

CALCULATION OF TOTAL PROJECT TIME

Activity	Expected Time	Precedence 1	Precedence 2	Task	Early Start	Early Finish	Late Start	Late Finish	Slack
A	10.00			A	0.00	10.00	0.00	10.00	0.00
B	6.17	A		B	10.00	16.17	12.17	18.34	2.17
C	7.67	A		C	10.00	17.67	10.01	17.68	0.01
D	6.00	B		D	16.17	22.17	18.34	24.34	2.17
E	6.67	C		E	17.67	24.34	17.67	24.34	0.00
F	3.00	D	E	F	24.34	27.34	24.34	27.34	0.00
G	4.00	F		G	27.34	31.34	27.34	31.34	0.00
				Project Time		**31.34**			

Figure 17-19

Project diagram

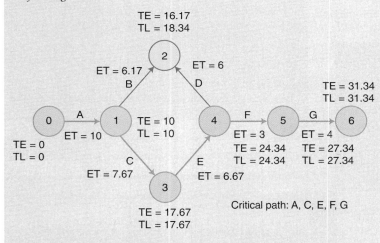

Critical path: A, C, E, F, G

We calculate the variance associated with activity A as

$$\sigma_A^2 = \left(\frac{p-o}{6}\right)^2 = \left(\frac{14-6}{6}\right)^2 = 1.78$$

All the variances are shown in Spreadsheet 17-2.

d. To determine the probability of completing the project in 30 weeks, we need to calculate the variance for each path through the project. We do this by summing the individual variances of each activity included on the path. For the first path, A, B, D, F, and G, the variance is 3.36 weeks. The variance for the second path A, C, E, F,

and G is 4.67 weeks. We use the following formula to determine the probability of completion by a specified time.

$$z = \left(\frac{D_T - T_E}{\sqrt{\sigma_P^2}}\right)$$

The probability that the first path (A, B, D, F, G) will be completed within 30 weeks is

$$z = \left(\frac{30 - 29.17}{\sqrt{3.36}}\right) = 0.45$$

A z-value of 0.45 equates to a probability of 0.6736, or a 67.36% chance of this path being completed in 30 weeks. The probability that the second path (A, C, E, F, G) will be completed within 30 weeks is

$$z = \left(\frac{30 - 31.34}{\sqrt{4.67}}\right) = -0.62$$

A z-value of -0.62 equates to a probability of 0.2676, or a 26.76% chance that this path will be completed in 30 weeks.

This problem can also be solved using a spreadsheet. This is shown in Spreadsheet 17.2.

■ Solved Problem 3

You are in charge of a new project that needs to be completed within 24 weeks. Figure 17-20 shows the network diagram and other relevant information.

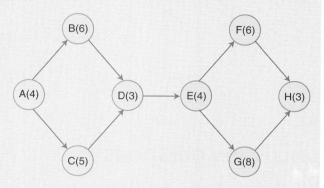

Critical path: A, B, D, E, G, H

Figure 17-20

Project diagram

Activity	Normal Time	Normal Cost ($)	Crash Time	Crash Cost ($)	Maximum Weeks Crashed	Crash cost per week ($)
A	4	4,000	3	4,500	1	500
B	6	9,000	6	9,000	0	0
C	5	1,500	3	2,000	2	250
D	3	6,000	2	9,000	1	3,000
E	4	8,000	2	16,000	2	4,000
F	6	3,000	5	3,500	1	500
G	8	4,000	6	6,000	2	1,000
H	3	3,600	2	4,800	1	1,200

Solution:

First we need to determine the completion time for the project. Using Figure 17-20, we can identify the four paths through the project and calculate the project completion time. The first path (A, B, D, E, F, H) takes 26 weeks (4 + 6 + 3 + 4 + 6 + 3). Each of the paths and its completion time are shown here.

Path	Completion Time (weeks)
A, B, D, E, F, H	26
A, B, D, E, G, H	28
A, C, D, E, F, H	25
A, C, D, E, G, H	27

We determine the time to finish this project by the connected path that takes the longest time to complete. In this case, the completion time is 28 weeks. The critical path of this project includes activities A, B, D, E, G, and H.

Given the crash costs, we need to reduce the completion time from 28 weeks to 24 weeks. To do this, we consider the activities on the critical path and their associated crash cost. We do not need to consider crashing activities C or F because they are not part of the critical path and we cannot crash activity B because it cannot be reduced. Of the remaining activities, the least expensive activity to crash is A, which we can crash 1 week at a cost of $500. Since we want to reduce the project by 4 weeks, we have to find additional reductions. The next least expensive activity to crash is G, which we can crash 2 weeks at a total cost of $2000. We need only one more week of reduction. Activity H is the next least expensive activity to crash, at $1200 per week. By crashing these three activities, we can finish the project in 24 weeks. The additional cost for crashing the project is $3700 ($500 for A, $2000 for G, and $1200 for H). Figure 17-21 shows the crashed project diagram.

Figure 17-21

Crashed project diagram

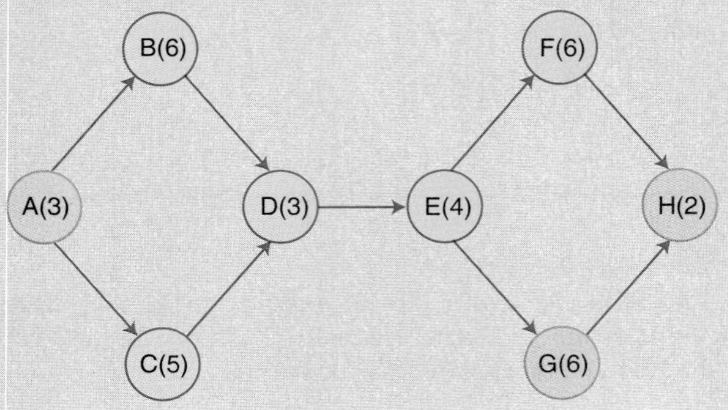

DISCUSSION QUESTIONS

1. Identify some projects that are currently underway in your community. Is there a new hospital being built, a new retail store being opened, highway construction being done? For at least one project, try to identify the major activities.
2. Visit a local organization. Learn about the kinds of projects they are working on and how they manage these projects.
3. Identify a personal project that you have recently completed or are in the process of completing—for example, a research paper, or organizing a social event. Identify the major activities you had to complete.

4. Explain the advantage of using probabilistic time estimates.
5. Explain the role of dummy activities.
6. Explain how we calculate the expected time value.
7. Explain the phases of a project's life cycle.
8. Describe the life cycle of a project you have done.
9. Provide an example of precedence relationships from your personal life.
10. Explain why determining the critical path is important in project management.

PROBLEMS

Use the following project information for Problems 1 and 2.

Activity	Activity Time (weeks)	Immediate Predecessor(s)
A	3	none
B	4	A
C	2	B
D	5	B
E	4	C
F	3	D
G	2	E, F

1. Construct a network diagram using AON notation.
2. Using the network diagram constructed in Problem 1:
   a. Calculate the completion time for the project.

   b. Determine which activities are included on the critical path.

3. Jack's Floating Banana Party Company is planning to add a new party vessel for the upcoming season. Jack has identified several activities that must be finished before the start of the season. Using the following information:

Activity	Activity Time (weeks)	Immediate Predecessor(s)
A	6	none
B	5	none
C	3	A
D	3	B
E	6	C, D
F	9	D

a. Draw the network diagram for this project.
b. Identify the critical path.
c. Calculate the expected project length.

Use the following project information for Problems 4 through 8.

Activity	Optimistic Time Estimate (weeks)	Most Likely Time Estimates (weeks)	Pessimistic Time Estimates (weeks)	Immediate Predecessor(s)
A	3	6	9	none
B	3	5	7	A
C	4	7	12	A
D	4	8	10	B
E	5	10	16	C
F	3	4	5	D, E
G	3	6	8	D, E
H	4	6	10	F
I	5	8	11	G
J	3	3	3	H, I

4. Using the information given, construct a network diagram using AOA notation.

5. Using the information given, calculate the expected time for each of the project activities.

6. Using the information given, calculate the variance for each of the project activities.

7. Using your results from Problems 4, 5, and 6:
   a. Calculate the completion time for this project.
   b. Identify the activities included on the critical path of this project.

8. Using your results from Problem 7:
   a. Calculate the probability that the project will be completed in 38 weeks.
   b. Calculate the probability that the project will be completed in 42 weeks.

Use the information provided in Table 17-12 here and the network diagram in Figure 17-22 for the next 4 problems.

Figure 17-22

AON network diagram

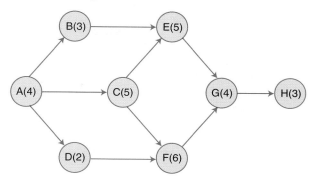

9. Using the information given:
   a. Calculate the completion time of the project.
   b. Identify the activities on the critical path.

10. Using the information given and the project completion time calculated in Problem 9 (a), reduce the completion time of the project by 3 weeks in the most economical way.

11. Using the information given and the project completion time calculated in Problem 9 (a), reduce the completion time of the project by 5 weeks in the most economical way.

Figure 17-23

AOA network diagram

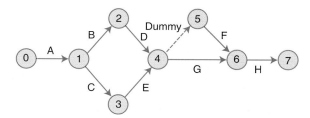

Table 17-12

Activity	Normal Time (weeks)	Normal Cost ($)	Crash Time (weeks)	Crash Cost ($)	Maximum Weeks Reduced	Crash Cost per Week ($)
A	4	800	3	1200	1	400
B	3	900	2	1000	1	100
C	5	1250	3	2250	2	500
D	2	800	2	800	0	0
E	5	1500	4	2000	1	500
F	6	2000	5	3000	1	1000
G	4	600	3	900	1	300
H	3	900	3	900	0	0

12. Using the information given and the project completion time calculated in Problem 9 (a), calculate the minimum time for completing the project possible.

Use Figure 17-23 and the following project data for the next 2 questions.

13. Using the information given:
   a. Calculate the expected time for each of the project activities.
   b. Calculate the variance for each of the project activities.
   c. Evaluate the connected paths through the diagram to determine the expected project completion time.

Activity	Optimistic Time (weeks)	Most Likely Time (weeks)	Pessimistic Time (weeks)
A	8	10	12
B	4	10	16
C	4	5	6
D	6	8	10
E	4	7	12
F	6	7	9
G	4	8	12
H	3	3	3

14. Using the information given and expected project completion time from Problem 13 (c):
   a. Calculate the probability of completing the project in 36 weeks.
   b. Calculate the probability of completing the project in 40 weeks.

15. The accounting department at Northeast University is offering a combined 5-year B.S./M.S. in accounting. The senior accounting professor has identified the project activities and any precedent relationships, as shown in the following Table 17-13. Three time estimates for each activity are included.
   a. Develop a network diagram for this project using AOA notation.
   b. Calculate the expected time for each of the project activities.
   c. Identify the critical path for the project.
   d. Calculate the expected project completion time.

16. The dean of the business school wants to start offering this program starting 32 weeks from now. Using the information provided in Problem 15:
   a. Calculate the probability of the program starting on time.
   b. If the dean needs a 95% probability of being done on time, how long can the expected project duration be?

Table 17-13

Activity	Description of Activity	Immediate Predecessor(s)	Optimistic Time Estimates (weeks)	Most Likely Time Estimates (weeks)	Pessimistic Time Estimates (weeks)
A	Design general curriculum requirements	none	4	8	16
B	Develop program brochure	A	2	3	6
C	Identify prospective students	none	3	6	3
D	Develop advertising campaign	B, C	4	7	10
E	Design specific curriculum content	A	8	16	20
F	Send brochure and student application	D	2	3	4
G	Evaluate applications	F	2	4	6
H	Accept students, notify students	G	1	2	3
I	Schedule rooms for classes	H	1	1	7
J	Designate professors to teach courses	H	1	2	3
K	Select texts for courses	J	3	5	7
L	Order and receive texts	K	6	8	17

CASE: *The Research Office Moves*

Jeannette, the senior administrative assistant, has just learned that she is in charge of the upcoming move of the Research Office at Southwest University. She has coordinated several such moves before and immediately begins organizing her thoughts. Determining what needs to be done, when it needs to be done, and who needs to do it are critical to a successful move. From past moves, Jeannette knows the first step is having the management team allocate the offices available to the different departments. She knows that each department manager fights for the best office space. Because of the politics, Jeannette expects this activity to take 3 weeks.

After the management team finalizes departmental allocations, each department manager allocates office space to individuals within the department. This is also quite political and typically takes 2 weeks. Individuals often take the office space allocations personally and each manager needs time to smooth any ruffled feathers. The allocation decisions are returned to Jeannette so that she can develop an overall layout for the move. She normally does this in about 4 weeks. During the first week of this phase, Jeannette sends each individual a printout of the floor space they will have and requests that they determine how the furniture be arranged. Individuals inform her of any additional or replacement office furniture needs. They indicate where phone jacks and computer hookups should be. Each individual requests the packing supplies needed to pack up their office items. These requests are returned in 3 weeks.

When Jeannette receives the individual requests, she consolidates the requests to form lists of packing supplies and furniture. She orders the supplies from the university-approved supplier and the supplies arrive in 2 weeks. She chooses between three approved office furniture suppliers. Jeannette selects and orders the office furniture, which is scheduled to arrive in 6 weeks. When the packing supplies arrive, Jeannette distributes them to each individual so that packing can be done. This normally takes a week to sort and distribute supplies. Every individual packs their office items and tags their office furniture that is to be moved. Individuals are expected to complete their packing in 2 weeks.

After ordering the furniture, Jeannette makes arrangements for the movers to move the items, the telecommunications office to move or install telephones, and computer services to provide Internet hookups. The movers require 3 weeks notice but move the items in a single day. The phone installers demand 2 weeks notice but complete the work in 1 day. The computer services technicians require 4 weeks notice and complete the hookups in 1 day. The final activity is moving day. All three of these groups—the movers, the phone installers, and the computer technicians—are there on the same date to minimize office disruption and minimize the time the office is unable to provide customer service.

In past moves, Jeannette has had trouble making sure that everything flows smoothly. She believes that there must be a method available to help her manage this office move.

a. Why are office allocations so difficult? What factors must be considered when planning an office layout?

b. Offer Jeannette a method for monitoring the office move. Explain why this method or approach would be reasonable.

c. How long should it take from the day the decision is made to move until the move is completed? Employees only work Monday through Friday. All of Jeannette's activity time estimates assume a 5-day workweek.

d. What are the critical activities for the timely completion of this office move?

e. What recommendations could you make to Jeannette to make this easier in the future?

INTERACTIVE LEARNING

Enhance and test your knowledge of Chapter 17 using the interactive CD.

1. Spreadsheet *Solved Problem 3*

   Visit our dynamic Web site, www.wiley.com/college/reid, for more cases, web links, and additional information.

2. Company Tour
   Halliburton Company (Kellogg Brown & Root), www.halliburton.com/kbr/kbr.asp

3. **Additional Web Resources**
   Project Management Institute, www.pmi.org
   The Project Management Site, www.projectmanagement.com/main.htm
   Project Management Today, www.projectnet.co.uk/pm/pmt/pmt.htm

4. **Virtual Company Consulting Case**

5. **INTERNET CHALLENGE:** *Wedding Bells*

Your Internet challenge is to help plan the wedding described at the beginning of this chapter. Use the list of activities the couple identified for their wedding preparation and search the Internet for information on each activity. Complete the following:

1. Find time estimates for each activity. You can add to the list but you must include all the activities.

2. Develop a project schedule for the wedding. You can use either PERT or CPM. You can use PERT with single time estimates but you will not be able to calculate the probability of on-time completion.

3. Determine the critical path for the wedding.

4. Based on the wedding date, determine when activities on the critical path must be started and finished.

BIBLIOGRAPHY

Denzler, David R. "A Review of CA-Super Project." *APICS—The Performance Advantage* (September 1991), pp. 40–41.

Goldratt, Eliyahu M. *Critical Chain*. Great Barrington, Mass.: The North River Express, 1997.

Kerzner, Harold. *Project Management for Executives*. New York: Van Nostrand Reinhold, 1984.

Meredith, Jack R., and Samuel J. Mantel, Jr. *Project Management: A Managerial Approach*. New York: Wiley, 1985.

Moder, J. E., E.W. Davis, and C. Phillips. *Project Management with CPM and PERT*. New York: Van Nostrand Reinhold, 1983.

Smith-Daniels, Dwight E., and Nicholas J. Aquilano. "Constrained Resource Project Scheduling." *Journal of Operations Management*, Vol. 4, No. 4 (1984), pp. 369–87.

Waiting Line Models

Before studying this supplement you should know or, if necessary, review

1. Competitive advantages, Chapter 2, pages 28–32.
2. Priority rules, Chapter 16, pages 488–489.

LEARNING OBJECTIVES

After completing this supplement you should be able to

1. Describe the elements of a waiting line problem.
2. Use waiting line models to estimate system performance.
3. Use waiting line models to make managerial decisions.

CHAPTER OUTLINE

Waiting in lines is part of everyday life. Whether it is waiting in line at a grocery store to buy deli items (take a number) or checking out at the cash registers (find the quickest line), waiting in line at the bank for a teller, or waiting at an amusement park to go on the newest ride, we spend a lot of time waiting. We wait in lines at the movies, campus dining rooms, the Registrar's Office for class registration, and at the Division of Motor Vehicles. We wait in lines at the end of the school term to sell books back. Think about the lines you have waited in just during the past week. How long you wait in line depends on a number of factors. Your wait is a result of the number of people served before you, the number of servers working, and the amount of time it takes to serve each individual customer.

▶ A **waiting line system** includes the customer population source as well as the process or service system.

Wait time is affected by the design of the waiting line system. A **waiting line system** is defined by two elements: the population source of its customers and the process or service system itself. In this supplement we examine the elements of waiting line systems and appropriate performance measures. Performance characteristics are calculated for different waiting line systems. We conclude with descriptions of managerial decisions related to waiting line system design and performance.

■ ELEMENTS OF WAITING LINES

Any time there is more customer demand for a service than can be provided, a waiting line occurs. Customers can be either human or inanimate objects (a machine requiring service, a customer order waiting to be processed, or a pick list waiting to be filled).

LINKS TO PRACTICE
Waiting for Fast Food

Fast-food restaurants illustrate the transient nature of waiting line systems. Waiting lines occur at a fast-food restaurant drive-through during peak meal times each day. There is a temporary surge in demand that cannot be quickly handled with the available capacity. In an effort to speed up delivery, some restaurants use an extra window—the first window for paying and the second window for picking up the food. At other times of the day, the restaurant uses a single window and may have no waiting line at the drive-through window.

The challenge is designing service systems with adequate but not excessive amounts of capacity. A fast-food restaurant experiences variable demand and variable service times. The restaurant cannot be sure how much customer demand there will be and it does not know exactly what each customer will order—each order can be unique and require a different service time. It is important to understand the different elements of a waiting line system. These elements include the customer population source, the service system, the arrival and service patterns, and the priorities used for controlling the line. Let's first look at the primary input into the waiting line system: the customers.

The Customer Population

The customer population is defined as finite or infinite. When potential new customers for the waiting line system are affected by the number of customers already in the system, the customer population is **finite**. For example, if you are in a class with nine other students, the total customer population for meeting with the professor during office hours is ten students. As the students waiting to meet with the professor increases, the population of possible new customers decreases. There is a finite limit as to how large the waiting line can ever be.

▶ **In a finite customer population** the number of potential new customers is affected by the number of customers already in the system.

When the number of customers waiting in line does not affect the rate at which the population generates new customers, the customer population is considered **infinite**. For example, if you are taking a class with 500 other students (a relatively large population) and the probability of all the students trying to meet with the professor at the same time is very low, then the number of students in line does not significantly affect the population's ability to generate new customers.

▶ **In an infinite customer population** the number of potential new customers is not affected by the number of customers already in the system.

In addition to waiting, a customer has other possible actions. For example, a customer may balk, renege, or jockey. **Balking** occurs when the customer decides not to enter the waiting line. For example, you see that there are already 12 students waiting to meet with your professor, so you choose to come back later. **Reneging** occurs when the customer enters the waiting line but leaves before being serviced. For example, you enter the line waiting to meet with your professor, but after waiting 15 minutes and seeing little progress, you decide to leave. **Jockeying** occurs when a customer changes from one line to another, hoping to reduce the waiting time. A good example of this is picking a line at the grocery store and changing to another line in the hope of being served quicker. The models used in this supplement assume that customers are patient; they do not balk, renege, or jockey; and the customers come from an infinite population.

▶ **Balking**
The customer decides not to enter the waiting line.

▶ **Reneging**
The customer enters the line but decides to exit before being served.

The Service System

The service system is defined by the number of waiting lines, the number of servers, the arrangement of the servers, the arrival and service patterns, and the service priority rules.

▶ **Jockeying**
The customer enters one line and then switches to a different line in an effort to reduce the waiting time.

The Number of Waiting Lines

Waiting line systems can have single or multiple lines. Banks often have a single line for customers. Customers wait in line until a teller is free and then proceed to that teller's position. Other examples of single-line systems include airline counters, rental car counters, restaurants, amusement park attractions, and delis. The advantage of using a single line when multiple servers are available is the customer's perception of fairness in terms of equitable waits. That is, the customer is not penalized by picking the slow line but is served in a true first-come, first-served fashion. The single line approach eliminates jockeying behavior.

The multiple-line approach is best when specialized servers are used. For example, in a grocery some registers are express lanes for customers with a small number of items. Using express lines reduces the waiting time for customers making smaller purchases. Sometimes these express lanes are limited even further to cash only or debit card transactions. Examples of single and multiple line systems are shown in Figure A-1.

The Number of Servers   System capacity is a product of the number of service facilities and server proficiency. In waiting line systems, the terms server and channel are used interchangeably. It is assumed that a server or channel can serve one customer at a time. Waiting line systems are either single server (single channel) or multi-server (multi-channel). Single-server examples include small retail stores with a single checkout counter, a theater with a single person selling tickets and controlling admission into the show, or a ballroom with a single person controlling admission. Multi-server systems have parallel service providers offering the same service. Multi-server examples include grocery stores (multiple cashiers), drive-through banks (multiple drive-through windows), and gas stations (multiple gas pumps).

The Arrangement of the Servers   Services require a single activity or a series of activities and are identified by the term phase. Waiting line models refer to single-phase and multi-phase systems. In a single-channel, single-phase system, the services

Figure A-1

Examples of waiting line systems

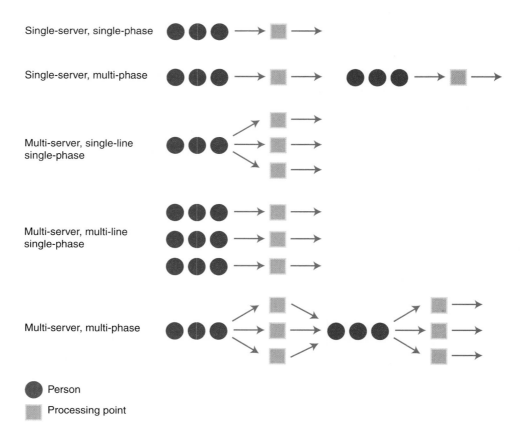

Single-server, single-phase

Single-server, multi-phase

Multi-server, single-line single-phase

Multi-server, multi-line single-phase

Multi-server, multi-phase

● Person

■ Processing point

required by the customer are done by a single server. A good example is a drive-through car wash. An example of a single-channel, multiple-phase system is the drive-through service at a fast-food restaurant, where the order is placed at the first service point, paid for at the second service point, and the food picked up at the third service point.

A multi-server, single-phase system is used when volume dictates that one server cannot accommodate customer demand. In this situation, identical servers increase the system's capacity. A good example of a single-line, multi-server, single-phase system is a bank with a single waiting line that feeds customers to multiple identical servers. Multi-line, multi-server, single-phase systems are often used in grocery stores. Each register has its own line and a server capable of providing the single activity required.

Multi-server, multi-phase systems have customers entering the system through any one of a number of identical servers and then proceeding through to a subsequent server. One such system might be found in a men's custom clothing store. First, a sales clerk assists the customer in selecting the material and style. After the customer picks the material, one of the tailors measures the customer to ensure a custom-fitted suit.

Arrival and Service Patterns

Variability in arrival and service patterns are the cause of waiting lines. Lines form when several customers request service at approximately the same time. This surge of customers temporarily overloads the service system and a line develops. Waiting line models that assess the performance of service systems typically assume that customer arrival times are represented by a Poisson distribution and service times are described by an exponential distribution. The Poisson distribution specifies the probability that n customers will arrive in T time periods (such as per hour). The exponential distribution describes the service rates as the probability that a particular service time will not exceed T time periods.

Waiting line models require an **arrival rate** and a **service rate**. The arrival rate specifies the average number of customers per time period. For example, a system may have ten customers arrive on average each hour. The service rate specifies the average number of customers that can be serviced during a time period. The service rate is the capacity of the service system. If the number of customers you can serve per time period is less than the average number of customers arriving, the waiting line grows infinitely. You never catch up with the demand!

▶ **Arrival rate**
The average number of customers arriving per time period.

▶ **Service rate**
The average number of customers that can be served per time period.

Problem Solving Tip: Make sure the arrival rate and service rate are for the same time period—that is, the number of customers per hour, or per day, or per week.

Waiting Line Priority Rules

A waiting line priority rule determines which customer is served next. A frequently used priority rule is *first-come, first-served*. This priority rule selects customers based on who has been waiting the longest in line. Generally customers consider *first-come, first-served* to be the fairest method for determining priority.

"Congratulations, keep moving, please. Congratulations, keep moving, please. Congratulations . . ."

However, it is not the only priority rule used. Other rules include *best customers first, highest profit customer first, quickest service requirement first, largest service requirement first, earliest reservation first, emergencies first,* and so on. Although each priority rule has merit, it is important to use the priority rule that best supports the overall organizational strategy.

You must understand how the priority rule used affects the performance of your waiting line system. As an example, first-come, first-served is generally considered fair, yet it is biased against customers requiring short service times. When checking out at a store that is using first-come, first-served as a priority rule, a customer waiting behind another customer with a large number of items waits longer than a customer waiting behind a second customer with only a few items. Although processing was sequential, the wait times varied because of the preceding customer.

■ WAITING LINE PERFORMANCE MEASURES

Performance measures can be used to gain useful information about waiting line systems. These measures include:

1. *The average number of customers waiting in line, or in the system.* The number of customers waiting in line can be interpreted in several ways. Short waiting lines can result from relatively constant customer arrivals (no major surges in demand) or by the organization having excess capacity (too many cashiers open). On the other hand, long waiting lines can result from poor server efficiency or inadequate system capacity.

2. *The average amount of time customers spend waiting, or the average time a customer spends in the system.* Customers often link long waits to poor quality service. When long waiting times occur, one option is to change the demand pattern. That is, the company can offer discounts or better service at less busy times of the day or week. For example, a restaurant offers early bird diners a discount so that demand is more level. The discount moves some demand from prime-time dining hours to the less desired dining hours.

   If too much time is spent in the system, customers might perceive the competency of the service provider as poor. For example, the amount of time customers spend in line and in the system at a retail checkout counter can be a result of a new employee not yet proficient at handling the transactions.

3. The *system utilization rate* is a measure of capacity utilization that shows the percentage of time the servers are busy. Management's goal is to have enough servers to assure that waiting is within allowable limits but not too many servers as to be cost inefficient.

We calculate these measures for two different waiting line models: the single-server model and the multi-server model.

SINGLE-SERVER WAITING LINE MODEL ∎

The easiest waiting line model involves a single-server, single-line, single-phase system. The following assumptions are made when we model this environment.

1. The customers are patient and come from an infinite population.
2. Customer arrival is described by a Poisson distribution, with a mean arrival rate of λ.
3. Customer service rate is described by an exponential distribution, with a mean service rate of μ.
4. The waiting line priority rule used is first-come, first-served.

Using these assumptions, we can calculate the operating characteristics of a waiting line system using the following formulas:

λ = mean arrival rate of customers

μ = mean service rate

$p = \dfrac{\lambda}{\mu}$ = the average utilization of the system

$L = \dfrac{\lambda}{\mu - \lambda}$ = the average number of customers in the service system

$L_Q = pL$ = the average number of customers waiting in line

$W = \dfrac{1}{\mu - \lambda}$ = the average time spent waiting in the system, including service

$W_Q = pW$ = the average time spent waiting in line

$P_n = (1 - p)p^n$ = the probality that n customers are in the service system

---

∎ Example A.1 Single-Server Operating Characteristics at the Help Desk

The computer lab at State University has a help desk to assist students working on computer spreadsheet assignments. The students patiently form a single line in front of the desk to wait for help. Students are served based on a first-come, first-served priority rule. On average, 15 students per hour arrive at the help desk. Student arrivals are best described using a Poisson distribution. The help desk server can help an average of 20 students per hour, with the service rate being described by an exponential distribution. Calculate the following operating characteristics of the service system.

a. The average utilization of the help desk server
b. The average number of students in the system
c. The average number of students waiting in line
d. The average time a student spends in the system
e. The average time a student spends waiting in line
f. The probability of having more than four students in the system

Solution:

a. Average utilization: $p = \dfrac{\lambda}{\mu} = \dfrac{15}{20} = 0.75$, or 75%.

b. Average number of students in the system: $L = \dfrac{\lambda}{\mu - \lambda} = \dfrac{15}{20 - 15} = 3$ students

c. Average number of students waiting in line: $L_Q = pL = 0.75 \times 3 = 2.25$ students

d. Average time a student spent in the system: $W = \dfrac{1}{\mu - \lambda} = \dfrac{1}{20 - 15} = 0.2$ hours, or 12 minutes

e. Average time a student spent waiting in line: $W_Q = pW = 0.75 \times (0.2) = 0.15$ hours, or 9 minutes

f. The probability that there are more than four students in the system equals one minus the probability that there are four or fewer students in the system. We use the following formula.

Problem Solving Tip: Any term raised to the zero power is equal to 1. By definition, zero factorial equals one.

$$P = 1 - \sum_{n=0}^{4} P_n = 1 - \sum_{n=0}^{4}\left(1 - p\right)p^n$$
$$= 1 - 0.25(1 + 0.75 + 0.75^2 + 0.75^3 + 0.75^4)$$
$$= 1 - 0.7626 = 0.2374$$

or a 0.2374 (23.74%) chance of having more than four students in the system.

■ MULTI-SERVER WAITING LINE MODEL

In the single-line, multi-server, single-phase model, customers form a single line and are served by the first server available. The model assumes that there are s identical servers, the service time distribution for each server is exponential, and the mean service time is $1/\mu$. Using these assumptions, the operating characteristics can be described with the following formulas.

$p = \dfrac{\lambda}{s\mu}$ = the average utilization of the system

S = the number of servers in the system

$P_0 = \left[\displaystyle\sum_{n=0}^{s-1}\dfrac{(\lambda/\mu)^n}{n!} + \dfrac{(\lambda/\mu)^s}{s!}\left(\dfrac{1}{1 - p}\right)\right]^{-1}$ = the probability that no customers are in the system

$L_Q = \dfrac{P_0(\lambda/\mu)^s\, p}{s!(1 - p)^2}$ = the average number of customers waiting in line

$W_Q = \dfrac{L_Q}{\lambda}$ = the average time spent waiting in line

$W = W_Q + \dfrac{1}{\mu}$ = the average time spent in the system, including service

$L = \lambda W$ = the average number of customers in the service system

■ Example A.2 Multi-Server Operating Characteristics at the Help Desk

State University has decided to increase the number of computer assignments in their curriculum and are concerned about the impact on the help desk. Instead of a single person working at the help desk, the university is considering a plan to have three identical service providers. It expects that students will arrive at a rate of 45 per hour, according to a Poisson distribution. The service rate for each of the three servers is 18 students per hour, with exponential service times. Calculate the following operating characteristics of the service system:

   a. The average utilization of the help desk
   b. The probability that there are no students in the system
   c. The average number of students waiting in line
   d. The average time a student spends waiting in line
   e. The average time a student spends in the system
   f. The average number of students in the system

Solution:

   a. Average utilization: $p = \dfrac{\lambda}{s\mu} = \dfrac{45}{(3 \times 18)} = 0.833$, or 83.3%

   b. The probability that there are no students in the system:

$$P_0 = \left[\sum_{n=0}^{s-1} \frac{(\lambda/\mu)^n}{n!} + \frac{(\lambda/\mu)^s}{s!} \left(\frac{1}{1-p} \right) \right]^{-1}$$

$$= \left[\frac{(45/18)^0}{0!} + \frac{(45/18)^1}{1!} + \frac{(45/18)^2}{2!} + \left(\frac{(45/18)^3}{3!} \left(\frac{1}{1-0.833} \right) \right) \right]^{-1}$$

$$= \frac{1}{22.215} = 0.045, \text{ or 4.5\% of having no students in the system}$$

   c. The average number of students waiting in line:

$$L_Q = \frac{P_0(\lambda/\mu)^s p}{s!(1-p)^2} = \frac{0.045(45/18)^3 \times 0.833}{3! \times (1-0.833)^2} = \frac{0.5857}{0.1673} = 3.5 \text{ students}$$

   d. The average time a student spends waiting in line: $W_Q = \dfrac{L_Q}{\lambda} = \dfrac{3.5}{45} = 0.078$ hours,

   or 4.68 minutes

   e. The average time a student spends in the system:

$$W = W_Q + \frac{1}{\mu} = 0.078 + \frac{1}{18} = 0.134 \text{ hours, or 8.04 minutes}$$

   f. The average number of students in the system:

$$L = \lambda W = 45(0.134) = 6.03 \text{ students}$$

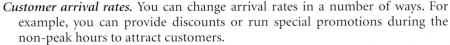

■ CHANGING OPERATIONAL CHARACTERISTICS

After calculating the operating characteristics for a waiting line system, sometimes you need to change the system to alter its performance. Let's look at the type of changes you can make to the different elements of the waiting line system.

Customer arrival rates. You can change arrival rates in a number of ways. For example, you can provide discounts or run special promotions during the non-peak hours to attract customers.

Number of service facilities. You can either increase or decrease the number of server facilities. For example, a grocery store can easily change the number of cashiers open for business (up to the number of registers available). The grocery increases the number of cashiers open when lines are too long.

Another approach is to dedicate specific servers for specific transactions. One example would be to limit the number of items that can be processed at a particular cashier (ten items or less) or to limit a cashier to cash-only transactions.

Changing the number of phases. You can use a multi-phase system where servers specialize in a portion of the total service rather than needing to know the entire service provided. Since a server has fewer tasks to learn, the individual server proficiency should improve. This goes back to the concept of division of labor.

Number of servers at each facility. You can assign additional people at service facilities to speed up service time. A good example is at a grocery store where a grocery bagger is at each cashier so the customer is processed more quickly.

Server efficiency. You can improve server efficiency through process improvements. For example, cashier accuracy is significantly improved through the use of scanners. You can also improve server efficiency by providing additional technical training to upgrade server skills.

Changing the priority rule. The priority rule determines who should be served next. There are priority rules other than first-come, first-served. If you want to change priority rules, consider the impact on those customers who will wait longer.

Changing the number of lines. Changing to a single line model from a multi-line model is most appropriate when the company is concerned about fairness for its customers. A single line ensures that customers do not jockey in an attempt to gain an advantage over another customer. Multi-line models easily accommodate specialty servers (express lanes).

Once changes are suggested, evaluate the impact of the changes on the operating performance characteristics of the waiting line system. Changes in one area can require changes in other areas. For example, if you achieve a more constant customer arrival rate, you may be able to reduce the number of service facilities. Not reducing the number of service facilities could have a negative effect on the system's average utilization. When proposing changes, calculate the operating performance measures to better understand the impact of the changes.

OM ACROSS THE ORGANIZATION

Waiting line models are important to a company because they directly affect customer service perception and the costs of providing a service. Several functional areas are affected by waiting line decisions.

Accounting is concerned with the cost of the waiting line system used. If system average utilization is low, that suggests the waiting line design is inefficient and too expensive. Poor system design can result in overstaffing or unnecessary capital acquisitions in an effort to improve customer service.

Marketing is concerned about response time for customers—how long customers must wait in line before being served and how long it takes to be served. Quick service or response can be a competitive advantage. Long waits suggest a lack of concern by the organization or can be linked to a perception of poor service quality.

Purchasing must be sure to buy capital equipment capable of achieving the proposed service rate.

Operations uses waiting line theory to estimate queues or waiting times at different processing points, to allow for a better estimate of lead time and improve due date delivery promising. Operations is also affected by the system design. When single-phase systems are used, operators must have greater skills. The organization needs to hire employees with higher skill levels or provide training to upgrade the workforce.

Within an organization, waiting line analysis can be done by the manufacturing engineers or the operations manager.

OM IS EVERYWHERE ■

It is unlikely that you calculate operating performance characteristics in your personal life, but it is likely that you will be faced with waiting lines. Even without using the formulas, you know enough to rationally consider system design changes. We know that people do not like to wait, but we also know that it is too expensive to serve every customer immediately. Although you may hate the long lines when you sell back your books at the end of the term, you can at least understand why the wait occurs. When you visit an amusement park, consider the way waiting lines are structured and evaluate their effectiveness. Think about how you can better use the time you spend waiting in line.

SUPPLEMENT HIGHLIGHTS

1. The elements of a waiting line system include the customer population source, the patience of the customer, the service system, arrival and service distributions, waiting line priority rules, and system performance measures. Understanding these elements is critical when analyzing waiting line systems.

2. Waiting line models allow us to estimate system performance by predicting average system utilization, average number of customers in the service system, average number of customers waiting in line, average time a customer spends in the system, average time a customer waits in line, and the probability of n customers in the service system.

3. The benefit of calculating operational characteristics is to provide management with information as to whether system changes are needed. Management can change the operational performance of the waiting line system by altering any or all of the following: the customer arrival rates, the number of service facilities, the number of phases, the number of servers per facility, server efficiency, the priority rule, and the number of lines in the system. Based on proposed changes, management can then evaluate the expected performance of the system.

KEY TERMS

FORMULA REVIEW

For Single-Server Waiting Line Models

$p = \dfrac{\lambda}{\mu}$ is the average utilization of the system

$L = \dfrac{\lambda}{\mu - \lambda}$ is the average number of customers in the service system

$L_Q = pL$ is the average number of customers waiting in line

$W = \dfrac{1}{\mu - \lambda}$ is the average time spent waiting in the system, including service

$W_Q = pW$ is the average time spent waiting in line

$P_n = (1 - p)p^n$ is the probability that n customers are in the service system

For the Multi-Server Waiting Line Model

$p = \dfrac{\lambda}{s\mu}$ is the average utilization of the system

$P_0 = \left[\displaystyle\sum_{n=0}^{s-1} \dfrac{(\lambda/\mu)^n}{n!} + \dfrac{(\lambda/\mu)^s}{s!} \left(\dfrac{1}{1-p} \right) \right]^{-1}$ is the probability that no customers are in the system

$L_Q = \dfrac{P_0(\lambda/\mu)^s p}{s!(1-p)^2}$ is the average number of customers waiting in line

$W_Q = \dfrac{L_Q}{\lambda}$ is the average time spent waiting in line

$W = W_Q + \dfrac{1}{\mu}$ is the average time spent in the system, including service

$L = \lambda W$ is the average number of customers in the service system

SOLVED PROBLEMS

■ Solved Problem 1

The local Division of Motor Vehicles (DMV) is concerned with its waiting line system. Currently the DMV uses a single-server, single-line, single-phase system when processing license renewals. Based on historical evidence, the average number of customers arriving per hour is 9 and is described by a Poisson distribution. The service rate is 12 customers per hour and is described by an exponential distribution. The customers are patient and come from an infinite population. The manager of the DMV would like you to calculate the operational characteristics of the waiting line system.

a. What is the average system utilization?
b. What is the average number of customers in the system?
c. What is the average number of customers waiting in line?
d. What is the average time a customer spends in the system?
e. What is the average time a customer spends waiting in line?

Solution:

a. Average utilization is 0.75 or 75%

$$p = \frac{\lambda}{\mu} = \frac{9}{12} = 0.75$$

b. Average number of customers in the system is 3.

$$L = \frac{\lambda}{\mu - \lambda} = \frac{9}{12 - 9} = 3 \text{ cutomers}$$

c. Average number of customers waiting in line is 2.25.

$$L_Q = pL = 0.75 \times 3 = 2.25 \text{ customers}$$

d. Average time a customer spends in the system is 0.33 hours or 20 minutes.

$$W = \frac{1}{\mu - \lambda} = \frac{1}{12 - 9} = 0.33 \text{ hours}$$

e. Average time a customer spends waiting in line is 0.25 hours or 15 minutes.

$$W_Q = pW = 0.75 \times 0.33 = 0.25 \text{ hours}$$

These operational characteristics can be calculated as shown in Spreadsheet A.1 Using a spreadsheet allows the modeler to vary parameters quickly and see the resulting operational characteristics.

Arrival Rate	9
Service Rate	12

Results	
Average system utilization	75%
Average # of customers in system	3
Average # of customers in line	2.25
Average time spent in system (hours)	0.33
Average time spent waiting in line (hours)	0.25

■ Solved Problem 2

The county has decided to consolidate several of its DMV facilities into a larger, centrally located facility. The DMV manager wants you to calculate the operational characteristics of a multi-server, single-phase waiting line system. The arrival rate is expected to be 72 customers per hour and follows a Poisson distribution. The number of identical servers is 7. Each server will be able to serve an average of 12 customers per hour. The service times are described by an exponential distribution. Your job is to calculate the following:

a. The average system utilization.
b. The probability of no customers in the system.
c. The average number of customers waiting in line.
d. The average time a customer waits in line.
e. The average time a customer spends in the system.

Solution:

a. Average system utilization is 0.857 or 85.7%

$$p = \frac{\mu}{s\lambda} = \frac{72}{7 \times 12} = 0.857$$

b. The probability that no customers are in the system is 0.004 or 0.4%.

$$P_0 = \left[\sum_{n=0}^{s-1} \frac{(\lambda/\mu)^n}{n!} + \frac{(\lambda/\mu)^s}{s!}\left(\frac{1}{1-p}\right) \right]^{-1}$$

$$= \left[\left[\frac{(72/12)^0}{0!} + \frac{(72/12)^1}{1!} + \frac{(72/12)^2}{2!} + \frac{(72/12)^3}{3!} \right. \right.$$

$$+ \frac{(72/12)^4}{4!} + \frac{(72/12)^5}{5!} + \frac{(72/12)^6}{6!} \right]$$

$$\left. + \left[\frac{(72/12)^7}{7!}\left(\frac{1}{1-p}\right) \right] \right]^{-1}$$

$$= \frac{1}{623.8} = 0.002$$

c. The average number of customers waiting in line is 9.31.

$$L_Q = \frac{P_0(\lambda/\mu)^s p}{s!(1-p)^2}$$

$$= \frac{0.002(72/12)^7 \times 0.857}{7!(1-0.857)^2} = 4.66 \text{ customers}$$

d. The average time spent waiting in line is 0.065 hours or 3.9 minutes.

$$W_Q = \frac{L_Q}{\lambda} = \frac{4.66}{72} = 0.065 \text{ hours}$$

e. The average time a customer spends in the system is 0.148 hours or 8.88 minutes.

$$W = W_Q + \frac{1}{\mu} = 0.065 + \frac{1}{12} = 0.148 \text{ hours}$$

DISCUSSION QUESTIONS

1. Describe the elements of a waiting line system.

2. Provide examples of when a single-line, single-server, single-phase waiting line system is appropriate.

3. Describe the operating performance characteristics calculated for evaluating waiting line systems.

4. Describe the implications on customer service and server skills when using a single-line, single-server, single-phase waiting line system.

5. Describe the implications on customer service and server skills when using a single-line, multi-server, single-phase waiting line system.

6. Describe the implications on customer service and server skills when a multi-server, multi-stage waiting line system is used.

7. Describe a situation in your daily life that could be improved by waiting line analysis.

8. Explain how the design of a waiting system can negatively affect customers.

9. Visit your local bank and observe the waiting line system. Describe the system in terms of number of lines, number of facilities, and number of phases.

10. On your next trip to the Division of Motor Vehicles, evaluate their waiting line system.

11. Describe any disadvantages of using waiting line models.

PROBLEMS

1. Melanie is the manager of the Clean Machine car wash and has gathered the following information. Customers arrive at a rate of 8 per hour according to a Poisson distribution. The car washer can service an average of 10 cars per hour with service times described by an exponential distribution. Melanie is concerned with the number of customers waiting in line. She has asked you to calculate the following system characteristics.
   a. Average system utilization.
   b. Average number of customers in the system.
   c. Average number of customers waiting in line.

2. Melanie realizes that how long the customer must wait is also very important. She is also concerned about customers balking when the waiting line is too long. Using the arrival and service rates in Problem 1, she wants you to calculate the following system characteristics.
   a. The average time a customer spends in the system.
   b. The average time a customer spends waiting in line.
   c. The probability of having more than 3 customers in the system.
   d. The probability of having more than 4 customers in the system.

3. If Melanie adds an additional server at Clean Machine car wash, the service rate changes to an average of 16 cars per hour. The customer arrival rate is 10 cars per hour. Melanie has asked you to calculate the following system characteristics.
   a. Average system utilization.
   b. Average number of customers in the system.
   c. Average number of customers waiting in line.

4. Melanie is curious to see the difference in waiting times for customers caused by the additional server added in

Problem 3. Calculate the following system characteristics for her.
   a. The average time a customer spends in the system.
   b. The average time a customer spends waiting in line.
   c. The probability of having more than 3 customers in the system.
   d. The probability of having more than 4 customers in the system.

5. After Melanie added the additional car washer at Clean Machine (service rate is an average of 16 customers per hour), business improved. Melanie now estimates that the arrival rate is 12 customers per hour. Given this new information, she wants you to calculate the following system characteristics.
   a. Average system utilization.
   b. Average number of customers in the system.
   c. Average number of customers waiting in line.

6. As usual, Melanie then requested you to calculate system characteristics concerning customer time spent in the system.
   a. Calculate the average time a customer spends in the system.
   b. Calculate the average time a customer spends waiting in line.
   c. Calculate the probability of having more than 4 customers in the system.

7. Business continues to grow at Clean Machine. Melanie has decided to use a second car washing bay, staffed with another identical two-person team. Clean Machine will now use a single-line, multi-server, single-phase waiting line system. The arrival rate is estimated to average 24 customers

per hour according to a Poisson distribution. Each of the car wash teams can service an average of 16 customers per hour according to an exponential distribution. Calculate the following operational characteristics.

a. Average system utilization.
b. Average number of customers in the system.
c. Average number of customers waiting in line.
d. Calculate the average time a customer spends in the system.

e. Calculate the average time a customer spends waiting in line.
f. Calculate the probability of having more than 4 customers in the system.

8. Melanie is very concerned about the number of customers waiting in line. Given the information in Problem 7, calculate how high the customer arrival rate can increase without the average number of customers waiting in line exceeding 4.

CASE: *The Copy Center Holdup*

Catherine Blake, the office manager for the College of Business Administration, has received numerous complaints lately from several department chairpersons. In the past few months, the chairpersons have insisted that something be done about the amount of time their administrative assistants waste waiting in line to make copies. Currently the college has two photo copy centers dedicated for small copying jobs, copy center A on the third floor and copy center B on the fourth floor. Both centers are self-serve and have identical processing capabilities. The copying machines are not visible to the administrative assistants from their offices. When copying is required, the administrative assistant goes to the copy room and waits in line to make the necessary copies. Catherine's assistant, Brian, was assigned to investigate the problem.

Brian reported that, on average, administrative assistants arrive at copy center A at the rate of 10 per hour and at copy center B at the rate of 14 per hour. Each of the copy centers can service 15 jobs per hour. The administrative assistants' arrivals essentially follow a Poisson distribution and the service times are approximated by a negative exponential distribution. Brian has proposed that the two copy centers be combined into a single copy center with either two or three

identical copy machines. He estimates that the arrival rate would be 24 per hour. Each machine would still service 15 jobs per hour. Currently, administrative assistants earn an average of $15.00 per hour.

a. Determine the utilization of each of the copy centers.
b. Determine the average waiting time at each of the copy centers.
c. What is the annual cost of the administrative assistants average waiting time using the current system?
d. Determine the utilization of the combined copy center with two copiers.
e. Determine the average waiting time at the combined copy center.
f. What would be the annual cost of the administrative assistants average waiting time using the combined two-copier setup?
g. What would be the utilization of the combined copy center with three copiers?
h. What would be the annual cost of the administrative assistants average waiting time using the combined three-copier setup?
i. What would you recommend to Catherine?

INTERACTIVE LEARNING

Visit our dynamic Web site, www.wiley.com/college/reid, for more cases, web links, and additional information.

1. **Additional Web Resources**
   Q Systems, www.queue.com.au

2. **Virtual Company Consulting Case**

3. **INTERNET CHALLENGE**   *Designing a New Copy Center*

In an effort to put more real-life experience in your education, you have been assigned a special class project. You must analyze the current photocopying procedures and make a recommendation for replacement copy machines. Currently, your school makes an average of 150,000 photocopies each month. The average copying job requires a 1-minute preparation time and the run time is determined by the number of copies. For your school, the average job requires 2,500 copies. Thus, if you use a photocopier that prints at 25 copies per minute (cmp), the average job would take 10 minutes for copying plus 1-minute for preparation, or a total of 11 minutes. Faster machines obviously decrease the copying time but the prep time remains constant. There are an average of 12 jobs per hour. Administrative assistants must remain at the copier while the copies are being made. The average hourly rate for the administrative assistants is $15.00.

You are to evaluate three possible options. The first proposal uses a single high-volume machine capable of producing a minimum of 45 copies per minute. The second proposal uses two medium–volume machines capable of producing between 20 and 44 copies per minute. The third proposal uses four low-volume machines capable of producing up to 20 copies per minute. The school operates 8 hours per day, 5 days per week, 50 weeks out of the year. Your job now is to find three such copiers on the Web to use in your analysis.

a. Determine the utilization of a high-volume, single machine copy center.
b. Determine the average waiting time for administrative assistants.
c. Calculate the total cost (equipment and wasted time) of this proposal.
d. Determine the utilization of a medium-volume, two-machine copy center.
e. Determine the average waiting time for administrative assistants.
f. Calculate the total cost (equipment and wasted time) of this proposal.
g. Determine the utilization of a low-volume, four-machine copy center.
h. Determine the average waiting time for administrative assistants.
i. Calculate the total cost (equipment and wasted time) of this proposal.
j. Make a recommendation for the new copy center. Be sure to address any additional issues that should be considered.

BIBLIOGRAPHY

Hall, Randolph W. *Queueing Methods For Services and Manufacturing.* Englewood Cliffs, N.J.: Prentice-Hall, 1991.

Moore, P. M. *Queues, Inventories and Maintenance.* New York: Wiley, 1958.

APPENDIX A
SOLUTIONS TO SELECTED PROBLEMS

Chapter 2

1. Productivity of worker 1 = 1000 labels/
30 minutes = 33.33 labels/minute
Productivity of worker 2 = 850 labels/
20 minutes = 42.5 labels/minute
Worker 1 is more productive than worker 2.

3. Productivity of first machine = 6 loaves/
5 hours = 1.2 loaves/hour
Productivity of second machine = 4 loaves/
2 hours = 2 loaves/hour
The second machine is more productive than the
first machine.

5. Productivity using old method = 3 walls/
45 minutes = 0.067 wall/minute
Productivity using new method = 2 walls/
20 minutes = 0.1 wall/minute
The painter is more productive using the new
method.

8. a. Multifactor productivity = $60/($15 + $20 +
$20) = $60/$55 = 1.09
Findings indicate that the average cost to each
patient is about 9% higher than the total overall costs per patient, which include labor costs,
materials costs, and overhead costs.

b. Labor productivity = $60/3 hours =
$20/hour

9.

Work Crew	Productivity
Anna, Sue, and Tim	10 homes/35 hours = 0.29 home/hour
Jim, Hose, and Andy	15 homes/45 hours = 0.33 home/hour
Dan, Wendy, and Carry	18 homes/56 hours = 0.32 home/hour
Rosie, Chandra, and Seth	10 homes/30 hours = 0.33 home/hour
Sherry, Vicky, and Roger	18 homes/42 hours = 0.43 home/hour

The crew made up of Sherry, Vicky, and Roger is
the most productive.

Chapter 3

1. a. Fixed costs (FC) = $40,000
Variable cost (VC) = $45 per unit
Selling price (SP) = $100 per unit
Break-even volume: $Q = FC/(SP - VC) =$
$40,000/(100 - 45) = 728$ units

Graphical Solution:
Total revenue $(TR) = 100Q$
Total cost $(TC) = 40,000 + 45Q$
The break-even volume is the point of intersection of
the total revenue and total cost functions.

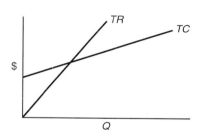

b. $Q = 200$ units
SP = $80 per unit
FC = $40,000
VC = $45 per unit
Profit = total revenue − total cost =
$(SP)(Q) - [FC + (VC)(Q)]$
Profit = $(80)(2000) - [40,000 + (45)(2,000)]$
= $30,000

c. $Q = 1,500$ units
SP = $100 per unit
FC = $40,000
VC = $45 per unit
Profit = total revenue − total cost = $(SP)(Q) -$
$[FC + (VC)(Q)]$
Profit = $(100)(1500) - [40,000 + (45)(1500)]$
= $43,500

The pricing strategy of $100 per unit yields a higher
profit contribution.

3. Fixed cost (FC) = \$200/year
Variable costs (VC) = \$0.20/unit
Selling price (SP) = \$1.00/hot chocolate
Break-even volume: $Q = F/(SP - VC) = 200/(1.00 - 0.20)$ = 250 hot chocolates

5. **a.** Total cost (process I) = $FC + (VC)(Q)$ = 80,000 + 75Q
Total cost (process II) = $FC + (VC)(Q)$ = 100,000 + 60Q
At break-even volume: total cost (process I) = total cost (process II)
80,000 + 75Q = 100,000 + 60Q
Q = 1334 units

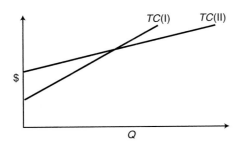

1 ≤ Q ≤ 1,334, choose process I
Q ≥ 1,334, choose process II
Q = 1,334, indifferent between process I and process II

b. At Q = 500
Total cost of process I = 80,000 + (75)(500) = \$117,500
Total cost of process II = 100,000 + (60)(500) = \$130,000
Process I yields lower total costs than process II.

6. F = \$25,000/year
VC = \$35/customer
Break-even quantity = 12000 customers
$Q = F/(SP - 35)$
$12,000 = 25,000/(SP - 35)$
$SP = \$37.08$

7. **a.** SP = \$20/unit
VC = \$18/unit
F = \$70,000/year
$Q = 70,000/(20 - 18)$ = 35,000 units

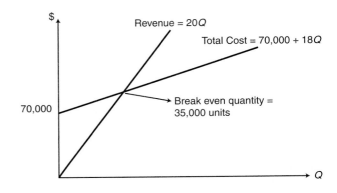

b. Increasing sales volume option:
Q new = (20,000)(1.35) = 27,000 units
Profit = (27,000)(20) − [70,000 + 18(27,000)] = −\$16,000
Reducing variables cost option:
VC new = \$16.2/unit
Profit = (20,000)(20) − [70,000 + 16.2(20,000)] = \$6,000
Reducing the variables cost option is the better option.

10. **a.** Profit without new equipment:
Profit = (35)(50,000) − [150,000 + 10(50,000)] = \$1,100,000
Profit with new equipment:
Profit = (35)(70,000) − [200,000 + 13(70,000)] = \$1,340,000
Easy Tech will increase their profitability by \$240,000 annually if they improve their software quality.

b. Profit = (40)(40,000) − [200,000 + 13(40,000)] = \$880,000
Easy Tech should not consider increasing their selling price as this pricing strategy results in lower profitability.

Chapter 4

1. **a.** Total cost of outsourcing = total cost of insourcing
120,000 + 2.25Q = 300,000 + 1.50Q
Q = 240,000 units

b. If Q = 300,000 units:
Total cost of outsourcing = 120,000 + 2.25(300,000) = \$795,000
Total cost of insourcing = 300,000 + 1.50(300,000) = \$750,000
Insourcing is a cheaper alternative.

3. **a.** Total cost at Downhill Boards = 125,000 + 0.90 (160,000) = \$269,000 per year

b. Total cost at Durable Finish $= 170,000 + 0.65$ $(160,000) = \$274,000$ per year

c. The point of indifference is when both costs are the same.

$125,000 + 0.90Q = 170,000 + 0.65Q$
$Q = 180,000$ snowboards

d. Annual demand must be greater than 180,000 units to justify outsourcing the process, which is an increase of over 20,000 units from the current annual demand of 160,000.

5. a. Total cost with in-house purchasing $=$ $85,000 + 15\,(1,450) = \$106,750$ per year

b. Total cost using Value-Buy $= 100,000 +$ $5\,(1,450) = \$107,250$ per year

c. Point of indifference is calculated by setting the total cost of in-house purchasing to the total cost using Value-Buy:

$85,000 + 15Q = 100,000 + 5Q$
$Q = 1,500$ purchases

d. Compare the two different costs at $Q = 1,600$:
Total cost using $VB = 100,000 + 5(1,600) =$ $\$108,000$

Total cost with in-house purchasing $=$ $85,000 + 15(1,600) = \$109,000$
They should use VB since the cost will be $\$1000$ cheaper than in-house purchasing.

e. Additional factors that should be considered are quality control issues, on-time deliveries, inventory costs, and the core competencies of the organization.

Chapter 6

1. a. Mean of sample $1 = (5.8 + 5.9 + 6.0 + 6.1)/4 = 5.95$

Mean of sample $2 = (6.2 + 6.0 + 5.9 + 5.9)/4 = 6$

Mean of sample $3 = (6.1 + 5.9 + 6.0 + 5.8)/4 = 5.95$

Mean of sample $4 = (6.0 + 5.9 + 5.0 + 6.1)/4 = 5.975$

b. The mean of the sampling distribution is the average of the sample means $\bar{x} = $ Mean $=$ $(5.95 + 6 + 5.95 + 5.975)/4 = 5.97$

The standard deviation of the sampling distribution is computed as $\dfrac{\sigma}{\sqrt{n}}$. The population standard deviation σ can be estimated from the 4 samples using the equation:

$$\sqrt{\dfrac{\sum_{i=1}^{n}(x_i - \bar{x})^2}{n-1}},$$ where $n = 16$, and $\bar{X} = 5.97$,

therefore $\sigma = 0.1138$. The standard deviation of the sampling distribution of the sample means is equal to 0.0569, which is estimated using $\dfrac{\sigma}{\sqrt{n}}$, where $\sigma = 0.1138$, and $n = 4$ (i.e., the number of observations in each sample).

c. Center Line (CL) $= \bar{x} = 5.97$

$$UCL = \bar{x} + 3\ \dfrac{\sigma}{\sqrt{n}} = 5.97 + 3\,(0.0569) =$$
6.14

$$LCL = \bar{x} - 3\ \dfrac{\sigma}{\sqrt{n}} = 5.97 - 3\,(0.0569) =$$
5.80

3. $\bar{x} = 19.8$ ounces, $\bar{R} = 0.4$ ounces, $A_2 = 0.58$ for $n = 5$

$CL = \bar{x} = 19.8$
$UCL = \bar{x} + A_2\bar{R} = 19.8 + 0.58\,(0.4) = 20.03$
$LCL = \bar{x} - A_2\bar{R} = 19.8 - 0.58\,(0.4) = 19.57$

4.

Sample	Sample 1	2	3	4	Mean	Range
1	16.40	16.11	15.90	15.78	16.05	0.62
2	15.97	16.10	16.20	15.81	16.02	0.39
3	15.91	16.00	16.04	15.92	15.97	0.13
4	16.20	16.21	15.93	15.95	16.07	0.28
5	15.87	16.21	16.34	16.43	16.21	0.56
6	15.43	15.49	15.55	15.92	15.60	0.49
7	16.43	16.21	15.99	16.00	16.16	0.44
8	15.50	15.92	16.12	16.02	15.89	0.62
9	16.13	16.21	16.05	16.01	16.10	0.20
10	15.68	16.43	16.20	15.97	16.07	0.75
				Mean	16.01	0.45

$\bar{x} = 16.01$
$\bar{R} = 0.45$

Control limits for X-bar chart:

$CL = 16.01$
$UCL = 16.01 + (0.73)(0.45) = 16.34$
$LCL = 16.01 - (0.73)(0.45) = 15.68$

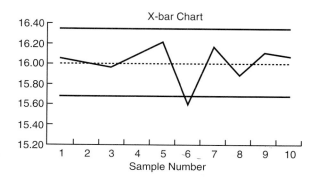

X-bar Chart

Control Limits for R-chart:
CL = 0.45
UCL = (2.28)(0.45) = 1.03
LCL = (0)(0.45) = 0

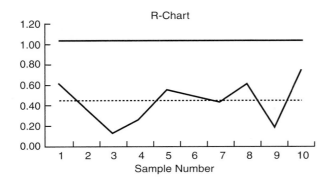

The process mean is not in control.
  b. The process is not capable of meeting the design standards. Design standards dictate that fill levels range between 16.3 and 15.7 ounces. There are nine observations that do not fall in this range.
5. $\bar{R} = 0.3$ ounces, $D_4 = 2.11$, $D_3 = 0$, $n = 5$
CL = $\bar{R}$ = 0.3 ounce
UCL = $D_4 \bar{R}$ = 2.11(0.3) = 0.633
LCL = $D_3 \bar{R}$ = 0(0.3) = 0

7. CL = $\bar{P}$ = $\dfrac{6}{100}$ = 0.06

$$UCL = 0.06 + 3\sqrt{\frac{0.06(1-0.06)}{20}} = 0.22$$

$$LCL = 0.06 - 3\sqrt{\frac{0.06(1-0.06)}{20}} = 0$$

(rounded to zero since the LCL value is negative)

9. CL = $\bar{C}$ = $\dfrac{10}{9}$ = 1.11

UCL = 1.11 + 3 $\sqrt{1.11}$ = 4.27
LCL = 1.11 − 3 $\sqrt{1.11}$ = 0 (rounded to zero since the LCL value is negative)

11. C_p(Machine A)
$$= \frac{USL - LSL}{6\sigma} = \frac{16.2 - 15.8}{6(0.2)} = 0.33$$
C_p(Machine B)
$$= \frac{USL - LSL}{6\sigma} = \frac{16.2 - 15.8}{6(0.3)} = 0.22$$
C_p(Machine C)
$$= \frac{USL - LSL}{6\sigma} = \frac{16.2 - 15.8}{6(0.05)} = 1.33$$
Machine A is the only capable machine since its C_p value is greater than 1.

13.

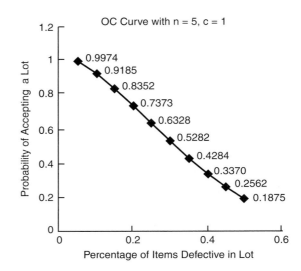

14. a. A c-chart should be used.
CL = $\bar{C}$ = 3 defects/day
UCL = $\bar{C} + 3\sqrt{\bar{C}}$ = 3 + 3$\sqrt{3}$ = 8.20

LCL = $\bar{C} - 3\sqrt{\bar{C}}$ = 3 − 3$\sqrt{3}$ = 0 (rounded to zero since the LCL value is negative)
  b. The process appears to be out of control since 9 defects exceed the upper control limit (UCL) value of 8.20.

15.

	Percentage of Items Defective (p)									
	0.05	0.1	0.15	0.2	0.25	0.3	0.35	0.4	0.45	0.5
	0.9138	0.7361	0.5443	0.3758	0.244	0.1493	0.086	0.0436	0.0232	0.0108

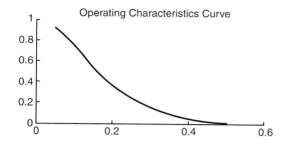

Operating Characteristics Curve

16. a. $n = 233$
$c = 17$
b. AOQL = 4.77%

Chapter 7

1. $D = 30$ packages per hour
$T = 20$ minutes $= 1/3$ hour
$C = 5$ packages per container
$$N = \frac{DT}{C} = \frac{(30)(1/3)}{5} = 2 \text{ Kanbans}$$

2. a. $D = 10$ thermostats per hour
$T = 30$ minutes $= 1/2$ hour
$C = 5$ thermostats per container
$$N = \frac{DT}{C} = \frac{(10)(1/2)}{5} = 1 \text{ Kanban}$$

b. $N = \dfrac{DT + \text{SafetyStock}}{C}$

$$= \frac{(10)(1/2) + 2}{5} = 1.4 \text{ Kanbans}$$

5. $D = (500 \text{ pounds/day})(1 \text{ day/8 hours})$
$= 62.5$ pounds/hour
$T = 1$ hour
$C = 10$ per container
$N = (62.5)(1)/10 = 6.25$ containers

Chapter 8

1. $F_5 = (A_2 + A_3 + A_4)/3 = (350 + 287 + 300)/3 = 312.33$

2. Naïve method: $F_6 = A_5 = 460$
Simple average: $F_6 = (A_1 + A_2 + A_3 + A_4 + A_5)/5 = (432 + 396 + 415 + 458 + 460)/5 = 432.2$
3-period moving average: $F_6 = (A_3 + A_4 + A_5)/3 = (415 + 458 + 460)/3 = 444.3$

3. a. 3-period moving average: $F_{\text{June}} = (A_{\text{March}} + A_{\text{April}} + A_{\text{May}})/3 = (38 + 39 + 43)/3 = 40$
5-period moving average: $F_{\text{June}} = (A_{\text{January}} + A_{\text{February}} + A_{\text{March}} + A_{\text{April}} + A_{\text{May}})/5 = (32 + 41 + 38 + 39 + 43)/5 = 38.6$

b. Naïve: $F_{\text{June}} = A_{\text{May}} = 43$

c. 3-period moving average: $F_{\text{July}} = (A_{\text{April}} + A_{\text{May}} + A_{\text{June}})/3 = (39 + 43 + 41)/3 = 41$
5-period moving average: $F_{\text{July}} = (A_{\text{February}} + A_{\text{March}} + A_{\text{April}} + A_{\text{May}} + A_{\text{June}})/5 = (41 + 38 + 39 + 43 + 41)/5 = 40.4$
Naïve: $F_{\text{July}} = A_{\text{June}} = 41$

8.3.d.

Month	Actual	3-Period Moving Average	Absolute Error	5-Period Moving Average	Absolute Error	Naïve	Absolute Error
January	32						
February	41					32	9
March	38					41	3
April	39	37	2			38	1
May	43	39.33	3.67			39	4
June	41	40	1	38.6	2.4	43	2

MAD(3-period moving average) =
$$\frac{\Sigma|\text{Actual} - \text{Forecast}|}{n} =$$
$(2 + 3.67 + 1)/3 = 2.22$

MAD(5-period moving average) =
$$\frac{\Sigma|\text{Actual} - \text{Forecast}|}{n} = 2.4/1 = 2.4$$

MAD(naïve) =
$$\frac{\Sigma|\text{Actual} - \text{Forecast}|}{n} =$$
$(9 + 3 + 1 + 4 + 2)/5 = 3.8$
The 3-period moving average provides the best historical fit using the MAD criterion and thus would be better to use.

e.

Month	Actual	3-Period Moving Average	Squared Error	5-Period Moving Average	Squared Error	Naïve	Squared Error
January	32						
February	41					32	81
March	38					41	9
April	39	37	4			38	1
May	43	39.33	13.47			39	16
June	41	40	1	38.6	5.76	43	4

MSE(3-period moving average) $=$

$$\frac{\Sigma(\text{Actual} - \text{Forecast})^2}{n - 1} =$$

$(4 + 13.47 + 1)/2 = 9.24$

MSE(5-period moving average) $=$

$$\frac{\Sigma(\text{Actual} - \text{Forecast})^2}{n - 1} : \text{Not possible to}$$

compute since there are not enough observations (i.e., $n = 1$).

MSE(naïve) $=$

$$\frac{\Sigma(\text{Actual} - \text{Forecast})^2}{n - 1} = (81 + 9 + 1 +$$

$16 + 4)/4 = 111/4 = 27.75$

The 3-period moving average provides the best historical fit using the MSE criterion.

5. Forecasts using $\alpha = 0.1$:

Week	Demand	Exponential Smoothing	Absolute Error
1	330	330	
2	350	330	20
3	320	332	12
4	370	330.8	39.2
5	368	334.72	33.28
6	343	338.048	4.952
		MAD:	21.89

Forecasts using $\alpha = 0.7$:

Week	Demand	Exponential Smoothing	Absolute Error
1	330	330	
2	350	330	20
3	320	344	24
4	370	327.2	42.8
5	368	357.16	10.84
6	343	364.748	21.748
		MAD:	23.88

Using $\alpha = 0.1$ provides a better historical fit based on the MAD criterion.

7.

Week	Demand	3-Period Moving Average	Absolute Error
1	20		
2	31		
3	36		
4	38	29	9
5	42	35	7
6	40	38.67	1.33
		MAD:	5.776667
		MSE:	65.88

Week	Demand	Exponential Smoothing	Absolute Error
1	20	20	
2	31	20	11
3	36	22.2	13.8
4	38	24.96	13.04
5	42	27.568	14.432
6	40	30.4544	9.5456
		MAD:	12.36352
		MSE:	195.2207

Regression model: Demand $= 21 + 3.857$ Time

Time (X)	Demand (Y)	X^2	XY
1	20	1	20
2	31	4	62
3	36	9	108
4	38	16	152
5	42	25	210
6	40	36	240
Total: 21	207	91	792

$\overline{X} = 21/6 = 3.5$

$\overline{Y} = 207/6 = 34.5$

$$b = \frac{\Sigma XY - n\overline{X}\,\overline{Y}}{\Sigma X^2 - n\overline{X}^2} = \frac{792 - (6)(3.5)(34.5)}{91 - 6(3.5)^2} = 3.857$$

$$a = \overline{Y} - b\overline{X} = 34.5 - 3.857(3.5) = 21$$

Week	Demand	Regression Line	Absolute Error
1	20	24.857	4.857
2	31	28.714	2.286
3	36	32.571	3.429
4	38	36.428	1.572
5	42	40.285	1.715
6	40	44.142	4.142
		MAD:	3.00
		MSE:	12.63

The linear regression model provides the best historical fit using the MAD and the MSE criteria.

8. $A_{December} = 1,100$ units/month
$S_{Nov} = 1,000$ units/month
$T_{Nov} = 200$ units/month
$\alpha = 0.20$
$\beta = 0.10$
Step 1: Smoothing the level of the series:
$S_{Dec} = \alpha A_{Dec} + (1 - \alpha)(S_{Nov} + T_{Nov}) =$
$0.20(1100) + 0.80(1200) = 1,180$ units
Step 2: Smoothing the trend:
$T_{Dec} = \beta(S_{Dec} - S_{Nov}) + (1 - \beta)T_{Nov} =$
$0.10(1180 - 1000) + 0.90(200) = 198$ units
Step 3: Forecast including trend:
$FIT = S_{Dec} + T_{Dec} = 1180 + 198 = 1378$ units

9. *Step 1*: Average demand for each season:
Year 1: 2840/4 = 710
Year 2: 3241/4 = 810.25
Step 2: Seasonal index for each season:

Season	Year 1	Year 2
Fall	200/710 = 0.282	230/810.25 = 0.284
Winter	1400/710 = 1.972	1600/810.25 = 1.975
Spring	520/710 = 0.732	580/810.25 = 0.716
Summer	720/710 = 1.014	831/810.25 = 1.026

Step 3: Average seasonal index for each season:

Season	Forecast
Fall	0.283
Winter	1.973
Spring	0.724
Summer	1.020

Step 4: Average demand per season = 4000/4
= 1000
Step 5: Multiply next year's average seasonal demand by each seasonal index.

Season	Forecast
Fall	283
Winter	1973
Spring	724
Summer	1020

11. a. The correlation coefficient is 0.9887. This high correlation indicates that there is a strong linear association between sales and training hours.
   b. Using a regression model:
   Sales = −16.6 + 4.455 training hours
   If training hours = 18, then
   Sales = −16.6 + 4.455 × 18
   = 63.59 (in thousands)

12. Regression model:
   enrollment = 196.8 + 22.4 × Year
   Year 6 forecast: 196.8 + 22.4 × 6 = 331.2
   Year 7 forecast: 196.8 + 22.4 × 7 = 353.6

13. a. Resort attendance = $a + b$ (average temperature)
   Using regression analysis, the estimated model is:
   resort attendance = 58.65 − 0.65 (average temperature).
   Resort attendance forecast when the average temperature is 45 degrees:
   = 58.65 − 0.65 (45) = 29.4 thousand attendees.
   b. The correlation coefficient is = −0.97. Since this value is very close to 1, it indicates that the average temperature is a strong predictor of resort attendance. Note that since the sign is negative, it indicates that an inverse or negative relationship exists between the two variables.

14. *Step 1*:
   Average demand for each quarter for year 1
   = (352 + 156 + 489 + 314)/4 = 327.75
   Average demand for each quarter for year 2
   = (391 + 212 + 518 + 352)/4 = 368.25
   Step 2:
   Compute a seasonal index for every season of every year:

Quarter	Year 1	Year 2
Fall	352/327.75 = 1.07	391/368.25 = 1.06
Winter	156/327.75 = 0.48	212/368.25 = 0.58
Spring	489/327.75 = 1.49	518/368.25 = 1.41
Summer	314/327.75 = 0.96	352/368.25 = 0.95

   Step 3:
   Calculate the average seasonal index for each season:

Quarter	Average Seasonal Index
Fall	(1.07 + 1.06)/2 = 1.065
Winter	(0.48 + 0.58)/2 = 0.53
Spring	(1.49 + 1.41)/2 = 1.45
Summer	(0.96 + 0.95)/2 = 0.955

Step 4:
Calculate the average demand per season for
next year = 1525/4 = 381.25
Step 5:
Multiply next year's average seasonal demand by
each seasonal index.

Quarter	Forecast
Fall	(381.25)(1.065) = 406.03
Winter	(381.25)(0.53) = 202.06
Spring	(381.25)(1.45) = 552.81
Summer	(381.25)(0.955) = 364.09

20. a.

Period	Actual	Forecast A	Absolute Error	Squared Error
1	10	10	0	0
2	8	11	3	9
3	12	12	0	0
4	11	13	2	4
5	12	14	2	4
		Total	7	17

$$MAD_A = (0 + 3 + 0 + 2 + 2)/5 = 7/5$$
$$= 1.4$$
$$MSE_A = (0 + 9 + 0 + 4 + 4)/4 = 17/4$$
$$= 4.25$$

Period	Actual	Forecast B	Absolute Error	Squared Error
1	10	9	1	1
2	8	10	2	4
3	12	8	4	16
4	11	12	1	1
5	12	11	1	1
		Total	9	23

$$MAD_B = (1 + 2 + 4 + 1 + 1)/5 = 9/5$$
$$= 1.8$$
$$MSE_B = (1 + 4 + 16 + 1 + 1)/4 = 23/4$$
$$= 5.75$$

Period	Actual	Forecast C	Absolute Error	Squared Error
1	10	8	2	4
2	8	11	3	9
3	12	10	2	4
4	11	11	0	0
5	12	12	0	0
		Total	7	17

$$MAD_C = (2 + 3 + 2 + 0 + 0)/5 = 7/5$$
$$= 1.4$$
$$MSE_C = (4 + 9 + 4 + 0 + 0)/4 = 17/4$$
$$= 4.25$$

b. Forecast method B is the naïve method.

Week	Actual Sales	Forecast	Deviation	Cumulative Deviation	Tracking Signal
				6	3
1	12	11	1	7	3.5
2	14	13	1	8	4
3	14	14	0	8	4
4	16	14	2	10	5

22. The forecast should be reviewed in weeks 2, 3,
and 4 because the tracking signal has reached or
exceeded +4.

Chapter 9

1. $Utilization_{Effective} = \dfrac{ActualOutput}{EffectiveCapacity}(100\%)$

$$= \dfrac{300}{250}(100\%) = 120\%$$

$Utilization_{Design} = \dfrac{ActualOutput}{DesignCapacity}(100\%)$

$$= \dfrac{300}{400}(100\%) = 75\%$$

The utilization rates show that the facility's current output is below its design capacity and considerably higher than its effective capacity. The facility can probably operate at the effective level
for only a short time.

3. a. Effective capacity = 60 brownies
Design capacity = 100 brownies

b. $Utilization_{Effective} = \dfrac{ActualOutput}{EffectiveCapacity}$

$$(100\%) = \dfrac{64}{60}(100\%) = 106.67\%$$

$Utilization_{Design} = \dfrac{ActualOutput}{DesignCapacity}$

$$(100\%) = \dfrac{64}{100}(100\%) = 64\%$$

The utilization rates show that the facility's current output is below its design capacity and considerably higher than its effective capacity. The facility can probably operate at the effective level
for only a short time.

7. a.

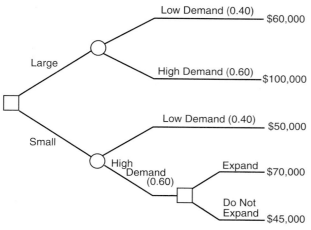

b. $EV_{small\ expansion} = 50,000(0.40) + 70,000\ (0.60)$
$= \$62,000$
$EV_{large\ expansion} = 60,000(0.40) + 100,000\ (0.60)$
$= \$84,000$
Company should opt for the large expansion.

8. a.

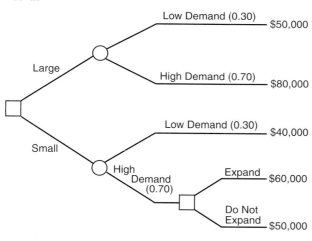

b. $EV_{small\ expansion} = 60,000(0.70) + 40,000\ (0.30)$
$= \$54,000$
$EV_{large\ expansion} = 80,000(0.70) + 50,000\ (0.30)$
$= \$71,000$
Company should opt for the large expansion now.

12.

Factor	Factor Weight	Factor Score for Location 1	Factor Score for Location 2	Weighted Score for Location 1	Weighted Score for Location 2
Proximity to airport	40	5	3	200	120
Proximity to road access	30	4	1	120	30
Proximity to labor source	10	3	5	30	50
Size of facility	20	2	4	40	80
			Total	390	280

Location 1 is the better location because it provides a higher factor rating score than location 2.

15. Load-distance score $_{Jasper} = \Sigma l_{ij}\ d_{ij} = (30)(15) + (6)(10) + (10.5)(12) + (4.5)(8) = 672$
Load-distance score $_{Longboat} = \Sigma l_{ij}\ d_{ij} = (12)(15) + (12)(10) + (30)(12) + (24)(8) = 852$
Warehouse should be located in Jasper.

16.

	Load (l_i)	$l_i x_i$	$l_i y_i$
	15	60	270
	10	120	20
	12	120	96
	8	64	120
Total	45	364	506

$$X_{c.g.} = \frac{\Sigma l_i x_i}{\Sigma l_i} = \frac{364}{45} = 8.1$$

$$Y_{c.g.} = \frac{\Sigma l_i y_i}{\Sigma l_i} = \frac{506}{45} = 11.2$$

17. Total Cost $_A = 70,000 + 1(2000) = \$72,000$
Total Cost $_B = 34,000 + 5(2000) = \$44,000$
Total Cost $_C = 20,000 + 8(2000) = \$36,000$
Total Cost $_D = 50,000 + 4(2000) = \$58,000$
Location C is best.

18. Total Cost $_A = 85,000 + (3000)(2) = \$91,000$
Total Cost $_B = 49,000 + (3000)(7) = \$70,000$
Total Cost $_C = 35,000 + (3000)(10) = \$65,000$
Total Cost $_D = 65,000 + (3000)(6) = \$83,000$
Location C is best because it provides the lowest total annual costs.

Chapter 10

1.

Departments	Number of Trips (*l*)	Current Layout Distance (*d*)	Current Layout Load-Distance Score (*ld*)	Proposed layout Distance (*d*)	Proposed layout Load-Distance Score (*ld*)
AB	15	1	15	2	30
AC	45	2	90	1	45
AD	25	1	25	2	50
AE	10	2	20	1	10
AF	50	3	150	3	150
BC	30	1	30	1	30
BD	16	2	32	2	32
BE	25	1	25	1	25
BF	25	2	50	1	25
CD	34	3	102	3	102
CE	15	2	30	2	30
CF	20	1	20	2	40
DE	40	1	40	1	40
DF	10	2	20	1	10
EF	20	1	20	2	40
Total			669		659

Proposed layout is the preferred one due to lower *ld* score.

2. The following departments have the highest number of trips between them and should be located close to each other:

A and F, which have 50 trips between them
A and C, which have 45 trips between them
Proposed layout:

A	C	D
F	B	E

Compute the *ld* scores for both the current and proposed layouts in order to make an evaluation.

Departments	Proposed Layout Number of Trips (*l*)	Proposed Layout Distance (*d*)	Proposed Layout Load-Distance Score (*ld*)
AB	15	2	30
AC	45	1	45
AD	25	2	50
AE	10	3	30
AF	50	1	50
BC	30	1	30
BD	16	2	32
BE	25	1	25
BF	25	1	25
CD	34	1	34
CE	15	2	30
CF	20	2	40
DE	40	1	40
DF	10	3	30
EF	20	2	40
Total			531

Proposed layout is the preferred one.

3.

Departments	Number of Trips (l)	Current Layout Distance (d)	Current Layout Load-Distance Score (ld)	Proposed layout Distance (d)	Proposed layout Load-Distance Score (ld)
AB	5	1	5	1	5
AC	20	2	40	2	40
AD	5	1	5	1	5
AF	8	2	16	2	16
BD	30	2	60	2	60
BE	10	2	20	2	20
BF	10	3	30	1	10
CD	20	3	60	1	20
CE	15	1	15	1	15
CF	5	2	10	2	10
EF	17	1	17	1	17
		Total	278		218

Proposed location is better based on the ld score.

7. To assign departments to specific storage areas, we progressively assign departments with the highest number of trips closest to the dock. Using this logic, the following block plan is developed:

	2	4	5
Dock			
	6	1	3

8. *Step 1:*
Compute the ratios of number of trips to the area needed.

Department	Trips to and from Dock	Area Needed	Ratio of trips to Area Needed
1	160	2	80
2	100	1	100
3	150	3	50
4	120	1	120
5	270	3	90

Step 2:
Use the ratios from step 1 to assign departments to storage areas

	4	5	5	1	3
Dock			Aisle		
	2	5	1	3	3

10.

Proposed layout Distance (d)	Proposed layout Load-Distance Score (ld)
1	6
2	24
1	18
1	1
3	3
2	8
1	19
1	3
1	0
3	15
1	0
1	0
2	14
2	38
2	0
Total	149

This plan is better because it yields a lower total ld score.

12. a. Task F is the bottleneck
b.

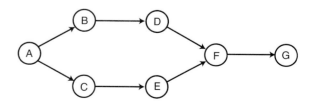

c. $C = (3{,}600 \text{ seconds/hour})/(60 \text{ units/hour}) = 60$ seconds/unit

13. a.

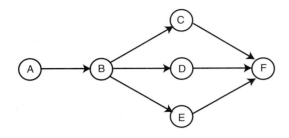

b. $C =$ (3,600 seconds/hour)/(50 units/hour)
$= 72$ seconds/unit

c. TM $= \dfrac{\Sigma t}{C} = \dfrac{225}{72} = 3.125$ or 4 stations

d.

Station	Task
1	A
2	B, E
3	D
4	C
5	F

e. Efficiency $= \dfrac{\Sigma t}{NC}$ (100%) $= \dfrac{225}{(5)(72)}$ (100%)
$= 62.5\%$

Balance Delay (%) $= 37.5\%$

15. a. Task A is the bottleneck.

b. $C =$ (3,600 seconds/hour)/(50 units/hour)
$= 72$ seconds/unit

c.

Work Station	Task Selected	Task Time	Idle Time
1	A	55	17
2	C	22	50
	E	50	0
3	B	30	42
	D	35	7
4	F	15	57
	G	5	52
	H	10	42

d. TM $= \dfrac{\Sigma t}{C} = \dfrac{222}{72} = 3.08$ or 4 stations.
Same number of stations as the theoretical
minimum stations was used.

e. Efficiency $=$
$\dfrac{\Sigma t}{NC}$ (100%) $= \dfrac{222}{(4)(72)}$ (100%) $= 77.08\%$
Balance Delay (%) $= 22.92\%$

17. a. $C =$ (3,600 seconds/hour)/(30 units/hour)
$= 120$ seconds/unit

b. TM $= \dfrac{\Sigma t}{C} = \dfrac{270}{120} = 2.25$ or 3 stations

c.

Work Station	Task Selected
1	A
	B
	D
	F
	C
2	E
	G
	H
	I
3	J
	K

d. Efficiency $= \dfrac{\Sigma t}{NC}$ (100%) $= \dfrac{3,270}{(3)(120)}$
(100%) $= 75\%$
Balance Delay $= 25\%$

18. a. $C =$ (3,600 seconds/hour)/(30 units/hour)
$= 120$ seconds/dress

b. Task D

c. Maximum output $=$ (available time)/(minimum cycle time) $=$ (3,600 seconds/hour)/
(100 seconds/unit) $= 36$ dresses per hour

d. TM $= \dfrac{\Sigma t}{C} = \dfrac{405}{120} = 3.38$ or 4 stations

e.

Work Station	Task Selected
1	B
	A
	C
2	D
3	E
	F
4	G
5	H

f. Efficiency $= \dfrac{\Sigma t}{NC}$ (100%) $= \dfrac{405}{(5)(120)}$
(100%) $= 67.5\%$
Balance Delay $= 32.5\%$

Chapter 11

1. With $z = 2.17$ and $e = 0.05$, the number of observations needed for each work element is:

Work element 1: $n = \left[\dfrac{2.17}{0.05} \times \dfrac{0.20}{1.10}\right]^2 = 63$

Work element 2: $n = \left[\dfrac{2.17}{0.05} \times \dfrac{0.10}{0.80}\right]^2 = 30$

Work element 3: $n = \left[\dfrac{2.17}{0.05} \times \dfrac{0.15}{0.90}\right]^2 = 53$

Work element 4: $n = \left[\dfrac{2.17}{0.05} \times \dfrac{0.10}{1.00}\right]^2 = 19$

Sample size needed is 63.

2. With $z = 2.57$ and $e = 0.05$, the number of observations needed for each work element is:

Work element 1: $n = \left[\dfrac{2.57}{0.05} \times \dfrac{0.20}{1.10}\right]^2 = 88$

Work element 2: $n = \left[\dfrac{2.57}{0.05} \times \dfrac{0.10}{0.80}\right]^2 = 42$

Work element 3: $n = \left[\dfrac{2.57}{0.05} \times \dfrac{0.15}{0.90}\right]^2 = 74$

Work element 4: $n = \left[\dfrac{2.57}{0.05} \times \dfrac{0.10}{1.00}\right]^2 = 27$

Sample size needed is 88.

5.

Work Element	Normal Time (NT)
1	1.14
2	0.85
3	0.88
4	0.99

6. $ST = (NT)(AF)$, where $AF = 1 + PFD$
   $= 1 + 0.15 = 1.15$
   $ST_{\text{element 1}} = (1.14)(1.15) = 1.311$
   $ST_{\text{element 2}} = (0.85)(1.15) = 0.978$
   $ST_{\text{element 3}} = (1.14)(1.15) = 1.012$
   $ST_{\text{element 4}} = (0.99)(1.15) = 1.139$
   $ST_{\text{job}} = (1.311 + 0.978 + 1.012 + 1.139)$
   $= 4.440$

7. $(1\text{ unit}/4.44\text{ minutes}) \times (60\text{ minutes/hour}) \times (8\text{ hours/day}) = 108.1\text{ units/day}$

8. $ST = (NT)(AF)$, where $AF =$
   $\dfrac{1}{1-PFD} = \dfrac{1}{1-0.15} = 1.176$
   $ST_{\text{element 1}} = (1.14)(1.176) = 1.341$
   $ST_{\text{element 2}} = (0.85)(1.176) = 1.000$
   $ST_{\text{element 3}} = (0.88)(1.176) = 1.035$
   $ST_{\text{element 4}} = (0.99)(1.176) = 1.164$
   $ST_{\text{job}} = (1.341 + 1.000 + 1.035 + 1.164)$
   $= 4.540\text{ minutes}$

11. **a.**

Element	Mean Observed Time
1	2.194
2	1.265
3	1.771
4	2.608
5	1.576

b. Normal time = (mean observed time)(performance rating factor)(frequency)
Normal time $_{\text{element 1}} = (2.194)(0.90)(1)$
$= 1.975\text{ minutes}$
Normal time $_{\text{element 2}} = (1.265)(0.80)(1)$
$= 1.012\text{ minutes}$
Normal time $_{\text{element 3}} = (1.771)(1.10)(1)$
$= 1.948\text{ minutes}$
Normal time $_{\text{element 4}} = (2.608)(1.05)(1)$
$= 2.738\text{ minutes}$
Normal time $_{\text{element 5}} = (1.576)(0.95)(1)$
$= 1.497\text{ minutes}$

c. $ST_{\text{element 1}} = (1.975)(1.20) = 2.370\text{ minutes}$
$ST_{\text{element 2}} = (1.012)(1.20) = 1.214\text{ minutes}$
$ST_{\text{element 3}} = (1.948)(1.20) = 2.338\text{ minutes}$
$ST_{\text{element 4}} = (2.738)(1.20) = 3.286\text{ minutes}$
$ST_{\text{element 5}} = (1.497)(1.20) = 1.796\text{ minutes}$
Standard time for job $= (2.37 + 1.214 + 2.338 + 3.286 + 1.796) = 11.004\text{ minutes}$

d. $(60\text{ minutes/hour})(1\text{ unit}/11.004\text{ minutes}) = 5.45\text{ units/hour}$

e. $(5.45\text{ units/hour})(0.90) = 4.9\text{ units/hour}$

14. **a.**

Element	Mean Observed Time (minutes)
1	0.582
2	1.515
3	0.759
4	0.319
5	2.1

b. Normal time $_{element\ 1}$ = $(0.582)(0.95)(1)$
= 0.553 minutes
Normal time $_{element\ 2}$ = $(1.515)(0.90)(0.25)$
= 0.341 minutes
Normal time $_{element\ 3}$ = $(0.759)(1)(1)$
= 0.759 minutes
Normal time $_{element\ 4}$ = $(0.319)(1.10)(1)$
= 0.351 minutes
Normal time $_{element\ 5}$ = $(2.10)(0.90)(0.20)$
= 0.378 minutes

c. ST $_{element\ 1}$ = $(0.553)(1.20)$ = 0.664 minutes
ST $_{element\ 2}$ = $(0.341)(1.20)$ = 0.409 minutes
ST $_{element\ 3}$ = $(0.759)(1.20)$ = 0.911 minutes
ST $_{element\ 4}$ = $(0.351)(1.20)$ = 0.421 minutes
ST $_{element\ 5}$ = $(0.378)(1.20)$ = 0.454 minutes
Standard time for Job = $(0.664 + 0.409 +$
$0.911 + 0.421 + 0.454)$ = 2.859 minutes

d. (60 minutes/hour)(1 unit/2.859 minutes)
= 20.99 units/hour

e. (20.99 units/hour)(1.10) = 23.09 units/hour

16. $n = (1.96/0.05)^2 (0.5)(1 - 0.5)$
= 385 observations

Chapter 12

2. a. AIT = $(15)(18000)/365$ = 739.7 units
b. AIT = $(2)(18000)/365$ = 98.6 units
c. Cost-related information is needed to compare the two alternatives. For example, transportation costs, insurance costs, and the speed and reliability of the mode of service delivery are important considerations in comparing the two alternatives.

4. a. Inventory turnover = $\$3,600,000/\$250,000$ = 14.4 inventory turns
b. Weeks of supply = $\$250,000/(3,600,000/52)$ = 3.6 weeks of supply

6. a. Annual holding cost rate = 20.5%
b. Annual holding costs = $(\$3,400,000)(0.205)$ = \$697,000

8. a. Annual holding cost rate = 10% + 4.5% + 10% = 24.5%
b. Total annual holding costs = $(0.245)(3,400,000)$ = \$833,000

9. a. Average inventory level = $\dfrac{Q}{2} = \dfrac{1300}{2} =$
650 units
b. Number of orders placed per year (N) =
$\dfrac{D}{Q} = \dfrac{5200}{1300}$ = 4 orders

c. Annual inventory holding cost = $\dfrac{Q}{2} H =$
$(650)(3)$ = \$1950
d. Total annual ordering cost = $(D/Q)(S)$ =
$(4)(50)$ = \$200
e. Total annual cost = $\$1950 + \$200 = \$2150$

10. a. Average inventory level = $\dfrac{Q}{2} = \dfrac{650}{2} =$
325 units
b. Number of orders placed per year = $\dfrac{D}{Q} =$
$\dfrac{5200}{650}$ = 8 orders
c. Annual inventory holding cost = $\dfrac{Q}{2} H =$
$(325)(3)$ = \$975
d. Total annual ordering cost = $(D/Q)(S)$ =
$(8)(50)$ = \$400
e. Total annual cost = $\$975 + \$400 = \$1375$
An order quantity of 650 units yields lower total annual costs than an order quantity of 1300 units.

11. a. EOQ = $\sqrt{\dfrac{2DS}{H}} = \sqrt{\dfrac{(2)(5,200)(50)}{3}} =$
416.33 units
b. Average inventory = $\dfrac{416.33}{2}$ = 208.2 units
c. Number of orders placed per year = $\dfrac{D}{Q} =$
$\dfrac{5,200}{416.33}$ = 12.5
d. Annual ordering cost = $(12.5)(50)$ = \$625
e. Annual inventory holding costs = $\dfrac{Q}{2} H =$
$(208.2)(3)$ = \$624.50
f. Total annual cost = $\$624.50 + \$624$
= \$1249.50
g. The economic order quantity provides the lowest total annual costs.

13. EOQ at price of \$18/bag = $\sqrt{\dfrac{(2)(1,560)(10)}{(18)(0.25)}} =$
83.3 bags (infeasible quantity)

EOQ at price of \$19/bag = $\sqrt{\dfrac{(2)(1,560)(10)}{(19)(0.25)}} =$
81.0 bags (feasible quantity)
Total cost at feasible EOQ amount = $(81/2)(19 \times 0.25) + (1,560/81)(10) + (19)(1,560)$ = \$30,025
Total cost at $q = 100$: $(100/2)(18 \times 0.25) + (1,560/100)(10) + (18)(1,560)$ = \$28,461
Optimal ordering policy is to order 100 bags at a time.

16.

Current total annual costs $= \dfrac{Q}{2}H + \dfrac{D}{Q}S =$

$$\dfrac{(650)}{2}(3) + \dfrac{(150 \times 52)}{650}(20) = \$1,215$$

17. a. $EOQ = \sqrt{\dfrac{2DS}{H}} = \sqrt{\dfrac{(2)(150 \times 52)(20)}{3}} =$

322.5 units

17. (*continued*)

b. Total annual costs $=$

$$\dfrac{Q}{2}H + \dfrac{D}{Q}S = \dfrac{(322.5)}{2}(3) +$$

$$\dfrac{(150 \times 52)}{322.5}(20) = \$967.50$$

c. Lost annual savings $= \$1,215 - \$967.5 =$
$\$247.50$

18.

		Demand (000)					Expected
		75	80	85	90	95	Profit (000)
	75	596.25	596.25	596.25	596.25	596.25	596.25
Order	80	573.75	636	636	636	636	626.6625
Amount	85	551.25	613.5	675.75	675.75	675.75	641.5125
(000)	90	528.75	591	653.25	715.5	715.5	637.6875
	95	506.25	568.5	630.75	693.00	755.25	621.4125

An order amount of 85,000 calendars maximizes expected profits.

23. a. $I_{max} = Q(1 - d/p) = 1,000,000(1 -$
$100,000/250,000) = 600,000$ pounds

b. Total cost $= \dfrac{(5,000,000)(200)}{600,000} +$

$$\dfrac{(600,000)(0.55/50)}{2} = \$4,966.67$$

24. a. $EPQ = \sqrt{\dfrac{(2)(5,000,000)(200)}{(0.55/50)(1 - 100,000/250,000)}}$
$= 550,481.85$ pounds or 11,009.64 bags

b. $I_{max} = Q(1 - d/p) = 550,481.85(1 -$
$100,000/250,000) = 330,289.11$ pounds or
6605.78 bags

24. (*continued*)

c. Total cost $= \dfrac{(5,000,000)(200)}{550,481.85} +$

$$\dfrac{(330,289.11)(0.55/50)}{2} = \$3,633.18$$

d. Penalty cost $= \$4,966.67 - \$3,633.18 =$
$\$1,333.49$

Chapter 13

1. a. Total aggregate production rate $= \sum_{i=1}^{6} de$-
$mand_i = 34,000$ units
Production rate per period $= (34,000 - 400)/6 = 5,600$ units

b. (5,600 units $\times$ 6 hours each)/160 hours per
employee $= 210$ employees

Ch. 13, 2. a.

Period	1	2	3	4	5	6	Total
Demand (units)	5,600	4,800	7,840	5,200	6,560	3,600	33,600
Cumulative Demand	5,600	10,400	18,240	23,440	30,000	33,600	
Period Production	5,600	5,600	5,600	5,600	5,600	5,600	33,600
Cumulative Production	5,600	11,200	16,800	22,400	28,000	33,600	
Ending Inventory	0	800	0	0	0	0	800
Back Orders	0	0	1,440	1,040	2,000	0	4,480

b. Total cost = regular-time labor cost + carrying inventory cost + back-order cost
Total cost = ($10.00 per hour × 160 hours per period × 6 periods × 210 employees) + (800 units × $10 per unit) + (4480 units × $20 per unit) = $2,113,600.

c. Roughly 13.3% of the total demand was not satisfied and had to be placed on back order. In specific, during periods 3, 4, and 5, demand is greater than production and back ordering is necessary. This could present a potential loss to the firm, and therefore customer satisfaction is not optimal under this plan. However, from operations and human resources perspectives, this plan is easy to implement as it uses a constant level of resources. Job security would most likely be high under this plan.

5.

Period	1	2	3	4	5	6	Total
Employees Needed	210	180	294	195	246	135	1,260

6. a.

Period	1	2	3	4	5	6	Total
Demand (units)	5,600	4,800	7,840	5,200	6,560	3,600	34,000
Employees Needed	210	180	294	195	246	135	1,260
Number of Hires	0		114		51		165
Number of Fires		30		99		111	240

b. Total cost = hiring cost + firing cost + regular-time labor cost
Total cost = (165 × $600) + (240 × $450) + ($10/hour × 160 hours/period × 1260 employees) = $2,223,000

c. This plan yields virtually no inventory carrying cost since it produces exactly what is needed. Moreover, customer service is high since no back orders are needed. However, from a planning perspective, this plan would be difficult to implement due to the high variability of resources needed each period. Moreover, employee morale would tend to be fairly low with such a plan due to lack of job security.

9. a. Regular-time production units possible each period given a workforce of 195:
(160 hours/employee/period)/(6 hours/unit) = 26.67 units/employee/period
(26.67 units/employee/period)(195 employees) = 5200 units/period

b.

Period	1	2	3	4	5	6	Total
Subcontracting Amount	500	0	1,000	0	1,000	0	2,500

10. a.

Period	1	2	3	4	5	6	Total
Demand	5600	4,800	7,840	5,200	6,560	3,600	33,600
Regular-Time Production Units	5,200	5,200	5,200	5,200	5,200	5,200	31,200
Subcontracting Amount	500	0	1,000	0	1,000	0	2,500
Ending Inventory	0	400	0	0	0	1,600	2,000
Units Short	0	0	1,240	0	360	0	1,600

b. Total cost = Regular-time production cost + subcontracting cost + ending inventory cost + back-ordering cost + firing cost
Total cost = (31,200 units × 6 hours/unit × $10/hour) + (2500 units × $84/unit) + (2000 units × $10/unit) + (1600 units × $20/unit) + (15 employees × $450) = $2,140,750

c. From an operations perspective, this plan provides stable use of resources throughout the production period. However, periods 3 and 5 will experience back-ordering costs since they will be short in the amounts of 1,240 units and 360 units, respectively. Therefore, this plan will not provide as much customer satisfaction.

12. a.

Period	1	2	3	4	5	6	Total
Demand	5,600	4,800	7,840	5,200	6,560	3,600	
Regular time units produced	5,200	5,200	5,200	5,200	5,200	5,200	31,200
Units produced in OT	1,040	1,040	1,040	1,040	320	0	4,480
Ending inventory	640	2,080	0	1,040	0	1,600	5,360
Back orders	0	0	560	0	0	0	560

b. Total costs = regular-time production cost + overtime cost + inventory cost + back-ordering cost
Total costs = (31,200 units × 6 hours/unit × $10/hour) + (4,480 units × 6 hours/unit × $15/hour) + (5,360 units × $10/unit) + (560 units × $20/unit) = $2,340,000

c. This plan maintains a constant level of workforce, thus providing a constant and predictable number of employees needed each period. However, under this plan anticipated demand cannot be met in period 3 without experiencing back-order costs. Also, this plan relies on building inventory in order to fulfill demand in subsequent periods.

13. Average weekly demand = 43.33 clients
Number of employees needed to meet average weekly demand:
43.33 clients × 12 hours/client = 520 hours
520 hours/40 hours per employee = 13 employees

15. Number of employees needed to meet peak demand:
50 clients × 12 hours/client = 600 hours
600 hours/40 hours per employee = 15 employees

16. a.

Week	1	2	3	4	5	6	Total
Number of Clients	48	36	50	40	38	48	
Service hours Needed	576	432	600	480	456	576	3,120
Regular-time Hours Available	600	600	600	600	600	600	3,600
Undertime Hours	24	168	0	120	144	24	480

b. Total cost = hiring cost + regular-time labor cost
Total cost = (3 employees)($2,000) + (3,600 hours)($25/hour) = $96,000

c. This plan provides a uniform use of resources. Thus, this plan will be easy to implement from an operational perspective. However, about 15.4% of the regular-time hours available are not fully utilized. The underutilized hours could perhaps be used to perform other administrative tasks to improve productivity.

21. a and b.

Week	1	2	3	4	5	6	Total
Temporary Workers Needed	3	0	3	0	0	3	9

22. a.

Week	1	2	3	4	5	6	Total
Number of Clients	48	36	50	40	38	48	
Service hours Needed	576	432	600	480	456	576	3,120
Number of Employees Needed	15	11	15	12	12	15	80
Number of full-time Employees Available	12	12	12	12	12	12	72
Temporary Workers Needed	3	0	3	0	0	3	9

b. Total cost = regular-time labor cost + temporary work cost
Total cost = (72 workers × 40 hours/worker × $25/hour) + (9 workers × 40 hours/worker × $40/hour) = $86,400

c. This plan provides the same level of full-time resources throughout the service periods. Thus, from an operational perspective, it is easy to implement. This plan may be more favored by management because it provides lower benefits costs, since excess service hours are covered by temporary employees. However, training costs may tend to be higher under this plan to elevate the skill levels of the temporary employees.

Chapter 14

1. a and b.

Week	1	2	3	4	5	6
Forecast	20	35	50	50	45	40
Proj Avail 15	67	32	54	4	31	63
MPS	72		72		72	72

c. 63 units in week 6
d. 4 MPS orders are needed.

2. a and b.

Week	1	2	3	4	5	6
Forecast	20	35	50	50	45	40
Proj Avail 15	115	80	30	100	55	15
MPS	120			120		

c. This plan provides higher average inventory per period and lower setup costs than the PMS developed in problem 1.

3. a and b.

Week	1	2	3	4	5	6
Forecast	20	35	50	50	45	40
Proj Avail 15	43	8	6	4	7	15
MPS	48		48	48	48	48

c. This plan provides the highest setup cost but the lowest average inventory per period.

6. a. Machine time required using existing machine:

Period	1	2	3	4	total
Machine Time (hours)	400	700	700	1,100	2,900

Machine time required using new machine:

Period	1	2	3	4	total
Machine Time (hours)	320	720	720	1,360	3,120

b. Total machine time requires 3,120 hours with new machine compared to 2,900 hours with old existing machine. Therefore, new machine will prove to be not beneficial to WAI.

8.

Period	1	2	3	4	5	6	7	8
Forecast	30	30	30	40	40	40	45	45
Customer Orders	35	15	20	18	12	0	15	0
Projected Available 50	15	85	55	15	75	35	90	45
Available-to-promise	15	47			88		85	
MPS		100			100		100	

9. Revised MPS schedule with new orders:

Period	1	2	3	4	5	6	7	8
Forecast	30	30	30	40	40	40	45	45
Customer Orders	60	15	30	18	52	20	15	0
Projected Available 50	−10	60	30	−10	38	−2	53	8
Available-to-promise	−10	37			28		85	
MPS		100			100		100	

From answer to Problem 8, we see that period 1 only has 15 units available, so we reject order #2. Order 1 is accepted since we have 47 available to promise. The new ATP would be 37 units. Accept order 3, change ATP to 48. Accept order 4, reduce ATP in period 5 to 28.

Chapter 15

1.

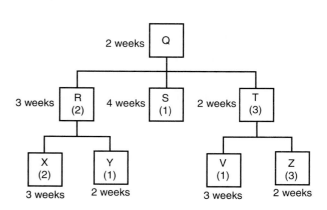

Note: numbers inside parentheses represent usage per parent while numbers outside the boxes indicate lead time in weeks.

2. The cumulative lead time is 8 weeks.

5. The cumulative lead time is 7 weeks.

8.

Component	Gross Requirement
A	2,500
B	5,000
C	2,500
D	7,500
E	5,000
F	20,000
G	10,000
H	22,500
I	15,000
J	5,000
K	25,000
L	10,000
M	60,000
N	120,000
O	45,000
P	25,000
Q	50,000

9.

Component	Gross Requirement
A	2,500
B	4,750
C	2,000
D	6,750
E	4,250
F	16,000
G	8,500
H	15,250
I	8,500
J	3,250
K	16,250
L	6,000
M	47,750
N	95,750
O	30,500
P	15,750
Q	31,500

12.

Product: AB501

Week	1	2	3	4	5	6	7	8	9	10
Gross Requirements	300	500	300	500	300	500	300	500		
Scheduled Receipts										
Projected Available 1100	800	300	0	0	0	0	0	0		
Planned Orders		500	300	500	300	500				

Product: AB511

Week	1	2	3	4	5	6	7	8	9	10
Gross Requirements	150	250	150	250	150	250	150	250		
Scheduled Receipts										
Projected Available 550	400	150	0	0	100	100	200	200		
Planned Orders	250	250	250	250	250					

Product: AB521

Week	1	2	3	4	5	6	7	8	9	10
Gross Requirements	450	750	450	750	450	750	450	750		
Scheduled Receipts										
Projected Available 1650	1200	450	0	1200	750	0	750	0		
Planned Orders		1950			1200					

13. Average inventory for AB501 = 1,100/10 = 110 units

Average inventory for AB511 = 1,150/10 = 115 units

Average inventory for AB521 = 4,350/10 = 435

14. Average inventory for AB501 = 1,100/10 = 110 units

Average inventory for AB511 = 550/10 = 55 units

Average inventory for AB521 = 1,650/10 = 165 units

19.

Orders	Setup + Run Time (hours)
LL110	14
LL118	14
LL131	66
LL140	14

Total time = 108 hours
Capacity needed = 108 hours

20. a. Available weekly capacity = (3 machines)
(8 hours/day)(5 days/week)(0.90 utilization)(0.90 efficiency) = 97.2 hours
b. Additional capacity of 10.8 hours is needed.

21. Available weekly capacity = (3 machines)(10 hours/day)(5 days/week)(0.90 utilization)(0.90 efficiency) = 121.5 hours
This new policy provides adequate capacity.

22. Available weekly capacity = (3 machines)(10 hours/day)(5 days/week)(0.90 utilization)(0.80 efficiency) = 108 hours
There is enough capacity to complete the orders.

Chapter 16

1. a.

	1	2	3	4	5
Planned input	40	50	50	60	60
Actual input	45	45	45	55	60
Deviation	5	−5	−5	−5	0
Cumulative Deviation	5	0	−5	−10	−10

	1	2	3	4	5
Planned output	70	70	70	70	70
Actual output	50	50	60	60	60
Deviation	−20	−20	−10	−10	−10
Cumulative Deviation	−20	−40	−50	−60	−70
Backlog 50 hours	45	40	25	20	20

b. If planned input is consistently below actual input, the work center may not have enough capacity to meet the planned input. The same is true when actual output is consistently less than the planned output.

4. a.

	1	2	3	4	5	Total
Planned input	40	50	50	60	60	260
Planned output	40	50	50	60	60	260

Total planned input/total planned output = 260/260 = 100.00%

b.

	1	2	3	4	5	Total
Actual input	25	35	35	40	40	175
Planned output	40	50	50	60	60	260

Total actual input/total actual output = 175/260 = 67.3%

c. Total actual output/total planned output = 250/260 = 96.2%
Work Center 2 is producing at 96.2% of its total planned output and appears to have a higher productivity level than work center 3.

5. a. Job sequence: B, F, E, C, A, D
b.

B done at end of day 5	F done at end of day 11	E done at end of day 18	C done at end of day 26	A done at end of day 35	D done at end of day 45

Make span = 45 days
Mean job flow time = (5 + 11 + 18 + 26 + 35 + 45)/6 = 23.33 days
Average number of jobs in the system = 140/45 = 3.11 jobs

Mean job lateness = 13/6 = 2.17 days
Mean job tardiness = 45/6 = 7.5 days
Maximum tardiness = 25 days

Job	Completion Date	Due Date	Lateness (days)	Tardiness
A	35	15	20	20
B	5	20	−15	0
C	26	30	−4	0
D	45	20	25	25
E	18	22	−4	0
F	11	20	−9	0
			Total = 13	Total = 45

6. a. Job sequence: B, F, C, E, A, D

b.

Make span = 45 days

Mean job flow time = (5 + 11 + 19 + 26 + 35 + 45)/6 = 23.5 days

B done at end of day 5	F done at end of day 11	C done at end of day 19	E done at end of day 26	A done at end of day 35	D done at end of day 45

Average number of jobs in the system = 141/45 = 3.13 jobs

Mean job lateness = 14/6 = 2.33 days
Mean job tardiness = 49/6 = 8.17 days
Maximum tardiness = 25 days

Job	Completion Date	Due Date	Lateness (days)	Tardiness
A	35	15	20	20
B	5	20	−15	0
C	19	30	−11	0
D	45	20	25	25
E	26	22	4	4
F	11	20	−9	0
			Total = 14	Total = 49

9. a.

Job	Job Time	Remaining job time at other w/cs	Due date	Slack Times	Remaining number of operations at other w/cs	S/RO
A	9	10	30	11	3	2.75
B	5	2	10	3	1	1.5
C	8	8	24	8	2	2.67
D	10	18	40	12	3	3
E	7	12	26	7	1	3.5
F	6	6	15	3	2	1

F done at end of day 6	B done at end of day 11	C done at end of day 19	A done at end of day 28	D done at end of day 38	E done at end of day 45

b. Make span = 45 days
Mean job flow time = (6 + 11 + 19 + 28 + 38 + 45)/6 = 24.5 days
Average number of jobs in the system = 147/45 = 3.27 jobs

Mean job lateness = 2/6 = 0.33 days
Mean job tardiness = 20/6 = 3.33 days
Maximum tardiness = 19 days

Job	Completion Date	Due Date	Lateness (days)	Tardiness
A	28	30	−2	0
B	11	10	1	1
C	19	24	−5	0
D	38	40	−2	0
E	45	26	19	19
F	6	15	−9	0
			Total = 2	Total = 20

10. a.

Wash

```
0    6   9  11    18  22    26
┌───┬──┬──┬────┬────┐
│ A │B │C │ D  │ E  │
└───┴──┴──┴────┴────┘
     ┌───┬──┬───┬───┬────┐
     │ A │B │ C │ D │ E  │
     └───┴──┴───┴───┴────┘
0    6    10  15  18  23   26
```
Press

b. Make span = 26 hours

Mean job flow time = (10 + 15 + 18 + 23 + 26)/5 = 18.4 hours

Average number of jobs in the system = 92/26 = 3.54 jobs

11. a.

Wash

```
0    2   5    9       15      22     27
┌──┬──┬────┬──────┬───────┐
│C │B │ E  │  A   │   D   │
└──┴──┴────┴──────┴───────┘
   ┌──┬────┬──┬─────┬────────┐
   │C │ B  │E │  A  │   D    │
   └──┴────┴──┴─────┴────────┘
0    2   5      10 13 15  19 22     27
```
Press

b. Make span = 27 hours

Mean job flow time = (5 + 10 + 13 + 19 + 27)/5 = 14.8 hours

Average number of jobs in the system = 74/27 = 2.74 jobs

12. a.

Wash

```
0    2   5      12      18  22    25
┌──┬──┬────┬──────┬────┐
│C │B │ D  │  A   │ E  │
└──┴──┴────┴──────┴────┘
   ┌──┬─────┬────┬────┬─────┐
   │C │  B  │ D  │ A  │ E   │
   └──┴─────┴────┴────┴─────┘
0    2   5   10  12  17     22    25
```
Press

b. Make span = 25 hours

Mean job flow time = (5 + 10 + 17 + 22 + 25)/5 = 15.8 hours

Average number of jobs in the system = 79/25 = 3.16 jobs

16.

Employee	M	T	W	Th	F	S	Su
1	OFF	OFF	X	X	X	X	X
2	X	X	OFF	OFF	X	X	X
3	OFF	OFF	X	X	X	X	X
4	X	X	OFF	OFF	X	X	X
5	X	X	OFF	OFF	X	X	X
6	OFF	OFF	X	X	X	X	X

17.

Employee	M	T	W	Th	F	S	Su
1	OFF	OFF	X	X	X	X	X
2	X	X	OFF	OFF	X	X	X
3	OFF	OFF	X	X	X	X	X
4	X	X	OFF	OFF	X	X	X
5	OFF	OFF	X	X	X	X	X
6	X	X	OFF	OFF	X	X	X

Chapter 17

1.

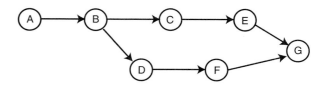

2. a. Project completion time = 17 weeks
   b. Critical activities: A, B, D, F, G

7. a. Path completion times:
   ABDFHJ = 32 weeks
   ABDGIJ = 35.5 weeks
   ACEFHJ = 36.83 weeks
   ACEGIJ = 40.33
   Project completion time = 40.33 weeks
   b. Critical activities: A C E G I J

11. Reduce G by 1 week, then A by 1 week, then C by 2 weeks, and then F by 1 week.
   Total additional cost is $2,700.

12. 17 weeks is the minimum project completion time.

15.

   a.

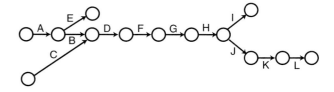

b.

Activity	A	B	C	D	E	F	G	H	I	J	K	L
Expected time	8.67	3.33	6	7	15.33	3	4	2	2	2	5	9.17

c. Path completion times:
AE = 24 weeks
ABDFGHI = 30 weeks
ABDFGHJKL = 44.17
CDFGHI = 24 weeks
CDFGHJKL = 38.17 weeks
Critical path: ABDFGHJKL

d. Estimated project completion time = 44.17 weeks.

16. a. $P(\text{project} \leq 32) = P(\text{critical path} \leq 32) =$

$$P(Z \leq \frac{32 - 44.17}{\sqrt{10.026}}) = P(Z \leq -3.84) = 0$$

b. $Z = \dfrac{X - \mu}{\sigma}$

$$1.645 = \frac{X - 44.17}{\sqrt{10.026}}$$

X = 49.4 weeks

Supplement A

3. a. Average system utilization = 10/16 = 0.625

b. Average number of customers in the system = 10/6 = 1.67

c. Average number of customers waiting in line = (0.625)(1.67) = 1.0417

4. a. Average time in the system = 1/(16 − 10) = 0.1667 hour or 10 minutes

b. Average time waiting in line = (0.625)(0.1667) = 0.1042 hour or 6.25 minutes

c. Probability of having more than 3 customers in the system = 0.1526

d. Probability of having more than 4 customers in the system = 0.0954

7. a. Average system utilization = 0.75

b. Average number of customers in the system = 3.4286

c. Average number of customers waiting in line = 1.9286

d. Average time a customer spends in the system = 0.1492 hour or 8.5714 minutes

e. Average time a customer spends waiting in line = 0.0804 hour or 4.8214 minutes

f. Probability of having more than 4 customers in the system = 0.2712

APPENDIX B
THE STANDARD NORMAL DISTRIBUTION

This table gives the area under the standardized normal curve from 0 to z, as shown by the shaded portion of the following figure.

Examples: If z is the standard normal random variable, then
Prob $(0 \leq z \leq 1.32) = 0.4066$
Prob $(z \geq 1.32) = 0.5000 - 0.4066 = 0.0934$
Prob $(z \leq 1.32)$ = Prob $(z \leq 0)$ + Prob $(0 \leq z \leq 1.32)$
$= 0.5000 + 0.4066 = 0.9066$
Prob $(z \leq -1.32)$ = Prob $(z \geq 1.32) = 0.0934$ (by symmetry)

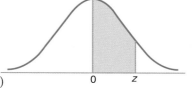

z	0.00	0.01	0.02	0.03	0.04	0.05	0.06	0.07	0.08	0.09
0.0	0.0000	0.0040	0.0080	0.0120	0.0160	0.0199	0.0239	0.0279	0.0319	0.0359
0.1	0.0398	0.0438	0.0478	0.0517	0.0557	0.0596	0.0636	0.0675	0.0714	0.0753
0.2	0.0793	0.0832	0.0871	0.0910	0.0948	0.0987	0.1026	0.1064	0.1103	0.1141
0.3	0.1179	0.1217	0.1255	0.1293	0.1331	0.1368	0.1406	0.1443	0.1480	0.1517
0.4	0.1554	0.1591	0.1628	0.1664	0.1700	0.1736	0.1772	0.1808	0.1844	0.1879
0.5	0.1915	0.1950	0.1985	0.2019	0.2054	0.2088	0.2123	0.2157	0.2190	0.2224
0.6	0.2257	0.2291	0.2324	0.2357	0.2389	0.2422	0.2454	0.2486	0.2518	0.2549
0.7	0.2580	0.2612	0.2642	0.2673	0.2704	0.2734	0.2764	0.2794	0.2823	0.2852
0.8	0.2881	0.2910	0.2939	0.2967	0.2995	0.3023	0.3051	0.3078	0.3106	0.3133
0.9	0.3159	0.3186	0.3212	0.3238	0.3264	0.3289	0.3315	0.3340	0.3365	0.3389
1.0	0.3413	0.3438	0.3461	0.3485	0.3508	0.3531	0.3554	0.3577	0.3599	0.3621
1.1	0.3643	0.3665	0.3686	0.3708	0.3729	0.3749	0.3770	0.3790	0.3810	0.3830
1.2	0.3849	0.3869	0.3888	0.3907	0.3925	0.3944	0.3962	0.3980	0.3997	0.4015
1.3	0.4032	0.4049	0.4066	0.4082	0.4099	0.4115	0.4131	0.4147	0.4162	0.4177
1.4	0.4192	0.4207	0.4222	0.4236	0.4251	0.4265	0.4279	0.4292	0.4306	0.4319
1.5	0.4332	0.4345	0.4357	0.4370	0.4382	0.4394	0.4406	0.4418	0.4429	0.4441
1.6	0.4452	0.4463	0.4474	0.4484	0.4495	0.4505	0.4515	0.4525	0.4535	0.4545
1.7	0.4554	0.4564	0.4573	0.4582	0.4591	0.4599	0.4608	0.4616	0.4625	0.4633
1.8	0.4641	0.4649	0.4656	0.4664	0.4671	0.4678	0.4686	0.4693	0.4699	0.4706
1.9	0.4713	0.4719	0.4726	0.4732	0.4738	0.4744	0.4750	0.4756	0.4761	0.4767
2.0	0.4772	0.4778	0.4783	0.4788	0.4793	0.4798	0.4803	0.4808	0.4812	0.4817
2.1	0.4821	0.4826	0.4830	0.4834	0.4838	0.4842	0.4846	0.4850	0.4854	0.4857
2.2	0.4861	0.4864	0.4868	0.4871	0.4875	0.4878	0.4881	0.4884	0.4887	0.4890
2.3	0.4893	0.4896	0.4898	0.4901	0.4904	0.4906	0.4909	0.4911	0.4913	0.4916
2.4	0.4918	0.4920	0.4922	0.4925	0.4927	0.4929	0.4931	0.4932	0.4934	0.4936
2.5	0.4938	0.4940	0.4941	0.4943	0.4945	0.4946	0.4948	0.4949	0.4951	0.4952
2.6	0.4953	0.4955	0.4956	0.4957	0.4959	0.4960	0.4961	0.4962	0.4963	0.4964
2.7	0.4965	0.4966	0.4967	0.4968	0.4969	0.4970	0.4971	0.4972	0.4973	0.4974
2.8	0.4974	0.4975	0.4976	0.4977	0.4977	0.4978	0.4979	0.4979	0.4980	0.4981
2.9	0.4981	0.4982	0.4982	0.4983	0.4984	0.4984	0.4985	0.4985	0.4986	0.4986
3.0	0.4986	0.4987	0.4987	0.4988	0.4988	0.4989	0.4989	0.4989	0.4990	0.4990
3.5	0.4998									

Source: Adapted from Robert Markland, Topics in Management Science (3rd Ed.) Wiley, New York 1989.

APPENDIX C
P-Chart

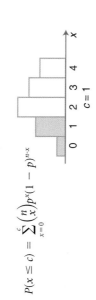

$$P(x \le c) = \sum_{x=0}^{c} \binom{n}{x} p^x (1 - p)^{n-x}$$

P

n	x	.05	.10	.15	.20	.25	.30	.35	.40	.45	.50	.55	.60	.65	.70	.75	.80	.85	.90
1	0	.9500	.9000	.8500	.8000	.7500	.7000	.6500	.6000	.5500	.5000	.4500	.4000	.3500	.3000	.2500	.2000	.1500	.1000
	1	1.0000	1.0000	1.0000	1.0000	1.0000	1.0000	1.0000	1.0000	1.0000	1.0000	1.0000	1.0000	1.0000	1.0000	1.0000	1.0000	1.0000	1.0000
2	0	.9025	.8100	.7225	.6400	.5625	.4900	.4225	.3600	.3025	.2500	.2025	.1600	.1225	.0900	.0625	.0400	.0225	.0100
	1	.9975	.9900	.9775	.9600	.9375	.9100	.8775	.8400	.7975	.7500	.6975	.6400	.5775	.5100	.4375	.3600	.2775	.1900
	2	1.0000	1.0000	1.0000	1.0000	1.0000	1.0000	1.0000	1.0000	1.0000	1.0000	1.0000	1.0000	1.0000	1.0000	1.0000	1.0000	1.0000	1.0000
3	0	.8574	.7290	.6141	.5120	.4219	.3430	.2746	.2160	.1664	.1250	.0911	.0640	.0429	.0270	.0156	.0080	.0034	.0010
	1	.9928	.9720	.9393	.8960	.8438	.7840	.7183	.6480	.5748	.5000	.4253	.3520	.2818	.2160	.1563	.1040	.0608	.0280
	2	.9999	.9990	.9966	.9920	.9844	.9730	.9571	.9360	.9089	.8750	.8336	.7840	.7254	.6570	.5781	.4880	.3859	.2710
	3	1.0000	1.0000	1.0000	1.0000	1.0000	1.0000	1.0000	1.0000	1.0000	1.0000	1.0000	1.0000	1.0000	1.0000	1.0000	1.0000	1.0000	1.0000
4	0	.8145	.6561	.5220	.4096	.3164	.2401	.1785	.1296	.0915	.0625	.0410	.0256	.0150	.0081	.0039	.0016	.0005	.0001
	1	.9860	.9477	.8905	.8192	.7383	.6517	.5630	.4752	.3910	.3125	.2415	.1792	.1265	.0837	.0508	.0272	.0120	.0037
	2	.9995	.9963	.9880	.9728	.9492	.9163	.8735	.8208	.7585	.6875	.6090	.5248	.4370	.3483	.2617	.1808	.1095	.0523
	3	1.0000	.9999	.9995	.9984	.9961	.9919	.9850	.9744	.9590	.9375	.9085	.8704	.8215	.7599	.6836	.5904	.4780	.3439
	4	1.0000	1.0000	1.0000	1.0000	1.0000	1.0000	1.0000	1.0000	1.0000	1.0000	1.0000	1.0000	1.0000	1.0000	1.0000	1.0000	1.0000	1.0000
5	0	.7738	.5905	.4437	.3277	.2373	.1681	.1160	.0778	.0503	.0313	.0185	.0102	.0053	.0024	.0010	.0003	.0001	.0000
	1	.9974	.9185	.8352	.7373	.6328	.5282	.4284	.3370	.2562	.1875	.1312	.0870	.0540	.0308	.0156	.0067	.0022	.0005
	2	.9988	.9914	.9734	.9421	.8965	.8369	.7648	.6826	.5931	.5000	.4069	.3174	.2352	.1631	.1035	.0579	.0266	.0086
	3	1.0000	.9995	.9978	.9933	.9844	.9692	.9460	.9130	.8688	.8125	.7438	.6630	.5716	.4718	.3672	.2627	.1648	.0815
	4	1.0000	1.0000	.9999	.9997	.9990	.9976	.9947	.9898	.9815	.9688	.9497	.9222	.8840	.8319	.7627	.6723	.5563	.4095
	5	1.0000	1.0000	1.0000	1.0000	1.0000	1.0000	1.0000	1.0000	1.0000	1.0000	1.0000	1.0000	1.0000	1.0000	1.0000	1.0000	1.0000	1.0000
6	0	.7351	.5314	.3771	.2621	.1780	.1176	.0754	.0467	.0277	.0156	.0083	.0041	.0018	.0007	.0002	.0001	.0000	.0000
	1	.9672	.8857	.7765	.6554	.5339	.4202	.3191	.2333	.1636	.1094	.0692	.0410	.0223	.0109	.0046	.0016	.0004	.0001
	2	.9978	.9842	.9527	.9011	.8306	.7443	.6471	.5443	.4415	.3438	.2553	.1792	.1174	.0705	.0376	.0170	.0059	.0013
	3	.9999	.9987	.9941	.9830	.9624	.9295	.8826	.8208	.7447	.6563	.5585	.4557	.3529	.2557	.1694	.0989	.0473	.0159
	4	1.0000	.9999	.9996	.9984	.9954	.9891	.9777	.9590	.9308	.8906	.8364	.7667	.6809	.5798	.4661	.3446	.2235	.1143
	5	1.0000	1.0000	1.0000	.9999	.9998	.9993	.9982	.9959	.9917	.9844	.9723	.9533	.9246	.8824	.8220	.7379	.6229	.4686
	6	1.0000	1.0000	1.0000	1.0000	1.0000	1.0000	1.0000	1.0000	1.0000	1.0000	1.0000	1.0000	1.0000	1.0000	1.0000	1.0000	1.0000	1.0000
7	0	.6983	.4783	.3206	.2097	.1335	.0824	.0490	.0280	.0152	.0078	.0037	.0016	.0006	.0002	.0001	.0000	.0000	.0000
	1	.9556	.8503	.7166	.5767	.4449	.3294	.2338	.1586	.1024	.0625	.0357	.0188	.0090	.0038	.0013	.0004	.0001	.0000
	2	.9962	.9743	.9262	.8520	.7564	.6471	.5323	.4199	.3164	.2266	.1529							

n	x	.05	.10	.15	.20	.25	.30	.35	.40	.45	.50	.55	.60	.65	.70	.75	.80	.85	.90
	3	.9998	.9973	.9879	.9667	.9294	.8740	.8002	.7102	.6083	.5000	.3917	.2898	.1998	.1260	.0706	.0333	.0121	.0027
	4	1.0000	.9998	.9988	.9953	.9871	.9712	.9444	.9037	.8471	.7734	.6836	.5801	.4677	.3529	.2436	.1480	.0738	.0257
	5	1.0000	1.0000	.9999	.9996	.9987	.9962	.9910	.9812	.9643	.9375	.8976	.8414	.7662	.6706	.5551	.4233	.2834	.1497
	6	1.0000	1.0000	1.0000	1.0000	.9999	.9998	.9994	.9984	.9963	.9922	.9848	.9720	.9510	.9176	.8665	.7903	.6794	.5217
	7	1.0000	1.0000	1.0000	1.0000	1.0000	1.0000	1.0000	1.0000	1.0000	1.0000	1.0000	1.0000	1.0000	1.0000	1.0000	1.0000	1.0000	1.0000
8	0	.6634	.4305	.2725	.1678	.1001	.0576	.0319	.0168	.0084	.0039	.0017	.0007	.0002	.0001	.0000	.0000	.0000	.0000
	1	.9428	.8131	.6572	.5033	.3671	.2553	.1691	.1064	.0632	.0352	.0181	.0085	.0036	.0013	.0004	.0001	.0000	.0000
	2	.9942	.9619	.8948	.7969	.6785	.5518	.4278	.3154	.2201	.1445	.0885	.0498	.0253	.0113	.0042	.0012	.0002	.0000
	3	.9996	.9950	.9786	.9437	.8862	.8059	.7064	.5941	.4470	.3633	.2604	.1737	.1061	.0580	.0273	.0104	.0029	.0004
	4	1.0000	.9996	.9971	.9896	.9727	.9420	.8939	.8263	.7396	.6367	.5230	.4059	.2936	.1941	.1138	.0563	.0214	.0050
	5	1.0000	1.0000	.9998	.9988	.9958	.9887	.9747	.9502	.9115	.8555	.7799	.6846	.5722	.4482	.3215	.2031	.1052	.0381
	6	1.0000	1.0000	1.0000	.9999	.9996	.9987	.9964	.9915	.9819	.9648	.9368	.8936	.8309	.7447	.6329	.4967	.3428	.1869
	7	1.0000	1.0000	1.0000	1.0000	1.0000	.9999	.9998	.9993	.9983	.9961	.9916	.9832	.9681	.9424	.8999	.8322	.7275	.5695
	8	1.0000	1.0000	1.0000	1.0000	1.0000	1.0000	1.0000	1.0000	1.0000	1.0000	1.0000	1.0000	1.0000	1.0000	1.0000	1.0000	1.0000	1.0000
9	0	.6302	.3874	.2316	.1342	.0751	.0404	.0207	.0101	.0046	.0020	.0008	.0003	.0001	.0000	.0000	.0000	.0000	.0000
	1	.9288	.7748	.5995	.4362	.3003	.1960	.1211	.0705	.0385	.0195	.0091	.0038	.0014	.0004	.0001	.0000	.0000	.0000
	2	.9916	.9470	.8591	.7382	.6007	.4628	.3373	.2318	.1495	.0898	.0498	.0250	.0112	.0043	.0013	.0003	.0000	.0000
	3	.9994	.9917	.9661	.9144	.8343	.7297	.6089	.4826	.3614	.2539	.1658	.0994	.0536	.0253	.0100	.0031	.0006	.0001
	4	1.0000	.9991	.9944	.9804	.9511	.9012	.8283	.7334	.6214	.5000	.3786	.2666	.1717	.0988	.0489	.0196	.0056	.0009
	5	1.0000	.9999	.9994	.9969	.9900	.9747	.9496	.9006	.8342	.7461	.6386	.5174	.3911	.2703	.1657	.0856	.0339	.0083
	6	1.0000	1.0000	1.0000	.9997	.9987	.9957	.9888	.9750	.9502	.9102	.8505	.7682	.6627	.5372	.3993	.2618	.1409	.0530
	7	1.0000	1.0000	1.0000	1.0000	.9999	.9996	.9986	.9962	.9909	.9805	.9615	.9295	.8789	.8040	.6997	.5638	.4005	.2252
	8	1.0000	1.0000	1.0000	1.0000	1.0000	1.0000	.9999	.9997	.9992	.9980	.9954	.9899	.9793	.9596	.9249	.8658	.7684	.6126
	9	1.0000	1.0000	1.0000	1.0000	1.0000	1.0000	1.0000	1.0000	1.0000	1.0000	1.0000	1.0000	1.0000	1.0000	1.0000	1.0000	1.0000	1.0000
10	0	.5987	.3487	.1969	.1074	.0563	.0282	.0135	.0060	.0025	.0010	.0003	.0001	.0000	.0000	.0000	.0000	.0000	.0000
	1	.9139	.7361	.5443	.3758	.2440	.1493	.0860	.0464	.0233	.0107	.0045	.0017	.0005	.0001	.0000	.0000	.0000	.0000
	2	.9885	.9298	.8202	.6778	.5256	.3828	.2616	.1673	.0996	.0547	.0274	.0123	.0048	.0016	.0004	.0001	.0000	.0000
	3	.9990	.9872	.9500	.8791	.7759	.6496	.5138	.3823	.2660	.1719	.1020	.0548	.0260	.0106	.0035	.0009	.0001	.0000
	4	.9999	.9984	.9901	.9672	.9219	.8497	.7515	.6331	.5044	.3770	.2616	.1662	.0949	.0473	.0197	.0064	.0014	.0001
	5	1.0000	.9999	.9986	.9936	.9803	.9527	.9051	.8338	.7384	.6230	.4956	.3669	.2485	.1503	.0781	.0328	.0099	.0016
	6	1.0000	1.0000	.9999	.9991	.9965	.9894	.9740	.9452	.8980	.8281	.7340	.6177	.4862	.3504	.2241	.1209	.0500	.0128
	7	1.0000	1.0000	1.0000	.9999	.9996	.9984	.9952	.9877	.9726	.9453	.9004	.8327	.7384	.6172	.4744	.3222	.1798	.0702
	8	1.0000	1.0000	1.0000	1.0000	1.0000	.9999	.9995	.9983	.9955	.9893	.9767	.9536	.9140	.8507	.7560	.6242	.4557	.2639
	9	1.0000	1.0000	1.0000	1.0000	1.0000	1.0000	1.0000	.9999	.9997	.9990	.9975	.9940	.9865	.9718	.9437	.8926	.8031	.6513
	10	1.0000	1.0000	1.0000	1.0000	1.0000	1.0000	1.0000	1.0000	1.0000	1.0000	1.0000	1.0000	1.0000	1.0000	1.0000	1.0000	1.0000	1.0000
15	0	.4633	.2059	.0874	.0352	.0134	.0047	.0016	.0005	.0001	.0000	.0000	.0000	.0000	.0000	.0000	.0000	.0000	.0000
	1	.8290	.5490	.3186	.1671	.0802	.0353	.0142	.0052	.0017	.0005	.0001	.0000	.0000	.0000	.0000	.0000	.0000	.0000
	2	.9638	.8159	.6042	.3980	.2361	.1268	.0617	.0271	.0107	.0037	.0011	.0003	.0001	.0000	.0000	.0000	.0000	.0000
	3	.9945	.9444	.8227	.6482	.4613	.2969	.1727	.0905	.0424	.0176	.0063	.0019	.0005	.0001	.0000	.0000	.0000	.0000
	4	.9994	.9873	.9383	.8358	.6865	.5155	.3519	.2173	.1204	.0592	.0255	.0093	.0028	.0007	.0001	.0000	.0000	.0000

n	x	.05	.10	.15	.20	.25	.30	.35	.40	.45	.50	.55	.60	.65	.70	.75	.80	.85	.90
	5	.9999	.9978	.9832	.9389	.8516	.7216	.5643	.4032	.2608	.1509	.0769	.0338	.0124	.0037	.0008	.0001	.0000	.0000
	6	1.0000	.9997	.9964	.9819	.9434	.8689	.7548	.6098	.4522	.3036	.1818	.0950	.0422	.0152	.0042	.0008	.0001	.0000
	7	1.0000	1.0000	.9994	.9958	.9827	.9500	.8868	.7869	.6535	.5000	.3465	.2131	.1132	.0500	.0173	.0042	.0006	.0000
	8	1.0000	1.0000	.9999	.9992	.9958	.9848	.9578	.9050	.8182	.6964	.5478	.3902	.2452	.1311	.0566	.0181	.0036	.0003
	9	1.0000	1.0000	1.0000	.9999	.9992	.9963	.9876	.9662	.9231	.8491	.7392	.5968	.4357	.2784	.1484	.0611	.0168	.0022
	10	1.0000	1.0000	1.0000	1.0000	.9999	.9993	.9972	.9907	.9745	.9408	.8796	.7827	.6481	.4845	.3135	.1642	.0617	.0127
	11	1.0000	1.0000	1.0000	1.0000	1.0000	.9999	.9995	.9981	.9937	.9824	.9576	.9095	.8273	.7031	.5387	.3518	.1773	.0556
	12	1.0000	1.0000	1.0000	1.0000	1.0000	1.0000	.9999	.9997	.9989	.9963	.9893	.9729	.9383	.8732	.7639	.6020	.3958	.1841
	13	1.0000	1.0000	1.0000	1.0000	1.0000	1.0000	1.0000	1.0000	.9999	.9995	.9983	.9948	.9858	.9647	.9198	.8329	.6814	.4510
	14	1.0000	1.0000	1.0000	1.0000	1.0000	1.0000	1.0000	1.0000	1.0000	1.0000	.9999	.9995	.9984	.9953	.9866	.9648	.9126	.7941
	15	1.0000	1.0000	1.0000	1.0000	1.0000	1.0000	1.0000	1.0000	1.0000	1.0000	1.0000	1.0000	1.0000	1.0000	1.0000	1.0000	1.0000	1.0000
20....	0	.3585	.1216	.0388	.0115	.0032	.0008	.0002	.0000	.0000	.0000	.0000	.0000	.0000	.0000	.0000	.0000	.0000	.0000
	1	.7358	.3917	.1756	.0692	.0243	.0076	.0021	.0005	.0001	.0000	.0000	.0000	.0000	.0000	.0000	.0000	.0000	.0000
	2	.9245	.6769	.4049	.2061	.0913	.0355	.0121	.0036	.0009	.0002	.0000	.0000	.0000	.0000	.0000	.0000	.0000	.0000
	3	.9841	.8670	.6477	.4114	.2252	.1071	.0444	.0160	.0049	.0013	.0003	.0000	.0000	.0000	.0000	.0000	.0000	.0000
	4	.9974	.9568	.8298	.6296	.4148	.2375	.1182	.0510	.0189	.0059	.0015	.0003	.0000	.0000	.0000	.0000	.0000	.0000
	5	.9997	.9887	.9327	.8042	.6172	.4164	.2454	.1256	.0553	.0207	.0064	.0016	.0003	.0000	.0000	.0000	.0000	.0000
	6	1.0000	.9976	.9781	.9133	.7858	.6080	.4166	.2500	.1299	.0577	.0214	.0065	.0015	.0003	.0000	.0000	.0000	.0000
	7	1.0000	.9996	.9941	.9679	.8982	.7723	.6010	.4159	.2520	.1316	.0580	.0210	.0060	.0013	.0002	.0000	.0000	.0000
	8	1.0000	.9999	.9987	.9900	.9591	.8867	.7624	.5956	.4143	.2517	.1308	.0565	.0196	.0051	.0009	.0001	.0000	.0000
	9	1.0000	1.0000	.9998	.9974	.9861	.9520	.8782	.7553	.5914	.4119	.2493	.1275	.0532	.0171	.0039	.0006	.0000	.0000
	10	1.0000	1.0000	1.0000	.9994	.9961	.9829	.9468	.8725	.7507	.5881	.4086	.2447	.1218	.0480	.0139	.0026	.0002	.0000
	11	1.0000	1.0000	1.0000	.9999	.9991	.9949	.9804	.9435	.8692	.7483	.5857	.4044	.2376	.1133	.0409	.0100	.0013	.0001
	12	1.0000	1.0000	1.0000	1.0000	.9998	.9987	.9940	.9790	.9420	.8684	.7480	.5841	.3990	.2277	.1018	.0321	.0059	.0004
	13	1.0000	1.0000	1.0000	1.0000	1.0000	.9997	.9985	.9935	.9786	.9423	.8701	.7500	.5834	.3920	.2142	.0867	.0219	.0024
	14	1.0000	1.0000	1.0000	1.0000	1.0000	1.0000	.9997	.9984	.9936	.9793	.9447	.8744	.7546	.5836	.3828	.1958	.0673	.0113
	15	1.0000	1.0000	1.0000	1.0000	1.0000	1.0000	1.0000	.9997	.9985	.9941	.9811	.9490	.8818	.7625	.5852	.3704	.1702	.0432
	16	1.0000	1.0000	1.0000	1.0000	1.0000	1.0000	1.0000	1.0000	.9997	.9987	.9951	.9840	.9556	.8929	.7748	.5886	.3523	.1330
	17	1.0000	1.0000	1.0000	1.0000	1.0000	1.0000	1.0000	1.0000	1.0000	.9998	.9991	.9964	.9879	.9645	.9087	.7939	.5951	.3231
	18	1.0000	1.0000	1.0000	1.0000	1.0000	1.0000	1.0000	1.0000	1.0000	1.0000	.9999	.9995	.9979	.9924	.9757	.9308	.8244	.6083
	19	1.0000	1.0000	1.0000	1.0000	1.0000	1.0000	1.0000	1.0000	1.0000	1.0000	1.0000	1.0000	.9998	.9992	.9968	.9885	.9612	.8784
	20	1.0000	1.0000	1.0000	1.0000	1.0000	1.0000	1.0000	1.0000	1.0000	1.0000	1.0000	1.0000	1.0000	1.0000	1.0000	1.0000	1.0000	1.0000

P

PHOTO CREDITS

Chapter 1
Pages 2 and 18: Walter Hodges/Stone. Pages 4 and 6: ©AP/Wide World Photos. Page 8: Charles O'Rear/Corbis Images. Page 11 (left): Courtesy Library of Congress. Page 11 (right): ©Stone.

Chapter 2
Pages 22 and 36: W. Sallaz/The Image Bank. Page 25: ©AP/Wide World Photos. Page 27: Ed Kashi/Corbis Images. Page 29: Courtesy Southwest Airlines Co. Page 31: AFP/Corbis Images. Page 33: Courtesy Ritz-Carlton Hotel Company, L.L.C.

Chapter 3
Pages 42 and 71: Chris Everard/Stone. Page 43: ©Vadem Allegro, courtesy of ZIBA Design. Page 45: Bob Daemmrich Photography. Page 50: Courtesy Association for Manufacturing Excellence. From "How Design Teams Use DFM/A to Lower Costs and Speed Products to Market" by John Ingalls, *Target* Vol. 12, no. 1, March 1996, pp. 13–19. Reproduced with permission. Page 53 (left): Richard T. Nowitz/Corbis Images. Page 53 (right): David Seawell/Corbis Images. Page 60: Michael Rosenfeld/Stone. Page 63: Steward Cohen/Stone. Page 64: Owen Franken/Corbis Images. Page 65 (top): Michael Rosenfeld/Stone. Page 65 (bottom): ©AP/Wide World Photos.

Chapter 4
Pages 78 and 99: Jon Feingersh/Corbis Stock Market. Page 85: Courtesy Lands' End. Page 90: Courtesy Timken. Page 91: Michael Newman/PhotoEdit. Page 94: Monika Graff/The Image Works. Page 96: Courtesy Fingerhut.

Chapter 5
Pages 108 and 132: AFP/Corbis Images. Page 110: Roger Ressmeyer/Corbis Images. Page 114: Taylor-Fabricious/Gamma Liaison. Page 125: Ted Horowitz/Corbis Stock Market.

Chapter 6
Pages 137 and 165: Jose L. Pelaez/Corbis Stock Market. Page 138: William Whitehurst/Corbis Stock Market. Page 148: Ed Wheeler/Corbis Stock Market. Page 154: Paul Amasy/Corbis Images. Page 155 (center): Courtesy Motorola. Page 155 (bottom): Jeff Zaruba/Stone. Page 163: William Taufic/Corbis Stock Market.

Chapter 7
Pages 176 and 200: ©Pictor. Page 177: Tom & Pat Leeson/Photo Researchers. Page 182: ©AP/Wide World Photos. Page 189: Courtesy Ryder System Inc. Page 194: Bruce Ayres/Stone. Page 197: Charles Thatcher/Stone.

Chapter 8
Pages 206 and 234: Patti McConville/The Image Bank. Page 208: ©AP/Wide World Photos. Page 209: Ralph Wetmore/Stone. Page 210 (left): ©Sidney/The Image Works. Page 210 (right): Courtesy IBM. Page 223: Marc Muench/Corbis Images.

Chapter 9
Pages 247 and 272: Stock, Boston/PictureQuest. Page 249: ©Stone. Page 253: ©William Waldron. Page 255: Richard Braine/Stone. Page 260: ©AP/Wide World Photos.

Chapter 10
Pages 283 and 308: Michael Rosenfeld/Stone. Page 284: Courtesy The Kroger Co. Page 285: HMS Images/The Image Bank. Pages 286 and 287 (left): ©AP/Wide World Photos. Page 287 (right): Mary Kate Denny/PhotoEdit. Page 288: ©AP/Wide World Photos. Page 296: Charlie Westerman/Stone. Page 298: Chuck Keeler/Stone. Page 305: Steve Raymer/Corbis Images.

Chapter 11
Pages 319 and 342: Andy Sacks/Stone. Page 320: Courtesy SAS Institute, Inc. Page 321: Henry Martin/The Cartoon Bank, Inc. Page 324: ©SUPERSTOCK. Page 325: Courtesy Herman Miller, Inc. Page 330: Julian Hirshowitz/Corbis Stock Market. Page 341: ©John Caldwell.

Chapter 12
Pages 352 and 385: ©Telegraph Colour Library/FPG International. Page 355: Mike Timo/Stone. Page 356: Palm ™VIIx handheld. Courtesy Palm, Inc. Page 361: ©AP/Wide World Photos. Page 369: Leif Skoogfors/Corbis Images. Page 374: M.L. Sinibaldi/Corbis Stock Market. Pages 378 and 383: ©AP/Wide World Photos.

Chapter 13
Pages 395 and 417: ©SUPERSTOCK. Page 403: Alex Farnsworth/The Image Works. Page 397: Courtesy Apple Computers. Page 398: John Davis/Stone.

Chapter 14

Pages 427 and 441: Tim Wright/Corbis Images. Page 428: Ross Whitaker/The Image Bank. Page 432: Anna Clopet/ Corbis Images. Page 437: ©1996 Ted Goff Cartoons.

Chapter 15

Pages 452 and 469: Christel Rosenfeld/Stone. Page 467: Ed Honowitz/Stone. Page 468: Richard T. Nowitz/Corbis Images.

Chapter 16

Pages 481 and 508: Frank Siteman/Stone. Page 482: Eric Sander/Gamma Liaison. Page 483: Ariel Skelley/Corbis Stock Market. Page 488: James Stevenson/The Cartoon Bank, Inc.

Page 490: Terry Vine/Stone. Page 499: David Young Wolff/ Stone. Page 501: Spencer Tirey/Gamma Liaison.

Chapter 17

Pages 520 and 544: Mug Shots/Corbis Stock Market. Page 521: ©AP/Wide World Photos. Page 522: ©Bettman/Corbis Images. Page 534: ©DILBERT reprinted with permission of United Feature Syndicate. Page 535: ©AP/Wide World Photos. Page 538: Mark L. Stephenson/Corbis Images.

Supplement A

Pages 554 (top) and 563: Chuck Savage/Corbis Stock Market. Page 554 (bottom): Kristin Sladen/The Image Works. Page 560: Barney Tobey/The Cartoon Bank, Inc.

SUBJECT INDEX

Page references followed by italic *t* indicate material in tables. Page references beginning with B, C, or D refer to Supplements B, C, and D which appear only on the CD-ROM that accompanies the text.

COMPANY INDEX

Note: Company names consisting of a person's name such as "Eddie Bauer" are not inverted, so this term will be found in the "E" section of the index as opposed to the B section. Company names beginning with articles like "the," such as "The Gap" likewise will be found among the "G" entries rather than under "T."

I